Salazar and
Modern Portugal

Salazar and Modern Portugal

HUGH KAY

HAWTHORN BOOKS, INC.
PUBLISHERS
NEW YORK

SALAZAR AND MODERN PORTUGAL

1   2   3   4   5   6   7   8   9   10

For the President,
Staff and Students of the
English College, Lisbon
with affection and
gratitude

Contents

Plates

MAPS

Acknowledgments and thanks for permission to reproduce photographs are due to: Associated Press for Plates 1, 2, 9, 18, 19, 26; STEF Agency, Lisbon, for 3; Isobel Soares for 11; 'Diario di Lisboa' for 12; L. Lourenco, Cascais, for 17; Press Association for 20; Information and Tourism Centre, Mozambique, for 27.

Abbreviations

BALL
: George W. Ball, *The Discipline of Power*, Little, Brown, Boston, 1968.

BOXER
: Professor C. R. Boxer, *Race Relations in the Portuguese Colonial Empire, 1415-1825*, Clarendon Press, 1963.

CHURCHILL
: Winston S. Churchill, *The Second World War*, vols. i-iv, Cassell, London, 1948-51.

CROZIER
: Brian Crozier, *Franco*, Eyre & Spottiswoode, London, 1967.

DAVIDSON
: Basil Davidson, *The Liberation of Guiné*, Penguin Library, 1969.

DELGADO
: Humberto Delgado, *The Memoirs of General Delgado*, Cassell, 1964.

DERRICK
: Derrick, *The Portugal of Salazar*, Sands, London, 1938.

DISC
: António de Oliveira Salazar, *Discursos e Notas Políticas*, vols. i-vi.

DGFP
: Documents on German Foreign Policy, 1918-45; Archives of the German Foreign Ministry, published by the British Foreign Office and the U.S. State Department.

D.D.IT.
: Italian Ministry of Foreign Affairs: *I Documenti Diplomatici Italiani*, 8th. series, 1935-9; Libreria dello Stato, Rome, 1952-3.

DOCUMENTS SECRETS
: (Eristov): *Documents Secrets du Ministère des Affaires Etrangères d'Allemagne*, Editions Paul Dupont, Paris, 1946.

D & A
: *Doctrine and Action*, Faber & Faber, London 1939; a collection of speeches by António de Oliveira Salazar, translated by Robert Edgar Broughton.

DUFFY
: James Duffy, *Portugal in Africa*, Penguin African Library, 1962.

EDEN   The Rt. Hon. the Earl of Avon, K.G., P.C., M.C., *The Eden Memoirs*, Cassell, London, 1960-5.

EGERTON   F. C. C. Egerton, *Salazar, Rebuilder of Portugal*, Hodder & Stoughton, London, 1943.

FERRO   António Ferro, *Salazar, Portugal and her Leader*, Faber & Faber, London, 1939.

FIGUEIREDO   António de Figueiredo, *Portugal and its Empire: the Truth*, Gollancz, London, 1961.

FRANCO NOGUEIRA   Dr Franco Nogueira, *The United Nations and Portugal*, Sidgwick & Jackson, London, 1963.

FRYER   Peter Fryer and Patricia McGowan Pinheiro, *Oldest Ally*, Dobson, London, 1961.

GARNIER   Christine Garnier, *Vacances avec Salazar*, 1952.

HAMMOND   R. J. Hammond, *Portugal and Africa, 1815-1910*, Food Research Institute, Stanford University, 1966.

HC DEB   British Parliamentary Debates (Hansard).

IND. DOCS.   *Vinte Anos de Defesa do Estado Português de India*, 1967. Published by the Ministry of Foreign Affairs, Lisbon, 1967.

LAWRENCE   Leo Lawrence, *Nehru Seizes Goa*, Pageant Press, New York, 1962.

LIVERMORE   H. V. Livermore, *A New History of Portugal*, Cambridge, 1966.

L.B. (*Livros Brancos*), *Dez Anos de Política Externa, 1936-47*, vols i-v, a collection of diplomatic documents published by the Ministry of Foreign Affairs, Lisbon, 1961-5.

MARINI   Emile Marini, *Goa as I saw It*, Les Cahiers de Voyage, Switzerland, 1956.

MEDLICOTT   W. N. Medlicott, *The Economic Blockade. Vols I & II*, published by Her Majesty's Stationery Office, 1952.

MÉGEVAND   Louis Mégevand, *Le Vrai Salazar*, Paris, 1957.

MONDLANE   Eduardo Mondlane, *The Struggle for Mozambique*, Penguin African Library, 1969.

PATTEE   Richard Pattee, *Portugal and the Portuguese World*, Bruce, Milwaukee, 1957.

PIDE	*Policia Internacional e de Defesa do Estado* (the Portuguese security police).
P. D'A.	Jacques Ploncard D'Assac, *Salazar*, published by La Table Ronde, Paris, 1967.
SCHLESINGER	Arthur M. Schlesinger Jr., *A Thousand Days*, Fawcett Crest, Greenwich, Conn., 1967.
SURVEY	Survey of International Affairs, 1939-46, *The War and the Neutrals*, Oxford University Press, 1956 (published under the auspices of the Royal Institute of International Affairs, Chatham House, London).
THOMAS	Hugh Thomas, *The Spanish Civil War*, Eyre & Spottiswoode, London, 1961.
WEST	J. George West, *The New Corporative State of Portugal*, A Lecture at King's College, London, 1937, published by SPN, Lisbon.
WOODWARD	F. L. Woodward, *British Foreign Policy in the Second World War*, Her Majesty's Stationery Office, London, 1952.

Preface

Few statesmen have lived as obscurely as Dr António de Oliveira Salazar. His personal life has always been withdrawn, his public appearances few. His speeches, during his public life, were sometimes hard to interpret, harder still to translate. His distaste for the personality cult has restricted him to a speech or two a year, an occasional interview with a foreign journalist. Far from unapproachable on the official level, he has always severely rationed his social life. Very few people have taken a meal with him, or addressed him by his Christian name. His private life is wholly his own: for him, exhibitions of self-analysis are a form of indecent exposure. Impatient of writing letters when the telephone would do, he was often at his best in writing memoranda for his ministers or ambassadors. There are few better sources for penetrating the mind and heart of the man than his wartime telegrams to Armindo Monteiro, Portugal's ambassador in London. Some of his best reflections, however, are contained in handwritten notes, decipherable only by faith and familiarity; and Portugal levies a fifty-year embargo on confidential state papers. After his illness ended his public life in September 1968, Dr Salazar's personal papers were entrusted to a group of 'elders' for classification. The task was bound to be a long one, and, as many of the documents relate to living persons and current policies, they will not be open to the chroniclers for some time yet.

These are some of the problems facing any biographer of Salazar. There are others. In a relatively 'closed' society where the voice of public criticism has been muted, there are few personal memoirs or published debates. Official departments today may speak very freely on an off-the-record basis, or, as they like to put it, 'to give you some background'. But most of them do not as yet employ a press and publicity officer with the necessary tested facts and figures to hand, and full discretion to use them. Within the limits of the system, correspondents are very well served by the foreign press departments of the Foreign Ministry and the National Secretariat of

Information, and are on easy and cordial terms with them. But they sense that the spokesmen are hampered by lack of co-ordination between government departments and an unsteady flow of information.

Portuguese statistics have become more sophisticated and reliable in recent years. The National Institute of Statistics and the research departments of the major banks are the best sources. The Institute has long since abandoned its optimistic viewpoint, and tends to err by understatement – to the chagrin of the houseproud ministries. But there are still large areas of research calling for more sociologists, statisticians and demographers. The last major drawback is the dearth of reliable studies in depth of the Salazar period, notably in regard to the post-war years. Sources are not lacking, but the data has to be gathered piecemeal and abounds in inconsistencies. Any inquirer must prepare himself for an abnormal amount of interviewing, elaborate use of questionnaires, and constant recourse to foreign sources for cross-checking.

My own documentary sources are detailed in the text, but special mention must be made of some of them. Departing from the fifty-year rule, the Foreign Ministry in Lisbon is publishing a large collection of diplomatic exchanges covering the period of the Spanish Civil War, Second World War, and the Goa crisis. The main series sheds new light on the significance for wartime Europe and America of Portugal's relationships with Britain and Spain. Its main effect is to write an almost unsuspected chapter in the complex history of the Anglo-Portuguese Alliance.

The other sources are self-explanatory, but anyone who works in this field cannot fail to acknowledge his special debt to the studies of wartime Portugal by Professor W. N. Medlicott and Sir Llewellyn Woodward; to the critiques of Portuguese colonial policy and race relations by Professors James Duffy (Brandeis), R. J. Hammond (Stanford), C. R. Boxer (now of Yale), Adriano Moreira and the staff of the *Instituto Superior de Ciências Sociais e Política Ultramarina* (Lisbon), Fernando Pacheco de Amorim (Coimbra), and the Brazilian sociologist Gilberto Freyre; to the histories of Portugal by Professor H. V. Livermore (Columbia) and Dr Richard Pattee (Quebec); and to Professor Marcello Caetano's studies of colonial affairs and the corporative state.

So many people of all shades of opinion have helped me by recalling their experiences or answering technical questions that an exhaustive list would make a short chapter. In particular I am indebted to Dr Salazar himself, with whom I had several long conversations, and to the present Prime Minister of Portugal, Professor Marcello Caetano, who received me twice in the year before he returned to high office; on the official side to the Portuguese Foreign Minister, Dr Alberto Franco Nogueira, who made all his department's facilities available to me; to his staff, especially Drs Caldeira Coelho, Pinto Mesquita and António Patricio; in other ministries to Drs Costa André, Ribeiro da Cunha, Ferreira da Silva, Nuno Murgado, Manuel Rino and Arnaldo Sampaio; and to the Portuguese Press Counsellor in London, Sr António Potier. I had the advantage of discussing the Spanish and World War years with Ambassador Pedro Theotónio Pereira, Portugal's envoy to Spain at that time, and with General Santos Costa, then Under-Secretary for War and later Minister of Defence; of talks with Dr Salazar's personal friends, including his physician, Dr Eduardo Coelho, and his 'flat mate' of Coimbra days, Professor Diogo Pacheco de Amorim; and with the former Overseas Minister, Professor Adriano Moreira.

On the side of the unofficial opposition, my thanks are due to many lawyers, doctors, academics and journalists who adopt the Republican, Socialist or Christian Democratic positions, including Drs Sousa Tavares, De Abranches Ferrão, Pires de Lima, Mario Soares, and above all, Dr Raul Rêgo, whose scrupulous objectivity and fairmindedness have always been of the utmost service. There is, in Portuguese life, an increasingly important stratum of 'technical', non-political critics, whose constructive commentaries are central to the process of modernisation and did much to sort fact from feeling for me in many controversial areas. I am particularly grateful to Dr Valentim Xavier Pintado, formerly economic adviser to the progressive *Banco Português do Atlantico* and now Secretary of State for Economic Affairs, and to Drs Jesus Nunes dos Santos, Manuel Domingues and Vitor Serra, of the *Associação Portuguesa das Empresas do Ultramar*.

Tradition prevents me from naming the diplomats of many countries who, in their embassies and consulates in Lisbon and Portuguese Africa, gave generously of their knowledge and wisdom. I have been treated with great kindness, too, by the resident foreign correspondents in Lisbon, especially those of the British press and the international news agencies. In this connection a special tribute must go to that great lady, Miss José Shercliffe, who has written and broad-

cast from Lisbon for twenty-nine years (notably for the London
Times, the B.B.C. and the Associated Press). In my visits to Portuguese
Africa I have received help on all sides, black and white, official and
unofficial, from the local clergy and from missionaries. Nor do I
forget the missionaries and African nationalists whom I have met
in London, often in controversy, but whose insights and experience,
they may rest assured, have not been wasted on me. The basic
differences between us so often turn on whether or not one believes
that an evolution, as distinct from revolution, can be authentically
fostered in their countries. I believe that it can, and that the process
has gathered momentum.

Finally, though far from least, my thanks to the Gulbenkian
Foundation for assisting the final stage of the work with a grant; to
Lieutenant-Colonel A. J. E. Cranstoun, of Corehouse, Lanark, who
first introduced me to Portugal; to Mr J. P. Donnelly, of St George's
College, Weybridge, to whom I am indebted for a brilliant analytical
job on much of the Portuguese documentation; to Mr W. J. Igoe,
who also, incredibly, found time to assist with research; and to
Senhora Ana Maria Ramos do Sacramento Monteiro Henriques
Pereira, without whose secretarial support in Lisbon I would have
lost my nerve.

There have been few public personalities more elusive than that of
Dr Salazar; few nations more individualistic than Portugal. The object
of this book is to dispense with passion and over-simplified judgments,
and to see beyond them to the multiple complexities in the life of a
man and a nation who, however they are judged, have been part of
one another for a very long time, with important implications for
the outside world. I am among those who think that Portugal today,
and even more tomorrow, has more to give to the world than either
the world or Portugal realizes: a contribution at once distinctive
and indispensable. But first Portugal must be known and understood
in the difficult transitional phase she finds herself in now. The urgency
of this is the only justification for a journalist's attempt to trace the
story of the past forty years.

LONDON AND LISBON
April 1967 to March 1970

Explanatory Notes

1. DR SALAZAR'S OFFICE

There is confusion at times over Dr Salazar's title and office. He was President of the Council of Ministers (i.e. Prime Minister), and not President of the Republic of Portugal, the title reserved for the head of state.

2. PORTUGUESE TERRITORY

Portuguese territory today consists of the mainland of Portugal; the Azores and Madeira islands in the Atlantic; the overseas provinces of Angola (West Africa) and Mozambique (East Africa); the Cape Verde Islands, and the islands of São Tomé and Principe (off the West African coast); Macao in China; Timor in the Indonesian archipelago; the Portuguese Indian provinces of Goa, Diu and Damão were occupied by India in 1961 and are no longer under Portuguese control.

3. FORMER EMPIRE

In the age of discovery the Portuguese Empire included Brazil, Morocco, part of the Congo (Portugal still retains the enclave of Cabinda), and many strongholds in the Far East. The discoverers established themselves in many parts of India, Burma, Ceylon, Siam, the Malayan peninsula, Indonesia, Indo-China, China and Japan.

Formosa is a Portuguese word. Portuguese family names are still common in India and Ceylon (Fonseca, Sousa, etc.). The Portuguese language can still be heard in dialect in the last two countries, notably in Bombay and on the Malabar coast; also in Java and Malacca; while Singapore and Timor retain the patois known as the *dialectico malaqueiro*.

Newfoundland was the Terra Nova of the explorers, and Labrador commemorates João Fernandes Lavrador.

4. PORTUGUESE MAINLAND

Portugal itself is virtually cut in half by the River Tagus which meets the Atlantic at the estuary where Lisbon stands.

> The *northern provinces* (with main towns) are: Minho (Braga, Guimarães), Trás-os-Montes (Braganza), Douro (Porto), Beira Alta (Viseu), Beira Litoral (Coimbra, Leiria, Fátima), Beira Baixa (Castelo Branco), Estremadura (Torres Vedras, Sintra); Ribatejo (the Tagus divides this province as it flows west to the Atlantic). Lisbon, on the Tagus estuary, stands physically in Estremadura.
>
> The *southern provinces*: Alto Alentejo (Evora, Portalegre), Baixo Alentejo (Beja), Algarve (Faro, Lagos, Sagres, Cape St Vincent).

The north is the land of mountains (the Serra de Estrela rises as high as 6,400 ft), forests and damp, fertile valleys. It includes industrial centres, the wine country, and the problematical structure of its agriculture is a multiplicity of small-holdings. In some parts the peasant farmers reveal a strong Celtic strain and the visitor feels as though he were in the Scottish Highlands. Porto (or Oporto) is a banking and manufacturing centre. Coimbra is the home of a 600-year-old university, where Dr Salazar studied and taught. Not far from Porto is the seaside town of Matosinhos, centre of the sardine fisheries and the fish-canning industry. Braga has been called Portugal's Canterbury. Fátima, where the Blessed Virgin is believed to have appeared in 1917, is a centre of world-wide pilgrimage.

The south is very different. On the hot rolling plains of the Alentejo, the peasant is usually, not a small-holder, but a farm worker on the vast estates of wealthy landowners. A vast irrigation scheme is developing here with German aid. The Algarve bears traces of the Moorish occupation and includes the tempestuous coastline where Henry the Navigator brooded over his charts.

Lisbon is a city standing on seven hills, with a population of about a million, and a booming industry. It has one of the largest harbours in Europe and also the largest dockyard. The Tagus was traditionally vital to imperial links, British and Portuguese, because of Lisbon's strategic position on the Atlantic seaboard: one of the reasons for the Anglo-Portuguese Alliance.

5. THE ALLIANCE

Anglo-Portuguese relations reached their first landmark in 1147 when English crusaders helped Afonso Henriques, founder of the Portuguese nation, to take Lisbon from the Moors. The Alliance involves twelve treaties based on mutual trading interests, early joint hostility to Castile, protection of the Atlantic shipping routes, the need to resolve Anglo-Portuguese disputes in Africa, and finally the British and American need of bases in the Azores in the Second World War.

The first treaty was signed in St Paul's Cathedral on 16 June 1373, when Anglo-Portuguese trade was very brisk. In 1385, John, the Master of Avis and bastard son of Pedro the Cruel, came to the Portuguese throne and defeated the Castilians at Aljubarotta. A year later, on 17 May 1386, a second treaty was signed in the Star Chamber at Westminster. The Portuguese king was to help John of Gaunt, who claimed the Castilian throne, and he married the Lancastrian's daughter, Philippa. Portuguese ships protected English interests in the Channel.

Further treaties in 1572, 1642 and 1654 were followed, after the Restoration of the Stuarts in England, by the famous treaty of 1661 with Charles II, who married Catherine of Braganza. Her dowry ran into two million cruzados, with Tangier and Bombay thrown in (Britain's first connection with India). More treaties followed in 1703 and 1810, the latter according to Britain 'most favoured nation' treatment. Portugal's grant to Britain of equal trading rights in Brazilian ports was the start of the financial decline which, over the following century, was to lead Portugal into catastrophe.

In 1884 Britain recognized Portuguese possessions on both sides of the River Zaire (now the River Congo) in return for free navigation rights and limited customs duties. In 1891, after the British ultimatum arrested Portuguese efforts to link Angola with Mozambique, a treaty was signed to establish a *modus vivendi*. (The intermediate area which Portugal sought to possess became Rhodesia instead. Britain's attitude was that Portugal could not claim territory over which she had not established effective control.)

In 1899, when Britain needed the help of Mozambique in the Boer War, she pledged herself 'to defend and protect all conquests of or colonies belonging to the Crown of Portugal against all his enemies, future as well as present'.

The treaty granting bases in the Azores to the British and United States forces in the Second World War was signed in 1943.

6. CURRENCY

The Portuguese escudo was worth 3d. in English money (80 = £1) until the devaluation of sterling in November 1967. Since then the rate of exchange has been approximately 69 escudos to £1.

One conto equals 1,000 escudos.

Salazar and Modern Portugal

Introduction

To most people outside Portugal, Salazar has always been a symbol rather than a man. Few would recognize his photograph or be able to tell you what sort of person he is. For some, he is the symbol of redemption, a man who restored his country's status and fortunes. For others, he is a symbol of repression at home and oppression in Africa. He has done little to illuminate his own image. For publicity he had only contempt, and, in the forty years of his leadership, he never travelled further afield than Spain. His foreign admirers and critics alike know he is in a class of his own, but find it hard to describe. Although, in the early days, he frankly accepted the label of 'dictator' and always admitted to being 'authoritarian', he was not like other dictators. Though he came to power on the wave of a military coup, he was not a soldier. In the first few years in which he held high office, he was sometimes acclaimed in the streets; but there is no record of the classical trappings of dictatorship, the chanting crowds, the demagogic threats and utterances, parades or displays. The initial coup was popular and achieved without bloodshed, and Salazar appeared as a donnish, austere ex-seminarian with one foot in the cloister, seemingly cold and cerebral, self-effacing. No one has ever accused him of hoarding private wealth. He lived the life of a bachelor peasant, leaving the pomp and the banquets to others. In September 1968 he lay in a public hospital, technically homeless, a state pensioner, with under £3,000 in the bank after forty years of power. For friends and enemies, he is incorrupt because in some sense he is inhuman: whether as the selfless ascetic is inhuman, or as the man of pride to whom wealth is nothing but power is all.

A biography of Salazar must, therefore, be an attempt to understand how this retiring, improbable character managed to gain the support of a turbulent nation, and maintain it for four decades. It must ask how a man of faith, his beliefs partly shaped by Leo XIII's *Rerum Novarum*, could incur the indictment of running a police state and denying essential human rights to his people; whether he was right to impose and maintain a monastic economy on the nation, to sacrifice growth and welfare to stability, and one generation to the next. Has the ferment of ideas in Portuguese life been so damped down as to surrender the nation to mediocrity?

It has been said that the measure of Salazar's success is that people have forgotten how bad the situation was when he came to power, and that his failure is reckoned by Portugal's political immaturity. He has, thus, to be judged partly by comparisons between 1928 and 1969, and, during that period, Portugal's home economy and her status in the wider world have changed for the better beyond recognition; but has the price, in terms of freedom, been too high? The answers would be simple if Salazar could be written off as a ruthless dictator, unconcerned for his people; but objectively such simplifications will not do. The wartime years reveal his shrewdness and judgment, his flair for playing off great nations against each other, and equally his tough, realistic decisiveness; yet his mind is unusually complex and abstract. Shortly before the end of his public life, Salazar told a journalist that Portugal had had a choice of being or becoming, and she had chosen to be. This sounds like the traditional *Homme du Midi* who rests content with what he is and what he has. Coupled with Salazar's early theme of the grace of poverty, it could be construed as a static choice of indigence, tutored and ennobled by its certainty of an ultimate future 'above'. But Portugal is an Atlantic, not a Mediterranean, power; and Salazar never was an *Homme du Midi*. He was more concerned to foster a slow evolution towards a future 'ahead', but one which defies advance definition, and has to be measured, not in decades, but in whole generations. Though capable of almost cynical pragmatism, it was in the light of abstractions which, for him, were larger than life itself, that Salazar sceptically warded off the mid-twentieth-century winds of change.

Central to Salazar's mind is an all-pervading, transcendent sense of history. Portugal was once a major power, commanding a far-flung empire of lands her sailors discovered. After the age of discovery, there followed the age of decadence; most of the Far East empire was lost, and Brazil proclaimed her independence unilaterally in the eighteenth century. In modern times, Portugal was seen as a small and impoverished nation, clinging for survival to what remained of her overseas territories, mainly in Africa, where Portuguese society was backward and the native peoples exploited and unenlightened. For five hundred years, from the days of Henry the Navigator, the

Portuguese had rarely known stable government, and, in the first quarter of the twentieth century, her army and finances were derided throughout Europe. Then Salazar came to power, promising a firm and effective grasp of the economic realities, untrained in either military or diplomatic skills, and with only a reader's knowledge of Portugal Overseas. He believed the spirit of endurance of the days of exploration was not dead, and rallied the nation to the effort and self-denial which encouraged the soundness of the escudo. In foreign relations, he took his stand on the one constant factor: his country's strategic position in the Atlantic and Indian Oceans, its importance to the alliance with Britain, and the implications of the alliance for the whole of the Iberian peninsula. Self-taught though he was in such matters, Salazar's handling of his wartime relations with Britain, America, Spain and the Axis powers was to form an important chapter in Western history. That story is not well known, and a great deal of new data has come to light which will be examined. Whose side was Salazar really on in the Second World War, and whom did he want to win? Did he play the game wholly for himself, responding to the Allies' needs only when it suited him, or did the ancient alliance mean more to him than this? How did he justify selling Portuguese wolfram, a mineral scarce but vital to the munitions industry, to both sides in the conflict, and which side did better out of him? No ally could have been harder to handle than Salazar was from London's point of view – Churchill called him 'impossible' – yet the gains from his co-operation were considerable. It is through a close examination of his wartime policies – Chapters 6-8 – that the student will most rapidly and thoroughly get to the root of the man.

If Salazar conditioned Portugal for forty years, it is equally true that his thinking and instincts were embedded in the Portuguese outlook and heritage. Though he could see the nation's problems with an outsider's eyes, he was never an alien seeking to alter the national character. Again, his attitude to Africa could be simply explained if he had been no more than a predatory, out-of-date colonialist, determined to use the overseas possessions as a means of feeding Portugal, and searching for spurious formulae to justify the colonial 'presence'. Yet world opinion, at least in informed circles, is aware that there is more to it than this, and that Salazar's policies cannot be separated from the Portuguese character. The world-wide hostility shown to the Portuguese in 1961, when trouble broke out in Angola, has in certain quarters tempered itself to a sceptical curiosity, a certain uneasiness that the point has been missed, a sense that, however the Portuguese are judged, Angola and Mozambique cannot be wholly understood in terms of the modern, anti-colonial stereotypes. The critics of nine years ago gave the Portuguese six months to live in Africa, yet they are still there, and today's critics are often willing to make distinctions between Portuguese 'colonialism' and South African 'racialism'. Visiting correspondents and observers from international agencies have indicated positive aspects of Portuguese African life on which, one feels, a future might be built, without denying African aspirations, provided that Portuguese policies mean what they say.

It is in regard to Portuguese intentions, of course, that the outside world remains to be convinced; and the relative friendliness to Portugal today of certain Western powers is not unconnected with strategic considerations and the vast new commercial potential opened up in Angola and Mozambique. Certainly, substantial changes have occurred since 1961. In most parts of the two major African provinces, life seems normal enough, with the frontier wars of attrition strangely remote. But the questions remain. Is this another lull before the storm? Has African education really progressed? What chance have the African peoples of effectively sharing in power, and in the right proportions? Is their apparent contentment due to their unenlightenment rather than real acceptance of the white man's presence? How far is the vaunted Portuguese flair for inter-racial relations a fiction or a fact? Is it imperilled by a tendency for the 'white powers' of southern Africa to close their ranks in the teeth of the freedom fighters and international disapproval? Are the Portuguese, or are they not, on the way to creating an authentic inter-racial nation? To answer these questions, it will be necessary to reach back into history, to examine the dream and the reality, to trace the story of slavery and labour exploitation, to recall the enlightened ideals lost in the wastelands of ineptitude, and the recent, more convincing reforms. What really happened in Angola in 1961, what has happened since, and where is it leading?

Finally, it remains true that most Britons and Americans really know very little of Portugal and her potential, so an attempt will be made to provide a basis for judging where she stands today in regard to her trading partners in Europe, and what she has to offer the investor. The positive side of the story leading up to this is often forgotten. When Salazar came to power, Portugal was a bad joke in the European chancellories, her currency worthless, her army an obsolete remnant, the nation fragmented and beggared. Within a few years, Salazar had balanced the budget, restored the currency, started to build a modern army, constructed thousands of homes. He kept his country out of the Second World War with not a little profit, and, in spite of German penetration into Portuguese society, pursued a policy which decisively contributed to keeping the Axis powers out of the Iberian peninsula, with obvious advantages for the Allies. After the war he led Portugal into NATO and the United Nations, and thus restored her to a place in the international comity which she had long since lost. Today, Portugal must rapidly outgrow his pre-Keynesian ideas, but his slow-grinding thrift, his *femme de ménage* economics at least brought the country to a point where, with expansionist policies, modernized management and more foreign investment, a major breakthrough need not be postponed for long.

The other side of the coin is the story of political repression and the frustrations of the opposition, with particular stress on police activity, censorship and allegedly rigged elections, the dangerous prolongation of deflationary measures, the slow development of education and health and welfare services, the dissonance between Portuguese and United Nations policy, the latter-day threat to the Anglo-Portuguese Alliance. It is, of course, essential to judge the Salazar regime in a Portuguese context, and not by reference to an arbitrary, external standard. Only so will it be seen how a new future, important to the Western world, may now be emerging in Portugal from past travails, built on the strengths and weaknesses alike of Salazar himself and the people he has ruled.

The problem of judging Salazar himself may be readily gauged from three quotations. Years ago, the Swiss writer Gonzague de Reynold could say of him:

> Salazar carried his responsibilities like Christ carrying his cross. . . . One would confess one's sins to Salazar, one would entrust one's whole future to him without asking for any acknowledgment, but one would hate to have him for an examiner.[1]

Dr Cunha Leal, a former Republican Premier, put it another way:

> Inexperienced, disinclined to enter into any relations with his fellow students, and a misogynist by nature, he [Salazar] took

[1] Gonzague de Reynold, *Portugal,* pp. 268, 284, Paris, 1936.

refuge in his pride as a snail within its shell. He always remained practically alone, pitilessly stifling his own dreams with the weight of a cold soul, sadly stripped of the illusions of youth . . .

There follows a parable about the devil taking Salazar to the top of a high mountain. Then, says Cunha Leal, just when Portugal stood in need of a man of genius, fate had installed in the *Terreira de Paço*

> a poor Benedictine lay brother, obstinate and of limited capacity, vain and irascible, petty and revengeful, with no knowledge of men or realities, looking at the world through a tube with a limited field of vision.[1]

A more moderate reaction comes from the U.S. statesman, Mr George W. Ball, who, in August 1963, as President Kennedy's Under Secretary of State, had two long talks in Lisbon with Salazar. Years later, he wrote:

> I found Dr Salazar a man of charm and urbanity, very quick and perceptive, extremely conservative in view, but profoundly absorbed by a time dimension quite different from our own, conveying the strong yet curious impression that he and his whole country were living in more than one century, as though Prince Henry the Navigator, Vasco da Gama and Magellan were still active agents in the shaping of Portuguese policy. Remembering something of the grand but pathetic story of Portugal, I was prepared for history to intrude itself, but not so vividly; yet later, mulling over what we had talked about, I found myself asking, why not?[2]

It may have been more than politeness that led Mr Ball to write 'living in more than one century' rather than 'living in the past'. No one could doubt Salazar's grasp of modern realities. What raised the dust was the way he defied the signs of the times and seemed to be telling the winds to be still: his persistent appeal to the perennial in an age of Heraclitean flux.

[1] *A Obra Intangivel do Dr. Oliveira Salazar*, Lisbon, 1930.
[2] Ball, p. 246.

CHAPTER I

The Setting

In one of his best-known novels,[1] *The Sin of Father Amaro*, Eça de Queiroz has drawn an ironic indictment of small-town life in Portugal towards the end of the nineteenth century: those selfish little societies, their scheming politicians, their corrupt priests, their smugness and snobbery. Lower middle-class drawing-room walls dripped with the symbols of piety. The ladies solemnly went to church, and later relished the clerical scandals, whispered in parlours. An inordinate number of minor officials, their duties neglected or nominal, gave themselves airs and intrigued for petty promotion. Irreligious males, revolted by clerical indolence, groped with high passion for secular faith. Their explosive wrangles rocked the coffee shops as they damned the past and the present, with only the future left to defend. There were high-sounding words about freedom and love and equality; monarchists vied with masons, republicans with socialists. The central theme was revolution, usually French or Spanish. Stifled for lack of a home-grown creed, serious writers were looking for sources further afield in Europe, and the small-town intelligentsia dropped even German and Russian names with splendid *insouciance*. The unifying topic was a common disregard for the overfed clergy, but, while the men talked, the beggars were left to crawl to the doors of the *Misericordia*. Yet, as in all things human, there were still the good pastors, the honest politicians, here and there, while deeper in the countryside the abiding values of peasant family life were never totally overlaid.

Salazar's birthplace was the hamlet of Vimieiro near the town of Santa Comba in the Dão valley, home of some of the finest Portuguese wines. Salazar himself was never to be a serious drinker, but his cottage at Santa Comba always had a few bottles of home brew for visitors, to whom it was offered apologetically. The town lies between Coimbra and Viseu in the province of Beira Alta, where the hills are

[1] Eça de Queiroz, *The Sin of Father Amaro*; English edition Max Reinhardt, London.

wooded, the valleys fertile, and the skyline is the Serra de Estrela.
The boy arrived in one of the less pretentious cottages on the Viseu
road on 28 April 1889. His father's name was António de Oliveira,
his mother was Maria do Resgate Salazar, and, as sometimes happened
in Portuguese families, the boy's definitive name was taken from the
maternal side. Salazar's father was already fifty when his son was
born; he died at the age of ninety-three in 1932, outliving his wife
by six years. In 1889, Maria was forty-three, and the couple already
had four daughters: Martha (later the village teacher for forty years),
Elisa, Maria-Leopoldina and Laura. They were a deeply religious
pair, the father rough and affectionate, the mother a woman of
character and intelligence, by far the greater influence on her son.
She was consulted when he came to office in 1926, and he later said
that, had she lived longer, he would have had to leave public life
and go back home, as 'she could not have lived without me'. The
description accorded to Salazar's mother by his French biographer
is somewhat unnerving. She was, he says, 'extremely intelligent,
active, far-seeing, rather austere, very pious'.[1] There was, however,
nothing sanctimonious about this down-to-earth woman, and family
relationships were tender. They had their own little plot of land, Sr
de Oliveira acted as bailiff on the lands of the local 'squire', while his
wife, as soon as a railway station appeared, opened a workers' café.

Salazar was born into a form of feudalism, locally benign, and the
sort of poverty where there was always something on the table,
but not very much. In his early life, the family values certainly
prevailed, and a Catholic religion taught in terms of the cross,
contemplative prayer and personal salvation. Its weakness was a
practical individualism, in principle condemned as a Protestant sin
by the Council of Trent; and it was only two years after Salazar's
birth that Pope Leo XIII's encyclical *Rerum Novarum* shocked the
complacent faithful by preaching the social virtues and working-
class rights. The implied message was that saving one's soul meant
dying for the brethren, a hard message nobody wanted to hear, and
three generations were to pass before the message was sufficiently
spelled out to allow for a tentative start to the Christian-Marxist
dialogue. One of the keys to Salazar's life is the problem he plainly
had in synthesizing his mother's faith with that of Leo: the two
primary influences on his youth. On the one hand, authority and

1 Ploncard D'Assac (henceforth, and in *Abbreviations*, P.D'A.) p. 12.

obedience, the grace of suffering, salvation in spite of the world, and charity; on the other, man's right to share in decisions that shape his life, social solutions for social evils, salvation by means of the world, and justice.

Salazar was not strong and the daily journey to Santa Comba primary school was hardly justified by results. It was overcrowded and he learned too slowly. His father transferred him to a village school where a Sr José Ribeiro taught a class of thirty in his cottage for a few shillings a month each. Later, Salazar went to Fr João Pimental's school at Viseu, and finally at the age of eleven won a free place in the Viseu seminary where he stayed for eight years. Like many who enter seminaries very young, he decided, after minor orders, not to proceed to the priesthood. There were practical reasons for this. On 1 February 1908, King Carlos had been murdered and a secularist republic was clearly on the way. What future there would be for priests was anyone's guess. Moreover, Salazar's theological studies had been completed, but he was still only nineteen, and could not be ordained until the canonical age of twenty-four. His scholarship was finished, and his family were in no position to maintain him indefinitely. Yet there may have been more to it than this. Patrons could be found for clever boys, and Salazar was in the event helped into the university by the family his father worked for. Finance as such need not have been prohibitive. There are at least two other possibilities, both with a bearing on future developments, which may have affected his decision to remain a layman.

It is a fair surmise that Salazar brought to Viseu from the pious feminine stronghold at Vimieiro a certain moral fussiness, a not uncommon feature of seminary and novitiate life which often relates to an over-prudish concern for chastity. In aggravated forms it is an index that the priestly vocation is lacking, suggesting as it does an obsessional sense of spiritual insecurity which in a priest is a pastoral menace. On the other hand, Salazar's niggling observance of the rules, which from all accounts must have been hard for his fellow students to bear,[1] may have held a deeper meaning: a subconscious

[1] Mario de Figueiredo, a future President of the National Assembly, was a fellow seminarian. He remembers receiving food parcels from home which he used to share with Salazar. It was against the rules for students to enter each other's rooms, so, having first asked a priest's permission, Salazar would stand at his friend's door, solemnly munching cakes on the safe side of the threshold. Many years later, Professor de Figueiredo related this story with an admiration that must surely have been a polite afterthought; Garnier, p. 43 (see Abbs).

fear that his real problem was a basic indisposition for living under obedience. One of his oldest friends has suggested that 'if Salazar had not been a Catholic, he would have been an Anarchist'.[1] His whole political life has been, subjectively, a matter of certainties. His faith in his own prescriptions has not wavered. He has always suspected trends or fashions in manners and policies. A man who would one day regard the winds of change as a tyranny would hardly have settled down to the sacrifice of personal judgment asked of priests in the days of the Modernist crisis by authoritarian hierarchies. His critics would say he was ambitious, and always reserved to himself alone the right of private judgment. Others would say that he simply obeyed the *diktat* of his own lucidity and confident sense of direction at a time when no one else in the country knew which way to go. However, even if he could not contemplate life under Church authority for himself, the attitudes of seminary life left a deep impression upon him and were discernible in the way he ran the country. In the midst of his public life he acknowledged his debt to that early foundation:

> Even if I had had the misfortune to lose the faith, I would never have forgotten the good Fathers who cared for me for eight years virtually free, and to whom I owe what is best in my moral formation and intellectual discipline.[2]

Contemporaries remember him in student days plunged in his books and easily bored by games. He does not, on the other hand, seem to have been remote, and he made enduring friendships. Academically, he was outstanding, and at this time began to acquire the knowledge of Thomist philosophy which finally marked him for life.

It was in 1910 that Salazar went to Coimbra University to study law and economics, and it was in that year, too, that the Republic was proclaimed in Lisbon. To ascertain what Coimbra meant to him, and how it interplayed with current events to shape his prescriptions for the future, there has to be some understanding of Portuguese history and tradition, and of what led up to a constitutional change which for Portugal, some would say, was out of character. When Salazar came to power in 1929, the country was in peril of disintegration, but it is less than fair to ascribe the whole of the

[1] In a private conversation with the author, December 1968.
[2] P. D'A., *op. cit.*, p. 13, quoting Luis Teixeira, *Profil de Salazar*, Lisbon, 1938.

blame to the Republicans who governed from 1910 to 1926. It is true that they failed to unify the nation or solve its financial problems, but instability had been endemic for centuries. How did this come about?

Ethnically, culturally, historically and geographically, Portugal stands at the cross-roads of continents, a link between Europe and Africa, Europe and South America. But, while ready to exercise a mediating role, she has never been prepared to diminish her own identity. Most Portuguese have always rejected the Spanish view that 'the Portuguese is a Spaniard with his back to Castile and his eyes on the Atlantic sea'.[1] His ancestors were Swabian, Phoenician, Greek, Celtic, Carthaginian, Visigoth, Roman and Moorish; but his distinctive Lusitanian identity has been self-conscious from almost uncharted times. Since the birth of the Portuguese nation in the days of Afonso Henriques, he has fought to preserve it in a struggle eight hundred years long. With a formerly predatory Spain and the Pyrenees between him and Europe, however, he turned his gaze outwards and became a discoverer. His land, in the words of the Spanish essayist Eugenio d'Ors, became his balcony on the infinite. It is a small land and the sea became his breathing space, a natural element linking the homeland with discovered territory in far-off continents. The wide world became his domestic milieu, and the lands across the sea an intercontinental projection of Portugal, central to his vision, not peripheral, and relevant to his survival. The view is subjective and has often been criticized even within the nation. Yet when Portugal argues today that what the United Nations call her colonies are really 'Portugal Overseas', there is more to it than a spurious legalistic device to evade their right to independence. Portuguese practice in the *ultramar* has not measured up to principle, but the 'Portugal Overseas' mentality is deeply embedded. It stems from the days when, once a man arrived in a new land, he and the land were stuck with each other. He either had to *plant* himself there, or face a sea journey of several months with a less than evens chance of surviving it. There were hopes of quick profits, but not to take home. The phrase 'my children were born here' became the symbol of commitment to the colonized land.

All this suggests adventure, not instability. But there are flaws in the Portuguese character. Unlike 'Mediterranean Man', the Portuguese is not content with what he is and has; but his *siso* and *loucura*,

[1] Salvador de Madariaga, *Spain*, p. 185, London, 1946.

his prudence and quixotic flair, are always at war within him, and deflect him from the path of single-minded progress. The concept of the hero-nation is the source of his pride in the age of discovery, when the fifteenth and sixteenth-century Portuguese mariners pioneered the sea routes to the Far East and South America; with it goes a melancholic yearning for past glories (*saudade*) and a secret belief in ultimate resurrection (*Sebastianismo*).[1] The touchiness and suspicion the Portuguese often shows in his international bargaining have much to do with the sense of shame he feels for the decadent age that followed the age of the *Lusiadas*,[2] the Portuguese poet Camões' great epic of the discoveries. But there is a dark side to his nature, a deep pessimism which, responding to French revolutionary thought blowing across the Pyrenees, saw the age of discovery as a time of monumental folly and dishonour, and repented of the sword the explorers took out with the cross. The clash of the old and new traditions, of the perpetuated mystery of Portugal's heroic age with the age of reason of eighteenth-century France, threw nineteenth-century Portugal into turmoil and drove her agonized lyrical poet, Antero de Quental, to such a state of despair that he died a suicide. So, while the Portuguese are gentle and generous, they can also be very tiresome. Conventions like keeping time or answering letters can be brushed aside with a kind of sublime contempt for the trivial. Equally their impetuosity hurls them into adventure or self-destruction. They are natural orators, easily get drunk on words, confuse them with solid policy. They can be sensual, petty and devious, and they can also be extremely tough. At times they quickly tire of what they have started, and seem to lack the staying power to see it through. Yet they are inured to hardship and rise to their best in hopeless situations, as Wellington found in the Peninsular War. It is not surprising that their uncertainties responded with relief to a Salazar who told them: 'I know quite well what I want and where I am going', or that today their special brand of nationalism brings them into conflict with the generalized prescriptions of the United Nations.

There were other, severely practical, reasons for the nation's rest-

[1] After King Sebastian, whose armies were cut to pieces by the Moors at the Battle of Alcaçer Kebir in 1578. He was not seen to die, and the legend arose that he would come back some day.

[2] Camões' epic poems celebrating the discoveries and the spirit of the nation. The *Lusiadas* first appeared in 1572. They proclaimed what has been described as a civic religion which gave pride of place to heroism, the Portuguese sense of mission, the man of duty, the qualities of manliness and nobility.

lessness. Few shoulders were ever broad enough to take the total load of a far-flung empire wobbling on the stalk of a nation of less than two million people (only nine million today). It was hard enough for Portugal to have to protect her sovereignty against her next-door neighbour, Spain, and to lose it to her for sixty years in the sixteenth and seventeenth centuries.[1] But that was not all. If the vaunted 'civilizing mission' seemed to achieve so little in Africa for so long, it was partly because the Portuguese were having to fight for survival on too many fronts. All the discovered lands were threatened at various times by Dutch, Spanish, Danish, German and English ambition. The Moors harried Portugal out of North Africa. One by one the Eastern possessions were whittled away. With the initial uprush of newly-found wealth, the national moral fibre at home had weakened. Then came the age of reason to challenge the older traditions. In Portugal, Pombal's despotic reforms attempted to marry liberal thought to a form of monarchical absolutism. His imaginative but alien institutions barely survived him,[2] but he left an indelible mark on his country's history. As Prime Minister, he virtually ruled the country from 1750 to 1777, rebuilt Lisbon after the earthquake of 1755, and some years later repelled a Franco-Spanish invasion with 15,000 men, a third of the enemy force.

Pombal was the product of a curious blend of influence: Anglican, Jansenist, English (economics), French (philosophy), and German (politics). But he never forgot his country's two-thirds dependence on British trade. He was both anti-clerical and anti-Catholic. His decision to expel the Jesuits[3] came shortly after the tragedy of the Paraguayan 'Reductions',[4] but was essentially an assault on Jesuit ultramontanism, the Society's conservative hold on education, as at Coimbra, and the Jesuits' role as 'the pope's men'. Jansenism was reactionary but it was also nationalistic, and as such it left its

---

[1] 1580-1640. With Europe splitting apart in the Reformation, Philip II of Spain wanted to ensure that the peninsula was 'solid' before the coming showdown with England. It was during the period of Spanish suzerainty over Portugal that he launched the Armada. In spite of the ensuing disaster, half his ships returned to Spain. They were, as Sir Winston Churchill was to notice, Portuguese built.
[2] J. Smith: *Memoirs of the Marquis de Pombal*, London, 1845; and João De Saldanha Oliveira e Sousa, *O Marques de Pombal, sua vide e morte cristã*, Lisbon, 1934.
[3] Carlos J. Menezes, *Os Jesuitas e O Marques de Pombal*, Porto, 1893; and Salvador R. de Madariaga, *Cuadro Histórico de las Indias*, Buenos Aires, 1950.
[4] R. B. Cunninghame-Graham, *A Vanished Arcadia, being some account of the Jesuits in Paraguay, 1607-1767*, London, 1901.

mark on Pombal. His chief aim was to let in some of the fresh ideas blowing across the Channel from English liberalism and over the Pyrenees from French revolutionary thought, but to adapt them to Portugal's specific needs. In effect, he was to uproot his country's traditions and modernize its intellectual life, with a new stress on science in the universities. Elbowing the aristocracy out of the way, he sought to establish a new prosperity based on the middle class, but he also set up large undertakings to supervise whole sectors of the economy. His schemes did not outlive him because they had been transplanted without due regard for Portuguese psychology, and simply failed to take root.[1] From this time on, Portugal was enfeebled by her inability either to synthesize the old traditions with the new, or to decide which she wanted; while England could not forgive, and has never really forgiven her for not embracing the English liberal forms. Thus the Anglo-Saxon, Protestant, liberal mind and the partly Latin, Catholic and dogmatic mind of Portugal have never really met.

Wellington freed Portugal from Napoleon's forces, having praised the resistance of the Portuguese as they fell back, burning their crops as they went, to the lines of Torres Vedras. But the Napoleonic invasion had wrecked the country's industry and arrested its rural development. The century had started with a favourable balance of trade, but by the end of the wars, Portugal was in steep financial decline, and did not recover for more than a century. The Treaty of Vienna (1815) did nothing for her either, and there followed a phase of unrest as thrones toppled and rival constitutions set the scene for political strife throughout the nineteenth century. Drawing their inspiration from the French Constitution of 1791, the Portuguese 'Septembrists' imposed one of their own on King João VI in 1822. In the same year, Brazil declared her independence under Emperor Pedro, João's son. Four years later, on João's death, Pedro became king of Portugal too, but stayed in Brazil. He gave Lisbon a new, more liberal Charter, drafted with the aid of Sir Charles Stuart and fostered by a group known as the 'Chartists', and abdicated his Portuguese throne in favour of his seven-year-old daughter Maria. She was ousted in 1828 by her reactionary uncle, Miguel, to whom she had been engaged. Five years later, Pedro lost his Brazilian throne, drove Miguel out of Lisbon with British aid, and, on Pedro's

---

[1] Pattee, pp. 145 *et seq.*

death in 1834, Maria became queen of Portugal again. Miguelists, Chartists and Septembrists continued to vie with each other for power, and it was a sign of the times that between 1839 and 1851 as many as eighteen colonial ministers were appointed. The second half of the century saw a regrouping of forces among the *Regeneradores* (a mixture of Chartists and Septembrists), the *Progresistas* (radical Chartists), and the Republicans.

In the first half of the nineteenth century, republicanism stood for an attitude, not a programme, and often meant no more than liberalism. Such trends, in fact, had fostered the constitutional monarchy. Republicanism strictly so-called came into its own with the wave of revolutions that marked the Europe of 1848. The concept was never a natural growth in Portugal, but was imported by a lively intellectual minority, alive to what was going on in the outside world. Two attempts to establish a Republican Party, in 1848 and 1873, were short-lived. It was only after the impetus given to European republicanism by the fall in France of the Emperor Louis Napoleon had made some headway that Portugal's Republican Party was firmly set up in 1881. It has been argued that Portugal adapted European revolutionary models whose spirit was alien to the Portuguese peasantry, and that in 1910 the Republic was foisted on an unwilling nation. It might be fairer to say that the experiment failed initially because it was planted in soil unprepared to receive it. The overall levels of education were low. The intellectuals themselves were enthused with noble theories and ideals, but lacked the leadership quality. As administrators they were just non-starters. Among them were men of whom Portugal could be proud, but there were also factions and corruption. With the monarchy plainly past hope, some attempt at radical change was needed. The tragedy is that the concept outstripped the achievement.

There were various strains of thought at work in the anti-Monarchist groups in the latter half of the nineteenth century. Marxism had its place, but, as Richard Pattee writes in his history of Portugal,[1] the minds of mid-nineteenth century Portuguese thinkers like Alexandre Herculano were moulded by Kantian rationalism, which ruled out the dogmatic metaphysics identified with traditional Christian philosophy. It allowed for a belief in freedom, immortality and God which was rationally legitimate, but scientifically

[1] Pattee, *op. cit.*, p. 176. See also Oliveira Martins, *Portugal contemporaneo*, ii, p. 308.

indemonstrable, and Kant opened up for his age a world-view in which science, morals and religion could be harmonized. As regards the social order, the Portuguese historian Oliveira Martins[1] was less interested in Marxism and collectivism than in a form of non-violent Proudhonism, envisaging the fusion of bourgeoisie and proletariat in a new social class. Meanwhile, Romanticism had fostered a minority dream of Iberian unity, a federal arrangement for the Spanish regions and Portugal, and the same idea appealed to Antero de Quental, the revolutionary poet who saw his country's independence as an 'unnecessary amputation . . . from the great body of the Iberian peninsula'.[2] He had been inspired by Proudhon, Hegel and Michelet, and by the Spanish Revolution of 1868. For him, the mission of the bourgeoisie, the establishment of freedom and industrial order, had been completed. The next stage called for militant socialism, based on justice and equality, with radical economic reform. One of the most important strains in the rich creative writing of this period was that of the realist school, the *vencidos da vida*, who reflected the pessimistic streak never far from the Portuguese surface. Oliveira Martins was among them, and he attacked the memory of the golden age of discovery. For this provocative mind, the memory spelled rapine and pillage, harsh conquest, greed and ambition, recklessness and exploitation, an abiding delusion of grandeur. Abuses had been attacked at the time by St Francis Xavier and others. Three hundred years later the theme was revived by Ramalho Ortigão and Eça de Queiroz, for whom a patriotism blind to historical truth was at best a fossilized survival.[3] Not all Republicans shared or share this view, but it has been an element in the opposition to Salazar's policies, and at the turn of the century was a powerful stick to beat the traditional Church and monarchy with.

In the second half of the century, England began to cast her eye on those parts of her ally's African colonies which, in her view, the Portuguese had not effectively occupied, and a dispute over two islands in the bay of Lourenço Marques had to be arbitrated, in Portugal's favour, by President MacMahon of France. In 1884-5, the Treaty of Berlin formally established the 'effective occupation

[1] *Historia de regime republicano em Portugal*, edited by Luis de Montalvor; vol. i, p. 246.
[2] Fryer and McGowan Pinheiro, *Oldest Ally*, Dobson, London, 1961 (henceforth Fryer and McGowan Pinheiro), pp. 243-9.
  Pattee, *op. cit.*, pp. 173-83.

principle, and made inroads into Portuguese territory by setting up the Congo Free State. Portugal, however, at that time was engaged in a phase of renewed exploratory energy which led to the expeditions, deep into southern Africa, of Andrade Corvo, Camelo and Ivens, Augusto Cardoso and Serpa Pinto. The Portuguese wanted the territories linking Angola and Mozambique, but Cecil Rhodes acquired the Mashonaland concession from Lobengula, Lord Salisbury issued his famous ultimatum to Lisbon, and in 1891 the disputed region became the Rhodesias. The new generation of administrators in Angola and Mozambique reached its high-water mark in the 1890s. Many of these men were authoritarian Monarchists, and some distinguished themselves by putting down native resistance. But their ultimate aims were humane enough, and genuine efforts were made to establish a Christian civilization. The great names of the period were Freire de Andrade, Paivo Couceiro, João de Almeida, António Enes, Eduardo Ferreira da Costa, and the greatest of them all, Mousinho Albuquerque. His programme included agrarian reform, health and hospital services, communications and infrastructures. Frustrated at every turn by the ruling clique in Lisbon, he finally lost heart, resigned and killed himself. In 1899, England concluded a secret pact with Germany to offer loans to Portugal on the security of her African territories. A neat device for getting hold of Angola and Mozambique, it was frustrated by the outbreak of the Boer War. In this campaign, England secured her ally's support through Mozambique by threatening a blockade, and the Treaty of 1899 reaffirmed the earlier ones of 1642 and 1661, while England pledged herself to defend Portugal's colonies, present and future.

At home, the monarchy was waning fast and the country was in confusion. Between 1828 and 1859 the national debt had grown from 40,000 contos to three times as much, and a chronic deficit set in. To pay these debts, a further 320,000 contos was borrowed between 1853 and 1892. By 1890 imports were double the value of exports. Then came the disastrous tobacco loan, the Barings called in their Portuguese credits, gold payments on the Bank of Portugal's notes were suspended. Speculative buying of foreign securities fanned the flames. The floating debt rose from 23,000 to 83,000 contos in the eighteen years before 1910, while the fiduciary circulation rose by 42,640 contos.[1] As Portugal moved into the twentieth century,

---

[1] Egerton, pp. 117-22; and Araujo Correia, *Portugal economico e financeiro*.

the forces of republicanism, freemasonry (with its militant Carbonaria), and anti-clerical agnosticism combined to attack the
Establishment. There were demands for suppression of the religious
orders, and again the Jesuits were selected for special treatment.
Republican leaders included António José de Almeida, Afonso
Costa, Alexandre Braga, and João de Menezes, who bore the
Republican theme to the working-class, combining it adroitly with
an appeal to class struggle. A patriarchal character was given to the
movement by Bernardino Machado, a former professor of Coimbra
and Minister of the Crown. He favoured a quiet revolution, in which
the Republicans would form a government and ease the monarchy
out of the picture gently.[1] But events were to overtake him. Unrest,
confusion and disorder were spreading fast. The Monarchists were
divided between the *regeneradores*, who supported the virtual dictatorship of João Franco, and the *progresistas* who aimed at a constitutional
reform arising from the will of the people, not bestowed from the
throne; but the latter group became more and more identified with
the forces of disorder. In 1908 the Carbonaria went to the heart of
the matter and murdered King Carlos and his elder son. Two years
later, bowing to events he could not control, Manuel II left the
country for England, and on 5 October 1910, the Portuguese
Republic was proclaimed.

[1] *De monarchia para e república*, Coimbra, 1912.

CHAPTER 2

The Formation

As the Republic 'arrived' in Lisbon, Salazar was beginning his scholastic career at Coimbra University, where he studied in the faculty of law. When the new Constitution was proclaimed, his fellow students rioted with delight, smashed up the *Sala dos Capelos* and riddled the pictures of Portugal's kings with bullets. Though Salazar was never an ardent Monarchist, he was, as an ex-seminarian, out of tune with the prevalent fashion in agnostic anti-clericalism. He was often seen on his own, book in hand, pacing up and down in the traditional Coimbra cloak which, once bought, was never replaced. The student's proud status symbol, it acquired honour with age, frayed edges and tatters, and for Salazar it became a kind of shell. He broke out of it once to protest against the conversion of a university church to the purposes of a museum, but consistently refused to join the Monarchist Party or any other. The law faculty was versatile, and he studied economics and public administration. To assist his scanty funds, he gave lessons in a curious school, the *Colegio de Via Sacra*, modelled by Canon Barreiros on English pedagogical principles.

Some years later, he was to write in *My Reply* that 'the superiority of the Anglo-Saxon, so strikingly demonstrated during the European War (1914-18), has to be ascribed to certain fundamental elements in his upbringing'. Portugal, he maintained, needed comparable education to develop a public spirit, a concern for the commonweal. Her difficulties were rooted, not in systems of government, but rather in the need to change men. Intellectual training was not enough. A harmonious development of the total personality was required. This theme of 'changing men' was becoming habitual to him. He had caused a mild sensation at Viseu, when he was only twenty, by a speech which indicted the pessimistic trend in Portuguese life and letters. His theme was the nobility of patriotism, the folly of defeatism. He attacked what he called *empregomania* (literally, the decadent pessimists, the prophets of dissolution, who were bent on extinguishing hopes of the country's regeneration).

While his philosophical background was Thomist, in terms of current thought he came under two main influences: the social teachings of Pope Leo XIII, and the *Action Française* of Charles Maurras. Leo's *Rerum Novarum* is usually called the workers' charter because it argued for the right to strike and the just family wage. More surprisingly, in an age of *laissez-faire* economics when the Church was seen as the patron of privilege, it was also a charter for state intervention, and as such was rejected by certain reactionary bishops. Unlike Marx, Leo did not believe that the total fabric of society was crumbling or that the lessons of experience were irrelevant. He called, not for violent revolution, but for control: it was the duty of those with political authority to see that justice was done, especially to the poorer classes. The solution to problems of private property was, not to abolish, but to share it equitably, and ensure that everyone had some. A capitalism based on belief in *absolute* property rights was as atheistic in practice as Communism in theory; the one ignored God while the other defied him, and between the two blasphemies there was nothing to choose. Capitalism was not evil, but could produce evil. The state was not inherently oppressive, but could oppress. Both had to be recalled to their proper function: the effective service of all the people. In general, private property was important to the fulfilment of human personality, and was also the best way of ensuring a decent living for all, but it should be controlled as to its nature, extent and use by the rulers of the state who had the care of the common good as their first and overriding obligation.

There were limits to the state's right of intervention, however. This theme was to be clarified in a later encyclical, *Quadragesimo Anno*, written in 1931 by Pope Pius XI, and which was to have even more importance for Salazar. It established the doctrine of subsidiarity: the state should not arrogate to itself any functions which can be as well or better performed by subordinate social bodies (an example would be that nationalization is justified only as a last resort when the common good can be served in no other way). Leo warred on uncontrolled industrial capitalism, Pius on financial imperialism. Both attacked what they saw as the dehumanization of the people through the more aggressive forms of atheistic socialism: the enslavement of human personality to an amorphous collectivity in which personal rights were sunk without trace.

The right-wing French movement, known as *Action Française* and associated with Charles Maurras, was a very different matter, though some of its content seemed to accord with Leonine teaching. It was an *intégriste* system of thought, a reaction against the French Republic and nineteenth-century liberalism. It was not a religious movement, and Maurras was an unbeliever. But it stood for austerity and the family virtues, a paternalistic view of society, and a social discipline which in principle contrasted with the confusion actually reigning in Portugal. It was, however, in conflict with current Catholic social teaching.

Leo XIII had been putting pressure on French Catholics to accept the Republic. His argument was that, although Christians were free to choose whatever political system they liked, they were bound to accept, without reserve, the authority of established governments, especially those which were elected democratically. In the encyclical *Immortale Dei*, he defended the sovereign rights of Church and State, each in its own sphere, and was moving in fact towards a Christian pluralist concept. Years later, in 1922, Pius XI condemned Maurras's movement for asserting that monarchy was the only legitimate form of government, and later, the French Jesuit Cardinal Billot was virtually stripped of his office for supporting it. Salazar, however, was preoccupied with the need for social order in the face of a chaotic situation, and, while not a Monarchist, his shelves were filled with the works of French right-wing authors. He was also affected by the *integralismo lusitano* of António Sardinha, whose aims were supra-political: the creation of an organic monarchy, traditionalist and anti-parliamentarian. Up to a point it accorded with Salazar's growing distrust of party strife as the author of Portugal's troubles, and eventually his suspicion of the party system as such.

He became a member of a non-party, Catholic movement known as the Academic Centre of Christian Democracy, which refused the title 'royal' and was attacked by left and right alike. He rejected the Monarchists because they opposed the doctrines of Pope Leo, and was out of sympathy with the main Catholic party because of its monarchical tendencies. At this time he was a frequent contributor to journals concerned with social studies, and especially to the weekly *O Imparcial*, directed by his friend Manuel Gonçalves Cerejeira, who later became Cardinal Patriarch of Lisbon.[1]

---

[1] P. D'A., *op. cit.*, pp. 19-20.

In May 1914 he made a speech at Oporto on the Church and Democracy which started a riot. The *form* of government, he said, was of secondary importance. Democracy was a historical phenomenon and was now irresistible. It could also be harmonized with Catholicism. But the nation needed instruction and education for this, and the government machine needed adaptation to conditions of time and place. Democracy became demagogy when it gave privileges to one class at the expense of another.[1] Delivered at a time when the new democratic republic was proving its repressive ineptitude, the speech caused a rumpus. Nevertheless, the local press noted the speaker's impeccable style and wide-ranging intelligence, and described him as 'one of the most powerful minds of the new generation'. Later that year he obtained his licentiate of law with 19 marks out of 20, and joined the university staff. The pay was scanty, and he had to give private tuition to eke it out. He declined to take a part-time advisory post in business as this, he said, would have taken up time he needed to plan his lectures. In 1917 he became assistant lecturer in the university's department of economics, and he published, during this period, three important studies which were remembered a decade later. First came *The Gold Agio; its nature and causes (1891-1915)*; then *The Problem of Wheat Production*; and finally *Some Aspects of the Commodity Crisis*. Coimbra gave him his doctorate in May 1918.

Between 1915 and 1928 he lived *en république* with Cerejeira and de Figueiredo, which meant that they shared an apartment and expenses, and were cared for by a little maid called Maria, who later followed Salazar to Lisbon and has been with him ever since. They were joined from time to time by others, including the future professor of mathematics, Diogo Pacheco de Amorim, who was to acquire an international reputation. He remembers Salazar as a quiet companion, sitting in a corner, often content to listen while the others argued, inserting a sobering comment here and there. Externally cold, always reserved, often alone, Salazar was yet never without friends, and his relationships were deep with unspoken affection. He remained prim: he was, for example, shocked to the core by the 'vulgar' suggestion that a public appeal should be made for funds to keep *O Imparcial* going, and he provoked his friend Diogo to language that has certainly never been used to him since. A friend who burst

1 Egerton, *op. cit.*, p. 105.

into his room without knocking came in for very short shrift. 'I might,' said the scandalized Salazar, 'have been disrobing.' If none of these incidents broke a friendship it was because of the sheer impossibility of ignoring Salazar. There was more to it than his intellectual power, absorbing though it was. From early years he seemed to acquire a curious hold over people, his students more than any. His manner was undramatic. What he said came out flatly, softly, didactically. His irony was not always kind. Yet those who were close to him seemed to over-react in his favour, just as those he excluded seemed to react with disproportionate bitterness. A little irreverent rough and tumble might have helped him, but Salazar's friendship had its practical side which was patently hard to resist. Towards the end of the First World War, Pacheco de Amorim fell dangerously ill. Everyone came to see him – except Salazar, who presumably feared an emotional scene. He wrote, instead, a note: 'I have a little money in a drawer. It is for you. You can repay it in the future if you like.' The last sentence probably meant: 'Don't die.' It was to the unpredictable moments in this creature of habit that people surrendered.

At this stage of his life, Salazar's solitary love affair ended. He was far from blind to feminine charm, as Cerejeira has testified in a penetrating summary of the contrasts which have baffled every student of Salazar's character:

Salazar walked on a straight road, oblivious of side turnings. He was a man for great issues, also for small detail. In his youth he had already developed his tenacity of will, his high intelligence and his absolute calm. Those of us who knew him recall his rare capacity for objectivity in discussion. He had the art of outlining a theme with fine irony, but was scornful of eloquence. Now, as then, he starts a thing with a timid gesture, hesitates before committing himself, needs to feel he is supported. But then he throws himself into action. I have never observed such contrasts in a man. He appreciates the company of women and their beauty, yet leads the life of a monk. Scepticism and zest, pride and modesty, distrust and confidence, the most disarming kindness and at times the most unexpected hardness of heart – all are in constant conflict within him.[1]

Salazar fell in love with the daughter of the estate-owners his father worked for; the parents were also the young scholar's patrons. One

[1] P. D'A., *op. cit.*, p. 28.

version is that the mother saw Salazar dancing with her daughter and decided that things had gone far enough. The other is that Salazar was tutoring the girl, and, by way of an exercise, told her to write an essay on love. Her mother saw it, and intervened. Salazar, it was felt, was of humble class, and had no future. The association must end. It was the only time his friends saw him cry. Years later, at his father's funeral, he saw the girl again. By this time he was Prime Minister, she was married to someone else. He spoke to her, but not, it seems, to her mother. In later years, his attitude to the family mellowed.

From the comparative shelter of the academic world, Salazar watched the country toss and turn as successive governments rose and fell. The sixteen years of Republican government have been described as a period of 'continual anarchy, government corruption, rioting and pillage, assassinations, arbitrary imprisonment and religious persecution.'[1] During that time, there were 9 presidents, 44 ministries, 25 uprisings, 3 dictatorships, and, between 1920 and 1925, a minimum of 325 bomb incidents.

The first Republican government was formed under President Teofilo Braga, the apostle of positivism and historian of Portuguese literature, with A. J. de Almeida as Minister of the Interior, Bernardino Machado in charge of foreign affairs, and Afonso Costa as Minister of Justice. The latter was, in effect, to dominate the scene in various posts, including the premiership, during the next six years. They were the three main elements in the Republican grouping. De Almeida led the Evolutionists and edited *A Luta*. Afonso Costa led the Democrats and wrote in *O Mundo*. The outstanding independent was Machado Santos, head of the Carbonaria, who wrote in a paper suitably called *Intransigente*.[2] There were many outstanding Republican figures, men of high culture and noble purpose, but lacking in administrative grasp, and forced to work with colleagues who were not in their class.

The enlightened labour legislation for Africa enacted in recent years must trace its genesis to a Republican ancestry first from the Native Labour Code of 1878 (which in theory established a free labour system for Africans), then through the *ultramar* statutes of

[1] S. George West: *The New Corporative State of Portugal*, Lecture at King's College, London, 1937; SPN Books, Lisbon.
[2] Machado Santos, *A Revolução Portuguesa*.

1914, the distinctive contribution to Angola by Norton de Matos, one of its finest governors, and the Native Assimilation Code of 1921. This is still a matter of pride in Portugal, even though the blueprints generously conceived at the time in Lisbon failed in the bush for want of an honest and efficient cadre of colonial officials, backed by a formative tradition. There have, moreover, been few more distinguished ministers of education in Europe than the brilliant man of letters António Sergio, who served under Teixeira Gomes in 1923 and died in 1968 as one of the surviving Republican father-figures.

One of the first moves of the new Republic was to curtail the influence of the Catholic Church.[1] Many bishops were exiled, including the Cardinal Patriarch of Lisbon, the Archbishops of Portalegre and Braga, and the Bishops of Oporto and Beja. The Jesuits and other religious orders were outlawed, likewise religious teaching in schools. It was Afonso Costa's boast that three generations would see the extinction of religion in Portugal. Divorce was introduced, legal status granted to illegitimate children, and the Church disestablished. No papal document could be promulgated without government permission, and the state assumed powers to supervise seminary staffs and textbooks. All Church property was transferred to the state. Protestant missions, which had been working in Portugal at home and overseas since 1885, were further encouraged. Bequests to the Catholic Church were forbidden, and pensions, offered to priests unable to earn their livelihood as such, were subtly aimed at thinning the ranks of the clergy. Most Catholics nowadays prefer separation from the state, and one of the Republic's better ideas was to make parish priests and their parishes wholly dependent on the offerings of the faithful, one-third of which were deducted for state charities. Church and parish administration was committed to the laity in *associações cultuais*, the kind of measure favoured by post-Vatican II progressives. The intention in the Republicans' mind, however, was not to foster the primitive spirit of Christianity, but rather to secularize the Church's institutions and to reduce the Catholic Church to comparative insignificance in the national life. Religion was to be made as 'personal' as possible, so that, lacking social co-ordination, it might gradually wither.[2]

[1] Fortunato de Almeida, *Historia de Igreja em Portugal*, Coimbra, 1920.
[2] Joaquim Maria Lourenço, *Situação Jurídica de Igreja em Portugal*, 1911; Coimbra, 1943.

The leading spirit in all this was Afonso Costa, a freemason of bitterly anti-Catholic persuasion. He was, however, a man of intellect and ability, but ran into trouble very early on when he tried to foster a programme of severe restraint in government spending. There were too many vested interests in the large numbers of sinecure jobs which padded the lives of civil servants unable or unwilling to work in competitive fields. The cafés in the *Rossio*, the best-known Lisbon centre of gossip and political argument, thrived on the wasted hours of officials with nothing to do. It was a mark of the government's lack of integrity that the grace and favour system of public appointments could not be swiftly abolished.

Another serious blot on the record was the treatment of political opponents. Not only Monarchists, but also radical Republicans, were among the unfortunates herded in shocking prison conditions, a source of concern to humanitarian feeling in England. London had been quick to recognize the Republic, if only to counteract the German influences which had played a decisive role in Republican plotting in the Rotunda, the traditional meeting place for the disaffected. But a British national protest was organized over Portugal's political prisoners, and in 1913 a powerful, detailed indictment was published by a group of notables led by the Earl of Lytton, the Duchess of Bedford (who had seen the Portuguese prisons), and many others, including the Hon. Audrey Herbert, M.P., G. M. Trevelyan, the historian, and W. G. Gladstone. The protest alleged that the victims numbered 2,000, all social classes included, and a quarter of them radical Republicans. The issue was raised in the House of Lords and in *The Times, Spectator, Daily Mail*, and *Morning Post*.[1] Evidence had been obtained from the Limoeiro prison and the *Penitenciaria*, from the Aljube prison near the cathedral, and from Terceira in the Azores. Political prisoners were often held for two years without trial. Sentences were long, the jails overcrowded. Convict clothes and cropped hair were prescribed. Food was bad and the cells were damp, medical attention scanty. Prisoners complained of being beset by rats, mice and lice. Punishments included floggings and solitary confinement in tiny cells, dark even in daytime. Prisoners were exposed, on their way to jail from court, to the jeers of the crowd. Women were jailed almost as often as men, and a particularly sad case was that of a young philanthropist, Dona Constança Telles

[1] *Spectator*, London, 8 March 1913.

de Gama, whose main offence seems to have been that she had been running relief services for people in prison and their families. Some of the worst cases included transfer to underground levels of fortresses, and there were those who did not survive, especially when they contracted tuberculosis. Protests about this kind of aggression are almost inevitably exaggerated. Rumour builds on fact, the isolated tragedy is reported in general terms. But when all allowances are made, there is no doubt that there was much arbitrary imprisonment in disgraceful conditions, and that the courts were meting out corrupt justice. The governments replied to foreign protests by assurances that all would be rectified in due time.

During the Republican years the Monarchists made unflagging efforts to unhinge the Republican Constitution. Prominent among the challengers were the old hard-liners of the 'African Generation' of the 1890s, notably Paiva Couceiro. But there were also deep and fatal divisions on the anti-Monarchist side, and the whole story was one of national fragmentation. There was also trouble abroad. Norton de Matos went to govern Angola in 1912. In the same year Britain sent Lord Haldane to Berlin to discuss 'the possibility of a rearrangement of interests in Africa'. Von Turpitz recorded that 'Haldane began to hold out hopes of a great colonial empire in Africa for us . . . exaggerated offers of colonial possessions which did not belong to England and which they had no right to dispose of.'[1] Once again, Portuguese Africa was in peril, and, once again, as in 1899, was saved by the bell, this time by the outbreak of the First World War in 1914. General Pimenta de Castro's government, formed in 1915, lasted four months. He was succeeded by Afonso Costa, and in 1916 Germany declared war on Portugal for impounding German ships at England's request, whereupon Costa sent an expeditionary force to France, where its record was undistinguished.

The end of that year saw the rise of a benevolent dictatorship when Sidónio Pais seized power, exiled President Machado and Norton de Matos, and arrested Afonso Costa. He formed a triumvirate with Feliciano da Costa and Machado Santos, and, though not a Catholic himself, restored relations with the Holy See and eased restrictions on the Church.[2] Sidónio Pais had served in the army and taught mathematics at university level. He had also been Portuguese envoy

[1] Livermore, p. 323.
[2] Cunha e Costa, *A Igreja Católica e Sidónio Pais*, Coimbra, 1921; and *Centro Católico Português*, by A. O. Salazar, Coimbra, 1922.

in Berlin. He was a freemason but moderate, and showed great energy in the face of acute social problems. He is remembered for his continual presence in the hospitals during an epidemic, and his vigorous organization of communal feeding and relief services. He was murdered on 14 December 1918. Strikes, riots, killings and confusion continued to reign. In 1921, António Granjo, then Prime Minister, with several colleagues, was abducted in a 'phantom waggonette' and brutally murdered. Between 1918 and 1926 only one president, A. J. de Almeida, completed his term of office.

After 1920, in fact, the situation became pure farce. The 1925-6 deficit, officially posted as 63,565 contos, was found by Filomena da Câmara to be more than five times as much. Then there was the Waterlow scandal in the early 1920s, when a group of tricksters, with fake Bank of Portugal paper, or possibly stolen originals, induced the British printing firm to produce 580,000 500-escudo banknotes, and launched a spurious bank, the *Banco de Angola e Metropole*, to offload this worthless paper into the national economy. The facts came to light when someone observed notes with duplicate numbers. The bank's surprisingly daring policies had also attracted attention, and it was realized too that the general trend to galloping inflation was growing even more acute than usual. The Bank of Portugal sued Waterlow's, and a House of Lords judgment awarded the bank £600,000 damages. Sinel de Cordes negotiated with Mr Winston Churchill a reduction of Portugal's debt to Britain, but even when this was scaled down to £24 million, Portugal could not pay it.[1] The League of Nations responded favourably to a Portuguese application for a loan of £12 million, little enough when compared with the money lent to nations defeated in the First World War, but only on condition that the League should stage an inquiry into Portugal's state finances and into the Bank of Portugal. This, in spite of the country's problems, was refused with some dignity by General Ivens Ferraz.

By 1926 the cost-of-living was thirty times its 1914 level. The currency was down to $\frac{1}{33}$ of its par value: the escudo, in fact, worth 4s. 5d. in 1891, was down to 2d. in 1925. The 1917-28 deficits totalled 2,574,000 contos as against a surplus of 1,963,000 in the first eleven years of Salazar's policies.[2] In the seven years prior to 1926, the fiduciary circulation rose from 87,767 contos to 791,024. In the

[1] Jesus Pabon, *La revolución portuguesa*, vols. i and ii, Madrid, 1941 and 1945.
[2] Pattee, *op. cit.*, p. 202; also *A obra de Salazar na pasta das finanças*, Lisbon, 1941.

Republic's first decade, prices multiplied by twelve times, wages by four and a half times. The whole period of open politics, both under the monarchy and afterwards, gave the country an important corpus of thought and writing, without which Portugal's literary record would have been much impoverished; but, from where Salazar viewed the situation at Coimbra, it seemed that Portugal was far from ready for a viable system of party government.

In 1919, Salazar and three of his colleagues had been suspended from teaching. They were charged with using their positions to insinuate Monarchist ideas in their students. Salazar prepared his defence in the form of a statement called *My Reply*, which, in places, was extremely cutting:

> No one can point to any known occurrence which could justify them in forming an opinion about my political convictions. I have never been condemned, judged, pronounced on, investigated or jailed. Not even jailed – and this is indeed remarkable when, in the course of a few years, half the population of Portugal – Monarchists, Catholics, Democrats, Evolutionists, Camachists, Syndicalists, Socialists, Sidonists, and those with no views at all – have entered the prisons and fortresses of the Republic, sometimes successively, sometimes alternately, and sometimes simultaneously.

His abstention from political activity was not due to lack of concern:

> I am convinced that politics alone can never solve the great problems calling for solution today, and that it is a grave mistake to expect everything to happen either as a result of political evolution or because of an arbitrary departure from the normal course of evolutionary politics. I am sure that the solution is to be found more in each one of us than in the political colour of a ministry. So far as I can, I try to make my students men. . . . Now men who are genuinely serious and studious do not confine themselves in an enclosed system of thought, ignoring or despising the progress of human intelligence, refusing to recognize . . . the facts of our own day, however greatly these may conflict with our own ideas and our most cherished convictions.[1]

He returned to his habitual theme of the country's need for 'a work of education in the sense of an integral and harmonious development

[1] Egerton, *op. cit.*, pp. 106-7; P. D'A., *op. cit.*, pp. 25-6.

of all the individual's faculties'. His judges were duly impressed, pronounced in flattering terms, and reinstated him.

In 1921 he was persuaded to stand for parliament, though he did so reluctantly and complained to Mario de Figueiredo that he lacked political imagination, and so distrusted himself. He was, however, returned from Guimarães as one of three Catholic deputies, made one appearance in the Chamber, and never returned there. The proceedings struck him as disorderly and futile. In the following year he wrote:

> Any political power which seeks to express itself in a form which truly represents authentic interests must be based on an organization which is not only political but also social, an organization of professions and classes.[1]

He was convinced that party politics had failed. Addressing the Second Congress of the Catholic Centre in Lisbon, he added:

> We are drawing near to that moment in political and social evolution in which a political party based on the individual, the citizen or the elector, will no longer have sufficient reason for its existence. Man in isolation is an abstraction, a fiction mainly created under the influence of the erroneous principles current during the last century.

In other words, liberal individualism had led to a fragmentation of society and a perversion of the democratic process. This was because the party system was based on a concept of man divorced from his social context. Distinct from his immediate and natural grouping, his family or his profession, man has an identity but not, in practice, an existence. The principal points of the address which so well expresses the basis of Salazar's future Constitution, may be summarized in this way:

1. The ultimate foundation of public order and the origin of all legitimate power is not the will of the people, but God. This is true even where democratic elections are held.

2. More immediately, the legitimacy of a government and the force of human law depend, not on the will of the majority, but on the common good.

---

[1] Egerton, *op. cit.*, p. 108.

3. Provided these principles are observed, the Church can accept historical variations in the forms of government, their relative good being conditioned by the circumstances. The Church also recognizes the right of the faithful to choose whatever mode of political organization they prefer.

4. Whatever form the individual Christian prefers, however, he has an explicit duty of unreserved obedience to the established government. Revolution and sedition, save in extreme cases of injustice, are inadmissible.

5. The Church has no rights over the State when the latter is acting within its own political sphere. Even if all the citizens are Catholics, all the Church can ask for is freedom to exercise her apostolate and liberty of worship.[1]

Salazar was, of course, presenting a summary of Leo XIII and Benedict XV, who were anxious to convince governments of the day that the Church had no designs on the political sphere. He was faithful to them, though convinced that there was a diametric contradiction between the people's right to choose their form of government and the subject's duty to obey the state. In later years he was to show himself extremely sensitive to any attempt by the Church or churchmen to judge his policies. As we shall see, the recognition of the two sovereignties of Church and State raised the dilemma of the 'overlap'. What was to happen when both jurisdictions had a stake in the same situation, as when a political issue raised a moral problem? Both Leo and Pius XI were explicit that social and economic questions should 'be brought within our supreme jurisdiction, insofar as they refer to moral issues'.[2] Doubtless Salazar accepted this in principle, but in practice he was to find it hard to distinguish between the Church's licit intervention and what he regarded, with varying degrees of justice, as the groundless interference of churchmen. For the moment, however, his preoccupation was the weakness of democracy as hitherto understood in Portugal. This weakness, as he saw it, was that a minority of the population could achieve sufficient power to overturn the institutions they disliked, whatever the majority felt. Anti-dogmatic democracy had not put an end to destructive strife. A democratic constitution based on the will of the people, and not on immutable principle, was by definition unstable.

[1] P. D'A., op. cit., pp. 30-4.
[2] Rerum Novarum, s.13; Quadragesimo Anno, Part II.

Salazar was speaking more and more freely now. At that time in Portugal, militant young Catholics showed a faith that was more cerebral than devotional, more concerned with social principles than with religious observance. Salazar's observance, however, was assiduous, reflecting no doubt the piety of his home. His contemporaries seem to have taken this for granted. They never questioned its authenticity, nor did they accuse him of confusing piety with pietism. It certainly raised no barrier between them and their punctilious friend.[1] Cerejeira, however, himself destined for orders, had detected the conflict between Salazar's doubts and certainties, his modesty and his pride. Was he, at this time, developing some sense of personal destiny, expecting to be called like a modern Cincinnatus from the fields to save the nation? If he had ambition, he concealed it well; in that context, his reluctant acceptance of office in 1926, his quick return for the second time to his academic shelter, and his strict conditions for returning to office in 1928 were brinkmanship of the coolest order. At Braga, in 1924, he stressed obedience as the path to peace. He rejected the notion that the proletariat produces while other classes are parasitic. There was a hierarchy in the work of production, and

> this hierarchy, the work of invention, organization, direction and actual execution, not only expresses a necessity inherent in material production, but is the image of the inequality imposed by nature upon individual capacity, something society cannot ignore and should not attempt to oppose.[2]

There were two kinds of wealth: egoistical and sacrificial. One was concerned with production for immediate consumption, answering both natural and artificial needs. The other was devoted to the progressive enrichment of the community and depended on foresight and sacrifice, on readiness to forgo the satisfaction of present needs for the sake of the future; in this way new wealth would be created from which the whole community would benefit. This remained a cardinal principle of his economic policy. Sacrifice, work and patience had to be the way to prosperity. The nation could not expect to have what it lacked the cash to pay for. The books must always balance. Living beyond one's means, even to meet the needs

---

[1] Author's conversation with Professor Pacheco de Amorím, November 1968.
[2] Egerton, *op. cit.*, p. 110.

of the poor, would destroy the whole economy and the poor along with it.

Together with this groping for a kind of productive poverty came his perennial anxiety about the relative claims of freedom and authority. At Coimbra, in 1925, Salazar spoke of the need for 'a perfect equilibrium between a necessary authority which is independent of human passion and a social justice which does not vary with the fluctuations of public opinion'. He argued:

A changing will which expresses and imposes itself in different directions endangers the State both as regards fundamental principle and constitution. The stability that is indispensable can be assured only in two ways. Either the State must withdraw itself from the fluctuations of public opinion, and this would be tantamount to a denial of its own position, or it must maintain a public opinion that is stable and consistent so far as the essential part of the doctrine is concerned.[1]

The speech reflects an effort to reconcile liberty and authority, idealism and realism. The difficulty of doing so in a non-party, organic democracy, as Salazar saw his system, is still as acute for his successor as it was for himself.

[1] *Ibid.*, pp. 112-13.

CHAPTER 3

The Invitation

The country's patience with the chaotic economic and political situation was ebbing fast. In the early months of 1925, a number of army and naval officers staged abortive coups. Some of the organizers were caught and arraigned in April, but it was the prosecutor, General Carmona, who asked the court to acquit them. He was a former Minister for War and was later to be President of the Republic. He told the court:

> If we see the authors of the evils from which the country is suffering travelling at large abroad, while here men of such great civic virtue are branded as criminals, there must be something wrong. . . . The country is sick . . .[1]

In February 1926, with Bernardino Machado back as President, the National Assembly paid tribute to the reigning pope, Pius XI, and peace was made once more with the Vatican. But the country's major problems remained unsolved, and groups of officers continued to meet and prepare for an effective revolution. Men like Colonel de Albuquerque, Sinel de Cordes, Raul Esteves, Commandant Filomena da Câmara and Mendes Cabeçadas planned a movement aimed at normalizing national life, defending the legitimate constitutional regime, establishing a government of military men and civilians which would govern the country only until the situation was sane enough to allow for fresh elections. They began to group themselves round General Gomes da Costa, one of the 'African Generation' and commander of the expeditionary force in Flanders during the 1914 War. By 27 May Gomes da Costa was in Braga to direct the uprising in the north, while Carmona went to Evora to move in from the south. Gomes da Costa based himself on the 11th Cavalry Regiment and the 8th and 29th Infantry Regiments. Two lieutenants were sent across Braga by tram to try and secure the aid of General Gomes Peres, commanding the 8th Division, but in vain. Gomes

[1] Egerton, *op. cit.*, p. 99.

Peres tried to stop the uprising, but was turned down flat not only by his own division but also by the Republican Guard. He then went off to Valença to try and raise a loyalist detachment in the Minho Alto to march on Braga. But it was no use.

> The revolutionary junta in Braga described their plan as the formation of a national ministry above and beyond national parties within the framework of the Republic for the purpose of restoring honesty and decency in public administration.[1]

On 28 May, Gomes da Costa issued this proclamation:

> Men of Portugal! To men of dignity and honour the present situation of the country is intolerable. The prey of a corrupt and tyrannical minority, the nation, filled with shame, feels that it is dying. For my part, I declare myself in open revolt. Let men of courage and of worth come to me in arms, if, with me, they are prepared to conquer or die. Portugal, to arms!

Moving into the area held by the 8th Division and finding himself unopposed, Gomes da Costa posted a further declaration:

> The nation . . . wants a strong government whose mission it is to save the fatherland, which concentrates in itself all power but only to restore it, at the proper time, to a truly national representative body: a Republic which is not that of political gangs, but which is concerned for the true interests of the nation, the vital and permanent interests of the nation, the vital and permanent interests of Portugal. . . . At the head of the Portuguese army, united in the same patriotic aspiration, I proclaim the national interest and oppose it to the infamous behaviour of the politicians and the parties, and I will hand over this sick country to a government able to confront her internal enemies with the same fighting heroism she displayed in the face of foreign hostility.[2]

Meanwhile, during the night, sympathizers had been posting a manifesto in Lisbon which pledged the military junta to reform of the public services, taxation, justice, the army, and the overseas territories. By 29 May, Oporto and nearly all the armed forces had turned over to Gomes da Costa. In Lisbon, President Machado accepted the *fait accompli*, invited Mendes Cabeçadas to form a government, abdicated his own office, and left the Palace of Belém on 1 June.

[1] Pabon, *op. cit.*, ii, p. 222.
[2] P. D'A., *op. cit.*, pp. 30-57.

Mendes Cabeçadas, though active in the military plot, was of a different mould from that of Gomes da Costa. He wanted to compromise with the party politicians, but knew there would be trouble over this with the generals. He proposed to retain for himself the posts of Prime Minister, and Minister of Marine, Justice and Culture. Gama Ochoa was to have foreign affairs and education. Gomes da Costa would be Minister for War, for the overseas territories, and for agriculture. This news was brought to Gomes da Costa as he marched towards Lisbon, and he saw the proposals as a move to divert his energies from central issues by loading him with the problems of potato growing. When, therefore, Mendes Cabeçadas met him at Sacavém, an alternative arrangement had to be made. Mendes Cabeçadas would be Prime Minister and Minister of the Interior. Gomes da Costa would take war and overseas territories only. Carmona would be Foreign Minister, while finance would be given to a promising young economist at Coimbra University called Salazar. On 6 June 1926 Gomes da Costa entered Lisbon. Six days later Salazar arrived to assume office as Minister of Finance.

It was on 6 June that the well-known Lisbon journalist António Ferro met the head of the new military junta, General Gomes da Costa, at the air force base of Amadora, a few miles outside the capital. The general was apologetic. 'The new government,' he said, 'is the best we can find at a moment like this. But the Minister of Finance is to be a man called Salazar from Coimbra. Everyone speaks well of him. Do you happen to know him?' The junta, of course, was composed of men who hardly knew a credit from a debit. They had had little or no experience of civil administration, and no respected civil service to rely on. Salazar's name, however, was known. His provocative critiques of the economy had been widely publicized, particularly his studies of the gold standard and wheat production. 'My Reply' had attracted considerable attention, too, and his call for a government above party interests put him solidly on the junta's wavelength. On the strength of his growing reputation and the advice given to the generals by their friends, tentative approaches had been made to Salazar, whose reactions were unenthusiastic. On 11 June a small group of officers drove up to Santa Comba to see him and to put the pressure on him to accept.

At that time, Salazar was staying with his mother, whose health had deteriorated sharply. She had, in fact, only months to live. The officers urged him, nevertheless, to go to Lisbon at once and to

accept the finance portfolio. Mégevand tells us that the ailing Maria
settled his doubts. 'Don't worry about me, son,' she told him. 'If
they've come for you it's because they need you. Accept. The
country's rights come before ours. Leave the rest to God.'[1] The
answer was wholly in character, and the next day Salazar arrived in
Lisbon in the middle of the afternoon, looking decidedly out of place.
Newsmen at the station observed the tall, thin figure, the big ears,
the bushy hair, the dark suit with trousers on the short side, the
watch chain over the waistcoat, the hands deep in the pockets. What
was his programme? Nothing, until he found out what the situation
was. Then he would try to satisfy his questioners' curiosity. He had
been told to come. Here he was. That was all. Salazar went first to the
Ministry of the Interior to see Cabeçadas, then to his own office.
He could hardly have come at a worse time.

The military government was in confusion. Its Monarchist and
Republican elements quarrelled over Gomes da Costa's proposals
for decentralization, the end of individual suffrage, corporative
organization, religious freedom and a restoration of religious teaching
in the schools. The garrison at Oporto was getting restive and
threatening to take action unless the ruling junta took decisive steps
to run the country, while the Sacavém garrison was pushing for
Cabeçadas's removal. Salazar spent five days in Lisbon. An un-
confirmed story is that he returned to Santa Comba after receiving
a phone call from someone who said he was Minister of Finance, the
post which Salazar thought was his. The more probable explanation
is that the government refused to accept his conditions for doing the
job: complete control over all spending, severe cuts in public expenditure, a share in all decisions affecting financial legislation. On
the very day that Cabeçadas gave up the unequal struggle and departed
from office, Salazar had his proposals flatly turned down, partly,
perhaps, because the government did not want to be inhibited in the
disposal of favours to those who had helped them into power.
After the refusal, Salazar asked a messenger when the next train for
Coimbra would be leaving. In two hours, he was told. He was on
the train.[2]

Gomes da Costa failed to cope with the mountainous problems
facing him. They were not a soldier's task and by 7 July he found
himself deposed and packed off to the Azores. He was later allowed

[1] Mégevand, *op. cit.*, p. 68.
[2] P. D'A., *op. cit.*, pp. 45-55.

to come back, promoted to marshal, allotted a state pension, and put out to grass. Meanwhile, in July, Carmona had taken over as acting president, but the country continued to flounder.

Salazar may well have realized that the government, or its successor, would have to come back to him. At any rate, he had no intention of working under impossible conditions and being blamed for what he could not control. He returned to his university work and was with his mother when she died on 17 November 1926. In the following summer he went to Liège for a meeting of the Jociste movement, Father (later Cardinal) Cardijn's Young Christian Workers, travelling by way of Lourdes and Paris, which enchanted him. He was to say, years later, that, had his mother lived, he could not have remained long in office: 'She could not have lived without me, and I was unable to work when I felt she was unhappy.'[1] But now Maria had died, and Salazar published an article in *Novidades* based on what he had learned of the national accounts during his days in the Ministry. On 28 March 1927, he made his famous speech on the 'Two Economies': one which regards financial success as the chief end of human activity, the other which professes to despise wealth and confuses virtue with poverty. Both positions were unsound. It was not production that corrupted people, but mistakes and lack of balance in consumption. The solution was the creation of wealth through hard work; the regulation of consumption in the light of man's moral, as well as physical and intellectual development; and judicious saving in both production and consumption. A morality of consumption needed to be devised. Public opinion was all too prone to criticize the burden of taxation and not the errors made in the spending of the revenue thus acquired. As to private consumption, public opinion seemed to have nothing to say at all. The attitude that a man could lawfully do what he liked with what was his own led to irrational consumption, with the same effect on the nation as the same approach on a housewife's part would have on the family.

In these early references to the domestic virtues of thrift, hard work and self control, Salazar was mounting his offensive against the endemic Iberian tendency to conceive expensive and elaborate schemes before attending to essential needs.[2] His own work was to start with a programme of infrastructures, without which the economy could not move, but these were to be strictly productive,

[1] P. D'A., *op cit.*, pp. 55-6.
[2] Egerton, *op. cit.*, pp. 115-17.

national necessities and not prestigious luxuries. Fifteen years later, António Sergio dismissed the achievement as 'propaganda, motor roads *de luxe*, budget surpluses and historic commemorations.'[1] Yet, without the roads and the surpluses, nothing at all could have happened. Critics like Cunha Leal, in fact, were making the reverse complaint that the policy was dull and unimaginative, but Salazar asked to be judged by the houses, jobs and rising new industries which were there to show that the policy, so far, had worked. It was in the post-war years that his critics more justly asserted that the thrift had been prolonged too far and was stunting the nation's growth.

Early in 1927 disorders broke out throughout Portugal. Eighty people were killed in Oporto, with 360 injured, while 100 died in Lisbon. Six hundred people were exiled. The revolution, initiated without a shot being fired, was plainly going wrong. On 25 March 1928, Carmona was confirmed as President of the Republic (he served three full seven-year terms, and died during his fourth term in 1951). If the movement was not to fail, he had to take some swift action. The government began to think again about Salazar. Salazar had made a strong impression on the ministers he had met in 1926, and while his conditions had seemed unacceptable at that time, it began to look, on reflection, as though he had had a point. His subsequent articles on the public accounts had also been widely read and commended – and there was nobody else to turn to. Carmona decided to try again, and Duarte Pacheco, soon to emerge as a brilliant Minister of Public Works, was sent to Coimbra to try to bring Salazar back. Salazar asked for a night to think it over, spent part of it on his knees like a squire on the vigil of knighthood, talked at length to Cerejeira, and served Mass in the morning for his confessor, Fr Crawley-Boevey.[2] In later years he told Christine Garnier:

> I hesitated all night. I did not know if I should accept the proposition that had been made to me. I was terribly depressed at the idea of leaving the University. I was fully aware of the distance between the man of study and the man of action. And then, I was afraid . . . naturally I was afraid. I foresaw the possibility of failure. Imagine, if I had failed to put the finances in order, what would my students have thought of me?[3]

[1] Preface to Gilberto Freyre's *O mundo que o Português criou*.
[2] Mégevand, *op. cit.*, p. 190.
[3] Garnier, p. 63; P. D'A., *op. cit.*, p. 59.

Eventually, he decided to go. He arrived in Lisbon on 27 April, eve of his thirty-ninth birthday, and this time started work on his own terms. To make this apparent, he made a speech at his installation which described his decision as

> such a great sacrifice that I could never have undertaken it just for the sake of obliging someone. It is a sacrifice which I am willing to make for my country, in serene and calm discharge of a conscientious duty.

Even so, he laid down his conditions, and a working arrangement was reached with the rest of the government. There were four points:

1. That each government department shall undertake to limit and to organize its services within the total amount allotted to it by the Ministry of Finance.

2. That any measures adopted by the various government departments which may directly affect the state's receipts and expenditure shall be discussed beforehand and an agreement arrived at with the Ministry of Finance.

3. That the Ministry of Finance shall be entitled to place its veto on all increases of current or ordinary expenditure, as well as on expenditure for development purposes, for which the necessary credit operations shall not be undertaken without the knowledge of the Ministry of Finance.

4. That the Ministry of Finance undertakes to collaborate with the other departments in such measures as may be adopted for the reduction of expenditure or collection of revenue, which will be organized as far as possible on uniform principles.[1]

That this rudimentary piece of common sense could have created traumas in the minds of certain ministers is the clearest index of the mess the country was in. Salazar promised to keep the country fully informed, but added a couple of sentences which left no one in any doubt about the man they were dealing with:

> I know quite well what I want and where I am going, but let no one insist that the goal should be reached in a few months. For the rest, let the country study, let it suggest, let it object, and let

[1] D & A, pp. 43-5.

it discuss, but when the time comes for me to give orders, I shall expect it to obey.[1]

Lest Catholics should think they had any special claim on him, Salazar had already told *Novidades*:

Tell the Catholics that the sacrifice I have made gives me the right to expect that they of all Portuguese, will be the first to make the sacrifices I may ask of them, and the last to ask for favours which I cannot grant.[2]

Two weeks after assuming office, Salazar issued a decree outlining the principles on which he intended to work:

Unity of the budget, that is, a single total of receipts and a single total of expenditure. This serves as a guarantee of the accuracy of the balance.

The ordinary expenditure of the state to be completely covered by ordinary revenue.

The concept of extraordinary expenditure to be restricted; any recourse to loans to cover such expenditure to be rigorously limited.

Control of payments on account of work completed.

Civil and penal responsibility of heads of departments for expenditure beyond that legally authorized.

No state financing of any private enterprise.

Suppression of the *ad valorem* tax which was embarrassing economic life by multiplying excise duties.

Defence of the budget against the pressure of colonial finances.

Obligation placed on self-governing bodies, local authorities and the colonies to balance their normal expenditure with their normal revenue.[3]

Normality was the word. The decree was so commonplace that the public found it hard to take seriously. Yet the truth is that these simple propositions had been ignored, because of corruption or muddle-headedness, for many years. The recuperative measures

[1] *Ibid.*
[2] *Novidades*, 27 April 1928.
[3] Egerton, *op. cit.*, pp. 124-5.

Portugal needed called for character and clear thinking rather than economic vision.

Public opinion changed as results became apparent. Salazar achieved a surplus in his first year – having promised it for the second – by pruning expenditure and applying new taxes.[1] In the eleven years preceding his appointment, the nation's deficits totalled 2,574,000 contos. Between 1928 and 1939, Salazar achieved total surpluses of 1,963,000 contos, then equivalent to about £20 million. This was devoted to public works, social assistance, re-armament, communications, ports, irrigation, hydro-electric schemes, and education. Extraordinary expenditure for that period[2] shows how Salazar saw his order of priorities:

	Contos
Repayment of national debt	613,843
Increase in national patrimony	86,175
Works and buildings (including hospitals and schools)	138,459
Roads, harbours, agricultural works and rural improvement	1,077,204
Colonial development	35,845
Social welfare (cheap housing)	68,444
Defence	860,093
Miscellaneous	376,106

It was in relation to the national debt and the building up of reserves that Salazar showed the more sophisticated side of his thinking,[3] and won European applause – Mr S. George West, lecturer in Portuguese in London University, referred to him in 1937 as 'one of the greatest finance ministers in modern times'.[4] The fact was that Portugal had come through the world depression relatively unscathed. In the seventeen years prior to 1927, the national debt had risen from 692,000 contos to 7,449,000, a third of it floating. Many loans had been negotiated under widely varying conditions, and nominal values bore little relation to reality. Salazar set himself

[1] Egerton, op. cit., pp. 125-33.
[2] Ibid., p. 126.
[3] A obra de Salazar na pasta das finanças, op. cit., pp. 50-1; Reports on the Economic and Commercial Conditions of Portugal: Department of Overseas Trade, London series; also Colonel Tomás Wylie Fernandes: President Oliveira Salazar's Record, Lisbon, 1939.
[4] S. George West, 'The New Corporative State of Portugal', a lecture at King's College, London, 1937, published by SPN Books, Lisbon.

to rationalize the muddle, partly by a series of conversion operations. By 1934 the floating debt was extinguished, and the overall total greatly reduced. Interest paid by the state fell from 6¾ to 3¼ per cent, gold reserves built up sufficiently to form a 30 per cent backing for the note issue, and foreign exchange balances began to accumulate. As public confidence grew, capital deployed abroad was gradually repatriated. The need to borrow dwindled, and with it the need for foreign exchange to pay debt charges. Some of the conversions involved no reduction in the interest payable, but the conversion in 1934 of the 6½ per cent gold loan of 1923 to a 4¾ per cent escudo loan reduced debt charges on about £8 million by £140,000 a year. By 1940 much of the external debt had already been returned to Portugal, and more than 80 per cent was now owned by Portuguese nationals or foreigners resident in Portugal.

But interest still had to be paid in foreign exchange, and to avoid this Salazar converted the appropriate bonds to a new consolidated escudo loan. To stimulate new initiatives and the purchase of new equipment, he altered the taxation system so as to lay the charge on average, rather than actual, profits. To make more credit available for productive investment, he reorganized the *Caixa Geral de Depositos*, a National Savings Bank, whose lending potential had been almost wholly absorbed by government access to 99 per cent of its funds. Salazar prescribed that the amount available for government use should be restricted to 22 per cent, and he opened two further institutions: the *Caixa Nacional de Credito* and the *Caixa Nacional de Previdência*. Between 1928 and 1934, voluntary deposits in the *Caixa*, now authorized to issue bonds, increased by £8½ million.

When there was enough gold available to back the note circulation, Portugal returned to the gold standard in July 1931, but when Britain abandoned it in the following September, Salazar devalued the escudo to keep in line with the pound. The connection between the two currencies was formally abandoned, and by 1939 the rate of exchange had been brought down from 110 (escudos to the £ sterling) to 100, where it was stabilized. Meanwhile, a national campaign to boost wheat production had been launched in 1929. Shortages had been costing the country 200,000 contos a year and the import figure for 1929 itself was £3½ million. Within a few years, Portugal had become self-sufficient in wheat, and special commissions had been established to supervise the growth of the fruit, sardines, rice and other export industries. With growing financial stability, a fifteen-year, £60-million plan was launched in 1936 to cover defence, communications, transport, colonial credit, education and other public services. At that time Salazar was able to say: 'We are doing our best to hold out against restrictions . . . and we are still one of the few countries which have not imposed any control on foreign exchange transactions.'[1]

Looking again at the 1928-39 figures for extraordinary expenditure, it may seem that the amount allotted for defence was disproportionately high, but Salazar was virtually starting from nothing, with a useless navy and the army's equipment obsolete. The times were dangerous and Portugal would have to show she was pulling her weight before she could invoke the alliance with England for assistance. In the event, Portugal's re-armament programme enabled her to provide adequate defence for the Azores where the Allies established their Atlantic bases in 1943. General Humberto Delgado, opposition leader in the 1950s, was to argue in his *Memoirs*[2] that Salazar's financial measures were initially right but, when prolonged and applied to 'every aspect of the nation's life which showed any lack of stability', simply became a restraint on national trade and growth. The needs of the poor were neglected. The end-product was a wealthy and stable state founded on 'poor, starving masses'. Delgado, of course, never distinguished himself for understatement, and his emotive terms, written in 1963, bore little relation to the situation at that time: a far cry from the days when beggars roamed the city streets and the countryside in their hundreds. By 1963 the new skilled worker and his equivalents were establishing an unfamiliar lower middle class, living standards were still low but wages were rising and keeping ahead of prices, Salazar's policies had become outmoded, some would say long outmoded, yet in absolute terms they had achieved a great deal. The escudo had become one of the world's hardest currencies, and without that stability there would have been no growth at all. The question is really one of tempo and balance, the order of priorities, the proportions to be allotted to conflicting demands.

But controversy over Salazar's economic policies really belongs to the post-1945 period. His position in the 1930s was that to increase economic expansion and welfare provision more than he was doing

[1] D & A, pp. 19-20.
[2] Delgado, cf. Preface.

would be tantamount to pouring boiling water into a delicate glass. The first task was to build up the basic services that would make increased production possible. The consequent rise in national and personal earnings would raise everyone's standards of living.

In restricting government spending, whether on welfare or industry, Salazar's motives were doctrinal as well as practical. The principle of subsidiarity was always with him. The state should not do things proper to subordinate social bodies if they were competent for the purpose. With this went a certain acknowledgment that in an age of growing complexity, voluntary effort and industry's social services *were* inadequate, and that the state's role in this field would have to develop:

> We avoid socialism as much as possible even in the domain of welfare, and we prefer that the action of the state should be confined to supplementing the shortcomings of individuals and of the organizations protecting them [e.g. social insurance run on a voluntary basis by industry]. Thus there is a double action: on the one hand, social insurance extending its field of activity and its plans; and, on the other, the increasing ability of the state to satisfy the needs which do not fall within the purview of social insurance, or which cannot be met by it.[1]

Underlying it all was Salazar's preoccupation with the family as the basis, and as an effective unit of society, and the right and duty of the head of the family to provide for it on a basis of free choice. For him, this went to the heart of human dignity. Modern Europe, of course, does not tend to equate, almost automatically, state activity with depersonalization. Popes John XXIII and Paul VI, while maintaining the subsidiary concept, give a much more positive value to state action than their predecessors did. But Salazar's view looks much less dated when one compares the parallel systems of state and voluntary welfare working in some European countries; the extent and success, for instance, of industrial family allowances paid by the worker's firm out of a common fund.[2] How far and how fast Salazar's policies worked is matter for a later chapter.

[1] *Catholic Herald*, London, 26 July 1963.
[2] Michael P. Fogarty, *The Just Wage*, Chapman, London 1961.

CHAPTER 4

Estado Novo

From the time of his appointment as Finance Minister, Salazar began to make his mark on every aspect of government. He dominated his colleagues, controlled the expenditure, was the man of ideas, and exerted an influence way beyond the scope of his portfolio. Events moved swiftly. The *União Nacional* was formally set up on 30 June 1930. This was to be, not a party, but a pressure group intended to bind all sections of the community in a corporative movement. It was to be an educative force, promulgating the corporative idea, and an integrating factor in the service of national unity. A Colonial Act was passed in the same year.[1] Exiled Republicans in the Atlantic islands and Portuguese Guinea staged an abortive uprising in 1931. A temporary alliance of Republicans and Freemasons with the Communists attempted a movement in Lisbon in the August of that year, and forty people died in the disorders. This too was unproductive, and an attempted alliance of the old parties in a Socialist-Republican coalition failed to win widespread support. Salazar continued to stand head and shoulders over his colleagues, who eventually accepted the facts and acquiesced in President Carmona's decision to appoint Salazar as head of the government. The scholar from Coimbra was by this time more sure than ever that he knew what he wanted and where he was going, and appears to have made no bones about his promotion.

Salazar became Prime Minister on 5 July 1932, and held that office until his health collapsed in the autumn of 1968. His key legislative act, the Corporative Constitution, was approved in a national plebiscite on 19 March 1933. A draft of the instrument had been published a year before, and the public were invited to state their objections in the press. Republicans complained that it excluded a restoration of liberalism, even in a modified or purified form. Socialists wanted far more consideration of social and economic

[1] Cf. Chapter 9 *infra*.

questions, especially the relationship of capital and labour. Some Catholics thought the document did not go far enough in restoring religion to its proper place in society. Elements in the army wanted a harder line. The objections, however, tended to stay in the realm of generalities. There have been conflicting accounts of the results of the referendum,[1] but the correct version of the official claim is:

For	719,364
Against	5,955
Abstentions	488,840
Registered electorate	1,214,159

Most men and certain women, such as graduates or heads of families, were entitled to a vote, but many of them failed to have themselves registered as voters. Fryer and McGowan Pinheiro state that the 1933 Constitution was railroaded through by 'not letting more than a handful of people vote "no" and counting all but a small number of abstentions as "yes" votes'; but in that case the 'yes' vote would have topped the million mark, as the total register was certainly of the order of 1,200,000.[2] Nor do the authors indicate how the potential 'no' voters were restrained, though it could well be that the known opponents of the regime found it hard to get their names on to the voting register (much more specific allegations were made, with reason, after elections in later years). What is quite clear is that, in March 1933, the number of abstentions was heavy, well over a third of the register; yet, in subsequent voting for the first National Assembly, the turnout was very high. This may be due to the nature of the question put to the electorate in 1933. They had to vote for a principle in a package deal, with no opportunity to accept one clause and reject another. Moreover, the niceties of constitutional reform evoke less interest than a contest between rival personalities. It is also possible that, after so many years of elections riddled with muddle, corruption and even violence, some electors were simply too disillusioned to bother with the ballot box, though this too contrasts with the higher polls in later elections.

The National Statute of Labour was passed in September 1933. Freemasonry was outlawed by decree in May 1934. By this time a

[1] Fryer and McGowan Pinheiro (p. 116) give the official figures as 580,379 in favour; 5,405 against; 11,528 abstentions, which indicate a total electorate of less than 600,000. Derrick (p. 110) gives even more improbable figures: For, 1,292,864; Against, 6,090; Spoilt, 660; Abstentions, 30,654. Egerton follows him.
[2] P. D'A., *op. cit.*, p. 93.

National-Syndicalist movement had arisen, under the leadership of Dr Rolão Preto. This was a variant on the National Socialist theme, members wearing blue shirts and a Maltese Cross instead of black shirts and a swastika. In August 1934 the movement's executive responded to Salazar's appeal to abandon their opposition and join the National Union, but their leader had taken another view. Two months before, he had written to President Carmona strongly criticizing the regime and demanding freedom of press and propaganda for all political parties. The government forestalled publication of the letter, and Preto and Count Monsaraz were arrested and deported to Spain. In December 1934 some 80 per cent of the electorate turned out to vote for the first National Assembly, which went into session in January 1935. In the autumn of 1936 Salazar established the Portuguese Legion, a kind of voluntary Home Guard dedicated to the ideals of the national movement. Today it is often seen as a forum for gentlemen wishing to play at soldiers, but in fact it includes a not insignificant cadre of hard-line reactionaries. Then came the *Moçidade-Portuguesa*, a youth movement sometimes compared to the Hitler Youth, but not realistically. It is, of course, wedded to the National Union's aims and controlled by the state. It is also a substitute for the Scout Movement, rejected by Salazar's suspicious approach to all international movements. The movement, however, has made a useful contribution to training youth in the service of the community. It runs camps, a variety of sports and outdoor activities, and modified endurance tests of a kind identified in Britain with the Duke of Edinburgh's Award.

Thus, in principle, the institutional framework of Salazar's regime was established. King Manuel had died in England in 1932. His body was brought back to Portugal and buried with full honours, and the Monarchist *integralistas* recognized D. Duarte Nuno of Braganza, descendant of the Miguel I who was displaced in 1834, as the legitimate pretender to the throne. Duarte declared himself in favour of a Christian monarchy based on the corporative state. Salazar showed respect and sympathy for the monarchy, but the question of restoration has never become a pressing issue. Duarte's supporters have continued to be a prop for Salazar's system.

Central to any understanding of Salazar must be a grasp of his corporative principle, compared with Mussolini's fascist philosophy and institutions. The two are frequently identified, yet the distinctions are considerable, and, even where the effects are similar in practice, there are differences of mentality which have a bearing on any dispassionate judgment of Salazar and Portugal's reaction to him. Shortly after he became Prime Minister, Salazar told the National Union that he was aware of the restlessness felt in certain sections of the community. There were, he said, two currents of thought which tended to divert the ship of state. One of them found nothing of value in the past or the present and sought to create a brave new world on a totally different model. This new world, however, would be 'an incongruous mixture of generous intentions, naive inexperience, and a regression to the sentiments of man's animal nature'. On the other hand there was a section which had become 'frozen stiff in the attitudes and ideas they have acquired and in the preconceptions of their generation'. They saw error and sin in the beckoning future. They opposed every attempt at renovation or reform because their traditional ideas and institutions 'have all the virtue and perfection of immutable truths'.[1] A middle way had to be found, one that would marry the best of the past to what the future seemed to hold in store, or at least those elements in it which answered 'the nature and needs of the present'.

Salazar's New State, the *Estado Novo*, is based on a system variously described as corporate or corporative. The first term has more often been used of Fascism which subordinates all to the state, while the second is supposed to denote a state which represents and thus serves the people, who contribute to the life of the state through their family, professional, vocational and municipal groups. Whatever his practice, Salazar's theory was corporative. Crudely, the idea is that the nation is unitary rather than pluralist, a family which achieves its aims and solves its disputes at a *round* table, not an aggregate of conflicting interests seeking a compromise through tensions *across* the table. The corporative system begins with a common political faith, within which there is room for divergence; it is not a co-operative system linking divergent faiths (though provision must be made for individuals who do not share the unitary faith to be integrated into the life of the state).

Whether this concept is viable or has ever really been tried is the subject of a debate whose genesis dates from the Holy Roman Empire. It has certainly not happened in Portugal, though some of

[1] *Egerton, op. cit.*, p. 186.

its elements are present, and the thinking behind it has marked Salazar's life and work. What Salazar was looking for was a system in which the people would be represented, not through what he saw as divisive parties coloured by class war,[1] but through corporations with some similarity to the medieval guilds. All those, for instance, engaged in a given trade, whatever their status or function in the production process, would be united in a single corporation, with separate infrastructures to provide for separate interests, e.g., workers and employers. The corporations would exert their influence nationally through a parliamentary Corporative Chamber composed of representatives chosen by each corporation from among its own ranks. There would also be a National Assembly, composed of individuals directly elected by the people at large, to represent the nation as a whole; it would include no party nor, as such, regional representation. It would also provide a pluralist element in the overall system: a means of expression for personal (as distinct from group) beliefs and interests. Thus there would be an interaction of warp and woof, of the vertical (Chamber) with the horizontal (Assembly). The role of the Chamber, a house of specialists, would initially be to advise. The role of the Assembly would be to legislate. The government would be empowered to make new laws by decree, but its action would be conditioned and criticized by parliament, and the Assembly's power to make new laws during its limited sittings would act as a check on executive legislation.

In his *Le Siècle de Corporatisme*, Michail Manoilesco distinguished three forms of corporatism. There was pure corporatism where the corporations were the sole source of legislative power; mixed corporatism, where they shared this power with a National Assembly; and subordinate corporatism, where they merely advised. In Salazar's Constitution the Corporative Chamber is always advisory, and Article 71 does not include it in the list of the nation's representatives (which are given as the Head of State, the National Assembly, the Government, and the Courts). But Derrick, in *The Portugal of Salazar*, already quoted, argues that Salazar's corporations are not to be

[1] 'The [pre-1926 governments were] constitutionally under the control of the Chambers. . . . Behind these Chambers, or rather above them, stood numerous political bodies with their directorates, supported by an electorate (managed by political bosses, corrupt, self-seeking, and without ideals) that was the supreme and final arbiter of the powers of the state. Under such conditions it cannot be said that we had free elections or that the electors knew what they were voting for.' Salazar in D & A, p. 14.

located in Manoilesco's third category, as Salazar once hinted that he meant in the end to abolish the Assembly altogether and give the legislative power to the Chamber. The result would be a full-fledged organic democracy based on functional associations. But Salazar also insisted on the voluntary nature of the corporations, and on the need for interests falling outside their scope to be represented. The more probable interpretation is that he meant eventually to strengthen the Chamber's role and involve it more directly in the power to legislate, but without dissolving the Assembly. Indeed, on hearing reports that Mussolini was planning to abolish the Italian Assembly, Salazar was critical. What has happened in practice is that, while the various professional, industrial, rural, municipal and educational sectors have their organizations and are represented in the Corporative Chamber, these organizations are still largely inchoate. Parts of them exist, such as unions, guilds and federations, but in many cases these have not been structured into complete corporations within the constitutional definitions. The practical result is that most of the Chamber's members are appointed and will not be elected until the 'completion' is achieved. Only then, presumably, would the question of increasing the Chamber's power arise.

At any rate, with corporatism dominating his mind, Salazar set out to resolve the intellectual clash between the demands of freedom and authority. However it is judged, the formula must be viewed in the context of Portuguese history and character, not in that of other countries which have worked conventional democracies with different results. Rightly or wrongly, Salazar thought that the party system had failed irrevocably in Portugal, and that parliamentary procedure had been hamstrung by long, inconsequential wrangling, while life had passed the nation by. The power of decision had to be restored, national interests given priority over sectional claims, albeit in a representative framework. As he put it himself:

> It [the former parliament] assumed the place of the executive, making this subordinate to itself, lessening its authority and paralysing its action. . . . Matters of secondary importance, rightly or wrongly regarded as scandals, took up all the time and all the energy.[1]

His idea of the separation of powers is unfamiliar to British ears, less so, perhaps, to Americans. Salazar did not envisage a legislating

[1] *Ibid.*, pp. 224-7.

parliament and an executive government (with ministers issuing Orders only within strict and specific limits granted by Acts of Parliament). He wanted a government with the right both to enact and execute, and a parliament confined to enacting 'general legal principles' (it was not to be concerned with administration nor even with detailed aspects of legislation). There would be no provision for the government to be answerable to parliament for its executive acts. Rather, its responsibility would be exclusively to the Head of State, and, through him, to the nation. As for liberalism:

> our liberalism did not ring true; it was always intolerant and Jacobin. If it were installed in power again, it would be even more shamelessly so. . . . It would no longer be merely indifferent to the things of the spirit but would become amoral in both theory and practice.[1]

Its 'fatal tendency to exploit the masses' and reduce all to a common low level would lead in the end to Communism, the fatal consequence of the revolt against reason, discipline and authority. Salazar pleaded again for a realization of the need for a social hierarchy which, he said, gave discipline to society and raised the social level by acknowledging the supremacy of the spirit. He described his regime as 'popular but not demagogic, representative but anti-democratic, strong but not tyrannical or all-absorbing'.

The Constitution of 1933 defines the Portuguese state as

> a unitary and corporative republic founded upon the equality of all its citizens in the eyes of the law, upon the free access for all classes to the benefits of civilization, and upon the participation of all the constituent forces of the nation in its administrative life and in the making of laws.[2]

Sovereignty is vested in the nation,[3] and the Head of State is the President of the Republic. He is elected for seven years, answerable to the nation, and empowered to hire and fire the Premier and other ministers. Under the Constitution as originally passed, the President was elected directly by universal suffrage. After the Delgado campaign of 1958, the Assembly changed the system by an amendment of Article 72. This now prescribes that the President should be

[1] D & A, pp. 224-7.
[2] Political Constitution of the Republic, Art. 5 (SNI, Lisbon).
[3] Ibid., Art. 71.

elected by an electoral college composed of the members of both parliamentary chambers, and representatives chosen by municipal and provincial councils.[1] The President is advised by a Council of State composed of ten members: the President of the Council of Ministers (Prime Minister); the Presidents of the Assembly and Chamber; the President of the Supreme Court of Justice; the Procurator-General of the Republic; and five public men of outstanding ability, appointed for life by the Head of State. The President of the Republic is bound to consult the Council of State before convoking, adjourning or dissolving the Assembly, and in all grave emergencies.[2]

The government is composed of the Prime Minister and the Council of Ministers. Its role is to advise the President of the Republic, legislate by way of its own decree-laws or of Bills presented to the National Assembly, and to control public administration.[3] The Assembly is composed of 130 deputies, each one with the same right as the government to introduce legislation, except that only the government can introduce legislation to increase state expenditure or limit revenue. The Assembly can suspend and abrogate laws, but sits only for three months in the year.[4] Decree-laws issued by the government during a session of the Assembly are subject to the Assembly's ratification.[5] All laws are subject to the assent of the President of the Republic. If he fails to promulgate an Assembly law within fifteen days, it must be returned to the Assembly. If a two-thirds majority of the deputies pass it again, the President can no longer withhold his assent. The Corporative Chamber is composed of representatives of local autonomous bodies, municipalities, the administration, and of industrial, agricultural, commercial, financial, cultural and religious interests. The Chamber works through specialist committees whose job it is to examine and report on Bills submitted to the National Assembly.[6] In 1934 a Corporative Council, composed of certain ministers and two academic lawyers, was set up. It appoints the administration's representatives in the Chamber, and also the representatives of those bodies which have not as yet completed their corporative organization. At present, a high proportion

[1] *Ibid.*, Art. 72 (as amended in 1959) to 82.
[2] *Ibid.*, Arts. 83, 84.
[3] *Ibid.*, Arts. 107-15.
[4] *Ibid.*, Arts. 85-101.
[5] *Ibid.*, Art. 109.
[6] *Ibid.*, Arts. 102-6.

of the members of the Chamber are appointees, as distinct from being elected by complete corporations. In Salazar's thinking,[1] the welfare of the collectivity transcends and includes the welfare of the individual. He exists socially, as the member of a group: his family, profession or municipal region. In this social quality all his essential rights are recognized. There are no abstract rights of man, only concrete ones. Thus representation is organized, not through 'artificial' groups or parties, but by 'real' and permanent elements in the national life. The smallest association is the family and, on the municipal level, only heads of families are allowed to vote for the parish council. This in turn has a corporative vote for the municipal council, and the latter has a similar vote for the provincial council.

The Constitution specifically provides for freedom of speech and association,[2] but also calls for special laws 'to prevent, by precautionary or restrictive measures, the perversion of public opinion in its function as a social force'. At a later stage it prescribes that 'public opinion is a fundamental element of the policy and administration of the country; it shall be the duty of the state to protect it against all those influences which distort it from the truth, justice, good administration, and the commonweal.'[3] (In practice the 'protective' clauses have been more in evidence than the substantive proposition of freedom.) In the economic field, property, capital and labour are all given their respective social functions, but the law is to 'determine the conditions of their use or exploitation in accordance with the community aim in view'.[4] There is special protection for small home industries,[5] and strikes and lock-outs are prohibited.[6]

STATUTE OF NATIONAL LABOUR

The legal forms of the corporative state are of considerable importance, even though they have not been properly worked. For one thing, while only the National Union is at present represented in the Assembly, and the corporations are still largely inchoate, the debates are not uncritical nor wholly without influence on events; and, in the field of industry, syndical bargaining has acquired some teeth.

[1] West, *op. cit.*, pp. 16-17.
[2] Constitution, *op. cit.*, Art. 8.
[3] *Ibid.*, Art. 22.
[4] *Ibid.*, Art. 35.
[5] *Ibid.*, Art. 32.
[6] *Ibid.*, Art. 39.

Moreover, there is reason to believe that Salazar's successor, Professor Marcello Caetano, does not propose to depart from corporative forms, for the present at least, but will try to give them a more dynamic expression.

In the year that the Constitution was promulgated, the document sometimes described as the Portuguese workers' Bill of Rights became law. The Statute of National Labour is part and parcel of the corporative theme. It lays down the principle that production must be regulated for the benefit of the nation as a whole, and that this calls for discipline and rationalization. The improvement of the working classes' living standards is not to be treated in isolation but should 'proceed simultaneously with the strengthening of the economic structure'.[1] Private enterprise is seen as the best means of social and economic progress, but the state must co-ordinate the nation's economic and social life in such a way as to establish an equilibrium between capital and labour, and between production and consumption. Thus the state is to

defend agriculture, industry and commerce from unfair exploitation, from wasteful competition and from parasitical growths, to keep the cost of living low and raise the standard of life of the working classes by perfecting technique and facilitating credits, and to inculcate in employer and employee alike, by organizing production on a corporative basis, a sense of interdependence and of solidarity.[2]

The corporative system thus aims to outlaw the class struggle, together with strikes and lock-outs.

In Section II, the Statute defends the right of private property but only insofar as it is compatible with the rights of other people and with the common good. It is for the management to manage: if the worker shares in the control and profits of the firm, it is only by free consent of the proprietors.[3] Normally, firms should not be

[1] West, *op. cit.*, pp. 17-18, quoting A. H. W. King's *Report on the Economic and Commercial Conditions of Portugal*, p. 2, London, 1936 (published by the Department of Overseas Trade).

[2] King, *op. cit.*, p. 65. See preceding footnote.

[3] This seems to be less generous than the social teaching of the Popes, who do not claim 'workers' participation' as an absolute right but strongly urge that the worker should have a share in both profits and management. Some Catholic thinkers argue that a rise in wages can be a share in profits and that consultation

compelled to employ more workers than they need, but in labour crises they must co-operate with the state for the public interest. Everyone has a right to work and to a wage consistent with personal and family dignity, and this is to be achieved through individual and collective bargaining. The Statute prescribes minimum standards to limit hours of work, secure an obligatory rest day, provide for 'double time' payment on Sundays and equivalent days, and oblige employers to grant annual holidays on full pay (which was enlightened thinking for 1933). Collective labour contracts are to be negotiated by the workers' syndicates (*sindicatos*) and the employers' guilds (*gremios*). When such contracts are sanctioned by the corporation linking both organizations, and are also approved by the government, they become binding on all employers and workers engaged in the trade, profession or industry concerned. Today, the position is more advanced. Bargains can now be concluded by syndicates and guilds without government sanction, but the government can be brought in if there is failure to agree.

The Statute's third section defines that a corporation comprises and co-ordinates the activities of all the subordinate organizations in its field: syndicates, guilds, federations and unions. The workers' syndicates and the employers' guilds represent all those engaged in a specific trade or industry. Both syndicates and guilds are (separately) grouped in federations, each of which is still concerned with *one* specific trade or industry. Then come the unions, which represent the interests of the syndicates or guilds (as the case may be) of *different but connected and affiliated* branches of trade and industry. At the top of the pyramid employers and workers join up their interests and send representatives to the Corporative Chamber. Juridical personality is granted to syndicates and guilds, which legally represent all persons engaged in the same branch of trade or industry, whether or not they are members of the syndicate or guild concerned.[1]

It is basic to the corporative concept that all these bodies are

through joint committees and trade unions can amount to a share in control; that the problem is often one of semantics. Others prefer to claim for the worker 'a property right in his job' as distinct from 'a property right in the firm's capital'. If the question is one of status – the worker seen as a partner and not as a hireling – then it seems to me that the Popes should demand participation in its fullest sense through shareholding and worker-directors. Salazar's position was marked by his preoccupation with the concept of hierarchy in society.

[1] West, *op. cit.*, p. 20.

voluntary associations. As strikes and lock-outs are prohibited, labour tribunals have been set up under the National Institute of Labour and Social Welfare to conciliate and arbitrate in regard to contracts of employment, accident claims, insurance schemes and labour legislation. Today the corporations run effective social security schemes for industrial workers, who in addition may benefit from health, housing and insurance schemes run by larger firms. While less powerful than British or American unions, the Portuguese syndicates are not ineffective in collective bargaining, and employers take them seriously. Social security and labour rights are supposed to be guaranteed for rural workers and fishermen by the organizations known as the *Casas do Povo* and the *Casas dos Pescadores*, which are also represented in the Corporative Chamber. In theory there should be one per parish, supported by local landowners, the municipality and the state. In practice the scheme has worked out patchily, and the rural workers are not compensated for the lack of a welfare state to the same degree as the urban worker, through his syndicates.

In August 1934, the *English Review* commented:

> People have a habit of writing about the corporate state as if it were a patent medicine invented by Signor Mussolini, of which the British market rights have been acquired by Sir Oswald Mosley – as if, in other words, it was something you had to take or leave as it is found in Italy.

In fact, the concept was canvassed in the 1870s and has appeared in Italian, Austrian and Portuguese forms. Otto Gierke discussed it in Germany under the heading of guild socialism and syndicalism, while F. W. Maitland was a leading British exponent. All were different. Salazar maintained that 'Portugal is directed by a system which, as befits her history and geography, themselves so different from all others, is an original one.'[1] Corporatism is not necessarily political and is mainly concerned for the identity, not the opposition, of workers' and employers' interests. It depends on a corporate mind, will and conscience.[2]

[1] António de Oliveira Salazar, *The Place of the New Portuguese State in Europe's Political Evolution*, D & A, p. 225 *et seq.*
[2] J. Steenkiste, 'The Corporative Ideal', *New Review*, p. 315, Calcutta, October 1935.

In the account he gives of Salazar's approach, West takes for his polarization the contrasting ideas of political pluralism and Fascism.[1] Political pluralism, he tells us, regards the state, not as something representing the whole of society's organized life, but as one of many social institutions on an equal footing. The Italian corporate state, on the other hand, made all functional associations subordinate contributors to the life of the state-nation, which was sovereign. Fascism reflected the Hegelian preference for order, and freedom was achieved in the freedom of the state, not in one's individual or corporative capacity. Salazar's functional associations are also common to political pluralism and Fascism, but they repudiate the *liberty without authority* stress of the former, and the *authority without liberty* stress of the latter. His formula is one which attempts a synthesis of *authority and liberties*. Though his corporations are subordinate contributors to the life of the state, it is through the corporations, and not through the state, that men are invited to find their freedom. Putting it another way, individuals are urged to realize their freedom in their corporative capacities, and, while in one sense subject to the state, they are to make the state what it is. Sovereignty resides in the nation, and the state is the nation's expression, not identical with or superior to it (cf. Articles 71-2 of the Constitution).

A modern way of putting this might be to say that the state's authority is an authority of service, and, if Jacques Maritain's distinction is acceptable, that the state is superior to the individual (man in his material aspect) but subordinate to the person (man in his spiritual aspect). The Portuguese corporations are not identical with the medieval guilds. They are designed to avoid the disorderly competition, monopolies and plutocracy prevalent in the Middle Ages and fostered by the guilds. The guilds, too, were ignorant of the modern class struggle and were not designed to cope with it. They were also locally based, while the worker of today lives in a nationally controlled economy. Salazar's system, therefore, claims to be *sui generis* and to differ from Fascism in that it recognizes the *personality* of the corporation, whereas

> the Fascist corporations have no juridical personality whatever, they are not self-contained economic entities, but organs of the public power.[2]

[1] Steenkiste, *op. cit.*, p. 315.
[2] Angelo Brucculeri, 'Italian Fascism', *New Review*, p. 317, Calcutta, April 1935.

Mussolini's system envisaged dictation from the top to all subordinate bodies, while Salazar's system presupposed, at least in theory, that the subordinate bodies would initiate ideas and enterprises whose effects would rise from below to permeate, change and regenerate the whole community, including the government and legislature.

A discussion of corporate personality today may seem remote from history's concrete realities, but it is essential to an understanding of Salazar whose motives were deeply embedded in abstractions, and whose tendency has been, not to depart from his principles, but to confuse the theory with the achievement. In an introduction to his translation of Gierke's *Natural Law and the Theory of Society*,[1] Professor Ernest Barker has a section on the personality of groups, and examines three theories as to what constitutes the personality of a corporation. In the *fiction or concession* theory, the unity of a legal group or corporation derives from state concession; but, as the personality of a group must lie somewhere in the fact of the many individuals composing it, the unity conferred by the state is only a pretence or fiction. The *collective contract* theory is based on the idea of aggregation; but aggregation does not of itself yield genuine unity. Finally, there is Gierke's theory of *real personality*.

This theory argues that, just as there is a human person behind the individual legal person, so behind the legal group-person is a real group-being. 'Legal group-responsibility is the shadow cast by real group-personality: it is the reflection of reality in the mirror of law.'[2] Social wholes are 'corporeal-spiritual', and their effects are spiritual processes which are corporeally mediated, as in the folk-soul, the class spirit, the family feeling, the *esprit de corps*. Gierke insists on the need for the articulation of contained groups in the containing state, and sees the life of the lower group as necessarily integrated in that of the higher.

Barker is doubtful about Gierke's doctrine of the distinct, corporative existence of the group: Gierke himself was not sure whether it constituted an organism or a mechanism. So Barker suggests a third possibility: 'the organization of men created and sustained by a common human purpose'. (He had found little personality and no autonomy in the Italian system; the only group-person really intended to act was the Italian nation as integrally realized in the Fascist state of Italy.) Pondering on Barker's problem, West comes to the rescue

---

[1] Introduction to Vol. 1, Cambridge 1934; see also West, *op. cit.*, pp. 25-8.
[2] Gierke, *op. cit.*, Introduction by Ernest Barker, p. lxvii.

by referring to an article by Steenkiste[1] which, he thinks, reconciles Barker's view with Gierke's. Steenkiste offers a definition, derived from Catholic sources, which sees the group as 'a symbolical representation of a collection of spiritual *relations*'. West adds: 'The group, consisting of a number of human beings linked by common spiritual bonds or relations, such as a common purpose, is a true moral person.'[2]

This view of the matter seems to make common cause with Salazar's discourse on *The Place of the New Portuguese State in Europe's Political Evolution*,[3] which represents the corporative state as consisting not only of economic groups, but also of spiritual groups:

> In the organization of the economic corporations, the interests which they pursue must be kept in view, or, better, the interests of production must be subordinated not only to the national economy as a whole, but also to the spiritual finality and higher destiny of the nation and of the individuals which constitute it.

West comments:

> The relationship implicit in the phrase 'of the nation and of the individuals which constitute it' would seem to bring the Portuguese concept of the legal personality of the corporation within the Catholic definition advocated by Steenkiste as 'a symbolical representation of a collection of spiritual relations'.

Certainly, in Salazar's theory, the state does not swallow up the groups. They are simply asked to acknowledge the state as a co-ordinating agent, 'regulating group-life insofar as the common welfare of the whole nation postulates a superior unifying moral power'.[4] For such reasons Salazar has always claimed that his regime, though authoritarian, is not totalitarian.

Michael Derrick makes a distinction between the Fascist *corporatisme d'état* and the Portuguese *corporatisme d'association*, in which the state is supposed to be society's servant. Salazar seems to have thought that this was a return to early Portuguese tradition, the age of the popular monarchy.[5] Derrick further argues that Article III of the Italian Charter of Labour explicitly subjected the syndicates to total

[1] Steenkiste, *op. cit.*, p. 461.
[2] West, *op. cit.*, p. 27.
[3] Salazar, *op. cit.*, D & A, p. 225 *et seq.*
[4] Steenkiste, *op. cit.*
[5] Derrick, *op. cit.*, pp. 137-40.

state control and turned them into an organ of administration.[1] Article VI confined state corporatism strictly to the economic field: 'the unitary organization of all the forces of production'. Salazar's system, on the other hand, took in all aspects of the national life: the Church, defence, the judiciary, the administration, the universities, music and fine arts, even the Olympic Games committee.

Salazar has always claimed that his thinking was based on the social teaching of the modern popes, which, for him, meant Leo XIII (in the last quarter of the nineteenth century) and Pius XI, whose great social encyclical *Quadragesimo Anno* appeared in 1931.[2] Was he faithful to them? Pius XI, who was basically suspicious of Mussolini from the outset, and was criticized by Montini (now Paul VI) for having any truck with him at all, described the Italian syndicates in his encyclical and expressed the fear that 'the state is substituting itself in the place of private initiative, instead of limiting itself to necessary and sufficient help and assistance'. He added:

> It is feared that the new syndical and corporative institution possesses an excessively bureaucratic and political character, and that, notwithstanding the general advantages referred to above, it risks serving particular political aims rather than contributing to the initiation of a better social order.[3]

In other words, Mussolini's corporatism was a threat to Pius's principle of subsidiarity. At the same time, however, Pius did preach the virtues of what has been called the vocational order of society. 'The aim of social legislation', he said, 'must therefore be the re-establishment of vocational groups' as a means of abolishing class war. He continued:

> Labour . . . is not a mere chattel, since the human dignity of the working man must be recognized in it and consequently it cannot be bought and sold like any piece of merchandise. None the less

---

[1] Benito Mussolini, *The Corporate State*, pp. 96-7, Vallecchi Editore, Florence, 1936.
[2] Salazar deeply respected Pius XII as well, but he regarded the reign of John XXIII (1958-63), and the Second Vatican Council summoned in 1962, as a disastrous episode in the Church's life. As he saw it, the Johannine liberalism and the Conciliar decrees combined to undermine the static and inflexible authority of the Rock of Peter, on which the Church had to stand. At least one of John's encyclicals appeared in Portugal in bowdlerized form!
Pius XI, *Quadragesimo Anno*, pp. 42-3, Catholic Truth Society, London, 1931.

the demand and supply of labour divides men on the labour market into two classes, as into two camps, and the bargaining between these parties transforms this labour market into an arena where the two armies are engaged in combat.

The search for a solution demanded

vocational groups binding men together, not according to the position they occupy in the labour market, but according to the diverse functions they exercise in society. For as nature induces those who dwell in close proximity to unite into municipalities, so those who practise the same trade or profession, economic or otherwise, combine into vocational groups. These groups, in a true sense autonomous, are considered by many to be, if not essential to civil society, at least its natural and spontaneous development.

Where, however, employers or workers needed separate representation to solve a clash between their respective interests,

separate deliberations will take place in their respective assemblies and separate votes will be taken as the matter may require.[1]

A good deal of Salazar's theory is consistent with this, and his view of the family's rights in regard to the state was derived from Leo XIII's *Rerum Novarum*:

A family, no less than the state, is, as we have said, a true society, governed by an authority peculiar to itself, that is to say, by the authority of the father. Provided, therefore, the limits which are prescribed by the very purposes for which it exists be not transgressed, the family has *at least* equal rights with the state in the choice and pursuit of the things needful to its preservation and just liberty. . . . Inasmuch as the domestic household is antecedent, as well in idea as in fact, to the gathering of men into a community, the family must necessarily have rights and duties which are *prior* to those of the community, and founded more immediately in nature.[2]

In the realm of theory, therefore, Salazar cannot be easily faulted in terms of papal teaching on workers' and employers' associations, the rights of the family, and the relation of the state to subordinate

[1] Pius XI, *op cit.*, pp. 38-9.
[2] Leo XIII: *Rerum Novarum*, s.10, Catholic Truth Society, London.

groupings. In practice, the great criticism of his regime has always been that stability was bought and maintained by the suppression of human rights and liberties. Everything said by Leo and Pius, for instance, was qualified by an overriding demand for free association as a basic human right, and political parties are examples of those 'private societies' of which Leo said that

> although they exist within the state and are severally part of the state [they] cannot be absolutely, and as such, prohibited by the state. For to enter into a society of this kind is the natural right of man.

There are, of course, exceptions, where questions of the common good arise:

> There are occasions, doubtless, when it is fitting that the law should intervene to prevent associations; as when men join together for purposes which are evidently bad, unlawful or dangerous to the state. In such cases public authority may justly forbid the formation of associations, and may dissolve them if they already exist.

But the pope adds a warning:

> Every precaution should be taken not to violate the rights of individuals and not to impose unreasonable regulations under pretence of public benefit. For laws only bind when they are in accordance with right reason, and hence with the eternal law of God.[1]

St Thomas Aquinas had put it even more strongly:

> Human law is law only by virtue of its accordance with right reason: and thus it is manifest that it flows from the eternal law. And insofar as it deviates from right reason it is called an unjust law; in such cases it is no law at all, but rather a species of violence.[2]

In terms of Leo's *dicta*, Salazar justified his prohibition of political parties on the ground that the past had proved the endemic danger to the state arising from the deep-rooted Portuguese tendency to behave irrationally when operating a party system.[3] Salazar's critics

---

[1] *Ibid.*, s.38.
[2] St Thomas Aquinas, *Summa Theol.*, 1a-2ae, Q. xciii, Art. 3, ad. 2.
[3] Efforts to work on the lines of the English parliamentary system had led to a 'chaos of *camarillas* and *caciquismo*, corruption, rotativism and revolution', as Derrick puts it (*op. cit.*, p. 108).

object that this approach may well have been justified in his early days in power when he had to unite and set to work an indolent, dispirited and fragmented people; but that what should have been at the most a temporary expedient became a national way of life, and as such ran counter to Leonine teaching. It will be said, and rightly said, that the British or American democratic models will never transplant to societies inherently unattuned to them,[1] and that the Christian ethic allows for any kind of government, provided it does not infringe the basic human rights. On that principle, Salazar's corporative state is not inherently objectionable. The question is how far it has lived up to its objective and allowed free scope for the human rights it asserts.

[1] 'One of the greatest mistakes of the 19th century was to suppose that the English parliamentary system . . . was a form of government capable of adaptation to the needs of all European peoples.' – Salazar, in an introduction to *Une Revolution dans la Paix*, Flammarion, Paris, 1936.

CHAPTER 5

The Mind of Salazar

Salazar came to power as the star of the Axis dictators rose over Europe. He was deeply impressed by Mussolini's organizing genius, which seemed to be doing for Italy what Salazar wanted to do for Portugal, and, despite their differing philosophies, there is no doubt that Il Duce's unitary theory, like Pius XI's 'vocational order of society', had a bearing on Salazar's corporate principle. He disliked and distrusted Hitler from the start, especially when the Führer started to cast a roving eye over Africa, and German influence gained ground in Portuguese business and intellectual circles. Salazar was extremely sceptical of the League of Nations and thought the Allies had mishandled Germany, whose pretensions after her treatment at Versailles he felt he could understand.[1] With regard to Hitler personally, however, he had no illusions at all. His feeling for Mussolini weakened as the latter was drawn more closely into the German net. In the League of Nations, Portugal opposed the Abyssinian adventure, and the Fascist dictator's confrontation with the Church was highly embarrassing. Il Duce's photograph stayed on Salazar's desk for a very long time, disappearing only when it was plain beyond doubt that the Duce was no longer his own man. By 1936, the Portuguese leader was making some acid distinctions between the totalitarian regimes and his own 'dictatorship of professors':

> Although Fascism and National Socialism differ from Communism in economic outlook and ideals, they are alike in their conception of the totalitarian state. In both, the party is the state, to whose ends all the activities of the citizen are subject, and man exists only for its greatness and its glory.

In Germany

> racial distinctions (are) so well-designed that juridically the distinction between a citizen and a subject becomes fraught with the

[1] See Chapters 6 and 7 *infra*.

most serious political consequences, both internally and externally.[1]

It was reasonable enough to grant freedoms in England which were inappropriate elsewhere because of the nation's highly developed public spirit, sense of responsibility and common sense, but Salazar wondered if

> an excessive subordination to public opinion does not deprive the (English) government of a great part of its initiative, at times so necessary to the vital interests of a great country.[2]

He was writing in those anxious pre-war days when he felt that England was dithering over re-armament and conscription while the German war machine was building up to immense proportions. England's tradition of parliamentary government was 'glorious' and the House of Commons rightly refrained from usurping the executive's function, but, Salazar felt, the House did sometimes hamper the executive. 'The great exertions of which England is capable', he added, 'usually follow a period of dilatoriness in political administration.'

However, this was no excuse for Nazi and Fascist errors, and what was wanted for the citizen of Portugal's New State was that he should have

> a clear-cut conception of his country and national unity; of the family as the social nucleus *par excellence*; of authority and those in authority; of spiritual values and the respect due to every individual; of the right to work, the excellence of virtue, and the sacred nature of religious belief.

Hence, Salazar declared:

> We are opposed to all forms of internationalism, Communism, Socialism, syndicalism and everything which may divide or minimize or break up the family. We are against class warfare, irreligion and disloyalty to one's own country; against serfdom, a materialistic conception of life, and might over right.[3]

While accepting, therefore, that there were things in common between the Italian view and his own, such as anti-democracy, Salazar urged that 'the methods of renovation' were different. The Fascist dictatorship, he said, was 'leaning towards a pagan Caesarism, towards a

---

[1] D & A, *op. cit.*, Preface, pp. 32-5.
[2] *Ibid.*, pp. 36-7.
[3] *Ibid.*, p. 26.

new state which recognizes no limitations of legal or moral order'. Mussolini was 'a magnificent opportunist' and it was not for nothing that he was 'a child of the country of the Caesars and of Machiavelli':

> I see him as perpetually drawn backwards and forwards between the elite he has created and which works so brilliantly for him, and the mob to whom from time to time he is forced to throw a sop. . . . The new Portuguese state, on the other hand, cannot and does not attempt to escape from certain limitations of the moral order which it deems indispensable as boundary lines in its work of reformation.[1]

What baffled Salazar was that, although Communism was an unnatural and uneconomic system, it should continue to attract liberals who by definition ought to hate it. The 'living example of Russia is powerless to destroy the mirage, the attraction of the abyss'.[2] Economically, Communism was on the downgrade, already discredited. Yet politically it was in the ascendant; even in England it had become 'the rallying cry of the revolutionary instincts of our age', and had done so 'by power of words, by sheer bluff, perhaps by the voluptuousness of contrast'. It was largely the success of Communist 'evangelism' that made Salazar so suspicious of all international movements. He had believed in the League of Nations' potential, but felt it had gone into decline because it had sought to become a kind of super-state in the face of a growing nationalism, and tried to impose a specific political creed on one and all. Thus a ring of great democracies had sought to dominate the League with 'ill-disguised demagogic ideas'. Salazar had always opposed the Treaty of Versailles and the folly of the victors' refusal to allow for the problems and resurgent aspirations of the defeated over the years.[3] In any case, the League had killed itself by adopting 'the worst features of the democracies' such as 'petty lobbying' and 'political jobbery'. Once its impartiality was lost, it could only become a tool for some countries to use against others.

Salazar went to considerable pains to distinguish between the totalitarian formula and his new Constitution. In a speech in which he described its intent to the people, he said it

> rejects everything which, directly or indirectly, proceeds from . . . totalitarian ideas, because these are incompatible with its objectives.

[1] Ferro, *op. cit.*, p. 176.
[2] *Ibid.*, pp. 50-60.
[3] Cf. Chapter 7 *infra*.

It begins by establishing morals and justice as something outside the limits of its own sovereignty. It imposes on the state the duty of respecting the natural rights of individuals, families, corporations and local autonomous bodies. It ensures liberty and freedom of belief and religious practices. It entrusts to parents and their representatives the instruction and education of their children. It guarantees property, capital and labour in an amicable relationship.[1]

In Salazar's Portugal there has never been any restriction on the practice of non-Catholic religions. In the field of education, however, Republicans and Socialists tend to favour the laicization of state schools. They would exclude religious teaching altogether, leaving this to specifically Catholic schools, to the home and the parish. Most practising Catholics would retain the religious character of the state schools, though many could call for reforms in the way religion is taught. In the 1930s, as now, however, the opposition's concern was for a restoration of parliamentary democracy on conventional Western lines. Salazar simply could not envisage it, and he was perfectly frank about it:

> We are anti-parliamentarians, anti-democrats, anti-liberals, and we are determined to establish a corporative state. Such statements may shock those nations which are used to adjusting the deficiencies of their own political systems by virtue of improved social conditions, and which are unable to appreciate the harm that may result from the application of similar methods in countries differently constituted. When all is said and done, we are merely trying to reach the same end by methods which are best suited to our particular needs. The most valuable attitudes we could wish for in our institutions is that they should be as thoroughly Portuguese as possible.

Commenting on the nineteenth-century tendency to apply English parliamentary ways to European countries, he asserted that, with the exception of Switzerland and some of the northern countries where special conditions obtained

> parliamentary democracy has resulted in instability and disorder, or, what is worse, it has become a despotic domination of the

[1] D & A, *op. cit.*, pp. 231-2.

nation by political parties. When matters come to a climax, dictatorships are created . . . so that a new beginning can be made.[1]

Liberalism in practice, he thought, had deprived people of the very
liberties it was supposed to safeguard, and the trouble with democracy
was that the people were considered only at election time: 'We want
to elevate, educate and rescue the people from the slavery of
plutocracy.' As for socialism, he told António Ferro:

> I am wholly against any development of state activity in any
> economic field in which the failure of individual effort has not
> first been proved. But I believe in . . . greater public power to create
> conditions, internal or external, material or moral, which are
> necessary to the development of production.[2]

Too many Portuguese were all too ready to hide behind officialdom,
he added, and would love to have state-controlled industries where
salaries were safe whatever the individual's performance. This had,
time and again, proved to be ruinous and opened the door to every kind
of corruption and dishonesty. State intervention should always be

> of an educational and moderating character; for there can be no
> progress if it attempts to extend its activities at the expense of the
> individual. Real progress can only be achieved when the state is
> prepared to abandon all forms of activity which can best be
> performed through private channels. . . . Not all advancement is
> progress, and backwardness may simply mean that we have not
> departed too much from the principles of rational economy.[3]

Private enterprise has always been the dominant factor in the
Portuguese economy under Salazar, but criticism in the post-war
years has turned on his credit restrictions and coyness towards
foreign investment, which many economists feel today went on too
long and extended too far. Salazar's thinking from the start was
dominated by the past: the undisciplined credit systems which had
brought the country to the brink of bankruptcy, and which he
described as a process of mortgaging the income of future generations.[4] He believed that the country was too inept in economic
judgment to be trusted with generous credit schemes, and thus laid

---

[1] *Ibid.*, Preface, p. 29 (1938).
[2] Ferro, *op. cit.*, p. 169.
[3] D & A, p. 168 (March, 1933).
[4] *Ibid.*, p. 311; Egerton, *op. cit.*, p. 152.

heavy restrictions on the life-giving flow of money required for industrial investment and expansion. It was, beyond doubt, the right way to begin, but the pathway out of deflation was to be grudging and slow.

From the beginning, too, Salazar's practice contrasted sharply with his proclamations of human rights. In the name of national security, critical voices were silenced through censorship, police and 'controlled' elections,[1] and some of the worst allegations of police brutality were made during the 1930s. It would be easy to say that Salazar simply said what he did not mean, but the truth is different and more complex. In the first years, when the memory of blood in the streets was alive, the hand that sought to unify a torn and tormented nation had to be firm and decisive, and, at a stage when Portugal's survival was still in question, some liberties were luxuries. Half the country was illiterate, and an easy prey to unscrupulous campaigners, and if there was anything that Salazar hated most, it was the irresponsible manipulation of untutored public opinion for political ends. The trouble is that the early ambulance measures turned into long-term treatment. This happened, not because Salazar's theory was spurious, but because in practice he was convinced that the people needed to be nursed for quite a long time before they could have their heads even within his system. He tried to cradle the nation by prescribing what he thought it ought to want, and went on doing this beyond the time when, by his critics' reasoning, the people should have been allowed to come of age and be given the key of the door.[2]

There is a close connection between Salazar's view of poverty, his apparent predilection for mediocrity, and his paternalistic mode of government. He has often been accused of expecting the nation to adopt his own preference for simple living. The condition of *abject* poverty revolted him, and in 1932 he spoke of himself as one who had 'to labour without rest and with rage in his heart as long as a woman went hungry or a child cried with the cold'. These expressions were common with him, and close associates who rebuked him for overworking were told: 'There's no other way as long as there remains a single person in Portugal who has to beg for a crust of bread.'[3] There was, however, a moderate form of poverty

[1] See Chapter 11.
[2] The story of the Portuguese opposition and its frustrations is told in Chapter 11.
[3] Ferro, *op. cit.*, p. 45.

which he raised to the national altars as a high social virtue: another adaptation from religious life. He was to tell the National Union:

I owe to Providence the grace of poverty; devoid of goods of value, very little binds me to the wheel of fortune. Not that I ever missed having lucrative posts, riches, ostentation. To earn my daily bread on the modest scale to which I have accustomed myself and in which I can live, I have no need to enmesh myself in the tangle of business or in embarrassing commitments. I am an independent man.[1]

Did this condition of mind tend to favour and foster a certain mediocrity in national standards? For instance, Salazar once said it was 'more humane and more Christian to work for a collective middle state where neither multi-millionaires nor paupers are possible'.[2] The answer seems to be that he was determined to snap Portugal out of the melancholy, self-depreciatory, fantasy world she had got herself into, despairing yet looking for miracles. He urged the people to learn to love their country even in its transitional state. To do so, one had to know her, yet one could not know her without doing a little loving first. For the rest:

Instead of either super-athletes or cripples, let us just have a nation of healthy men and women. Instead of supermen or frightened little men, instead of greedy and nervous men, let us have men with developed wills, calm, patient and tenacious. In the realm of the intellect, let knowledge be only an infinite capacity for study.[3]

The aim must be 'to make our lives real, not a series of dreams and mirages'; having achieved this, the nation could move on to greater things. It was in terms of this realism, too, that Salazar differed from Maurras. He was very sensitive to suggestions that his thought derived from *Action Française*,[4] and he told António Ferro that he disapproved of Maurras's insistence on the primacy of politics. It was through the work of ordinary men, not the high affairs of kings, that a nation's life developed:

There is something we need which we have never had, and the lack of which has been responsible for our ups and downs. We need a will to give our actions continuity. . . . Our country's past is

[1] Salazar, *My Deposition*, SNI, Lisbon, p. 6 (January, 1949).
[2] Ferro, *op. cit.*, p. 49.
[3] Ibid., p. 105.
[4] Cf. Chapter 2 *supra*.

full of glory, full of heroism, but what we have needed, especially in the past 100 years, has been less brilliance and more staying power, something less showy, but with more perspective.[1]

The contrast between past glories and the ensuing failures had given rise to the melancholic fatalism expressed in ballad form in the *fado*: 'We're removed from the realities of life because we're given to living in a sham heroism', Salazar added. To reform the nation 'we must reform the individual'.

He remained convinced, however, of Portugal's capacity for greatness, and that her action on the wider world should be that of a civilizing mission. The nation of the present was the depository of spiritual forces accumulated over generations, and a trustee for the future.[2] But all would depend on recognition of the family as the most essential institution, one that was entrusted above all others with the educative function:

> When the family breaks up . . . man stands alone before the state, a stranger, defenceless, morally no more than half himself. He loses a name and becomes a number, and social life immediately assumes a different aspect.[3]

Hence the dignity of the father of the family must never be weakened by reducing him to the status of a tool in the production line; and the dignity of the whole family is assailed when the wives are simply regarded as cheap labour in the service of production, and the children are seen merely as potential contributors to it:

> When production ignores the family, it begins by absorbing all the members who are capable of working, the wife and the children, and finds work for them. It might be imagined that the additional wages so obtained were a benefit, but this is far from being the case. . . .

The family virtues cannot be bought. Industry cannot produce them. On the contrary, it is the family virtues which, developed in their own sphere, reach out through the breadwinner to industry and make its wheels turn:

> Happiness, contentment and *joie de vivre* are sources of energy which increase both the quality and the quantity of the work produced.

[1] Ferro, *op. cit.*, p. 247 *et seq.*
[2] Egerton, *op. cit.*, pp. 159-61.
[3] *Ibid.*, p. 166.

The family is the purest source of the moral factors of production.[1]

The key to Salazar's thinking lies in his association of beauty and order. He identified his government with truths he saw as absolute, and felt that the relative quality of human affairs called for absolute standards somewhere:

> There is much in life which is contingent, but truth, as well as authority, is bound up with the notion of the absolute . . . no one can rule in the name of doubt.[2]

Salazar had in his time been the victim of other people's censorship which, he admitted to Ferro, had infuriated him. This did not convince him that censorship was wrong, only that it needed reform. Portuguese journalism had always been virulent, slanderous and misleading, whatever side it represented, and the effects of this on a largely uneducated country called, in Salazar's view, for control. He complained that Western liberals rarely attacked the Russian censorship, and he referred to 'the enslavement of thought by huge capitalist organizations, by private interests, by the brute force of wealth'. Even in liberal countries, prejudiced or unscrupulous newspaper owners and writers exercised in subtle form their own peculiar brand of censorship, if only through selectivity. So state censorship was 'a lawful means of defence' against other kinds, and also against Communism which waged 'a latent war' and represented 'a foreign invasion which is ever imminent'. Censorship in Portugal, he declared, was 'chiefly interested in preventing the infiltration of Marxist ideas, the propagation of lies, the malefic and often irreparable effect of slander'. However, public opinion was irrepressible. Censorship could not nullify it. It would always find ways and means of making itself felt. Public opinion, in fact, was

> indispensable to a government and is at times a great stimulus; yet a government should retain some measure of control over its formation, for the very sake of its quality.[3]

Just as men allowed traffic signals to limit their freedom, so 'let us place our liberty in the hands of authority; only authority knows how to administer it and protect it'.[4]

[1] *Ibid.*, p. 195 (1933).
[2] Ferro, *op. cit.*, p. 24 *et seq.*
[3] *Ibid.*
[4] Ferro, *op. cit.*, pp. 154-5.

For some people this attitude is simply Fascist. Others would see it as an example of what the American writers Gordon and Danger-field, in their book *The Hidden Weapon*, called Salazar's 'romanticized medieval paternalism', or, more simply, what a great English news-paper editor once called 'the fatal teaching mentality'. It has to be judged, however, in the context of time and place. Salazar inherited a situation to justify almost any restriction. It is the prolongation of the 'emergency' which has to be called in question, and the unusual factor is that strange quality of 'timelessness' in Salazar: a dimension in which a century seems like a generation, or a decade like a fleeting year. Unhappily, even at its best, state censorship soon acquires the bias and deviousness he attacked in other systems, and it was he him-self who said:

> Indigestion or a family squabble could lead to the bad-tempered cutting out of a bit of news or a part of an article. I myself have in my time been the victim of the censorship, and I can assure you that it has stung me, infuriated me to the point of wanting to start a revolution.[1]

Sensitivity to what he called 'disrespect for authority' is surpassed in Portugal today only by hypersensitivity to foreign press attacks. This is understandable when a country has stood alone for years and the world has denied her a full and honest hearing. Still, the fact remains that what would be shrugged off elsewhere becomes 'an in-cident' in Lisbon. Basically, what the writer is up against is Portugal's great open wound, the perennial sense of inferiority, the shame that the glory and the dream have passed. Yet, suggest to the Portuguese that, if the right things are done, the glory could revive in a more realistic form, and they quickly take heart – even to the point of listen-ing generously to your strictures. Some foreign journalists who have written critically have been surprised to find themselves regarded, by officials, as 'friends of Portugal'. This is because they have written 'objectively' or in a way that tries 'to see things in the round', as the Portuguese like putting it. Quite often, foreign papers carrying anti-Portuguese articles get through to the bookstalls, but this may be because the rank and file will not be able to read them; as often as not, however, it depends on the mood of the moment. A lot of foreign 'revolutionary' material gets into Portuguese bookshops today. The

[1] Ferro, *op. cit.*, p. 150.

big problems arose, as we shall see, when Portuguese citizens wanted to publish a critical work. They are much less acute in 1970.

Reverting to the 1930s, one finds the question of police brutality looming large, as it had done in the past and was going to do again. Ferro raised the matter with Salazar who replied that complaints had been investigated thoroughly, and that doctors had been appointed to examine alleged victims. It had been found that some accusations were unfounded, but that others were true. There had been, in consequence, a shake-up in the police force. Salazar added, however, that the ill-treated prisoners were

> always, or almost always, of the terrorist and extremist category; people who manufactured bombs, and who, in spite of all the questions of the police, refused to reveal where they had hidden their criminal and murderous weapons.

Even while putting down the abuse, he said, he found himself asking

> whether the lives of a defenceless crowd, the lives of little children, do not fully justify a little rough handling of half a dozen such wretches.[1]

However, 'a little rough handling' may have been a profoundly euphemistic way of putting it. But the greatest source of frustration among the intellectuals has always been the inability to form a viable opposition – even what has been called an opposition *à la Turque*, some kind of consultative assembly where young and provocative minds could air grievances and criticisms. Salazar would argue that the Assembly and Chamber have always offered a forum for this, and up to a point they have; but in most of the elections after 1945 the opposition candidates withdrew and candidates elected to the Assembly on the National Union list are supporters of the regime. They can at times be critical, and the *Opiniones* of the Corporative Chamber are searching and by no means without influence on decision. But, from an opposition point of view, this is all too much 'within the family'. In 1934 Salazar explained:

> The efforts of the government and of its departments, and the non-party spirit of the revolution, are incompatible with the existence of either majorities or minorities, or with the recognition of private, regional or doctrinal elements. . . . Opposition parties,

[1] *Ibid.*, p. 183.

even if they should be friendly and kindly disposed, who discuss and vote by rule of thumb, waiting for the government to fall, are things of the past.[1]

The list of candidates recently backed by the National Union, he added, would have been different if there had been oppositionists of greater experience to choose from. Those who presented themselves, he thought, were too involved with theory and too untrained for the practical tasks facing the nation. Old prejudices and ideals were 'still active in men who would otherwise have been suitable candidates'.

There really was, and is, a dearth of suitable men for public life. It really was important, too, for the issues to be tackled on their merits, and for Portugal to be saved from the tendency to oppose for opposition's sake and nothing more. The meritocracy concept is suspect, yet the Portugal of pre-war years was desperate for leaders who really knew what they were doing. Nor did the post-war opposition produce leaders of statesmanlike calibre. Their programmes were often accused of being unconstructive and even negative, rich enough in proposals for new structures but lacking in detailed blueprints for reshaping the national life and economy. Yet it is equally true to say that, unless men have a chance to practise politics, it is hard for leaders to emerge. The only way to break the vicious circle is to take a chance on someone and let him have a go. Sterner critics assert that national growth was arrested by Salazar's over-prudent adherence to mediocre standards and an insatiable love of power which, whether he started with it or not, grew on him over the years. It might be fairer and more accurate to put it in the form that Salazar's work became his whole life, and that his persistence in office derived, not from a greed for power, but from a conviction that after him would come the deluge. He could not make an act of faith in his potential successors. It is arguable that good ones were simply not in evidence until very recent years, yet it is also true that Salazar was so single-minded that his impatience with views that clashed with his certainties drove him to inconsistency. One or two brilliant younger men of humble origin, called to high office, ended up in a dignified form of cold storage once they began to run, as he saw it, too fast. The result was that, with certain exceptions, ministerial calibre in the 1960s was weaker than it had been in the previous decade.

From the beginning, too, Salazar expected his ministers and

[1] D & A, p. 254.

senior civil servants to accept a sacrificial form of living. Their salaries were not, and are not, far from the poverty line. It is one thing
to call for dedication in public servants, and an end to graft and
corruption. It has always, moreover, been true that former ministers
could expect comfortable jobs in commerce and industry when they
returned to private life. But no one can be surprised that, as the years
went by, the younger and better minds began to seek more immediate
rewards. Many dedicated men entered Salazar's service, but too many
of them had to take a 'spare time' job to make ends meet, and this was
not the best way to prepare a nation for responsibility. In the last
analysis, however, the basic complaint of the opposition in the pre-
war, as in the post-war, years was that the education programme was
too gradual and subservient to austere financial prescriptions, while
the intellectuals, anxious to make a contribution, were restrained
from creating a ferment of new ideas like the corpus of speculation
which marked the latter half of the nineteenth century.

Between 1932 and 1939, Salazar sometimes took charge of two or
three portfolios at once, and at that stage it was, perhaps, unavoidable
that his government should look like a one-man band. His working
day was unremitting. He breakfasted at eight, read the papers, worked
until two. Then lunch and visitors. From four to six a rest, and a walk
in the garden; then back to the desk until ten. A light supper, and
back to work until midnight. The routine rarely changed. Salazar
never smoked. With meals he would take a glass of wine, bottled
on his own little plot in the Dão valley, but he mostly preferred
coffee or water. He would glance at all the books that came his way,
settling down from time to time with the odd biography, or with a
favourite author, English or French, and usually a political commen-
tator. He made it his business to keep up to date with the foreign
economic journals, and liked to know what was happening in the
field of sociology. But man, he would say, does not change much.
The modern world saddened him, the West became for him a kind
of abyss, and while, in the 1960s, he was to welcome the tourists'
foreign currency, he feared the impact of pagan attitudes on Portuguese social life. He never married, perhaps because the first unhappy
taste of rejection had dealt a blow to his pride, perhaps because the
almost anarchical taste for having his own way hindered an all-
embracing commitment. Then there was his painful reserve: an almost
Manichaean fastidiousness implying, perhaps, a distaste for sex, and
always a total involvement in his job. He delighted in feminine

company, and some of the ladies who called on him may have seen themselves as confidantes. The probability is that Salazar told them less than nothing. It is doubtful whether they ever called him anything other than 'Doctor'. He would show courtesy, concern for the family, even a chaste tenderness; but always the iron curtain of protocol. He would talk for relaxation, and if anyone tried to divert him, on social occasions, to 'business', he was likely to look at his watch and reach for his hat. He dreaded being asked for favours which he had no right nor wish to grant.

At the same time he grieved for his childless state and lack of family life, and wept a little when on one occasion he told a friend that he knew he would never have the joy of fondling his own grand-children. His loneliness was met up to a point by Dona Maria, the remarkable peasant girl he brought to Lisbon from Coimbra. She has stayed with him to this day, a lively sprig from the Dão valley, perhaps a mother-substitute despite her junior years, and in many ways a prototype of the parish priest's housekeeper. She was not well schooled, but was always bright and alert, conscious of affairs of state but much too discreet to ask questions, concerned to anticipate Salazar's wishes and sometimes to soothe his peevishness.

When he was already fifty, there came a morning when he heard some sobbing in the kitchen. Maria had with her a little girl of six years old, the baby sister of her brother-in-law. The child's mother was dead, and she herself was due to go to an orphanage. The story was outlined, and Salazar asked the child's name. It was Micas. He picked her up: 'If that's all it is, Micas will stay with me.' The child was later joined by another, this time Maria's niece: her name was Maria Antonia, and Salazar called her *Arc de Triomphe* because of her bandy legs. Both children grew up in his home and lived there until they married: no special status, no artificial injection into 'society'. Their husbands are working men. There are photo-graphs in private collections showing the girls clinging to Salazar as if he were their natural father. They meant as much to him.

During the 1930s, Republican and Socialist opposition mounted, either over human rights or economic policy, but for many people the sense of relief at having a tidy administration prolonged the initial euphoria. An incident in July 1937 throws some light on popular feeling at the time and also on aspects of Salazar's character. Stepping out of his car to go to Mass in a friend's private chapel near Lisbon, he was nearly killed by a bomb explosion. He stood quite still, told the crowd to be calm, and then went into Mass. Afterwards, his host, Dr José Trocado, tried to make him rest, but was simply told: 'Since it is not God's will that I should die, I'm going back to work.' Back in Lisbon, a huge crowd gathered outside his house, and Salazar came to the window: 'Just a word, ladies and gentlemen,' he said, 'there can be no doubt about it, we are indestructible because Providence has willed it so, and you on earth also desire it.' The crowd roared back: 'We're here to hear you.' Salazar asked: 'Can there be any doubt that the Revolution should continue?' The reply was a massive 'no'. Then, thanking the people for 'this manifestation', Salazar added: 'I thank you, not for myself, I've no concern with vanity and glory, but for the consoling conviction you all give me that our work can now never die.'[1] This kind of demonstration was unusual, and undoubtedly provoked some cynical reaction in the coffee shops that afternoon, but the incident reveals the curious blend of confidence and insecurity in Salazar's personality which had troubled the observant Cerejeira. It also reveals, however, the kind of confidence Salazar could inspire.

He lacked the warm appeal of a national hero. Many people were too uneducated to worry one way or the other, provided the government seemed to know what it was doing. But they were also aware of growing employment and housing opportunities; and a realization filtered through that the country was winning new status abroad to redeem the national sense of shame. There was, in all, a certain recognition of Salazar's achievement which could from time to time break out in unexpected ways. Salazar's own unemotional front hardly encouraged acclaim. The cold, unsmiling face, the apparent disregard of the greetings of passers-by, the lack of reaction to cheers on public occasions – all this was puzzling and even resented. Leaders were expected to have a hint of theatre about them, and to know, or pretend that they knew, all whom they met by name. Ferro once asked Salazar whether he realized how bad an image he could project. The reply was another compromise between certainty and doubt:

I could not flatter the people without being a traitor to my own conscience. Our regime is popular but it is not a government of the masses, being neither influenced nor directed by them. Those good people who cheer me one day, moved by the excitement of the

[1] *Anais de Revolução Nacional*, pp. 16, 157.

moment, may rise in rebellion next day for equally passing reasons. How often have I not been moved by the obvious sincerity of certain demonstrations. How often have I longed to speak to the people, to express my gratitude and my love. But when I am on the point of doing so, something holds me back, something which seems to say: 'Do not commit yourself, do not be led by emotion, by the mood of the occasion, to promise today what you will be unable to fulfil on the morrow' . . . If I were swayed by passing influences, if my attitude or utterances were determined by the enthusiasm of the multitude or even of my friends, I should no longer be myself, and then it would not be honest for me even to go on governing.[1]

Salazar's achievement by 1937 was considerable. The administrative services had been drastically reorganized, and a system of inspection established to cut out the graft and corruption common before the New State was created. Roads and railways had been rebuilt, the telephone system extended, a broadcasting station set up, harbours reconstructed; electrical power was being developed, important drainage, flood protection and irrigation works had been started. The army was being modernized. Housing estates were appearing, to provide cheap homes for industrial workers. More than a thousand primary schools had been opened to cope with an overwhelming illiteracy rate. West added:

> It is probable that there has never existed in Portugal such intense internal activity as there is today, manifesting itself not only in public works, but also in increased agricultural and industrial production. One cannot enter the smallest village without being able to observe evidence of renewed endeavour. The number of registered unemployed on 31 December 1935 was 42,000, or less than one per cent of the population. Emigration had declined from 40,000 in 1929 to 9,000 in 1935, but this may be due to restrictions imposed in Brazil.[2]

To be more precise, 3,500 miles of first- and second-class roads were renewed between 1927 and 1938, and 1,000 miles of new road built. The number of telephone subscribers trebled. By 1933, some 200,000 uncultivated acres had been brought into production. By 1936 wheat

[1] Ferro, *op. cit.*, p. 77.
[2] West, *op. cit.*, pp. 13-14.

production had risen by 71 per cent and imports of 180,000 tons had turned into exports of 110,000. Rice production per annum had risen from 17,000 tons to 84,000. Similar growth had been achieved with maize, beans, wine, oil and potatoes. An adverse foreign trade balance of 2,000,000 contos in 1927 was reduced by 1938 to 1,336,000. Bank deposits between 1928 and 1939 rose from 2,800,000 contos to 6,894,000, and the discount rate fell from 8 to 4 per cent. Schemes for work and shelter for the homeless were under way, and by 1941 were reported by Associated Press to have made substantial headway. By the outbreak of the Second World War, Salazar's reputation for management was standing high.

Though his decisions have affected millions of lives and attracted world-wide wrath, Salazar could appear in almost any foreign capital and pass unnoticed. To the end of his public life he remained, in many respects, one of the world's least-known statesmen.

His way of reducing chaos to order seemed to some observers to hint at a character other than Portuguese. Reflective, slow to act, undeviating once the decision was taken, he appeared to know his country as only a foreigner could, a Disraeli without the panache. Some have seen him as one of the atypical redemptive spirits who have arisen from time to time in Portugal to solve a national crisis or open a new phase of history: John of Avis, Nuno Alvares Pereira, Henry the Navigator, Afonso de Albuquerque, João de Castro. Was he of that company, or the 'poor Benedictine laybrother' described by Cunha Leal? In his day-to-day living there was that about him which seemed to recall the princely, half-eremitical Navigator as he sat at Cape St Vincent brooding over the Atlantic and planning great journeys for his ships. But Salazar was no traveller. Biographies of statesmen usually whirl from airport to high-powered conference, from dramatic interventions in debate to public ceremonial. Salazar's life was spent very largely at a desk; he rarely visited other people's homes, was hardly ever seen at a cinema or theatre, and left ceremonies and banquets to the President. When Queen Elizabeth visited Lisbon he was photographed in evening dress, but one wonders whether he had ever worn it before or was destined to do so again.

Yet this was the man who, in the coming war years and the sub-sequent Portuguese agony in Africa and Goa, was to leave an indelible mark on the history, not only of his country, but of Europe and the wider world. This realization has always tempered his more tolerant critics' sense of social grievance to the point where they can discern in his character the contrasts of a mottled landscape, and even at times to see some kind of distinction between the man and his regime. A leading oppositionist has suggested to the author that if, at the end of the war, Salazar had resigned, led a conservative opposition for five years, and stood for election in 1950, he might well have been returned to power. The impression he made abroad at the time when the Second World War broke out is ably described by Professor Medlicott in his study of the wartime economic blockade:

> The advent of Dr Oliveira Salazar and his form of government, although unquestionably patriotic, had considerably modified the traditional relationship with Britain. Courteous, informal, self-effacing but by no means inaccessible, he was a dictator without arrogance, a benevolent despot, or, in Lord Templewood's words, a philosopher-king; there were those on the Allied side who regarded him with less enthusiasm, but all agreed that he was among the more sober and hard-working of modern dictators, and, although the immense personal responsibility which his sense of duty imposed on him made him somewhat unapproachable in mind, he was not so in person. Already before 1939, he had been responsible for great economic progress in his country, and he was particularly proud of the recent revival in the colonies, whose valuable products . . . not only helped his strenuous efforts to raise the standards of economic life at home, but yielded enough for a considerable re-export trade, which the Allies now wished to curtail.[1]

Some years later, the *Scotsman*, looking back, could say that Britain's ancient ally was in good fettle, governed by a regime of professors in a discreet dictatorship. The unitary, corporative state actually worked, and the whole situation 'seems admirably suited to the Portuguese temperament'.[2] The *Manchester Guardian*, too, found him to be, not a flamboyant autocrat, but 'a diligent and commanding national manager'. The paper added:

> He has gained stature in staying the course, and Portugal, though pervaded by feudal manners, looks from the outside a much cleaner and neater country than when he took over.[3]

[1] Medlicott, ii, p. 511.
[2] 9 February 1957.
[3] 4 July 1957.

If those commentators seem to have been unaware of the ferment of internal opposition in Portugal, or to have discounted it, the reason doubtless is that Salazar still commanded a high degree of popular support. Perhaps it was a certain sense of trust in a man who was keeping his country out of a world war, and to her economic advantage, that had prompted an incident in 1941, witnessed by Egerton, Salazar's first biographer. He tells us that, about the time of Salazar's birthday in that year, a huge crowd gathered near the Ministry of Finance, where he still had his office:

It was not at all the kind of demonstration which has become such a standard feature of the totalitarian countries. There was nothing staged about it. Some cheered, some sang; there was the inevitable explosion of fire crackers.

Salazar stood on a balcony, ignoring the drizzle, the photographers' flashlights, and the rose petals showered from an upper window by a group of sycophantic ladies. There were oratorical efforts by a worker and a student. Salazar replied, speaking of peace and war, calling the nation to confidence. A huge procession formed and wound its way past the balcony:

As they passed the building of the Ministry of Finance, they looked up at Salazar, and their faces expressed confidence rather than enthusiasm, reverence rather than blind devotion.[1]

In his office beforehand, Salazar seemed tired. With his people he seemed to Egerton to grow younger, stronger and happier. Back home, later that night, he was his calm and confident self once more. He was by then in the throes of his wartime diplomacy, which history may judge to have been his most notable contribution to Portugal, and of far more significance to the Western world than is often realized. The linchpin of the whole story is the position of Portugal's Iberian neighbour, Spain. We must, therefore, return to 1936 to examine Salazar's policies in regard to the Spanish Civil War and Spain's relations with the Axis dictators.

[1] Egerton, op. cit., pp. 144-5.

CHAPTER 6

War in Spain

It was because of Portugal's sympathy for General Franco's Nationalists in the Spanish Civil War that critics abroad began to attach the Fascist label to the Portuguese regime. For them it was a simple case of like responding to like; dictatorships were either of the left (and Communist) or of the right (and Fascist), with each side closing its ranks in face of the other. Life, however, in the peninsula has never been open to quite such a simplified reading. Its modern dictators, whether for better or worse, were always different from other autocrats and from each other. Their policies were less predictable, more pragmatic and more flexible than those of a ruler working within the limits of a dogmatic world view. Moreover the character, history and even location of the Iberian peoples dictate their own principles to even the strongest dictators. Salazar's foreign policy in the 1930s and 1940s was a response to those realities. It was essentially a Portuguese and Iberian response, undetermined by a creed or an 'evangelical' intent, save in the defensive sense that Salazar, as a pre-war Catholic, saw Communism as civilization's *primary* threat. One man who sensed all this more clearly than most in 1936 was Britain's Foreign Secretary, Anthony Eden. Though British and Portuguese policies often clashed, his grasp of Portuguese realities and his ability to deal with them were to prove of major importance to the Allied cause in the Second World War.

After a century of internal conflict, Portugal's standing in Europe was that of a poor relation. Many Portuguese in fact had come to accept a junior partner's dependence on the fourteenth-century Anglo-Portuguese Alliance – though the 1890s had shown how tenuous that could be – and to regard as imprudent any attempt to devise for Portugal an independent foreign policy. Salazar's approach was quite different.[1] If Portugal were to rediscover herself, she would have to re-establish her own identity, albeit within the Alliance. It

[1] Chapter 7 *infra*.

was a matter of self-respect, of course, but also of defending those special Portuguese interests which, unless and until they offered a hope or posed a threat to Britain, would be of small concern to the ancient ally. Salazar's basic respect for Britain was always at war with his resentment at his ally's flair, as it seemed to him, for a certain type of cynical patronage.

His approach to the Spanish conflict has been analysed by the man who in 1936 was his Under-Secretary for War, Colonel (now General) Santos Costa. There were, according to him, three possibilities open to Portugal. The first was indifference, or collaboration with the Spanish Republican government and the various left-wing forces, including the Communists. The second was to use the conflict to break up the unity imposed on Spain by Castile for more than two centuries, and to foster the division of Spain into small, separate states; in a word, Balkanization. The third was to work to establish the whole peninsula as a primary element in the defence of Christian civilization[1]: two separate nations allied in a solidarity pact.

On the first point, Santos Costa continues, Portugal could hardly be indifferent to anything which happened in the peninsula, let alone the bloodiest civil war in Spanish history. On the other hand, collaboration with the Republicans would have been of the utmost value to Communist world strategy. The peninsula separated the Atlantic from the Mediterranean, and Africa from Europe. The Pyrenees made communication with Europe difficult, but the nineteen kilometres of the Straits were no obstacle to contacts between Spain and North Africa. Iberia, in 1936, was a glittering prize for Communist strategists and might even have been worth more to them than what they eventually acquired at the end of the Second World War. More immediately, Portugal faced the prospect of being overrun by a victorious Republican force, and her integrity was threatened by an amalgam of international Communism and the imperialism of certain sections of Spanish society (notably in Catalonia) which favoured the absorption of Portugal into Spain. The Portuguese national instinct had to find a way to preserve its nationhood in the conflict that was tearing the peninsula apart.

Secondly, the 'Balkanization' concept has to be seen against the

[1] Dez Anos de Política Externa (1936-47), intro. to vol. III. This series is a collection of diplomatic correspondence, mainly relating to Anglo-Portuguese relations, during the years of the Civil War and the Second World War. It is published by the Portuguese Ministry of Foreign Affairs.

background of peninsula geography. Dominion over Iberia requires control of the central plateau and its means of communication with the richer lands of the coast. Iberian history, in fact, can be epitomized in the struggle between the *Meseta* and the coastal lands for political and economic power, and Portugal's strategic value in this context is that command of the Tagus and Sado estuaries offers natural access to the centre of the peninsula. For such reasons, residuary Spanish ambitions regarding Portugal, never shared by General Franco, have tended to die rather hard.

Iberia's mountainous terrain favours the individualist and regional character of its peoples, and a tendency to guerrilla warfare. In 1936, the fragmentation of Spain was an idea canvassed in Portugal and the European chancellories. As the war dragged on, deep-seated ambitions for regional autonomy, more or less suppressed for two hundred years, emerged again, and autonomous governments were in fact set up in the Basque country[1] and Catalonia. The question for Portugal was whether or not to favour the independence movements. Superficially, a fragmented Spain seemed to offer protection for Portuguese integrity within the peninsula, and a larger role in world affairs. But Salazar saw it differently. In his view, the shattered unity of the Spanish nation would be a constant threat to Portuguese well-being and peace; and a Balkanized Iberia would be an open invitation to a Communist invasion of Portugal. For comparable reasons, Eden also defended the principle of Spanish integrity.

In the upshot, Salazar chose the principle of a strong and united Spain, closely bound to an independent Portugal in a common strategy. The persistence with which he pursued this policy has been described by Santos Costa as one of the most brilliant phases of Portuguese diplomatic history. With the *Pacto Iberico* of 1939,[2] there developed a policy of collaboration between Portugal and Spain which was to be of crucial importance for the defence of the peninsula, now stronger than it had been for three hundred years in relation to the wider world. Thanks to her confidence in Portuguese friendship, Spain was greatly aided in her resolve to remain neutral in the Second World War, while Portugal, confident of her position within the peninsula, was able to concentrate her forces on the defence of her

---

[1] It was the Basques' desire for autonomy that brought them into alliance with the Republican government, which purported to accede to their demands. Hence the anomalous position of an intensely Catholic region allied to the extreme left.
[2] L.B., v, p. 667.

overseas territories. This has remained true to the present time, and represents the enduring importance of the Pact in modern geopolitics and geostrategy.

It was perhaps not easy for other countries, in the impassioned 1930s, to make subtle distinctions and consider the possibility that Salazar's primary motivation in foreign policy was the preservation of Portuguese sovereignty, together with an anti-Communism that did not *inherently* favour the Axis powers. His admiration for Mussolini's early work came to be tempered by his discomfort at Italy's growing relationship with Germany, and he was to show that he feared the prospect of a German-dominated Spain as much as he feared what he thought of as a Communist victory. On the other hand, he thought that a victorious Franco would resist domination by the Axis, but that a Republican success would certainly subjugate Spain to Communism and the Soviet Union. He always insisted that he was anti-Communist but not anti-democratic, but his difficulty in convincing the world of this has had its bearing on Portugal's foreign relations to this day. Reading today his correspondence with his ambassadors of thirty years ago, one sees why British and Portuguese perspectives were bound to be different. Though the war in Spain had practical implications for the whole of Europe, and Britain and France were greatly concerned to inhibit an 'escalation', the problems facing Portugal by reason of her proximity to Spain were more immediate and direct. For many earnest men all over the world the Republican cause in Spain was an apocalyptic symbol. But the actual conflict was on Portugal's doorstep, and her sovereignty was at stake. This was true in any event, for if a triumphant Spanish left would have turned its predatory eye on its neighbour, so would certain sections of the Falange. It was for such reasons that Portugal's participation in the non-intervention policy was less than enthusiastic. Salazar himself was to admit in a public speech at the end of the war how serious his misgivings over non-intervention had been.[1]

A clear exposition of his mind at this time appears from a record of a talk he had in Lisbon with the British Ambassador in May 1938. He set out to show why Portugal, in a certain sense, had always to be wary of Spain (though not of Franco personally). Salazar writes:

I reminded him of the imperialist tradition of the absolute monarchy in Spain, the federalist tradition of the First Republic, the

[1] Disc., iii, p. 137.

infiltration tactics of the Bourbon constitutional monarchy, and the attitude of the Second Republic . . . I explained to him the nature of the political elements prevailing in Spain since the start of the civil war, and the characteristics, mentality and (imperialist) tendencies of a section of the Falange.[1]

Salazar went on to argue that Britain was mistaken in not supporting the Spanish Nationalists, and in thinking that after the war, economic weakness would drive Franco into the British camp. This was a failure to see 'how much a nation is capable of when it resolves to suffer'. It was in Britain's interest to ensure that Portugal's relationship with Spain was strengthened so as to counterbalance German and Italian influences. This would reduce the risk of Spain being used as a means of attacking Britain through Portugal. As for France, her anti-Nationalist tendencies were stirring up anew the hostility felt for her in the peninsula since the time of the Napoleonic invasion. (Salazar contrives to make this sound as though it had happened in very recent times.)

In one respect events proved Salazar wrong, for Franco did turn to Britain for aid after the battle was won. His relations with Britain, however, owed much to Salazar's lubricating efforts, and the *Pacto Iberico* did to some extent, albeit indirectly, involve Franco with the Allied camp.[2] Moreover, it was perfectly true that a Portugal occupied by Britain's enemies would have posed a serious threat to Britain's Atlantic sea routes, and to her shipping travelling by the Cape and thus within striking distance of Angola and Mozambique.

It was in March 1936 that Armindo Monteiro, then Portuguese Foreign Minister, pointed out to Eden the growing importance of the Spanish Communist Party: its alliance with other extremist elements, its influence inside the Republican government, its probable dream of an Iberian Federation. After the civil war had broken out in July, Lisbon made repeated attempts to find out what London was really thinking, and how the British government would view a victory for the Spanish left.[3] The replies were at first evasive, though Eden did

[1] L.B., i, pp. 360-1.
[2] How Portugal helped Spain to stay out of the Second World War is discussed in Chapter 7.
[3] A definition of terms: Franco's *Nationalists* rose against the *Republican* government, a regime comparable to the French Popular Front. The Nationalists are thus sometimes referred to as the 'insurgents'. At first, the government carried on from Madrid, transferring to Valencia in November 1936; while Franco set up a rebel government at Burgos. Thus 'the Valencia government' means the

say that a Communist-dominated Spain would not be pleasing to his government.[1] The fact was that Eden was faced with a sharp division in British public opinion over the Spanish war, the Labour Party and the left-wing generally identifying themselves with the Republican cause as a struggle for social justice, freedom and democracy. But for Eden there was one thing sure: he saw that this currently localized struggle could easily bring the major European powers into conflict, and that it must at all costs be contained. The French Prime Minister, M. Blum, was under domestic pressure to aid the Spanish Republicans, with whom his own moral sympathies lay, but he too was restrained from outright intervention by the wider political realities. Eden asked him, on 23 July, whether he would supply arms to the Spanish government, and Blum replied that he would. Eden commented: 'It is your affair, but I ask one thing: be prudent.' Two days later Blum decided that France would not supply arms, but that a shipment would be arranged through Mexico, and no hindrances would be put in the way of private transactions.[2] Meanwhile, Salazar had cabled his minister in Paris to the effect that Portugal was not organizing a military force to go to Franco's aid, and he decided not to recognize the Burgos (Nationalist) government for the time being.[3]

Salazar could not do much for Franco in terms of actual military aid, but in the early phases of the war Franco received a lot of German aid through Portugal. Franco's elder brother Nicolás, aided by Gil Robles, was allowed to set up an office in Lisbon for the purchase of arms. In his classic history of the civil war, Hugh Thomas relates that Salazar stated on 1 August his intention of helping the insurgents 'with all available means', including the intervention of the Portuguese army if necessary. Professor Thomas adds:

> As a result, Spanish Republicans who escaped into Portuguese territory were usually handed over to the Nationalists. The Portuguese press served the Nationalists from the start. On

Republicans, 'the Burgos government' means the Nationalist insurgents. Portugal maintained technical diplomatic relations with the Republicans in Madrid until 22 October 1936, but Salazar did not even then recognize the Burgos government. He kept in touch with Franco through private intermediaries, and in November 1937 sent Dr Pedro Theotonio Pereira to Franco as a 'special agent'. When Salazar finally recognized the Nationalists, Pereira became a full Ambassador.

[1] L.B. iii, pp. 5, 14, 27.
[2] Thomas, pp. 219, 225.
[3] L.B., iii, pp. 35, 49-50.

August 20, the German Minister at Lisbon reported that war material brought from Germany in the steamships *Wigbert* and *Kamerun* had been despatched onwards to Spain most smoothly. Salazar, he said, had removed 'all difficulties . . . by his personal initiative and handling of details'.[1]

Hugh Thomas claims that eventually 20,000 Portuguese fought for the Nationalists, some of them unwilling conscripts, most of them volunteers, and quotes in support Sir Robert Hodgson's 'Spain Resurgent'. In a speech delivered in May 1939,[2] Salazar declared that 'several thousand' Portuguese had fought under Franco's banner.[3] The Spanish Republican Julio Alvarez del Vayo complains that late in August 1936 the Republican situation worsened and that this was largely due to foreign assistance to the insurgents. 'Badajoz', he says, 'was captured, thanks partly to the co-operation of the Portuguese frontier authorities, who, not content with allowing munitions lorries to be unloaded in Portuguese ports . . . handed over to them (the Nationalists) all Republican combatants who attempted to fall back into Portugal.'[4] The German Chargé d'Affaires in Lisbon, Count du Moulin, informed Berlin on 22 August that 'the Portuguese government determined on the clear policy of complete support for the rebels as far as it was possible to do so and maintain the semblance of formal neutrality'.[5]

All this was very disturbing to the Foreign Office in London where it was felt that all outside intervention in Spain risked inflating the civil war to European proportions. At the end of July, Eden flatly told Monteiro that he found Fascists and Communists equally displeasing, to which Monteiro replied that an insurgent victory in Spain would not necessarily mean a regime of the German or Italian type, while a Communist victory would be a triumph for anarchism, with grave consequences for France and Europe.[6] By this time German

---

[1] Thomas, p. 231.
[2] Disc., iii, p. 137.
[3] I have made searching inquiries about this in Lisbon, especially among British residents living there at the time. The general impression is that the numbers were very much less than 20,000; that volunteers were recruited for a *Legion Viriato* which was organized in Spain; and that some of the Portuguese who crossed the border joined the Republicans. No one recalls any conscripts.
[4] Alvarez del Vayo, *Freedom's Battle*, London-Toronto, 1940, p. 35. Also p. 99 *infra*.
[5] DGFP, p. 54.
[6] L.B., iii, p. 56.

and Italian military aid was flowing fast to the Spanish Nationalists, while Russia was supplying the Republican side with money and materials. At the instigation of Foreign Minister Yvon Delbos, the French government decided to appeal urgently to countries likely to aid either side in Spain for a general agreement not to intervene: in other words, for a Non-Intervention Pact. On 31 July, Delbos announced that France would ban the supply of arms to Spain, and the Minister of Commerce announced that all Spanish credits in France would be blocked. The French proposals began to go out to the various embassies, and Eden in London committed all his energies to the non-intervention cause. Within a few days the Soviet government had agreed to join in the Pact in principle, but urged that Portugal should be asked to join the subscribing states. This request was issued at once, and Monteiro reserved his judgment.

On 7 August, he talked to the British Chargé d'Affaires in Lisbon, and pointed out that Russia's reference to Portugal had to be seen in the light of her own blatant intrusion in the civil war. It was not the first time, he said, that European blocs had formed behind the opposing factions in a Spanish civil war, and on the last occasion Portugal had had to serve as a battleground. Hence her need to preserve the utmost liberty of action now, and the proposal that she should do nothing to avert the catastrophe threatening her showed a lack of understanding of the sacrifice she was being asked to make. Portugal naturally wanted to harmonize her policy with Britain's, but could Britain guarantee immediate protection by land, sea and air if Portugal were attacked from Spain? As a Bolshevist victory there would isolate Britain between the Communist and Fascist blocs, could not Britain regard the Spanish insurgents, if not with favour, at least without antipathy?[1]

Even Eden seems to have found this anti-Communist fear a shade neurotic, yet the fact was that Portuguese ambassadors, having sounded out opinions in various capitals, were sending home ominous and uniform messages, whether from Paris or the Vatican. The minister in Madrid spoke for most of them when he said that 'in the event of the defeat of the insurgents, I consider a Soviet regime will be inevitable; there will in consequence be an attempt to foment revolution in Portugal, and a war against Portugal is to be expected'.[2] However, by the middle of August, Portugal had accepted the

[1] *Ibid.*, p. 89.
[2] *Ibid.*, p. 95.

non-intervention policy in principle, reserving liberty of action if her border should seem to be threatened by the progress of the war.[1] At the same time, Britain and France exchanged Notes undertaking to ban the export of arms from their countries to Spain, and to enforce the undertaking as soon as agreement had been signalled from Rome, Berlin, Moscow and Lisbon. Monteiro then wrote to the British Ambassador in Lisbon, setting out the terms for Portugal's entry into the Pact. His conditions certainly read as though he intended to play for time. For instance, no action was to be construed as intervention if it were dictated by one of the following:

1. Defence of the lives, property and liberty of Portuguese subjects.

2. Application of international decisions occasioned by the war.

3. Mediation between the contending parties.

4. Defence against any 'regime of social subversion' which may be set up in Spain 'if the necessity of safeguarding Western security demands such defence'.

5. Maintenance of relations with local or central authorities exercising *de facto* power in Spanish territory.

6. The formal recognition of either contending party as 'belligerents', or of a new Spanish government.

Not only should there be a ban on the export of arms, but it would be contrary to the spirit of the Portuguese conditions if other countries allowed volunteers to go to the theatre of war, the opening of subscriptions to aid the contestants, or the despatch of money to them. It was a tough list, but the reason for Monteiro's caution may lie in the references he makes to the continuing supply by France of 'arms, munitions, aircraft and warships' to the Spanish government forces.[2]

On 21 August Italy signalled her agreement to the French proposals to ban the supply of arms, but reserved her right to send money and volunteers to Spain. Russia followed with a ratification of her agreement-in-principle, and Stalin issued a ban on the export of war materials. Germany signed the French proposals, and Eden adopted Italy's suggestion for a commission to supervise the working of the Pact. A Non-Intervention Committee was set up, the first meeting

[1] L.B., iii, p. 136.
[2] *Ibid.*, p. 176.

to be held in London on 9 September. Under pressure from London, the Portuguese government published a decree on 27 August, prohibiting the export of arms to Spain, subject to the usual reservations. Feeling between Portugal and France was now running high, and Britain was putting pressure on Portugal in an effort to bring her into the Non-Intervention Committee. Monteiro explained his attitude to this in a Note to the French minister in Lisbon on 1 September.[1] He evidently felt that to join the Committee would to some degree imply a surrender of national sovereignty. He preferred the principle of direct commitments between governments rather than an international organism without juridical standing. However, Portugal would not withhold her support from this proposal, provided the competence of the commission would be rigorously delimited, that the reservations and conditions notified by the various governments would be respected, and that the commission's impartiality would be guaranteed. Portugal would enter into the commission's work if this would consist of correlating information from responsible sources and transmitting it to individual governments which alone could decide how best to fulfil their contracted obligations.

It was early in September 1936 that the crews of two Portuguese warships in Lisbon locked up their officers and prepared to sail to Spain to join the government forces. Salazar ordered the ships to be destroyed by gunfire and issued a statement on 9 September[2] to the effect that the Spanish war was an international struggle on a national battlefield; that the left-wing press in Britain and France was campaigning against the Portuguese state; that people of position in Portugal, including civil servants, had been guilty of undercover subversion, and that the offensive against Communism would now be reinforced in defence of Portugal and Western civilization. The next day he issued a decree requiring service personnel and civilian public servants alike to declare allegiance to the social order of the *Estado Novo*, and that they repudiated Communism and all revolutionary ideas. The oath to the flag, already in use in the army and navy, would no longer be deemed sufficient. A week later the Portuguese Legion was founded. This had nothing to do with the Spanish war as such, and must be plainly distinguished from the *Legion Viriato*. It was and remains today a voluntary 'Home Guard' devoted to combating Communism and anarchy.

[1] *Ibid.*, p. 224.
[2] *Ibid.*, pp. 255-8.

Meanwhile, the first meeting of the Non-Intervention Committee[1] had taken place in London with twenty-six countries represented, but not Portugal, who, according to her ambassador in Berlin, was waiting for other countries to ban the departure from their countries of volunteers for Spain before she would take her seat. He added that the German ship *Usamoro* had been refused facilities for unloading a cargo of arms in Lisbon.[2] The London meeting agreed on 9 September on a general embargo of arms for Spain. A week or so later, Monteiro was in Geneva where he addressed the League of Nations.[3] Portugal, he said, was prepared to support the non-intervention policy, while safeguarding herself by reservations appropriate to her special circumstances. In an attack on the legality of the Spanish Republican government, he argued that, without non-intervention, some countries might be tempted to help a government which, he claimed, did not represent the will of the Spanish people and was not exercising effective authority. Its legitimacy was more a matter of appearance than of legal substance. The Portuguese had only one desire: to see the end of a terrible struggle in a country for whom they had profound feelings of friendship. By this time Monteiro had come to believe that Eden was right and that Portugal should now join in the NIC. Salazar was harder to persuade, and in fact issued a distinctly acidulous *Nota Oficiosa* on the subject.[4] The Spanish uprising, he wrote, was an army movement against Communism, not against parliamentary democracy. The anti-Portuguese campaign in Europe had nothing to do with the 'reasonable conditions' she had outlined for her entry into NIC, but arose from the frustration of those who had plotted to tie Portugal's hands, while leaving to others complete freedom of action. Had Portugal been opposed to the Spanish Nationalists, there would have been no such anxiety to get her to the table. However, he concluded, perhaps surprisingly, Britain at least understood the delicacy of Portugal's position.

Eventually, Monteiro's counsels prevailed, and Portugal took her place at the NIC meeting in London on 28 September, by which time Lord Plymouth had succeeded Mr W. S. Morrison as British representative. Within twenty-four hours, the Spanish government's delegate to the League of Nations was protesting that Germany was

[1] Hereinafter referred to as NIC.
[2] Thomas, p. 278.
[3] L.B., iii, p. 378.
[4] *Ibid.*, p. 311.

supplying planes to Franco and that German cargo ships were unloading petrol, light tanks, dismantled planes, hand grenades and
various arms in Lisbon, whence they would be transported by land
to Spain. In a Note to the Portuguese government, the Spanish
Republicans complained that 'three rebel planes remained after
landing in Portugal for one night, before going on to bomb Badajoz
next day'. A few days later, at another meeting of NIC in London,
the Soviet Ambassador, Maisky, alleged that Portugal was letting her
territory be used as a Nationalist base of operations, and demanded
a special commission to patrol the Spanish-Portuguese frontier.
The Russian charges, outlined in a letter of 6 October,[1] detailed
complaints from Alvarez del Vayo, then Spanish Republican Foreign
Minister in Madrid. These stated that a train carrying fourteen
aeroplanes came through Portugal and travelled via Carceres to
Seville; that the Portuguese munitions factory, Barcarena, had sent
machine-guns to the insurgents under the guise of scrap iron; that a
consignment of asphyxiating gas and other Italian war materials
had been sent from Lisbon to the Spanish frontier. Maisky quoted
reports in the *New York Times* and the London *Daily Herald* to show
that the Spanish insurgents were negotiating for the purchase of
war materials from an office in Lisbon, which the former paper
designated as No. 28, Rua Castilho. Its correspondent, Frank
Kluckholm, added:

> Watchers can see caravans bearing oil and other unknown products,
> covered carefully by sheets of canvas, rumbling towards the
> Spanish frontier, and no secret has been made of the fact that these
> shipments go into Spain.[2]

When the allegations came before NIC on 9 October, the Portuguese Ambassador, Calheiros, walked out, but later showed sympathy
to a request from Eden for an early reply to the Russian charges.
Meanwhile, Monteiro instructed Calheiros to warn the French
Ambassador discreetly that Portugal had a complete dossier on the
details of French intervention on the side of the Spanish Republicans.
On 18 October, the Portuguese Chargé d'Affaires in Alicante reported
that Russian arms and men for Spain were still arriving via Levantine
ports, while the Spanish Nationalists' mission in Lisbon reported aid
to the Madrid government by Russia and even Mexico. Stories from

[1] *Ibid.*, pp. 413-17.
[2] *Ibid.*, p. 416.

Geneva, travelling via London and Paris, suggested that Soviet Foreign Minister Litvinov was involved in planning a Communist Catalan state.

On 22 October Monteiro replied to the Spanish and Russian charges in two long and detailed letters addressed to the chairman of NIC. These documents were devastating, yet few writers who repeat the charges bother to examine the answer. In a somewhat ostentatious gesture, the letters were rushed from Lisbon by special train to be in time for the NIC meeting, and the idea apparently was to stress that Portugal was responding to her ancient ally's request. Only a few days before, in a speech to army and navy officers, Salazar had declared that nothing could alter the Anglo-Portuguese Alliance.[1]

The reply to the Spanish Republicans[2] pointed out that the Non-Intervention Pact related only to an arms embargo, and that Portugal adhered to the Pact only on 21 August. Hence some of the charges were either outside NIC's competence or related to dates prior to Portugal's commitment. Nevertheless, said Monteiro, he would deal with all the points raised. His answers may be summarized thus:

1. The three aircraft which 'stayed the night' were unarmed, were forced down by an emergency, and in one case needed repairs. They landed on the evening of 13 August and took off for Spain on the morning of 14 August. But the bombing of Badajoz took place on the morning of 13 August. Hence it could not be said that the three aircraft had flown from Portugal to bomb Badajoz, nor was there any indication that they had been involved in that bombardment before they landed in Portugal. Whenever armed Spanish planes landed in Portugal they were interned. This had already happened on two occasions, once to a Republican and once to a Nationalist plane. Both were still being held at the Alverca military aerodrome.

2. The ship *Kamerun*, supposed to be carrying tanks, aircraft, bombs and grenades for Spain, arrived in Lisbon from Gibraltar, an innocent port, on 21 August and sailed again the same day for Hamburg, arriving there on 27 August. (The dates could be confirmed from Lloyd's Shipping List.) The ship did not approach a quay but was unloaded up-river by a tender. It would have been impossible to discharge planes, tanks, bombs and grenades in this way. The cargo was one of petroleum, an item not prohibited by the arms ban.

[1] Disc., ii, p. 209.
[2] L.B., iii, p. 473.

3. It was quite untrue to say that Spanish insurgents were given the run of Portugal while Republican refugees were interned there. Thousands of refugees of both persuasions had been received in Portugal, and only armed combatants crossing the border were interned. Many of these, moreover, had been released at the request of the Spanish Republican Ambassador in Lisbon, who on 10 April had written to Monteiro:

> I have always rendered justice, and in my previous Note I paid tribute to the noble attitude by which the government of Portugal had given shelter to a number of Spanish refugees whose political ideals clash with those of Portugal's *Estado Novo*. Your Excellency's government have thus honoured one of the most noble international traditions . . .

4. Monteiro hotly denied that any Republican refugees had been handed over to the Nationalists, and pointed out that the charges named no names, dates or places.[1] On the other hand there had been incidents like that of 13 August when a group of armed Republicans crossed into Portugal and shot a Spaniard living there.

5. Monteiro also denied the assertion that the Spanish insurgents were given unrestricted transit through Portugal, which enabled them to find aircraft, arms, munitions, etc. The charges, he said, did not attempt to say how or when they had managed to find such things in a country which lacked them herself.

6. The Republican Ambassador in Lisbon was in no way restrained, and was allowed not only his freedom to move about as he wished but also all the usual honours and guards to protect him from his hostile compatriots. Two Spanish policemen attached to the embassy and alleged to have been forced back over the border into Spain had in fact returned of their own free will to join the Nationalists. They had written to their ambassador telling him they had done this, and the story appeared in the Spanish press. By way of contrast to all this, the Portuguese Embassy in Madrid had not been protected by the Republicans, and had had to move to Alicante.

Monteiro made equally short work of the Russian allegations.[2] The famous train allegedly carrying aircraft was supposed to have been made up of twenty-three platform wagons and to have travelled

---

[1] On one occasion the Portuguese ship *Nyassa* returned 1500 Republicans to their own side at Valencia (L.B., iv, p. 140).

[2] L.B., iii, p. 494.

via Carceres. But in fact no trains of this kind had travelled on the appropriate lines at all since 18 August, when the Carceres route was re-opened. Barcarena was not a munitions factory at all, but a place where fireworks were made, and it certainly was not capable of producing machine-guns. A careful check had been made and Portugal's supply of machine-guns, all obtained either from Vickers-Armstrong in England or Madson in Copenhagen, was found to be intact. Nothing was known about asphyxiating gas being supplied to Spain, but if proof could be adduced and names given, Portuguese authorities would ensure that the persons concerned were severely punished. Why, Monteiro asked, should Franco want to make use of Portuguese ports for his supplies, when he controlled major Spanish ports like Vigo, Corunna, Ferrol and Cadiz?

There is only one point on which Monteiro is evasive, and that relates to the alleged headquarters in Lisbon for recruiting men and purchasing arms. All he says is:

> It is often repeated that there is a Spanish Military Committee working in Lisbon. But no names are mentioned. Yet how can credit be given to an information in which Señor Gil Robles is termed a Fascist, when he became a cabinet minister in the Spanish Republic under the 1931 Constitution? The other names mentioned in the accusation do not refer to persons at present in Portugal.

He is on stronger ground when he points out that arms are not manufactured in Portugal at all; that Portugal is currently working on her own re-armament programme and cannot supply war material for anyone else; and that Portuguese law prohibits private persons from importing arms. One is left with the feeling that the house in the Rua Castilho probably did contain some kind of military mission, at least at one stage, and that perhaps its job was to establish contacts with sources of supply in a number of foreign countries. Lisbon has always been a catchpoint for that kind of activity, and still is.

But Monteiro is not concerned to remain on the defensive. The letter contains a long, detailed and documented indictment of the way in which the Russians built up in Spain, well before the civil war, 'a vast organization supplied with rich means of propaganda and action'. The civil war, Monteiro alleges, is the outcome of Soviet influence in Spanish affairs. In this he quotes French Foreign Minister Yvon Delbos's book *L'Experience Rouge*[1] and says that a

[1] Yvon Delbos, *L'Expérience Rouge*, pp. 185-6, Paris, 1933.

number of French and Portuguese newspapers have already given
precise details of the way armed cells were built up in the south of
Spain with minute instructions for 'the first day of the revolution',
including lists of names of those who were to be murdered – usually
headed, for some obscure reason, by the local medical practitioner!
The letter also quotes the French paper *Le Matin*, which in March
outlined the programme decided on at the February meeting of the
Comintern. This included sending two highly skilled revolutionary
technicians, Bela Kun and Losovski, to the peninsula to organize a
workers' government, institute mass terror, form a Red Army and
provoke war against Portugal. Monteiro adds that Bela Kun with
several assistants – Losovski, Janson, Riedel, Primac (or Primakoff),
Berzine and Neumann – arrived in Barcelona in March.[1] Russian
arms began to arrive and an increasing flow of Russian advisers and
experts followed. Monteiro names some of the ships carrying arms
and the ports they arrived at. He also gives more names of the
infiltrated Russian 'technicians'. Soviet Ambassador Rosenberg is
named as the 'hidden spirit' of the Madrid government. Ten
deliveries of Russian aircraft, tanks and munitions to the Spanish
Republicans during the civil war are carefully identified with precise
description. Certainly these charges are much more specific than
anything levelled at the Portuguese by the Russians. As Eden was to
tell the House of Commons a week later:

> Almost the whole burden of the criticisms of Soviet Russia is
> addressed against one country, and that the smallest of the three
> Powers, Portugal. . . . Nor have we any information whatever to
> support the Soviet charges . . .[2]

The Italian Chargé d'Affaires in Alicante told his Portuguese opposite
number earlier in October that he was sure the Madrid government
would not be pressurizing Portugal so hard were it not for the
influence of Rosenberg.

Monteiro's document was presented to NIC on 27 October, a few
days after Maisky had reserved his government's right to supply

---

[1] Professor Hugh Thomas insists in *The Spanish Civil War* (p. 104f.) that Kun
could not have been in Spain at this time, as he was ill and weak, and was soon
afterwards shot. However, Thomas adds, it is possible that 'Erno Gero, the
Hungarian Communist who under the name of "Singer" had been for a time
"instructor" to the French Party, did visit Spain at this time'.
[2] Eden, *Facing the Dictators*, p. 412.

arms to Madrid as other countries were in breach of the Pact. He informed Plymouth of this on 24 October, the day on which Portugal broke off diplomatic relations with the Madrid government because of its involvement with the Russians. Britain had argued against this step, for Eden thought it would only serve to create a new imbalance in the international comity. But while Salazar spoke of the break as painful and regrettable – 'we and Spain are two brothers with separate houses in the peninsula' – he felt it was essential. Portugal was defending international order against Communist Party designs, and she had given proof of her political, moral and intellectual independence in the face of the 'intolerable Pharisaism' of international life.[1] Shortly afterwards, Portugal, Brazil, Chile, Argentina and Peru agreed that they would all unite in recognizing Franco's government as soon as Portugal decided that the time was ripe to do so.[2] Italy and Germany did so on 17 November. Meanwhile, on 8 November, the Republican government had moved from Madrid to Valencia, and Salazar took over the Portuguese Foreign Ministry in addition to his other duties, while Monteiro prepared to go to London as ambassador. This step was to prove of the utmost importance for Anglo-Portuguese relations during the Second World War.

So far, the best that could be said about the non-intervention policy was that it amounted to an attempt to limit the risks of war. Eden called it 'an improvised safety curtain' which was, as he wrote years later, tattered and full of holes, but 'better than total war in Spain and a European war out of that'. Efforts to strengthen the policy by inspection and effective control mechanisms were bound to run into trouble, not only because the purveyors of arms and personnel did not want to be controlled, but also because, with a country like Portugal, all sorts of sensitivities were certain to be aroused by any suggestion that she needed to be invigilated. Even apart from her basic desire for Franco's success – which meant she could hardly be *sorry* that he was getting reinforcements from abroad[3] – she saw any suggestion of inspection by a NIC team as an intrusion into her sovereignty, possibly by the very people she had accused of being the real instigators of the war. Nor can one discount the special touchiness of a nation still struggling with an inferiority complex.

[1] Disc., ii, p. 221.
[2] L.B., iii, p. 577.
[3] *Ibid.*, pp. 607-8.

That she had nothing much to hide appears from her ultimate readiness to invite British observers to come and stand guard over her. Britain was the old ally, and there was something less humiliating about British 'overseers' than about any sort of mixed team. These delicate considerations, of course, were lost on British and European public opinion, and Portugal simply appeared as an obstructionist working for the 'Fascist' group. When NIC approved, on 12 November, Lord Plymouth's plan to uncover breaches of the Pact by posting observers on the Spanish frontiers, Portugal, together with Germany and Italy, argued that before the plan could be put up to the two Spanish contestants, control by air would have to be included. This was virtually to ask for the impossible and seemed to reflect a wish to prolong the argument, not to reach quick conclusions.

The position, however, was deteriorating. German and Italian troops were now pouring into Spain. Germany accused Russia of having 50,000 troops in Spain. Russia reported that Germany was about to send an additional 60,000. Something had to be done. At the end of October, when Franco was threatening to blockade the Republican ports, Eden told the House of Commons that neither of the Spanish sides would be granted belligerent rights, that the Royal Navy would protect British ships against either Spanish side, in waters outside the three-mile limit, and that he was going to introduce legislation banning all British ships from carrying arms for Spain.[1] Then on 2 December, NIC decided to submit Plymouth's control plan to both Burgos and Valencia (Portugal abstaining from the vote). Two days later, Britain and France put up a mediation plan to Germany, Italy, Portugal and Russia. Eden's idea was that these leading powers should call an armistice, send a commission to Spain, hold a plebiscite, and then set up a government of men like Salvador de Madariaga, who had kept out of the civil war. The replies were not exactly heart-warming. Russia and Portugal agreed to support any mediation plan which could be devised. Germany and Italy said much the same but added that they thought the idea would be unacceptable to both Spanish sides.

By the time Britain and France had sent an *aide-mémoire* to Salazar on 5 December,[2] there were really three main British proposals before the NIC: (1) for a control system to stop arms being sent to Spain;

[1] Eden, *op. cit.*, p. 415.
[2] L.B., iii, p. 591.

(2) for a mediation plan; and (3) for banning recruitment of 'volunteers' in NIC countries. Salazar's reply to all these proposals was trenchant.[1] What it amounted to was that, first, NIC members were infringing the Pact at the moment, and public agreements seemed to mean little in practice; secondly, that whatever happened in Portugal would be controlled by Portuguese authorities and by nobody else; thirdly, a distinction had to be made as regards mediation. If the Spanish problem were merely one of an armed conflict between two political parties seeking power, the NIC view of mediation would make sense. But if, as Salazar himself believed, what was taking place was a struggle between civilization and barbarism, then the NIC view of mediation was simply incomprehensible. Salazar continued with the revealing remark that what Spain needed was an indisputable victory followed by strong but generous rule of a kind she had lacked for so long. 'The important thing to look at in Spain,' he added, 'is not the war, but the peace.' However, he concluded duly, if both sides showed that they wanted mediation, Portugal would co-operate. At the turn of the new year he followed this up by a letter to the British Embassy and French Legation in Lisbon, supporting the ban on recruitment, adding that Portuguese participants in the Spanish war were mostly revolutionaries who were involved in plots against Portugal under the Spanish Republic. Thus 1936 ended with Portugal pledged in principle to ban recruiting on her soil for the war in Spain, and to help with mediation efforts if both Spanish contestants were to show a desire for it. The question of supervision to ensure that the arms ban enshrined by the Pact was observed remained very prickly, and for the moment Salazar would have none of it. Here was the start of the many major problems lying ahead for Portugal in her endeavours to balance her peninsula policy with her wider international obligations and her special alliance with Britain.

January 1937 opened inauspiciously. Eden had been working for some time to try and improve Anglo-Italian relations in the Mediterranean without showing the sort of weakness some of his colleagues were prone to. He was in no doubt at all that Mussolini would respond only to strength, and that the League of Nations' failure to impose sanctions strong enough to deter the Italians from their Abyssinian adventure had brought Mussolini, whose bluff had worked, closer to

[1] L.B., iii, pp. 603-8.

Hitler, who admired success. On 2 January, Eden concluded with
Italy a gentleman's agreement which ought to have halted Italian
intervention in Spain. In fact, only two days later, another 4,000
Italian troops were on their way there. Eden then knew that it was
absolutely useless to negotiate with Mussolini again unless he first
carried out the engagements he had already entered into.[1]

By 7 January 1937, it was already plain enough that the non-intervention policy had run into very heavy weather, and Eden told the
House of Commons:

> The Spanish civil war has ceased to be an internal Spanish issue
> and has become an international battleground. The character of the
> future government of Spain has now become less important to
> the peace of Europe than that the dictators should not be victorious
> in that country.[2]

The object of Germany and Italy clearly was 'to secure General
Franco's victory whether or not it represents the will of the Spanish
people'. But Eden went on trying, and January and February saw an
exchange of correspondence between Britain and Portugal which at
times became positively waspish. The general tenor of Salazar's
remarks was that England was much too inclined to take Portugal for
granted and that Portugal had every intention of maintaining her
right to an independent line.[3] The question of the volunteers was
disposed of without too much difficulty. On his arrival in London
as ambassador, Monteiro urged Salazar to play for time on this
issue but certainly not to resist the idea too strongly. If he did,
Portugal would have to bear the blame for the policy's ultimate
failure. Salazar issued a Note on 16 January,[4] however, saying that
Portugal would join in concerted action with other powers in taking
stringent measures to prevent the enlistment and transit of recruits for
the Spanish theatre of war, but would await the promulgation of such
measures in other countries first in order to 'draw inspiration from
them'. When the Portuguese decree was issued, it would be expressly
conditional on a strict fulfilment of the other signatory powers'
engagements to ban recruiting. The decree was finally issued on

---

[1] A little more than a year later when Chamberlain insisted on passing an appease-
ment policy over Eden's head, the latter resigned.
[2] Eden, *op. cit.*, p. 433.
[3] L.B., iv, pp. 1-160.
   Ibid., p. 13.

20 February. It forbade Portuguese citizens and anyone living in or passing through Portugal to enlist for either Spanish army, or to engage in propaganda relative to the civil war; and it ordered Portuguese citizens fighting in Spain to return home. Two years later, Salazar was to say how proud he was of the 'several thousand' Portuguese who had evaded the vigilance of the authorities in countless ways and made their way to fight and sometimes die for Spain.[1] It was, he said, as if the pledges he had given to NIC 'ran counter to the thought and inmost feelings of the people'.

Negotiations over the supervision of arms control was a much more difficult matter. The opening salvo came on 14 January when the British Foreign Office expressed its anxious concern that Portugal should accept the principle of control and receive a team of invigilators on Portuguese soil. Salazar replied by telling the British Ambassador that Portugal was not in the position of other states which could not ensure law and order within their own frontiers. He offered to keep special watch on Portugal's boundary lines, but would not accept international control. Britain by this time was becoming really impatient. The ambassador told Salazar that the NIC's sub-committee was proposing to extend the control system to volunteers as well as the passage of arms, and that this would mean control of all Spanish frontiers and all vessels approaching Spain. France was prepared to accept the necessary measures to implement the plan, and so was Britain in regard to Gibraltar. Why couldn't Portugal? The ambassador indicated that if Salazar was really going to be difficult, then the sub-committee might have to contemplate checking on vessels approaching Portuguese ports as well. A swift and favourable response would be appreciated.[2] Eden followed this up with a frontal assault on Monteiro on 2 February. He was very disapproving and said he simply could not see what advantage it was to Portugal to refuse co-operation.

Salazar's rejoinder is of considerable importance for the light it throws on Portuguese psychology, and it does serve to show that there were perfectly authentic considerations in Salazar's mind apart from his wish to see Franco victorious. Perhaps only those who have lived with the Portuguese will find this assertion convincing. At any rate, on 4 February, Salazar wrote an exceptionally long letter to the British Ambassador. He wanted, he said, to follow up their recent

[1] Disc., iii, p. 137.
[2] L.B., iv, p. 31.

talk as his own French was not all that good and he might have given some wrong impressions.[1] Portugal, he said, was very touchy about her national soil:

> I refer to the reaction of the Portuguese conscience towards any foreign supervision. Portugal is not more touchy about her honour, nor does she claim to be more jealous of it, than England or France; but she understands it in a different manner. Her sensitiveness is different. She has a feeling of national dignity, perhaps a wrong one, perhaps in an exaggerated form: but what matters are the questions whether the feeling exists and whether the government can modify it within days or months. . . .

> To consider the Portuguese refusal as almost insulting to the honour of England and France is – we can now say it on our side – to fail to understand the problem of the mentality and habits of the peoples in question, who are not obliged to react collectively in the same manner towards the same events or towards the same decisions by their respective governments. And those who, like the British government, value so highly and conform to the expressions of public opinion, should be the last to be surprised if others attribute due importance to it.[2]

Salazar cited the occasion, several years before, when Portugal was at her lowest economic ebb and refused a loan from Geneva because the condition was that she should accept outside supervision of her financial policy. He then turned to feelings in London that Portugal actually opposed England's policy and complained:

> But in the first place we almost always remain entirely ignorant as to what is the policy of England. Nobody tells us and our efforts to inform ourselves are almost always practically useless . . . we continue only to be informed of what is made public.

Referring to the grave implications of the Spanish crisis for the peace of the peninsula and the independence of Portugal, Salazar went on:

> We cannot believe that, in face of the Communist menace in Spain, of the plans for an Iberian Soviet Federation, or at least of the danger to the peace of other people arising from its establishment in the

[1] Salazar reads and understands English but does not speak it. He uses French as his second language and in my experience seems to speak it very well.
[2] L.B., iv, pp. 41-4.

peninsula, British policy can be merely to go on supporting in any way possible the non-intervention agreement which has already failed . . . it cannot be expected that we should with closed eyes participate in English policy in questions which we consider to be matters of life and death for us, whatever may be the confidence we repose in the nobility, clear-sightedness and energy with which the English government would defend Portugal, should occasion arise.

Finally, with regard to the threat of a quasi-blockade of Portuguese ports, Salazar pointed out that Britain seemed to be behind other pressures recently put on Portugal by Germany, Italy and France. This sort of thing, he said, was not necessary. Portugal would do her best. As to what she could not do, force would be useless.

Notwithstanding these strictures, Salazar wrote to Monteiro a few days later intimating that, while he would still refuse to have international control officials in Portugal, he would be prepared to accept English *observers* attached to the British embassy or consulate in Lisbon. The offer was a private affair between Portugal and Britain, and had nothing to do with NIC. There followed a series of heated exchanges in which Britain laid down her conditions for accepting the invitation to send observers, and again urged Portugal to co-operate in maritime control and not to insist on working outside the framework of NIC. At one stage Ribbentrop, then German Ambassador in London, told Monteiro that Salazar's attitude was, by holding up a settlement, keeping the French frontier open for aid to the Republicans, and that the sufferer was Franco. As proof of this, one had only to observe the mildness of the Russian and French committee members in face of the Portuguese stand. Monteiro himself wrote to Salazar, pleading with him to drop the idea of British observers: 'We shall be a spectacle of the dependence which your whole work was freeing us from: the world press will proclaim our subordination to England.' If Portugal would agree to international control, she would join in the supervisory work and could exercise control over Gibraltar and the Pyrenean area.[1] Salazar, however, stuck to his guns and eventually an agreement was finalized for 129 British observers to observe the roads, railway stations and frontier with Spain. Their task would be to ascertain what materials and how many people were crossing the frontier, and they would be entitled

[1] L.B., iv, pp. 55-89.

to secure whatever information they needed to help them in their task from Portuguese officials. They would have diplomatic status and would make their reports to the British Ambassador. The matter was concluded by the end of February, but only after some hard bargaining and, at one stage, a threat by Salazar to walk out of the NIC for good. He was determined, too, that the expenses of the operation should not be borne by the Committee, emphasizing the bilateral nature of the agreement, and it was finally agreed that Britain would pay salaries and contingencies, while Portugal would pay travel, maintenance and residence.[1]

Outlining the scheme in the House of Commons on 11 March, Eden described it as 'very satisfactory'. He also secured agreement at NIC level on international observers for Spanish frontiers other than the Spanish/Portuguese boundary (the Committee accepted that this was covered by the Anglo-Portuguese agreement); for all merchant vessels belonging to NIC countries to carry an observer who would watch the unloading of the cargo at Spanish ports; and maritime observation of the Spanish coast by the British, French, Italian and German navies. They would, however, have power only to board and warn ships. Eden's original idea had been to offer the services of the Royal Navy to supervise all sea approaches to ports and harbours in Spain and her overseas possessions, to prevent volunteers or war materials entering these territories. The Royal Navy ships would have had a right to search merchant ships and divert them to appropriate ports if a proper search could not be made at sea. But the British cabinet shrank from the idea, and the emasculated scheme put up to the NIC ran into many delays and arguments which might have been obviated by a scheme entrusting operations to the British navy, in which there was much international confidence. Now, patrolling vessels would merely be entitled to board and warn merchant ships which had not submitted to observation. A disregarded warning would simply be *prima facie* evidence of a breach of the Pact. Finally, Maisky's refusal to have Spain's external assets discussed heightened the suspicion that Spanish gold had found its way to Russia, and it blocked all possibility of shortening the civil war by curtailing financial aid to the contesting parties. Maisky's attitude, of course, gave the Germans and Italians a clear excuse for stalling on the issue of volunteers.[2]

[1] *Ibid.*, pp. 91-188.
[2] Eden, *op. cit.*, pp. 438-9.

Having started his peace-making work as a 'neutral', Eden came to fear a Nationalist victory more than a Republican success, because, he said, the foreign powers backing Franco were themselves a menace to peace. However, he did not believe that Spain would ever be dominated for long by another power. He told the House of Commons:

> That strong partisans on one side or the other will feel gratitude to those who have helped them in the civil strife is likely enough, but, unless the whole past history of Spain is belied in this conflict, the great mass of the proud Spanish people will feel the least ill-will to those nations which have intervened the least.[1]

Here was a point of profound disagreement with the Portuguese who believed that a victorious Franco would not be dominated by the Axis, but were equally convinced that a Republican victory would mean a Communist, Moscow-oriented Spain.

Difficulties arising between Britain and Portugal over the Spanish war were not eased by parallel differences over Portugal's re-armament programme and an apparent British willingness to appease Hitler by offering him Portugal's overseas possessions (all this is described in the following chapter). Yet, although Salazar's complex policies ran into trouble on almost every point of detail, they were basically constructive and almost visionary. Briefly, he envisaged an Iberian solidarity between an independent Portugal and Nationalist Spain which would interlock with the Anglo-Portuguese Alliance. In this way, Franco's interests would be drawn Westwards and away from the Axis, with the peninsula secured against the forces of Communism, and Russian ambition denied a strategic base in South-West Europe. With the likelihood of war between the major powers, Britain could help Portugal to re-arm, while Portugal would serve British interests through her control of the Atlantic islands and vital ports in East and West Africa. A peninsula looking towards Britain would safeguard the latter's entry to the Mediterranean and, if anything should go wrong with Suez, ensure for her an open road to the Orient. The former would be Spain's contribution, the latter Portugal's. Nothing infuriated Salazar more than Britain's apparent tendency to treat Portugal as a poor relation (*coisa pouca*), and Monteiro was told to make it very plain that, where the advantages of the Alliance were concerned, the traffic was not one-way.

[1] Eden, *op. cit.*, p. 437.

Obviously, however, interests were bound to conflict from time to time, no matter how close the Alliance. As Bianchi, the Portuguese Ambassador in Washington, explained to the U.S. Secretary of State, Mr Cordell Hull, in February 1937, Portugal tried to take British and international feeling into account by adhering to a Pact which she felt was really illusory. But because of her own special problems, she also had to pursue an individual policy which at times ran contrary to the collective view. Bianchi instanced violations of the border by armed Republicans who kidnapped Nationalist refugees on Portuguese soil and took them back to Spain to be shot; and the hostility shown in the Republican sector to a Portuguese ship which, at the Madrid government's request and Portugal's expense, was repatriating Republican refugees. Thus Portugal, living at close quarters with the Spanish problem, was bound to take a specialized view of it.[1]

In the spring of 1937, Salazar's suspicions became acute. He saw that events were favouring Franco and took the view that attempts at mediation now would simply be an Anglo-Franco tactic aimed at saving their own interests along with the Spanish Popular Front. He insisted that the bombing of open cities was a question to be discussed together with, and not in isolation from, the other problems involved in 'humanizing' the war: treatment of prisoners, killing civilians for political reasons, People's Courts, the burning and mining of towns and villages, massacres of whole classes of persons (like priests). The bombing of Guernica, he said, was one of many atrocities committed during the Spanish war, and as such did not rate a special inquiry. Other suggestions for reducing the war were made, especially by Britain, but for Salazar a temporary cessation of hostilities enabling volunteers to be withdrawn, for instance, would simply be an interference aimed at the winning side. Collective action in this matter would have to be severely impartial, he insisted, and a precondition would be acceptance of the proposals by both sides in Spain. Eden's plan for an outright armistice he saw as a manœuvre to halt the Nationalist advance. The Valencia government's bombardment of German and Italian ships had been dictated by Russia, Salazar told his ambassadors, and Russia was out to smash NIC and gain total freedom of action. This must be stopped. When Germany and Italy, after disputes among the powers operating the naval control of arms exports, decided to withdraw from the international patrol,

[1] L.B., iv, p. 140.

Salazar seems to have thought erroneously that they were withdrawing from NIC altogether, and decided that Portugal must continue to serve to ensure that impartiality was maintained.[1]

There were elements of truth in these suspicions, but sometimes they seemed to become obsessional. At one stage, for example, Salazar thought that Britain and France wanted to establish Bilbao as a Republican centre of resistance, like Madrid, with the Royal Navy keeping Nationalist ships at bay while Republican war materials sailed right through under cover of the Red Cross. (All British ships actually did was to rush food through to a starving city.) It comes, too, as a shock to read that a man with a proverbial love of children should have suspected the evacuation of the Basque children to be an assault on family unity, the basis of the state.

Preoccupied with an unstable France and the arrogant cynicism of Mussolini, Britain became extremely irritated by Portugal's attitude, and tended to write it off as 'Fascism'. Indeed, Salazar had openly avowed that Portugal's task was not to allow the non-intervention policy to be weighted against the Nationalists.[2] Some sections of British opinion believed that the attitude of the Portuguese government did not represent the Portuguese national will. Monteiro felt that Britain had become so used to Portugal trailing along at her skirts that a sudden show of Portuguese independence had come as a shock. 'Our destiny was to be obedient in all things' – *estavamos destinados a obedecer sem limites* – the ambassador complained in a telegram to Salazar.[3] Indeed, from a severely Portuguese point of view, the one merit of the whole situation was that Portugal really was emerging as a country with a mind of its own. This is probably one of the keys to Salazar's mind. Consciously or otherwise, he was partly consumed with a determination not to have Portugal treated as a hanger-on, whether hired or unpaid. There was a great deal, moreover, in his feeling that the Spanish story was being told in a one-sided way (only a year later the Vatican was to condemn Franco's bombardment of cities, rightly enough, but without a mention of the other side's performances). Italy, too, had compiled an extensive dossier on French and Russian intervention in Spain, so that Salazar's complaints about lack of partiality at NIC level were far from groundless. Finally, while Britain was responding very slowly to Portugal's

[1] L.B., iv, pp. 265-365.
[2] Disc., ii, p. 301.
[3] L.B., iv, pp. 544-51.

efforts to re-arm herself through purchases of British armaments, some sections of British opinion were undoubtedly considering the prospect of buying Hitler off with Angola.

Hints of a more constructive role for Portugal, however, began with a telegram Salazar sent to Monteiro on 18 June,[1] in which he discussed the prospects of acting as a link between Franco and various governments, especially London. Through an intermediary, Salazar had obtained a statement of aims from Franco himself. These were: close understanding with Portugal; collaboration with Britain; and Spanish independence from Germany and Italy (their aid would not be repaid in political terms, it had been a 'commercial' agreement). Franco would co-operate in the withdrawal of volunteers provided Valencia would do likewise, and provided the Moors were excepted from the withdrawal. Conscious of his military supremacy, Franco would not consider an armistice. That being so, Salazar commented, Portugal must try to prevent Britain from putting Franco in a position where he would be bound to refuse an armistice and thus attract the label of an enemy of peace. The Portuguese leader added a Note about the 'strange confusion in English public opinion regarding the generic term "fascist", which is given to anything that is non-parliamentary or anti-Communist'.

Franco's position was at once communicated to Eden who was evidently much impressed. Salazar allowed Monteiro to tell him that the contact with Franco was a former Portuguese minister of state who was very close to the Nationalists and in a position to receive Franco's reactions swiftly. The possibility of Portugal acting as an intermediary between Britain and Franco's Spain had occurred to others as well, and by the early part of July was being discussed in the British press.

Britain was by this time pressing hard for a withdrawal of foreign volunteers from both sides in Spain. Meanwhile, by 19 June, Franco felt sufficiently sure of himself to ask for belligerent rights. The two questions became interlocked. What made it all the more urgent to achieve some means of running the civil war down was an ugly incident arising from the system of NIC maritime control. In May, Republican aircraft attacked an Italian ship lying, perhaps illicitly, in the Bay of Majorca, killing six of the crew. A few days later, a

[1] *Ibid.*, p. 407.

similar attack was made on the German battleship *Deutschland* as she lay at anchor off Ibiza: thirty-one of the crew were killed and eighty-three wounded. Subsequent talks led nowhere and towards the end of June, the Germans and Italians withdrew their ships from the patrol.[1] This left the whole of the Republican coastline without supervision: ships heading for it would be wholly free from international control. But British and French ships would still be controlling Franco's coastline. So to restore this 'equilibrium', Portugal withdrew facilities from the British land observers on her territory. These were later restored, but Eden's immediate reaction was sharp: why had there been no prior consultation? The Foreign Office pointed out that so far the patrols had reported no ships belonging to the NIC countries as being in breach of the Pact, and the only ships getting through with war supplies belonged to countries not in NIC. This situation was unlikely to change. So where was the disequilibrium?[2] This was on 27 June, a week or so after Franco's plea for belligerent rights. So when Salazar then replied that it was useless to discuss the withdrawal of volunteers from Spain until the observer question had been settled, Eden retorted that until the volunteers were disposed of there could be no question of according belligerent rights to Franco.

After reading British press attacks on Portugal, and after talks with Eden, Grandi (the Italian envoy in London) and Ribbentrop, Monteiro urged Salazar to get Franco to let his volunteers go. It was essential, Monteiro argued, that Franco should make this move as a matter of prestige before the suggestion came from Rome. Determined to try and steer Franco away from anti-British policies, Monteiro suggested – perhaps at Eden's instigation – that Franco could make a useful gesture by removing the guns now trained on Gibraltar. Salazar did not reject the proposal out of hand, but thought it 'presented difficulties'. Valencia would never do anything comparable, and it would amount to a unilateral demilitarization of the Gibraltar zone. Still, Monteiro returned to the charge, defining Portugal's interests as threefold: a Franco victory; liberation of Spain from Italian and German military and political influence; a Spanish policy that is not anti-English. He added: 'Leagued as we cannot fail to be for a long time to the English military and hence political system, I judge that it is not in our interest to do anything

[1] L.B., iv, p. 454.
[2] *Ibid.*, p. 462.

hostile to it, but rather to strengthen it, and strengthen ourselves within it.'[1]

Attacks on shipping in the Mediterranean far from any Spanish port brought Italy under acute suspicion. Portugal protested when Eden's brilliantly successful Nyon Conference, called to establish pledges of mutual security among the Mediterranean powers, did not include her. But she was not geographically a Mediterranean country, and there were other problems for her to study. On 20 November, Franco agreed in principle to the NIC proposals for the withdrawal of volunteers, but hedged his acceptance round with reservations that left the question still open. The Republican acceptance in principle, for what it was worth, followed in December. As Franco's successes built up, a number of countries, including Britain and Japan, began to face the prospect of having to grant him formal recognition. By this time his government was working from Salamanca, and it was there, early in December, that Salazar sent Dr Pedro Theotónio Pereira, till then his Minister of Commerce, as a resident 'special agent'. This, Salazar told London, did not amount to *de jure* recognition, and, while Franco appreciated the move, he was not satisfied by it.

At the start of 1938, Salazar's feeling was more and more in favour of a *conclusive* end to the Spanish war. A Republican victory would mean that Spain was dependent on Russia, and that Russia, through Spain, would aim to control France. On the other hand, France need not fear that a victory for Franco would mean Axis domination in the peninsula, if only because British influence would temper the situation. A compromise, however, would leave the international situation in regard to the peninsula in confusion; which in the long run would make it harder for France to cope with her own problems, and Salazar could not understand why she wanted an equilibrium in Spain.

Sickened by Chamberlain's wooing of Mussolini, Eden resigned as British Foreign Secretary in February, and was succeeded by Lord Halifax, to whom Monteiro outlined Portugal's scheme for trying to enlarge the circle of Franco's friends: the best means, as he saw it, of avoiding Italo-German predominance in Spanish affairs. An early Portuguese recognition of Franco, he added, would be a first step in this direction. Monteiro made it plain that Portugal was not looking

[1] *Ibid.*, p. 590 *et seq.*

for guidance, but simply keeping Britain informed out of friendship. Halifax said he would take time to think about it,[1] and Monteiro reported to Lisbon: 'The [British] press, dominated by the Jews, will continue to give the world the idea that England ardently desires the victory of the Left in Spain; this does not correspond to 60 per cent of the truth.'[2] Halifax answered through Sir Alexander Cadogan at the end of March. Although Britain felt she could not recognize General Franco as long as the Republicans controlled a considerable portion of Spanish territory, the question of Portugal's recognition of Nationalist Spain was a matter for her alone. However, His Majesty's Government 'would consider it a matter for regret if the policies of the two governments could not be identical in this matter'.[3] So far as Monteiro was concerned, a wink was as good as a nod. Eventually, on 28 April, Salazar addressed the National Assembly on the subject. He condemned the inchoate idealism of the League of Nations, repudiated the equally obnoxious 'policies of realism' (a clear reference to Germany), re-affirmed the Anglo-Portuguese Alliance and welcomed the visit of the British Military Mission to Lisbon, and announced Portugal's recognition of Franco's Spain. Conditions in Spain were such, he said, that the Republicans could no longer claim to be in control, especially in view of the separate governments set up in the Basque country and Catalonia. While in Republican territory there was disorder, on Franco's side there were order and growth. Employment was on the increase and the people were being cared for. No one could say these regions were under the sway of rebel generals.[4, 5]

Monteiro's state of mind at this time is of special interest, as he was swiftly developing the Anglophile mentality which was to bring him into ultimate conflict with Salazar, and also an acute scepticism towards Franco's Spain. The wariness he displayed in this respect, however, was rooted in something almost older than time. After a conversation with the distinguished Spanish exile, Salvador de Madariaga, he called him 'a man with rootedly Spanish opinions, profoundly Spanish, and therefore not always able to understand Portuguese independence'. The remark reflects a permanent factor in

[1] L.B., v, p. 226.
[2] Ibid., pp. 230-7.
[3] Ibid., pp. 245-6.
[4] Disc., iii, p. 59.
[5] The wide implications of this speech are discussed in Chapter 7, infra.

all Spanish-Portuguese relationships; and now Portugal had cause to fear the rising tide of Falangist imperialism. What irked Monteiro was his belief that Portugal's aid to the Nationalists would be quickly forgotten. He regarded Portugal's diplomatic activity in NIC as a basic element in the Nationalist victory, but in fact, he argued bitterly, the credit for this had gone to Germany and Italy. He predicted that indifference and ingratitude would characterize the new Spain's attitude towards her peninsular neighbour. A very different note had been struck by General Franco's brother, Nicolás. When Salazar recognized the Franco government and raised Theotónio Pereira to full ambassadorial rank, Franco sent his brother to Lisbon as Spanish Ambassador. Presenting his credentials to President Carmona, Don Nicolás said that 'Spain will never forget the hand of friendship stretched out to her in her hour of bitterness'. In the event, Salazar pressed on with his plan to build an enduring relationship between himself and Franco, and thus between their two countries. Franco responded. Between them they overrode history.

Meanwhile, new proposals for withdrawing volunteers from Spain had been worked out in NIC under pressure from Britain. In July 1938, Franco indicated that he was disposed to reject them, and Monteiro reacted angrily. This, he said, would have a deplorable effect on foreign opinion. Couldn't Franco at least agree in principle once more? Even then he would be able to gain a few months' grace. Had the man no sense at all of diplomacy? In all these matters there had to be a certain amount of bluff, if only to calm the left in other countries. At this time, too, Theotónio Pereira was urging Salazar to make himself felt with Franco to obviate the dangerous influences pressing on the Spanish leader, especially from Germany. Pereira also felt with Monteiro that unless Portugal established her influence at that stage, Spain would go on ignoring her 'if only from habit'. Salazar reacted by advising Franco to accept the proposals in principle, and to phrase his objections, 'not as statements of dogma, but rather as questions'.[1]

On the eve of the Munich conference, when a war of the major powers seemed inevitable, Salazar was acutely conscious of the need to establish a right sense of direction for Spain. He feared two possibilities. One was that Italy and Britain might find themselves at war, in which case Spain would cease to be neutral. The other was worse.

[1] L.B., v, pp. 395-6.

If Italy sought to attack France through Spain, Britain might attack the Italians in Spain by moving through Portugal. The solution, he told Nicolás Franco on 16 September, was for both Spain and Portugal to make up their minds to keep right out of the impending conflict, and exchange mutual assurances. Salazar's fears were not imaginary. As the Spanish writer Fernandez Flores said to Pereira, 'If there is a war, we will be on opposing sides – a horrifying prospect.'[1] Franco's Foreign Minister, General Jordana, also agreed with Pereira on the desirability of a mutual guarantee of frontiers. In that case, Pereira pointed out to Lisbon, Portugal could concentrate on the defence of her overseas possessions, knowing that her domestic frontiers were safe. He also hinted to Jordana that any abuse of Spanish bases by the Germans would have very serious consequences. Salazar's next move was to ask London's opinion about an Iberian Pact, binding Spain and Portugal in a relationship of solidarity without absorption. Monteiro did not like this. He wanted Portugal to keep her hands free, secure the armaments she needed from Britain, and stay strong enough to intervene in Spain if necessary as an *elemento do equilibrio*. But London favoured the idea of a Pact, and Salazar made up his mind. On 27 October, he announced that a Spanish Nationalist victory would form an indestructible basis for the mutual security of the peninsular countries.[2]

He then set himself to urging London to enter into *rapprochement* with Franco. He felt that time was running out and that, unless Britain quickly improved her relations with Spain and to some degree modified her support for the French Popular Front, the Axis would seize its opportunity. 'It is evident', he wrote, 'that if England does not modify her position, she will see Spain, willingly or unwillingly, become a hostile element or camp in the event of war, and this is of great importance to us.'[3] Franco himself was aware of the dangers and started pressing hard for a non-aggression pact with Lisbon. In a most revealing Note to the Foreign Office, dated 18 January 1939, Monteiro declared:

> The truth is that foreign pressure is being felt more than ever in Spain and that certain countries have of late considerably strengthened their positions of political and economic influence.

[1] L.B., v, p. 448.
[2] Disc., iii, p. 103.
[3] L.B., v, p. 568.

My government have even noticed that such influence is being actively exerted in the press. The longer the civil strife continues, the more that influence will tend to consolidate itself.

My government feel . . . that it would be relatively easy for Great Britain to improve the situation. This is clear from the Nationalist government's insistence with Lisbon that a non-aggression pact should be concluded; *they allege among various other reasons, that such a pact would facilitate their defence against certain of their friends. I mention this fact in the strictest confidence.* (Author's italics)

My government fear that Spain may not remain neutral at a moment of grave crisis, if Great Britain maintains her present position.[1]

By the last week in February, Britain was ready to accord recognition to Franco, and the Spanish Ambassador in London, the Duke of Alba, was generous in his thanks to Monteiro. The latter, however, remained unimpressed to the last, declaring himself 'entirely convinced that the services of Portugal (to Spain) will be entirely ignored after the victory'.[2] Finally, on 17 March 1939, Spain and Portugal signed the Treaty of Friendship and Non-Aggression, which was to be known as the *Pacto Iberico*.[3] The parties pledged themselves to respect each other's territories and frontiers, and not to commit any act of aggression against each other; to refuse help to any future aggressor against either country, and to refuse to allow any act of aggression to be launched from either territory against the other; and not to enter into any pact or alliance involving aggression against either country.

The ink was hardly dry on the paper when Spain also adhered to the Anti-Comintern Pact formed by Germany, Italy and Japan. Salazar was not very happy about this, and declined to join the Pact himself. But he took the view that Franco's move was little more than a symbolic gesture of gratitude, and he told London that Portugal would try to make sure that the Pact would not lead to any further solidarity between Spain and the two totalitarian powers. By April the Spanish war was over. In a long conversation with Pereira,[4] the victorious Franco insisted that Spain was not unconditionally linked with the Axis, though Serrano Suñer, his close associate and

---

[1] *Ibid.*, p. 578.
[2] *Ibid.*, p. 650.
[3] *Ibid.*, p. 667.
[4] *Ibid.*, p. 726.

a man of strong pro-Axis sympathies, told Pereira that a logical follow-up to the Treaty with Portugal would be another with Italy. Meanwhile, Monteiro was reporting that London had little confidence in Spain's neutrality in the event of a major war. Moreover, it was being said in some circles that one of the obstacles to a much needed *rapprochement* between London and Moscow was the Anglo-Portuguese Alliance. It was therefore of the utmost importance that Portugal should do nothing to give rise to any suspicions about her motives and intentions. In fact, the eve of the Second World War found Salazar trying to prevent a breach of diplomatic relations between Spain and France. On 1 September, both Spain and Portugal declared their neutrality, and two days later the Second World War was under way.

Five months before, Salazar had established Portugal's foreign policy in unambiguous terms: the two basic elements would be Iberian solidarity and the Anglo-Portuguese Alliance. How he was to reconcile local solidarity with a wider neutrality and an alliance with Britain is the subject of the next chapter. But before turning to it, it is worth recalling how, in that crucial speech of 22 May, Salazar spoke about Spain:

> Spain succeeded in drowning in her own blood the virus which threatened the peace and civilization of the peninsula; bowed down by suffering, in her martyrdom she must have penetrated in deepest meditation to the inmost recesses of her being; and from the thought of her past, from her blood and indomitable courage, she will draw the principles of a new social and political order and in their name be able to declare that, having risen against Communist enslavement, she did not fight so bravely in order to mortgage her independence and destiny in any other way. There is but one restriction to her full liberty of external action today: her treaty of friendship with Portugal.[1]

The speech was not well received in Berlin.

[1] Disc., iii, p. 137.

1. Salazar at the age of forty-eight (in 1937), five years after becoming Prime Minister, wearing the ill-fitting, funereal suit that became a kind of uniform for him in those days.

2. Salazar addressing a mass meeting of the Portuguese Legion in Lisbon on 11 March 1938, and giving the Legion salute.

3. Salazar's historic meeting with General Franco at Seville on 12 February 1942 may have had decisive effects in keeping Spain out of the Second World War. In the background, Salazar talks to Franco's brother Nicolás while waiting for the Generalissimo. In the foreground, Spain's General Jordana talks to Portuguese Ambassador Theotónio Pereira.

4. Professor Mario de Azevedo Gomes, Minister of Agriculture in 1923, was imprisoned several times under Salazar's government. Between 1960 and 1965, when he died, he was Portugal's leading oppositionist.

5. Dr Cunha Leal, the only forme Portuguese Premier, apart from Salazar to be alive in March 1970. He wa always one of Salazar's bitterest critics.

6. The distinguished historian, Jaime Cortesão, exiled under Salazar. He returned to Portugal in 1958, and died two years later.

7. Dr António Sergio, Minister of Education in 1923 and a man of letters in his own right. During Salazar's regime he was exiled for a time and several times imprisoned. He died in 1969 at the age of eighty-five.

8. The Cardinal Patriarch of Lisbon, D. Manual Gonçalves Cerejeira, Salazar's flat mate in student days at Coimbra.

9. Salazar welcomes Mr Anthony Eden, Britain's Foreign Secretary, at a reception for NATO delegates at the Queluz Palace near Lisbon on 23 February 1952.

10. Salazar with Dag Hammarskjöld, U.N. Secretary-General, who later died in an air crash in N. Rhodesia in 1961.

11. Three Portuguese Socialist oppositionists pictured together in Oporto in February 1969. The ageing lawyer in the centre is Oporto's Antonio Macedo. With him are Raul Rêgo, the Lisbon author and journalist who was imprisoned three times under Salazar's government for interrogation without trial, and the Lisbon lawyer Mario Soares who was imprisoned fourteen times and exiled to São Tomé in 1969. Salazar's successor, Marcello Caetano, had Dr Soares freed and brought home to Lisbon before the end of the year.

12. Holden Roberto, leader of the UPA guerrilla movement which has been attacking Angola from camps in the Congo since 1961. It first struck in March of that year. Thousands died in the ensuing massacre and retaliation.

13. Marshal António Oscar Fragosa Carmona, President of the Portuguese Republic, who brought Salazar into the government in 1928 and later named him Prime Minister.

14. Salazar with Queen Elizabeth during the state visit of the Queen and the Duke of Edinburgh to Portugal in 195

15. Dr Alberto Franco Nogueira, Foreign Minister of Portugal from 1961 to 1969, who made his name in his speeches to the U.N. General Assembly over Portugal's African policies.

16. Professor Adriano Moreira, the young Overseas Minister who introduced, in 1961, a body of new legislation for the overseas provinces, and ended the *assimilado* system.

17. Professor Marcello das Neves Alves Caetano, Salazar's successor as Prime Minister.

18. Dr Eduardo Mondlane, leader of the FRELIMO guerrillas in the north of Mozambique, pictured here at his home and headquarters in Oyster Bay, Dar-es-Salaam, Tanzania, in 1968. In February 1969, he was murdered by a time-bomb sent to him by post in a parcel of books.

19. General Humberto Delgado, candidate for the presidency of the Republic in 1958, acknowledges his supporters' cheers at the height of the campaign. The election was won by Admiral Tomás.

20. Captain Henrique Galvão (left foreground), whose supporters hijacked the Portuguese liner *Santa Maria* in the Caribbean in January 1961, is seen on board the vessel after its arrival in Recife, Brazil.

21. Rhodesia's Prime Minister, Ian Smith, calls on Salazar.

22. Salazar in cheerful mood in the garden of his home.

23-24. Salazar with his adopted daughters Micas (left and below) and Maria Antónia in the garden of his Lisbon home. They were both brought up by his housekeeper.

25. The woman all Portugal knows quite simply as Dona Maria, Salazar's housekeeper in his Coimbra days and throughout his public life. She still looks after him in his retirement.

26. Students of Coimbra University visiting Salazar in his home on the eve of his eightieth birthday in 1969. The didactic wag of the finger is typical, the quilted jacket quite out of character.

27. Professor Caetano, Prime Minister of Portugal, inspects a guard o
honour at Beira on 17 April 1969, during his first visit as Premier to th
Province of Mozambique.

28. Professor Caetano, the Portuguese Premier, visiting Portugues
Guinea in April 1969, moves freely among the crowds of welcomin
people, white and black. The Portuguese government argues that ther
is still majority support for the present regime among the African people
of this province, where guerrilla forces have had far more success tha
in Angola or Mozambique.

CHAPTER 7

World War

There was never any way of insulating Portugal from any major war in the West. Her mainland position on the Atlantic seaboard was strategic enough; much more so her dependent Atlantic islands, notably Cape Verde and the Azores. Early in the Second World War supplies for Germany travelled from Portugal through Spain and Italy. After the German occupation of France the route ran straight into France from Spain. Portugal's attitude to the war was bound to affect Spanish policy, and the late Winston Churchill always acknowledged the blessings conferred by Spanish neutrality on the Allied landings in North Africa. Germany looked to metropolitan Portugal not only for re-exports (of produce from Portuguese Africa and elsewhere) but also for her indigenous tin, wool, skins, sardines and olive oil: above all for her wolfram, that essential component for modern weapons of war. Sweden, the only other European source of wolfram outside the Iberian peninsula, could offer only a tenth of Portuguese production, and Iberian wolfram was of even greater concern to Germany after the Trans-Siberian route to Far East sources was cut.

In the years before the war, Salazar had sought to strengthen Portugal by broadening her international friendships. While always asserting fidelity to the alliance with Britain,[1] he laid new stress on Portugal's links with Brazil, and worked for a relationship with Spain appropriate to independent and sovereign states, and sought a reconciliation with the Holy See, leading to the Concordat of 1940. But he soon ran into a series of dilemmas. He favoured the cause of the Spanish Nationalists, fearing a Communist invasion of Portugal if the Left were to triumph in Spain, yet was also uneasy at the thought of a Spanish government enjoying strong ties with Germany and Italy. The Portuguese Foreign Minister, Senhor Armindo Monteiro, was even more suspicious of Spain and laid the dilemma bare to Mr Anthony Eden at the Foreign Office in London soon after the

---

[1] Disc., ii, p. 301; iii, p. 61; iii, p. 137.

Spanish war had broken out.[1] Salazar's dislike of the Nazi regime and its ambitions, however, was tempered by his view of the German Reich as a bastion against the spread of Communism. In spite of the Abyssinian war – the Portuguese delegate had presided at the meeting expelling Italy from the League of Nations – Salazar's admiration for Mussolini died very hard. When the world war did break out he hoped (without believing) that it would be short and that neither side would be completely defeated.[2] There were other complications: Portugal's own endemic fight against poverty, for instance, and the Germans' use of the Spanish civil war to infiltrate into Portugal where they acquired a growing influence among the intelligentsia. Above all, Portugal's neutrality and independence had to be preserved. How could the demands of alliance and neutrality both be served? What follows is an attempt to describe how Salazar set about reconciling all these conflicting pressures in a six-year piece of tightrope diplomacy and relentless bargaining that would have been difficult for a man less sure of himself.

On the political and financial levels his concessions to the Allies were made without undue strain, but his captiousness and dogged calculation in the negotiations over wartime trade drove British officials to the verge of despair. Even Mr Eden, who made so many allowances, was once driven to speak of 'conduct incomprehensible in an ally'. As Salazar saw it, however, the Allied blockade had struck heavily at struggling Portugal's export trade; so, if there had to be a war and belligerents had to come shopping in Portugal, the latter might as well extract from all customers such profits as the traffic would bear. Equally, too much overt favour to either set of belligerents would imperil Portugal's neutral status. In the words of Professor Medlicott:

> His [Salazar's] desire to maintain with both sides a sufficient and indeed a prosperous level of wartime trade was as much an assertion of the rights and dignity of a neutral as a matter of expedient profiteering. When he made concessions it seemed only right that the Allies should pay for them.[3]

At the end of the day, the various agreements signed by Salazar sent far more wolfram into Allied hands than ever reached the

[1] Eden, *Facing the Dictators*, p. 400.
[2] *Survey*, p. 320.
[3] Medlicott, ii, p. 608.

Germans', as we shall see, but his policy obstructed the Allied pre-emptive campaign. The Allies needed *some* Portuguese wolfram but it was every bit as important to stop the other side from getting any. However, in January 1943, the British Ambassador in Lisbon, Sir Ronald Campbell, told the Foreign Office that in all the tedious arguments he had with Salazar, the latter had repeatedly asked whether Britain was invoking the Alliance or just appealing to its spirit. Like his predecessor, Sir Walford Selby, Campbell believed that Salazar was fundamentally loyal to the Alliance and that he 'would answer the call if it were made on grounds of dire necessity'.[1] Six months later the call came, when the British invoked the Alliance in their plea for bases in the Azores. Salazar responded favourably and virtually at once. The detailed joint-planning that followed ran into heavy weather until Churchill nearly ordered an invasion of the islands, but Eden, with his curious instinct for understanding a foreign statesman he had never met, simply warned the Portuguese that the whole Alliance was being imperilled by the delays. Soon after, agreement was finalized.

It is often said that Salazar waited to see who was winning before helping the Allies. Apart from the fact that some of his services were rendered early in the war, this is too facile a reading of a complicated character in a complex situation. Actually, he tended to form his very definite views well ahead of events and to stay with his own judgments in spite of changing appearances. One piece of evidence suggests that he made up his mind about the victory at a very early stage in the war. The American journalist Henry J. Taylor is the source:

> As early as Hitler's attack on Poland, in 1939, and even after France fell, Dr Salazar told me privately that he foresaw a very long struggle and the war ending in an Allied victory, instead of a short war and a German peace. He was convinced that England would stand, immensely hurt but undefeated, that the U.S. would come in and that victory would go to us. I found not another continental European leader who then agreed with him.[2]

What is quite certain is that in February 1942, when the Allied fortunes were still at a low ebb, Salazar insisted at his Seville meeting with Franco that the Allies would win in the end – and this in spite of

[1] *Ibid.*, p. 583.
[2] *Milwaukee Sentinel*, 2 October 1968.

Franco's deep scepticism and Serrano Suñer's energetic pro-Axis advocacy.

One of Salazar's major services to the Allied cause was the part he played in making it easier for Franco to resist Hitler's pressures upon him to bring Spain into the war. Salazar, of course, had a vivid grasp of what it would mean for the world, and especially for Portugal, if a Communist (or even Communist-supported) regime were to be established in the south-west corner of Europe, and for this reason he could not understand why Britain had failed to accept Spanish Nationalism as a force to impede the Communist advance. His grievance, moreover, was double-edged: Britain's refusal to aid Franco was not only a failure to combat Communism but also had the deplorable effect of driving Franco into the arms of Hitler and Mussolini. Monteiro, now Portuguese Ambassador in London, wrote in July 1937, to the Permanent Under-Secretary at the Foreign Office, Sir Robert Vansittart, to explain the first half of Salazar's grievance in somewhat dramatic terms:

> As you are aware, my government have always looked upon the so-called Spanish Civil War as an international war – a clash between nations upholding divergent ideologies. . . . My country has been directly menaced; the Spanish [Republican] government at Valencia have not failed to indicate their intentions once the victory is theirs. In Portugal there are no illusions as to the consequences of such a victory: they would represent the fulfilment of long-standing revolutionary ambitions. And indeed it cannot be denied that the establishment of an Iberian Soviet Republic would amount to a formidable stroke for Russia. Caught between the claws of the Communist pincers, how long could Europe resist?[1]

The implication was that it was all very well for Britain to be insular and blithe. Only a few years ago, Monteiro argued, Communism had amounted to nothing in Spain. Now it was 'epidemic' there and had worked its way into the vanguard of 'the enemy' well before the day of mobilization.

As regards German activity in Spain, Salazar, who had now taken over the conduct of foreign affairs himself, wrote to Monteiro on 29 September, in more matter-of-fact terms:

[1] L.B., i, p. 82.

Spain is anxious to free herself from the interference of Germany and Italy. Only two things are to be feared: continued economic influence which will only grow if the war goes on much longer, and the danger of political domination of the Falange by the Germans.[1]

He added his particular misgivings about German influence in the section of the Falange that was hostile to Franco, and reported that this trend had already provoked clashes within the movement.

Salazar's solution for some of the problems at least was to try and bring Spain and Portugal closer together so that they could find enough security in their mutual guarantees to be less dependent and less exposed to outside intervention. It was on the basis of proposals initiated by Salazar just before the Spanish Nationalist victory, that Portugal signed with the Franco government on 17 March 1939 the *Pacto del Bloque Iberico*, a Treaty of Friendship and Non-Aggression. In 1940 an important Protocol[2] was added to this treaty which formally recognized Portugal's alliance with Britain and made it clear that the Iberian Pact was in no way prejudicial to it. By adhering to Portugal within the context of the Anglo-Portuguese Alliance, Spain took a fairly substantial step away from the Axis – to the great annoyance of Berlin and Rome. Nor was Franco a reluctant partner. On 28 April 1939, he had a long talk with the Portuguese Ambassador, Dr Theotónio Pereira, at San Sebastian,[3] in which he dropped the wariness and reserve he had shown on previous occasions. He said it was quite wrong to see Spain as unconditionally leagued to the Berlin-Rome Axis. She felt gratitude to the Axis, of course, and more sympathy than she felt for 'the England-France-Russia bloc'; but she remained mistress of her own actions and proposed to go on doing so.

Perhaps the clearest exposition of Salazar's mind and policy in those perilous days appears in an important telegram he sent to the Portuguese Ambassador in Washington on 11 April 1939.[4] He starts with the familiar refrain that Portugal has drawn attention for three long years to the true character of the Spanish war: the defence of the West against Bolshevism. A complete Franco victory was necessary to give Spain peace and order under a strong government. Again

[1] *Ibid.*, v, p. 76.
[2] 29 July.
[3] L.B., v, p. 725.
[4] *Ibid.*, pp. 700-2.

and again, Portugal has warned Britain and France against driving
Franco into the arms of Hitler and Mussolini, and she has recently
been authorized by the Spaniards to make it clear that the future of
Spain has not been mortgaged and that the latter wants friendship
with France and England. Salazar then proceeds to give France and
England a thorough dressing-down for subordinating their foreign
policy to the interests of home politics. He adds:

> Portugal has the right to recall the errors made by others, because
> despite our correct behaviour and loyalty to England (publicly
> recognized more than once by England herself), the Portuguese
> attitude was not understood by third powers and was opposed by
> them, and we therefore had an unpleasant and dangerous time of it.
> The Portuguese government believes that Spain should now be
> left to choose her own regime without any pressure from outside.
> Franco should be given moral aid to carry out the great work of
> reconstruction, and it must be kept in mind that resentment over
> the attitudes of certain powers is bound to remain in the hearts of
> the Spanish people for quite a long time.

> The treaty of friendship with Portugal, signed after the victory,
> in which our obligations under the Alliance with England are
> respected, proves Franco's wish to guarantee peace in the Peninsula
> and that he is free of any anti-British intentions. Spain's adherence
> to the anti-Communist pact [of the Axis powers], which we were
> informed of in advance, must be regarded as a public manifestation
> of gratitude by Spain towards the two totalitarian powers which
> helped her win in the name of the struggle against Communism.
> It should be noted that Spain would not conclude that pact before
> entering into the treaty of friendship with us. . . .

> The position of England and France right to the end was of no
> help at all, on the contrary it was a great hindrance to the policy
> pursued by us on behalf of all the Western powers.

Against the background of these overtures to Spain there lingered
in more cynical and suspicious Iberian minds the history of antagonism
between the two countries of the peninsula. This had to be put in
perspective and Salazar did so brilliantly in his May address to the
Portuguese National Assembly. One of the most telling of his
arguments was the frank reference he made to the Portuguese
volunteers who had fought with Franco and had been a major bone

of contention in the non-intervention conferences. Salazar began[1] by pointing out that while Portugal and Spain, or Spanish kingdoms, had often fought each other, they had also fought side by side against the common foe. He went on:

> For some reason the liberty and independence of Spain appear to be a postulate of Portuguese policy; and during the recent crisis the voice of history was heard again and Portugal remained faithful to this tradition. Contrary to the pledges given by the government for sufficiently obvious political reasons, and as if those pledges ran counter to the thought and inmost feelings of the people, several thousands of Portuguese, evading in countless ways the vigilance of the authorities, left their life and interests and ease and went to fight for Spain, to die for Spain. It is a source of pride to me that they should have died well. . . .

Portugal had guaranteed security and order on the frontier, Salazar continued; she had confronted 'the blindness and incomprehension of Europe', and her people were 'faithful friends of Spain and true sons of the peninsula'. England should appreciate the fact that Spain had emerged from the civil war with only one foreign commitment, namely her treaty with Portugal, which meant that a true zone of peace had been created in the Iberian peninsula. True to the fixed principles of her history, Portugal would remain faithful to the Anglo-Portuguese Alliance, while 'in matters that lie outside the Alliance we reserve our freedom of action and the right to form many friend-ships'.

So a certain pattern begins to emerge. Spain is to stand with Portugal against Communism. The Anglo-Portuguese Alliance is to be for both Portugal and Spain an antidote to predatory Nazism. Yet it cannot be forgotten that the disliked German Reich is also an anti-Communist bastion. Salazar's adherence to the Alliance with Britain was proclaimed in three major speeches in successive years from 1937 onwards,[2] but if love affairs seldom run smoothly, this was no exception. To begin with, England showed little interest in Portugal's urgent need to re-arm virtually from scratch, and left-wing opinion in Britain during the civil war had been severely critical of Portugal even to the point of demanding an end to the old Alliance. Moreover,

[1] Disc., iii, pp. 146-52.
[2] Ibid., ii, p. 301; iii, p. 61; iii, p. 137.

Germany was making a decided effort in these pre-war years to seduce Portugal into her orbit. Thanks to German salesmanship and cheap prices, England lost a lot of her Portuguese trade, and Englishmen, it seems, had already begun to drink less port. Making the most of their presence in Spain during the civil war, the Germans infiltrated themselves across the border and gradually built up considerable influence with the Portuguese upper classes, the universities, the para-military legion, the youth movement and the press; and it was in Germany that the Portuguese security police were initially trained. Whether by accident or with a view to keeping up appearances with Berlin, Salazar's wartime government included a number of strongly pro-German ministers – an added complication for his conduct of diplomacy. Many intelligent and highly placed Portuguese, while revolted by Hitler's barbarous methods, were deeply impressed by Germany's enormous technical prowess, and could hardly fail to compare the sense of order, strength and mastery generated by the Reich with the poverty-stricken morass from which Portugal was slowly emerging.

Britain, moreover, appeared to be reverting to her nineteenth-century pastime of dividing up the Portuguese African territories with Germany. It was less than fifty years since Salisbury's ultimatum to the Portuguese to withdraw from the lands of the Makololos and Mashonas; forty years since Salisbury and Balfour divided Portuguese Africa between Britain and Germany in anticipation of Portuguese collapse; and less than thirty years since Haldane's conversations in Berlin on the same topic. It became known that when Lord Halifax went to Berlin in November 1937, the Nazis expected him to make an offer of Angola as a substitute for one of the former German colonies lost in the First World War. When Halifax suggested no such thing, Schacht took the initiative and suggested that Portugal might be persuaded to accept a repartition of colonies in Africa.[1] It also seems that Chamberlain would have been willing to talk about Angola or the Congo – as a substitute for the former German territory of Tanganyika – as part of a general settlement.[2] This actually got into the European press in December 1937, and was denied to the Portuguese minister in Berlin by Goering,[3] while in the House of

[1] DGFP, i, no. 19, p. 32; no. 31, pp. 59, 60, 63, 65; and British Foreign Office document no. FO 371/21682/C 13657-G.
[2] Feiling, *The Life of Neville Chamberlain*, p. 333.
[3] L.B., i, p. 218; DGFP, i, nos. 50, 51, 60, 61.

Commons on 21 December, Eden also denied any intention of reviv-
ing the 1898 and 1912 negotiations.[1] For all that, secret British proposals presented to Hitler on 3 March 1938, included a redistribution
of colonies between the latitude five degrees south and the Zambesi,
but Hitler rejected this as an alternative to the return of the former
German colonies because, he argued primly, Belgium and Portugal
might think he was asking for something he had no right to.[2] There
the matter uneasily rested; Sir Walford Selby, the new British
Ambassador in Lisbon, having explained to the Portuguese on the
same day that Britain had no intention of bargaining with Germany
at Portugal's expense. The astonishing thing is that anyone in
Whitehall should ever have entertained the idea that Dr Salazar
would peacefully acquiesce in any attempt to redistribute Portuguese
territory. It seems, in fact, that it was fostered far more by Schacht
and the British Ambassador in Berlin, Sir Nevile Henderson, than by
their respective governments.

Britain's failure to supply arms to Portugal until well after the start
of the war was partly due to indifference and partly to Britain's own
re-armament problems. One British firm offered Lisbon some
distinctly obsolete material, and in the end Portugal started to buy
small arms from continental sources, including Germany, hoping
the heavy equipment would eventually come from England. This
drew reproaches from London, and matters grew worse when a
British military mission came to Lisbon in 1938 and some of its
members seemed to be getting involved with Portuguese elements
bent on removing the Salazar government. But other members
eventually arrived and made an excellent impression on the Portuguese
Under-Secretary for War, Colonel Fernando Santos Costa. Service
attachés were later appointed, and, at Salazar's request, British naval
and military experts came to Lisbon to help plan coastal defences.
When Hitler signed a pact with Communist Russia and then invaded
Catholic Poland, even Portugal's pro-German elements were given
some pause: but the factor which more than any other gave authenticity
to Portugal's value as a wartime ally was that, whatever the upper
classes might think and however they might be divided, the ordinary
people of Portugal were fervently pro-British. One of the better
memories of that terrible war is that of the Portuguese people, who

[1] HC Deb., 5th Ser., vol. 330, coll. 1880-1.
[2] DGFP, nos. 138 (pp. 242-3, 246-7), 141; see also *Survey*, p. 316 *et seq.*; for
British documentation, see Public Record Office, London, series FO 371.

had little enough for themselves, lavishing kindness and hospitality on refugees from all parts of Europe, military escapees and the survivors of ships torpedoed near the Portuguese coast.

The difficulties over re-armament and Portuguese suspicions of the Anglo-German discussions on her African colonies, revealed the weakness in the old Alliance. They showed that Salazar, for all his basic admiration of British traditions and achievements, was becoming exceedingly critical of what he saw as the growing decadence of British political institutions. Britain, for her part, not only disliked Portugal's predilection for the Spanish Nationalists but grew increasingly suspicious of her intentions, resenting in particular the anti-British tone of the German-influenced Portuguese press, and sometimes accusing Portuguese leaders of outright bad faith. Salazar lacked sympathy for Britain's internal political problems: the disputes over Spain and disarmament, for instance. The preservation, too, of Portugal's sovereignty loomed over all else in his mind. Equally, the British press not only conveyed a sense of hostility to 'Fascist' Portugal – this really annoyed Salazar – but also of indifference in some high quarters: Portugal, it seemed, was not important. There were, of course, individual exceptions and history will recognize its debt to the friendship between Monteiro, whose passion for England proved a little too much for Salazar in the end, and Eden, who had not met Salazar but developed an unerring instinct for dealing with him. Monteiro brilliantly interpreted the British mind to his difficult superior. Eden's recognition that Salazar was not a man to be bullied, cajoled or bought was to prove an inestimable blessing in the Allies' bid for bases in the Azores.

Salazar undoubtedly regarded his ally with unsentimental realism, and Portugal's own unhappy democratic experiments did not predispose him to understand the march and countermarch of democratic procedures elsewhere. Reading the telegrams, one is tempted to feel that his head was in the Alliance but not his heart. Monteiro, however, genuinely loved the British way of life, admired the Foreign Office, esteemed Eden, and respected Parliament. He was the complete Anglophile and even liked English guile. For all his tendency to hyperbole and his abiding suspicion of France and Spain, he was a shrewd diplomat with a judgment that went quickly to the heart of things. Eden, as Lord Avon, was to write in his *Memoirs* about a conversation he had with Monteiro at the Foreign Office in London in the summer of 1936:

Monteiro was one of the first to think that France might be shattered because the hatreds within the country were greater than the hatred of some Frenchmen for the common enemy. The *Comité des Forges*, for instance, was so anti-Blum that it had scarcely time to be anti-German. Monteiro and I saw this, with regret, Hitler with satisfaction.[1]

It was in September 1936 that Salazar explained to the British Ambassador the need to re-arm the Portuguese army as soon as possible with the most modern weapons available, but he added that any equipment bought from Britain would have to be of the same standard as the equipment used by the British army, and there would have to be a guaranteed delivery date.[2] Monteiro followed this up in London and warned Eden and Vansittart of the dangers of German infiltration in Spain and, as he saw it, Britain's failure to understand the situation.[3] The new year, 1937, started badly. Britain, with plenty of re-armament problems of her own, was less than energetic in dealing with Portugal's, and Portuguese officials began to notice the difference between Foreign Office correspondence and 'the clarity and precision of the very good offers in the German Memorandum of 14 November 1936'.[4] A major snag was that Britain could not give advance guarantees that export licences would be granted for aircraft destined for Portugal, as certain theoretical contingencies had to be allowed for. The Foreign Office indicated, however, that it was inconceivable that any such licences would in practice be withheld. This was not good enough for Salazar, who told Monteiro that the British attitude was always thus, grudging and unsatisfactory;[5] while Vansittart eventually came clean with Monteiro and told him that the Foreign Office attached little importance to Portuguese re-armament.[6] On 14 June 1937, Monteiro complained to Eden, with a good deal of justice, that his country's initial orders should have fitted in easily with the British production lines and taken no more than a matter of days or weeks to fulfil. In fact, however, attempts to place aircraft orders had been met with intimations of long delays, and Vickers had said they could

[1] Eden, *op. cit.*, p. 401.
[2] L.B., pp. 16-18.
[3] *Ibid.*, p. 28.
[4] *Ibid.*, p. 46.
[5] *Ibid.*, p. 51.
[6] *Ibid.*, p. 61.

not start supplying a few thousand rounds of 4.5-inch howitzer ammunition for seven months, and even then only at the delivery rate of 2,000 rounds a month.[1]

In this atmosphere, Salazar delivered a speech to army and navy officers on 6 July,[2] in which he plumped firmly for the British Alliance but rejected the all too prevalent Portuguese attitude that the Alliance implied Portuguese dependency and was to be welcomed as such. This, said Salazar, was a false position which could end up with Portugal becoming a kind of protectorate; and, what was more, the Alliance would not prevent Portugal from holding her own views in matters such as the Spanish Civil War. Traversing the history of the Alliance over the past one hundred and fifty years, he quoted the praises and gratitude bestowed on Portugal by British political and military leaders, including Palmerston. He described the attitude of 'certain people of England' who had 'invited the British government to re-examine the Anglo-Portuguese Alliance' as placing their personal feelings and resentment before great national and international interests, and added:

> I have no doubt that from the British point of view the continuation of the Alliance should be examined, but only when the British Empire comes to an end or when some cataclysm destroys Britain's insular position.

The classic arguments for the Alliance, Salazar continued, had come from British sources. Palmerston had spoken of the advantages to Britain as 'many, great and obvious; commercial, political, military and naval', the loss of which would place formidable weapons in the hands of the enemy. Quite apart from Portuguese military assistance, Britain must maintain her communications in the South Atlantic, along the Mediterranean, and with the East, via the Cape. 'Portugal, with her islands and colonies, stands at the cross-roads of the great maritime routes, offering shelter and security within her ports.' What it all boiled down to was that Portugal fully intended to be loyal to the Alliance, but that the advantages were not one-sided, and that Britain should remind herself of this. If an Englishman may be forgiven for finding this a shade arrogant, he can take comfort from Monteiro's qualification:

---

[1] L.B., i, p. 64.
[2] Disc., ii, p. 301.

We have absolute need of support in international matters and in spite of everything England is still the only valid one we can find.[1]

In the midst of Portugal's preoccupation with her alliances, the American Secretary of State, Mr Cordell Hull, issued in July 1937 what has come to be known as the Hull Memorandum. This was a plea for the renunciation of force and of interference in other nations' affairs, and a peaceful solution of disputes through negotiation, loyalty to international agreements, economic stability and a reduction of armaments. Salazar reacted sharply in the following month, in a statement which is of special interest because it indicates his basic distrust of world organizations and is not without some bearing on the problems of communication in recent years between Portugal and the United Nations. The statement included this comment:

> The idea of supra-national organization and the tendency towards citizenship of the world are essentially wrong and humanly impossible, or are so remote from conditions as they really are that they can only operate . . . as subversive factors.[2]

Salazar's scepticism of idealism in politics, together with his consciousness of the international implications of Communism, inspired in him a deep suspicion of anything which managed, in the name of an ideal, to establish itself as an international network. His pragmatism rejected what seemed to him to be the unreality of idealistic policies, his hatred of Communism was enhanced by the Western powers' impotence to 'contain' it. In his already quoted speech to the officers[3] he had referred to 'systems of ideals which are literally systems of crime' and which, even when confined to a particular state, were in fact supra-national because of the 'tremendous idealistic and political interests which dominate the nations'. He was convinced that 'Western civilization is at stake'. His scepticism emerged again in the following year, when he spoke of the League of Nations in almost scornful terms:

> There was a time when we believed in such illusions as 'a universal and lasting peace', 'collective security', 'agreements and pacts within the framework of the League of Nations'; and, since the League has broken down beyond recovery, the so-called policy

[1] L.B., i, p. 170.
[2] Ibid., p. 111.
[3] Disc., ii, p. 301.

of realism is acclaimed. . . . Personally, I mistrust all these policies. . . .[1]

A more encouraging factor in the Anglo-Portuguese Alliance occurred in July 1937 when Salazar welcomed British proposals to send a military mission to Portugal. It could hardly come too soon, especially as Portugal was about to sever diplomatic relations with Czechoslovakia, after the latter's change of heart about supplying arms for the Portuguese army. In the following month, Salazar was again threatening to place more armaments orders outside Britain if the latter would not give the required guarantees about delivery. A partial guarantee was offered by London in October, which Monteiro advised Salazar to accept, despite the qualifying clause covering the remote possibility of Portuguese aggression attracting League of Nations condemnation. But Salazar would not have it,[2] as in his view, one of the clauses, relating to perils of war, was worded in such a way as to leave Britain free to interpret it as she wished at any time.

Salazar, it is clear, thought in terms that were pre-eminently neither pro-British nor pro-German but simply pro-Portuguese. He said a good deal about the implications of current trends for Western civilization, but his basic position was always that of a leader of a small and poor but proud nation fighting to re-establish itself again after generations of humiliating inadequacy. It was a fight for survival and Salazar's naturally suspicious mind saw every move so clearly in the context of Portuguese history that every decision he took was weighted with an excess of caution. But Britain could do her share of the haggling, too, and Salazar complained to Monteiro in November 1937[3] that British awkwardness over the exact wording of the military mission's terms of reference suggested such anxiety to avoid firm commitment, that one could see how meagre the mission's results were likely to be.

Anglo-Portuguese tensions continued to be reflected in the British press and on 3 December, Monteiro was complaining to Eden, without getting much change, about Lord Beaverbrook – *esse maldito homen*. More importantly, it was in this interview that Monteiro broached the question of Anglo-German conversations over the

[1] Disc., iii, p. 59.
[2] L.B., i, p. 165.
[3] *Ibid.*, p. 204.

African colonies,[1] and pointed out that it was fundamental to the
interests of Britain to keep the Portuguese possessions in Portuguese
hands. He was, of course, right. The mineral wealth of central
Africa lay mostly in Katanga and the Rhodesias, and exports travelled
by railways (to the Atlantic and Indian Oceans) which ran through
Angola and Mozambique. Also, if the Suez Canal were closed and the
Cape route had to be used, oil from the Middle East would travel
round South Africa and be exposed to attacks from any hostile powers
occupying the Portuguese territories. On reporting this conversation
back to Salazar, however, Monteiro was told[2] to be very careful
about showing opposition to Germany at the Foreign Office in
London and not to get involved in other people's negotiations.
Certainly, Monteiro had not told Eden anything that Salazar did not
believe himself, but Salazar evidently feared that Monteiro might
have given Eden an excuse for telling the Germans that it was the
Portuguese who were making all the trouble over Africa. To make
matters worse for poor Monteiro, the Foreign Office circulated a
record of the 3 December conversation to the embassies, perhaps
with a view to finding out, through the embassy in Lisbon, how far
Monteiro's position really represented Salazar's. At any rate, the
matter came up in a talk between the chargé d'affaires in Lisbon,
Mr Bateman, and the secretary-general of the Portuguese Foreign
Ministry, Dr Teixeira de Sampayo, who pointed to British press
references to the Anglo-German negotiations of 1898 and 1912, and
to the fact that no official source in London had said anything to
indicate that such references were irrelevant to the present situation.
This had created much discomfort in Portugal. The secretary-general
also criticized Britain's favourable attitude to the Valencia (Republican) government in Spain without regard for Portugal's position
in the Spanish affair.

Outlining this conversation to Salazar, however,[3] Teixeira de
Sampayo injected some politely acidulous comments on 'our
ambassador' in London. By telling Eden: 'If we give peace to Europe
by the return of Germany to Africa, we shall have caused Africa to
lose her peace', he had revealed Portuguese distrust of Germany and
it must have appeared to Eden that Portugal was trying to discourage
British negotiation with the Reich. Monteiro had also said that

[1] *Ibid.*, p. 217.
[2] *Ibid.*, p. 220.
[3] *Ibid.*, p. 518 *et seq.* (and Appendix).

Abyssinia was a millstone round Italy's neck, and this seemed to have diminished the strength of the Italian peril in Eden's eyes. If this Foreign Office document (reporting the Eden-Monteiro discussion) were to fall into the hands of the Germans or Italians, it could harm Portugal. Teixeira de Sampayo added that Eden had told Monteiro that British public opinion was against a cession of colonies to Germany unless this could guarantee to Europe a tranquillity not enjoyed at present (but this, according to Bateman, meant British colonies, not Portuguese).

On 21 December, the British government denied in Parliament that there was any question of a colonial deal with Germany.[1] Meanwhile, Salazar, after reading his secretary-general's report had forwarded it to Monteiro and indicated to the latter that he (Monteiro) had gone too far with Eden. Britain's cautious attitude towards Portugal, he went on, justified Portugal in not being too eager to go beyond the call of loyalty or self-interest. Monteiro came swinging back at this on 30 December.[2] His talk with Eden, he said, had been private and the Foreign Office's tortuous stratagem in circulating a note of a confidential conversation could only mean that they wanted to get official confirmation of Monteiro's personal view. Salazar must see that the preservation of the political balance in Africa was vital for Portugal and that she could not detach herself completely from any discussion of Central and Southern Africa. The prevailing temper in Britain was against the expense of re-armament and in favour of a 'just settlement of outstanding claims', or, in other words, giving Germany just what she asked. The danger to Portugal's African possessions was clear and there was no point in trusting fair words or treaties. Monteiro made four suggestions: oppose any agreement modifying the present division of power in Africa; prove to the British and French that any alternative arrangements would be detrimental to British and French interests; approach Belgium and South Africa for mutual protection; build a strong army in Portuguese Africa.

The British programme for the forthcoming military mission was submitted towards the end of January 1938.[3] It proposed talks on:

(*a*) Measures for improving British facilities for joint defence.

---

[1] Whitehall preferred to talk to Berlin about a general reappraisal by *all* the colonial powers in Africa. But Portugal's position was plainly a key issue. (See British documents, series 371, quoted *supra*.)

[2] L.B., i, p. 248.

[3] *Ibid.*, pp. 277-9.

(b) Measures for improving Portuguese coastal defences so that, in case of war, Portugal could provide facilities for the British fleet, and also air bases on land.

(c) Collaboration between the industries of the two countries in supplying munitions to either.

(d) Comparison of the organization and equipment of the two armies.

In conveying this to Salazar, Monteiro commented that it was a case of the old, old story: Britain wanting naval and air supremacy while leaving her allies to cope with weakness on the ground; and there was thus no guarantee that Britain would help in the defence of Portugal's national territory.[1] It is hard to see how Britain, desperately unprepared herself and trying to stave off a general war, could have committed herself at this stage to the land defence of Portugal itself, let alone the overseas territories; and in fact it was shortly after this that a number of anxious questions were asked in the House of Commons to see just how far Britain's treaty obligations went. Was she, one Member of Parliament asked, supposed to take on the defence of the world by herself? Monteiro's judgment may have been a shade clouded at this time by his resentment at the way his private talk with Eden had been retailed, but his next despatch to Salazar was on firmer ground.[2] He plainly saw that Britain was going to need Iberian friendship in relation to the Mediterranean area, and may even have been prescient enough to suspect that one day Portugal's allies would be attempting a North African landing. At any rate, he argued that the radiant treatment being given by the Portuguese press to the forthcoming mission was unsound. England should be given to understand that the advantages cut both ways. If Franco were to win the war in Spain, Portugal would be Britain's only point of support in the Peninsula. This was the type of long-term situation that would count with Britain, Monteiro added, where the tendency was still to see the existing Portuguese system as something that would disappear with Salazar. All this made sense to Salazar but he decided to accept the British programme,[3] on the strict understanding that the mission would be concerned with preliminary talks and not with mutual commitments. This was in February. In mid-March, the Germans occupied Austria.

[1] *Ibid.*, p. 282.
[2] *Ibid.*, p. 289.
[3] *Ibid.*, p. 298.

By the end of March 1938, the mission had given strong advice that Britain and Portugal should use identical types of weapon. At a meeting between Salazar and the British Ambassador, Sir Walford Selby,[1] a tentative scheme for an agreement was sketched out. Britain would help Portugal to place with British firms all her orders for arms and ammunition heavier than rifles and light machine-guns, and for ships and aircraft, but His Majesty's Government must have the last word on delivery dates. However, it would be firmly stated that the integrity and independence of Portugal and her empire was of primary importance to Britain, and Portugal could accordingly be assured of adequate protection while waiting for her arms to arrive. At first, the idea was to establish these points in an exchange of Notes but in the end, without the slightest sign of ill-temper on either side, Salazar held back – evidently because once again he felt that Britain was relying far too much on her sea power, while he wanted what was in fact virtually impossible for Britain: a firm promise of military help on land. In his impatience to re-arm, Salazar was already shopping round Europe for small arms, and he explained to Sir Walford Selby[2] that what Britain had to offer was not always the best, nor what Portugal precisely required; that weapons from other sources were sometimes cheaper, facilities for payment were easier, and with Britain there was always the problem of delivery dates. This impatience on the Portuguese side had much to do with uncertainties in Spain: the possibility that the 'Iberian unity' merchants might prevail on Spanish policy or that Germany might push Spain into doing what she otherwise would not do. If in a major war Germany threw Spain into the ring against Portugal, Salazar told Sir Walford in May,[3] a sudden land attack against unarmed troops would take the invaders to the Atlantic ports in a matter of days, and Britain's sea power would be powerless to do anything about it. Portugal, historically speaking, had to be suspicious of Spain, though not of General Franco. Nor was it any use thinking that if Franco succeeded and could not get enough economic aid from Germany and Italy, he would turn to Britain for loans. Some people simply did not realize 'what a nation is capable of when it resolves to suffer'. What it all boiled down to was that Salazar was more interested in British arms supplies than in promises of military aid, and said as much.

[1] *Ibid.*, i, p. 334 *et seq.*
[2] *Ibid.*, p. 346.
[3] *Ibid.*, p. 361.

It was while these exchanges were going on that Salazar made his April 1938 speech to the National Assembly, already quoted, in which he spoke of the failures of the League of Nations. This speech contains some of the few pointed references he ever made in public to his disapproval of the Axis powers. Even these were closely hedged around. Again, this has to be understood in the context of a nation in no position to quarrel too much with anybody other than an ally, and certainly not with a power likely to be a major belligerent in a forthcoming war. For those with ears to hear, however, the April speech was a fair indication of which way the wind was blowing. First, he dismissed the 'policy of idealism' which usually was not the same thing as 'a policy with an ideal'. It was, he went on,

> characterized by its divorce from reality, by its indifference to facts, and by its attachment to theoretical systems which ignore the realities of life and the changes created by other doctrinal systems and events in history. Its aim is to convert the world to its abstract way of thinking, regardless of what may happen or of the forces which are antagonistic to it, and thus its record is one of successive failures.

The policy of idealism, taking refuge in the belief in the goodness of human nature, the abolition of war and the possibility of a general disarmament, had become lifeless and inert. It disregarded the difference between sentiment and interest on the one hand, and agreements and obligations on the other, and it was indifferent to events in Spain, Prague, Geneva and elsewhere.

In contrast to all this, Salazar continued, some nations had adopted the equally dubious policy of realism:

> With a complete grasp of existing circumstances, of their own capabilities and those of others, they have applied realism to the Saar, the Rhineland, Danzig, and to the policy of the Anschluss. In other fields, the realistic policy has been in force on the Brenner since 1934; in the Nyon agreement in 1937 for the patrolling of the Mediterranean; in the recent Anglo-Italian agreement; and even in tacit acceptance of the disappearance of Austria.

Shortly, he warned, 'people will become so fascinated with the policy of realism that there is a danger of their being forced to acquiesce in what I see as the corruption of realism – the *fait accompli* and the use of force'. Finally in this context:

We deplore the existence of systems which ignore the rights of others and are lacking in ideals of justice – we deplore them, but in accordance with realities, we must also be prepared. These are then our reasons for our re-armament, for our friendships within and outside Europe, and for our Alliance with Great Britain.[1]

The Portuguese Premier then referred to left-wing British papers – 'it is true these papers are not of high standing' – which were advocating abandonment of the Alliance and the 'occupation of Portuguese territory as a measure for safeguarding British interests'. He was inclined, he said, 'to attribute these attacks to the fact that the methods which have always characterized Continental democracies are beginning to pervade English policy'. In any event, Portugal had chosen her policy and would stick to it.[2]

As the months drew on towards Munich – Eden had resigned in February – Monteiro commented ironically in July,[3] that Portugal's overseas possessions had been saved in 1898 by the Boer War and again in 1914 by the Great War, but that 'we cannot go on indefinitely counting on disasters to save us'. (In fact, yet another world war was to do so.) But he urged the desirability of a new treaty of alliance with Britain and the conclusion of a military agreement between the two countries. But Salazar was not in the mood. He was getting restive about the continuing activity of the British military mission in Portugal, which, he believed, was dabbling in local politics hostile to himself.[4] When Monteiro urged him not to sign a pact with Spain but to keep his hands free for Britain, Salazar wrote:

> The worst hypothesis would be if Italy utilized Spanish ports as bases and caused Spain to lose her neutrality as regards England: our services on the English side would be required and there would be a clash between our duty as allies and our sympathy for Nationalist Spain and Italy.[5]

It was partly to offset this peculiarly embarrassing peril that Salazar later signed the Iberian Pact and the ensuing Protocol with Spain which provided for Iberian solidarity within the context of Portugal's engagements with Britain.

[1] Disc., iii, p. 59.
[2] Ibid.
[3] L.B., i, p. 396.
[4] Ibid., p. 414.
[5] Ibid., p. 454.

Far from settling anything for the small European powers with large overseas possessions, the Munich crisis of September 1938 left the Belgians, Dutch and Portuguese deeply concerned that a re-division of Africa to Germany's advantage was still possible. Monteiro and the Dutch Ambassador in London agreed that even the Foreign Office in Whitehall had not been fully informed about what happened at Munich, and that the costly British intelligence service was not much good. Meanwhile, Pirow, the South African Minister of Defence, who was notoriously pro-German, was urging that, in any deal supporting Germany's claims, the territory of South-West Africa should be left to the Union. Rumours were rife that Hitler was after Angola again.[1]

Salazar's own attitude to the Munich settlement was expressed in his October speech to the National Assembly.[2] It was a strange performance: a curious blend of perceptiveness and miscalculation, of principle and of something verging on the cynical. He showed no concern for Czechoslovakia at this time: possibly his unforgiving nature was still smarting at the breakdown of the arms deal; and his feeling for Mussolini seems to have warped his judgment of a futile sell-out. He considered it was 'Chamberlain's undoubted glory' to have found 'a compromise between reason and necessity', but that the British Prime Minister had probably been aided 'by the great political ability of the head of the Italian nation'. He missed the point, so painfully clear to Winston Churchill, that the neutralization of Czechoslovakia had freed twenty-five German divisions to menace the Western front, and had opened up for the Nazis the road to the Black Sea. Still, Churchill was very nearly unique in his grasp of current realities, and while Salazar believed that an opportunity for peace had been secured, he did not believe it would be seized. Peace, he said, was still too dependent on fear, and intensive military preparations were going on 'hand-in-hand with the solemn exchange of friendship and peremptory declarations that never again would the nations have recourse to war'.

The Portuguese leader was on firmer ground when he blamed the post-war unrest on the Treaty of Versailles, whose economic clauses had been condemned by Churchill as malignant and silly. It would be senseless, said Salazar, to say that no conditions should have been imposed on vanquished Germany; but it was equally senseless to suppose that Germany would be 'resigned to occupy indefinitely

[1] *Ibid.*, ii, pp. 15-32.
[2] Disc., iii, p. 103.

a secondary place', which was contrary to her national conscience, and which would deprive Europe of the extraordinary organizing ability and highly trained skills of scores of millions of men. For these reasons, a German regime had emerged which at least promised the country a new unity, full sovereignty and the recovery of former greatness. Other European nations had then proclaimed their 'loud aversion' from that regime, tried to seal it off, and to set up ideological barriers round it 'which were hardly consonant with the interests of the Allied countries'. What irked Salazar even more was that the 'great democracies' actually boasted of Soviet help in ostracizing the Germans. The net result was that Germany had 'affected the role of victim in perhaps an exaggerated way' and had 'built up an immense military power which, without a shot being fired, enabled her to expand her frontiers'.

The speech is obscure and in some ways inconsistent. Salazar could hardly have meant that Europe should have embraced the National Socialist philosophy with all its practical implications. As we shall see, although his determination to establish Portuguese neutrality restrained him from forthright condemnations, his dis-approval of German policy emerged in a number of his public speeches, albeit wrapped up in his somewhat tortuous style. Pre-sumably he was trying to say that, had Europe tried to understand the phenomenon of Hitler's rise to power, the Nazi regime might have been saved from itself and its excesses. Whether he was right or wrong in this, he was not alone in his view. But having complained that it had been wrong to try and segregate Germany from the European family, he then proceeded to defend Portugal's policy in 1936 of opposing Russian membership of the League of Nations. Russia, he said, would have disrupted the League which was 'already suffering from too much ideology of the socialist and international variety' and would have driven countries with different ideas right out of the League altogether. How right, he now said, that view had been. With Russia excluded from the talks, the Munich settlement had discarded the Versailles mentality and re-established the principle that solutions to disputes should be sought through friendly understanding. Yet Churchill, an anti-Communist up to the hilt, and one without illusions over Russia's reliability, took a very different view. Writing in later years he argued that Russia's presence at Munich would have acted as a substantial deterrent to Hitler, and that her exclusion, almost with disdain, was something that rankled afterwards in Stalin's

mind, and Britain was to pay dearly for it. Churchill and Eden argued
in similar vein in 1939, when the Chamberlain government's feeble-
ness in their talks with Russia ruined an initiative which might otherwise have averted the Russo-German pact and might have made
Hitler think again before marching on Poland.

The fact is that, in his more irritable moments, Salazar could be
perverse and untrue to himself. In the difficult years that lay ahead
he was to show a sureness of touch that contrasted sharply with the
limited sentiments he displayed in his April speech of 1938. In it,
his pragmatism wars with his principles. His disregard of the rights
and wrongs of the Sudeten question comes oddly from one who has
already denounced those nations which interfere in other nations'
affairs, and who seven months later was to condemn the whole of
Hitler's policy in regard to the German communities living abroad.[1]
He loses his temper with international idealism, as in other contexts
with democracy, because he feels it is too concerned with concepts
and not enough with what is likely to work; yet his pragmatism
surrenders to his inflexible conviction that nothing good can ever
come out of Moscow. His diagnosis of how Europe contrived to bring
the worst out of Germany is by no means without substance; the
Allies did better after the Second World War. But the implication
that as late as 1938, Germany still needed to be 'understood' while
Russia was still beyond the pale was a strange sentiment for one whose
own country was in peril because of other people's attempts to
appease Hitler by offering him Angola and Mozambique.

Only a few weeks later, Salazar was complaining to Monteiro that
certain British interests kept suggesting a colonial 'readjustment' in
Germany's favour.[2] In November, the Portuguese Chargé d'Affaires
in Pretoria, Dr Ferreira da Fonseca, had a conversation with the
South African Premier, Dr Hertzog, which left him bristling with

---

[1] In his speech to the National Assembly on 22 May 1939 (Disc., iii, 143-4),
Salazar rebuked the use of the *lebensraum* plea as a stepping-stone to political
domination, and then turned to emigrants working in foreign countries: 'So
long as groups of emigrants work in a foreign country, to whose economic life
and hospitality they have turned in their need, no one will complain if they
receive the protection of their native country; but if Europe adopts the principle
that those groups amount to real enclaves and represent a prolongation or
affirmation of an alien sovereignty, it will be objected at once that this attitude is
a first step towards political invasion, and the disposal of excess population will
run into new obstacles.'
[2] L.B., ii, p. 39-52.

suspicion. At first, Hertzog had shown great interest in a suggestion that Portugal and South Africa should collaborate for defence purposes in Africa, and that a Portuguese minister should visit Pretoria for negotiations; but all of a sudden he seemed to cool off and to be anxious to avoid giving a firm opinion about the German colonial problem. Suspecting once more the influence of certain British elements, among whom he named Sir John Simon, Ferreira da Fonseca wrote to Salazar:

> The campaign now in progress in London shows clearly that certain influential English circles, and not only an irresponsible section of the press or a 'society of Jews' as the South African minister picturesquely puts it, would welcome the sacrifice of the Portuguese territories.[1]

Meanwhile, however, and by way of contrast, the British government had given great pleasure to Salazar by issuing, on 3 October, a statement of goodwill to the effect that Britain would stand by all the obligations of the treaties with Portugal. This was followed in November,[2] by a suggestion from London that the Anglo-Portuguese treaties should be revised, and Monteiro saw this as an index that Britain's recent approximation to Germany, and her feeling that she had no need of Portugal, was undergoing revision. True, on the Labour benches in the House of Commons, Arthur Henderson and others were asking whether Britain was bound by the fourteenth-century treaties and their successors to fight in defence of the Portuguese colonies, and whether the Anglo-German Treaty of 1898 had any validity.[3] But on government level a distinct change of tone was discernible. The British military mission to Lisbon had ended with the usual round of congratulations and the exchange of decorations. At the turn of the year, Vickers offered to supply Portugal with Spitfires at an early date. When Portugal ordered the Bofors but, for technical reasons outlined by Teixeira de Sampayo, went to Germany and Italy for other classes of artillery, London was really dismayed and took the situation very seriously. Monteiro cabled to Lisbon that there were strong political reasons for buying only from Britain and America, despite the technical or financial reasons to the contrary; but, even more importantly, the British

[1] L.B., ii, p. 71.
[2] Ibid., p. 64 et seqq.
[3] Ibid., pp. 89, 153.

Ambassador in Lisbon went to Salazar, confessed that Britain had failed Portugal over the arms question, and that she would make amends. He added that Britain was attributing increasing importance to the Alliance with Portugal and wanted to remedy past deficiencies.[1] The *New York Times* of 31 March 1939 commented on the strategic importance of Portugal and the Alliance to Britain, and noted the transformation of the British attitude from one of paternal toleration to responsible consideration:

> In the present state of confusion in which Europe finds itself, little Portugal is influencing events more strongly than on any occasion since the epoch of her explorations and her Empire.

By this time, of course, Hitler had marched on Prague. The Munich settlement was already in ashes.

Salazar, for his part, was shortly to come out with his most important speech to date in defence of the Anglo-Portuguese Alliance, yet it was at this time that he clashed badly with Monteiro over British suspicions of Portugal, which Monteiro was disposed to understand. For some time Salazar had felt that the ambassador was becoming a little over-identified with the liberal English outlook, and to make matters worse Monteiro kept on harping on his own suspicions of Spain – even to the point of suggesting that General Franco should accommodate himself to France, despite the latter's hostility to him in the Spanish Civil War. Monteiro, too, seemed remarkably unperturbed by moves for an Anglo-Russian rapprochement in the face of German aggression. The angry exchanges between the two friends, as indeed they were, reveal a good deal about both of them; while Salazar's incisive diagnosis of Britain's weaknesses has to be read against his May speech when he re-affirmed the Alliance within a few months of world war.

Having praised Chamberlain after Munich, Salazar must have been put out by Monteiro's despatch of 31 March 1939, which analysed Chamberlain's failure in foreign policy. Monteiro attributed this to Chamberlain's habit of trusting only to his own instinct and the advice of two or three men who 'on the international board could only figure as modest amateurs'.[2] The ambassador reinforced this view by quoting Mussolini: 'There is no room for originality; foreign policy is never original.' Monteiro, after all, was Eden's friend too;

[1] *Ibid.*, p. 170.
[2] *Ibid.*, p. 227.

Eden had been excluded from Chamberlain's confidence, his advice
had been ignored, and he had resigned over Chamberlain's appease-
ment policies. At any rate, when Monteiro reported on 15 April[1]
what the London press was saying about Spain, Salazar's hackles
rose in earnest. The papers had referred to a concentration of Italian
troops in Logrono, disembarkations at Cadiz, and intensive military
activity at Vigo. All this well after the end of the Spanish Civil War.
Moreover, the London editors wrote, German troops were still on
Spanish soil, and Portugal's attitudes were suspiciously pro-Axis.
Monteiro underlined the danger of a German invasion of Portugal
which would prevent the Allies from attacking Spain from a Portuguese base. Firmly established in Iberia, the Germans could then
emerge as potential masters of the Mediterranean, assail the British
lines of communication, and neutralize Gibraltar. The German navy
was already nosing around the Portuguese coast, and Monteiro
envisaged the possibility of a German naval occupation while German
troops marched in from Spain. Would it not be wise, he urged, for a
strong detachment of the British navy to visit the Tagus and show
the flag?

Salazar had no illusions about what the Germans could do, but he
was highly sceptical of the press reports about the Italian landings,
and in any event he reacted sharply against what he saw as a British
attack of nerves. He ascribed this to feelings of inferiority, the decline
of British institutions, and the enfeebling effect on government of the
democratic process. His reply to Monteiro is a litany of criticism of
British deficiencies which is by no means wholly misplaced; but its
secondary interest lies in what it reveals of Salazar's endemic inability
to put faith in popular 'participation' in government:

> I cannot avoid the impression that the French and especially the
> English allow themselves to be panicked, and give credit to the
> wildest rumours. . . . In Lisbon, members of the British embassy
> and the French legation are only too ready to spread alarming
> rumours. . . . One deduces that they do this either to frighten
> small countries into acting as instruments of their policy, or be-
> cause they are scared themselves. I believe the latter to be the case.

> England feels particularly the inferiority of her political machine.
> Everyone can see that the rivalry between the two parties and the
> decadence of British political institutions diminish the power and

[1] L.B., ii, pp. 268-87.

speed of government decisions: the government, when trying to deal with strong centralized powers, is hampered by childish questions. At the same time, deplorable publicity is given to the deficiencies in her defence organization, as against the image of strength propagated by her enemies.

Secondly, England feels her military inferiority because, due to internal political difficulties, she cannot impose obligatory military service; and she cannot step up arms production for fear of disrupting ordinary industrial production. A third cause of the present panic is the difficulty some states have in forming a common anti-aggression policy precisely because they lack confidence in British military power; thus they prefer to reach agreement with Germany and Italy rather than make things harder for themselves by adhering to the Anglo-French bloc.[1]

Next day, the Spanish embassy in Lisbon denied the rumours of an Italian landing in Spain, and asserted that Spain was not concerned with Axis policy.

Monteiro was not going to let Salazar get away with this Note, however. England, he retorted, 'does not accept new ideas very easily and is therefore slow to move: but once on the move, these people will not stop until they win'. He rejected the assertion that British institutions were weak; and as for military weakness, this was being repaired. It was up to Portugal to prove that *she* was reliable. The British government was not quite convinced of this, one very good reason being the pro-Axis propaganda in the press closest to the Portuguese government, while the other was the inadequacy of Portugal's own re-armament programme.[2] Salazar was furious. The telegram, he wrote back, provoked the suspicion that 'our representatives abroad let themselves be absorbed by their milieu and prefer their own private information to that provided by their government'. Did Monteiro think the present re-armament programme in Portugal could be boosted without throwing the whole country into misery? Did he think that in any event Portugal could really stop a powerful enemy violating her frontiers? Could he quote one single fact to justify the slightest doubt about Portugal's fidelity to England? Did he think the treaties with England obliged Portugal to follow British policy indiscriminately and go to war by her side in any situation?

[1] *Ibid.*, p. 287.
[2] *Ibid.*, p. 337.

Ambassadors 'must have absolute confidence in the political information furnished to them with the greatest care by their government', if they were to carry out their mission properly.[1] Monteiro replied with detailed explanations of British suspicions. First, he said, the principle had been established that arms used by the two countries should be as similar as possible, yet Portugal had gone against Britain's express wish and adopted light arms of German calibre, while the artillery also rejected British in favour of German and Italian models. Then, having persuaded England to take 'unprecedented interest in our affairs, we either reject her political proposals or neglect them as if they were of no value, as happened with her request for suggestions about the Treaty of Alliance'. Finally, Portugal gave equal standing in her press to the hostile propaganda of anti-British countries side by side with British propaganda: 'we show no preference and so we lose any authority to protest against the frequent outbursts in the British press'.[2]

One can almost feel Salazar quivering with controlled wrath as he composes his rejoinder. The government cannot allow its representative to attack its own policy. It is beyond comprehension that Monteiro should do this with such injustice and ignorance of the facts. England, says Salazar, has never shown him any sign that she lacked confidence in Portuguese fidelity, and as for the armaments question England has herself to blame. It is *her* fault that the Portuguese army lacks artillery.[3] The next move was obvious. Monteiro asked to be relieved of his post. Before reacting to this, Salazar then delivered an important speech to the National Assembly on 22 May, adhering in unambiguous terms to the Alliance with England, declaring it to be an unchanging principle of Portuguese policy. Whether or not he strengthened his words to appease Monteiro, the speech undoubtedly had that effect.

The National Assembly had been summoned to authorize the head of state to visit the Union of South Africa at the invitation of King George VI of England. Taking a broad look at current European problems, Salazar declared:

> Just as a victory of the Reds in Spain would have brought a constant risk of collision between French and English interests in the

[1] L.B., ii, p. 345.
[2] *Ibid.*, p. 347.
[3] *Ibid.*, p. 355.

Peninsula on the one hand and the Anglo-Portuguese Alliance on the other (by virtue of the conflict of ideas and politics), so it is also clear that only through Nationalist Spain, bound by fraternal ties with Portugal, can France and England hope to work for the security of their interests and frontiers, and an improvement in their relations. Seen thus, our treaty with Spain is truly the crowning of a great work and the keystone of a policy.

During the civil war, of course, the English Alliance with Portugal was put to a severe strain. Yet, while some sections of English public opinion seemed unable to understand Portugal's attitude to Spain, the Portuguese and British governments were considering the problems arising from the Alliance and, in friendly collaboration, were studying their joint defence problems. The contacts established in the work of the military mission had been maintained and would have to be continued:

> This simple fact, confirmed by many other demonstrations of high esteem, clearly proves that we are resolved to abide by the fixed principles of our history and, remaining faithful to the Anglo-Portuguese Alliance, to secure the defence of our common interests, while in matters that lie outside the Alliance we reserve our freedom of action and the right to form many other friendships.

A distinction had to be made, Salazar continued, between 'alliances deeply rooted in geographical and historical reasons' and 'temporary agreements due to passing interest or momentary attraction, which are as fragile, artificial and precarious as many modern marriages'. He went on:

> For my part, and I know that I am speaking in the name of my country, I am as determined faithfully to fulfil the duties of the alliance as I am determined, for the honour and in the interests of both parties concerned, not to suffer it to be corrupted or debased.[1]

Chamberlain was so delighted with this that he sent a personal message of thanks to Salazar, and Monteiro then readily accepted Salazar's plea to him to remain at his post in London.

In the telegram rejecting the resignation, Salazar explained that he did not question Monteiro's sincerity and that he had dealt with

[1] Disc., iii, p. 137.

Monteiro's accusations through the medium of official telegrams only because he wanted to ensure that the historical record would be straight. He hoped that Monteiro would one day, in the light of subsequent events, officially retract his groundless suspicions. It would be disastrous, Salazar indicated, if the Portuguese Ambassador in London were to resign immediately after Chamberlain's message and statement in the House of Commons confirming Britain's obligations to Portugal, for this would look as though Monteiro disapproved of the Alliance. Moreover, given his exceptional gifts, background and training, Monteiro had a duty to show some dividends on the 'capital' thus invested in him.[1] This telegram did not exactly glow with warmth, nor did Monteiro's reply in which he agreed to stay where he was but accused Salazar of having been harsh and unjust. His own attitudes, he said, had been dictated by the need to defend the Portuguese government from perils which were perhaps not clearly seen in Lisbon, but were all too plain in London. He accepted the suggestion that he should meet Salazar shortly in Lisbon, and ended with a declaration of friendship.[2]

Earlier in the year, in April, tentative moves were made between Britain and Russia with a view to a possible alliance, now that the Munich Agreement was in ashes and the Nazi aggressor still unsatisfied. It was recognized in Britain that this would distress some of the smaller powers, especially Portugal, but on 29 May, in the House of Commons, Mr Churchill suggested a way out of the dilemma. Speaking of Portugal in warm terms, he suggested that any Anglo-Russian alliance should contain a proviso excluding molestation of any ally of Britain's by Russian intrigues or Communist propaganda. In the long run, Churchill hoped, an alliance with Russia would be to the smaller powers' advantage because of Russia's strong antagonism for Germany. Never mind the motivation behind it; the point was that Russia was anti-German. Eden also backed the idea because he felt it was the only way to peace. The Munich Agreement had been made without consulting Moscow and, Eden feared, this must have gravely undermined Litvinov's position as Soviet Foreign Minister (as a Jew, Litvinov had been the butt of constant and vicious attacks from the Germans). Eden saw that, unless forestalled by a determined British approach, Stalin might come to terms with Hitler at any time, as such a *volte-face* was perfectly feasible between dictatorships. On 3

[1] L.B., ii, p. 382.
[2] *Ibid.*, pp. 401-6. Monteiro was recalled three years later.

May, Eden was proved right–to his own dismay–when Litvinov was sacked and succeeded by the bland and ruthless Molotov who was in favour of rapprochement with the Nazis. The British government's approach to the talks with Russia was weak and vacillating, and Eden, though now out of of office, offered to go personally to see Stalin whom he had met before. This offer was rejected by Chamberlain. The Churchill-Eden line was echoed in the House of Commons by the Liberal Party leader Sir Archibald Sinclair, who told the House that the 'ideological prejudices' even of 'so valued an ally' as Portugal should not stand in the way of an agreement with Russia which could be a vital buttress for peace. Salazar remained unconvinced and told London that, whatever his new relationship with Britain might be, he would disagree with any arrangement made with Russia, whose promises of help would be valueless.[1]

With the German-Polish dispute now coming to a head, a British Note delivered in Lisbon on 16 August, testified to 'the fact that the re-armament of Portugal has in large measure been delayed by the goodwill shown by the Portuguese government in desiring to purchase British materials'. The Note offered four 3·7-inch anti-aircraft guns at once with another twelve to follow at the rate of one a month. Portuguese officers due shortly in London would be given a demonstration of the new 25-pounder guns, and early consideration would be given to Portugal's request for 'certain coast defence equipments'.[2]

Once Moscow became convinced that talks with Britain were getting nowhere, and that not even a tripartite alliance of Britain, France and Russia would of itself be enough to stop Hitler now, the volte-face predicted by Eden occurred and the Russo-German Non-Aggression Treaty was signed on 23 August. With only a matter of days to go before the outbreak of war, Portugal put pressure on Spain to keep her head and stay out of it. Dr Theotónio Pereira, the Portuguese Ambassador at San Sebastian, saw that the Spanish government was divided, the pro-Axis group being led by Serrano Suñer, with Beigbeder, the Foreign Minister, representing the opposite pole. So on 31 August, the ambassador got to work on Serrano, urging him to get rid of the notion that, once hostilities had commenced, France would attack Spain. Britain and France, he insisted, would give Spain every guarantee, and the real danger for

[1] *Ibid.*, pp. 363-6, 388; Eden, *The Reckoning*, pp. 53-6.
[2] *Ibid.*, p. 455.

Spain would be to act like Italy and follow Hitler blindfold. Pereira came away convinced that Beigbeder, to whom he also spoke, would impress upon General Franco the importance of adhering closely to Portugal and the policy of Iberian solidarity.[1]

Meanwhile, the British Ambassador in Lisbon had been discussing Portugal's position if war should now break out. According to Salazar, he made it plain that Portugal's right to keep out of the war was recognized and the Ambassador's own view was that 'if Portugal can keep Spain neutral in the event of war, it is the best service she can render'. Salazar duly reported this to Monteiro in a telegram dated 25 August 1939.[2] At the turn of the month both Portugal and Spain declared their neutrality, and on 3 September, Britain was at war with Germany. The Alliance was now to face its greatest test.

Whatever the pro-German sections of the upper strata thought, for most Portuguese people the Russo-German Pact and the invasion of Catholic Poland were the last straw. German claims to be Portugal's protector against Communism were now derisory. Portuguese neutrality suited Britain well, if only because in her own ill-prepared condition she could not have carried the extra burden of fighting for Portugal's territorial integrity: which is what it would have come to if Portugal had declared war on Germany and then invoked the Alliance. Salazar enforced his country's neutral behaviour with a strictness sometimes irksome to both sides. But it kept German submarines out of Portuguese territorial waters and ports, which would otherwise have provided useful bases for the German navy. At times outward observances were hard to maintain. Portugal, and Salazar himself, was full of admiration for the British resolution to fight on after all her co-belligerents had fallen, and the Portuguese people were highly enthusiastic when the Duke of Kent arrived in Lisbon in June for the celebration of Portugal's eight hundredth anniversary as an independent state. After protests from the German Embassy, the authorities tried to stop people wearing Spitfire and Churchill badges, and the taxi drivers from flying Union Jacks on their radiators. But the manufacturers were not daunted, and eventually another badge appeared which consisted simply of a hat and a cigar! German propaganda intensified its efforts and tried to spread the rumour, especially among the intelligentsia, that Britain

[1] L.B., ii, p. 518.
[2] Disc., iii, pp. 123-4; L.B., ii, p. 487.

would eventually get rid of Salazar's regime: so much so that Eden, early in 1941, had to issue a denial from the floor of the House of Commons.

Salazar's philosophy of neutrality was that it would be wrong to involve the whole of Europe in the conflict. Europeans not involved should set out to create and consolidate zones of peace. An Iberian peace zone would be decisive and Spanish neutrality was therefore most welcome. The Germans, moreover, a few days before war broke out, had promised to respect Portugal's integrity on the condition of Portuguese neutrality. Salazar, however, seemed to make it quite clear whose side he was really on by publicly praising 'the heroic sacrifice of Poland' and proclaiming once again, on 9 October, 'our friendship and our complete fidelity to the English Alliance'. He spoke, too, of the current crisis as one in which the Latin and Christian civilization of Europe was at stake. He was not, however, ready to admit that Russia was in any way qualified to restore those values. He deplored the creation of ideological blocs and the habit of interfering in other nations' internal affairs.[1] Some of the strongest denunciations of Nazism, their meaning clear even when they were not quite specific, came from Salazar's friend the Cardinal Patriarch of Lisbon, and one of the more outspokenly anti-Nazi newspapers was the Catholic daily, *A Voz*, though it could also be critical of the Allies and especially of the United States.[2]

Salazar found himself at the catchpoint of many conflicting hopes and duties. He certainly had no time for Nazi Germany and had every reason to fear her African ambitions, but he was also acutely conscious that one outcome of the war could be the spread of Communism[3] (he had little faith that the Russo-German Pact would last for long). However, when in June 1941, Germany reneged on her ally and attacked Russia, Cardinal Cerejeira told the Lisbon clergy not to identify the Communist heresy with the Russian people. He was trying to say that there need be no insoluble dilemma created in the Portuguese conscience by an alliance between Russia and Britain: it was the people, not the creed, that mattered in the context of the struggle against Hitler. There was nothing immoral in supporting the Russian war effort. This attitude was in striking contrast to that

[1] *Ibid.*, pp. 177-90.
[2] *Survey*, pp. 319-20.
[3] D.D.It., ser. VIII, vol. xii, no. 592; and Hugh Muir, *European Junction*, Harrap, London, 1942.

of the more Germanophile newspapers which simply declined to publish anything about the Russian war effort and thumped away at the need to resist Communism. Worse than any of this, however, was the balancing act to be performed by Salazar, if he were to maintain his dual role of 'adjacent neutral' and Britain's ally: a task that would certainly have daunted less subtle (some would say less devious) minds than his. It was here that his tranquil sure-footedness served him and the Allies well. His attitude to Britain was to be constant: admiration for her traditions and powers of endurance; impatience with her parliamentary processes; hard bargaining in matters of detail; fidelity once the Alliance was invoked. As will be seen, his calculating stubbornness in wartime negotiations over, for instance, the blockade or the distribution of wolfram made him a much tougher customer to deal with than Franco ever was from the Allied point of view.[1] He was, for a start, in a much stronger economic position, and he 'was a man of remarkable tenacity who was always liable to revive a disputed point after agreement seemed to have been reached'.[2]

After the fall of the Low Countries and of France in 1940, refugees swarmed into Portugal and the big question was whether or not the Germans, aided by Spain or otherwise, would cross the Pyrenees into the peninsula. One of the factors restraining them may have been the usefulness of Portugal's neutrality to both sides. German and Italian, as well as British and American airliners landed at Lisbon airport, and Lisbon became the chief distribution port for Red Cross relief supplies to prisoners-of-war and internees, much of the material travelling in Portuguese ships on the last stage of the journey. The Lisbon of those days has been described as one of the world's busiest financial black markets. Moreover:

To travellers from countries at war, Portugal seemed an incredible oasis of peace and prosperity: no blackout; no ration cards till much later in the war; shops full of food and luxuries, for those who could afford to buy them; hotels full of wealthy refugees killing time till they could get a place in the Pan-American Clipper; a skulking place for spies (real, or more often fancied) of all the nations at war.[3]

[1] Chapter 8, *infra*.
[2] *Survey*, p. 320.
[3] *Ibid.*, p. 321.

It was in this situation, however, that Salazar took a number of steps, long before it was clear who was going to win the war, that were to prove of great value to the Allies. The first two involved a healthy slice of self-interest, the third was generous. First, he set about doubling the Portuguese army's strength to 80,000 between 1940 and 1941, many of the troops being deployed in the Atlantic islands and the Azores. By the time the Allies arrived to establish bases in the Azores in 1943, some 40,000 Portuguese troops were there to provide a security framework. Secondly, in July 1940, Salazar supported Britain's policy of economic assistance for Spain by joining in a three-cornered agreement for produce to be supplied to Spain from Portugal's overseas territories, payment to be made through the Anglo-Spanish clearing. At Britain's request, Salazar asked for and obtained from the Spaniards suitable assurances of their willing and able neutrality. Thirdly, in October 1940, Salazar agreed to supply Britain with escudos for the duration of the war in return for sterling credits; while other neutrals were prepared to sell their currencies only against gold. Under this agreement Britain's wartime debt to Portugal rose five or six times higher than anyone had expected. Salazar never tried to get out of the bargain, and at the end of the war spent all the acquired credit in England. As will be seen, this arrangement was an important contribution to the British pre-emptive campaign in the economic war.

It would be tendentious to argue that Salazar kept Spain out of the war, as though no other considerations were involved. But it is fair to say that Franco was surrounded by pressures that could have forced him into co-belligerency with the Axis, and that his success in keeping Spain out of the conflict owed much to Allied economic assistance and to Salazar's activity as a link between the Allies and Spain. Moreover, Salazar's whole concept of Iberian solidarity and neutrality relieved Franco's fears of an Allied landing in the Peninsula through Portugal. At the start of the war, Salazar had good cause to be worried about Spain, especially as, very shortly after the signing of the Iberian Pact in March 1939, Franco had joined with the Axis in the Anti-Comintern Pact. Salazar was to say later that he had been told about this in advance and that it was only a symbol of gratitude for what the Axis had done for the Spanish Nationalists; all the same, it must have exercised his mind at the time. It gave new emphasis to the fact that the Axis were in a position to demand returns for past favours to Franco and that they were quite capable, whether Franco liked it or not, of invading Spain. From there it would have been an easy leap to move into neighbouring Portugal.

Then there were the internal pressures on the Caudillo; some Falangists opposed him personally, some were pro-Axis, and some strongly favoured the absorption of Portugal into Spain. Nor was this last issue confined to a lunatic fringe. Spanish newspapers like *Arriba* and certain radio commentators dwelt constantly on the closely interwoven history of the two peninsular countries, who were said to share the same soul, sometimes described as *Hispanida*. On 15 November 1939 the *Diario de Burgos* said outright that, had it not been for British meddling, the union of Spain and Portugal would already have been achieved and was a geographical necessity. The threat was taken sufficiently seriously for the Portuguese archbishops to issue a joint pastoral letter to the effect that it was wrong to oppose the decree of providence which gave to each nation its own destiny.

Franco, however, was not an imperialist, and favoured a good neighbour policy on the lines of Salazar's own thinking. He was, moreover, a severe pragmatist and a skilful strategist who was to rule Spain not so much by dictation as by a subtle manœuvring of opposing forces – a process of quiet manipulation, establishing his policies almost imperceptibly. He knew what the traffic would bear and worked within the facts. If Salazar was to perform a rare balancing feat in his external diplomacy during the war, Franco's corresponding expertise was to handle the complex and competing forces within his own country, while alternately encouraging and stonewalling Hitler on the periphery. It is said that he would have preferred an Axis victory, but only a limited one. A major German victory might have returned Gibraltar to Spain and widened her scope in North Africa, but it might also have menaced her independence. In any event, he obviously wanted to keep his own exhausted country out of the war if he could. There was much more likelihood of obtaining economic aid from the Allies than from the Axis, and Franco was only too conscious of British sea power in his own vicinity. Finally, a belligerent Spain would be putting at risk her Atlantic islands and African territories. A swift look at the chronology of events will show how Franco steered, and was helped to steer, his way through all the shoals:

September 1939: Spain sends a military mission to Portugal.

March 1940: The basis of Britain's policy towards Spain is established in agreements whereby Britain is to finance Spanish purchases from the sterling area and to make a loan to Spain of £2 million. Spain promises not to re-export a range of important imports.

May 1940: Portugal supplies Spain with 10,000 tons of wheat and 6,000 tons of maize. On 22 May Halifax writes to Salazar asking him to take to Spain an offer of 100,000 tons of wheat from Britain and to secure assurances about Spanish neutrality. Salazar succeeds on both counts. After the fall of France the dominating thought in the peninsula is the possibility of the German army crossing the Pyrenees.

3 June 1940: Franco offers Hitler Spain's co-operation in whatever form is convenient to Germany.

12 June 1940: After Italy's entry into the war, Spain changes her neutral status to one of non-belligerency, and provisionally occupies Tangier.

19 June 1940: Spain indicates to Germany her willingness to enter the war but hedges this round with an unacceptable set of conditions. She wants Gibraltar, French Morocco, the department of Oran in Algeria, an enlargement of Rio de Oro and of Spanish Guinea, plus military and economic aid.

6 July 1940: The Portuguese Ambassador in Madrid, Dr Theotónio Pereira, secures from General Franco a promise to go as far as possible with a Spanish guarantee of Portuguese Iberian independence. For Britain, Mr David Eccles in Lisbon secures the three-cornered agreement for produce from Portugal's overseas territories to be supplied to Spain.

17 July 1940: In an aggressive speech, Franco lays claim publicly to Gibraltar and an expansion of Spain's African holdings.

29 July 1940: A Protocol, drafted by Salazar, is added to the Iberian Pact. It provides for close consultation between Spain and Portugal in the event of circumstances arising which threaten the security or independence of either country. Commenting on the Protocol, Professor Medlicott says:

> As it re-affirmed treaties, conventions, and undertakings with third states, and so recognized the obligations of Portugal towards England under the ancient Alliance, it was a noticeable strengthening of the impulse towards neutrality by the two powers.[1]

In the same month Hoare hears reports that Mussolini has put pressure on Franco to enter the war, but that Franco has replied to the

[1] Medlicott, ii, p. 514.

effect that he is 'in no position' to do so. Meanwhile, Britain's determination to fight on alone, together with the joint economic incentives
coming from Britain and the United States, is beginning to tell on
Franco.

September 1940: Britain promises more aid to Spain. Serrano Súñer
goes to Berlin only to be told that Hitler wants a continental bloc with
Spain's economy managed from Berlin. Serrano's suggestion that
Hitler should offer Spain some territorial accretions in North Africa
is coldly received. Franco again refuses to enter the war.

17 October 1940: Serrano is appointed Foreign Minister, but Spanish
policy does not change in favour of the Axis.

23 October 1940: Franco meets Hitler at Hendaya on the Spanish
border and leaves the Fuehrer saying he would rather go to the
dentist than go through another round of negotiation with Franco
(whose droning voice reminded one observer of an Arab at prayer).
According to Hoare's reports, the Caudillo refuses to grant bases on
Spanish soil to the Germans, nor will he give them a right of passage
through Spain. He repeats his conditions for entering the war, stress-
ing the need for heavy guns.

Between the Hendaya meeting and the end of January 1941,
Franco is said to have had the German request repeated to him several
times and to have maintained his position as before, though promising
to make preparations for entering the war as soon as possible.
After meeting Franco at Bordighera on 12 February, Mussolini told
Hitler that Spain was really in no position to go to war and that
Franco would have to be thought of as a political ally. During 1941,
both in public and in private discussions with Allied ambassadors,
Franco manifested great unfriendliness to the Allied powers. He was
a prey to all kinds of doubt and told the United States' Ambassador,
Carlton Hayes, that while Spain was neutral in the quarrel between
Britain and Germany, for instance, she was not neutral in the struggle
against Communism.[1] Hence the despatch of the Spanish Blue
Division to fight with the Germans on the Russian front. He still
believed that the Axis would ultimately win, in spite of the tough
Russian winter campaign of 1940-1. On the other hand he realized
that the war was going to be long drawn out and he could not afford
to wait for an Axis victory. Spain could collapse economically or a
Republican rising might occur. He also feared an Allied landing in

---

[1] Crozier, p. 369.

the peninsula through Portugal and the influence of Salazar's solidarity/neutrality policy was always there to weight him towards the Allies.[1] The Allies, too, had done their best to see that he got the supplies he needed, while the Germans had bullied the Spanish government, charged exorbitant prices and taken little care to see that Spain was supplied with what she really wanted.[2]

With the fear of an Allied landing in his mind, Franco asked Salazar for talks under the provisions of the 1940 Protocol, and in the gravity of the circumstances, Salazar decided to go to Seville to meet his opposite number in Spain. The meeting took place on 17 February 1942. Serrano was there but was already on the way out of Franco's favour. Moreover, speaking in his Gallego dialect which closely approximates to Portuguese, Franco commanded the conversation without benefit of interpreters. Many years later the Caudillo was to tell a French journalist that Salazar was 'the most accomplished and worthy of respect of all the statesmen I have known'.[3] Unfortunately, the only record of the Seville talks is contained in a report to Berlin by the German Ambassador, Stohrer, who obtained his information from Serrano.[4] Both men had their reasons for glossing the story to suit their own ends. As far as one can see, however, the Spanish side took the line that, if the Allies landed or were allowed to land in Portugal, Spain would regard this as an act of aggression against herself and proceed accordingly. There was no reason to fear a German landing in Portugal, and Germany was going to win the war. Serrano alleged that the British were determined to get rid of Salazar and his regime. Salazar flatly refused to believe this and urged his own belief that victory would go to the Allies, notwithstanding appearances. He is supposed to have said that he regarded Britain with esteem though without deep sympathy,[5] and argued that an Allied victory was less to be feared than an Axis success. If Germany won, he said, he was afraid of Europe being Germanicized. If the Allies were to win, he thought they would want to keep Germany

[1] Ibid., p. 359.
[2] Woodward, p. 366.
[3] Georges Groussard in Le Figaro, 20 June 1958.
[4] Documents Secrets (Eristov), vol. iii (Espagne), no. 30.
[5] Former Ministers who worked closely with Salazar for many years – including Dr Theotónio Pereira and General Santos Costa – have told me of their impression that Salazar, in spite of all the ups and downs, felt for Britain a deep friendship that went beyond admiration and endured until he unsuccessfully invoked the Alliance over Goa. He was then disappointed and hurt. See Chapter 10 infra.

going as a bastion against Communism. He saw no danger of an Allied invasion, though he is said to have shown some anxiety about the United States, which he accused of sabotaging Portugal by a niggardly policy in issuing Navicerts. In the end, the two leaders pledged themselves to defend their countries' integrity and independence, and to come to each other's aid in the event of aggression. They also planned to strengthen their economic ties.

Was this interview decisive for Franco? If so, it is because it was part and parcel of a developing Iberian association in which Salazar, to say the least of it, played a notable part. Henry J. Taylor was in Lisbon and spoke to Salazar on the night of his return from Seville. Salazar told him: 'Spain will turn back from a ghastly, incalculable mistake.'[1] The turning point of the war came towards the end of 1942 with the Battle of Alamein and Operation Torch, the Allied landings in North Africa, in which Franco acquiesced and earned Churchill's gratitude. After this, the Iberian peninsula's importance faded – but not that of the Azores.

The Azores is the name given to nine islands extending over 500 miles in the Atlantic Ocean, a third of the way from Lisbon to New York. In his study of Portugal,[2] Mr John Eppstein tells us that those islands are the peaks of a volcanic range, and that some volcanoes are still active. The largest island is São Miguel, and its port, Ponta Delgada, is the capital, with 20,000 residents. Today, a large commercial airport stands on Santa Maria, while the United States and Portuguese air forces share a military air base on Terceira, and a new French missile-tracking station has been set up on Flores.

From early on in the war both sides, foreseeing the Battle of the Atlantic, were interested in the Azores and also in the Cape Verde islands lying 1,000 miles further to the south-west (350 miles off Africa's western bulge); all of which were Portuguese territory. Hitler wanted bases to attack Atlantic shipping including vessels travelling by the Cape route or from South America. The Allies wanted bases for anti-submarine activity and stages for the Atlantic air ferry. After the collapse of France in 1940, Hitler was well placed to launch an occupying force on the Azores from the French ports, and it now seems that he was restrained only by his admirals who thought the project too costly and difficult. They wanted to con-

[1] Henry J. Taylor in *Milwaukee Sentinel*, 2 October 1968.
[2] John Eppstein, *Portugal*, Queen Anne Press, London, 1967.

centrate all their forces on attacking Allied shipping as quickly as possible and without diversions. Not knowing this at the time, however, Churchill wanted to forestall the enemy by simply seizing the Azores and Cape Verde, but the Foreign Office prevailed on him not to take action until it was clear beyond doubt that the Germans were attempting an occupation.

Salazar was never very worried about a German invasion of the islands, if only because he trusted the British navy. But he did fear an invasion of mainland Portugal by way of Spain, and in December 1940 he asked for secret talks with the British government, sending a military mission to London for the purpose in February 1941. On the assumption that the Germans would invade the peninsula without Spanish co-operation, Britain offered to supply Portugal with defence equipment, and to send active military aid if Portugal asked for it as soon as the Germans crossed the Pyrenees. This would have involved abandoning neutrality before it was absolutely necessary, as Salazar saw it, and his reply was that he did not want to invoke military aid until Portugal herself was attacked. This, of course, would have been too late for aid to be effective. So Britain simply suggested that, if Portugal were attacked, Salazar's best course would be to stage a token resistance only, and to move his government to the Azores. He accepted this advice and began at once to reinforce the defence of the islands.

United States policy over the Azores tended to be impatient.[1] While the British press carefully avoided hints about occupation, American opinion was less alive to Portuguese sensitivities. On 18 April 1941, however, the U.S. Secretary of State, Mr Cordell Hull, told Portugal's Ambassador Bianchi in Washington, that America would not occupy the islands unless the Germans moved (he did not make it clear whether this meant a German move into Portugal or even into Spain). It was with this sort of threat hanging over him that Salazar went to Coimbra University on 19 April to meet a detachment of Oxford dons who conferred a doctorate on him, Mr T. J. Higham giving the Latin address, and Salazar replying in kind and not without some elegance.

While Roosevelt did not hide his determination to seize the Azores if the Germans as much as made a move towards them – he even asked Brazil to help in this temporary and preventive operation – he behaved

[1] *Survey*, pp. 331-6; Woodward, pp. 375-6.

discreetly enough during April. He ordered patrols to cover areas of the Atlantic, including the Azores, with a view to warning British convoys of the presence of German raiders and U-boats; but, in deference to Portuguese feeling, he would not allow aircraft to fly directly over the islands. He also urged Churchill not to consider an invasion unless Portugal were attacked or a German assault on the islands imminent. Even then, he insisted, Portugal should be guaranteed that her sovereignty over the islands would be restored to her eventually, unimpaired. But then came the news that Darlan was negotiating with Hitler, and there was a strong likelihood that German aircraft and shipping would be able to use Dakar, a prospect which lent new and heightened importance to the Azores. On 6 May, Senator Pepper delivered a speech to the U.S. Senate in which he openly referred to a possible U.S. occupation of the islands. Salazar moved swiftly and secured an explicit declaration from the U.S. government that the senator's views were his own and that government policy was one of strict respect for Portuguese sovereignty.[1] It was in this month, too, that the U.S. government agreed to leave negotiations over the Azores to Britain, in view of her Alliance with Portugal. Still, on 23 May, Roosevelt ordered a force of 25,000 men to be ready in a month to make for the Azores,[2] and then on 27 May, the President broadcast a fireside chat in which he spoke of the threat to America involved in a German occupation of the islands, and of his resolve to be on guard against any attempt to set up German bases in the Atlantic.[3] This, coming on top of press recommendations that the U.S. forces might have to seize the Azores without waiting for Lisbon's permission, aroused indignation in Portugal, together with a certain fear that the Germans might now be tempted to forestall the Allies and to swoop on the islands at once.

A rapid series of exchanges between Lisbon and Washington[4] began with a Portuguese Note pointing out that Portugal's neutrality, approved of by both Britain and America, had been unimpeachably observed and had provided Europe and the Americas with their last direct contact. To maintain this, the Portuguese government had tried to set up an adequate defence system in Cape Verde and the

---

[1] *Diario de Noticias*, Lisbon, 9 May 1941.

[2] Langer and Gleason, *The Undeclared War*, p. 369.

[3] *Documents on American Foreign Relations*, 1940-1, pp. 51, 53, 54.

[4] Archives of the Portuguese Foreign Ministry (to be published shortly); Langer and Gleason, pp. 588-9.

Azores. The President's references to the islands were 'involved with the expounding of the thesis that it devolves on the United States to define and decide whether, and when, and where they are threatened and how their forces are to be used'. In expounding this thesis 'there is not the slightest reference to the fundamental respect for the sovereignty of others exercised and maintained without prejudice to anybody'. Cordell Hull wrote a less than reassuring reply on 10 June, which stated that the President had referred to the strategic importance of the islands 'solely in terms of their potential value from the point of view of attack against this hemisphere', but also referred to 'the inalienable right of self-defence'. Bianchi told Hull that this was not good enough, and a state of unease persisted in Portugal, notwithstanding the German attack on the Soviet Union which might have been taken as a sign that Germany's powers of occupation were now fully stretched elsewhere. The Portuguese mood was to receive some justification in July, when the Americans occupied Iceland.

At any rate, on 8 July 1941, Roosevelt wrote a long personal letter to Salazar which was presented in Lisbon on 21 July, in which he stated flatly:

> In the opinion of the government of the United States, the continued exercise of unimpaired and sovereign jurisdiction by the government of Portugal over the territory of Portugal itself, over the Azores and over all the Portuguese colonies offers complete assurance of security to the Western Hemisphere insofar as the regions mentioned are concerned. It is, consequently, the consistent desire of the United States that there be no infringement of Portuguese sovereign control over those territories. This policy of the United States I made emphatically clear in the message which I addressed yesterday to the Congress of the United States concerning the steps which had been taken to assist the people of Iceland in the defence of the integrity and independence of their country.

The President spoke of his government's gratification at the steps taken by Salazar to strengthen the defence of the Azores, and added that the United States would stand ready to assist Portugal in the defence of those possessions against any threat of German aggression, 'should your government express to me its belief that such aggression is imminent or its desire that such steps be taken'. All this would be done in full recognition of Portugal's sovereignty and with categorical assurances that American forces sent to the Azores would be withdrawn immediately at the end of the war. The letter then takes on a personal note in which the President refers to his own experience, during the First World War, of visiting those ports in the Azores which Portugal made available to the Allies; it was then that he saw for himself how close and friendly the relations between the Portuguese people and the U.S. navy had become. Salazar replied to this letter on 29 July, in equally cordial terms, but indicated that all he might do would be to ask the United States for some defence materials if they could not be obtained from Britain.

It seems that at the subsequent Atlantic Conference in August, Churchill was told that Salazar had gone further than this, indicating his willingness to accept United States protection if a German invasion drove him to the Azores and the British were preoccupied elsewhere.[1] It sounds highly unlikely that Salazar said any such thing. However, the Conference decided that the United States would be responsible for the Azores in any such emergency, subject to British support, and also to British responsibility for occupying Cape Verde. Whatever the ambiguities behind all this, it came to nothing in practice.

There the Azores rested until 1943, but meanwhile another threat to Portuguese neutrality emerged in the Far East. The island of Timor is the largest of the Lesser Sunda Islands in the Malay archipelago. It lies roughly midway between Java and New Guinea, and directly north of Western Australia. In 1941 it was divided between the Dutch and the Portuguese (today the Dutch half belongs to Indonesia), with the Portuguese occupying the eastern half together with the enclave in Dutch territory known as Ocussi-Ambeno. The province of Timor has belonged to Portugal since the sixteenth century and today numbers half a million residents. Its strategic importance was obvious in November 1941, when Monteiro told Eden that Portugal would resist any Japanese attempt to seize the island, and might have to ask for help under the Alliance. Discussions with Australia and the Dutch authorities had not been concluded when the Japanese swooped on Pearl Harbour on 7 December. Four days later, with Australian and Dutch agreement, Britain told Portugal that Australian and Dutch forces would come to her aid in case of emergency, and the Governor of Timor should be told to ask for that aid if the occasion arose – or accept it if there was no time for an invitation to be sent. Portugal agreed to this arrangement at once.

[1] Churchill, iii, pp. 388-9.

On 16 December, the British Ambassador in Lisbon, now the distinguished Sir Ronald Campbell who had been ambassador in Paris, told the Portuguese government that the Dutch had reported the presence of a Japanese submarine near Timor. It had been arranged with Australia that Dutch and Australian officers should see the Portuguese Governor of Timor and that, in anticipation of his invitation, it had also been arranged that 350 Dutch and Australian troops would arrive in the Portuguese province two hours after the interview. Salazar's reaction was violent. He ordered the Governor not to agree to the landing of Allied troops unless he was attacked by the Japanese, otherwise Portugal's neutrality would be in ashes and the Japanese might well retaliate by attacking the Portuguese island of Macao, off the coast of China. Meanwhile, however, the troops had already landed and Salazar protested that the Allies had violated his country's sovereignty. This was clearly a change of mind on his part in the light of his original agreement that the landings should take place without invitation if there was no time to send one. Eden, however, was reluctant to take this line with Salazar in view of the Allies' need of his islands, his wolfram and his services with Spain. So he formally apologized, indicating that the move had been made only because the Portuguese forces in Timor were unable to cope by themselves, and he promised that the Allied troops would withdraw if Portuguese reinforcements arrived. Salazar continued to make appropriate noises, but in fact accepted the situation. The Japanese attacked on the night of 19-20 February, before Portuguese reinforcements could get there, and the Japanese Ambassador in Lisbon explained that it was necessary to expel the 'foreign troops'. The Allied force retreated inland and held on in the hills. Portugal transmitted a Japanese suggestion that, if the Allied troops surrendered the Japanese might withdraw. But the offer was rejected and a guerrilla war of attrition dragged on. In the event, Timor was lost to Portugal until the end of the war.

The Azores question was much more critical, and in 1943 Admiral Sir Dudley Pound revived an earlier proposal to *ask* Portugal for facilities in the islands, with a view to combating the U-boat menace which was ravaging the Allies' Atlantic convoys. Even a single aircraft over a convoy was enough to hamper the attackers, but without the Azores and to obtain the utmost air protection, the convoys had to follow an icy, northerly route beset by bad weather, and an open book to the enemy. A more benign southerly route with air protection would be of special value in winter and would facilitate variation of convoy routes when U-boats were concentrated in the north. More direct sailings across the Atlantic would economize shipping. Naval escorts could be fuelled in the islands, which could also be used as a staging-post for the air-supply route.[1] From island bases the Allies could strike at the Bay of Biscay and at the area near the Azores where, from 1942 onwards, U-boats met their supply submarines which enabled them to remain at sea for long periods. Fewer escort carriers would be needed. It was also reckoned that the shortening of the air-ferry route might save the Allies a million tons of shipping a year, not to mention 100 million gallons of fuel.[2]

As long as there was any danger of Germany invading Portugal, Salazar was afraid that a grant of bases to the Allies would be an open invitation to Hitler to retaliate by marching on Portugal through Spain. After Alamein and Torch, however, the risk of German invasion gradually disappeared. By 1943 it was clear that Spain was not going to enter the war, and Hitler had enough on his hands without trying to force his way through that unwilling country. It was, in fact, on 14 May 1943, that he finally decided to abandon the idea of crossing Spain to attack Gibraltar, remarking that the Axis must face the fact that it was saddled with Italy.[3] So the time had plainly come to tackle the Azores question head on, and Eden was never in any doubt that the way to do this was to ask Salazar for facilities in the name of the Alliance. For this reason he had disliked the report he had received in February from the British Ambassador in Rio de Janeiro to the effect that Roosevelt had been suggesting to the Brazilians that they should defend the Azores. Eden was sure that Salazar would reject the proposal out of hand.

On 10 May, on his way to Washington for the Trident Conference, Churchill cabled to London that he wanted to talk to the Americans about a combined approach to Portugal, adding that he was willing to tell the Portuguese that, if they refused, the Allies would invade. Eden and the Foreign Office were completely against this formula which seemed to them immoral and bad politics, and warned the Prime Minister that it would lose the Allies a world of goodwill on the Portuguese side as well as the required facilities. The Defence

[1] Woodward, pp. 378-83; Eden, *The Reckoning*, p. 390.
[2] *Survey*, p. 336.
[3] Eden, *The Reckoning*, p. 390; Fuehrer Conferences on Naval Affairs, 1943, cap. iii.

Committee took the same view. Churchill wired back that he could see no substance in the moral argument. Pound and Admiral King were willing to invade and it was worth it if it was going to save a million tons of shipping and thousands of lives. Small nations depended on an Allied victory, so what he proposed was in Portugal's interest too. On 24 May, Eden and Clement Attlee cabled again, begging Churchill to wait till he got back to London before deciding the issue. Back came another wire accusing them of paralysing action. But the War Cabinet supported them and thus, reluctantly, Churchill acquiesced. The central theme of the Eden-Attlee cable is a testimony to all that Eden had learned from Monteiro about the man the Allies had to deal with in Lisbon:

> . . . His Majesty's Ambassador, when here, told us he thought there was a chance of Salazar giving us what we want. Salazar's temperament being what it is, he is less likely to give way to an ultimatum. We feel it would be better to invoke the Alliance and state our case. If he rejects that he will have shown that the Alliance is of little value. We should then be in a better moral position than if we, without any approach, suddenly threatened to seize the territory of an Ally. . . .[1]

The approach to Salazar was eventually made on 18 June, in a two-pronged movement. In London, Eden saw Monteiro and explained Britain's case in great detail, gave him two papers setting out the facilities required and the reasons for asking for them. Eden also offered in return to discuss measures of assistance against possible German air attacks on the Portuguese mainland, and protection for Portuguese shipping and trade. Britain also 'gave assurances about the maintenance of Portugal's sovereignty over all her colonies'.[2] Basically, the British request was for reconnaissance aircraft facilities at São Miguel and Terceira, and fuelling facilities for naval escorts at São Miguel or Fayal.[3] Churchill cabled Roosevelt saying he would like to associate the United States with both the requests and the assurances. Roosevelt replied identifying himself with the former, but saying nothing about the latter.

Meanwhile, in Lisbon, Sir Ronald Campbell was tackling Salazar, who seemed surprised but promised sympathetic consideration.

[1] Eden, *ibid.*, p. 392.
[2] *Ibid.*, p. 393.
[3] Woodward, p. 379f.

After Campbell had gone, he sent for his Under-Secretary for War, Colonel (now General) Santos Costa, who began by opposing the request because it would demolish Portugal's neutrality. Salazar's answer was simple. The Alliance had been invoked and Portugal could not refuse. The only question was how to strengthen Portugal's defences and what military equipment to ask the British for. 'How long do you need to prepare, and how much material do you require?' Salazar asked Santos Costa, who knew exactly what he wanted. 'Three months,' he said, 'and enough for three divisions.' Salazar nodded.[1] On 23 June, Salazar granted the British request in principle, but asked for talks on conditions of the grant and on provision for Portugal's defence. As Campbell had predicted, Salazar answered the call when it came, though he was still to prove difficult over provision for American, as opposed to British, ships and aircraft. It will be said, of course, that Salazar by this time had nothing to lose by responding to his ancient ally. But this sort of observation loses force when viewed in the perspective of the previous seven years. Portuguese neutrality had served the Allies well, especially in the matter of Spain, and in protecting itself it had now ensured that the Allies would be moving in to well-defended islands. A belligerent Portugal, on the other hand, already extremely poor, would have destroyed herself and proved to be no more than a running sore in Britain's side. Finally, when the argument with the Americans was in full swing, Eden told Churchill

> . . . that the Americans did not understand that modern Portugal was not a country from which they could get everything by threats or bribes, and that Dr Salazar was not the kind of man who wanted to 'climb upon the Allied bandwagon in good time'.[2]

From the start, Salazar made it plain that he still wanted to keep Portugal technically neutral and thus wanted to restrict facilities to those who had a right to claim them under treaty. In other words, he wanted only British troops in the island, and even these should at first arrive quietly in modest numbers, though they would be completely free to expand thereafter. Eden decided to 'play it cool'. He was convinced that, once the British were in, it would be easy enough to work the Americans in as well. As even Churchill later

[1] Author's private conversation with General Santos Costa in Lisbon, January 1968.
[2] Woodward, p. 382.

put it to Eden: 'The great thing is to worm our way in and then, without raising any question of principles, swell ourselves out.'[1] Indeed, Salazar agreed at an early stage that it would be very hard to discriminate between British and American shipping as the convoys were mixed, and he quickly allowed the refuelling facilities to be extended to American warships and merchant vessels. As for Britain, the Foreign Office was only too glad that Portugal wanted to stay out of the war, for her entry would have made demands on British assistance which at that time could not be met.

Detailed conversations began on 6 July, and, so far as Britain was concerned, Portuguese co-operation was wholly satisfactory. Problems arose over the Americans, however. Churchill and Eden tried again to extract American guarantees for Portugal's territorial integrity but, although on 13 August Mr Winant was encouraging about this, he seemed to be linking promises of assurances with a Portuguese grant of American demands. The Foreign Office urged the Americans not to press, at that stage, for air landing facilities (the U.S. had asked in July that these should be made available to them under cover of commercial operations). The Foreign Office told Washington that there would in the event be no trouble about getting facilities for United States aircraft *en route* to Africa, but that it would be unwise to press the point explicitly while the British talks were going on. But these had slowed down, even after the required defence equipment had arrived. The islands' defences must be completed, Salazar argued, and he was not to be rushed. On 2 August Churchill and Eden had a 'shouting match' over this. The Prime Minister claimed that he had been right all along, the islands should just have been taken, and that Salazar was fooling Eden. The latter, supported by Sir Alan Brooke, hit back hard and pointed out that Britain could not have launched an expedition against the Azores before the end of August, anyway. In the end, Churchill apologized but said he felt that Salazar was 'intolerable'.[2] It was decided to give Salazar a deadline for 15 September. This was later changed to 1 October. Salazar insisted that the islands' defences would not be ready until 15 October, but agreed that the British could move in on 8 October. The agreement was signed on 18 August, and the British arrived in the Azores on the arranged day.

Portuguese co-operation continued to be satisfactory but the United

[1] *Ibid.*, p. 381f.
[2] Eden, *The Reckoning*, p. 400.

States asked in September to put a force of about 10,000 men on the islands. London took the view that this would be duplication and explained the difficulties implicit in the proposal. The British chiefs-of-staff added that they were concentrating first on plans for American aircraft which could be put into effect under British cover. Churchill was inclined to support the immediate American demands, though he did understand Portugal's fear that, once the Americans were in, they might want to stay. It was at this point that Eden delivered his already quoted defence of Salazar and pointed out that Portugal's behaviour contrasted well with that of other neutrals, notably Eire and Turkey. In October, the Americans made a direct approach to Salazar who repeated that, without breaking his neutrality, he could not give to America what he had given to Britain under treaty. But he granted the Americans similar facilities, though only within the framework of the British agreement, and theoretically all American units had to work on the basis of being on loan to the British government. He made slight objection to the extension of facilities for American naval patrols operating against U-boats, but it was not until July 1944 that he allowed a U.S. naval air squadron to operate from Lagens airfield. Even then the crews had to wear both British and American insignia. Protracted negotiations over a U.S. air base on the island of Santa Maria were concluded in time to be of use to the Allies in the Far East campaign.[1] The Azores agreement concluded with the British in 1943, however, was in time to be of very great value to the Allies, even though it would have been more useful still had it been signed at an earlier stage of the Battle of the Atlantic.

[1] Relations between Portugal and America were never easy after Roosevelt's fireside chat in 1941. True, the latter's personal letter to Salazar helped, and after Torch, which Salazar welcomed, Roosevelt wrote to President Carmona with assurance about the territorial integrity of Portugal. But neutrality continued to be interpreted strictly and when, in January 1943, eleven American fighter aircraft were forced to land in Lisbon, they were impounded and the crews interned.

CHAPTER 8

The Economic War

It was in the economic war that the dual role of neutral and ally underwent its severest moral and practical tests, and that the character of Salazar emerged in all its contrasts.[1] From his point of view, he was fighting for his country's economic life and to keep her out of a war that would otherwise destroy her. He accepted the ally's role in the military and political sphere to a degree which painfully stretched the meaning of neutrality, but seemed to feel that, unless the Alliance were specifically invoked to the contrary, wartime trading required him to wear, for much of the time, his neutral hat. The tenacity with which he bent the major powers to the needs of his own small nation must command admiration, however grudging; nor did Britain and America do all that badly out of him. Yet, in the eyes of his ancient ally, he at times fought less than fair, was always more prone to complain than understand, and, while out to extract the last ounce of profit he could from both sides, seemed to forget that the context was that of a war that ought to be shortened. It was as though the seminarian in him had given way for the duration to the *saloio*, the horny-handed peasant son of an ungenerous soil.

One of the main weapons of economic war is the blockade, which aims to stop neutral countries, especially those adjacent to the enemy, from exporting too much to their belligerent neighbours. This means limiting the adjacent neutrals' imports and thus their re-exports to the enemy countries. The more agreeable way of working this is to agree with the neutrals on the quantities of imports they require for their domestic needs, and to get them to promise not to import any more. The nation setting up the blockade has to point out gently that its navy will be happy to stop any excess supplies from reaching the neutrals, and to seize it as contraband. To achieve a minimum

---

[1] Medlicott, vol. I, Chap. XV, pp. 509 *et seq.*; vol. II, Chap. XI, pp. 314 *et seq.*; vol. II, Chap. XXII, p. 582 *et seq.* This monumental work takes the reader through a labyrinthine tangle of highly technical negotiation with great clarity and even contrives to make it an intensely human and dramatic story.

of inconvenience for all concerned, the Allies in the Second World War used a system of what were called Navicerts, a kind of commercial passport. The overseas exporter in, say, Brazil would advise the local British embassy of his intention to consign goods to, say, Portugal; and would give full details. Having checked with the Ministry of Economic Warfare (MEW) and found the proposed consignment to be within the limits of the ration, the mission would issue a Navicert guaranteeing exemption from seizure by Allied navies.

The other major factor in the economic conflict was known as pre-emption: buying from neutrals not only what you need for your own war effort but also such quantities as would otherwise be bought by the enemy. In this way the Allies sought to control the neutrals' indigenous products which could not be related to their imports. In this connection the leading Portuguese product was wolfram, the mineral vital for modern munitions and one of Portugal's few abundant natural resources. Apart from Spain, the only other European source of wolfram was Sweden, whose output was only a tenth of Portugal's. After the Russo-German war cut Germany's Trans-Siberian route to Far East sources, Iberian wolfram became extremely important to the Reich, and this continued to be true even after 1941 when Germany could call on Japanese supplies.

In March 1940, Britain had concluded her war trade agreement with Spain, and on 24 July, the tripartite agreement between Britain, Spain and Portugal had been signed by David Eccles in Lisbon.[1] This was of considerable help to the Allied cause and in the following October, Salazar extended certain financial facilities to Britain which were to prove to be of great value to the Allies in the pre-emption campaign. This, it will be remembered, took the form of an agreement whereby Portugal undertook to make escudos available to Britain *against sterling* for the duration of the war. By way of contrast, Sweden and Switzerland would sell their currencies only against gold, a commodity Britain was rapidly running short of. Moreover, sterling repayments of Britain's accumulated debt to Portugal would not fall due until five years after the end of the war. When the agreement was made, Salazar thought the debt would rise to something under £15 million. In fact, by the end of the war it had reached a total of £80 million, but Salazar did nothing to get out of his contract; and

[1] Chapters 6 and 7 *supra*.

when Portugal was finally free to draw her sterling balances, she spent the lot in England.

In the field of the blockade and pre-emption campaign, however, the course of the Alliance ran less smoothly. On 13 July, the British war cabinet decided to ration Spain and Portugal. The Iberian peninsula, after all, was the most convenient transit route for Germany's overseas supplies. Britain was Portugal's biggest customer and supplier, but the proposed blockade was none the less a considerable burden for a small country still trying to reach a decent standard of living. Her efforts had been helped by a recent upsurge in output and trade in her African possessions; and colonial produce – notably coffee, maize, sugar, cocoa, oilseed, cotton and sisal – had been feeding a brisk re-export trade with the Axis powers and countries now overrun by the Germans. Virtually defenceless, Portugal was afraid of anything that might be construed as an invitation to German reprisals, and after the strenuous work of the past few years it was painful to have to face the accumulation of what the Allies termed 'colonial surpluses'. Salazar was in no mood to enter into restrictive agreements.

But Britain had to pursue her war effort, so in August 1940 she unilaterally applied a ration list to Portuguese imports, and in September clamped down altogether on Portuguese imports of oil. Though much more complex issues had been solved with Spain in a very few weeks, it took from September 1940 to February 1941 to get Salazar to agree on an oil quota. To resolve an impasse, it was agreed that the level for Portugal's stocks of oil could be raised from 50,000 to 78,000 tons; but that she should not re-export any oil.

Import quotas were agreed for other rationed commodities, but there was constant trouble about existing stocks. After Britain had applied pressure by closing down certain quotas in October 1940, Salazar undertook to control the re-export of certain goods, but argued that existing stocks should not be taken into account. He simply refused to consider the matter at all, and the MEW replied that it would just have to debit the stocks against the domestic ration. Britain was not without understanding of Portugal's plight, especially in regard to colonial surpluses. Some of them would plainly rot if kept too long in a tropical climate; and the Lisbon banks, while willing to grant credit against stocks held in Lisbon, would not do as much for those in Africa. Portuguese colonial exporters were becoming restive. From the Allies' point of view, however,

Portuguese exports were still reaching Germany and had to be stopped. Such were the occupational hazards of being a neighbour of Britain's enemies.

In January 1941, the new ambassador, Sir Ronald Campbell, tried to get a fresh start by presenting a comprehensive statement of policy asking for an agreed quota system, a ban on re-exports to specified destinations, and no excessive stockpiling. It referred to the recent agreements revising various quotas and made suggestions on how to dispose of colonial produce. Sterling was to be offered to Spain to enable her to buy Portuguese sisal, sugar and maize. Salazar accepted this package deal and promised to give a guarantee that overseas goods (other than colonial produce) would not be re-exported. As regards colonial produce, he was willing to promise not to grant export licences, but refused to give *written* guarantees. He wanted, he said, to be trusted for once, and he hoped his ally would refrain from looking 'under saddles or in the ears of donkeys as they cross and re-cross the Spanish border'.[1] This agreement-in-principle, however, was finally established in an exchange of Notes in which, among other things, Salazar promised that a full Navicert system would be introduced in the colonies and that Portugal would take her own steps to control colonial products. Interpretation of the Notes, of course, offered generous scope for trouble in the years that lay ahead. Some colonial and other goods continued to be re-exported, with the MEW closing import quotas in retaliation. Evasions of the agreement arose from bureaucratic inefficiency and private smuggling every bit as much as from legalistic calculation from on high. But Salazar really did do some extraordinary things, such as announcing suddenly, in February 1941, that the agreement did not cover goods lying in the free port of Lisbon. If this shocked the MEW, there was more to come; for the next thing was a memorandum from Salazar in which he at last gave some figures relating to stocks, but revealed for the first time that he had issued certain Orders in the previous December which exempted from the Export Licensing Order of October 1940 goods already cleared by the customs before that Order came into force, and goods not destined for Portugal which had reached her ports before 1940. He then set out some practical suggestions and a settlement was eventually reached, but not without notable sacrifices on the Allied side.[2]

1 Medlicott, i, p. 521
2 *Ibid.*, p. 523.

Salazar always maintained that he fully accepted the principle of the blockade but objected to the means of enforcing it, which he once compared to the 'schoolboy practice of twisting arms'. Arguments over the application of the January agreement dragged on during 1941. Salazar, of course, was in a difficult situation. He had to maintain his neutrality in German eyes, keep Franco sweet, watch his own economy, and avoid inflaming domestic tempers through arduous legislation. Nor were his fears groundless. In October 1941, the Germans gave him a gentle prod by sinking one of Portugal's finest ships, the *Corte Real*, while another, the *Cassequel*, was torpedoed two months later. Then came the Allied occupation of Timor which subjected the Alliance, in Campbell's view, to the heaviest strain since 1890. The big Portuguese wolfram boom had the demerits of its virtues. Workers needed in agriculture were downing tools to join the rush. These were days when scraping, or 'fossicking', buckets of wolfram in one's own backyard secured a new prosperity for men who had worked in the fields for a couple of shillings a day. Britain and Germany between them were spending £1 million a week on wolfram and sardines, and the resultant enhanced domestic purchasing power was dragging the country into inflation.

But the Allies had their problems, too. Britain's balance of trade with Portugal was heavily adverse. American help was needed to supply Portugal with the oil, coal, steel and fertilizers she needed. But the United States suspected Portuguese intentions, and preferred to get her wolfram from South America, where the prices were less inflated. Meanwhile, Salazar went on quarrelling over detail. The big wolfram row was on. He complained that Spain was getting preferential treatment, and around the turn of the year he declared in outraged tones that, while Portugal was faithful to the Agreement-in-Principle, Britain was not. This was too much for the poor MEW which bitterly retorted that Portugal was jeopardizing the whole spirit of the agreement, that the blockade was being evaded, and that the Portuguese government was exhibiting an uninspiring amalgam of hypersensitivity and deviousness. Salazar and Campbell, in spite of all, seem to have had a good deal of basic respect for each other, and they were correspondingly frank. Neighbours would see them, through Salazar's uncurtained windows, walking up and down in heated exchange. Campbell reported an argument which occurred 'in a charged atmosphere' on 4 March 1942. It was over the interpretation of the phrase 'similar products' in relation to olive-oil and oilseeds. Salazar worked himself into a minor passion and declared that 'if he was expected to use olive-oil for soap-making, he was not, in the present state of the world, going to commit such a wicked crime'. Not to be outdone, the ambassador retorted that the MEW regarded Portugal as 'the spoilt child in the family of neutrals', and left the Portuguese leader in 'a very black mood'.[1] The incident, it seems, was not untypical.

Relations improved in some respects in 1942, though it was in this year that the wolfram affair reached its first embattled heights. After a wolfram agreement was reached with the British, however, Salazar seems to have felt a little ashamed of himself. The Americans had now joined with the British to try and solve the balance of trade predicament, and on 23 November 1942, Portugal signed with the Allies a Supply-Purchase Agreement which gave her coal; copper and ammonium sulphate; and products from petroleum, rubber, iron and steel. In return, Portugal supplied wolfram, tin, skins, wool, cork, rubber, sisal and sardines. Five days later, on 28 November, this was followed by a War-Trade Agreement covering issues arising from the blockade. Even this did not prevent new problems arising, especially when the Allies raised their prices to keep abreast of rising prices in Portugal, and to offset the wolfram export tax. The psychological war of attrition between the Allies and Portugal continued to drag on, albeit in a minor key; and the wolfram affair had yet to enter its final and toughest stage.

Competition for wolfram yielded rich rewards for a time to Portugal, especially when it raised the price to almost astronomical levels. Salazar did not fail to seize his advantage. Equally, he was genuinely afraid that if the Germans were not supplied with wolfram, they would come and get it. His general approach was to try and cater for both sides in proportions consistent with his plea of neutrality. In the summer of 1941, Portugal was producing 3,000 tons of an annual world supply of 37,000 tons, while Sweden, the only other European sourcé, bar Spain, was turning out only 300 tons. The Portuguese deposits lay to the north of the Tagus. The largest mine, Beralt, was British-owned; the second largest, Borralha, belonged to French interests. Then came the German-owned Silvicola mine; a few independent concessions in which Germans had notable interests; and finally there was much individual, often illicit, production and

[1] Medlicott, ii, pp. 322-3.

trafficking, with some colourful cloak-and-dagger performances by British and German agents. As prices rose in Spain even more steeply than in Portugal (£7,500 a ton at one stage) it became highly profitable to smuggle wolfram over the border for sale. In the early part of 1941, Britain was extracting wolfram at the rate of 1,600-2,000 tons a year from Beralt, 600 tons on a contract basis from Borralha, and about 50 tons a month from independent sources. But the Germans were stepping up their activity and in the first half of May alone secured 330 tons. By 10 June, prices were up to £1,250 a ton and the Vichy government was planning to secure control of Borralha. By the end of the year, however, Britain had acquired a total of 3,845 tons, while Germany secured 2,000-2,500 tons. In a matter of months prices had multiplied and now stood at the staggering figure of £6,000 a ton.

Early in 1942, the Portuguese government began thinking about state control of wolfram, ostensibly to control prices, stop fossicking and induce workers back to the land, but also doubtless to ensure that the Germans secured their required quotas. First, however, on 24 January 1942, Salazar signed an agreement with the Germans guaranteeing them export licences for 2,800 tons a year. This was, of course, the Allies' darkest hour of the war, and they were unable to supply Portugal with the steel and fertilizers abundantly available from the Germans. Salazar had just been promised 60,000 tons of steel by the German Ambassador, and the wolfram agreement may have been a *quid pro quo*. Even so, the British were still going to get the greater part of the Portuguese wolfram market, and on 10 February, a Portuguese court found in favour of Britain's claim to 900 tons of wolfram contracted for 1941-2 from Borralha, whose Vichy-controlled masters had tried to opt out of the deal. Meanwhile, Salazar had set up a Commission for the control of the mineral. All production had to be sold to the Commission for £1,500 a ton, and the Commission would buy from no one but recognized concessionaires. The idea was to divide the spoils in equal shares between the two sides. Each was to get 2,800 tons, to be made up of production from their own mines and up to 50 per cent of the 'free' wolfram. If either side did not need as much as 50 per cent to reach its total allotment, then the balance would go to the Commission to be bartered against commodities obtained from abroad. This concept of neutrality through equal division of products supplied to belligerents was different from that of the Northern neutrals who worked on the basis of 'normal pre-war supplies'. The MEW was appalled, not least because the scheme would open the door to more clandestine operations, and demanded an absolute 50 per cent of the free production. The Germans also bitterly complained, though in one sense the agreement gave them an advantage over Britain. The British had much more in the way of mining concessions in Portugal, and Germany had to rely largely on what could be bought from the independent sources. Through the 'pool' arrangement she would benefit from British production, though Britain would also benefit from independent sources in which German interests had some stake. On balance, the MEW felt, the Germans were getting the best of the deal, though the end-of-year figures for quantities actually acquired were to come out firmly on Britain's side.

Once again the exhausting round of hard bargaining began, with matters made worse by the simple fact that men with the right sort of training and ability could not be found to run the Commission. Salazar explained his position to Campbell. If he did not fulfil his commitments to Germany, he said, they would sink his ships again and thus cut off his trade with the United States, in which American ships took no part. Campbell's attitude was that, if Salazar told the Germans he would cut off all supplies after the first sinking, he would have them at his feet. But Salazar was beyond reasonable argument. He had, said Campbell, 'gone sour on us'.[1] When agreement had almost been reached, another row exploded over the interpretation of the phrase 'free mines', and British officials thought Salazar was deliberately trying to keep open a loophole the Allies were trying to block. Finally, however, a settlement was reached and an agreement signed on 24 August 1942:

> Export licences were to be granted to Britain and the United States for up to 4,000 tons a year.
>
> Seven concessions were recognized as British, one as American and five as German (these had yielded 945 tons in 1941).
>
> The Germans were to get 75 per cent of the free wolfram, the Allies 25 per cent.
>
> Britain, America and Germany were each to sell to the Commission at £800 a ton and buy back at £1,200.
>
> All exports of wolfram should bear a tax of £300 a ton.

[1] Medlicott, ii, p. 332.

Salazar was still determined to ensure that the Germans got their quota, even if he had to dip into Allied production to ensure the German supplies before the Allies received theirs. The Allies, too, at one stage thought they were being fobbed off with inferior-quality wolfram. Still, at the end of 1942, British acquisitions totalled 3,353 tons against 1,900 acquired by the Germans.

Salazar was not going to let go of Portugal's new-found wartime prosperity and 'with considerable subtlety and some genuine passion he maintained the rightness of a neutrality which extracted abundant profits from both sets of belligerents'.[1] One American critic said of him that men of principle always cost more to buy, but Salazar told the British Ambassador of his difficulty in teaching the Americans that Portuguese sovereignty and neutrality were not for sale for all the dollars in the world, and that it had been easier to teach even the most refractory pupils at Coimbra.

At the end of 1943, he hurled another bombshell by entering into yet another agreement with the Germans, a performance which even the tolerant Eden described as conduct incomprehensible in an ally. It may have been prompted by the difficulty he had in getting the supplies promised by Britain and America under the Supply-Purchase Agreement, whereas the Germans seem to have done what they said they would, especially with deliveries of iron and steel. The price-raising disputes were still going on as well. In any event, the new German agreement was in no way disastrous to the Allies because it limited the Germans to 2,100 tons and left the Allies all the production of their own mines plus an outright 50 per cent of the free wolfram.

The United States was none the less furious, and oil reprisals were hinted at. But strategic considerations intervened and a wave of goodwill went out to Portugal after the grant of the bases in the Azores at not a little risk to herself. The Germans were furious and many Portuguese sat tight for several weeks waiting to be bombed. It may be that Salazar kept the Germans at bay by promising them that their wolfram quota would not be reduced, and even Churchill apparently said that there was no harm in sending wolfram to Germany, even in higher quantities, if it would keep the Nazis quiet.[2]

[1] *Ibid.*, p. 582.
[2] *Ibid.*, pp. 590-2.

In a speech on 26 November 1943,[1] Salazar paid high tribute to Britain for not demanding the Azores at an earlier stage, even at a time of urgent need, and for asking even now no more than was absolutely necessary. He had less kind words for the MEW, which he accused of thinking in terms of self-interest rather than law and principle.

In January 1944, Campbell opened the final stage of the wolfram affair, and attempted to secure a complete embargo on supplies to Germany. He argued that the Nazis were getting nearly all their basic requirements from Portugal, and that this was prolonging the war. Salazar was amiable but unconvinced that Portuguese wolfram was making all that difference to Germany. A personal letter from Churchill, whom he greatly admired, made little difference. All he could do, he replied, was to promise a reduction of the German quota. But other pressures were brought to bear. Spain gave a lead in reducing wolfram exports. The Brazilians really upset Salazar by complaining that their young men were being killed by Portuguese wolfram. General Smuts sent a cable from Pretoria. Salazar then made an offer which was unacceptable to the Allies; and the Americans, who had just named the first full U.S. Ambassador in Portugal, were all for taking a very tough line. But Churchill and the Foreign Office warned that force would be futile, and meanwhile Campbell had been talking to the Duke of Palmella who had explained Salazar's problems with his own domestic critics. These were all for maintaining the spoils of war, and Salazar was really in a certain amount of trouble.

Eventually, Campbell went to him again on 24 May, and poured out a heartfelt *cri-de-cœur*, after which he had to sustain a long and searching cross-examination. A week later Salazar gave way and agreed to embargo wolfram exports to Germany altogether. The final decision was taken on 5 June, that is to say before the Allied landings in France, as Eden later testified in the House of Commons. Campbell's achievement was one of the finest in modern diplomacy and one of the toughest. He knew, too, how hard the decision had been for Salazar. Closure of the wolfram mines not only meant a loss of £2 million to the Portuguese treasury, but also put 100,000 people out of work. At the end of the day, however, the Allies had acquired 15,000 tons of wolfram in all from the peninsula at a cost of 170 million dollars, perhaps ten times its 'normal' worth.

Throughout the war, Salazar had maintained the neutral principle

[1] Disc., iv, p. 31.

even to the extent of clamping down on public manifestations of satisfaction at either side's successes. He stood doggedly by his 'juridical neutrality' to the last, and, as though to rub it in, ordered flags to be flown at half mast on the death of Hitler (the only other neutral to do as much was Eire). But popular rejoicing was not to be restrained, and Portugal drank an appropriate toast, which lasted for several days. The government did not intervene. It did solicit an invitation to the service of thanksgiving in the English community's Church of St George in Lisbon. The press was full of praise for the Allied achievement. On 8 May 1945, Salazar addressed the National Assembly. He spoke of his joy that the conflict was over, thanked God for keeping Portugal 'in the margin', and added that, of course, she had the satisfaction of knowing that she had come to the aid of her friends and allies whenever they had called on her. He was happy that England was in the vanguard of the victors, and could not help pointing out that he had said this would happen all along . . . though hope had become certainty only when he saw what the British war effort would really be like. That effort, he said, was something characteristic of the English, but was also quite unparalleled in history. Rising, bloodstained, in the midst of her ruins, England emerged not only victorious but unconquerable: worthy to be, as she was, the teacher of peoples, the mother and guide of nations. 'Let us bless the peace,' he ended, 'let us bless the victory.'[1]

It was a moving, if slightly exasperating speech, and it would be a gross misreading of Salazar's character to write it off as bogus or cynical. If perhaps some former backroom boy of the MEW, reading it in retrospect, finds it a little hard to take, he may regain his sense of humour in a corollary. In his *Memoirs*, Lord Avon recalls the day when Mr Churchill threatened to invade the Azores, lambasted Salazar as quite 'intolerable', and had a shouting match with his closest colleagues over it all. Shortly afterwards, the negotiations over the island bases were successfully concluded, and Churchill had to announce this in the House of Commons. He made 'splendid use of the opportunity,' says Lord Avon, 'and no listener could have guessed that any other thought had ever crossed his mind but to embrace our oldest ally in enduring affection.'[2] As for Portugal, whatever reservations she had about her leader in other respects, she must have known that, in the Second World War, Salazar had done her proud.

[1] *Ibid.*, p. 93.
[2] Eden, *The Reckoning*, p. 400.

CHAPTER 9

Portugal and the U.N.–Africa

In the year after the end of the war, Portugal met a series of reverses. The wheat crop and sardine catch were disastrous, and the hitherto healthy balance-of-payments weakened. When the United Nations formed their new organization, many countries, including Spain, Ireland and Italy, were left out. Among them was Portugal, less heavily censured than Spain, but touched nonetheless by the Fascist smear. Britain and America, concerned to establish a counter-weight to the Communist bloc, urged Salazar to apply for United Nations membership, but the application was undermined by the Soviet veto. Salazar tried again in 1947, when most of the member states favoured Portugal's entry, but once again the Russians stood in the way.

In the same year, India secured her independence, and Portugal's fears for her Indian enclaves mounted; the question of Goa's future became acute. In the summer of that year, however, Portugal was invited to the Marshall Plan Conference in Paris, and in 1948 she was able to bid successfully for financial cover for her balance-of-payments to the end of 1950. Her inclusion in a number of international aviation agreements was followed in April 1949 by her entry into the North Atlantic Treaty Organization, to which she has energetically contributed ever since. To this end, Salazar quickly increased his military budget, and entered into agreements with the United States for its continued use of bases in the Azores. On 25 July, however, Salazar told the National Assembly that, while Portugal was bound by the substantive terms of the NATO Pact, she did not subscribe to some of the thinking in its preamble, which posited uniform principles for the member states' internal regimes. Once again he referred to the material *and moral* reserves of Africa as a primary source for Europe to draw on in rebuilding her historical role. He deplored the exclusion of Spain from NATO, and on 23 September, received General Franco in a visit which the Caudillo paid to Portugal as a sign of Iberian solidarity.

Salazar was not unduly depressed by America's involvement in the Korean War of 1950, which would not, he thought, expand to world war dimensions. But he was very disturbed about the spread of Communist propaganda, and was almost obsessed with the theme of a battle of ideas. Britain and America, he felt, had involved themselves closely with Russia during the war without giving sufficient thought to the way the Russians would use the post-war situation to disseminate Communism. It was a mistake, he urged, to think of the Communist organization as simply another party. The West should be building up a *front d'intelligence* to take the initiative on the ideological battle-ground. As for Portugal, Salazar took what steps he could to repress the Communist underground movement, and relations with Spain, where the Communists had been vanquished, were systematically cemented. But for Franco, as Salazar saw it, the Russians would have had an invaluable outpost in South-West Europe, commanding the Mediterranean, and providing a European base for Marxist evangelization in the West. Salazar and Franco met for talks at Ciudad Rodrigo on 14 April 1952, and this was followed by a visit to Spain in 1953 by the Portuguese President Craveiro Lopes, who had been elected in 1951, after the death of President Carmona. Finally, in 1955, Portugal was admitted to the United Nations as part of a package deal which brought in sixteen new members, some fostered by the Western powers, others by the Soviet Union. Salazar was under no illusions about this. Kruschev, he would wryly say, was the only foreign statesman who understood him: understood, that is, that Salazar had seen through Kruschev.

When Salazar led Portugal into the United Nations, however, it was only to precipitate the conflict which has isolated his country politically, and brought her into a bracket with South Africa and Rhodesia, whose racial views, in fact, are not those of the Portuguese. The 1950s saw the dissolution of the British, French and Dutch empires, and Salazar viewed with extreme scepticism the British hope of transforming the empire into the commonwealth. His own policy was clear. Portugal's overseas territories were 'Portugal Overseas', an extension of Portuguese soil, and not colonies. To a hostile world, this proposition was simply a device for evading Portugal's obligation under the U.N. Charter to lead her subject peoples to independence and thus to terminate her empire. However, as has already been suggested, the Portuguese mentality is far more complex than that. The Portuguese sees his position as something totally different from that of other 'colonizing' powers. He was in Africa and the East five centuries ago, a century before the other Western powers (bar Spain) even started to think in terms of an overseas empire. He took with him an unusual capacity for 'belonging' to places he discovered and settled in. They were not outposts. They were ground he took to himself and in which he *planted* himself and his maritime nation. His simplicity and directness in his attitudes to other races, coupled with the fires of a healthy concupiscence, gave birth to his concept of miscegeneity, which, in the early days, implied an acceptance, at least in theory, of racial equality; a toleration of other cultures and an interest in cultural intermingling; and a facility for going to bed with native women 'naturally'. If later colonizers of other races showed ample prowess in their sexual relations with natives, the difference is said to be that the Portuguese did so without the sense of shame. Nor did the woman in Portuguese territory always have to accept the role of slave-concubine, a chattel to be relished in secret. She was often, for practical purposes, a girl friend or unofficial wife, and in varying degrees achieved social acceptance. In the Portuguese view, the definition of a colony does not hinge on questions of race or geography, but on attitude: on what the discovered territory meant to the discoverer and he to it, and the subsequent historical relationships between the homeland and the dependent peoples. All this colours today's reality. As the British writer Austin Coates has put it:

> It is often said that Portugal should have adapted herself to more modern concepts of empire. To some extent she has. But such adaptations in the history of nations are seldom complete. From their inception events develop in their own distinctive way. A shoot appears above the earth, puts forth an oak leaf, and into an oak tree it develops, not into beech or pine.[1]

The Portuguese themselves were a mixed race. They were also Catholics. Their inter-racial attitudes overseas, and their Christian civilizing mission, both emerged and developed naturally. They were later modified, and, says Mr Coates, eventually used as a justification. Both were betrayed, yet neither was basically spurious, and neither was wholly lost. The sense of belonging that the Portuguese settlers felt was quickly reflected in Portuguese law. The use of the word

[1] Austin Coates, 'Portuguese roots in Africa', *Optima*, Johannesburg, March 1965.

'province' in relation to the *ultramar* was not a device concocted in 1951, as is often alleged. A Royal Charter of 1518, declared that the people of Goa enjoyed the same rights as the Portuguese people at home in the metropolis, and that Goa was a province like any in the homeland. In 1612, a Council of India edict declared:

> India and other lands beyond the seas whose administration is dealt with by this Council are neither distinct nor separate from this kingdom [Portugal], nor do they belong to it by way of union, but are members of the same kingdom like the Algarve and any other of the provinces of Alentejo and *Entre Douro e Minho*; for they are ruled according to the same laws and by the same magistrates and enjoy the same privileges as those provinces of the said kingdom, and therefore a man who is born or lives in Goa or in Brazil or in Angola is as Portuguese as anyone who is born and lives in Lisbon.

Dr Alberto Franco Nogueira, then Portuguese Foreign Minister, told the U.N. General Assembly in 1961 that, in relation to the *ultramar*, the term 'province' was first used in Portuguese common and customary law about the year 1576. It appeared in statutory law on 12 March 1633; again in the modified Constitution of 1820 (Art. 132); in the Constitutions of 1832 and 1842 (Title X, in both cases); in the overseas legislation of 1867; in the Republican Constitution of 1911 (Title V), and in Salazar's Constitution of 1933. The word 'colony' appeared in some of the legislation of the 1930s, however, but this was for a specific reason. Portuguese law is based on Roman law, which uses 'colony' to denote equivalent status with the home base. Thus Salazar's draughtsmen favoured a restoration of this usage. It was promptly misunderstood and read in its modern connotation, with the result that in 1951, the government decided to amend the Constitution and restore the traditional 'province'.[1]

Portugal's legal case for claiming exclusion from the modern process known as decolonization is well set out in Franco Nogueira's book *The United Nations and Portugal*.[2] To understand it, we shall have to retrace the cumulative effect of events in the United Nations, which have common effects on both the Goan and the African questions,

---

[1] This special meaning of 'colony' may have some bearing on the tendency of the Portuguese to use 'colony' and 'province' almost indiscriminately in the history of Portuguese Africa. They probably regarded the words as straight alternatives for much the same thing, even if practice often fell short of the unitary ideal.

[2] Sidgwick and Jackson, London, 1963.

in spite of the many differences between the two. United Nations policy has turned on two concepts: internationalization and self-determination. Both elements appear in Chapter XI of the U.N. Charter which concerns the non-self-governing territories. Under Article 73, member nations with responsibilities for the administration of territories whose peoples have not attained a full measure of self-government recognize the principle that the interests of the inhabitants of these territories are paramount, and they accept a number of obligations towards them. These are to ensure the political, economic, social and educational advancement of the peoples concerned; to develop their capacity for self-government, taking account of their political aspirations and helping them in the progressive development of free institutions; to promote their progress in co-operation with the specialized agencies of the United Nations. A further obligation, under Article 73 (e), is to

> transmit regularly to the Secretary-General for information purposes, subject to such limitations as security and constitutional considerations may require, statistical and other information of a technical nature relating to economic, social and educational conditions in the territories for which they are respectively responsible.

The language of the Article seems to reflect the tensions already apparent between the colonial and anti-colonial nations. It seems to have been a concession to the former that the information to be supplied fell short of the 'political', and covered only statistical and technical information on social, economic and educational matters; and that it could be limited by security and constitutional considerations. Nevertheless, Franco Nogueira argues, the general tenor of the Article implies that sovereignty in non-self-governing territories is to be seen as residing in the colony itself. The administering power may be exercising that sovereignty, but only provisionally.

What constituted a non-self-governing territory? Articles 73 and 74 provide no specific definition.[1] In the early days of the U.N.'s life, the Secretary-General wrote to administering countries like Britain, Belgium, France, Denmark, Holland, the United States, Australia and New Zealand, asking them to list the territories under their control which they held to be covered by Article 73. They

---

[1] This discussion is solely concerned with colonies, not with territories covered by the Trusteeship system, in regard to which the U.N. has considerable powers. None of Portugal's possessions is a trust territory, and no one suggests that any of them is.

complied, and began to transmit the required information about them. Their replies were accepted as definite, and their lists were not queried. It seemed to be generally accepted that it was for the member state itself to say whether or not the Article covered any of its possessions.[1]

Even before Portugal came on the scene, the United Nations began the process of extending its own rules. The Fourth Committee assumed the right to pass judgment on the information submitted by administering powers, and it set up an *ad hoc* committee with the right to make recommendations on the information to the General Assembly. After agreeing to this for a year, the colonizing powers protested, ineffectively, at the continuation of the committee's work, but the Committee on Information from Non-Self-Governing Territories became a permanent institution. The General Assembly then passed a resolution giving itself the right, and the exclusive right in fact, to determine at what point information need no longer be transmitted. It created the Committee of Factors with the task of listing the conditions which, if the General Assembly held them to exist, would permit a ruling that a non-self-governing territory had become self-governing.

It was at this stage that Portugal, after hovering in the ante-room for ten years, was finally admitted to the United Nations. She had been held back by the Russians, and, as Salazar wryly put it, admitted at last as small change. It was clear that the Communist bloc was likely to associate itself with the Afro-Asian bloc in hostility to the Portuguese presence overseas, wherever it might be. The Secretary-General wrote the usual letter, and Portugal replied that none of her territories came within the scope of Article 73.[2] She relied in part on the passage in the Article which allowed security and constitutional considerations to limit the information a member state should supply about its

---

[1] The United States' list said nothing about Alaska, Hawaii, the Virgin Islands, Guam and Puerto Rico. India omitted the Andaman and Nicobar Islands. No one objected. Yet all these territories were (a) overseas and (b) inhabited by people ethnically different from the population of the administering power. It was only years later, and in order to cover Portuguese Africa and Goa, that the U.N. introduced the rule that overseas possessions inhabited by ethnically different people must come within the meaning of a non-self-governing territory. In *Nehru Seizes Goa*, Lawrence argues that no one sought to apply the rule to Pakistan's eastern half, and that, while changing its rules, the U.N. might have done something to help India's 60 million untouchables, the 20 million aborigines in reservation areas, and the Nagas who were clamouring for self-government.

[2] Franco Nogueira, *op. cit.*, pp. 139-88 for full argument.

territories, and argued that, as Portugal by her Constitution was a unitary state comprising all her territories in the homeland and overseas, none of them could be regarded as non-self-governing. Portugal further relied on Article 2 of the Charter which prohibited the United Nations from intervening in matters essentially within the domestic jurisdiction of any state.

Between 1956 and 1960, the General Assembly passed a series of measures designed to bring Portugal to heel. The first step was to require administering countries to set and announce time limits for the accession to independence of the administered territories. Further resolutions declared that there must be no pretext for postponing independence. Neither the lack of technicians, nor economic difficulties, nor a lack of elite groups and cadres could be a reason for delay. Whereas the original aim of Article 73 had been read as autonomy or independence for the colonies, it was now made plain that nothing but total independence would do. The Assembly further resolved that the administering powers were to include, in their annual reports, information of a political and constitutional character.

The crux of the matter was reached on 12 December 1959, when the General Assembly passed Resolution 1467 (XIV) which set up a committee (the Committee of Six) to study and enumerate the 'principles which should guide members in determining whether or not an obligation exists to transmit the information called for in Article 73(e)'. As of this moment, in the eyes of the Portuguese, the General Assembly was purporting to arrogate to itself the right, and the exclusive right, to decide which territories were non-self-governing, and to demand information thereon. A year later, on 14 December 1960, the Assembly passed Resolution 1514 (XV), the Declaration on the Granting of Independence to Colonial Countries and Peoples, which called for 'immediate steps to be taken by member states to transfer all powers to the peoples of dependent territories'. Within twenty-four hours came Resolution 1541 (XV) establishing 'the 12 principles which should guide members in determining whether or not an obligation exists to transmit the information called for under Article 73(e) of the Charter'; the 12 principles being based on the Report of the Committee of Six, set up the year before.[1] Essentially, the 12 principles sought to establish that

---

[1] See Appendix A for text of the Report of the Committee of Six, which includes principles first approved by the Assembly in 1953.

1. Chapter XI of the Charter was meant by its authors to relate to territories 'then known to be of the colonial type'.

2. Chapter XI envisages non-self-governing territories as being 'in a dynamic state of evolution and progress towards a "full measure of self-government"'. Until this end is reached, the obligation to transmit information continues.

3. This obligation is binding in international law.

4. *Prima facie* there is an obligation to transmit information in respect of a territory which is geographically separate and is distinct ethnically and/or culturally from the country administering it.

5. Once a *prima facie* case has been made out, other elements can be brought into consideration: for example, administrative, political, juridical, economic or historical. If these considerations 'affect the relationship between the metropolitan state and the territory concerned in a manner which arbitrarily places the latter in a position or status of subordination, they support the presumption that there is an obligation to transmit information under Article 73(e)'.

6-9. Territories reach a full measure of self-government either by emergence as a sovereign independent state; or by free association with an independent state; or by integration with an independent state. Free association and integration must be reached as a result of free choice by the peoples of the dependent territory. In free association these peoples must retain the right to modify the territory's status by constitutional processes. In a case of integration, the General Assembly may, if it thinks fit, supervise the processes by which the decision to integrate is reached.

10-12. The administering powers' duty to transmit information may be limited by security or constitutional considerations. This limitation does not relate to the principle of transmitting the information, but only to the quantum. A limitation for constitutional reasons applies only where the constitution of the dependent territory gives it self-government in economic, social and educational matters, and precludes the administering power from receiving statistical or technical information about economic, social and educational questions.

The Portuguese argument sees all this as a direct follow-up to the Bandoeng Conference and Manifesto[1] whose positions were later institutionalised by the U.N. in the 12 principles, the subsequent Anti-Colonialist Declaration, and the Committee of Seventeen.[2] In short, the Assembly demanded an end to any system involving what it regarded as non-self-governing territories. It also ruled that petitioners from non-self-governing territories could be heard even if the administering power were against it in any given case, and it determined that visits of inspection could be carried out in non-self-governing territories by teams appointed by the Assembly. The Charter envisaged such steps, but only in regard to trust territories. Finally, decisions were taken by the Assembly to authorize direct contacts between itself and groups or parties in opposition to a government and thus, in the Portuguese view, placed the latter on the same footing as the former. As regards the Portuguese territories themselves, the General Assembly, having approved the 12 principles, moved swiftly to pass Resolution 1542, also on 15 December 1960; this declared that the nine Portuguese overseas territories were non-self-governing within the meaning of Chapter XI of the Charter; called on Portugal to transmit the information required by Article 73(e); and invited her to share in the work of the Committee on Information from Non-Self-Governing Territories. A particularly painful twist was given to the Resolution by including in it a reference to Spain's indication, at the 1,048th meeting of the Fourth Committee, that she was ready to transmit information about her overseas possessions. This reference looks like an effort to drive a wedge between the Iberian partners, and it has succeeded in injecting a certain 'sensitivity' into peninsular relations, though Spain is always careful to insist that she respects Portugal's overseas policies. As, however, Spain's African possessions were comparatively slight, and she was not giving much away, the impression arose that she had made her decision in a bid for the U.N.'s backing of her claim to Gibraltar.[3]

[1] The conference held at Bandoeng, Indonesia, in April 1955. President Sukarno of Indonesia described it as 'the first inter-continental conference of the so-called coloured peoples in the history of mankind'.
[2] To which Britain, the U.S. and Russia were elected.
[3] Spain has given full independence to Spanish Guinea. She retains Spanish Morocco, where phosphates lie richly under the soil, but indicates that, in accordance with the appropriate U.N. resolutions, she will negotiate the future of this territory with the kingdom of Morocco, once the latter has sorted out

Portugal had fought, virtually single-handed, for five years to maintain her case in the United Nations, and Franco Nogueira's two major speeches in December 1960 are recognized, even by his opponents, as classical examples, at least, of forensic ingenuity. By Christmas 1960, Portugal felt her isolation acutely. She was very much alone. The world, it seemed, was against her. As has been said, it is precisely at such times that her toughness becomes apparent. Many of Franco Nogueira's arguments might seem, at least to the layman, to be somewhat academic, a traditional lawyer's concern for the letter as distinct from the spirit. But Franco Nogueira answers this himself by describing what the General Assembly's steps lead up to, the position they leave us in. The cumulative effect of these step-by-step measures, he argues, is to hold that the sovereignty of the administering power is illegal, and to transfer it instead to the U.N. Organization until the dependent territory is independent. During the interim period, the General Assembly assumes responsibility for the broad lines of the territory's administration, and groups or parties, in or out of the territory, which disagree with the homeland government are given the means of influencing U.N. voting in their favour.[1] This, in Franco Nogueira's argument, goes far beyond the wildest dreams of the authors of the Charter, and in a legal context their intention is of prime importance. The minister argues, too, that the philosophy behind the Report of the Committee of Six is in sharp contrast with the highest human ideals (and hence with the U.N.'s fundamental purposes). In effect, he says,

> we have here an expression of a school of thought which suggests that all ethnical groups, no matter how small they may be, should constitute a different and autonomous entity with a separate and autonomous political power; and that such groups shall necessarily have to be in conflict with and reacting against other groups. This philosophy seems to my delegation as being rather outmoded, and it represents a flagrant denial of the reality we find in the great and progressive nations of the world, where a combination of many races and cultures has made possible their outstanding contributions to civilization. On the one hand, we find a group or

---

an agreement with its rival claimants to the Spanish territory, namely Algeria and Mauretania. The question of the two Spanish enclaves on the north coast of Morocco, Ceuta and Melilla, has not yet come to the fore.

[1] Franco Nogueira, *op. cit.*, pp. 34-5.

society which has only one race, one culture, one language, one religion, may seem to be fairly happy, but it is certainly stagnant and dormant and does not contribute anything to mankind.[1]

So far as matters of interpretation are concerned, Franco Nogueira's basic complaint is that the General Assembly has been systematically changing the Charter without using the procedures which the Charter enjoins, and that the Assembly has arbitrarily revoked principles established by practice and tacit acceptance. Resolution 66(1), passed on 14 December 1946, accepted the original lists of colonies submitted by the administering powers without demur, and made no complaint about the territories omitted. All states continued to think for a decade that it was up to them individually to decide which territories came within the scope of Article 73. Even the Resolution establishing the 12 principles refers to them as a *guide* to members, which could be taken to mean for their individual guidance. Again, the Charter allowed for issues concerning the non-self-governing territories to be decided by simple majority vote. In practice, however, the Assembly submitted such issues for years to a two-thirds majority principle which, again, was accepted tacitly with no exceptions allowed. It went back on this in 1953. In 1956, Portugal reopened the question, and, on a Swedish motion, the Assembly reverted to the two-thirds rule. Portugal fought to maintain this, successfully, for three years, but again the procedure was reversed with the advent of more 'anti-colonial' members in the Assembly. Portugal asserts that, even if individual changes are inherently licit, frequent and arbitrary changes have the effect of making the law meaningless. To establish a law and then to keep on varying it is the same as having no law at all. It cuts the ground from under the Charter's feet. No one can feel confidence in what it lays down. It virtually has no force. Laws are established by keeping them, not just writing them down.

It is said in rejoinder to this that the U.N. is dynamic, not static. It is a living organism which grows, changes and develops to meet the needs of changing times and circumstances. Franco Nogueira would not deny that this may imply the need to change the Charter from time to time, but he points out that Chapter XVIII lays down special procedures for its own revision or amendment, and that the changes affecting the non-self-governing territories have by-passed

[1] Franco Nogueira, *op. cit.*, p. 158.

these channels. He refers to Mr Vyshinsky who, as Soviet Foreign Minister, denounced, in a different context in 1947, those who, meeting the obstacles created by Chapter XVIII, adopt a policy which

> under the guise of various amendments and resolutions, seeks to amend the Charter in the direction which one or other of the delegates represented here believes necessary or important. Since they are unable, or simply think it too difficult or troublesome, to amend the Charter in the prescribed manner or to raise questions about amending the Charter or one or other of its parts, these delegations, representing their respective governments, evidently consider it much more convenient to resort to various roundabout methods and manœuvres. Instead of amending the Charter, they try to get their own individual decisions or recommendations adopted on some specious question of academic or limited importance, as often happens with legal questions, and thus to carry out the necessary changes in practice without making the relevant changes in the Charter.[1]

Overriding everything else, however, is Franco Nogueira's insistence that, in terms of the fifth of the 12 principles, the relation of Portugal Overseas to the homeland is not 'subordinate'. Nothing has been done, arbitrarily or otherwise, to make it so.[2] When all the legal wrangling is done, what we are really dealing with here is a clash of irreconcilables. Whatever view one takes of Portugal's thinking and record, it has to be understood that she means what she says when she tells the world, in effect: 'We know what you mean by colonies, but our territories are different; they do not belong to that category.' It would be simple to write this off by accusing Portugal of seeking excuses for keeping possessions she needs for her economy. But, as will be seen, the loss of the African territories, while creating substantial short-term problems, would in no way be a long-term disaster. The explanation of Portuguese policy lies deeper than this in that curious 'sense of belonging' in alien lands; in the outward-bound, Atlantic vision which cannot accept that the sea is a bar or a boundary; in the facility for inter-racialism which even the sins and errors of Angolan history never succeeded in killing, and for which a hybrid culture or ethnic structure is simply the mark of a Teilhardian evolution. This is not to say that Portugal's inter-racialism was or is

[1] *Ibid.*, pp. 153-4.
[2] *Ibid.*, pp. 172-2.

absolute, or that she never betrayed her ideals. But a serious effort must be made to analyse a unique set of relationships, developed in Portuguese countries, which may yet have something to offer the world, albeit in new and changing forms, which the world dare not be without. Portugal's African history is very different from that of her impact in India, where circumstances allowed for a far more self-conscious and effective interpenetration of races and cultures, as we shall see in the next chapter. In missionary terms, too, the two stories are dissimilar, though in both cases the turn of events was anomalous and produced results which should have been precluded by all the normal canons. In India, the European Christian culture encountered that of the Hindu, ancient, profound and permeating. A Hindu society offers the Christian a forum for dialogue rather than conversions. Common ground needs to be sought, not through convergence of dogmatic systems, but in the contemplative traditions of East and West.[1] In the spirit of De Nobili and Ricci, the Christian missionary should see his task in the East, not as a bid to win the infidel for Christ, but rather to search for 'news of God' in the Hindu, Buddhist or Confucianist. While he hopes to attract them to the Christian Church through the gospel message, he aims at a marriage rather than a conquest. This 'adaptation' will be slow,[2] and in most oriental societies where the great non-Christian religions flourish, the Christian Churches command a scant minority, not least because the oriental believer is unimpressed by what the Christian has made of the West. Gandhi loved Christ, but not the Christian. By the standards of 'adaptation' the Portuguese mass conversion methods were all wrong and should have failed totally. Yet at least two-fifths of the Goanese people today are Catholics, possibly more. This is partly due to the impetus given by Francis Xavier, who stood in a class of his own, and also to the fact that the Portuguese settler learned to live in terms of a cultural give-and-take. The settler in Goa thus achieved in day-to-day living what the missionary in other lands found hard to do, although the latter's technique was in principle more realistic than that of his Portuguese counterpart.

[1] Viz. the work of Bede Griffiths, formerly a monk of the Benedictine Priory of Pluscarden in Scotland, who for many years now has been running a Christian monastic community, partly inspired by the Hindu tradition, in Kerala.

[2] In North Africa, too, Lavigerie told the first White Fathers that they would have to work for a century before they secured their first Moslem convert. They actually did a little better than that, but the principle was sound.

In Africa, seen as a whole, or at least in those parts where Islam did not prevail, the overall missionary drive has attracted more converts than in the East. The pagan or animist cults, based on the tribal system, were less resistant to Christianity than the 'national' religions of the East with their rich written traditions; and there is an obvious correlation between the tribal ideal and the early Christian sense of community. Where missionaries truly stood for that primitive sense of mutual support and love, the African road was wide open to them. Yet until comparatively modern times, the Portuguese missionary effort was not successful in Africa.[1] By 1800, the African population was hardly touched by the Church's work, and Duffy tells us:

> The principal reason was that the missionary offered nothing to the Africans but a disembodied doctrine, many of whose disciplines were distinctly distasteful. Where were the superior advantages of European civilization which went with this faith? They were not to be found in the slave trade, in the armed excursions into the interior, or in the example of the Portuguese traders who often led a life more African than European.[2]

There were many reasons for the weakness of the early missionary effort in Angola and Mozambique. Money and personnel were short. European priests, if they found the courage to go there at all, easily fell prey to the then uncontrolled tropical diseases. Some of them were dedicated and examplary, but many were not, and they tended to work more in centres like Luanda than to penetrate the interior. Many of the settlers were exiled malcontents or criminals, but they held in contempt the more primitive Africans living south of the Bengo River. Then, too, Portugal, with a home population of only a million (in the sixteenth century), was trying to maintain commitments in Asia and South America as well as Africa, and was constantly preoccupied with fending off the Spanish invader at home and

---

[1] Today's Catholic missions in Angola and Mozambique make a much better showing, but it is still sufficiently restricted to confirm that a lot of time was wasted in the first three centuries of the Portuguese presence. In 1963 there were 1,910,000 baptized Catholics in Angola (38.1 per cent of the population); and 895,000 in Mozambique (13.2 per cent). These percentages are roughly average for the central and southern regions of Africa respectively, and compare well with the Western region average of 4.9 per cent and the Eastern region average of 18.4 per cent. (Source: *Pro Mundi Vita, Centrum Informationis*, No. 13, Brussels, 1966.)

[2] Duffy, *op. cit.*, pp. 66-7.

overseas, not to mention her British and Dutch competitors in the colonial areas. But there can be no doubt that, while a certain amount of good was achieved, much of it was undone by the involvement of settlers and even missionaries in the slave trade when they should really have been leading the chiefs, who sold the slaves, to higher things. Even the Jesuits were involved in the Angola-Brazil slave traffic. Duffy tell us that for 250 years they gave Angola whatever dim enlightenment it possessed, and that on occasion they were the conscience of Angola, the only buffer between the African and his oppressor.[1] Even David Livingstone, who severely criticized Catholic practice in Portuguese Africa, had praise for the Jesuits' accomplishments. They provided the education that there was, trained an artisan class, a native clergy and a half-caste administrative class; and for their pains were accused by local whites of 'meddling'. But many of the Jesuits in Angola

> subscribed to the prevalent belief that the best way to convert the Negro was to sell him, so that he might be introduced to Christianity through the dignity of labour on American plantations.[2]

It is true that some seventeenth-century Dutch observers thought the Portuguese *tumbeiros* were more humane than the slave-trading ships of other nationalities. Some comfort, too, may be derived by relating these events to their own historical context and not to what Professor Hammond has called 'some arbitrary external standard'. But no son of St Ignatius today can fail to be appalled at the thought of a Jesuit selling slaves for profit. Even at the time, some of the wiser of their number were complaining to Rome that the practice was ruining missionary efforts;[3] while in South America, St Peter Claver, also a Jesuit, was teaching Christianity in his own way: namely by nursing dysentery-ridden Negroes in reeking huts where nobody else would go, and kissing their leprous sores. Not even the context of the time can offer a total absolution from the practice of slavery.

---

[1] Their systematic and successful adoption of this role in South America, and the story of the Jesuit 'Reductions', makes one of the finest chapters in missionary history.

[2] Duffy, *op. cit.*, pp. 54, 60.

[3] João Alvarez, S.J., *apud* Francisco Rodrigues S.A., *Historia de Companhia de Jesus na Assistência de Portugal*; vol. iii (2), Porto, 1944, p. 458: 'I personally feel that the troubles which afflict Portugal are on account of the slaves we secure unjustly from our conquests and the lands where we teach.'

Much enlightened legislation was passed in Lisbon from time to time to protect the indigenous African peoples, but Lisbon's writ too often failed to run in the bush. There were great prime ministers, overseas governors and explorers throughout five centuries whose reputations stood up to and even surpassed their counterparts of other colonial nations: Sà de Bandeira, Sousa Coutinho, Paiva Couceiro, Lacerda e Almeida, Silva Porto, António Enes, Mousinho de Albuquerque, Norton de Matos and many others. But the settler society as a whole too frequently failed to live up to such leadership. Yet, again, even Livingstone testifies that the Portuguese got on with the African better than any other colonizer did, and they showed the same propensity for living with or marrying native women as their fellow countrymen did elsewhere. The pregnancy of an African maid by the white man's son posed only a minor problem, without the connotation of guilt, says Austin Coates. It was not unknown for the slave to move into the family by such means.[1] It was, after all, the Portuguese who used to say that they won Brazil, not on the battlefield, but in bed.

But before looking more closely at the achievement or failure, it is only right to see the ideal as it presented itself to the best and most thoughtful Portuguese over many generations, and continues to do so. The concept of 'adaptation', they felt, though tried for a time successfully on the old Kingdom of the Congo, was not on the whole a feasible proposition for Africa, where there were no highly systematized cultures. What the African offered for baptism was rather a way of life; certain habits of mind and a social orientation arising from the tribal system; a facility for understanding the interplay of nature and supernature; a great, if inchoate, capacity for God; a potential awaiting cross-fertilization. For a philosophy Africans would have to look to other continents; their intuitive perceptions could be rationalized only by an alien intellectual discipline. The aim, however, should be, not a contented African enclave, but an integrated inter-racial society. The Christ the idealist worshipped would be neither white nor black, but a mulatto. But because the essential mainspring of this community would be Portuguese, the integrating factor should also be Portuguese, starting with a *lingua franca* transcending tribal

[1] At the 1960 census, there were 53,529 people of mixed blood in Angola (as against 172,529 whites), while the Mozambique figure was 31,455 (as against 97,245 whites). Source: *Annuário Estatístico: Vol. 11., Provincias Ultramarinas, 1966*; published by the *Instituto Nacional de Estatística, Lisboa.*

boundaries. The African should be slowly incorporated into the European ethos, retaining the best of his own tradition and enhancing his European brethren with it, but acquiring a share in a Christian civilization which, whether one liked it or not, was Judaeo-Greco-Roman, and hence European. In this view, Europe is not an imperial source but an ideological centre comparable to that Rome which the nomadic invaders sought, not to destroy, but to belong to; the 'Rome' that transcended and survived the purely political Roman structure.

Today, the Portuguese would say, the process must depend, neither on the theories of an imported democracy which cannot take root as it stands in African soil, nor on Western concepts of national-ism, which are ill-adjusted to tribal peoples, but on personal merit. It is an integrated man, an individual, that the Portuguese, at his best, cherishes; not an amorphous mass, and not a system. There can be no sudden and total *bouleversement* in African society, but a gradual evolution based on cross-fertilization and acquired merit. The entire evolution of the human race, biological, historical, philosophical, is the story of nature's aptitude for enrichment through the spawning hybrid, constantly fanning itself out through mergers, marriages and mixtures. The Portuguese is in many ways an easy-going character. For him it can be enough to conceive a noble ideal and to let it take its time. The Portuguese sense of mission is more than sounding brass.[1] As will be seen, some of Portugal's severest critics once thought that she stood a chance of achieving a situation in Africa that had eluded everyone else. The question today is whether, by confusing the ideal with the achievement for so long, she has lost that chance, or whether the rapid developments of more recent years could still offer hope for the race against time.

In the sixteenth and seventeenth centuries, the Portuguese presence in Upper Guinea was characterized by abandonment to the slavery, gold and ivory trade. Many of the settlers went native (*lançados*),

[1] Duffy quotes Boxer's comment on the seven-year Dutch siege of the Portuguese garrison at Massangano: 'The men who held out so stubbornly at Massangano . . . were inspired by something more than the expectations of securing slaves. The crusading spirit in its good and bad aspects was still far from dead in Portugal, and war against the Moslem, the heathen, and the heretic was still regarded as a sacred duty. Despite the violence, greed, and cruelty with which the history of Angola is stained, the fact remains that they sincerely believed that they were fighting God's battles and saving Negro souls from the fatal infection of heresy.' Duffy, *op. cit.*, pp. 54-5.

inter-married freely, and supplied a *lingua franca* for the coastal regions. The Dutch, French and English traders of the day tried hard to supplant the Portuguese, and envied the influence they acquired, partly by marrying into the ruling African families. On the Gold Coast of Lower Guinea they centred themselves in forts, and, while they also practised miscegenation energetically, an endemic African practice of abortion and infanticide in these areas restricted the number of mulatto children. On the whole, the local peoples stayed loyal to the Portuguese in the face of incursions by the other Europeans. A really dense mulatto population arose, however, in Cape Verde, São Tomé and Principé islands, with the Negro physique predominating. Writing in 1652, Fr António Vieira, S.J., wrote warmly of the Cape Verde islanders' intelligence and ability, adding

> There are clergy and canons here as black as jet, but so well-bred, so authoritative, so learned, such great musicians, so discreet and so accomplished, that they may be envied by those in our own cathedrals at home.[1]

Free Negroes and mulattoes were also prominent among the São Tomé clergy, and were doubtless better able to stand the climate than their white fellow priests. It was a strange island, peopled, so far as the whites were concerned, with forcibly baptized Jewish children, and the usual run of convicts. The Crown gave Negresses to the white men, but there were also many cases of Africans marrying white women. There were elements of racial prejudice, however, and in 1528 the governor was reprimanded by Lisbon for opposing the election of mulattoes to the Town Council. In Guinea, missionary work came a distinct second to the search for wealth, and here the Portuguese, though envied for the influence they attained in some areas, were at a disadvantage in others. French traders reported in 1725 that, at the coronation of the king of Wydah, Portuguese guests were forced to stand bareheaded behind other Europeans who were allowed to sit and keep their hats on;[2] and later the rulers of Dahomey imprisoned or deported to Brazil those of the Portuguese directors at São João Baptista de Ajudá (Whydah) who displeased them. The French reporter from Wydah also said that no Portuguese would dare strike a Negro who insulted him for fear of receiving twice as

---

[1] Quoted by Boxer, p. 14.
[2] *Ibid.*, p. 18.

much in return. However, the Portuguese language was more in use than others and became the basis for a number of Creole dialects.

The Portuguese ideal, however, found concrete expression for a time in the old Kingdom of the Congo, an area now in northern Angola between the Rivers Dande and Zaire (Congo). From Lisbon, King John II and his successors in the House of Aviz regarded the kings of the Congo as their brothers-in-arms, allies and not vassals. Congolese youths were sent to study in Portugal, while Lisbon sent to the Congo, artisans, farm workers, ladies to teach domestic economy, and missionaries. A Congolese prince, sent to Europe for his education, later became the Titular Bishop of Utica in 1518, after Portuguese pressure to this end had been exerted on a reluctant Pope. Mbemba-a-Nzinga, the local African king who ruled from 1506 to 1543, took the style of Dom Afonso I. He was a holy and intelligent convert, whose people really wanted to learn the European way of life. His court at São Salvador was modelled, in externals at least, on the Lisbon court. Schools were opened and the potential was high. But Portugal's lack of personnel and money, and her commitments in other continents, coupled with the spread of the slave trade brought the promise tumbling down. Even before his death, Afonso was writing desperately to the Portuguese king to ask for teachers, priests and protection against marauding adventurers, and begging 'Your Highness not to leave us unprotected or allow the Christian work done in our kingdom to be lost, for we alone can do no more'. The missionaries were of poor quality, racial prejudices developed, the local mulatto clergy became bitterly anti-Portuguese in the end, and in the 1640s supported the Calvinist Dutch invaders. It was a great tragedy, for the experiment was one in which Portugal's defenders find examples of sincere efforts to educate and Christianize the African with his consent,[1] and a programme of relatively disinterested economic and military assistance.

It was in Angola that the slave trade reached its height, and it is estimated that between 1580 and 1836 some 4 million Africans were exported, three-quarters of them from Angola. For 250 years, in fact, that country was the principal slave market for the South Atlantic Portuguese empire and for Spanish America. South of the Bengo, the African peoples were very primitive, and settlers and

---

[1] Duffy, op. cit., pp. 37-46, and also in his Portuguese Africa, Cambridge, Mass., 1959, pp. 5-23; Boxer, op. cit., pp. 19-20; Fr A. Brasio, Monumenta Missionaria Africana (Africa Ocidental), 1646.

missionaries alike saw them as savages on whom enlightenment would have to be imposed by force. From the sixteenth to the nineteenth centuries, the colonizers' efforts were severely hampered by a plethora of tropical diseases, and the history of this time is peppered with inter-tribal feuds and settlers' wars against the natives. As Manuel Severim de Faria wrote in 1625:

> There has been nothing but fighting in Angola from the beginning of the conquest until now, and very little has been done for the conversion of the inhabitants of that great province, the majority of whom are in the same state as when we first entered therein, and more scandalized by our weapons than edified by our religion.[1]

Lisbon tried to curb the excesses, and in 1649, King John IV severely modified a treaty imposed by the governor of Angola on the king of the Congo, but Lisbon was far away and the settlers did not shrink from executing many intractable chiefs. None of this prevented the usual pattern of miscegenation; it is thought likely that mulattoes served on town councils, and in 1684 the Crown ruled that no attention should be paid to colour in making military appointments. The treatment of mulattoes varied. At times, it seems, they could not sit down in the white man's presence, yet towards the end of the eighteenth century they were certainly treated as being on an equal footing with whites when, as officers of the militia, they attended the governor-general's receptions. The Italian Capuchins severely criticized the Negro and mulatto clergy, accusing them of unchastity, simony and slave-trading. The Jesuits had trained a number of Negro priests, but found it hard to find the right material and to get the training across. This may not have been due to prejudice on the missionaries' part, however, as the Capuchins seem to have won veneration for themselves in the seventeenth century, when they became the only missionaries to penetrate the interior and stay with it, and were conspicuous for their dedication. They taught arts and crafts, and seem to have been distinguished horticulturalists. But the overall picture was not a happy one, except in the region of the Dembos, whose chieftains mostly became Christians, freely embraced the Portuguese language, and often had white men serving under them. By and large, however, there was evidence by 1688 that the

[1] Noticias de Portugal, Evora, 1655, *Historial Geral das Guerras Angolanas*, A. de O. Cadornegas, 1681-3.

African in Angola was full of hostility to the white man, and discouraging reports were presented to King Pedro II. Boxer tells us that the Portuguese did not at this time establish in Angola a white-dominated, multi-racial society on the pattern of their achievement in Brazil. This was partly because the African tribes were stronger and more resistant to penetration than the Amerindians; partly because of a high mortality rate in the 'white man's grave', which resulted in fewer mulattoes, and especially because of the slave trade. Most of the tribes retained their way of life, while the coastal regions produced a powerful slave-owning and trading white class; a stratum of detribalized Negroes who co-operated in that trade; and a class of mulattoes and *mestiços*, some of whom attained important positions. The overriding spirit, in Boxer's view, was one of 'conscious white superiority'.[1]

In terms of what was done for the African, the civilizing mission, by 1800 or thereabouts, does not appear to have got very far. In view of the type of man who settled in Africa in those days, this is not surprising. The best Portuguese, who really had something to give, were all too often trying to do it in four continents at once, and Portugal was too small for this. Yet the first three centuries in Africa can hardly be written off. *Some* Negroes had benefited, and a class of successful mulattoes had arisen. Education, arts and crafts had arrived, if only in embryo. The note of Christianity had been struck, albeit faintly and off-key. Not all the settlers were bad, and the easy-going Portuguese, while tolerant of grave abuses, were also apt for relations with other races which frequently went beyond the mere relief of lust. By the nineteenth century, cohabitation and inter-marriage had sufficiently intertwined the roots of black and white to make the Portuguese *different* from other colonizers, whether for better or worse. Whatever his past performance, the white man in Angola in 1961 felt entitled to say that he belonged to the African soil in a way that his colonizing rivals had never done, and that Angola was, in consequence, unlike the British, French or other colonies. It is important not to confuse the fact of his 'belonging' with the blots on his escutcheon. He may not have deserved to be Angolan, but Angolan he had become. The modern winds of change, he would say, can fell a tree, but they cannot disentangle its mutually

[1] Boxer, *op. cit.*, pp. 38-40.

ingrowing roots. As for being in a small numerical minority, he claims to have imprinted Portugal on African society to such an extent that, if the white Angolans are comparatively few, the black Angolans are Portuguese; their tribes had not been welded into a new nation, but into Portugal, whereas, by way of contrast, Africans in British territory were not invited to think of themselves as Englishmen. Portuguese feeling about this is a psychological fact, and some observers would say is not without objective truth. The psychology must, at least, be grasped if, in seeking to urge the Portuguese to courses new, the rest of us are to find a viable means of communication with them.

Mozambique, on the East African coast, looked towards India as Angola looked towards Brazil, and, from Vasco da Gama's arrival in the harbour of Moçambique island[1] at the end of the fifteenth century to the year 1752, was administered from Goa. The pattern of the first three centuries in Mozambique was very different from that in Angola. The Portuguese arrived in much smaller numbers after a much longer and more perilous journey round the Cape, only to be ravaged by fever in areas where even food was hard to find. The terrain resisted penetration save by heroic efforts, and for some time the Portuguese confined themselves to the Swahili[2] coast where they traded with the Arab-Swahili city states, setting up forts and factories, resorting to force when necessary. By 1600, Moçambique was flourishing. In the early days they established themselves north of Cabo Delgado, the northern frontier province of Mozambique today, but after the Omani expeditions and the fall of Fort Jesus, Mombasa, in 1698, they were finally 'contained' in what is now Mozambique itself. They penetrated only that part of the interior which lay behind the coastline from Sofala to Quelimane, mainly up the Zambesi valley where the Cabora-Bassa dam is now to be constructed. They built interior towns at Sena (1531) and, a few years later, at Tete, which today gives its name to the province which includes the Cabora-Bassa scheme.

In the first three centuries of occupation, the slave trade was less

[1] I shall use the spelling Mozambique for the country as a whole, and the alternative Moçambique for the island capital town of the early period.
[2] This coastline ran from Somalia in the north, down the coasts of Kenya and Tanganyika (as they later came to be called), and down the coast of what came to be Mozambique, ending roughly at Sofala, where Beira stands today.

important than in Angola. The Portuguese exported slaves from Mozambique, but there was a heavy emphasis on domestic slavery, especially on the *prazos*, or plantations, in the interior. The main theme was a search for gold and silver, especially in the Manica and Mashona territories, and in the lands ruled by the great chieftain who was known as the Monomotapa. The results were not negligible, but on the whole were disappointing. The most prosperous years came in the first half of the seventeenth century, and in 1752 the Portuguese positions in Mozambique were given their own Governor in the person of Francisco de Melo e Castro. The second half of the century was much more troubled, with the Portuguese involved in inter-tribal wars and holding on partly by the ascendancy they secured over the Monomotapa. The tendency noted in parts of West Africa for the Portuguese settler to 'go native' showed itself in Mozambique as well, and an edict of the Goa Inquisition against a mixture of Christian, Moslem and pagan practices in 1771 bore witness to this.[1]

The missionary effort suffered severely from a shortage of personnel and the difficulty of surviving the climate.[2] St Francis Xavier spent six months in Mozambique in 1541, preaching and working in a hospital. Nineteen years later, one of the most famous of all pioneering missionaries arrived in the person of Fr Gonçalo da Silveira, S.J., who converted the Monomotapa but was later ungratefully strangled by his orders. The Dominicans then moved in and enjoyed a certain success with the African chiefs. Their work was cut short by tribal raids towards the end of the century, but they returned later and so did the Jesuits. Many of the Dominicans came from Goa and were not of the best quality, and indeed their history in Mozambique is fairly liberally peppered with scandals. Two of their most successful men, who seem to have won the devotion of the Africans, were the famous Fr João de Menezes and Fr Pedro Trindade, who ran estates with slaves, and, in the case of the former, died leaving an impressive batch of progeny,[3] having refused his superiors' orders to return to Goa. By the end of the eighteenth century, the missions were at a pretty low ebb, the religious orders having been suppressed by Pombal. After a temporary resurrection, they were again suppressed by the liberals in 1834.

[1] Boxer, *op. cit.*, pp. 45-6.
[2] Duffy, *op. cit.*, pp. 89-94.
[3] Boxer, *op. cit.*, pp. 48-9.

The extraordinary phenomenon of the *prazos* survived into the 1880s.[1] The plantation owners in the Zambesi valley and thereabouts were sometimes absentees, but those who stayed in Africa married African wives and often lived in luxury in splendid homes, surrounded by private armies and regiments of slaves or *colonos*, a brand of servant technically free but enslaved for practical purposes. In time, of course, a number of mulatto *prazeros* emerged. These local lords strenuously resisted Lisbon's attempts to curb their powers and make them behave properly to the Africans, but they were also useful to Lisbon as the only effective means of maintaining the Portuguese presence, and stemming tribal invasions. They profited from collecting taxes and fines, but, as in most things human, there was good and bad in the system. Fr Barreto, S.J., comes out with the extraordinary remark that some of them were 'very lavish in giving and very fierce, even cruel, in chastising, which are two qualities that will make any man adored by the Kaffirs'.[2] They resisted a number of edicts from Lisbon, in 1832, 1838, 1841 and 1854, aimed at suppressing them or cutting them down to size, and were finally suppressed, or their operations drastically modified, only in 1890. The nineteenth century saw a boom in the export of slaves, as the New World could not get enough to supply its needs from Angola and the Congo.[3] The slave trade, of course, had been a feature of local life before the Portuguese arrived, but they entered into it vigorously, and it was only under pressure from English colonial and humanitarian sources in the 1840s, admittedly with Lisbon's full co-operation, that the slave trade died away between 1850 and 1865. In this process, Lisbon was up against French interests, and the practice died hard. Duffy tells us that Livingstone, who had praise for the Portuguese in Angola, had none at all for what they had done in Mozambique.

David Livingstone was contemptuous of Portuguese exploration, but in fact the Portuguese had done better than he thought.[4] By the middle of the nineteenth century they were certainly the foremost among the European explorers, most of whom were late-comers,

[1] A. A. Lobato, *Evolução Administrativa e Economica de Moçambique, 1752-62*, pp. 209-33.
[2] Boxer, *op. cit.*, pp. 49-50; *Informação do Estado e Conquista dos Rios da Cuama*, by Fr Manuel Barreto, S.J., d. Goa, 1667.
[3] Duffy, *op. cit.*, pp. 95-8.
[4] *Ibid.*, pp. 103-16.

whose record stretched back to only sixty years before. The Portuguese had a line of forts through Angola, in Zambesia and the lands of the Monomotapa. Traders, priests and individual explorers had reached many of the more distant African communities. Lacerda had led an expedition to the lands of the Kazembe, so had Gamitto and Monteiro, and Pedro João Baptista and Amaro José had crossed the continent; Lacerda, a Brazilian mathematician, was one of the early campaigners against slavery. It was he, too, who foresaw the British presence in Southern and Central Africa, which was to establish a permanent separation of the Portuguese possessions in Angola and Mozambique. Silva Porto, one of the finest examples of the Portuguese patriarchal tradition at its best, reached Luanda in 1839 and established a new trade route from Bié to Benguela by way of Bailundo and Chisanji. After the formal ending of the slave trade and the termination of the Crown monopoly in ivory, this area of Angola became a flourishing centre of commerce, with the development of the ports of Luanda and Benguela. In 1852, Silva Porto crossed the continent to Barotseland and met Livingstone, though neither seems to have had much time for the other. His vision ran to more missions, extended trade routes, more settlements in the interior, and a reformed administration, but his country could not support him, and disillusioned by forces he could not control, he blew himself up in 1890. By this time, however, the Geographical Society of Lisbon had been founded in 1875, and there followed the Serpa Pinto expedition across Barotseland and down to Durban, and the two great journeys of Hermenegildo Capelo and Robert Ivens: from Bié to Cassanga, Malange, the upper reaches of the Cuango, and thence to Luanda; and, in 1884, from Moçamedes in southern Angola to Mozambique, via Lealui, Katanga, south to Zumbo and down the Zambesi to Quelimane. Serpa Pinto and Augusto Cardoso established the Portuguese presence in the Niassa region of north-west Mozambique, while Henrique Augusto Dias de Carvalho pushed the eastern frontier of Angola to the Kasai River.

Britain's attitude to Portugal in this period was a mixture of humanitarian disapproval and colonial ambition.[1] It took the line that the degenerate Portuguese should yield to the forces of enlightenment, and that their territorial claims were unsupported by 'effective occupation' of their alleged possessions in Africa. In 1884, an abortive

[1] Duffy, *op. cit.*, pp. 109-10.

Anglo-Portuguese Treaty was meant to secure the Portuguese on both sides of the Congo River (which today divides Angola from Congo-Kinshasa) for a distance of fifty miles. Britain was allowed the right of free navigation, granted generous fiscal concessions, and 'most favoured nation' treatment. The Portuguese gain was short-lived. The Berlin Conference of colonial powers in 1884-5 arose from a Portuguese suggestion but did Portugal little good. She had France, Belgium and Germany to contend with as well as Britain, and lost the northern shores of the Congo River, though retaining the enclave of Cabinda, as she does to this day. In a sense, Portugal could not win. The Berlin Conference established the 'effective occupation' criterion, and, while this undoubtedly had its point, it seems to have worked very oddly. The Portuguese presence on the north of the Congo River was sufficiently strong to justify her claim, even in terms of effective occupation.[1] But it failed to save her. To make matters worse, the standard of effective occupation, imposed on Portugal, was not so strictly applied to successful Belgian claims in the Congo nor to British claims in East Africa.

The Portuguese dream of a transcontinental empire remained. In 1886 and 1887, in fact, France and Germany signed treaties which gave Portugal 'rights of sovereignty and civilization in the territories which separate the Portuguese possessions of Angola and Mozambique, without prejudice to the rights which other powers may have acquired there'. Barros Gomes drew his rose-coloured map of Portuguese Africa stretching from Luanda to Lourenço Marques, but Portugal had still to reckon with Lord Salisbury and with Cecil Rhodes's acquisition of the Mashonaland concession from Lobengula, not to mention the British South African Company's takeover in Bechuanaland. In 1890 Britain sent gunboats to the straits of Lourenço Marques and delivered an ultimatum to Portugal to stay out of what was to be the Rhodesias. Portugal could not resist and in 1891 signed a treaty with Britain which gave the latter in effect the whole of the territory reaching from the Transvaal in the south to Katanga and German East Africa. By 1894, Portuguese Africa was established within the borders effective to this day. In 1899, Britain entered into an arrangement with Germany for lending money to Portugal on the security of her African territories, but this subtle form of 'invasion' was aborted by the Boer War. In 1899, a further Anglo-Portuguese

[1] See Chapter 1 *supra*.

Treaty provided that Britain would protect the Portuguese overseas territories in confirmation of the position established by the Treaties of 1642 and 1661. Portugal was to forbid the importation of arms for the Boers through Portuguese African territory, and Britain was to have the use of the ports of Mozambique for landing troops.

Although Portugal ended up with half of what she had hoped for, the events of 1884-90 left her with more territory than she would have had if the 'effective control' criterion had been applied to the full. Part of the credit for this goes to the Portuguese explorers who carried the flag to distant borders, and partly to Portuguese diplomacy which, at the Berlin Conference, played the colonial powers against each other. The results could have been much worse.

The last decade of the nineteenth century and the first decade of the twentieth saw a series of small wars to subdue insurgent natives, and it was not until 1920 that the whole of Portuguese Africa was subdued, with the British and Germans decisively kept out. Five years before the end of the last century, however, the famous 'Generation of 1895' arose.[1] This was a group of determined, authoritarian but responsible men, who worked for fifteen years to reform the administration in the African possessions and to disentangle them from intrigue, patronage and politics. The best-known governors and leading colonial officials in those days included Antonio Enes, Mousinho de Albuquerque, Freire de Andrade, Henrique de Paiva Couceiro, Eduardo Ferreira da Costa (the group's outstanding 'philosopher'), and Pedro Francisco de Amorim. Broadly speaking, they favoured free trade, foreign investment and systematized native labour, civil rather than military government, decentralization from Lisbon but a highly centralized internal regime. The African had to be made to work. His easy-going willingness to live by subsistence farming would not do for countries trying to move into a modern world. To the 'Generation' in general, it seemed farcical to talk about African equality, and Costa envisaged two legal codes, one for the whites and another for the blacks, the latter to be varied according to district traditions and needs. The concepts were admittedly despotic, but aimed at a just, humane and civilizing tutelage of the black man, with little stress on tribal government or African cultures, but rather an effort to inject Portuguese cultural values into tribal

1 Duffy, op. cit., pp. 120-4.

life. It was felt that the African best understood a system in which the administration, the judiciary and the military power were centralized in a governor-general who would be a kind of *paterfamilias* or paramount white chief. This type of paternalistic *administrador* replaced the *prazero* in importance and achieved a great deal more. Miscegenation was tolerated rather than fostered, and eventually used as a justification for the colonizing presence. Results were mixed, of course, much depending on the personal sense of order and incorruptibility of the individual governor-general. The Republican Regime, in the troubled years of 1910-26, wanted to protect the African, and Norton de Matos, an outstanding Governor-General of Angola, wanted to put more stress on giving the African culture than on using him as productive labour. But personnel were lacking, health and education services minimal. Most of the education depended on the missions, some Catholic, some Protestant – the latter including the Swiss Mission in Mozambique, the joint American Board of Commissioners for Foreign Missions in Angola, and the English Baptist Missionary Society.

The first real Native Labour Code was published in 1878 under the name of the *Regulamento para os Contratos de Serviçais e Colonos nas Provincias de Africa*. Its object was to replace forced labour by a system of labour under free contract, though a vagrancy clause was inserted to secure the labour of the 'backsliders'. In practice, what happened was that employers of labour secured their labourers from the tribal chiefs as before, but entered into a contract with them instead of just putting their money down; but the African worker had no practical way of opting out of the bargain struck by his chief. A Regulation of 1899 reasserted the moral and legal obligation of all to work, and Africans were liable to be recruited for work by public authorities unless they were earning salaries for a minimum number of months in the year, had sufficient capital to keep themselves, owned their own land, or produced commodities for export. Freire de Andrade made the position clear in 1907[1] when he declared his opposition to slavery, but saw no reason why the African should not be made to work, nor why he should be allowed to avoid work by exerting his own form of slavery on his womenfolk. In 1911, fresh legislation restricted the period of the labour contract to two years and penalties were prescribed for employers resorting to corporal punishment. Still further

---

[1] Hammond, pp. 324-5.

legislation in 1914 reflected the Republic's honest intent to humanize the African's way of living, but, as in other parts of Africa, the native was not in practice 'ennobled through work', and it was the white community which reaped the major benefits. It may be right to call this outright exploitation. Yet in a sense it may have been the only way to begin to modernize Portuguese Africa, and, had all the employers been humane, there would be less grounds for criticism. It is the way the employer so often behaved in practice that forms the basis of an indictment, one that applies to other colonial powers, no doubt, as well as to the Portuguese; but this does not amount to justification. Again, as in all human affairs, there were good employers and bad, and humanity rode side by side with cruelty and injustice.

Certainly, an impressive start had been made. At the end of the nineteenth century, the ports of Luanda, Lobito, Lourenço Marques and Beira had begun to come into their own. In Mozambique the great land companies began to transform the interior into an area of production. More white settlers began to come out under special schemes. In Angola the phenomenal Benguela Railway started to spread its tracks in 1903. In addition to serving huge areas of southern Africa, it was to develop in later years an exemplary range of social services, and for the first fifty years of the company's existence no dividends were paid. Scores of small towns appeared, and, under Norton de Matos, thousands of miles of roads were built. The Generation of 1895 established principles which were to have their bearing on Salazar's legislation, and, as under his regime, the policy was to get the economy going so that its growth would gradually pull up everyone's standard of living with it.

The criticism must be that so little was done at this time by direct intervention, *pari passu* with economic growth, to improve African standards. It may be said that Portugal herself was small and poor, and much had to be left to the initiative of trading companies and individuals. The perennial problem of personnel also accounted for the dearth of social services. The trouble was, however, that, despite the enlightened blueprints issued in Lisbon, forms of neo-slavery persisted to the end of the nineteenth century and into the twentieth, which were exemplified by the scandal of the São Tomé cocoa plantations.[1] By 1908, between 70,000 and 100,000 Angolan workers had been transported to São Tomé and Principe, and the reports of

[1] Duffy, *op. cit.*, pp. 134-7; See also *A Question of Slavery* by the same author (Oxford, 1967).

Henry W. Nevinson in *Harper's Magazine*, of the Cadbury brothers, of Charles Swann and John Harris spoke of the skulls and shackles littering the old slave trails, of murder and devastated lands, of cruelty and brutality to shock the humanitarian conscience of the Western world. Hammond tells us[1] that, according to reports by British Consuls, conditions on the cocoa islands were tolerable enough, and he thinks that the attacks by Harris and others on the island planters were based on the flimsiest evidence. Cohen visited the islands in 1882 and found the native workers well fed and well cared for when sick, though there was a lot of illness and a good many deaths. In 1905-6, Nightingale found the workers well treated in every respect, and living without any sort of police force. The evil, Hammond argues, was the way in which the labour was obtained, and in the failure to repatriate the workers to Angola. Eventually, pressure of world opinion, and co-operation between London and Lisbon, combined to bring the scandal to an end, though not before the British chocolate companies had imposed a boycott on the islands' products. By 1917, repatriation was complete.

The first four hundred years of Portuguese Africa offers a bewildering set of contrasts. On the one hand, the paucity and poor quality of the settlers and missionaries, the failure of Lisbon to assert itself in the bush, the horrors of climate and terrain, the exploitation of the African, so often seen as a primitive sub-human. On the other hand, a sense of civilizing mission, a genuine paternalism, free miscegenation, in many cases a relationship between black and white which even Livingstone thought to be unique; above all, the laying of foundations for a new and better order of things. Hammond, the most objective of scholars in this field, passes this judgment on the 1895 Generation:

> It was not so much that the African territories left to Portugal by treaty had almost all been effectively occupied, some for the first time in history, [but] that sufficient courage and tenacity had been forthcoming to confound both foreign critics and domestic prophets of disaster; and that the results were an encouragement – indeed, a commitment – to persevere in the task. It was no longer necessary to invoke the spirits of Vasco da Gama and Afonso de Albuquerque so as to confute the rationalism of Ferreira d'Almeida and Oliveira Martins, now that one could point to the governance

[1] Hammond, *op. cit.*, pp. 318-34.

of Enes and Freire de Andrade and the exploits of Mousinho de Albuquerque, Paiva Couceiro and João de Almeida. These men indeed brought a fresh infusion of strength to the Portuguese mystique of empire at a time when empire and mystique seemed sick beyond recovery.[1]

What we have now to consider is, not only whether conditions have improved, but whether the paternalistic view of the African has yielded to recognition of him as an equal. People are not fulfilled by mere cohabitation or legislation alone, valuable though these contributions are.

Salazar's approach from the start was to embrace the concept of a Pan-Lusitanian community, geographically scattered but spiritually united. In spite of the hyperbole and the hitherto scant achievement, there were genuine foundations for this position, as testified by the enduring bonds between Portugal and Brazil,[2] though it presumably meant very little to the mainly uneducated African populations. The Colonial Act of 1930 was the work of Salazar himself, who for a short time held the Overseas portfolio, and his successor, Armindo Monteiro, who later became Portugal's Ambassador in London. This Act, coupled with the Statutes of 1926 and 1929, the Imperial Organic Charter of 1933, and the Overseas Administration Reform Act of 1933, established the main theme until the early 1950s.

It was conceived against an unpromising background. Early in the nineteenth century, liberal elements had aimed at an *assimilação uniformizadora*, in which all the Africans would be brought into the fullness of Portuguese culture and citizenship. What happened in practice, however, was that the handful of white settlers tended to be assimilated to African ways of life. Antonio Enes and the Generation of 1895 certainly wanted to civilize the African, but they thought it a humanitarian pipedream to talk at that stage of African equality with the European. Hence their unified system of local government, and the patriarchal status of the governor-general, strong in paternalistic authority. Some of them also favoured, however, a certain decentralization from Lisbon, but it was not until the early 1920s that the Republic tended to offer more financial and political autonomy to the overseas provinces. Unfortunately, the administration was not up to it, the situation in the homeland was catastrophic,

[1] Hammond, *op. cit.*, p. 340.
[2] Duffy, *op. cit.*, p. 152.

and the result was financial chaos, in Africa as in Portugal. Moreover, when Salazar came to power, he found no highly trained cadre of dedicated colonial officials with a tradition behind them. Such officials as were there had all too often yielded to temptations of patronage and corruption. Whatever else has happened in Portuguese Africa, it is to Salazar's credit, and even his critics admit it, that he fostered the growth of a new, responsible, incorruptible and wholly committed generation of colonial servants, whose work has since been admired by the journalists of many countries. It did not happen in a day, but by the 1960s, when the present writer began to visit Portuguese Africa, the quality of local administration had reached impressive levels.

In the confusion prevalent at the time, Salazar reversed the trends of the 1920s and showed signs of being influenced strongly by the policies of António Enes. The Colonial Act began by unifying provincial administration and binding it tightly to Lisbon's control. A few deputies from Angola and Mozambique represented the provinces in the National Assembly in Lisbon, but the real power lay with the Council of Ministers there and with the Overseas Ministry. The Act forbade the use of forced labour by private companies and asserted the African worker's right to wages, paid in cash. But, again in the tradition of António Enes, it provided for special statutes to govern the native communities. This approach preserved the tribal traditions and usages, but at the same time it served to separate natives from Europeans. The ultimate objective was that all the natives should be assimilated into Portuguese society, but it is clear that, in Salazar's view, this would be a very long process. For some observers, this was realism. For others, it was a prognostication of the African's right to be rapidly trained to run his own country and affairs. While it may seem that Salazar was determined to grapple the African provinces to the motherland with hoops of steel, it is equally certain that he foresaw the turbulence awaiting many countries in their early days of independence, and believed in a lengthy incubation or novitiate for peoples under tutelage.

Thus the Colonial Act and associated statutes established two sorts of community: the *indigenas*, or the vast majority of the native peoples, and the *não-indigenas*, a group made up of whites, mulattoes and 'assimilated natives' (*assimilados*). Only the latter would be citizens of Portugal in the fullest sense, while the rest were to be led, 'by means appropriate to their rudimentary civilization' to a 'profitable development of their own activities and to their integration into the life of the colony, which is an extension of the mother country'.[1] To qualify as an *assimilado*, a native had to be eighteen years old, with a sufficient income for himself and his family, a birth certificate, a certificate of residence, good health, and two testimonials; he had to sign a declaration of loyalty, and was then exempted from forced labour (recruitment by public authorities) and was allowed to vote. The assimilation principle has always had its admirers, but by 1950 only 30,000 *assimilados* could be counted among Angola's population of 4,000,000, while the figure for Mozambique was 4,353 out of 5,733,000. By the time of the 1961 war, less than 1 per cent of the African population had been assimilated. The whole tenor of Salazar's policy was a slow, deliberate economic and social growth, and Africa was no exception.

The years before 1961 were peaceful in Portuguese Africa, but too much confidence was placed on the plainly easy terms on which the white minority lived with a black minority, while most of the Africans had yet to benefit from or even experience inter-racial society. In recounting the developments of the post-Second World War years, it should be remembered that for four and a half centuries, the Portuguese in Africa inspired themselves with a disembodied metaphysic. Certain foundations were laid, but most of the African population remained in their backward conditions. In the peaceful years before 1961 they were quiet, partly because of strict control, partly because there was insufficient education to make them interested in nationalist aspiration. The Second World War inevitably held up progress, and in the decade before the war Salazar had been preoccupied with the massive problems of re-establishing the homeland. Nevertheless, his financial and economic policies allowed for a restricted growth between 1928 and 1945, but it was not until the 1950s that what Duffy calls 'the golden decade of Portuguese African history' opened. It was to be, he says, 'a period of the most genuine prosperity and vitality that the colonies had ever known'.[2] What happened was that the disembodied ideal began to acquire an incarnation, and, as an American resident of Luanda told the author in 1963: 'The Portuguese can sit around confusing ideals with achievement for four centuries, but when they really get down to work, they do it right.' There is no doubt that it was the Angolan War of 1961

---

[1] Introduced in 1926 by Overseas Minister João Belo: *Estatuto político civil e criminal dos indigenas das colónia de Angola e Moçambique.*
[2] Duffy, *op. cit.*, p. 191.

that acted as a massive stimulant. For the first time the Portuguese began to admit their mistakes and inadequacies, and they started to work with incredible energy. The result was that between 1961, when the author first visited Portuguese Africa, and 1963, when he went for the second time, the difference even to the naked eye was dramatic. The question was: had it happened too late?

It is, however, an error to think that nothing was done before the dreadful shock of the Ides of March in 1961. Whatever the subsequent effort, none of its achievements would have been humanly possible without a degree of evolution in the 1950s. This does not alter the fact that in 1961 there were still many evils to rectify, and that the African's status and conditions were still minimal. It was the Galvão Report of 1947 and its sequel that first began to awaken world opinion to the weaknesses of life in Angola and Mozambique. Henrique Galvão was a Colonial Inspector and Deputy for Angola in the National Assembly in Lisbon. His revelations of corruption, forced labour and bad administration were at first ignored. He then delivered a speech in the National Assembly in 1948 which led to his downfall, and in 1952 he was arrested for subversive activities.[1] The report attacked the retarded development of Angola and Mozambique, the absence of health services, forced labour and undernourishment, the migration of 2,000,000 African workers to the Congo, the Rhodesias, and the Union. The report put the infant mortality rate at 60 per cent, the workers' death rate at 40 per cent. The natives, it said, were simply regarded as beasts of burden, and special condemnation was reserved for the practice of herding workers off to government projects huge distances from their villages.

The 1950s saw a dramatic upsurge in the African provinces, comparable to the first decade of Salazar's policies in the homeland. The first National Development Plan (1953-8) and its sequel (1959-64) provided for the development of extensive infrastructures in Africa. New roads, bridges, hydro-electric schemes, railways, factories, ports, airfields and farming settlements appeared, and exports boomed. The lower Limpopo Valley was reclaimed from swamp, and a plan to irrigate 250,000 acres (ultimately for 10,000 families) was put into operation. As other African countries broke out in frenetic revolt, Angola and Mozambique seemed like oases of quiet, with much talk of a new Brazil. Towards the end of the decade,

[1] See Chapter 11 *infra*.

foreign capital was admitted, mainly for heavy construction and mining, and notably for a multi-million German-backed project in Angola for iron and manganese production. Between 1953 and 1958, the Lisbon government spent £57 million in Africa, while the 1959 figure was £98 million, half from Portugal and international sources, the rest raised locally. In 1960, Portugal joined the International Monetary Fund and the International Bank for Reconstruction and Development. Between 1958 and 1960, goods passing through the port of Lourenço Marques leaped from 4½ million tons to 6 million, and Mozambique's exports rose mainly in sugar, cotton, cashew nuts, tea, copra, and sisal. Angola's growth was spectacular. Fine modern cities and towns stand in Luanda, Lobito, Benguela, Nova Lisboa, Malange, Sà de Bandeira, Silva Porto and Vila Luso. The main exports were agricultural, primarily coffee, but iron and diamond mining grew in importance. Iron was first exported in 1957, and between 1959 and 1960, iron exports doubled to 700,000 tons. The sense of accomplishment as a world power which Portugal acquired from these developments played a significant part in her determination to stay where she was in 1961.

The immediate beneficiaries in Africa were, of course, the white communities. The condition of the African peoples was still relatively unimproved. In 1958-9 there were only 94,529 pupils in Angolan schools, though Mozambique showed up better with a total of 406,528 African pupils. The vast majority, however, were undergoing what was called *ensino de adaptaçao*, a special system of education for unassimilated Africans in which they were taught Portuguese, reading, writing, arithmetic, a little history, with another year or two of further studies to follow. This form of education was mainly in the hands of the Catholic missions, and many of the teachers were Africans who had not reached a very high level of education themselves. Figueiredo tells us that in Mozambique about this time the illiteracy rate was still about 99 per cent.[1] This would seem to be a little exaggerated, but not very much. Portugal's standing in the international community was relatively high. She had joined NATO in 1949, won the admiration of American statesmen like Dean Acheson and President Eisenhower, and was gaining confidence. But in the mid-1950s the weaknesses of the African situation were exposed by the British journalist Basil Davidson, and the American anthro-

[1] Figueiredo, pp. 112-13.

pologist Marvin Harris.[1] What concerned them more than anything else was the system of forced labour, much of it illegal and conducted by corrupt local officials in league with tribal chiefs who often enough had no option but to co-operate.

The 1926 Statute had eliminated the old vagrancy clause, and, so far as the law was concerned, Africans could be forced to work only under three headings: (a) the authorities could compel them to work on public works of local importance such as road-building; (b) if an able-bodied male African was not working under contract with an employer he could be forced to work for the state for six months in the year; and (c) he could be forced to work if he did not pay his head tax. All other labour was in principle freely contracted, and African workers were known either as *voluntários*, who contracted directly with an employer, or as *contratados*, who entered into such contracts with the assistance of state officials. Contracts were for six months at a time, though in special cases for up to two years. There are different views about the principle involved. Some observers saw it as neo-slavery, others thought it reasonable to expect all able-bodied men in a developing country to work for the common good, and that the worker stood a better chance in life if he got into industrial or plantation employment than if he continued to eke out a pittance by subsistence farming on his own little plot. So much for the theory, but the allegations of neo-slavery turned largely on the abuses of the system which the administration had not as yet reformed. Much of the recruitment was illegal, workers were conscripted who ought to have been left alone, contracts were illegally extended under pressure, conditions of work were thoroughly miserable, pay was extremely low, workers were not always given transport to go home to their villages, there were instances of child labour, and workers were punished by beating with the *palmatorio*, a wooden instrument with holes in it for beating on the hands. Under international treaties, Africans were transported to neighbouring countries for labour, some of them having been recruited ostensibly for public works at home.[2] In 1958, the level of wages for many contracted workers was about £20 a year, according to some reports. Africans engaged on public works could earn from 15s. to 35s. a month, plus board and clothing.

[1] Marvin Harris, *Portugal's African 'Wards'*, New York, American Committee on Africa Inc., 1958; John Gunther, *Inside Africa*; Basil Davidson, *The African Awakening*, London, 1955; Eduardo Mondlane (cited later in this chapter).
[2] Fryer and McGowan Pinheiro, *op. cit.*, pp. 169-70.

Cotton growers bringing their produce to the concessionary markets were alleged to be earning less than £4 a year, though compelled to turn much of their land to cotton from food production. In 1950, Bishop Sebastião Soares de Resende of Beira wrote:

> After the cotton campaign was begun there, the fertile fields ceased to supply food for the neighbouring populations and the people of the region itself also commenced to feel hunger. There belongs to my diocese a region in which for six months the black spectre of hunger reaped the lives of the inhabitants. . . . I know of districts in which the native . . . received as payment for his harvest from 50 to 90 escudos [12s. 6d. to £1. 2s. 6d.]. And in the same region, and in the same locality, if the native worked at planting other crops, he could grow in an equal area of land, and perhaps with less effort, from 2,000 to 4,000 escudos [£25 to £50] worth of products.[1]

Some of the better employers, of course, were liberal enough with payments in kind, and would speak of the native's lack of interest in money, provided he could grow or be given his food. But that state of affairs was hardly an advertisement for a civilizing mission. Moreover, in centres like Luanda, where wages were more realistic and dignified, Africans were paid less than white men for doing the same work. In Luanda, in 1961, for instance, a European carpenter earned £39 a month, an African £21. 2s. 6d. An electrician earned £38. 10s., if he was white, £12. 15s. 6d., if he was black. The contrast for cooks was between £41. 7s. 6d. and £6. 5s., and for stokers between £50 and £5. 3s. 6d.[2] The number of state doctors at this time is said to have been of the order of one for 22,400 inhabitants, though there were others practising privately (mainly in the towns) or attending to the employees of the larger companies.

Among critics of the labour system over the years were missionaries of different denominations.[3] The English Baptists sometimes secured redress of wrongs by private representations, but when, in 1932, the Rev. A. A. Lambourne and his sister, in the Bembe district, incurred dislike and suspicion because of their attitude to official corruption,

---

[1] Fryer and McGowan Pinheiro, *op. cit.*, p. 171; Figueiredo, *op. cit.*, pp. 97-8; Sebastião Soares de Resende, *Ordem Anticomunista*, Lourenço Marques, 1950.
[2] *Anuário Estatístico de Angola*, 1958; Fryer and McGowan Pinheiro, *op. cit.*, p. 174.
[3] *Informations Catholiques Internationales*, Paris, no. 145, 1 June 1961, for Catholic protests.

they were ordered to leave the country, and only intervention by the Foreign Office saved them. In 1936, the Rev. A. E. Guest of Quibocolo protested at the injustices practised by certain government officers; he was indicted and required to leave Angola. In 1957, the Catholic Bishops of Portuguese Africa jointly issued a statement demanding equal treatment for African workers. They declared:

> No one can, under any pretext whatsoever, be compelled to leave family, home, village and goods, except in the case of a very grave public need and only while it persists, or in execution of a sentence for a crime.

The damage done to families by the removal of the male members to regions far away from home for extended periods incensed the Bishop of Beira, who wrote in 1953:

> To impose on native workers a stay of more than six months away from their families leads to first stirrings of revolt among the masses, and completely ruins their family life. . . .

The bishop demanded that the spectre of forced labour should be outlawed for good. If equal pay were granted, he said, there would be no problems about recruitment. His colleague, the Bishop of Malange, argued that, while there was no racism in Portuguese law, the same effect was produced by white men out to get rich quick, who found it in their interest to keep the black man down. The conflicts flaring up in other parts of Africa, he said, should be a warning of what this could lead to. A further sign of growing racial cleavage appeared in the fact that the new white settlers coming out from Portugal seemed to turn in on themselves, and it was noted that the proportion of mulattoes to whites was dwindling. The figures for Angola showed:

	Whites	Mulattoes
1900	9,000	7,000
1930	30,000	13,560
1955	109,600	30,400

By the end of the 1950s, however, much needed reforms were already under way, and the report of the International Labour Office in 1962, as will be seen, had a different tale to tell. The Bishop of Beira himself told the present writer in 1963 that he had said what had to be said, and would say it again if he had to, but that by the time of this conversation the material conditions of the Africans in Mozambique had substantially improved and even compared well with their counterparts under colonial rule in other countries. The testimony is significant, coming as it did from a man who had been in trouble with the Portuguese authorities, who had more than once suppressed his pastoral letters.

The peace of the 1950s, however, was rudely shattered in 1961. Already the spread of African nationalism elsewhere had overspilt in a small way into Angola, and in 1953, a riot of discontented workers on the island of São Tomé had led to the death of one hundred Africans. In 1956, pictures of President Nasser and small nationalist groups were appearing in Angola, while support there for Delgado in the 1958 presidential campaign reflected the white community's urge for more decentralization from Lisbon. In 1959, forty-five Africans and *assimilados*, and seven Europeans, were arrested. In 1960, fifty-two arrested Africans and mulattoes included the Chancellor of the Archdiocese of Luanda, Fr Joaquim Pinto de Andrade, whose brother Mario was leader of the nationalist *Movimento Popular para a Libertaçao de Angola* (MPLA). The arrest, too, of Dr Agostinho Neto provoked a protest march to Catete, in which thirty were said to have been killed, with two hundred wounded; it was also reported that the Portuguese troops involved destroyed two native villages. By this time the hydro-electric scheme at Cambambe, shortly to become the third largest dam in Africa, was under way, and 11,000 subsidized settlers were coming out from Portugal annually. *The Times* reported on 22 June 1960 that the past five years had seen the benefits of economic growth beginning to filter down to the African people. Two-thirds of the whites, the correspondent thought, were anti-Salazar, but few wanted to fly from the bosom of Mother Portugal. For all this, discontent among the Angolan Africans over low cotton earnings flared into riots in February 1960. These were quickly put down, but more was to come.

On the evening of 4 February 1961, three groups of Africans with sub-machine guns attacked a police barracks and two prisons in Luanda. They were beaten off with sixteen casualties, roughly half on each side. Many arrests ensued. Next day, at the funeral of one of the policemen killed, another incident flared up, and another twenty-four people were killed. The Portuguese claimed to have taken a prisoner who spoke only French (implying that he had been sent in from the Congo side of the northern border) and to have captured arms which had been made in Czechoslovakia. That night, a band of young whites roamed into the African township on the outskirts of the city, beating up natives and, according to the *Johannesburg Star*, killing ten of them. By 10 February, official figures stated that seven Portuguese had been killed so far, together with twenty-six Africans, while fifty-three had been wounded and one hundred arrested, including three whites. In a suicide raid on a Luanda prison on 12 February, seven Africans were killed, seventeen wounded and twenty arrested, and by the next day one hundred and sixty-six paratroopers had been sent to Angola from Lisbon. During the peaceful 1950s, the total number of soldiers and police in the huge stretches of Angola, many times the size of Portugal itself, was only 8,000, of whom 5,000 were Africans. By the middle of February 1961, the *Daily Telegraph* correspondent thought the total had reached 12,000, half of them coloured.[1] They were making a sweep of villages and suburbs round Luanda, with many arrests. Some of the rumours rife at this time spoke of hundreds and even thousands of deaths, but the reports of reliable foreign correspondents show that this was a gross exaggeration.[2]

If, after all this, there was any residual complacency, it was rudely ended on the Ides of March when the terror struck in the north of Angola: in Maquela do Zombo, Uige, Quitexe, Quibaxi, Nambuangongo and Carmona. The trouble was said to have started when farm workers at Primavera killed a manager who had refused them their pay and spurned their demands for humane treatment. But it is now beyond question that the main thrust came from the Congo side of the border, with well-trained nationalist fighters under the direction of Holden Roberto and his *União das Populações de Angola* (UPA). Most of the UPA fighters belonged to the Bacongo tribe which straddled the Congo-Angola border, constantly crossing and re-crossing the frontier areas, and living a semi-nomadic life without deep roots in either country. Roberto himself, however, was one of those with well-settled family homes in Angola. He is black, and an authentic African nationalist leader in the accepted sense. The nationalists[3] killed hundreds, possibly up to two thousand men, women and

---

[1] *Daily Telegraph*, London, 14 February 1961.
[2] *Ibid.*, by Martin Moore, 20 February 1961.
[3] Terms like 'terrorist' or 'freedom fighter' are emotive, and I prefer to describe the insurgent Africans as 'nationalists'. Even 'rebel' is unsuitable, as the outbreak was at least as much an 'invasion' as a 'rebellion'.

children, white and black; indeed it seems that most of the victims were black. Many were hideously mutilated, and methods of killing included crucifixion and the gouging out of eyes. Pangas were used to slit open the wombs of pregnant women, and the bodies were set alight. Much of the mutilation was inflicted after death, but cases of children being burned alive and of men hacked slowly to death were reported. At Madimba, for instance, 450 miles north of Luanda, settlers concealed their families in the grass, went to São Salvador for help, and returned to find their families slaughtered. Insane with anger and fear, the settlers struck back, and thousands of Africans, some of them innocent, died. The tension reached a level where the settler tended to shoot at every shadow. The reprisals were morally inexcusable, but it is still fair to point out that they had been in-itiated by a wave of horror that outstripped that of the Mau Mau. Later reports, as will be seen, show that the Portuguese army, as it moved in, acted as a restraining influence, disarmed the settlers and set up social service units to reclaim the local African communities, scattered by terror into the bush. There are insuperable problems about assessing numbers. Some reports said that nationalist fighters had killed 6,000 blacks; others that the reprisals accounted for 30,000 deaths. Both estimates seem unlikely, but once a figure was stated, it quickly gained currency in the foreign press. The question is how anyone managed to estimate precisely what happened in those huge tracts of bush and forest where even the population statistics had no reliable base. After hearing the versions of army and intelligence officers, local settlers, British missionaries caring for refugees in the Congo, and others, this writer would venture to say that in the first few months after the Ides of March the nationalists' victims totalled about 2,000, while the victims of reprisals and subsequent military action may have reached anything from 6,000 to 10,000.[1] The small numbers of settlers, their scattered locations, their handful of shot-guns and limited ammunition, and the paucity of troops and police in the early stage[2] seem to argue against the higher figures.

What is certain is that, by the summer, while perhaps 10,000 refugees made their way to Luanda and the Portuguese 'umbrella', up to 150,000 of them arrived in the Congo. Portugal's critics alleged that the refugees were fleeing from Portuguese brutality. The Portu-

[1] Robert H. Estabrook, *Washington Post*, inserted in U.S. Congressional Record, 87th Congress, 2nd session, on 13 March 1962.
[2] Reinforcements in strength from Lisbon did not arrive until June.

guese maintained that the refugees were fleeing, not from the army, which villagers welcomed everywhere, but simply from the area of fighting, and often more specifically from the nationalists. They were bewildered and simply ran; for most of them the natural escape route, geographically, was over the Congo border. In the Congo, Baptist, Methodist and Catholic missionaries joined with the Red Cross and other agencies to look after the wave of exhausted arrivals. From the refugee camps some grim reports were sent to Britain, claiming that Portuguese troops had bombed, machine-gunned and tortured villagers, burned their homes, and killed and wounded many.

Before looking at this in detail, it will be as well to examine quickly the events leading up to the summer months. In mid-March, the United States joined Russia in a demand for an inquiry by the United Nations Security Council. The resolution failed, but the incident marked a turning-point in Portugal's relationship with the U.S. government. In the 1950s she had won American approval, not least because of her stand against Communism, and the two countries were linked by American reliance on air and naval bases in the Azores under a ten-year lease from Portugal, not to mention their common membership of NATO. President Kennedy, however, whose term of office had opened at the beginning of 1961, was to become a champion of African nationalism, and, while duly concerned for Portugal and NATO solidarity, he favoured Liberia's resolution calling on Portugal to comply with U.N. anti-colonial policies and proposing a U.N. inquiry into the Angola situation. Salazar was warned, a week in advance, that America would support the resolution, and, in the Security Council debate, Adlai Stevenson politely insisted that America 'would be remiss in its duties as a friend of Portugal' if she failed to encourage the gradual advancement of all Portugal's subject peoples towards full self-determination.[1] The move failed, but the same resolution came before the General Assembly a month later, and this time was passed, again with U.S. support. There were anti-American demonstrations in Lisbon and Luanda at this time, but, as Schlesinger puts it, President Kennedy's administration was now 'free of automatic identification with colonialism' and in the third world 'was acclaimed as the friend of oppressed peoples'.[2] Kennedy's biographer goes on to record that the U.S. continued to be in a dilemma. The Azores base was seen as essential to American security

[1] The term was 'self-determination', not 'independence'.
[2] Schlesinger, pp. 472-3.

in case of trouble over Berlin. At the same time the U.S. administration was now committed to an anti-colonialist policy. In this situation, the Americans only had one choice: a moderating policy in the U.N. over Portugal, 'never enough for the nationalists in Africa, and always too much for the Pentagon and Dr Salazar'. They took part in the drafting of Afro-Asian resolutions on Portugal with a view to toning them down and consistently opposing the use of sanctions against her. At the same time, diplomatic pressures were exerted on Lisbon to change its 'colonial methods'. Finally, Salazar decided 'to extend American access to the facilities (in the Azores) without formal renewal of the agreement'. Thus, the Americans have remained in the islands for nearly eight years on a day-to-day basis, which has worked out well enough in practice, and tacitly acted as a bargaining factor in Portuguese hands. Meanwhile, Schlesinger tells us, 'Kennedy's effectiveness in making his African visitors understand the American dilemma over the Azores base limited the harm that restraint on the Portuguese colonies did to our general position in Africa.' The middle course, however, was not just a matter of cynical pragmatism but 'did express substantive conviction as well as tactical necessity'. Kennedy always 'mistrusted U.N. resolutions which promised big things but could not be carried out'.[1]

Taking stock of events at the end of March 1961, the Associated Press correspondent, writing in the *New York Herald Tribune*,[2] evidently felt that what had happened bore little relation to any widespread upsurge of spontaneous discontent. He spoke of the African majority as a happy, lazy and indifferent people living in a pleasant land, and, two days later, writing in the *New York Times*, Benjamin Welles reported overwhelming evidence that the attacks had been led by foreign African revolutionaries timed to coincide with the United Nations debates on Angola. It was true that local Africans had joined in, but the February outbreak in the Luanda slums was the work of detribalized, rootless elements, while the discontent on the coffee plantations, the result of a 66 per cent drop in prices over the previous three years, had provided fertile ground for militant organizers and witch-doctors to work on. The nationalist fighters were centred on training camps in the Congo, near Leopoldville, which enjoyed support from Ghana and Guinea. Welles discerned links with the Congo's African Solidarity Party, formerly led by Mr Gizenga

[1] Schlesinger, pp. 518-19.
[2] *New York Herald Tribune*, 28 March 1961.

and Mr Cleophas Kamitatu. There is no doubt that the whole affair had been thoroughly well planned and prepared, and correspondents were to report that the subsequent campaign bore all the hallmarks of sophisticated guerrilla tactics, with subtly contrived ambushes of a kind already familiar in Algeria and Malaya. The organizers appear to have made the most of superstition and fetish in their recruiting techniques, and the Portuguese suspicions of missionary activity derived in part from the interaction of Christian with pagan motifs in the guerrillas' behaviour. There was a morbid preoccupation with crucifixion. Prisoners confessed that they had been promised resurrection on the third day if they were killed in the fighting, and had been assured that the white man's bullets would turn to water inside them. The unhappy victims of these inducements even proclaimed their own immunity as they ran, fatally, towards the Portuguese firing lines. Their marching tunes included Christian hymns.

The attitudes of the Catholic African clergy were mixed. In the Luanda province, with 1,600,000 Catholics, there were only 70 African and 17 Goanese priests out of a total of 539. Laybrothers included 87 Europeans and 38 Africans, and there were 415 European and 88 African nuns. However, before the troubles, the vicar-general and the chancellor of the archdiocese were men of mixed blood, and three of the canons, including the dean, were Africans. White and black priests received the same scanty pay, teachers and students in the seminaries were roughly divided equally between white and black and preference was given to Africans in sending students to Rome for their theology, with the costs mainly borne by the government. Some of the priests were certainly active in the nationalist movement. In April 1961, the vicar-general, Mgr Canon Manuel Joacquim Mendes das Neves, a man of mixed blood, was arrested on suspicion of playing a leading role in the attacks. He was sent to Portugal, first to prison, then to residence under supervision in a religious house. He was not brought to trial. Some of the accusations against him were hysterical, and he was even accused of poisoning communion wafers to effect mass murder in church. His archbishop, Mgr Moises Alves de Pinho, a white Portuguese, publicly defended him and denounced his accusers. It remains true, however, that Mgr Neves had supported the nationalist movements, and the archbishop admitted as much to the present writer in the following August. He seems to have found money for them and to have used the confessional to pass messages, but no more. April also saw the arrest of four other African priests,

Frs Alexandre do Nascimento, Vicente Rafael, Martinho Campos and Alfredo Osorio. Mgr Neves died in a Jesuit house at Braga in 1967, and in the same year it was reported that, in all, eight deported Angolan priests were under supervised residence in Portugal, including Frs Pinto de Andrade, do Nascimento and Osorio.[1] After the 1961 outbreak, a large number of African catechists, trained by foreign Protestant missions, were rounded up, and were alleged to have been, in some cases, tortured and even killed. There was said to be evidence that Protestant mission stations had been used as strategic centres for nationalist attacks, and, while two Catholic priests and some Catholic teachers were killed, the Protestant missions remained untouched. In protesting against the closure of some missions by the authorities, the Protestants, it was said, seemed confident of their personal safety so far as the nationalists were concerned. Some British and American missionaries were arrested and expelled. The English Baptists were ordered to vacate their missions, ostensibly for security reasons and their own protection. It is true that the Protestant missionaries fostered African aspirations as a matter of principle, and it would be natural enough for African fighters, ploughing their way through perilous terrain, to seek occasional help from their missions. Those organizing the attacks may well have made use of Christian groups as a rallying point and played on a mixture of paganism and Christian sentiment. One would not feel confident about going bail for all the catechists. But to suggest that, for instance, the English Baptists allowed their missions to be used as centres of terrorist planning is to accuse them of acting wildly out of character. Their view of Angola and their account of the events in 1961 have been the subject of controversy, and the present writer has had his differences with them. But no one will seek to impugn their Christian dedication to the African or their pacific traditions. The Rev. Clifford Parsons, then secretary of the Baptist Missionary Society, has more than once spoken of his once-held belief that the Portuguese could achieve something in Africa that had eluded the rest of us, and of his respect for the high ideals and heroic mould of an earlier Portuguese history. The pity is that the Baptists' help was not invoked in 1961 towards establishing peace.

What happened in March was that a hard core of hundreds of well-trained nationalist fighters led the attacks, their ultimate head-

---

[1] *Informations Catholiques Internationales*, Paris, no. 300, 15 November 1967.

quarters being in the Congo. They recruited local help by threat and inducement but often met resistance from the African tribes. Their attacks, in the upshot, affected a fraction of Angola variously put at one-seventh to one-fourteenth of the whole terrain, and less than 1 per cent of the population. Mr George W. Ball, the former U.S. Under-Secretary of State, who is a constructive critic of Portuguese policy, tells us:

> The leaders of the insurrectionary movement come predominantly from two tribes (in Angola and Mozambique), each of which is an unpopular minority within its own territory; and any effort by these men to assert hegemony over the other tribes (many of which have been armed by the Portuguese) would be followed swiftly by civil war.[1]

On 16 April 1961, Tom Stacey reported in the *Sunday Times* that there were three factions involved: members of the former *Force Publique* of the Congo who took to the bush after the July mutiny of 1960; Angolan-African dissidents, including a few whites and coloured Communists, with headquarters at Leopoldville; and a mixed group led by Portuguese whites answerable to Delgado and Galvão. The second group wanted all the Portuguese out of Angola and an all-black government, while the third group favoured separation from Portugal and a democratic government of mixed races on a qualitative franchise. The *Christian Science Monitor*, the next day, reported that the president of Holden Roberto's UPA, Sr José Gilmore, was a native of São Salvador and was linked through the Nguizako tribe of that area with the Congolese President Kasavubu, who belonged to the Bacongo tribe. On the same day the *Daily Telegraph* reported that the African fighters had been trained in the Lumumbist areas of the Congo, and that their leaders included *mistos* and *assimilados*, deprived of lack of advancement, who were willing pupils of African nationalists and Communist agents. The paper added that five Angolan Catholic bishops had issued a joint pastoral letter showing some sympathy with complaints against the Portuguese administration, deploring 'criminal acts', but urging consideration for the Africans' legitimate and just aspirations. On 15 April, hundreds of nationalists attacked Cabinda, Quitexe and Malange. Others attacked the Bembe region and Pungo Alaquem. In Lucunga they poured

[1] Ball, *op. cit.*, p. 249.

petrol on houses and burned them down, and a refugee told the *New York Times*[1] that 'the terrorists fell on us as if they were demon-possessed, dancing and singing and shouting that the bullets of the whites did not kill'.

On 18 April, *Le Soir* reported an African male nurse's account of a massacre of Portuguese planters and the bombing of a village by the Portuguese by way of reprisal. Chief Sengele of Nkanda, near Quibocolo, had been killed by African fighters for refusing to join them. The paper added, however, that on 27 March, at Maquela, two lorry-loads of sixty black men and women prisoners had been murdered and thrown in the river by Portuguese, and that the villagers had recovered the mutilated bodies of some of the women. On 21 April, Richard Beeston reported in the *Daily Telegraph* that a senior Portuguese official had told him: 'We are now having to use armed forces to prevent the white population from avenging itself on the blacks.' Meanwhile, the Methodist Board of Missions in New York was asserting that eight Methodist black pastors had been killed by Portuguese troops and civilians after a hurried trial, that half their one hundred and fifty African pastors were in prison, had fled or been killed, and that seven schools and chapels had been destroyed in Luanda alone. *The Times* reported attacks on Nambuangongo, Quibumbo and Quicunzo. It added that the Bailundo tribe, wearing white handkerchiefs on their heads for recognition, were fighting bravely beside the whites.[2] Robert Targett, writing in the *Sunday Times* of 23 April, spoke of the nationalists as ferocious bands ravaging the northern areas in attacks far bigger and bloodier than the Mau Mau incidents in Kenya,[3] with thousands of Africans dying on both sides. Four tribes at the most were involved. There were still only 15,000 troops and police available. By the end of the month, settlers were complaining that the Portuguese authorities were not supplying

---

[1] *New York Times*, 18 April 1961.

[2] *The Times*, London, 22 April 1961.

[3] In an interview with Pierre de Vos which appeared in *Le Monde* on 5 July 1961, the UPA leader Holden Roberto, frankly admitted that massacres and tortures had been perpetrated on Portuguese men, women and children, and De Vos, working from Leopoldville, met some of the Africans who had committed atrocities, including the use of a circular saw to split people lengthwise. Those questioned seemed very blithe about it all. Holden Roberto argued that UPA had called a strike for 15 March, and that on the Primavera plantation the Portuguese had responded by shooting twenty workers, which was why the black response had been so savage. 'No one', he insisted, 'suspects the conditions in which my people are living.'

them with arms. An official campaign, however, had been mounted against the Protestant catechists.[1]

Some of the most vivid accounts of this period came in despatches to the *Daily Telegraph* from their correspondent Richard Beeston, who in June was the only foreign correspondent to have secured an entry visa to Angola in two months.[2] At the beginning of May he told us that thousands of local Africans had joined the nationalists, many through fear and intimidation. In the thick jungle of the Quizaxe region, indescribable atrocities had been committed against those refusing to be recruited. At the same time, the Portuguese, in a bid to burn the terrorist bands out of the forests in which they were hiding, sent in the air force with napalm bombs to destroy deserted villages; but rockets and machine-guns were also used against villages simply in order to demoralize. The Portuguese were waiting until the grass and trees were dry. They would then burn the terrorists out on a big scale, shoot them as they ran, and leave the escapees to starve. Discrimination would be impossible. An air force officer had said: 'We will hunt the terrorists down like game. We have no alternative but extermination.' After this, Portugal's critics began to accuse her of genocide.

It is extremely hard to judge whether and how far Portuguese tactics went beyond the conventions of 'jungle' war. All guerrilla war in

---

[1] It was estimated at the time that 20,000 Africans were receiving free education from Protestant missions, especially from the Americans. The total number of American Protestant clergy in Angola was about two hundred. At least one Catholic bishop in Angola has testified to the powerful contribution made by American missionaries.

[2] At the start of the troubles, the Portuguese officials, totally untrained and unprepared for handling an influx of newspapermen, became flustered and angry when some of the reports going out of the country seemed to them to be distorted. They were also upset by the hustling energy of the American correspondents, some of whom undoubtedly went a little too far. So the foreign press, apart from Beeston, found itself barred. When I got in at the end of July, the Portuguese told me that pictures from the Congo had been despatched from Luanda to foreign papers on the pretence that they had been taken during the fighting in Angola, and that the American pressmen were 'Teddy Boys'. So, too, were the Swedes. While I was in Luanda, the U.S. Assistant-Secretary of State, Mennen Williams arrived. This time the Americans sent their crack correspondents who did a brilliant job, often to Portugal's advantage. 'Soapy' Williams himself, recognizing good as well as bad in Angola, rebuked the Portuguese gently for their hypersensitivity – which was their own worst enemy – and read them a tactful lecture on the art of public relations. He plainly felt it was their own fault that they had not had fair play in the international press, and said so.

heavy forest and long grass involves the use of napalm or its equivalent. The bombs are aimed, not at people, but at clearing the terrain to uncover and destroy the enemy's hideout. It is admitted that, if the enemy uses an innocent village for shelter, it may be impossible to force him out without injuring and killing civilians. Such are the terrible fortunes of war, it is said, and the guilt lies with those who start it. An infantry detachment approaching an apparently deserted village can, and in Angola often did, discover to its cost and when it is too late that the innocent looking grass and trees are infested with enemy waiting to mow them down. From the refugee camps in the Congo, however, came fearsome reports from missionaries and others who were tending the wounded, hungry and exhausted arrivals. The gravamen of the reports was that Portuguese troops had massacred tens of thousands of African civilians without cause. Many refugees had arrived showing signs of bullet wounds and napalm burns. The Rev. David Grenfell, a Baptist missionary working with the refugees was to write to the *Guardian*[1] that there was overwhelming evidence of 'mass wilful murder'. The Baptist Missionary Society's report, issued in June 1961, spoke of women and children being mown down as they fled, of a crowd gathered together by troops at Sanga and then mown down with machine-guns, of 300 similarly killed at Tumbi, while at Tomboco, women and children were lined up to watch men and boys being put to death. The PIDE[2] had arrested 1,500 Africans in one area alone, and were out to seize especially those who showed the slightest sign of being educated. To have a primer in one's possession was perilous. Many prisoners had simply disappeared. Some had been thrown to crocodiles. Pastors had been shot. A boy had been bayoneted. A few matches applied to the dry grass in a few days' time would ensure the death of another 50,000 people. On 25 July, Beeston reported that in one town the PIDE had beaten up and driven into hiding all the educated Africans. Two days before, he had spoken of thousands of arrests, and of prisoners who died without trace. At the end of July, a British Labour M.P., Mr George Thomas, went to the Congo-Angola border with a Baptist missionary, the Rev. Eric Blakebrough, to question refugees. These two investigators sent home yet another account of mass extermination and the wholesale destruction of villages, and prepared lists of witnesses to give precision to the indictment.

[1] *Guardian*, 15 August 1961.
[2] Security Police (see Abbreviations).

On the other hand, in May, Dr Adriano Moreira, the new Portuguese Overseas Minister, had announced that white vengeance would not be tolerated. 'Under no circumstances,' he said, 'shall the innocent be made to suffer for the crimes of the guilty.' On 24 June, Beeston wrote that officials had vehemently denied the missionaries' account, and added:

It is admitted that punitive raids have been made on villages suspected of harbouring terrorists, but Western diplomats and observers I have spoken to believe that reports of large-scale massacres of civilians are either baseless or highly exaggerated.

Ten days later, on 4 July, he told us that forecasts about burning the terrorists out had proved to be unrealistic as thick forest 'does not burn'.[1] On 5 July, Beeston wrote that the army was stamping out mob law and that neutrals in the country also thought that the missionaries' estimates were exaggerated. By 24 and 25 July, he was comparing the ruthlessness of the PIDE with army policy, which was setting up psycho-social units in the north to reclaim Africans who had fled to the bush. They were being urged to return to their villages, and were promised full protection. On 8 August, the *Guardian* carried a letter from a Mr William Stanton, a British national in Angola, asserting that one accusation, relating to the arrest and murder of 500-600 people at Mavoio where he lived was unfounded. The incident had just not happened. Four days later the same paper reported that, speaking at Leeds, a Dr D. H. Wilson, just back from the refugee mission in the Congo, had said that he had encountered only one case of napalm burning. He suspected that some of the refugees had actually been wounded by the rebels, even when they said it was the Portuguese. He produced a crude lead bullet which would have been out of place in any modern armoury, but which, he said, according to an African, had been fired from an aeroplane. Whoever did it, the fact remains that at the Kimpsese hospital alone there were 120 refugees suffering from machine-gun wounds. An interesting sidelight on Dr Wilson's account is that even the letter of Mr David Grenfell, which was so critical of the Portuguese and which controverted some of Mr Stanton's statements, spoke of the

[1] Everyone in Angola knows this. The author was told that the farmers would be only too glad if someone *could* find a way of getting the grass alight at times. It seems highly unlikely that anyone in authority ever seriously set out to do it, though the agony of the situation may have provoked a wild threat.

difficulties of translating and interpreting witnesses in the Congo-Angola border region.

The Portuguese argued that many of the refugees were simply terrified, bewildered people who only knew that a war was raging round them, and could not always distinguish between the two sides. Arriving exhausted and often wounded, they were all too prone to say what they sensed was expected of them. If the Africans were so afraid of the Portuguese, why had thousands of them, where the movements of the nationalists conduced to it, chosen to seek Portuguese protection in Luanda and elsewhere.[1] By 1963, when the present writer returned to Angola for another visit, this argument had gathered weight, for by that time some 300,000 refugees had crossed to the Congo, but half of them had returned, and more were coming daily, in spite, the Portuguese claimed, of inducements to stay where they were. One was able to inspect some of the scores of new villages being built for them by the Portuguese with the active help of the refugees themselves, and to observe the cordial relations between the army and the returning African families, the beginnings of an educational 'crash' programme in remote areas, the miles and miles of piping bringing water to the villages, and the new medical services. It was pointed out to the author that the warfare had followed a pattern similar to the British campaign in Malaya and the French campaign in Algeria, and, while allowing that gross irregularities had doubtless taken place in patches, perhaps when an individual officer lost his head, Western diplomats said plainly that they discounted stories of planned massacre and genocide. In talking to these diplomats, to settlers who had fled the terror, and to foreigners of many nationalities living and working in Angola, one found a general tendency to make distinctions between the ruthlessness of the police and the rehabilitation programmes of the army, which was generally admitted to have made an impressive job of pacification. The author met Captain Ruy Mendoza, for instance, an officer charged with organizing the psycho-social services. As the army moved up and cleared the terrorists out of a given area, the psycho-social unit would move in to set up welfare and educational services, and to persuade the frightened Africans to return to village life. It is also true that, later in the year, when comparative peace had been established, the number of arrested persons confined in a huge camp

---

[1] The author himself saw large numbers of refugees housed and cared for by the Red Cross, Caritas and others in Luanda, which he reached at the start of August.

specially opened in the south at Moçamedes totalled about 10,000. Yet there was a stage in the Mau Mau crisis, an affair of much smaller proportions, when as many as 90,000 Africans were interned. By 1963, a number of Western ambassadors and journalists had been to Angola and had visited Moçamedes, where they found the internees living in farming communities with considerable freedom, and substantial numbers being released each year.

So much of what was alleged, while intelligible to a certain degree in terms of the general panic, seems to have been out of character. The *Guardian*, commenting in May 1961,[1] had said:

> The Portuguese have extolled the virtues of hard work for them-selves as for the Africans: the peasant families who have emigrated to Angola have not gone to manage African labour but themselves to plant and till. The Portuguese have always been on more equal terms with Africans than have, say, the British in Kenya.

Writing in the *Sunday Times*,[2] the Rev. Clifford Parsons, secretary of the Baptist Missionary Society, had warned that the influx of immigrants had created tensions. It is true that many of them were in no better circumstances than many Africans, and some of them were taught by Africans to read and write; but, while in some ways this was beneficial to race relations and suggested a certain crude equality, it is certainly true that rivalries did emerge in regard, for instance, to employment. At the same time, Mr Parsons, while severely condemning forced labour and brutality, was fair enough to say that, ten years before, the Portuguese had stood a better chance than any other colonial power in Africa of moving into the mid-20th century with a viable racial policy. The assimilation principle, he thought, still commanded the Africans' confidence at that time. But he plainly felt that the chances had since been lost. The Baptist Missionary Society's report of June 1961 also said:

> Until recently, in spite of forced labour and other injustices, racial relations have been surprisingly harmonious. . . . There has been no colour bar, nor have Africans been prevented from holding office. Some Africans have in fact achieved a higher standard of living than some of the Europeans in Angola.[3]

---

[1] *Guardian*, 6 May 1961.
[2] *Sunday Times*, 4 June 1961.
[3] *Ibid.*

An interim statement issued at the time of Mr George Thomas's visit stated:

> We do not believe that the Portuguese people are generally unfair and unkind. It is the Government of Portugal which is responsible for the legislation and administration which makes the present labour practice in Angola possible.[1]

Perhaps it is fair to comment that the Portuguese army was composed of ordinary Portuguese people, and most of the 20,000 troops in Angola by the end of July were conscripts. It is hard for one who knows these people to feel that they could be led into *wholesale* viciousness. As to the legislation, it was shortly to earn the approval of the International Labour Organization, though the latter still found ground for criticism of certain aspects of the practice as distinct from the theory. Finally, in this connection, it is useful to recall an International Red Cross report on the refugees, published in the *Observer* on 21 May 1961. This estimated that at that time 40,000 refugees had arrived. There were no signs of serious or contagious disease among them. Two German doctors had spent four or five days examining them, and only ten people were found to be ill. This is an encouraging commentary on the general living standards of the Africans in Angola at that time.

Early in July, a British mission of inquiry went to Northern Angola to see the situation at close quarters. The British Consul-General in Luanda was accompanied by the British military and air attachés from Lisbon. On 31 July, Mr Edward Heath, M.P., then Lord Privy Seal, told the House of Commons that the mission had sent a report to London, and, while such reports were confidential, he could give an indication of its contents. The mission had talked to Europeans, Africans, Portuguese officials, members of the forces and missionaries. The Portuguese had co-operated in making facilities available and the mission had received a great deal of information. Much of it was second-hand and hearsay, but on this they had formed the best judgment they could. The consul-general reported his belief that the senior Portuguese authorities had done what they could to stop the white civilian reprisals, though they were hampered in this by the small number of security forces in Angola at the time. The rebel

---

[1] Angola Action Group, Southend-on-Sea, 16 August 1961.

bands had now become smaller and better organized and were concentrating on cutting roads and communications, and on attacking the coffee plantations which were at this time being harvested. The consul-general had seen African villages and European settlements which had been burned to the ground. Some of it had been caused by military operations, some by the rebels themselves. There had been severe fighting and 'harsh methods were used'. The consul-general's view was that the majority of the refugees had fled to avoid being involved in any way in the operation. 'If they had stayed, they would have been faced with the choice either of joining the rebels or risking rebel reprisals if they remained loyal to the Portuguese.' The consul-general had no doubt that there had been 'cases of arbitrary and repressive conduct by civilians and by some members of the police', but 'he has reported very favourably on the sense of duty amongst senior officials and military commanders whom he met on these visits'. Mr Heath continued that the consul-general

> found that they [Portuguese officials and commanders] were attaching great importance to the task of rebuilding racial harmony, of restoring confidence, and of trying to meet the needs of the Africans. Both the civilian and military authorities were trying to create conditions in which the Africans could safely return to their villages, and they were trying to persuade them to do so.

In particular, the consul-general

> flatly denies the other allegations which have been made, namely that the Portuguese forces are following a deliberate policy of burning out the Africans. He deliberately denies that they are following a policy of extermination.

In answer to questions, Mr Heath said that the mission had been able to talk to Africans and missionaries in perfect freedom, and he did not think the report had been influenced by Portuguese officials 'watching while these discussions were being carried out'. He was not saying that there was no basis of grievance behind the revolt, as Lord Home had explained to the Portuguese government in Lisbon. Mr Heath thought that the best hope lay in a policy of reform producing a rallying point for moderate opinion in Angola. He referred to a statement made by Salazar to the National Assembly on 30 June, indicating that far-reaching administrative reforms and changes in the Africans' status would be brought about. This, Mr Heath commented, could make a profound difference to the course of events.[1]

But the reports from the refugee camps still leave one with a deep sense of disquiet, especially the allegations that women and children were shot at, and that many arrested Africans disappeared (whether they were moved south to the detention camp or whether some of them were killed remains obscure). Refugee camp workers and others tried to get at the truth, but, without casting the slightest reflection on the questioners, it may not be unfair to reiterate the problem of interpretation when the languages involved are African dialects and Portuguese. Those familiar with colonial Africa also know very well that the subservience imposed on Africans by the whites in many countries did create a tendency for the less tutored subject to respond to the situation he found himself in, in the way he thought he was expected to. But the fact remains that, when a savage war is unleashed, even the best, and not only the Portuguese, security forces can be led into excesses and harsh, indiscriminate action, quite apart from sheer error and confusion in a climate of panic. Undoubtedly, too, the urgent need to track the trouble to its source leads all too easily to brutal interrogation and wholesale arrests. Neither side comes out of the story with an unsullied record.

On 11 October 1961, Governor-General Deslandes announced that the crisis was over. The war, however, continues even now on a much restricted scale, confined largely to attacks by small forces on Cabinda and in the north and east of Angola, with casualties on the Portuguese side working out at about 120 military deaths a year. It is reckoned that the nationalist forces on the Angola side amount to 5,000 to 7,000, still based on camps in the Congo and Zambia. You can travel the length and breadth of the province without being conscious of a state of war, and most of the skirmishes take place at military points in rural areas, or when patrols are ambushed. It is a war of attrition, promising an interminable 'nuisance' value, but because of the huge areas to be policed, some 50,000 to 60,000 troops are held down in Angola alone.

In June 1960, penal sanctions for breach of work contracts were replaced by civil sanctions. Later, minimum wages and a system of

1 Hansard, vol. 645, no. 159, 31 July 1961, cols. 959-64.

labour inspection were introduced. International conventions regarding working ages of minors, days of rest, and the abolition of forced labour were ratified, though contract labour continued. In May 1961, the government abolished the compulsory growing of cotton, and the Mozambique Legislative Council began to consider the abolition of compulsory rice-growing. Native land laws were strengthened. Dr Moreira introduced a series of statutes to expand the voting lists of the provincial Legislative Council and to increase its authority.

Most importantly, a decree of 6 September 1961 ended the *assimilado* system.[1] This means that the Portuguese Constitution and codes of law now extend to all the inhabitants of the provinces, Africans get the vote on the same conditions as whites, more Africans can now vote for members of the Legislative Council and in national elections. In effect, the African is now, by birth, a full Portuguese citizen. Beginning in January 1962, a programme for the gradual abolition of tariffs between the mother country and the provinces began. There is now virtually a single 'common market' for Portugal and her overseas possessions. Each province now operates its own independent budget, but all belong to the escudo area, and all are involved in the National Development Plans. Efforts have also been made to curb the power of Portuguese monopolies in the *ultramar*.[2]

A cynic might say that the end of 'assimilation' is a recognition that Antonio Enes and his paternalism were wrong, and that the more liberal tendencies of the early nineteenth century were right; or alternatively, that Portugal was compelled in the end to make a show of bowing to some degree to the twentieth-century's winds of change. But, in differing degrees, both Salazar and Moreira envisaged a blend of ideas. In the constitutional and legislative fields, in education, employment and social services, African development should move up into a higher gear; but the basic aim would remain, namely a marriage of races and cultures, not an exclusive Africanization, nor a total repudiation of things African in favour of the European ethos. Moreira's vision in all this was younger and deeper than Salazar's. He is typical of the brilliant young men of modest origin whom Salazar favoured, but was inclined to curb when they seemed to be running ahead of time. Adriano Moreira was still in his middle thirties when he became Overseas Minister at a desperate time, in

[1] Decree 43,893; see also Decree nos. 43,895 and 43,730 for Provincial Settlement Boards and Municipal Institutions.
[2] Duffy, *op. cit.*, pp. 225-9.

1961. He brought a furious energy to bear on the crisis, and began to secure results quickly. That there are two flourishing universities in Luanda and Lourenço Marques today is largely due to his driving initiative, and to the stimulus injected by the man who, at first, was Governor-General of Angola under him, General Deslandes. Moreira *believes* in the African, and seems to favour the concept of a Portuguese Commonwealth of independent, multi-racial nations, including the present overseas provinces, and creating new links between Portugal and Brazil. There is a touch of genius about him, his defect being the sort of hypersensitive dynamism that easily offends other people and protests angrily when others offend him. When Deslandes sought to force the pace in regard to higher institutes of learning, he was acting in harmony with Moreira's policy, but the day-to-day detail of their relationship ran into difficulty. Moreira sacked Deslandes, and incurred the hostility of certain powerful military circles. Not long afterwards, Salazar 'translated' Moreira to the academic sphere, and he became Director of the Institute of Overseas Studies. In his conversations with the author, Salazar showed that he was by no means out of sympathy with Moreira's ideals and objectives, but he evidently thought the pace too abrupt, and that it would take a long time yet to educate the African for the highest responsibilities. Some African students' discomfort in the more abstract disciplines, like mathematics, troubled the former professor, and, in one of the last interviews he gave to a foreign correspondent, he spoke of the development of the subject peoples in terms of long generations ahead. Happily, there are men in the present government who, like Moreira, realize that history will not wait for this.

The men who started the rebellion in Angola were of different kinds, and, despite the protestations some of them made in 1961, leaned heavily on assistance from outside.[1] What seems to have happened was that early in 1960, the Russians sent as ambassador to Guinea a brilliant organizer and expert in the tactics of infiltration and subversion. This was Daniel Semenovich Solod, who had already done much to foster Soviet influence in the Middle East and North Africa. He now took control of affairs on the Atlantic coast of the African continent, and set to work on the Portuguese provinces. One of the first of the Portuguese dissidents he contacted was Mario

[1] Pieter Lessing; *Africa's Red Harvest*, 1962, Michael Joseph, London, pp. 11-24.

Pinto de Andrade, who was born in Angola of mixed parentage in 1928. Educated in Lisbon, Paris and Frankfurt, he was at one time involved with the Portuguese and French Communist Parties, and in 1955 his studies took him to Warsaw and Moscow. In 1958 he was a delegate at the Afro-Asian Writers' Conference at Tashkent, and at one time wrote for *Pravda*. He is a man of high intellect, and a poet. His movement, the MPLA, was originally more political than military, and, hinging as it does on men of mixed blood, its concern is rather to infiltrate and revolutionize the Portuguese system than simply to get rid of the Portuguese presence in Africa.

Holden Roberto, on the other hand, leader of the UPA, was African, and saw the future in terms of African rule. He has been known variously as José Gilmore and Ruy Ventura, and has always been a militant. Born in Angola in 1923, the son of an African peasant farmer, he attended a mission school in the Congo and later went to France where he made contact with the Communist Party. He has visited Britain and has Baptist affiliations. In 1954, he went to Leopoldville, where he seems to have been responsible for disseminating Communist literature in the Portuguese provinces. He was helped by former members of the disbanded Angolan Communist Party, and was well known to President Nkrumah of Ghana and President Sekou Touré of Guinea. Though both revolutionary leaders have been helped by the Communist bloc, Andrade has much more in common with Communist ideology than Roberto. Solod's other contact in 1960 was Viriato Francisco Clemente da Cruz, born in Angola in 1928, who later joined the French Communist Party, spearheaded a movement of Angolan intellectuals, and became well known in London. In 1959, he went to Conakry.

The UPA army was trained at a camp at Thysville, sixty miles north of the Congo-Angolan border. Roberto maintained, in 1961, that his operation was simply an attempt to save the day for a programme of strikes in Angola which had misfired. But, six months before the Ides of March in 1961, Communist radio stations in China, Prague and Bucharest were warning Africa about what was going to happen in Angola. It was in 1960, too, that Andrade and Da Cruz spent a lot of time in Russia and other Communist countries, and are believed to have arranged for arms to be sent to Angola from the Lenin works at Pilsen. On 3 December, a UPA message from Leopoldville declared: 'Long live UPA. Long live Nikita Kruschev. Long live Angola.' UPA, it said, was ready to open fire. 'Russia will provide weapons, and Lumumba will help us. Let us kill the whites. Lumumba has given the authority.' On 7 December 1960, the Peking *People's Daily*, a few days after the Communist 'summit' in Moscow, again foretold the eruption in Angola, and added that the call had gone out to rise and fight. On the eve of the terror in the following March, a UPA Order of the Day stated that 'our comrade the Devil (the U.S.S.R.) is standing by with a watchful eye. Long live Communism. Down with concentric tribalism.' By the middle of 1961, Radio Peking was broadcasting for seven hours a week to Portuguese Africa, and was joined by Moscow Radio in August.

There had been a certain amount of friction between MPLA and UPA, partly because one was based on a mixture of blood while one was Black Nationalist, and partly because Andrade was in effect a Communist, while Roberto was not.[1] UPA's aid came, not only from the East, but also from the American Committee for Africa and the British Movement for Freedom of Peoples in the Portuguese Colonies, who actually maintained that Roberto was anti-Communist. There had also been a hitch in the arrival of arms negotiated by the MPLA, and Roberto began his war with inferior arms, including rifles supplied by the Congo and some bought from soldiers of the United Nations there. Solod tried to help matters by arranging for arms to be sent from Conakry in trawlers which sailed direct to the Angolan coast. But this was a risky procedure, and early in May they were being despatched through Ghana, Soviet and Polish ships having delivered them at Takoradi. The UPA were soon using modern arms manufactured in Czechoslovakia, together with two-way radios. Reporting from Lisbon at this time,[2] Douglas Brown reported in the *Sunday Telegraph* that there was ample evidence that both Russian and Chinese arms were being used. Documents emanating from Nkrumah had been intercepted, and some of the prisoners captured spoke no language known in Angola. Help was coming from the Congo, Ghana, Guinea and Mali. Also in an endeavour to cement divisions, Solod arranged for a meeting at Conakry of a group known as FRAIN (*Front Révolutionnaire Africain pour L'Indépendence Nationaliste des Colonies Portugaises*). This included Amilcar Lopes Cabral, later to be the rebel leader in Portuguese Guinea, but Roberto was not represented. However, on 18 April, a conference of Portuguese nationalist movements took place at

[1] Duffy, *op. cit.*, p. 218.
[2] *Sunday Telegraph*, 21 May 1961.

Casablanca, where Russians and Chinese were joined by delegates from Ghana, Guinea, Morocco, Egypt and elsewhere. A telegram was despatched to Kruschev, and a permanent secretariat set up, to be based on Conakry. The conference also established a Common Front of Angolan Partisans in Leopoldville, which both the UPA and the MPLA joined, and which spawned three smaller movements. Roberto emerged from this as the *supremo* for Angola, and this was confirmed in an intercepted letter written by Lev Souhanov, of the Soviet Committee of Anglo-Asian Solidarity, to the Permanent Secretariat of the Nationalist Organizations of the Portuguese Colonies. The letter stated that Russia was setting up an organization to help the Portuguese nationalists. Later, Kruschev replied to the Casablanca telegram (on 19 June), indicating that the U.S.S.R. was ready to help Angola. After Casablanca, the UPA's finances were eased, as they were now able to draw on the Afro-Asian Solidarity Fund. Roberto and Andrade both visited the United States, and Roberto visited Britain.

When the author went to Angola in 1967, the position was that Andrade, after further dissensions, was in Rabat running an organization known as CONCP (Conference of Nationalist Organizations of the Portuguese Colonies) to co-ordinate the various Communist movements in Portuguese Africa. The MPLA was being run by Agostinho Neto, with headquarters at Brazzaville in the former French Congo, military headquarters at Dollizi, and with centres also in Zambia. The MPLA's job was to attack Cabinda, the Portuguese enclave on the Congo side of the border, and, from Zambia, to launch assaults on Lumbala and Gago Coutinho. The organization was relying for help mainly on Russia and the Eastern European countries. The UPA, on the other hand, while training in Bulgaria and other Communist countries, and receiving equipment from, for example, Yugoslavia, also enjoyed the support of the Organization of African Unity and a number of Western countries. Help was being received from Tunisia, Ghana, Egypt and Zambia, while the Congo was supplying logistical support and troops to recruit members in Angola. Roberto had established a Revolutionary Government of Angola in Exile (GRAE) in 1961.[1]

By 1967, it was estimated that the fighting had upset life in northern Angola enough to account for a total of 700,000 refugees, of whom,

---

[1] All this information comes from local Portuguese military intelligence.

the Portuguese claimed, 500,000 had returned. There were still 250,000 in the Congo. Two-fifths of the Portuguese army was composed of Angolans, of whom nine-tenths were black. There were dozens of black officers and hundreds of black sergeants. It was stated that since 1961, military deaths had totalled 600-700, with twice as many civilians, mostly Africans. The number of prisoners in 1967 was 2,000, half of them at São Nicolau. The policy was to reclaim captured guerrillas and re-incorporate them into the national life as quickly as possible.[1]

A recent *Sunday Telegraph* investigation by its 'Close-up' team[2] reported that seventeen Africans had been killed and thirty wounded in a guerrilla attack on a group of labourers cutting wood fuel for the Benguela Railway. President Mobutu of the Congo was reported to have been angered by the attack, for the Congo relies on the Benguela Railway to export Katangese copper. The Organization for African Unity in Addis Ababa, publicly congratulated the raiders, but a senior official told the 'Close-up' team that whoever had ordered the attack 'was an ass'. There are increasing signs that some African leaders are privately becoming restive about all guerrilla activities launched from their territories. For while their ideals dictate antipathy to the white-ruled 'southern third', their economic needs still force them to some degree to 'look south'.

Reactions to the Angola crisis in Britain and the U.S. were overwhelmingly hostile to Portugal. It was, after all, the age of decolonization and Salazar's dogged refusal to follow the trends created by Britain, France, Belgium and Holland was badly received. Newspaper

---

[1] Important corroboration of this comes from the Catholic Archbishop Alves de Pinho, a man much respected for his denunciations of violence by white or black of either side and for his spirited defence of Mgr Neves. In a statement issued in Rome, on 21 November 1962, during the first session of the Vatican Council, the archbishop confirmed that the Portuguese army had put a stop to civilian reprisals in the Angola trouble spots, and was trying to win the confidence of Africans who had panicked and taken refuge in the forests or crossed the frontier. 'Before coming to the Council,' he said, 'I was able to see, during my last pastoral visit to the regions where there had been disturbances, that the people were little by little resuming normal life on returning to the villages,' where, he said, they were 'received with benevolence and assisted by the civil and military authorities.' Archbishop Alves de Pinho and his fellow bishops had also denounced white Portuguese who had levelled indiscriminate 'vile rumours' against the African priests.

[2] *Sunday Telegraph*, 11 May 1969.

articles proliferated with details about the Angolan labour system and accounts of the savagery with which the Portuguese were alleged to have put the uprising down.[1] There was a basis of truth in them all, but some seemed to the present writer to be overstating their case. A brief visit to Angola in the summer of 1961 had been enough to suggest that there was another side to the coin, and that the truth of the matter was complex. The controversies of those days were heated, but a degree of coolness and light was to come in the following year, when the International Labour Office published its Official Bulletin in April 1962, and devoted Supplement II to a 'Report of the Commission appointed under Article 26 of the Constitution of the International Labour Organization to examine the complaint filed by the Government of Ghana concerning the observance by the Government of Portugal of the Abolition of Forced Labour Convention, 1957 (No. 105)'.[2]

This came about because, on 25 February 1961, Ghana had filed a complaint with the ILO to the effect that Portugal had not secured, in Mozambique, Angola and Portuguese Guinea, the effective observance of the Convention, which both Portugal and Ghana had ratified. This Convention outlawed all forms of forced or compulsory labour, either as a means of political coercion or education, or as punishment for holding or expressing views opposed to the established system of the country concerned. Such labour, moreover, was not to be used for economic development, discipline, punishment for strike action, or as means of racial or other discrimination.[3] The ILO accordingly appointed a Commission to investigate and report. The members were Mr Paul Ruegger (Switzerland), Chairman of the ILO Committee on Forced Labour, Mr Enrique Armand-Ugon (Uruguay), a former President of his country's High Court of Justice, and Mr Isaac Forster (Senegal), First President of his country's Supreme Court. The Commission held sessions in Geneva and also during visits to Angola and Mozambique. By way of witnesses, Ghana pro-

---

[1] Mr William Stanton, already quoted, wrote to *The Times*, a letter published on 4 July 1961, which said that Africans in Damba had asked him to protect them against the guerrillas whom they described as 'the bad men who are killing us'. He added: 'Press and radio raise their voices in fury when an African is bayoneted by a Portuguese soldier. But when Africans cut the hands and feet off a Portuguese child, pluck out her eyes and stick her mother's head on a pole, no one says a word.'

[2] International Labour Office: Official Bulletin, vol. XLV, no. 2, Supplement II, April 1962, Geneva.

[3] *Ibid.*, p. 2.

duced in Geneva Mr Dias Martins, an Angolan; Mr Basil Davidson, the well-known writer on African Affairs; and four Baptist ministers, the Rev. Eric Blakebrough, Max Hancock, Clifford J. Parsons and William D. Grenfell. Portugal produced the witnesses whom the Commission asked to hear (but did not avail herself of the opportunity to call witnesses of her own choosing). Those whose evidence was heard included government officials and members of firms employing labour in Portuguese Africa. During the African tour, the Commission was able to talk to many African workers. Other witnesses heard in Geneva included a representative of the South African mines which recruit labour in Mozambique, and two Angolan students who appeared at the request of the Anti-Slavery Society. The United Arab Republic also made representations. The Galvão Report was referred to, especially regarding the allegation that government officials in Angola acted as recruiting and distributing agents for labour on behalf of private employers, who wrote to the Department of Native Affairs for a supply of workers, and who cared little if the workers fell sick or died, as they could easily obtain others. Various other works were also consulted. The Commission, however, noted that the Galvão Report dealt with facts prior to 1949, and stated that it could not take account of allegations concerning the situation long before 23 November 1960.

The Commission felt that its work was not hindered by linguistic difficulties. Its members were able in many instances to talk to workers in the absence of management and the Portuguese authorities. When a worker did not speak Portuguese, they were normally able to choose another worker to interpret, and exceptionally made use of local Portuguese interpreters. The greater part of the visit, in fact, was devoted to this end, and the Commission, which decided for itself where it would go in the undertaking visited, would stop without prior warning to talk to groups of workers as it encountered them. The overall itinerary was chosen by the Commission itself.[1] Both in Angola and Mozambique the Commission

> asked workers whether they had been subjected to corporal punishment. All the workers stated that they had never been beaten by their employer; only one worker stated that he had sometimes been struck by an employer for whom he had worked previously and whose employment he had left long ago. Workers indicated

[1] ILO, *op. cit.*, ss. 79-82, pp. 29-30; s. 58, pp. 22-3.

that disciplinary penalties took the form of a loss of a part of their wages, for example, in the case of unjustified absence. . . . The cotton growers questioned by the Commission in Angola and Mozambique stated that they had never been beaten to make them grow cotton.[1]

The Portuguese authorities fully co-operated to enable the Commission to secure the information it required.[2] It was

> favourably impressed by the degree of freedom exercised by a very large majority of those with whom it came into contact in both Angola and Mozambique (government officials, employers and workers alike, and Africans no less than Europeans) in expressing their views to it without constraint or inhibition; it has noted in its report the few exceptions which it feels it necessary to make to this generalization.[3]

The report found that far-reaching changes had occurred in Portuguese policy, legislation and practice in connection with the ratification, on 26 June 1956, and 23 November 1959, respectively, of the Forced Labour Convention, 1930 and the Abolition of Forced Labour Convention, 1957. The report added:

> The Commission is fully satisfied of the *bona fides* of these changes of policy, legislation and practice, and rejects as entirely without foundation the suggestion made in support of the complaint that 'Portugal only ratified the Convention as a cover to continue her ruthless labour policies'.[4]

The Commission was not satisfied that all of the obligations under the 1957 Convention had been implemented in full from the date when the Convention came into force for Portugal (23 November 1960). This had to some extent been remedied since Ghana had filed her complaint, but further steps were necessary. On the positive side, and since November 1960, a number of measures had been enacted which, in law and practice, represented substantial changes. The general effect had been

> to provide new administrative machinery for the enforcement of labour legislation, to abolish the previous special status of natives,

---

[1] *Ibid.*, ss. 660-3, p. 220.
[2] *Ibid.*, s. 708, p. 229.
[3] *Ibid.*, s. 718, p. 232.
[4] *Ibid.*, s. 725(4), p. 234.

to modify or abolish arrangements concerning the cultivation of cotton, rice and castor-oil which had been alleged to involve an element or danger of forced labour, and to terminate systems of recruitment of workers through the administrative authorities which had continued to exist in certain cases after 23 November 1960.[1]

The Commission now urged the formal repeal of some of the legislation of the past which gave scope for forced labour and still remained on the statute book, including provisions regarding the moral obligation to work contained in the Native Labour Code of 1928.[2]

Citing the economic importance of the Benguela Railway, which it described as one of the world's great engineering achievements, the Commission wholly and forcefully exonerated the company from the charge of recourse to forced labour, and was fully satisfied that no recruited labour was now employed, though it had been until recent years, notably for work in sparsely populated areas. The Diamond Mining Company had continued to recruit labour through government officials and tribal chiefs in a manner liable to constitute forced labour, but the practice had been changed by orders of the governor-general and the governor of the Lunda district in 1961. Workers, however, came forward spontaneously to work in the diamond sorting centres, despite strict security conditions, because of the favourable remuneration. They were well fed, housed, and were cheerful. They were released before the end of their period of service if they asked for it.[3] Publicly owned railways and ports in Angola (i.e. not including the Benguela Railway) had continued to recruit through administrative channels and the chiefs after November 1960, and all unskilled labour in the ports of Luanda and Lobito and on the Luanda railroad had been recruited in this way. They remained in this employment contrary to their wishes. Again, instructions had been issued to bring this to an end, and the Commission called on the government to ensure their enforcement. Publicly owned railways and ports in Mozambique, on the other hand, were clear of such charges, and their conditions of employment and social services were 'in certain respects exemplary'. The Commission also cleared light industry and commerce in both countries of all

[1] ILO, *op. cit.*, ss. 726-31, pp. 234-6.
[2] *Ibid.*, ss. 729-36, pp. 236-7.
[3] *Ibid.*, ss. 737-40, pp. 237-8.

suspicion of forced labour. It pointed out that the difference between publicly owned railways and ports in the two countries was that in Angola, where objectionable forms of recruitment had been deemed necessary, the workers concerned were earning half the wages of their counterparts in private industry, whereas in Mozambique, where the wages of the employees concerned were as good as they were in other industrial sectors, there was no such recruitment.[1] The Commission also stated that recruitment of labour in Mozambique for South Africa was based on the economic attractiveness of employment in South Africa, together with the social status it conferred. It involved no element of compulsion under Portuguese jurisdiction. The operations of the Witwatersrand Native Labour Association were both efficient and humane. The Commission, however, thought that negotiations should be opened to alter the worker's liability, while in South Africa, to penal sanctions for breach of contract.[2]

The Commission was satisfied that labour had not been recruited for São Tomé and Principe for a decade or more. Nor, in general, was plantation labour in Angola and Mozambique recruited in a manner inconsistent with the 1957 Convention. The Commission had visited large European plantations growing coffee, sugar, coconuts, cotton, sisal and tea. The only one it criticized was the Cassaquel sugar plantation, whose management seemed concerned to display its technical processes and take credit for its social services rather than help the Commission investigate recruitment methods. The management had been less than frank, though the Portuguese liaison officer, who had tried to help the Commission in every way, tried to make the management understand the nature of the inquiry and the Portuguese government's wish that every facility should be extended. The Commission was unable to form a conclusion and urged the government to investigate Cassaquel thoroughly.[3] The Commission found that some low-paid workers were liable to tax amounting to more than a month's wages in the year, and some workers had spoken of the need to work in order to pay their taxes.[4]

---

[1] *Ibid.*, ss. 741-3, p. 238; ss. 741-3, p. 238; s. 764, p. 243.
[2] *Ibid.*, ss. 745-6, pp. 238-9.
[3] *Ibid.*, ss. 747-9, p. 240.
[4] Many Africans who have their own smallholdings and earn part of their living from their produce, supplement their earnings by working on a plantation for part of the year.

The government's attention was drawn to an ILO recommendation that this type of indirect way of urging workers to seek wage-earning employment should be avoided.[1]

Expressing satisfaction at Portugal's ratification of the Labour Inspection Convention, 1947, and describing it as a major step, the Commission offered detailed recommendations as to how the new inspectorate should work. It strongly endorsed the view of the Director of Native Affairs in Mozambique, 'whose evidence was outstanding for its comprehensiveness, precision and frankness, that the extent to which employers have difficulty in securing labour depends largely on the conditions of employment which they offer, and their general reputation for reliability, fairness and humanity'.[2]

While recognizing the enlightened and progressive personnel policy of some of the companies, the Commission pointed out that there could be no guarantee that grievance procedures would operate effectively or cases of forced labour brought to book unless there were 'some form of effective trade union organization embracing workers of all races and different grades'. The African trade unions were run on similar lines to their counterparts in Portugal itself, and, while there is no element of racial discrimination in Portuguese trade union law, the Commission felt that 'the existing trade unions do not in fact effectively represent the African worker'. This, however, was a matter for a separate inquiry.[3] In its concluding observations, the Commission spoke of 'the policy of abolishing forced labour to which the [Portuguese] government is so completely committed, and in the implementation of which it has already made such substantial progress'. But this, it added, could not be made fully effective 'in a context of social and cultural backwardness in which for many people, freedom and compulsion are equally impalpable and it is very difficult for the government to know much of what happens in the minds of those most directly affected by the measures which it takes'. The Commission was thinking here of a complex of economic, social and cultural pressures which result in people doing what they are told to do simply because they are so told. The report went on:

> Their lives are a series of conditioned reflexes which are less than human. It becomes at times impossible to say whether their labour

[1] ILO, *op. cit.*, s. 751, p. 240.
[2] *Ibid.*, s. 764, p. 243.
[3] *Ibid.*, ss. 767-9, pp. 244-5.

is the result of a compulsion which makes it technically forced
labour because they are so incapable of any choice or of the exercise
of any independent judgment that compulsion is unnecessary.
An order is an order; a suggestion is indistinguishable from an
order. . . .

The Commission did not say that this situation was universal in
Portuguese Africa, but it was satisfied that it did represent the actual
state of affairs 'in certain places, and particularly at the Cassaquel
sugar plantations'. In such places the workers were at 'so backward
a stage of development that freedom and economic opportunity
belong to a world so wholly beyond their grasp that the question
whether the labour exacted from them is forced labour becomes
virtually meaningless'. The Commission had been impressed 'by
the many signs of constructive economic and social development in
both Angola and Mozambique, but a great intensification of measures
of economic and social advancement is necessary to eliminate this
element in the problem of the effective abolition of forced labour'.
Portugal was 'rightly proud of the absence of any racial discrimination
in her territories', but there were as yet few Africans in positions of
responsibility, and the absence of trained African elements in the
administration made it difficult, especially because of the linguistic
difficulty, for the government to know what really takes place, for
instance, between the chief and his villagers. This was of great
importance because, where workers were recruited for employment
at some distance from their homes, the structure of African society
made some consultation of and co-operation with the local chiefs
indispensable:

A substantial and rapid advance in the training of African cadres
in both government and economic life would appear to be entirely
consistent with Portuguese policy as it has been explained to the
Commission and . . . would afford the best possible guarantee that
the policy of the government to make the abolition of forced labour
fully effective is not frustrated by a cultural and social background
which excludes either real knowledge or proper control.[1]

This report, by men of the highest qualifications, seems to the
present writer to put its finger on the heart of the matter. In his own

[1] *Ibid.*, ss. 771-7, pp. 245-7.

visits he has been impressed by the extent and efficiency, for instance, of the social provisions – in housing, dispensaries, schooling, domestic training services, infant care and the like – made by some of the companies, in Angola and Mozambique, for their workers. Industry is responsible for some outstanding medical services, and the Diamond Mining Company's schools and hospitals, for instance, cater for a population of about 90,000, many of whom are in no way, strictly speaking, the company's concern. Each plantation is bound by law to have its own small hospital now, and one has seen at first hand that the quality of the treatment is not stinted. All the visitor has to do is to examine the drugs cupboard and records which are strictly kept and open to frequent inspection. The Benguela Railway's schools, community centres, maternity clinics and nursery schools are models of their kind. The Institutes of Labour have to inspect all labour contracts today, to ensure that old practices do not creep in despite the new laws. But, while the worker's material conditions have improved out of recognition, it remains true that in human terms he remains immature, not because of a lack of capacity, but because, in the main, he does not as yet enjoy a liberal education or play a major role in national decision. The note of paternalism and tutelage is still strongly marked, and the fact that most of the Africans do not support the nationalists owes as much to their lack of enlightenment as to any contentment they feel. This position, however, is far from stagnant, and the African's opportunities are increasing.

The abuses of the old contract system stemmed from the fact that arrangements were made between employers and native chiefs, often through administrative officials, for a bulk supply of labour. Nowadays, every contract is personal, between the employer and the employee. Moreover, no written contract is valid until it has been passed by the Labour Department. The new labour laws and the Labour Department itself are among the toughest in the Portuguese world. Most Angolan workers have a contract, but most of them are *not* contract workers in the sense that they work for a set contract period outside their normal home territory. Urban development in Angola is such that in the main centres supply keeps up with demand, or the demand for labour tailors itself to whatever supply is available. The same is not true in Mozambique, where the railway and port authorities have to bring in additional labour. The Angolan mines, with their relatively high wage levels, can usually count on the workers coming to them unasked. The only areas in that country showing a labour shortage are the prosperous coffee-growing regions. Here the local Africans are usually small planters in their own right. So the big plantations have to seek their labour force elsewhere, usually in the Bailundo area, where the population density is highest. The African workers they employ can quite comfortably live on their own subsistence farming, but choose to earn more money, or, as we have seen, have to earn more to pay their taxes, by serving for part of the year on the big plantation.

The rural worker's position today does not substantially differ as between Angola and Mozambique, so Angola may be chosen for special treatment, if only because of the many specific complaints levelled against the Angolan system at the time of the crisis eight years ago. The Labour Statute of Angola is, in many respects, a model workers' charter. It goes into minute detail about labour contracts, family subsidies, overtime, paid holidays (extended by law to all workers), welfare, compensation, accidents, pensions and the penalties to be imposed on employers for infringements.[1] What makes all the difference to this measure and the detailed regulations passed every year is that now the inspectorate system has real teeth, and, if anyone is scared in Angola today, it is the defaulting employer. The Institute of Labour breathes down the companies' necks, in town and on plantation alike, and one only has to go to Luanda to hear the less conscientious managements squeal. Rural workers are now recruited by the companies themselves under strict government control, not in the sense that officials act any more as go-betweens, but simply in the sense that officials are posted to see that the rules are kept. Regulations are now so tight and detailed that employers commit an offence if workers are transported to plantations away from home even in trucks with seats. They may only travel in motor coaches. If this sounds a little obvious, it has only to be remembered that not long ago the recruited worker travelled in open trucks, exposed to the weather and cruelly jolted for hours.

The plantation worker who takes a job away from home will agree to work for six, nine or twelve months as he wishes, with food and housing found. If he brings his family, the employer must send the children to school. According to the worker's preference, his contract may provide for his wages to be paid partly to himself, partly to his

[1] Approved by Legislative Diploma No. 2827, 5 June 1967.

family at home, and partly in a lump sum when the contract is ful-filled. Food, clothing, lodging, health and education services have to be provided over and above the monetary wage. Minimum cash wages in Angola for rural workers, since 1966, are 17.5 escudos a day (about £1. 2s. a week), but the tax on it amounts to no more than £3. 10s. a year and the worker need spend none of his money while he is employed. Where rural workers are employed away from home, however, most employers pay substantially more than the minimum.

Most plantation owners also offer incentive payments for extra work, but only the most industrious take advantage of this. Hours are fixed by law at a maximum eight per day, with fines of up to 5,000 escudos for employers who try to force a harder pace. Most contracts assure the worker of a 21-day month. Even the basic minimum, so low by Western standards, is normal for Africa, and, when the 'fringe' benefits are added, compares very favourably with other African countries. Rural wage statistics are notoriously hard to obtain, above all in comparative international terms, but, taking into account all that the Angolan rural worker now receives, his rewards are certainly among the highest in the continent, bar Rhodesia and the Republic of South Africa. Recruiting, incidentally, was a harsh business in the days when the African was not attracted to employ-ment, but today, with more sophisticated purchases within his reach, his labour is not hard to secure. If the rural African's status symbols in Angola are the transistor radio and the bicycle (sometimes the motor-cycle), he can hardly be described as affluent; but he is not the semi-slave of previous years.

The labour situation in Angola was analysed in 1963, in a report for foreign companies by an English business consultant in Luanda, Mr Michael Chapman.[1] In an up-dated version (1967) he estimated that 75,000 workers had written contracts of employment, but he was satisfied that, even where the contract was verbal, inspection was tough enough to ensure that the same conditions obtained. The total number of employees in industry and agriculture was about 450,000, most of them, of course, in agriculture. Given a million or so family units, this meant that there were 600,000 self-employed farmers or herders, not unlike the European peasant, but mostly enjoying a somewhat lower standard of living. Some produced no more than

[1] Michael Chapman, *The Role of Labour in the Angolan Economy*, Angola Consultantes Lda., Luanda, 1963.

enough for their family needs, others produced for sale in the rural markets, while at the top end of the scale there were Africans owning up to 10,000 head of cattle, or cotton or coffee plantations employing labour. In the northern resettlement villages, thousands who had fled into the bush to escape the terror (and some who had returned from the rebel side to government protection) were being encouraged to settle and plant crops. Not untypical of the most successful of these villagers was a man who in one year sold 100 bags of coffee and made well over £350. This type of farmer, on the eve of Angola's industrial explosion, was the country's economic backbone.[1]

Plantations are compelled by law to provide housing consistent with certain minimum standards; required amounts of clothing including shoes, six shirts, four pairs of shorts, and a short coat where it is cold at night. Minimum food allowances are prescribed, and any company employing more than ten persons must provide medical care ranging from a first-aid expert to full-scale hospital facilities, according to the company's size. Smaller companies are bound to arrange comprehensive medical insurance. If workers muster more than twenty children among them, and if there is no school within five miles, the employer must provide both school and teacher, together with minimum facilities for recreation. Most areas have permanent labour inspectors now, and the worker can take his grievances to Labour Courts without cost to himself. Industrial firms often run social welfare programmes far and away beyond the legal minimum. The Benguela Railway Company assigns one-eighth of its annual budget to social welfare, excluding its superannuation benefits. It runs nine social centres like that at São Miguel which

---

[1] A United Nations committee reported in 1968 that the Angolan government was trying, without much success, to encourage the extension of the market system and the trading of a wider range of products, possibly because the fixed market prices were too low. An African cotton grower trading in rural markets on average earned 4,200 escudos a year (126 U.S. dollars). But there was evidence that many Africans preferred growing cash crops because it gave them more freedom. Thus, in areas where Africans could engage in this type of farming, it was reported that wage rates had gone up. (This section of the report seems to have been working on the basis of the position in 1966, and more recent inquiries in Angola reveal that the appeal of the market economy is catching on in African circles. This is in part evidenced by the proliferation of new branches of the banks in rural areas.)

(Cf. October 1968 Report of the Special Committee on the situation with regard to the implementation of the Declaration on the Granting of Independence to Colonial Countries and Peoples; Chapter VIII; pp. 64-5.)

houses 381 families, with bathing and laundry facilities. There is a first-aid station and consulting clinic where drugs and treatment are free. The centre also has a kindergarten, primary school, swimming pool, advisory service, dressmaking school for adult women, and a visiting team to advise families on hygiene, household management, and to give pre- and post-natal treatment. The houses all have at least three rooms, and there are shops and canteens where workers can buy what they need at cost plus 5 per cent. Post-primary school-children go to one of the company's apprentice schools, and there is a high-school and university scholarship scheme. The Diamond Mining Company employs twenty-three doctors and a total medical staff of 1,000, with a trained nurse for every 100 persons in its area. The *Companhia Mineira de Lobito*, with a labour force of 5,000, has a large hospital in Nova Lisboa, with an aircraft for emergency cases, and another in a less active area which was erected for the benefit of the whole of the local population. The CADA (coffee and palm oil) company employs 11,000 workers and runs fifteen elementary and primary schools, industrial and agricultural apprentice schools, one of the country's finest housing schemes, co-operative retail stores and a group of five hospitals with an additional fourteen first-aid posts.

Generally, the right to paid holidays, family subsidies, social security, rigid protection of minors, suppression of sex discrimination and the abolition of 'punishment' are established facts for all workers. Only about 10 per cent of the labour force in Angola is unionized, however, and the syndicates cater mostly for the lower ranks of the administration, workers in communications, the ports, and state-owned railways and road-building projects. They are, however, growing in importance and strength, and assuming more and more the responsibility for negotiating labour contracts. Industrial wages in Portuguese Africa, though, once again, hard to compare with other countries for lack of international data, are reckoned to be among the highest in Africa outside Rhodesia and the South African Republic. In 1965, the average industrial wage in Angola was estimated at 3,489 escudos (about £43. 10s. a month at the time). A selection of monthly wage rates in Luanda showed:[1]

---

[1] Instituto de Trabalho, Previdência e Acção Social de Angola: *Estatística Comparativa dos Salarios.*

Workers	*Escudos (then* 80 *to the* £)
Senior office staffs	5,028
Agriculture and fishery processing	4,006
Hotels	1,372
Civil engineering	2,919
Mining	7,140
Chemicals, hospitals	4,025
Paint	2,695
Metal industries	2,785
Textiles	3,578
Electricians	3,035
Theatre and cinema	2,132

These figures plainly relate to skilled grades and are the highest in Angola, though even unskilled workers in the enclave of Cabinda can earn twice as much as their counterparts elsewhere. The average overall figure for industrial wages in Angola is probably £3 a week, as good as most African countries, better than some. Add to this the range of social security and 'fringe' benefits prescribed by law or superimposed by the bigger firms, and the worker's standards in Angola are among the highest in Africa. It remains true, of course, that the vast majority of the workers are engaged in agriculture. But the situation today compares well with 1958 when the *Anuário Estatístico de Angola* showed that an African carpenter earned £21. 2s. 6d. against £39 for his European counterpart, and an African electrician earned £12. 15s. 6d. while a European commanded £38. 10s. The labour inspectorate now strictly enforces regulations compelling equal pay for all races.

Developments in the labour field in Mozambique have roughly paralleled those in Angola. The ILO Report of 1962 said nothing to suggest racial discrimination in either country's wage rates, or that the rates were abnormally low. It was not concerned with wages as such, but it refers to them here and there, and could hardly have disregarded wholesale exploitation or inequalities if it had found them.

In his recently published book[1] the late Dr Eduardo Mondlane, leader of the Mozambican nationalist movement FRELIMO,[2] outlines the major weaknesses in Mozambican society and bitterly attacks

---

[1] Mondlane, pp. 43-4.
[2] Frente de Libertação de Moçambique.

the whole of the Portuguese system. He complains that, although the *Estatuto dos Indígenas* of 1961 gave all races full Portuguese citizenship, distinctions continued to be made in practice. Official control of Africans was ensured by making them carry a *Cartão de identidade* bearing the name of the province and the man's place of residence. Such details were omitted from the *Bilhete de identidade* carried by those who were formerly known as non-indigenous citizens. Though the 1961 crop of legislation theoretically gave everyone more representation in the provincial legislature and in elections to the National Assembly in Lisbon, what happened in practice was different. Article XLV (s. 11) of the New Overseas Organic Law, for instance, provides that 'transitorily, in regions where the economic and social development deemed necessary has not been reached', municipalities may be replaced by administrative districts, except where the creation of 'parishes' proves possible. In other words, the administration could carry on much the same as before, while singling out the whites for special treatment in parishes. In the 1964 elections, Mondlane claims, there were only 93,079 voters out of a population of 6,592,994. Yet the total of non-indigenous people, that is, whites and the former *assimilados*, alone amounted to 163,149. Hence the limited franchise extended to very few Africans in practice.[1] Provincial decrees remained liable to cancellation by the Overseas Ministry in Lisbon, where the province's general economic policy was also drawn up.

Mondlane also describes the educational system which runs on similar lines to Angola's. For Africans, he says, there is the *ensino de adaptaçao* (three grades for teaching the three Rs and the Portuguese language), followed by three years' primary schooling, the last year being a preparation for admission to the secondary level (*liceal*).[2] Europeans and *assimilados* have traditionally had a different system and different schools: a five-year primary course followed by a secondary course of seven years, the highest grade being a preparation for university. Many Africans completed the pre-primary course only between the ages of twelve and fourteen, whereas the maximum age for entry to primary school was thirteen. Thus, many Africans stood no chance at all of anything but the most rudimentary schooling. In 1959, of 392,796 pre-primary pupils, only 6,928 started in primary school. In 1963, there were three state and three private secondary

[1] Many Africans entitled to vote fail to register because of political 'unawareness' and bureaucratic procedures.
[2] This system was abolished in 1964.

schools in Mozambique, and only 6 per cent of the 3,050 pupils were black. The Catholic missions, entrusted with education of the Africans, had no secondary schools at all. All the emphasis in education was on Portuguese language, history and culture, with no concern for African traditions.[1] As for the missions, there were, in 1959, 800,000 Catholics in Mozambique, catered for in 100 missions by 240 priests, only three of whom were Africans. In economic terms, Mondlane takes the view that Portugal gains from her association with Angola, but not from that with Mozambique.

Turning to the problems of the cotton-growers, he asserts that in the mid-1950s half-a-million people in Mozambique were involved in the growing of cotton, and were producing 140,000 tons a year, and that the textile industry in Portugal took 82 per cent of its raw materials from the overseas provinces. In 1930, forced cotton-growing was ensured by an instruction of the Cotton Export Board, and the subordination of the small African cotton-grower to the Portuguese monopolists had been described in 1958 by Professor Marvin Harris. Twelve Portuguese companies held monopolistic concession rights over cotton production in various parts of the country. Africans within such areas were allotted cotton acreage by the administration and ordered to plant, cultivate and harvest. They then sold the raw cotton to their local concession company at prices fixed by the government far below international levels. In 1956, the cotton-sellers received an average of 11.17 dollars per person as their family's reward for an entire year's work, says Harris.[2] Though the system was changed in 1961, Mondlane quotes examples to show that compulsion continued in practice, and involved brutality, chaining, and even deportation.

[1] The Missionary Agreement signed between Portugal and the Holy See in 1941, provides that, in missionary schools for natives, tuition in the Portuguese language is obligatory, except that vernacular languages can be used in the teaching of the Catholic religion. When there are not enough Portuguese missionaries, the Church may call on foreign personnel (but only then, it seems). The state does not pay salaries to missionaries, but, by the Missionary Statute, also passed in 1941, supports the missionary Church with substantial subsidies. Cf. Decree-Law No. 31,207, which is more explicit than the Agreement with Rome and provides that in principle missionary staff shall be of Portuguese nationality. Foreign Catholic missionaries must renounce the laws and courts of their country of origin and declare that they submit to those of Portugal. Article 68 of the Statute also provides that missionary education will be 'nationalist' in character. This means that it will be directed to building the native into the integrating, Portuguese concept of the nation.

[2] Ibid., pp. 83-7; Marvin Harris, op. cit.

The ILO Report already quoted tells us that the concessionary system relating to cotton and rice growing was abolished in May and August 1961, and a free system substituted. New supervisory arrangements had been set up to protect the small grower and defend his prices, and substantial changes had been effected.[1] The present writer, during his 1963 visit to Mozambique, found that the abuses, especially those relating to price, had not all been reformed. Bishop de Resende had complained about this in 1962 to Dr Adriano Moreira, while the latter was still Overseas Minister. By the time this writer returned to Mozambique in 1967, the situation seemed to be well under control and reasonable prices guaranteed. It is hard to say whether the cruel practices cited by Dr Mondlane were extensive, or whether, by the mid-1960s they were simply the work of an evil residue. It is, however, perfectly true that Portuguese legislation has always had a way of being among the most humane in the world, yet slow to effect concrete historical changes.

By the beginning of the present decade, some of the best and most progressive policies were exemplified by the agricultural co-operatives in Portuguese Africa, but in 1960, Mondlane complains, they accounted in Mozambique for only 12,000 farmers, or one-twentieth of 1 per cent of the population. Meanwhile, discontent had been breaking out in dock strikes in 1947, which resulted in strikers being deported to São Tomé, and in 1956, when forty-nine people were killed. Mondlane also refers to an incident in 1960, when 500 people were shot down, in a demonstration at Mueda, by Portuguese troops, an incident which 'though passing unnoticed by the rest of the world, acted as a catalyst on the region'.[2] In the 1940s, a movement of former secondary school pupils had been formed (NESAM) and a new generation of insurgents arose. They inspired an artistic movement which in Mozambique was represented by the painters Malangatana and Craveirinha, the short-story writer Luis Bernardo Honwana, and the poets Craveirinha (uncle of the painter of the same name) and Noemia de Sousa. Three movements among exiled Mozambicans emerged in Salisbury, Rhodesia; Malawi; and Kenya and Tanganyika (as it then was). Then in 1963, the FRELIMO movement itself was created.

Eduardo Mondlane was born in the south of Mozambique in 1920 of African parentage. He was educated by Protestant missionaries

[1] ILO, *op. cit.*, s. 242, p. 94; s. 727, p. 235; s. 750, p. 240.
[2] Mondlane, *op. cit.*, pp. 116-18.

and later went to a North Transvaal high school. He studied at Witwatersrand University and then, with the help of an American scholarship, in Lisbon. Finally, he secured a number of degrees in the United States, including an M.A. and Ph.D. in sociology. After a research studentship at Harvard, he joined the U.N. Department of Trusteeship, returning to Mozambique in 1961. His achievement in the next two years was to integrate various insurgent forces which, under his tutelage, came together in a congress in Tanganyika, as it then was, in 1962. Military operations began in 1963. FRELIMO's headquarters were established in Dar-es-Salaam, and a number of camps set up in South Tanganyika, some of them directly under Tanganyikan control, the rest run independently by FRELIMO itself. These are the bases for training and launching the guerrilla operations against Mozambique. Although he accepted aid from the Communist bloc, and FRELIMO's arms came from Russia, China and Czechoslovakia, Mondlane was not a Communist and he commanded considerable respect and support in the West, financial aid coming from bodies as respectable as the Rockefeller Foundation and the World Council of Churches. FRELIMO also enjoyed the support of the Organization of African Unity. Mondlane's chief collaborators were Uria Simango, a former Protestant pastor, a man of mixed blood, later trained in Peking; Marcelino dos Santos, a Communist, trained by the Party in Europe and a former student of Lisbon University, also of mixed blood; and Lazaro Kavandame, FRELIMO's link with the Dutch Catholics in the East of Mozambique, and the Catholic and Anglican missions in the West. Shortly after Mondlane's death early in 1969, Kavandame surrendered to the Portuguese and urged his supporters to follow him.

FRELIMO receives much more overt support from the Catholic foreign missions than any other Portuguese African rebel movement. This is partly because, although the guerrillas have killed many Africans, this particular movement has worked largely on conventional military lines without wholesale terrorism. Mondlane has been seen as a man of high culture and vision, leading a legitimate nationalist assault on a power denying the African his human rights. The Anglican and Swiss Protestant missions take much the same view. On the Catholic side, a number of Belgian White Fathers have been expelled from Mozambique by the Portuguese authorities for direct involvement with FRELIMO. One priest, whom the author met in London after his expulsion, had been in correspondence with

Dar-es-Salaam and smuggling Africans there from Mozambique to ensure a secondary education for them. He was convinced that the Portuguese, though fast developing primary and technical schools, were deliberately holding back on higher education for fear that a new generation of educated Africans would arise too quickly, on the pattern of other African countries, become malcontent, and prove an easy prey to insurgent recruiters. Many of the Catholic missionaries make it plain to the Portuguese that they feel their job is to help the African to independence, and not to educate him to become a Portuguese citizen. At first they generally show reluctance even to co-operate in the Portuguese social services, but in some cases, after some months' experience, enter into a grudging partnership with the authorities for the sake of the education and social welfare of their charges. Their complaint is that there is no clear programme of 'Africanization' in Mozambique, to which the Portuguese retort that the priests arrive with a generalized concept of the need to foster African independence, but without adequate knowledge of Portuguese Africa's special circumstances. With time, the Portuguese assert, some of the priests acquire a more mellow outlook. It is not government policy to get rid of them wholesale, and action is taken only where there is evidence of direct involvement with the nationalists.

By 1967, FRELIMO's training programme seemed to depend largely on Chinese instructors, while their arms were mostly Czech. They operated from ten camps in Tanzania, with Tanzanian government support, a little to the north of the Ruvuma River which divides Tanzania from Mozambique. Inside Mozambique, they were operating in the north-east Cabo Delgado district, working through the Maconde tribe which straddles the frontier; and in the western Niassa district, bordering on Lake Malawi and centred on Vila Cabral, mainly with the Nianja tribe. The Portuguese stated that the insurgents were boxed up in a 40 × 40 kilometre area in the east, and in a western area of 200 × 30 kilometres. The whole of the northern border (500 miles long) had to be guarded, however. The limitations on the FRELIMO thrust derived in part from the antagonism between the Maconde and the Macua, who account for half the population of Mozambique. Parallel movements were operating from Zambia: Jonas Savimbi's UNITA which strikes at Angola and COREMO, which had emerged as a rival to FRELIMO. Mondlane, in his book, asserts that by 1966, his movement was running 100 bush schools in Cabo Delgado, serving 10,000 pupils, and that by the end of 1967 another 2,000 pupils were being taught in Niassa. FRELIMO has frequently claimed that it has effectively occupied anything from a third to a quarter of Mozambique. In March 1968, however, *The Times* news team, after investigating the area, concluded that 5 per cent would be nearer the mark.[1] It found evidence that FRELIMO was running schools in the area, and it is clear that there was a FRELIMO 'presence' on Mozambican soil in the summer of 1968, when it held a congress there. Earlier that year, on the other hand, the British M.P., Mr Desmond Donnelly, visited the area and reported[2] that, in Vila Cabral, alleged to be FRELIMO's 'capital', he had walked about unescorted at night. Writing in *New Africa*,[3] Patrick Orr quoted the Anglican missionary at Messumba, Fr John Paul, to the effect that the Nianja had become disillusioned. Orr then referred to a phenomenon which was also witnessed by Donnelly, and has now been observed by a series of correspondents, visiting Ambassadors and British M.P.s. This was a series of fortified villages, visited early in 1967 by John Osman of the B.B.C.,[4] into which the local Africans, scattered and disrupted by the war, had been regrouped. At the time of Osman's visit there were 160,000 Africans in a ring of 140 villages, and a year later the numbers had doubled. These villages are overwhelmingly populated by Africans, who have actually been armed by the Portuguese and who, if they so wished, could at any time wipe out the handful of officials posted there. Donnelly found, wherever he went and especially in the new villages, that the easygoing manners of the Africans were equally characteristic of the Portuguese, and the two races enjoyed a relaxed relationship. If a majority of the Africans in the country had really sympathized with the nationalists, the Portuguese, in Donnelly's view, would not have stood a chance. Osman learned from missionary sources that many Africans who at first had gone over to FRELIMO were returning, and, already in the summer of 1967, when the author visited Mozambique, he was told that defectors were returning to Portuguese

[1] *The Times*, 11 March 1968.
[2] *Daily Telegraph* (colour supplement), 19 January 1968.
[3] November-December 1967.
[4] Despatch to B.B.C., London, dated 15 February 1967, and broadcast on B.B.C. 2 (television); see also United Nations: 'Report of the Special Committee on the situation with regard to the implementation of the Declaration on the granting of independence to colonial countries and peoples', 1968, pp. 100-6.

cover at the rate of hundreds a month. FRELIMO's continuing strength was estimated at something between 5,000 and 10,000.

Some of the villagers, in fact, were disillusioned FRELIMO nationalists, who had been enticed to the rebel side by promises of higher education and the like, but had returned when the promises did not materialize. Living and training conditions in the FRELIMO camps were hard, and the hearts of many recruits were not in the fighting. Some 80 per cent of the villagers were said to be getting an education, and the social and health services were impressive. On the general issue of African support for FRELIMO, it is significant that one-third of all the armed Portuguese forces in Mozambique are black. Despite the 60,000 troops required to guard the border regions, the size of the war may be discerned from the number of military deaths, which, between January 1964 and June 1967, totalled 226 on the Portuguese side, while the latter claim that several thousands of FRELIMO fighters have been killed.

Mondlane's book claims that, from the early days of FRELIMO activity, the PIDE made wholesale arrests, and resorted to torture and private execution. In 1966, a group of African intellectuals were given two-year sentences, including Malangatana, Craveirinha and Rui Nogár, while José Monteiro received five years plus security measures. About a dozen came to trial at this time, and some were acquitted by a local court which plainly disbelieved the police; but the Supreme Military Tribunal in Lisbon reversed the verdicts, and acquitted only one of the accused. There were a number of trials in 1967 of men accused of active involvement with FRELIMO. Two received sentences of eight and five years respectively, while twenty-eight others received sentences ranging from six months to three years. There have also been reports, admittedly unsubstantiated, that a number of African students who tried to leave the country were being held illegally as late as 1968. Early in that year, a group of Portuguese and foreign priests at Beira petitioned the bishops to use their influence in favour of foreign missionaries, Catholic and Protestant, who, the signatories claimed, were being harassed by the police.

The police act as an intelligence unit, and sometimes get killed in the process; the ordinary non-violent dissentient is left alone as a rule these days, and, as regards insurgent Africans, the emphasis now seems to be laid on reclamation rather than punishment, which, the police have come to see, only serves to foster fresh discontent. Their pictorial propaganda, disseminated in the bush, invites FRELIMO fighters to surrender their arms for payment at fixed prices. Those who surrender, as *The Times* news team suggested, are treated leniently and often go to resettlement villages. Those who are caught and jailed are often released before the end of their sentences and restored to village life. In August 1967, the author saw batches of petitions to the governor-general for early releases to be granted. They were signed by the chief of the PIDE on the basis of reports of individual prisoners' attitudes.

Dr Mondlane's visit to London in March 1968 was interrupted by reports of trouble within FRELIMO, and he flew back quickly to deal with it. It was well known that the movement had its internal rivalries, with the pro-China faction particularly restive. In July, Mondlane was re-elected president of FRELIMO at a congress inside Mozambique, but during that summer the FRELIMO headquarters in Dar-es-Salaam were raided, and, although the Tanzanian police made local arrests, nothing was proved. Finally, on 3 February 1969, Mondlane was killed by a time-bomb sent to him in a parcel of books. Whether the assassins were PIDE agents, who work effectively inside FRELIMO, or whether they were Mondlane's rivals may never be known. On the one hand, it would have been the height of folly for the Portuguese to create a martyr, one would think, and to displace a pro-Western leader open to civilized argument in favour of hardline Communists looking towards Peking. On the other hand, Simango, who succeeded Mondlane, was not of the same calibre, and this could have been foreseen. After Mondlane's death, Kavandame defected, and Simango has been replaced by the more dynamic, pro-Peking, Samora Machel, and expelled from Tanzania.

One does not have to agree with Mondlane's methods and policies to regret that Portugal failed to find a place for a man of his talent, energy and imagination. It is equally tragic that he could not have brought himself to work patiently within the Portuguese system as it began to adapt to realities. In an official post today, he could have done far more for his people than he stood much chance of doing through FRELIMO. He freely admitted that military success alone could be many years away, and it has to be asked: with the entire Portuguese infrastructure removed by his victory, what would he have put in its place? Many other questions arise. Did he, like Roberto's UPA in Angola, want the white man out of Mozambique? Or did he, like Andrade's MPLA, think in terms of independence from Portugal,

African majority rule, and a place for the compliant white man? Was he, indeed, a patriot or just a contender for power? Why was he at loggerheads with other Portuguese African nationalists? It may be too early to attempt answers to these questions, but there is no doubt about his organizing ability and his power of uniting diverse elements in his cause. He was far superior to his rivals, and, by comparison with him, a character like Delgado appears a poor joke. It may be said that, if Mozambique is moving forward today, it is partly because FRELIMO forced the authorities to action. There is a good deal of truth in this, though the initial impetus came from Angola in 1961. But what is left in the final analysis is a sorry story of waste: men of ability warring against each other at a time when Portugal needs their civilian talents as never before.

Mondlane argues, in his posthumously published Penguin book, that, while the educated African or mulatto may progress quite far in Portuguese society, there comes a point beyond which he may not pass. There is no doubt that similar convictions have contributed to the frustrations prompting other nationalist leaders. In Angola, half the civil servants or more are African. There is a black provincial secretary of education (whose rank is ministerial), a black director of finance, a black director of the judicial police, and a black head of customs. In Angola and Mozambique alike, there are plenty of African mayors and professional men, and there are Africans among the wealthiest men in both countries. This is even more true of men of mixed blood. Both groups are represented in the provincial assemblies, which are very far from being the rubber stamps they are often alleged to be. A governor-general without the backing and confidence of the local assembly would in practice find himself in trouble. But one does not as yet meet black bishops, for instance, though the percentage of Catholics in the Portuguese overseas provinces is higher than anywhere else in Africa,[1] and in other African countries African bishops abound. There are even four black cardinals. So in this respect Portuguese Africa lags behind, nor does one meet black ministers in Lisbon,[2] black generals, or black

---

[1] In Portuguese Africa there are 2,500,000 Catholics out of a population of 11,374,000; while in the whole of Africa the Catholic proportion is only 27 million out of 264 million. Thus the Portuguese provinces have nearly twice as many Catholics, proportionately, as the whole of the African continent.

[2] There are, however, a number of men of mixed blood in the highest ranks of the civil service.

heads of universities. African students in the homeland universities are increasing, and whereas a black face was uncommon in the streets of Lisbon several years ago, quite a lot may be seen today. The blockage of which Mondlane speaks, however, is certainly there and arises from many factors, including the lack of higher education, retarded in the past by metropolitan poverty; and there is the element of distrust fostered in the African whites by the nationalist wars on their own frontiers, coupled with the turmoil they have seen in the Congo, Rwanda and Burundi, the Sudan, and Nigeria. It is also true that the Portuguese freedom from racial prejudice is relative. Social barriers may be much less due to racial considerations than elsewhere, much more related to differences of wealth and education. But miscegenation usually takes the form of liaison rather than marriage. Working-class whites would not be unduly disturbed by a racially mixed marriage in the family, nor would some of the middle-class. But there are plenty who, while capable of accepting it, would be deterred at first, if only because of the practical problems it might yield. Given the ability to pay his way, no African is barred from any hotel or other public place, but, in overall terms of social standing, the African has not yet 'arrived'. The white man, too, remains sceptical of the African's ability to acquire the skills that will take him to the top in the foreseeable future. It is, however, common enough to see white labourers under African foremen, and even white illiterates receiving instruction from an African teacher. Education is now developing apace, and more and more of the younger men in official circles, at home and overseas, are coming to see the urgency of bringing the African peoples to an early fulfilment. A *Times* correspondent in Lourenço Marques wrote in 1966:

> The rebels have had difficulty in winning over the population, largely because of the economic and social reforms the Portuguese instituted after the 1961 uprising in Angola. These efforts have been helped by the relative lack of colour-consciousness among the Portuguese, and this has kept the war from becoming a racial conflict.[1]

There are sixty-eight distinct ethnic strains in Mozambique, most of them outside the war, but honest white men there will freely admit that the wars forced them to face reality. As one of them told the author: 'We ought to erect a monument to the *terroristas*.' What

[1] *The Times*, 21 November 1966.

matters is that the capacity for an improvement in the direction of racial equality is inherent in the Portuguese character, far more, in the author's view, than in other Western societies. But there is a race against time, and time is now very short.

Portuguese Guinea is an island-fringed enclave between Senegal and the Guinea of President Sekou Touré. It is difficult terrain, criss-crossed with rivers and liable in the rainy season to become a massive swamp. Its population of 600,000 live almost entirely on agriculture, and the Portuguese whites are mostly officials. This is not settler country, and it is surprising that the conscripted army from home stands up as well as it does to the gruelling, humid climate. The Portuguese lean heavily on the Moslems for support, notably tribes like the Mandinga and Fula, who account for 30 per cent of the population, while the remainder belong to various African cults. Visitors observe easy relationships in many areas between the whites and the Africans. Army officers teach in understaffed schools. Soldiers build houses and mosques. The temper of the population may to some extent be grasped from a comment made by President Sekou Touré at a Brazzaville Conference in 1966. Speaking of Portuguese Guinea, he remarked: 'If these people do not want to be liberated, we who are free and conscious have a duty to liberate them.' However, the distinguished writer on Africa, Basil Davidson, reported in 1967[1] a high degree of support and success for Amilcar Cabral's PAIGC, the African Independence Party of Guinea and Cape Verde, which had been waging war on the Portuguese since 1963.

Cabral was born of a Cape Verde father and a Mandigo mother at Bafata, in Portuguese Guinea. At Lisbon University he met Agostinho Neto and Mario Pinto de Andrade, and was a founder member of the MPLA. He returned to Bissau, capital of Portuguese Guinea, in 1956, and, after going underground, began to establish his movement. It called for several years' hard political preparation in the villages, but its military efforts over the past six years have presented the Portuguese with their most effective challenge to date. After an extensive tour of rebel-held territory, Davidson told us in November 1967,[2] that the Portuguese had no hold on four-fifths of the land frontiers

[1] *The Times*, 10 November 1967; see also Basil Davidson's Penguin Book (cf. Abbs).
[2] *Ibid.*

or half the coastlines. Although there were 33,000 Portuguese troops, aided by 3,000 African 'mercenaries', the rebel guerrillas, with strong peasant support, held half the villages and rural areas. The Portuguese held the towns and forty isolated rural posts. The rebels were composed, Davidson thought, of 6,000 guerrillas and 3,000 in regular formations. They obtained military supplies and instructors from Russia, Czechoslovakia, Yugoslavia and East Germany, but Cabral and his collaborators remained 'independent'. Davidson complained that, unlike the rebels, the Portuguese were using napalm, and that they imported this, as well as their jet bombers, from their NATO allies.[1]

In addition to military successes, the nationalists claim to be running schools and clinics in the regions they command, and to have nearly 500 men and women in Europe training as doctors and technicians. The Portuguese, on the other hand, have established resettlement villages (they claim 400) in the rural areas still under their control, with the usual anti-guerrilla defences and an African militia. It is difficult to pass a judgment on the conflicting claims about rebel progress or otherwise, though it is plain that Cabral's offensive, proportionately speaking, has dug itself into Guinea in a way that its counterparts in Angola and Mozambique have not achieved. Support appears to be coming from China and Cuba, and the rebels are well equipped with anti-aircraft guns and long-range bazookas. Cabral, whose competence is beyond question, is understood to work from Conakry in neighbouring Guinea, to recruit troops in Mali, and to be in touch with dissentients in Senegal who oppose the government of President Senghor. To refute some of the rebels' claims about the extent of the ground they hold in Portuguese Guinea, Portuguese officials point to the visit of President Tomás, early in 1968, when he came from Lisbon to tour the province and received an enthusiastic

---

[1] Some critics, writing more loosely than Davidson, seem to imply that NATO as such supplies weapons to Portugal. But members of NATO are not beneficiaries of some central supply. On the contrary, NATO has only such weapons as its members manufacture or buy for themselves, and for their NATO commitments. Portugal's munitions industry is modest and she buys a lot from her allies. As regards napalm, a distinction must be made. Horrible though it is, napalm is a conventional device used, like the older flamethrower, to clear bushland, forest or jungle where the enemy may be concealed, and whence he can launch his attacks while remaining invisible. There may be no alternative to using napalm unless the exposed troops are prepared to sustain excessive casualties. To use napalm punitively, on the other hand, would be indefensible

welcome. A report in the London *Economist* at that time,[1] claimed that during the President's visit the rebels had 'breached the fortress of Bissau island and bazookaed Bissau airport'. A corrective letter from the Portuguese press counsellor in London was published subsequently. It stated that the quoted incident had not occurred at all, and that Bissau, incidentally, was not an island. The President had travelled for six days in an atmosphere demonstrating 'the prevailing normality of life'. From Bissau in the west to Nova Lamego in the east, and back to the Bijagos islands in the west and south, 'he was greeted by large and enthusiastic crowds, mixing freely with them and without military guard or escort, even when only fifteen miles from the hostile frontier – inside the area which the terrorists claim to control'. Foreign correspondents had accompanied the president, and the representative of United Press International had reported:

> In Nova Lamego, and the same day in nearby Bafata, also in East Guinea, the President was preceded, accompanied and followed by singing and dancing Africans, Christians, Moslems and Animists. In the Bijagos islands he received the same welcome. . . . In the places visited by President Tomás, anti-Portuguese elements were not strong enough to make a show of open hostility. This leads observers to say that even if PAIGC controls certain parts of the territory, it does not control the masses.[2]

A military expert had told the correspondent, in fact, that of all the arms controlled by the Portuguese in Guinea, 45 per cent had been handed over to the local population for self-defence. It has also been reported, by correspondents touring the country on the Portuguese side,[3] that many of the Majako tribe round Teixeira Pinto, who early on had fled to neighbouring Guinea and Senegal, later returned to the Portuguese umbrella, deeply disillusioned. Rice co-operatives were said to have doubled the local crops in areas like Mansoa, and, while African planters were certainly exploited in the past, it seems that prices are now strictly controlled at a fair level. At one stage, the Portuguese military effort seemed to be weakening, but early in 1968, the air force rooted out the anti-aircraft nests round Quitaline, paratroopers moved into the south, naval patrols in assault craft

---

[1] *The Economist*, 27 April 1968.
[2] *Ibid.*, 4 May 1968.
[3] John Biggs-Davison, M.P.: *Yorkshire Post* (31 May 1968), *Daily Telegraph* (25 June 1968); Patrick Orr: *Glasgow Herald* (3 and 4 July 1968).

started patrolling the Cacine River, army posts were established near the Guinean border, and the rebels were being driven back to the border areas. Rebel assaults in the south had plainly lost momentum by the summer, and the guerrillas were pulling out of Oio (a populous southern region where the Portuguese last year collected 80 per cent of their taxes), and concentrating more in northern areas like the neighbourhood of Teixeira Pinto. It has often been argued that the Portuguese have little to gain from staying in Guinea, but, even apart from the encouragement their withdrawal would give to nationalist forces elsewhere, the fall of Portuguese Guinea would at once imperil Cape Verde, and the adjacent islands. If Communist-backed forces were to install themselves in the archipelago, the implications would be extremely serious for Western Atlantic strategy. NATO, as well as Portuguese, interests are at stake, says Lisbon.

Salazar's stable regime and the new-found strength of the Portuguese currency inspired confidence in the white populations of Angola and Mozambique, and the post-war economic upsurge in those provinces was the result. Today, the economic prospects seem exciting, but there are many imponderables, including the continuing influx of foreign capital, and the need to establish a balance between overall economic growth and the urgent importance of social and educational services for the ordinary citizen, at home and overseas alike. In a critical paper written in 1962, Professor Hammond argued that to contemplate the early withdrawal of Portuguese sovereignty over Angola and Mozambique would be to contemplate the economic disintegration of those provinces and 'the abrupt reassertion of more primitive forms of society'.[1] It was true that Portugal was taking only 20 per cent (by value) of Angolan exports and about 25 per cent from Mozambique. But to assess the economic significance of Portuguese control in terms of trade figures was as specious as to assess its civilizing effects solely in terms of the number of *assimilados*, and for the same reason: 'it neglects the evidence of observation in favour of that derived from statistics'. Hammond continued:

> The Portuguese, to an extent unmatched by other Europeans in tropical Africa, have established there not merely a governing and managerial class, but a whole urban civilization. More especially,

[1] R. J. Hammond, *Portugal's African Problem, Some Economic Facets*, Carnegie Endowment for International Peace, New York, 1962.

there exists a class of skilled European artisans ranging from plasterers to fishermen, from tailors to engine-drivers, which is to be found in the urban settlements up-country as well as in the coast towns.

As Hammond saw it, the towns, and the *lingua franca* they disseminated, were a major cohesive force in those vast and thinly populated territories, without which they would 'crumble into tribal fragments'. The whole exchange sector of the provincial economies and thus their prospect of further economic development depended on Portuguese participation. The Portuguese language had become an indispensable means of communication, so that a sudden withdrawal of the Portuguese and a wholesale injection of foreign advisers and technicians would not have worked. On the other hand, there was no reason why the existing monolithic, centralizing system should not develop into a different and less oppressive form.

For Portugal herself, on the other hand, separation from Africa would be serious but not catastrophic. Hammond pointed out that the emergence of Angola and Mozambique as major earners of foreign exchange for the escudo area had made the post-war development plans possible both at home and overseas. But in 1962, Portugal was in no position to finance much-needed large-scale development in the overseas provinces (which would have to go on relying on their exports and foreign capital); moreover, if Portugal were to place the welfare of the common man in the forefront of her economic policies, she might not be able to justify even the comparatively small amount of her then current resources devoted to the overseas provinces. Following Dr Luiz Teixeira Pinto, who later became Minister of the Economy, Hammond thought that Portugal herself was running hard to stay in the same place, with all the marks of underdevelopment: low incomes and savings, hidden unemployment, low diversity in industry, low technical accomplishment, relatively high population growth, and an internal economy based partly on subsistence, partly on exchange. To make a breakthrough in the home economy, the first development plan (1953-8) should have been three times its size. But this would have meant severe taxation of the wealthy minority, a step for which Portuguese society was ill-prepared. So Portugal herself needed foreign capital, but this was not in keeping with the mind of Salazar, who severely controlled injections of foreign money, and had subordinated economic development to financial and political stability. The system had, in Hammond's view, become an anachronism. All of which seemed to suggest that Portugal might be better off without her African involvement, and there are sectors of opinion in Portugal today which would argue much the same way. This, however, would seem to disregard the fact that the situation in Angola and Mozambique has changed out of all recognition in the past seven years since Hammond wrote his paper, a period which has seen extensive oil strikes and the opening up of massive deposits of iron ore, not to mention the plans for Cabora Bassa and the Cunene River scheme. It is worth attempting a profit and loss account of the African involvement from the point of view of Portugal and of the provinces themselves.

Withdrawal or expulsion from Africa would hurt Portugal in the short-term, mainly in the transport and textile sectors, and in the possible need to absorb up to half-a-million repatriated whites, including the returning army. In the long-term, however, manpower and investment would be released for expansion at home, and a substantial strain removed from the budget. For the reasons outlined in Hammond's report, industries in Angola and Mozambique would still need Portuguese personnel and know-how, so the Portuguese companies there would presumably carry on in one way or another, under arrangements made with the new local governments. As matters stand today, military costs in Africa, borne mainly by Lisbon, amount to 7 million contos a year (£90 million), and are not offset by Portugal's earnings from exports to the overseas provinces, which in 1967 amounted to only 5 million contos.[1]

The economic advantages Portugal derives from her presence in Africa include the substantial profits reaped by Portuguese companies based on the homeland but operating in the overseas provinces. The escudo area (covering all Portuguese territories) helps the homeland's balance of payments, partly by way of metropolitan re-exports based on imports from Africa. Portugal's balance of payments in relation to the overseas provinces yielded, in 1967, a surplus of £30 million, an increase of £5 million over the year before:

---

[1] Military expenditure accounted, in 1967, for 36.9 per cent of the state budget, and between 1963 and 1967 rose half as fast again as the budget's rate of growth. Portugal's total military expenditure, including commitments to NATO, amounts to 10 million contos a year (£120 million).

1967: Metropolitan balance of payments with
overseas provinces in millions of escudos[1]

Cape Verde	— 13
Guinea	— 308
São Tomé and Principé	+ 44
Angola	+1,634
Mozambique	+1,120
Macao	+ 23
Timor	— 83
Total	+2,417

Balancing these economic pros and cons, one would be inclined to say that there is every reason for staying in Africa, if it were not for the cost of the military operations. It is true that this money is not wasted. Soldiers' pay boosts private consumption and savings. Military operations call for infrastructure, research and training in skilled trades. Apart from the purchase of arms, all the money spent on the wars stays in the escudo area. But there is also an inflationary effect, and many would like to see the money now spent on defence diverted to public investment, improved welfare services, education; and the personnel engaged in fighting are urgently needed by a homeland economy seriously short of young and skilled labour. As against all this, however, there are the prospects opened up by the recent economic boom in Angola and Mozambique, by inventive planning, and by the discovery of rich new resources. Finally, there is Portugal's responsibility not to abandon to post-colonial anarchy the countries where her civilizing mission has not yet been fulfilled. Portuguese policy, therefore, remains as it was. It must be noticed, however, that Portugal now sells far more to Europe than she does to her overseas provinces. If, in 1967, her dealings with the latter yielded a surplus of 2,417m. escudos in the balance-of-payments, her balance vis-à-vis foreign countries showed a surplus of 3,958 escudos.

It is the white population of the African provinces which is restive for decentralization. They are doing well and want to run their own affairs, not in the sense of a total break with Portugal, but certainly in the sense of a much higher degree of economic and political autonomy. It can, for example, be embarrassing if financial regulations passed in Lisbon for the whole escudo area compel Angola to limit

[1] *Annual Report of the Bank of Portugal* (1967), published 1968, Lisbon, p. 174.

its imports from, say, the United States, and the latter in retaliation reduces its imports from Angola. For the time being, however, Angola and Mozambique urgently need the Portuguese army and investment, and membership of the escudo area, based on such a strong currency, makes it easier to borrow money abroad. The big Portuguese companies, so often accused of milking Africa, put far more into it than they are given credit for. We have seen that last year the Benguela Railway Company paid the equivalent of £500,000 in tax, and, as the provinces now have separate budgets, this money went to the Angolan treasury for local development. We have also

1967
(millions of escudos)

Transactions	Imports	Exports
Direct investments	35	87
Applications	13	87
Settlements	22	—
Transactions in securities	30	82
Credits connected with trading operations	61	13
Financial loans	89	761
Loans granted	—	761
Repayments and amortisations	89	—
Movements of capital of a personal nature	46	—
Sundries	45	8
Total	306	951

seen that the companies not only give employment, but run a private version of a welfare state. The African provinces, too, have the advantage of belonging to a Portuguese 'common market', with the abolition of tariffs between them and the homeland virtually complete. All imports from Africa, too, are paid for now at normal world prices. A special scheme for cotton was discontinued precisely because it worked out to the detriment of the African producer, and the sugar scheme has been made more flexible to ensure not only fair, but even advantageous prices as against those paid elsewhere. Foreign investment has been attracted in recent years by substantial tax concessions, loans and credit schemes, easy regulations for repatriation of capital, and factory location assistance. The Germans, the French, the Americans, the Swedes, the Swiss, the British and the Japanese are in Portuguese Africa now. As for Portuguese investment, the above table outlines the medium- and long-term private capital transactions between the metropolitan area and the overseas provinces.[1]

This shows an export surplus of 645 million as against 92 million for the previous year.

The government's current contribution may best be seen from the Third Development Plan (1968-73), involving a capitalization of 44,480 million escudos for the overseas provinces alone. This total shows a proportionate rise of 54 per cent over the figures for the Interim Plan (1965-7). It is expected that 36 per cent will be financed by the public sector, 30 per cent by credit institutions, companies and individuals, and the rest from foreign credit. The contribution of the central government (in Lisbon) to this scheme is about 15 per cent, i.e. 6,717 million escudos.[2] Taking the Plan as a whole, that is, for the homeland and the overseas provinces together, the programme is 80 per cent larger than the Interim Plan, five times larger than the Second Development Plan (1959-64), and fourteen times the size of the First Development Plan (1953-8):

Investments programmed for the overseas provinces
(millions of escudos)

Agriculture, forestry, stock-raising	5,057
Fisheries	836
Mining and manufacturing	21,205
Rural Improvement Schemes	116
Electrical power	2,268
Trade	281
Transport and communications	10,144
Housing and town planning	654
Tourism	196
Education and research	2,700
Health and assistance	1,023
	44,480

This shows a proportionate increase of 172 per cent in education and research and of 208 per cent in health services as against the Interim Plan.

---

[1] *Annual Report of the Bank of Portugal* (1967), published 1968, Lisbon, p. 175.
[2] Dr A. J. Da Motta Veiga, *Draft of the Third Development Plan, 1968-73*, National Information Office, Lisbon, 1967.

The two large African provinces show an 80 per cent rise in exports since 1960. Industrial output and money supply have been doubled. Some 20 million tons of freight pass through the ports each year, and the railroads linked to them provide Central Africa with vital outlets to the sea. Self-confidence has developed largely because of the newly discovered oil and iron deposits in Angola, the prospect of oil in Mozambique, and the breathtaking Cabora Bassa scheme. In Angola, imports connected with oil and mining development turned the traditionally favourable trade balance to a deficit of 1,068 million escudos in 1967, but the first half of 1968 reduced the gap to a half of what it had been for the same phase in the previous year, mainly because of a 19 per cent upsurge in exports, with the EEC, EFTA, United States and Japan as leading customers. Nearly 2,700,000 tons of iron was produced in 1968 as against 780,619 tons the year before, and, with reserves of 120 million tons of iron deposit at Cassange, Angola is fast becoming one of the world's largest exporters of iron ore. Plans are now well advanced for producing steel. Vast new deposits of iron have been discovered about 100 miles from Luanda, and the *Companhia do Manganes de Angola* aims to produce 500,000 tons a year. At the time of writing it is expected that the output of oil for 1968 will prove to have reached the 1 million ton mark, thanks to the strikes in Cabinda and offshore (where Gulf Oil has secured major concessions); and, with PETRANGOL turning out 600,000 tons a year near Luanda, it is estimated that Angola will very soon show an oil output of 7½ million tons a year. The cotton output for 1968 was twice that for 1967, and, to obviate the need for imports, more light industries are springing up, mainly in food, textiles and chemicals. The current development plan allots 11,500 million escudos for mining in Angola, 3,400 million to manufacturing, and 1,800 million to roads.

Coffee leads in agricultural production, with heavy stress on maize, wheat, palm and cattle breeding, and finally on irrigation and community farming. Diamonds are a traditional source of wealth, and Angola is the world's fourth largest sisal producer. The gross output in billions of escudos may be seen at a glance in this way:

	1967 (Jan.-Dec.)	1968 (Jan.-June)
Manufacturing	3.6	2.05
Mining	0.86	1.5

All this, however, represents a growing advantage to the white minority, while 90 per cent of the population continues to live by farming at or near subsistence level. The danger could be an ultimate confrontation between urban unemployment and rural under-employment, the curse of many African countries. That being so, the Plan's allotment of 2,250 million escudos to Angolan agriculture seems parsimonious. However, an agreement has now been signed with South Africa to develop a joint irrigation and power project on the Cunene River, which will benefit southern Angola up to Nova Lisboa. It involves an extension of the Cambambe Dam, and the plan is to irrigate 150,000 hectares directly by natural flow and another 350,000 by piping. The project should ultimately settle half-a-million people, with less than a third of them employed in the primary sector, and this could be an important step in leading the African population into a market economy. The Cunene scheme will involve the construction of no less than twenty-seven dams. The Benguela Railway, which links the Angolan port of Lobito on the Atlantic coast to railways in the Congo, Zambia, Rhodesia and Mozambique, is to spend 24 million dollars over the next four years on building an extension between Lobito and Cubal, and the end-product should be to double the annual freightload to four million tons.

Mozambique's balance of payments would be favourable if it were not for the losses arising from the sanctions on Rhodesia, including the closure of the oil pipeline from Beira to Umtali. The year 1967, however, showed an improvement in the trade deficit, which fell from 2,755 million escudos to 2,226 million. Traditionally, coal is Mozambique's most prolific mineral, but the development plan envisages increased production of asbestos, bauxite, beryl, lepidolite, colombo-tantalite, and montmorillenite; while Mozambique also produces small quantities of mica, microlite, bismuth, gold, silver, quartz and tourmaline. Twelve companies, Portuguese and foreign, are prospecting for oil, and already the SONAREP refinery expects to treble its output to 2.5 million tons a year. Other prospectors are looking for manganese, diamonds, and fluorite. Iron-ore extraction is to start at Mirrote, and rich deposits have been found at Malema and Bibane. Natural gas has been discovered at Buzi and Pande, and copper deposits at Maniaca. The Plan continues to lay heavy stress on railways, ports and roads; after all, Mozambique provides Zambia and Malawi with their only rail and port outlets to the Indian Ocean, and Rhodesia in part depends on her for the same services. But there is also encouragement for more light industries, while at Nampula a large co-operative runs the biggest cotton ginnery in southern Africa, with a throughput of 2½ tons of raw cotton an hour. The highlight of the future, of course, is the scheme to dam the Zambesi at Cabora Bassa in the Tete district of Mozambique. Within a decade, the scheme will be yielding well over twice as much power as the Kariba, and will certainly be the largest in Africa. The planners anticipate a capacity of 2,000 MW, and the present supply of 60 million kWH a year to South Africa will be multiplied by a hundred. The project, which includes extensive irrigation systems for the Tete region itself, offers enormous potential for Mozambique, and it is being said openly that the country could comfortably take another million settlers on the strength of it. The FRELIMO and COREMO freedom fighters based in neighbouring Zambia have declared war on Cabora Bassa and threaten to harass and block its construction. FRELIMO attacks in Tete, in fact, began early in 1968. But there is sufficient international confidence in Portugal's ability to handle this threat, and a number of countries tumbled over each other to secure the construction contracts. In the upshot, Portugal accepted a bid from Zamco, a Franco-German consortium, largely because of the generous credits offered by French and German sources to help the Portuguese to pay the bill. South Africa has a minority investment in the construction.

The economics of the African provinces will continue to depend mainly on agriculture and mining, with manufacturing industries accounting for no more than 10 per cent of the overall output. There is a lack of capital and liquidity, and an exchange problem arising from the tendency to treat these economies on a dual basis. For some purposes, they are treated on a basis of integrity with the homeland, but there are separate currencies, and, although the Angolan and Mozambican escudos are supposed to be exchanged at a par value with the metropolitan counterpart, there have been cases in Angola of a 16 per cent loss in exchange on the black market. This happens because the Lisbon government, in an effort to block the rate of escape of capital from Africa, slows the normal exchange procedures down (at any rate where Portuguese firms and individuals are concerned; foreigners receive substantial concessions). More foreign investment is needed, and the monetary system calls for urgent reform.

Some of the finest work in Africa has been done in the context of land settlement. The Limpopo Valley settlement is a brilliant achievement, and, by 1967, accounted for about 1,200 families, black, white and mixed, living in community, with a series of churches, schools, community centres and social services, but with each individual family owning its own plot of land. The principle is that the settler is given land, tools, his first seeds or cattle, and advice from first-class agronomists. If he comes from Portugal, he receives an aided passage. He repays what he is given by slow instalments, and eventually becomes the owner of his plot. Some of these families have done extremely well and delight in showing the visitor their refrigerators and cars. In Angola, where about 11,000 settlers come out every year, there are settlements like the famous one at Cela, which found it hard at first to pay their way, but have now achieved precarious viability. Cela is mostly white, but Limpopo offers an almost unique example in Africa of easy community relationships between white and black on roughly identical economic levels, and is all the more remarkable when it is remembered that fifteen or sixteen years ago the valley was simply a massive swamp 'all set around with fever trees'. The government in Angola is now planning extensive resettlement projects for Africans and whites alike. The U.N. Special Committee Report[1] tells us that the plans have suffered severe delays due to the complexity of the necessary surveys, legal procedures and methods of demarcation. In 1967, the total area under or pending concession was still only 7.3 per cent of the territory. As matters stood in 1967, the average European *per capita* occupation of land was sixty times that of the African. However, to speed things up, large areas were being demarcated by aerial photometric methods into blocs for directed settlement, free concessions and African occupation. The project's administration had been strengthened and the provincial settlement boards were putting more emphasis on setting up agricultural settlement nuclei. As the establishment of a multi-racial society was one of Portugal's basic objectives, new regulations had dropped terminology tending to emphasize racial contrasts. Two kinds of re-grouping were envisaged. For most Africans now living under customary law, land would be specially set aside and demarcated as not available for individual ownership. Africans would be organized there in model *regedorias*, the basic rural unit of administra-

[1] Report of U.N. Special Committee, *op. cit.*, pp. 65-71, 110-14.

tion, and government services would be extended to help increase productivity and stimulate social evolution. There would also be *enraizamentos*, permanent settlements, for more developed rural populations, where there could be a 'fusion of different ethnic groups'. Similarly, Mozambique envisaged European-type *colonatos* and, one-tenth of the size, African-type *ordenamentos*, but the difference would be one of more or less sophisticated farming, not of race. Official statements had indicated that a member of a less-advanced settlement could, if he showed ability, graduate to a *colonato*, and this had already happened in existing settlements. In the Magagade *colonato*, which already includes Africans, it had been estimated that a single settler family would be able to earn as much as 485,000 escudos in the year, while the same family, if in an *ordenamento*, would stand to earn 18,000 escudos. Even this, however, is an enormous increase on what the lone subsistence farmer or industrial worker can hope for.

Before discussing the growth of education in Angola and Mozambique, it will be as well to set out the population statistics for both countries. The *Anuário Estatístico*, Vol. 11, 1966, published by the *Institúto Nacional de Estatística*, projected estimates from the 1960 census to show that by 1966 there were 5,223,000 people in Angola and 7,040,000 in Mozambique. The only available breakdown of the population into races is dated no later than 1960, but it is worth citing to give a fair enough picture of racial distribution:

Angola		*Mozambique*	
White	172,529	White	97,245
Black	4,604,362	Black	6,455,614
Mixed	53,392	Mixed	31,355
Others	166	Indians	17,241
		Chinese	2,098
	4,830,449		6,603,553

In the past fifteen years, the educational programme has speeded up with extraordinary rapidity, at least at primary level. In 1958-9, the situation in Angola was very backward indeed:[1]

---

[1] Duffy, *op. cit.*, p. 179.

Grade	Pupils
Adaptaçao	55,779
Elementary (private)	13,226
Elementary (state)	16,771
Secondary-Academic (private)	2,355
Secondary-Academic (state)	3,006
Seconday-Technical (private)	288
Secondary-Technical (state)	3,074
	94,499

Between the school years beginning 1965 and 1966, however, the Angolan totals leaped from 255,690 pupils to 305,759.[1] The latest official figures relate to 1966-7, but from investigations made in 1967, the author would expect to find well over 500,000 pupils in Angola today, and well over 600,000 in Mozambique; and these estimates are conservative. The division of grades in 1966-7 was as follows:[2]

1966-7 Grade	Angola	Mozambique
University	644	662
Middle Level (commercial, technical, teacher training, etc.)	960	589
Secondary (academic, technical, teacher training for pre-primary schools in resettlement villages etc.)	31,437	23,480
Primary	295,508	439,658
Infants	1,474	1,051
Public services formation	619	633
Elementary technical	1,035	4,087
Art schools	195	230
Seminaries	715	485
Others	—	1,012
	332,587	471,887

The predominance of primary pupils over secondary totals is obvious. In Mozambique, in 1964-5, there were 381,456 students,

[1] Estatística de Educação, 1966-7, Luanda.
[2] Preview of figures to be published by the Overseas Ministry, Lisbon.

but 359,548 of them were in infant and primary schools, with only 21,908 in the others.[1] There was a big leap in the following year with 31,178 above primary level. But the position of the Africans was still very backward. In 1964-5, there were 333,699 Africans in primary school, but only 4,189 in higher grades. Of the 5,817 students in academic secondary schools, only 636 were black. As for Angola, suffice it to say that in Luanda, in 1965-6, only 15 per cent of the primary pupils reached the fourth grade. The United Nations Special Committee Report, already quoted, indicates that the bottleneck lies in teacher training.

However, education has certainly got into orbit now, and the sweep of developments in Angola is quite dramatically illustrated by the American specialist Michael Samuels in the following table:[2]

Angola

	No. of pupils in 1955	No. of pupils in 1966	Growth since 1955 (%)	Growth since 1960 (%)
Pre-Primary and Primary	68,759	225,145	227	113
Secondary-Academic	3,729	14,577	291	95
Secondary-Technical	2,164	13,220	512	194

Africa as a whole, in 1966, had 88 per cent of its students in the 5-14 age group, and 11 per cent in the 15-19 age group.[3] The figure for Angola at this time was, by the author's reckoning, 91 per cent in the first group, and it is certainly less now. So that, by overall African standards, the Portuguese showing is not all that bad. The FAO Africa Survey of 1962, moreover, shows that Angola and Mozambique had more students undergoing technical training than Kenya, Uganda, Ghana and Nigeria.[4] Today, if teacher training is one bottleneck, another is the difficulty of establishing secondary education in rural areas. Various reasons for this have already been explored, but

---

[1] *Estatística de Educação, op. cit.*
[2] Michael Samuels, 'The New Look in Angolan Education', published in *Africa Report*, New York, November 1967, and quoting the Angolan Education Department's *Sintese das Actividades dos Servicos (1964-65) and Reparticao de Estatistica Geral.*
[3] UNESCO: Statistical Year Book, 1966, p. 47.
[4] Food and Agricultural Organization: African Survey, 1962, Rome.

it is only right to add that part of the trouble lies in distances. Rural children at present can only go to secondary school if they are prepared to make long journeys into town or to board there, and, although there is government aid to this end, it is not an easy prospect for an African child in a developing country to become a boarder in what are, after all, white men's towns. Secondary education must be carried into the bush, and this entails the cost of road-building. Government expenditure is at present concentrating on the primary and technical levels, and the author found high enthusiasm among the African pupils in technical schools in Luanda and Lourenço Marques, which are run on the most up-to-date lines, and it was in this sector that government aid for lodging, clothing and subsistence was most apparent. However, the missionaries' insistence on the urgency of secondary school development cannot be denied, if the Africans are to take their proper place in government. In secondary schools throughout both countries there is always an admixture of children who are black or of mixed blood, and, while in a small minority, they are plainly and fully integrated into the life of their schools, and there seems to be no hint of racial discrimination.

The Portuguese have an exceptionally good record in the fight against tropical disease, and, while there is still ample room for improvement in the number of medical centres, the quality is of the highest, and has attracted significant praise from the World Health Organization. Some comparisons with other African countries show, however, that even in the size and scope of medical services, Angola and Mozambique show up quite well:

1961-4

Country	No. of hospital beds per 1,000 population[1]
Angola	2.5
Mozambique	1.5
Ghana	1.0
Nigeria	0.4
S. Rhodesia	4.1
Zambia	2.8
Tanzania	1.9

[1] World Health Organization: Third Report on World Health Situation, 1961-4.

Then, as to the number of doctors:

1964-6	
Country	No. of persons per doctor[1]
Angola	13,140
Mozambique	17,990
Cape Verde	8,800
Congo-Kinshasa	31,250
Malawi	49,250
Nigeria	44,230
S. Rhodesia	7,570
Sierra Leone	16,440
Tanzania	18,240
Uganda	11,600
Zambia	21,820
Ethiopia	68,520

In 1962, the World Health Organization sent a team to investigate medical services in Angola and Mozambique. The report was not published, as the Portuguese government withheld its consent. This is another example of the way in which the Portuguese, stung by certain criticisms, can spite themselves by refusing publication to a document which in fact does them a lot of good. The broad outlines of the report are public knowledge, however, and criticism seems to have related to insufficiencies rather than lack of know-how. It is also probable that there may have been some differences between the government and the WHO on some of the related economic and social data. However, a summary of the favourable points in the report appeared in the *Boletim Geral do Ultramar* in April-May 1963. The WHO team found that while some of the medical services were defective in organization, others were exemplary, and the local people plainly had complete confidence in them. Hospitals were well-equipped, with good staffs, and special praise was due to the leprosy services. The team visited one leprosy centre which it described as impeccable. It was also apparently impressed by the midwifery services, and found that most births were attended at least by a midwife. It also visited Portuguese Guinea, where it described the campaign against tuberculosis as magnificent. In Portuguese Africa generally, it was found that the rural labour code was strictly enforced,

[1] United Nations Statistical Year Book, 1967. Even Eduardo Mondlane once wrote that the Mozambique health department 'is one of the most forward looking and most successful in Africa'. (Cf. *Africa in the Modern World*, Ed. C. W. Stillman, Chicago, 1955.)

U

so that medical services were available to all workers, and that there were good prospects of a rapid rise in living standards. The hospitals were first-class, and first-aid centres were prolific enough to ensure that immediate aid was available almost anywhere. Most of the medical workers were Africans, and there was no sign of racial discrimination. The author, who has visited many hospitals in Angola and Mozambique, can add his testimony to the devotion of the doctors and nursing staffs, and to the presence of white and African patients in the same wards. In August of 1968, Dr Marcolino Candau, director-general of the WHO, visited Angola and Mozambique, and in his public speeches and broadcasts, praised the schools of medicine and the emphasis laid by the government on fresh-water supplies to the rural populations.

In its Third Report on the World Health Situation (1961-4) the WHO stated that in Angola there was piped water available for 308,285 people in urban areas, and for 1,074,679 in the countryside, with similar figures for sewerage. Nearly 2 million people had been inoculated against smallpox and nearly 380,000 against polio. In Mozambique, 80 per cent of the population had been immunized against smallpox, and 2.6 million penicillin injections were given in 1959 by way of immunization against yaws. The United Nations Economic Survey of Africa and the FAO Africa Survey show that in 1965, the average level of calorie intake was substantially higher in Angola than in Guinea, Ghana, E. Nigeria and Sierra Leone. Angola's infant mortality rate of 82 per thousand live births in 1957 also compares favourably with other African countries. It is estimated that sleeping sickness will have been wiped out in Angola by the early 1970s.

If much of this detail is tedious, it is nonetheless necessary. So much has been said to suggest that Portuguese Africa is still a region of harsh oppression, while in fact there is so much evidence, unpublished or unstressed, to show that in recent years, Angola and Mozambique have made dramatic strides. No one can deny the significance of the ILO Report, yet it received scant coverage in the world's press. Material conditions have improved to the point where it can certainly be said that the Portuguese African's living standards are as good as anywhere else on the continent, in some cases very much better, always excepting the paradoxically higher standards of the apartheid states. The visitor cannot fail to be struck by the dedication of the Portuguese teachers, agronomists, doctors and social workers he meets on his way, some of them working a fourteen-hour, seven-day week in the service of Africans with whom they enjoy the closest relations. The author recalls a visit to an orphanage in Carmona where sixty white, black and mulatto children of the terror's victims were growing up as a mixed family. They were cared for by a devoted married couple and closely watched over by the district governor, Major Rebocho Vaz, now Governor-General of Angola. Here in the town, and further afield in the scores of villages built by Rebocho Vaz for returning refugees, relationships were exemplary. A great many things can be laid on to impress visiting journalists, but atmosphere is not one of them. There was nothing contrived about the way white army officers and village leaders talked as equals, sitting down to discuss the social and economic programme for the neighbourhood – in which the army has constantly played a leading role. One watched the officers' children safely enjoying the freedom of these villages, though the roads between them were not free of rebel snipers, and the crash programmes for pre-primary education, with young African teachers keeping a year or two ahead of their pupils, young and old, by spending their summer holidays in town on special training courses. There is, at last, a local civil service outstanding for its integrity and commitment: no more shady deals between the *chefe de posto* and the dishonest or intimidated African chief for contract labour. American journalists like Robert Estabrook of the *Washington Post* and Drew Middleton of the *New York Times*, and now a series of British writers and M.P.s, have followed the same trail and seen the resurgence for themselves. It is noticeable, too, that even the more critical sources today make a clear distinction between 'racial discrimination' in South Africa and 'colonialism' in Portuguese Africa.

If there is material progress, is it still paternalistic? And, if 'Africanization' calls for special interpretation in Portuguese Africa, where a multi-racial meritocracy is the aim, can it be said that the Africans there really are being trained for the fullest participation in government, the economy's higher rewards, and the social order? There is no doubt about the theory. As Salazar once put it to the author, it was Lenin who made 'colonizing' disreputable by substituting the term 'colonialism', and Portugal's critics include those who, under the cloak of anti-colonialism, pursue neo-imperialism. Yet there is still both virtue and necessity in the colonizing principle. There is much available space in under-populated Africa on which, for instance, an over-populated Asia casts a legitimate eye. The right of every man to share in the earth's fruits, whoever owns them, is prior even to the right of private property. The whole race has an equitable easement over the whole world. Hence the need to ensure fair means of distribution and exchange in world markets, and to encourage migration. Moreover, inter-racialism has a positive content of its own, far loftier than co-existence. History has proved the excellence of the hybrid, to which the Portuguese mulatto, handsome, intelligent and successful, is no exception. Hence the notion of *Eur-Afrique* is something the world needs if it is not to divide along racial lines and is to evolve to the fullness of its capacity. President Senghor's vision of African socialism and a perfected *négritude* – the inner quality of the African character as expressed in its community traditions – is related to a Teilhardian view of evolution; and the Portuguese claim to understand how a marriage of that *négritude* with Europe's civilization can give the world something unique, something it cannot do without.

Salazar himself has always undoubtedly felt that African maturity depends on a continuous inter-breeding with Europeans, and though this suggests scant respect for Africa, he envisaged a two-way traffic. In more than one of his speeches he has referred to Europe's need of Africa in the field of political culture and ideology. Men of the Moreira school would set a much richer value than Salazar would on the African's potential contribution, and it may be that the Portuguese facility for getting on with the African could offer a crucible for a unique cultural exchange. The question is whether the corporativist system, even if brought to life by Marcello Caetano, could serve the African's need for political awareness and expression, and supply the formula for which many African one-party states are searching. Corporativism, however, has not as yet really been tried.

It was the Brazilian sociologist Gilberto Freyre who said that the Portuguese is a Ulysses, restless with the restlessness of Moor and Jew, restless within his narrow Iberian homeland. For him 'the tropics were mother lands, native lands, and strange lands to which he returned with very special rights – almost the rights of a tropical expatriate who has wandered in Europe, absorbing her qualities in his blood, being and culture, until Europe has also become intimately his.'[1] This grandiose language, and the talk of a new Brazil, is not wholly unreal, but, as Boxer constantly warns us, the Portuguese is

[1] John Biggs-Davison, M.P., 'Colour Blindness, a Portuguese Virtue'; *The Tablet*, 6 July 1968.

often misunderstood because he is viewed either as angel or devil. In fact he is simply a man, whose motives and morals are mixed. Over 140 years ago, a British naval officer could report a governor's ball in Mozambique where the guests 'included every grade, from highly polished civilization to the just-fledged savage'. Yet many years later it was also possible to complain that natives hardly ever rose above the rank of captain in the army. Slaves were treated badly in Angola and Brazil, yet, says Boxer, by the end of the eighteenth century, slavery on many Angolan rural estates had become little better than a farce, and at least one widow felt she could re-marry only if her slaves approved of her choice. Slaves in Brazil were much more likely to be granted manumission by the Portuguese than by anyone else, and the Portuguese were perfectly capable of caring for slaves they flogged. They were hard, too, on the Amerindians, yet could still fire guns in salute at an Amerindian wedding. It can be said categorically that systematic apartheid does not enter into their thinking, and colour bar as such means nothing to them. The Continental Hotel in Luanda is as open to the African as the Ritz in London is open to a street vendor – if he can pay the bill, and does not imagine that everyone is staring at him. One has seen black guests in Portuguese hotels, black teachers instructing adult white illiterates, black foremen over white labourers (though, oddly enough, never a black taxi-driver). If the inter-racial liaison is much more common than outright marriage, it is often because the white man may be subject to recall, and the black woman does not want to go with him. One knows families in Lisbon where some of the children are white and others coloured. The husband has worked in Africa, where his African mistress gave him children. On his recall, she has chosen to return to her tribe and has let him take the children with him to give them an educated future. He has married a white woman who has taken the hybrid children for her own and, when the time came, brought them up with her own without distinction. To the Portuguese there is nothing odd about this.

As has been said, the sense of white superiority is not absent, but it has much in common with what the Englishman used to feel about the immigrant Irish labourer. Such feelings are not irreversible. Freyre's 'luso-tropicalism' is not imaginary. The Portuguese does understand the tropical man. If he has not allowed scope for the African culture as he did for the Indian, it is because the former is more inchoate, less easy to define, more a way of life, and not a written heritage: a way of life which is hard to preserve in modern structures, but whose values are far from lost on the Portuguese. If the preservation of the African's customary laws once had a look of 'separate development', the door to full integration in the Europeans' way of life has begun to open a little wider. The test of Portuguese sincerity today is how quickly and authentically it is prepared to educate the African to capacity, and give him his full share of control. There is no doubt that the story of unrest in the African continent, the local wars, and the rivalries of immigrant and native workers has imperilled the unique advantages of having a racially mixed working-class. The frontier wars have driven the Portuguese further into the arms of the South Africans and white Rhodesians, for whom one detected a certain admiration in white Mozambican society after UDI was declared in Salisbury. Although Portugal rejects the apartheid system, her trade links with Rhodesia and South Africa are inevitable, and today there are certainly informal discussions at fairly high level from time to time on the subject of defence; probably close collaboration among police forces, and easy access for army officers. It would be disastrous, indeed, if South African and Rhodesian mentalities were to rub off to any great extent on the whites in Angola and Mozambique; and the danger is real. One of the best hopes, on the other side of the coin, lies in the new universities in Luanda and Lourenço Marques which have already produced their first crop of mixed graduates. Men like the present Minister of Education, Dr Veiga Simão, a scientist who secured his doctorate at Cambridge, are plainly determined to give the African his chance. With local universities now established, fewer Africans may now be sent to Europe and America (there have always been a few score of them in Lisbon, Coimbra and Oporto). On the other hand, there should now be a chance for many more of them to graduate. The African universities are at present concentrating on civil engineering, medicine, veterinary medicine, and the sciences. This is largely because these are the subjects most vitally needed in Africa now, but there is also no doubt a nervousness about letting Africans study law and politics. African students are still in a small minority but already number 100 in Luanda. At least a start has been made.

One of the wisest commentators on Portuguese Africa, Robert H. Estabrook of the *Washington Post*, wrote in 1962[1] that a multi-racial

---

[1] Estabrook, *op. cit.*

society with equal rights for Africans 'has not developed so comprehensively as the Portuguese claim, but there is a chance that they will. It seems to offer the best hope of amicable, psychologically satisfying relationships between Africans and Europeans.' Estabrook warns that nostalgic talk about Brazil's mixed culture overlooks the fact that developments in that country occurred without an overwhelmingly large indigenous population and at a time when world communications as we know them today did not exist. Critical world opinion could neither be formed nor felt. He concludes:

> Thus the net picture of Portuguese relations with Angola and Mozambique is one of contradictions of aim and performance – of failings and abuses, of reforms and ameliorations, of promises and hopes. The evolution as the Portuguese say they want it to be is preferable, at least to this observer, on the basis of what seems realistically possible, to either black nationalism that would exclude the Europeans or apartheid that would discriminate against the Africans.

> We are not an evil people, said one government official in Lisbon plaintively, in pleading for an objective assessment. This seems abundantly true, and some Portuguese are working hard to accommodate themselves to change. But the world will not stand still waiting for Portugal to prove her intentions.

The present writer's conviction is that, after nearly five centuries of confusing ideals and achievements, Portugal's civilizing mission has begun to find a viable incarnation, and that it is better to build on what is there than to uproot it all, with disastrous effects on white and black alike, and start all over again. The problem with most revolutions is that they tend to pose more problems than they solve. But if evolution is to be preferred, the Portuguese must have done with fears and start taking more calculated risks. It was a grave error to lose men of the calibre of Agostinho Neto, Mario Pinto de Andrade, Amilcar Cabral and Eduardo Mondlane; and they lost them largely because of a fear of the educated African or mulatto as such. One does not pretend that these men were above reproach, that their motives were unmixed, or that they were free from external pressures. But they were men of character and ability, and their aspirations were fostered abroad largely because the scope available to them at home was limited. Although he had Communist help, Mondlane was plainly not a Communist. Neto and Cabral depend on such help much more, and their ideologies are impregnated with Marxism. Yet their intentions would seem to suggest an independent African socialism, and, after all, whether they like it or not, they still bear a Portuguese stamp, especially those who were born of mixed parentage.[1] It may be that, given success, they would not be able to resist the dictates of the Communist bloc. In any case, military success continues to elude them, and the irony is that, having jogged Portugal's elbow, they have now lost much of their relevance. As we said of Mondlane, they could today fulfil their legitimate ambitions, for themselves and their people, better within the Portuguese structure than they can ever, on present showing, hope to do outside it. This waste could have been avoided had they found their proper place in their own society.

It is a great pity, however, that the Afro-Asian bloc in the United Nations seems to find it so very hard to see any merit at all in the Portuguese position, though their representatives at times show less intransigence in the corridors than they do in the General Assembly. Some of them are not blind to the other side of the coin, but have to point out that their policy is to foster African nationalism. Soon after the Angolan flare-up in 1961, Portugal refused to allow U.N. observers in, on the ground that this would be inconsistent with her argument that Angola was not a non-self-governing territory. But since then the government has allowed WHO and ILO teams in, and given the fullest co-operation. It has also issued repeated invitations to U Thant and the leaders of the various African states to 'come and see for yourselves' what life in Portuguese Africa is really like. These invitations have all been rejected. Over the past eight years, repeated resolutions of the General Assembly and the Security Council have called on the Portuguese to withdraw their forces from Africa, to negotiate with the revolutionary forces, to allow political parties and free institutions, and to prepare to give early independence to Angola and Mozambique. Other countries have been called upon to boycott Portugal, especially in the supply of arms, and attempts have been made to stop international agencies from helping her financially. Most states belonging to the Organization of African Unity have severed or refused diplomatic relations with Portugal; in 1963 she was expelled from the Economic Commission for Africa, and two years later was excluded from UNESCO-sponsored conferences.

[1] Unlike Neto and Andrade, Holden Roberto is wholly African and, according to those who have interviewed him, a better French than Portuguese speaker.

Malawi is an exception from OAU policy, having established formal relations with Portugal, on whose African railways and ports her landlocked economy so much depends. Portugal, in fact, at the Malawi government's request, is linking the new railway line in Mozambique (from the Port of Nacala to Vila Cabral) with Nyasa Railways (Cuamba to Balaca). Portugal is also seeking to establish diplomatic relations with Zambia, and off-the-record contacts are known to have taken place. There are also suggestions that Zambian and Angolan Railways may be contemplating arrangements to improve the Zambian copperbelt's link with outlets on the Atlantic seaboard. Already, Zambian Railways connect with the Benguela Railway which runs 800 miles across Angola to the Atlantic port of Lobito, and performs similar services for Katanga by its link-up with the Congolese Railways. The projected Chinese-built rail link between Zambia and Tanzania has only completed the survey stage, and, for multiple reasons, is an uncertain project. Moreover, Zambia obviously needs western as well as eastern outlets for her exports. She might, of course, find the answer in the railway which the British firm Lonrho, in conjunction with its Japanese partners, wants to build in the Congo, in connection with its hopes of concessions to develop the Congo's untapped mineral wealth. This line would run from Port Franqui via Kikwit, through Kinshasa, and on to the western sea-board at Matadi. This project might, on the face of it, make the Congo, and ultimately Zambia, independent of the Benguela Railway which, incidentally, is also owned by a British concern, Tanganyika Concessions, though managed by a Portuguese company. Yet there is much to be said for building on existing networks rather than waiting for long-term developments. Moreover, in the natural order of things, the economies of Zambia and the Congo must look south for most of their trading associations. Only a fraction of Zambian trade is conducted with her much poorer neighbours to the north.

Attempts are also being made to re-establish diplomatic relations with the Congo. The May 1969 manifesto of the Organization of African Unity, moreover, reserved its worst strictures for South Africa and excluded Portugal from the charge of apartheid. Rather, it urged that, given self-determination and independence, African governments in Angola and Mozambique should accept compliant white Portuguese as citizens, and added that 'an independent Mozambique, Angola or Portuguese Guinea may choose to be as friendly with Portugal as Brazil is'. This was not intended to reflect any weakening of OAU resolve, but it does indicate a genuine sympathy for the multi-racial ideal. The dilemma, however, remains. The Portuguese African's future cannot be determined in solely economic terms. He has still to attain his ultimate dignity as master of his own fate, and even the most prosperous form of subservience to the Portuguese falls short of this. In the work already quoted,[1] Mr G. W. Ball puts a lot of the responsibility on to Western shoulders. Portugal, he thought, should be received into the European Economic Community so that she would no longer be in any way dependent on her African possessions. Since he wrote, economic prospects in Angola and Mozambique have greatly improved, and yet, at the same time, and for reasons already given, it has become clear that Portugal without Africa could survive and develop at home. Ball feared that Africa was a dumping ground for Portuguese peasants unable to scrape a minimal living at home, and that Portugal's inclusion in EEC would obviate this. Certainly, Portugal's participation in Europe is of crucial importance, but one wonders whether there might be a way of giving the African his independence and at the same time preserving for him the advantages of a relationship with Portugal. Many thoughtful Portuguese today, at home and in Africa, favour the concept of a Portuguese Commonwealth of independent states in which Angola and Mozambique would enjoy what used to be called, in British terms, dominion status. This would mean real independence, but the advantages of the Portuguese 'common market' and the escudo area would be preserved for both sides; there could also, perhaps, be some form of strengthened association with Brazil. Portugal would have to establish at once a firm deadline for self-determination, and boost her educational drive to prepare her subject peoples to run their own show if they want to. The present writer would venture to prophesy that the ultimate vote would favour independence, but not total severance from metropolitan Portugal if some form of continuing association were available. But it would have to be a partnership of equals, and the local boss-class mentality still all too apparent in Mozambique, though less so in Angola, would have to die the death forthwith.

Why should this be preferable to simple independence on the familiar pattern? Because, however slow his approaches, Salazar rightly discerned the unique factors at work in Portuguese Africa.

[1] Ball, *op. cit.*, pp. 250-3.

First, a continuing relationship with Portugal would seem to be a natural outcome of a long evolution. Secondly, if the Portuguese really have a capacity for a degree of inter-racial living that has eluded the rest of us, neither they nor the Africans should be encouraged to discard what might become a dynamic exemplar. Thirdly, no country's future can be seen in isolation from its international role. The strategic position of Portugal's overseas possessions is important to Western defence, and thus the inclusion of Portuguese Africa in the Western defence network is a contribution to world peace. Finally, it seems as though history has been preparing Portugal for the role of a natural link between Europe, Africa and South America. As common markets develop throughout the world, they will need such special links or the world will become a series of inverted groupings with little sense of the family solidarity the whole human race ought to feel.

Such were the thoughts which strengthened Salazar in his stand against world opinion in 1961. No one visiting Lisbon in that year could miss the sense of shock as events in Africa jolted the nation out of its complacency, the feverish activity on government level to try and repair a long past in a few months, the tendency even for many of the government's critics to close their ranks with the national leaders in the teeth of the common threat. But this was not true of all the opposition. In the end of year elections for the National Assembly, some of them repeated, as Salazar saw it, 'the arguments of our enemies'. On 9 November, he broadcast to the nation in a tone of characteristic exasperation:

> Meanwhile, our people fight and die in Angola, as they have already fought and died elsewhere in the overseas territories. Are they fighting and dying for the present government? What a thought! Will they fight tomorrow for democracy? What an illusion! They fight and will continue to fight, under this or any other government, to defend the Nation, the tangible reality which the common folk, unaffected by the twisted philosophy of intellectuals, clearly feel through their pure patriotic instinct.

Even as he spoke, he was steeling himself for what he now knew to be imminent: the invasion of what was left of Portuguese India by the armies of the Indian Union.

CHAPTER 10

Portugal and the U.N. – Goa

Portugal had only five more weeks to wait before the second blow to fall on her in 1961 ended her residual dominion in what she still called Portuguese India. In the general climate of anti-Portuguese feeling, the Indian leader, Pandit Nehru, seized his opportunity in December, and invaded Goa and the other remaining Portuguese Indian enclaves. He was not, however, acting as an agent for the United Nations. One of his major complaints had certainly been that Portugal represented an outdated colonialism, but although strongly backed for this reason by the Afro-Asian bloc, he was not proposing to grant the Goanese their independence. He was proposing to absorb Goa into India, where, he argued, it belonged; and that is precisely what he did. Thanks to the Russian veto, he was able to do this without hindrance so far as the United Nations was concerned.

The Portuguese State of India, to use its official Portuguese title, is composed of three districts, Goa, Damão and Diu, situated on the west coast of India. Goa and Damão are adjacent to the state of Bombay, while Diu, further north, lies near the state of Saurashtra. The entire territory, in the mid-1950s, amounted to a population of 637,591, living within an area of 1,537 square miles. Goa itself is divided into Old and New Goa, the former comprising the principal island of Goa and the smaller islands at the mouth of the Mandovi and Zuari Rivers, several islands more distant, and the three districts of Bardez, Mormugão and Salsete. Damão, on the Gulf of Cambay, is constituted by three subdivisions: Damão itself, Dadrá and Nagar Aveli. Diu is a very small island south of the Katiawar peninsula, plus a little bit of land on the continent called Gogola. The population of 1955 was distributed as follows:

Goa	547,448
Damão	69,005
Diu	21,138

From a religious point of view the division was:

Hindus	388,488
Christians	
(mostly Catholic)	234,275
Moslems	14,162

Thus the Catholic population amounted to 36.7 per cent of the total, having fallen by emigration between 1881 and 1950 from an earlier 50 per cent. There was also a substantial *diaspora* of Goanese, roughly estimated as:

In Bombay	80,000
Elsewhere in India	20,000
In Pakistan	25,000
In Kenya	30,000
In the Middle East	20,000

Thus there were 175,000 Goanese abroad, 100,000 of them in India. Agriculture was the basic way of life for Goa itself, though in recent years mining developments, mainly in iron and manganese,[1] had begun to flourish richly. Portugal, however, enjoyed no more than a 10 per cent share in Goa's balance of trade. The entire trade between European Portugal and Portuguese India represented 0.75 per cent per thousand of metropolitan trade. The mother country was spending a basic 7,000 contos a year in the province, plus tens of thousands of contos in aid of Goanese shipping. Which hardly sounds like exploitation.[2] Nearly all office holders in Goa were Goanese, and Goanese held important governmental, military, judicial, ambassadorial and ecclesiastical posts in metropolitan Portugal and her other overseas provinces. They still do, and they have included many bishops and senior professors in institutes of higher learning. If the Governor-General and the Patriarch of Goa were always Portuguese, the policy was not unrelated to the problems posed by the Hindu caste system which affected even the Christian community. As one writer put it years ago, a Brahmin sacristan might feel some discomfort in dealing

[1] Between 1949 and 1955, iron-ore exports rose from an annual 49,188 tons to 1,500,000 tons; while manganese exports rose from 11,197 tons to about 180,000 tons.
[2] Pattee, *op. cit.*, pp. 263-6; António de Oliveira Salazar, *Goa and the Indian Union*, Lisbon, 1954.

with an archbishop of less distinguished origin; though, as this did not seem to matter in the lower ranks of public life, the argument cannot be pressed too far. The province was, by and large, well off, though the lack of varied opportunities had led to a substantial emigration. Many Goanese, too, are seamen. Goanese missionaries have played an important role in Africa.[1] In 1955, the Portuguese National Assembly granted substantial autonomy to Goa in administration and fiscal matters. At that time there were 339 elementary schools run by the state, and 177 mission schools, some of which gave instruction in Marathi, Gujarati and English. There were sixty-seven institutions teaching in English, and they catered for 12,000 students. A further ten establishments catered for industrial and agricultural training.

It was in 1510, that Afonso de Albuquerque finally secured Goa for Portugal. The Portuguese had met with heavy resistance from the local Moslem overlords, though the Hindus varied in their attitude, but the Moslems were eventually defeated in an act of harsh conquest, in which 6,000 of them died. Nevertheless, Albuquerque's policy, once he was established there, was based on the maintenance of local organization in the economic and social spheres, followed by integration into the political, administrative and religious institutions of Portugal. The native peoples were to run their own affairs as far as possible, but Albuquerque hoped that the region would naturally evolve, through contact with Portuguese settlers and missionaries, into Christian civilization. He organized municipal structures on the Lisbon model, established laws and courts, and proclaimed the principle of religious liberty. His 'policy of marriage' aimed at settling in Goa a Portuguese population whose blood would be generously mixed with the local peoples through inter-marriage, but he was selective about this. He was not out to create a population of mulattoes, and, in assisting 'mixed' families to establish themselves, favoured Moslem and Turkish brides who were of Aryan stock.[2] As time went on, however, more and more of the preponderantly Hindu population became Christians, and marriage between Hindu and Christian became commonplace, as the Portuguese names of many Goanese of mixed race still bear witness. The twin notions of becoming a

---

[1] Goa and Portuguese Africa, *Révue du Clergé Africain*, Mayidi, Belgian Congo, May 1956.
[2] Marini, pp. 25-8; Boxer, pp. 57-85; and Boxer quotes A. C. Germano da Silva Correia, *Historia de Colonização Portuguesa na India* (6 vols., Lisbon, 1943).

Christian and marrying a Portuguese undoubtedly appealed to some Hindus as a means of advancement and of attaining a higher degree of social acceptance. Yet there were many genuine conversions to Christianity, and the Catholic Goanese seaman is to this day regarded by seaport chaplains as a man of outstanding fidelity to his religion. The Hindu culture and religion, however, were not repressed. There was a massive attempt to do this in the latter half of the sixteenth century, but the mood passed, leaving a surprising number of Christians who kept the faith but acquired a kind of anti-clericalism. From the latter half of the eighteenth century onward, a new and more widespread toleration developed, and the Portuguese Code of Civil Law, passed in 1868, explicitly exempted Hindus from some of its provisions which seemed inconsistent with their traditions.

The Portuguese theory of racial miscegenation was noble enough. It hoped for a Christian society, but made ample room for co-existence and dialogue between Christian and non-Christian cultures. In many respects, it achieved a marriage of cultures in Goa, quite apart from the marriages of blood. Theory and practice, however, were often far from consistent. Discussion about this difficult topic usually fails because it turns on point-blank alternatives: either the Portuguese were wholly free from racial prejudice, or they set out to downgrade other races the better to exploit them. The truth, in fact, is far more intricate. As Professor Boxer puts it:

> For practical purposes, it can be said that the racial toleration and [relative] absence of a colour bar, of which the present-day Portuguese so proudly boasts, dates from the time of that Jekyll-and-Hyde character, Sebastião Joseph de Carvalho, Marquis of Pombal. This in itself is no mean achievement; but it does not square in historical fact with the claim so often made by and on behalf of the Portuguese that they never had the slightest idea of racial superiority or of discrimination against their subject peoples. [1]

The corollary to this was recently expressed by a Portuguese expert on the *ultramar* in a simple sentence: 'We Portuguese are not without racial prejudice, but we've less of it than most.' Albuquerque himself showed it by encouraging inter-marriage with Aryans only. Certainly, miscegenation was the general rule with the male Portuguese in India, as in Africa and Brazil, and this was due partly to his character, partly to force of circumstance. Fr Nicolas Lancilotto, an Italian

[1] Boxer, *op. cit.*, p. 84.

Jesuit, writing acidly to St Ignatius Loyola from India in 1550, said that the Portuguese 'adopted the vices and customs of the land without reserve'. They bought slaves, slept with them all, and then sold them.[1] Lancilotto's language is so intemperate in parts that one suspects his Italian blood of some anti-Portuguese bias, but there was a good deal in what he said. There were, however, plenty of formal mixed marriages and respectable Indo-Portuguese families. Moreover, even when the Portuguese ravished his slave, he frequently treated her more as *amiga* than *cativa*, it seems; that, at least, is how Professor Boxer sees the feeling of Camões for Barbara, the slave who held him in thrall. But there was plenty of evidence that slaves, both male and female, were often cruelly treated, and the children of slave mothers stood little chance of proper upbringing or education.

The picture, during the first 200 years or so of Portuguese occupation of Goa, is extremely varied and confused. The note of white superiority is inescapable, and mulattoes (*mestiços*) were looked down upon, not only by the whites, but also by the children of European fathers and Eurasian mothers (*castiços*). The religious orders, after some initial and rather unhappy experiments, declined to admit half-castes and Indians to their ranks; while the bishops gave only lowly posts to half-caste or Indian secular priests. This was not all due to prejudice. The marriage of an intuitive, oriental tradition with a metaphysical, occidental religion was bound to pose problems, and the weakness of character attributed to the native peoples by Church and state officials alike was not wholly without foundation. Attitudes varied widely. Some of Albuquerque's followers supported his selective approach to inter-marriage, while others completely rejected it and married or lived with Indians. On the whole, the Portuguese kings maintained a relatively progressive intention and at least tried to enforce the rule that full Portuguese citizenship should depend only on embracing the Christian religion, and not on colour. But Lisbon's writ did not always run in India, and viceroys and governors resisted its objectives when it came to making local appointments. By the second half of the eighteenth century, however, new trends had set in. The Vatican department for the missionary Church, *De Propaganda Fide*, and Pombal himself[2] put pressure on the

---

[1] Boxer quotes A. da Silva Rego, S.J., *Documentação para a historia das missões do Padroado Português do Oriente (India)*, 12 vols., Lisboa, 1947-58, vol. vii, pp. 32-8.

[2] His famous decree of 1761 not only insisted that colour was no bar to citizenship, but made the use of derogatory terms for natives a penal offence.

religious orders to admit Indians; indeed the scarcity of vocations demanded it. There had also been changes within the missionary Church in Goa. In 1638, the Portuguese refused to accept the juris-diction of a Christian Brahmin bishop, who promptly retorted by inciting the local Sultan and the Calvinist Dutch East India Company to attack Goa. For his pains, he was described by the Portuguese Patriarch of Ethiopia as a 'bare-bottomed nigger'. But, as the century went on, a new enlightenment appeared among the missionaries, and much was done to reduce discrimination in Church and State by the devoted work of Father Joseph Vaz and his Goanese Oratorians, who had saved the Catholic Church in Ceylon.[1]

Propaganda Fide was anxious to extricate the Church from involve-ment with the state's colonizing activities in missionary lands. It envisaged there, in other words, a formal separation of Church and State. This policy came into head-on conflict with the *Padroado*, the system whereby the Portuguese had undertaken to collaborate in the Church's missionary effort in foreign parts in return for certain privileges, such as the nomination of bishops. The conflict was long and bitter and has left a heritage which still affects Church-State rela-tions in Portuguese Africa, though the *Padroado* ended in 1951.

The problem is one, not only of spheres of influence, but of missionary method. The sixteenth-century Portuguese approach in Goa and elsewhere in India was one of aggressive proselytizing.[2] At one stage, as we have seen, there was a frontal assault on non-Christian religions and a vigorous effort to stamp them out. The linking of citizenship to acceptance of Christianity was a factor to make conversions suspect. Even the great Jesuit missionary St Francis Xavier, a Basque operating under Portuguese 'cover', has been accused of 'baptizing by hosepipe'. This, of course, is not quite fair. He was a saint, a prophet, and a servant of his people: one of those men who now and then walk into history with a flair for attracting the masses; but the enduring special quality of Goanese Catholicism, coupled with its devotion to his memory, hardly suggests that Francis Xavier's converts were just victims of mass hypnosis. At the same

[1] Boxer quotes Letter of Fr Pietro Avitabile, d. Goa, 31 Dec. 1645, apud Carlos Merces de Melo, S.J., *The recruitment and formation of the native clergy in India, 16th-19th century*, an historico-canonical study, Lisbon, 1955, pp. 247-58.
[2] Boxer, 'A note on Portuguese missionary methods in the East, 16th-18th century'; *Ceylon Historical Journal*.

time, the general tone of his evangelization was that of a Christian preaching to the infidel. The Portuguese missionaries, partly from principle and partly because of their involvement with the secular arm, saw their civilizing mission in terms of turning the indigenous peoples into good Christian Portuguese, and of imposing a European quality upon them. This was often badly received. Boxer quotes a Franciscan chronicler, writing in Goa in 1722, who speaks of Indian hatred of the conqueror, of being stampeded into Christianity, and of 'some of our friars'. He adds:

> I dare say this feeling endures to this day, not out of hatred of our religion, for by the mercy of God they have become very good Christians, but withal they still have a certain antipathy for us, as is frequently seen . . . we cannot find any other cause but that it originated in the beginning of our missions.[1]

Here again is the same familiar pattern of good and bad. Portuguese missionary method, understandable in its time, was nonetheless ill-conceived, yet the Goanese who were converted 'have become very good Christians', and it was Portuguese priests who helped to make them so. No doubt the missionaries themselves modified their attitudes as time went on and experience taught its lessons. In countries where Portugal's civil writ held no sway, Portuguese missions adopted very different methods from those identified with the *Padroado*. It is reasonable to suppose that their colleagues in Goa were also able to acquire a developing degree of flexibility, if not to the same extent.

The alternative method, resisted at first by *Propaganda Fide* but finally accepted by it and now the common coinage of Catholic mission theology, was that propounded by the two great Jesuit missionaries, Robert de Nobili and Matteo Ricci, who carried the Christian faith in the seventeenth century to India and China respectively. The principle was known as 'accommodation', though the term is misleading, as it implies no devious compromise with essential Christian conviction. What it amounts to is that Christianity offers a universal salvific gospel to all men, and that, since no one is asked to abdicate his own identity, it must express itself in and through diverse cultures and traditions. There is truth, nobility and 'news

---

[1] Boxer, p. 82, and he quotes António de Noronha, *Os Indús de Goa e Republica Portuguesa*, in *A India Portuguesa*, 2 vols., Nova Goa, 1923, vol. ii, pp. 211-368.

of God' in the Eastern cultures and religions. So the European missionary must see his task, not in terms of 'Europeanization', but of seeking common ground between the Christian and non-Christian dispensations, and then implanting the gospel within, say, the Hindu or Buddhist context. There will be a two-way traffic, for the Hindu has much to contribute to developing Christianity: a unique contribution without which the Christian faith and community will be poorer. The Western Church, for instance, which came to express its faith in metaphysical terms, a heritage of Greco-Roman philosophy, may restore its contemplative tradition. Certainly, if the Hindu is to embrace Christianity, he must be convinced that the claims of the Christian dogma and Church are authentic, and in the process he may be discarding some of his prior beliefs. But baptism does not imply a total rejection of what he once was. With this in view, De Nobili became a Brahmin, and both missionaries sought to marry the Christian liturgy to Indian and Chinese rites. Though they were to be discredited at Rome, their inspiration remained. At the twentieth-century Vatican Council, their principles were formally enshrined in constitutional form, though they have not yet been universally established in practice; which doubtless explains why, in some oriental countries, the Christian religion still accounts for only 1 or 2 per cent of the population, despite centuries of missionary endeavour. If the initial work of the *Padroado* system was not later lost, it is precisely because the Portuguese found a facility for a marriage of cultures in which the Hindu did not, after all, lose his identity, even though it also acquired a significant European facet.[1]

In spite of early resentments, the position in Goa by the middle of the eighteenth century appears from the fact that, during the Maratha invasion of Bardez and Salcete in 1939-40, the native Christians stayed loyal to the Portuguese, and Indian Christians and Hindus alike found the ransom money to keep the victorious invaders out of Goa. A forced loan was raised, but seemingly without creating resentment. Most of the Portuguese Indian territory seized by Nehru's India in 1961, was acquired between 1763 and 1788. Its residents were explicitly guaranteed complete freedom of worship

---

[1] A different situation developed in Portuguese Africa, where there was no great non-Christian religious culture comparable to Hinduism. Hence the problems of Europeanization *v*. Africanization continue to account for tensions, not only in the secular sphere, but also between Portugal and the Holy See.

and respect for their religion, and full toleration in all but a few details came with the new Constitutional era opening in the 1820s.

The interaction of the Portuguese and Hindu cultures is described by the Indian writer B. K. Boman Behram of Bombay in his book *Goa and Ourselves*.[1] The Portuguese, he says, did more than govern Goa:

> They had initiated a historic process which in the fullness of time made the Goan people a close-knit unit of the Lusitanian family. It is a true eastern capital of the Portuguese nation, in which was formed a society with very positive Portuguese characteristics, wholly integrated in the national spirit. In the result, one finds that a true Goan feels a bond of kinship with distant Portugal which he does not with his great neighbour on the other side of the frontier. . . .

The Christians, says the author, are 'an orientalized neo-Latin type', whereas

> The Hindus, by reasons of their customs and usages having been protected by special Portuguese law, and by the fact that they constantly intermingled with their neighbouring co-religionists, did not integrate so much in the sociological ethnography of Goa, and it cannot be said that the process of Lusitanization is complete in them. But, it is pointed out, the Hindus of Portuguese India . . . are a Portuguese type [and] definitely differ from Hindus inhabiting the adjoining territories.

Such impressions are consistent with those of writers like André Siegfried, Gilberto Freyre and Arnold Toynbee. The Goanese has his own identity and character and cannot willingly be a pawn in anyone's game. The question is how far, in the 1950s, he saw his future in terms of continuity with the past, or whether he wanted to move under Indian jurisdiction.

Some light on this matter was shed in an interview given in 1954 by Archbishop T. D. Roberts, S.J., who in 1937, had been sent to India to take charge of the Bombay archdiocese. By that time, the *Padroado* had been reduced, but, as a return for lost privileges, the Holy See had agreed that successive archbishops of Bombay should be alternatively English and Portuguese, Roberts, who has since become

[1] Quoted by Lawrence, p. 21.

famous, not only for his work in India, but also as a champion of liberalization in the Roman Catholic Church, at once came into contact with Salazar and the Cardinal Patriarch of Lisbon, and found them co-operative. In his book *Black Popes*,[1] a study of the use and abuse of authority, he shows great understanding of Salazar's early policies and pays him this tribute:

> He put Portugal – chaotic as he found his country – firmly on the path traced by Christian civilization; he has been justified by twenty-five years of peaceful prosperity. His name I link with Leon Harmel's because his three loves are the same: love of the worker, lover of the worker's family, the service of Jesus Christ . . . his alliance with Christianity is less proclaimed than implicit in reverence for all the Christian values – the dignity of the free individual, of the family, of the school, of patriotism.[2]

As befits a great apostle of freedom, Roberts had his reservations about even benign dictatorships; he felt that the corporate state had yet to be tested by time, and he was not at one with Salazar's European approach to the missionary Church. But he was grateful to Salazar's government for acknowledging that the *Padroado* was outmoded, and co-operating in its demise. When Roberts arrived in Bombay after his Lisbon detour, he found that the Portuguese Consul-General had been instructed to help him in every way. One of the first problems was that of the extra-territorial, Goanese parishes in Bombay, the residue of the *Padroado* parishes which once had virtually been at war with others in the vicinity which depended on *Propaganda*. What it came to in 1937 was that Goanese Catholics in Bombay belonged, not to parishes in their neighbourhoods, but to the two special parishes which cut across normal parochial boundaries. To get the archdiocese on to a rational footing, Roberts had to reorganize it on a territorial basis, but he could only do so with Portuguese agreement. This was accorded, and the parishes redistributed. He then set to work to build up the indigenous clergy, but soon saw that alternate Portuguese and English archbishops could not give the Bombay archdiocese the character and stability it needed, especially if India was to be convinced that Christianity was not a European preserve and alien to her soil. Robert's historic achievement was to convince Pope Pius XII of the need for an Indian archbishop, and

[1] Longmans Green & Co., London, 1954.
[2] P. 48.

he proved the feasibility of his scheme by leaving the diocese for four years in the competent hands of a priest who was named auxiliary bishop for the purpose, Mgr Valerian Gracias; he had been born in Karachi, but was of Goanese origin. Eventually, on 18 July 1950, Portugal and the Holy See signed an Accord which further reduced the *Padroado* to territory where Portugal's civil writ ran. The Archbishop of Goa was to be Portuguese, but his diocese was to be delimited to exclude areas within the Indian Republic. He remains Patriarch of the Indies, but this means Portuguese India – if that phrase has any meaning today. The way was open for an Indian to take Bombay. In December 1950, Roberts resigned and was at once succeeded by Gracias, who later was named Cardinal.

It was to Roberts that the London *Catholic Herald* turned in December 1954 for an opinion on the dispute between India and Portugal.[1] Roberts very properly declined to comment on the political aspects, but expressed the view that probably the majority of Goanese inside Goa wanted to stay with Portugal, while a majority of the *diaspora* favoured the inclusion of Goa into the Indian Union where they had now established themselves. Whatever the rights and wrongs of the dispute, however, Roberts took the view that the absorption of Goa into India would be to the Church's advantage. Already the incumbents of half the Indian Republic's Catholic Sees were of Indian or semi-Indian stock, most of them Goanese, and there were many Goanese priests at work in Indian dioceses. Their position would be strengthened if the taint of European control were removed more quickly from the Catholic community of the sub-continent, and Goanese bishops and clergy in India became Indian subjects. At that time the Church in India was on the most cordial terms with the Indian government, but the more intransigent Hindu movements like the Mahasabha were mounting an offensive against the presence of foreign missionaries in the country. With all this in view, it is understandable that *Propaganda* must have wanted to see Goa absorbed into India, though the Holy See skilfully avoided any involvement in the political crisis, and no view was expressed. Salazar, however, believed that *Propaganda* influenced Catholic circles in a number of foreign countries in the direction of supporting India's claim.

So far as the Goanese themselves were concerned, however, the London *Times* correspondent reported, on 22 March 1954, that 'there

---

[1] London *Catholic Herald*, 17 December 1954.

are no outward signs in Goa of dissatisfaction with the present regime or with conditions in general'. In August of that year, the Indians planned a 'peace march' of anti-Portuguese Goanese, who would enter Goa from India to demonstrate in India's favour. The *Daily Telegraph* correspondent on the spot reported:

> Despite all the agitation of recent months, with rival bands of 'liberators' recruited on Indian soil, some under Communist auspices, the miserable trickle of demonstrators who crossed the Portuguese frontier on Sunday can leave no doubt that the notion of 'Goa irridenta' is purely an Indian fantasy.[1]

The Times correspondent also reported that Indian sources had intended to urge masses of volunteers to bring freedom to the 'oppressed brothers' groaning under Portuguese rule. He added:

> The 'oppressed brothers', seemingly unattracted by this prospect, resorted in almost unprecedented numbers to the shrine of St Xavier with petitions to be saved from the disturbances which threatened their way of life. The Portuguese authorities made ready to meet 'peaceful penetration' by equally peaceful but no less determined moral resistance, keeping their very small resources of physical force firmly in the background.[2]

He also testified that the incoming volunteers were only a small number of Goanese living in India. The two reports seem to suggest that, not only were the residents of Goa unexcited at the prospect of Indian sovereignty, but that even the *diaspora* was less enthusiastic than the Indian government was prone to suggest. Pattee tells us:

> There seems little doubt that, of the emigrés, some of those who have achieved a position of some importance in India (that is, the elite), are favourable to annexation. It must be emphasized, however, that of these almost all have lost contact with affairs in Portuguese India and cannot claim to speak for their former compatriots. . . . Most Goans in India, and especially those in modest circumstances, seem to have remained passive or positively loyal to Portugal up to date. The confusion of parties and movements and the doubtful character of some of the leadership has not been such as to inspire unreserved ardour for liberation.[3]

[1] 17 August 1954.
[2] 17 August 1954.
[3] Pattee, *op. cit.*, pp. 281-2.

Pattee goes on to quote the *British Survey* which, in November 1954, noted that 'there seems to have been a remarkable consensus of opinion among responsible foreign reporters who have been in Goa that the general feeling of the population is against any change'.[1] He adds that Roy Trumball of the *New York Times*, André Siegfried of *Figaro* and others concurred in the view that 'the population of Goa is quite unaware of the reality of the Indian contention that it suffers from "oppression"'; and the British writer Evelyn Waugh had noted after a visit to Goa that the Goanese tended to compare their relatively high standards with India and were not impressed by what they saw across the frontier.[2] In August 1955, *The Times* correspondent reported that most Goanese in India tended to retire to their co-operative villages in Goa, where the only social division was represented by a certain residual Brahminism in recent converts to Christianity. African troops, Goanese police and European officials cohabited with the population and with each other comfortably, and without any sign of racial tension. Domestic consumers were not governed by heavy taxation and foreign exchange control. Consumer goods of all kinds were on sale in the shops. Exports of manganese to America and iron ore to Japan were earning high profits. Cigarettes sold at a quarter of the Indian prices, a dazzling display of textiles was on show, the overall standard of living was higher than in India, and in fact many Indians chose to live in Goa. It was very hard to find Goanese who favoured the Indian Union.[3]

Goanese in India who had various reasons for wanting Portugal, or the Portuguese regime, out of Goa formed a number of militant groups which were active in Portuguese Indian territory, and we are told that in the eleven years from 1946 to 1957, some 2,000 nationalists were arrested by the Portuguese, 300 were sentenced, and thirteen were deported to Portugal, Angola or Cape Verde.[4] The Goa League claimed that eighty-seven had been tortured or shot, but in view of the testimony by many European journalists that the propaganda emanating from India was highly exaggerated, this piece of information needs to be treated with reserve. In 1954, *The Times* reported that political prisoners in Goa were well treated, that most of them

---

[1] *British Survey*, London, November 1954, no. 68, p. 20.
[2] Pattee, *op. cit.*, p. 281.
[3] *The Times*, London, 26 August 1955.
[4] Fryer and McGowan Pinheiro, *op. cit.*, p. 176.

belonged to the *Azad Gomantak Lal*,[1] and that they included Indian agitators. The correspondent visited a prison and, referring to allegations from the other side of the border, concluded that the Indian press 'must be writing about another Goa'. He found no dungeons, truncheons or starvation of the kind alleged by Portugal's critics. The prisoners spent their time in gardens, were addressed by their first names by the lieutenant in charge, were housed in large rooms with clean sheets on the beds, wore ordinary clothes and spoke freely. Some said they had been knocked about by the police when they were first arrested. There were two Indian 'professional' prisoners and one agitator of the Praja Socialist Party.[2] Emile Marini, an Italian journalist who toured Goa in 1956, was able to examine all the prisons and found only 163 political detainees – not the thousands alleged by the Indian press. They were all in conditions identical with those described by *The Times* correspondent, and those whose religion required it were allowed special diets. None of them made any complaints, and some of them questioned by Marini showed little understanding of the issues leading to their activities and arrest.[3]

The militant groups included the *National Congress (Goa)*, founded in 1946, and later led by Peter Alvares, an Indian socialist or Goanese origin. It produced a number of offshoots, and one of its members was Antonio Furtado who was to be named administrator of the enclaves of Dadrá and Nagar Aveli when they were occupied by the Indians in 1954. Another group active in those areas was the *Goan People's Party*, run by Divakar Kakodkar and George Vaz, which was closely linked with the Indian Communist Party. The *United Front of Goans* was formed in 1950 to fight for an autonomous State of Goa within the Indian Union. Tristão Bragança Cunha, a Goanese Marxist, founded the *Goan Action Committee* to co-ordinate the 'liberation' movements. The *Goan Liberation Council*, formed in August 1954, by A. Soares, was predominantly Catholic. Soares had been active in the struggle against British rule, and then turned his attention to what he described as the Fascist regime in Portugal. None of these groups attracted substantial numerical support from

---

[1] This 'Free Goan Group' was formed early in 1954 by V. N. Lawande, who had been expelled by the Indian Congress. He was helped by the Hindu extremist Mahasabha and the Jan Sangh. These groups have been described as 'Hindu communalist'.
[2] *The Times*, 16 August 1954.
[3] Marini. *op. cit.*, p. 91 *et seq.*

the Goanese living in India, but they were energetic and often effective in rousing world opinion to their cause, and they offered Nehru a wedge to break through the Portuguese resistance.

The Indian Independence Act of 1947, which ended the British Raj, created the Indian Union and Pakistan out of what had been British India. This covered only a third of the Indian sub-continent, and the Act left intact the sovereignty of the 561 Indian states which occupied the remaining two-thirds. Most of these decided to move in with either India or Pakistan, but a few did not, and the Indian Union annexed them at gunpoint. The Kashmir story is well enough known, but little attention has been given to Moslem states like Bhopal, Junagadh, Hyderabad and others which, despite their people's wishes and their geographical contiguity to their fellow Moslems in Pakistan, were forced into the Indian Union's sector. Pakistan had yet to create its army, and could not help them. India had inherited an excellent army from Britain. The Indian dream was to recreate a sub-continental empire, and there was talk of Ashoka, the Gupta Emperor who ruled from the north two centuries and more before Christ.

Between 1947 and 1950, India's relations with Portugal were cordial. The Goanese co-operative organizations on Indian soil, named after the 'village republics' back in Goa, were respected and accorded privileges. When a movement for unhinging the Salazar regime was started by the Indian Socialist, Dr Ram Manohar Lohia,[1] Nehru simply commented that it was for the Goanese themselves to decide their own future. Various factors, however, combined to alter his position. As a leading figure in the anti-colonialist, Afro-Asian groupings he was doubtless under pressure from abroad to make the first move in unhinging Portugal from her empire. At home, the longing for national unity and an Indian world completely freed from European suzerainty was genuine and profound. Less noble considerations, perhaps, were the need to divert the Indian people's attention from Chinese activities on the northern border, and the attractions of Goa's iron and manganese.[2] Accordingly, on 27 February 1950, the Indian Legation in Lisbon delivered an *aide-*

---

[1] He spent four years (1946-50) as a deportee in Portugal for his activities in Goa.
[2] See Lawrence, *op. cit.*, p. 179. Leo Lawrence, a distinguished Goanese lawyer expelled from India in 1959 and an eye-witness of the 1961 invasion of Goa, tells of his conversation with an American journalist who, when asked why the Western world seemed to support India's case, and why Goa could not be

mémoire to the Portuguese Foreign Ministry.[1] It expressed satisfaction that the Portuguese were negotiating with the Holy See to bring the *Padroado* to an end, and suggested that the time had come to discuss the Portuguese colonies in India. The Indian nationalist movement was not confined to what had been British India, as the historical and cultural unity of India transcended political frontiers. Popular feeling in the French settlements and Portuguese colonies in geographical India was in favour of union with the new and free India of the Republic. The interruption of India's fundamental unity by a few hundred years of foreign rule over various segments of the country could not, in the perspective of history, be more than a transient phase. That unity, though often interrupted, had always remained an inspiration and, again and again, had been effectively restored. The union of the remaining foreign 'settlements' with the Indian Republic was part of the historical process. France had shown willing. It was hoped that Portugal would react in a similar spirit.

Salazar's reply, in a note dated 15 June 1950, was a polite but emphatic refusal. Goa, Damão and Diu were not colonies but an integral part of Portugal. There was no popular sentiment in those territories in favour of reunion with independent India. Portugal was unable to discuss, let alone accept, the solution proposed by the Indian government.[2] There followed over the next few years a series of exchanges in which charges and counter-charges were made about repression of Indian sympathizers in Goa and the bullying of the Goanese in India. In view of India's membership of the British Commonwealth, Portugal hoped that Britain, her ally, would help her. The diplomatic exchanges on this crucial and delicate aspect of the Goa story are not yet available to the public. But it is certain that Britain's advice to Portugal was to come to terms with Nehru. If she herself had been forced to leave India, what chance could there be for Portugal? Britain had her own troubles, too, with the Afro-Asian bloc. The 1950s were the years which saw the Suez crisis, the great decolonization phase in Africa, the ill-fated Central African Federation. Nehru was being hailed as the great apostle of peace and honorary leader of the third world.

---

left alone to decide her own future, offered this terse reply: 'And let you exploit these mines haphazardly? No, Goa is too small for that, I am sorry for you. But Goa is too small.'

[1] IND. DOCS., vol. i, p. 187.

[2] *Ibid.*, p. 219.

Salazar's attitude was that he was prepared to negotiate with India on any and every problem arising out of her presence in the sub-continent bar one thing: sovereignty over Goa. This topic could not even appear on an agenda. The question was a non-starter. Members of the opposition in Portugal who urged negotiations on the government not only got into trouble with the police but also with the greater part of public opinion. If it be said that this was just another instance of Portuguese obstinacy and extremism, then it is worth comparing the Goa crisis with the current Anglo-Spanish dispute on Gibraltar. Britain has made it plain to Madrid that she is ready to talk about anything – bar sovereignty. As with Goa, the power in possession is there by way of legal title and has no intention of relinquishing it. If, as India and Spain have both sought to argue, the issue is one of decolonization under the U.N. Charter, then the paramount question is the will of the colonized people. Portugal argued that the Goanese will was to stay Portuguese. Britain has proved by referendum that the Gibraltarians want to stay British. There are, of course, important differences between the two cases. Spain is not concerned with the Gibraltarians' wishes, claiming that the overriding factor is Spain's right to have her territorial integrity restored to her. Nehru, on the other hand, though concerned with the territorial question, put much more stress on what he asserted to be the Goanese wish to return to the Indian fold. There was, however, scant evidence for this. In the end, the anomalous truth was that the Afro-Asian and Communist blocs totally disregarded Principle IX of the United Nations Twelve Principles which declares that the integration of a territory with an independent state (in the case of Goa, with India) should be the result of

> the freely expressed wishes of the territory's peoples acting with full knowledge of the change in their status, their wishes having been expressed through informed and democratic processes, impartially conducted and based on universal suffrage. The United Nations could, when it deems it necessary, supervise these processes.[1]

Thus even assuming that India had the right to invade Goa, the annexation should have been ratified by a successful appeal to the people's wishes. After all, they might still have plumped for total independence. They were given no chance to decide. The conduct

[1] See Appendix A.

of the U.N., however, is not always explicable. In the case of Gibraltar, the General Assembly has called on Britain to surrender the Rock to Spain despite the explicit wish of nearly 100 per cent of the local people to stay British. If it is said, for both Spain and India, that the demands of territorial integrity are prior to the will of the people, the answer is that the principle is not proved. It was just this point which Britain offered to take to the International Court in 1968.

On 26 March 1954, India announced that in future Goa's officials would need a permit to enter Indian territory, as restrictions had been placed on Indians entering Goa. In June, India closed her mission in Lisbon, though the Portuguese mission in Delhi continued. The Indian government, in announcing the closure, argued that 'the withdrawal of British power from the former Indian empire left no justification for these vestiges of a colonial past to continue to exist in a free India', and the note accused Portugal of 'progressive curtailment of political liberties and a determined attempt to suppress by violence the deep-seated desire of the people of the Portuguese possessions for union with India'. There had been censorship, arrests, deportations and imprisonment, and Indian businessmen had been harassed. Portugal was reminded that a year before, India had told her that 'political borders artificially created by an accident of history for which no justification existed at the present moment' could 'no longer stem the rising tide of the national urge for unity'.[1] Earlier in the year, Nehru had had a meeting with Cardinal Gracias, who threw his significant weight behind the Indian claim. The cardinal prepared a manifesto stating the case for merger, and the idea was to get all the Goanese people in India to sign it. There were about 100,000 of them. Only ninety-six signed.[2] What has been described as a reign of terror was then let loose on the Goanese community in Bombay: police raids at night, arrests, threats, beatings-up, fruitless pressure on Goanese nationals to change their nationality, and many arbitrary expulsions.[3] Hundreds of people were taken to police headquarters and a number of prosecutions were staged. The pro-Portuguese paper *Anglo-Lusitano* had its offices set on fire, and its editor was deported. In July 1954, the enclaves of Dadrá and Nagar Aveli were occupied by irregular Indian forces, alleged on the Indian

[1] Keesing's Contemporary Archives.
[2] Lawrence, *op. cit.*, p. 34.
[3] *Ibid.*, pp. 37-40; Marini, *op. cit.*, p. 97 *et seq.*; IND. DOCS., *op. cit.*, pp. 359-62.

side to be Goanese, but apparently backed by regular Indian troops.[1] The Indian government then cut all communications between the enclaves and Damão, and Portugal subsequently took the issue to the International Court. Although world feeling was anti-Portuguese, and some of the judges came from very hostile countries, the preliminary judgment of 26 November 1957, decided that Portugal had the right of sovereignty in the two disputed territories. The final judgment confirmed her right or passage over Indian territory from coastal Damão to Dadrá and Nagar Aveli so far as private individuals, civil servants and goods were concerned, subject to the control of the Indian Union; but it found that Portugal had no right to send armed forces, police or ammunition across the intervening Indian territory.

It was in August 1954 that the Indians planned a demonstration by *satyagrahis*, demonstrators adopting the method of peaceful protest and 'conversion by goodness' associated in the past with Gandhi. The idea was that a large 'pilgrimage' of Goanese should cross the border into Goa in non-violent protest on 15 August. The organizers were supposed to be unofficial, and some connected them with the Communist Party, but in any event the programme misfired. As already noted, foreign observers crowded to the scene only to find a few straggling 'volunteers' preparing to cross the border into Goa instead of the thousands planned for, while thousands of people inside Goa went off with the Patriarch, Archbishop Vieira Alvernaz, to pray for deliverance from Indian harassment.[2] The most pungent comment came from the *Glasgow Herald* which took the view that the Portuguese had been guilty of repression in Goa, but added:

> Nevertheless, the easy-going and comfortable inhabitants do not seem to mind very much . . . the world has enough iniquities to make it an intolerable irony that so much energy should be frittered away in inflicting freedom on Goa.[3]

There was little to suggest any hope of solutions, however. In an exchange of notes, India had accepted a Portuguese proposal that neutral observers should visit Goa, but when it came to settling details, Portugal wanted to know precisely what subjects would be on the agenda for any formal meeting of officials, insisted that the

---

[1] Lawrence, *op. cit.*, pp. 65-84.
[2] *The Times*, 16 and 17 August 1954; *Daily Telegraph*, 17 August 1954 and 16 August 1955; *New York Times*, 16 August 1954; Marini, *op. cit.*, p. 102.
[3] *Glasgow Herald*, 19 August 1954.

question of sovereignty must not be raised, and finally expressed the view that an exchange of Notes was a quicker way of doing business than conferences. The *Guardian* correspondent thought that the Portuguese were shying away from direct contact and that both sides were playing to the gallery.[1]

In spite of all the evidence to the contrary, Nehru felt no difficulty in telling the Lok Sabha on 25 August 1954, that 'internally, in the Portuguese settlements, the opposition and resistance to foreign and colonial rule has gained momentum. This is an entirely Goan movement, popular and indigenous.' However, 'we may not adopt, advocate or deliberately bring about situations of violence', and, like the government, 'the great majority of our people' had no intention of departing from India's non-violent principles. These were 'the foundation on which our very nationhood rests'. When Goa became part of the Indian Union, it would enjoy the freedom of conscience, worship and religion guaranteed by the Indian Constitution. Moreover,

> the special circumstances of cultural, social and lingual relations and the sense of a territorial group which history has created will be respected. Laws and customs which are part of the social pattern of these areas and which are consistent with fundamental rights and freedoms, will be respected and modifications will be sought only by negotiation and consent.[2]

The language is strange in view of previous assertions that the Hindus of Goa and the adjoining Indian territory shared an identical culture and character. An interesting sidelight on this issue comes from the former French Resistance hero, Colonel Rémy, who visited Goa about this time and later reported an incident when an Indian minister had, to the surprise of local officials, arrived in Goa. He was shown round a school where Moslems, Christians, Parsees, Brahmins and Untouchables were sitting side by side. His question was: 'How do you manage to get them all together?' It was a senior boy who answered that the integrating factor was their common Portuguese character.[3]

By the end of the year India had ordered the Portuguese legation to get out of New Delhi and the Indian consulate was closed in Goa. It was on 30 November 1954, that Salazar delivered a solemn address

---

[1] *Guardian*, 16 August 1954.
[2] Lok Sabha Debates, part II, vol. V, no. 3, p. 230.
[3] Pattee, *op. cit.*, p. 285; *Diario de Noticias*, Lisbon, 27 July 1955.

on the situation to the National Assembly in Lisbon.[1] For the Indian Union to claim to turn the clock of history back to the sixteenth century and argue that she already existed potentially at that time, or to set herself up as the rightful heir of the people the Portuguese found in the country when they arrived was 'a fancy of static dreamers', not for men who wanted to shape history. On the Indian plea, no present-day sovereignty or frontier could lay claim to continued existence. As for self-determination, there were Goanese people in Portuguese territory, in India, in other countries where Portugal had no influence at all, but

> neither the material and moral pressure exerted within the Indian Union herself nor the thousand and one forms of inducement and enticement used outside her borders – as in Kenya or Tanganyika or Pakistan – have managed to dissuade these peoples from professing the fact that they are Portuguese. And here I want to place on record a word of heartfelt admiration for the patriotic loyalty which has been displayed, sometimes in very difficult circumstances, by such large numbers of individuals, to so many of whom Portugal has given only the honour of a name and the prestige of a history.

Salazar then shed some light on why the proposals to send neutral observers to Goa had come to nothing. Portugal's proposal had been that the observers should ascertain the facts of what had happened in Dadrá and Nagra Aveli. What the Indians agreed to was

> the principle of conversations to negotiate the sending of international observers to ascertain the overall situation in the Portuguese State of India, and the Portuguese proposal was thus speciously enmeshed in a cobweb of negotiations with no precise subject matter and no limitation of time.

The Indians had in effect imposed a blockade on all trade between Goa and the Indian Union and had supported decisions 'imposed by extremists on the Indian dockers' Unions' to extend the blockade to trade with third parties by refusing to handle ships which had or would touch at Goa. Goanese working in India were being prevented from sending money to their families at home. Goa's fishing and cargo boats had been boarded and subjected to acts of piracy. As for the *satyagrahis*, this form of demonstration had been severely put

[1] António de Oliveira Salazar, *Goa and the Indian Union*, Lisbon, 1954.

down within the Indian Union itself, and the participants in the marches on Goa had been 'organized, ordered and paid for at so much a martyr'. In Dadrá and Nagar Aveli men had been killed, wounded and taken prisoner, and the intervention of Portuguese personnel anxious to restore order had been prevented by armed forces posted along the borders. 'Non-violence', therefore, meant anything short of formal war.

Turning to accusations of colonialism, Salazar showed disdain for what he described as 'geographical imperatives'. He went on:

> Switzerland was constituted by Germans, Frenchmen and Italians, who retain their original tongues. . . . The Magyars have been in Hungary for 1,000 years, in the heart of a Europe that is linguistically and racially different. . . . In what respect is the existence in Hindustan of a people that has a western culture and is part of a European nation more shocking to the mind than the other illogicalities just cited?

Colonialism in its pejorative sense meant inequality of races and cultures and a purpose of economic exploitation expressed in a distinction between citizens and subjects. But,

> There is no colonialism where strategic, economic or financial advantages are not derived and where the running of public services even adds a heavy charge to the mother country's budget. A status or condition of colony is inconceivable where standards of living are similar, the culture is the same, public law contains no discrimination, individuals are equal before institutions and laws. There can be no colonialism when the people are an integral part of the nation, when the citizens actively co-operate in a footing of equality in forming the state, and when individuals hold public office and move about and engage in their occupations throughout the Portuguese territories.

Salazar then launched a frontal assault on *Propaganda Fide*. There had to be, he said, a minimum of relations and co-operation between governments and missions even when, as in the Portuguese system, the state is not denominational and there is no union with the Church apart from a Concordat with the Holy See:

> In the face of the ardent nationalism breaking out in Asia and Africa against the sovereignties and positions which Europe is continually abandoning, *Propaganda* believes it must try to save its achievements

by dissociating itself from the state, and, on the other hand, recruiting the clergy as far as possible among local converts: political independence and a native clergy are the distinguishing marks of the new tendencies, the former helping to emphasize an earlier trend.

To say that freedom is necessary to the Church was fair enough, but it was not true to argue that freedom is enough for the Church, especially when 'competing religious systems act in any way as factors of social cohesion of the peoples in question and as such receive special protection, direct or indirect, from the state'. So far as native clergy were concerned, Portugal had been a pioneer. There had been Indian priests in her territory in 1530, and all the clergy of Goa had been Goanese for two centuries. Moreover, they had laboured even beyond the *Padroado* in the service of the whole Church. But without the aid of foreign missionaries, Salazar saw little future for Christianity in the East. If the distinction between religious freedom and missionary freedom were accepted to the disadvantage of the latter, the next step would be to establish exclusively national Churches cut off from the universal Christian community, and this in turn would lead to a final disintegration of the local Christian bodies in a state of religious chaos.

As to what should be done, Salazar ruled out negotiations with India on the issue of sovereignty, though he was ready and willing to talk about anything else:

> We would be giving or selling . . . the Portuguese of India, the lands of Afonso de Albuquerque and our epic achievements in the Orient, the saints of the Church, our country's martyrs. For how much? For how much?

As to the suggestion that Portugal should give Goa full independence within a Portuguese federation or commonwealth, Salazar argued that in 1926, Portugal Overseas was suffering from the very same ills that afflicted the homeland, with the difference that the results overseas were worse. Remedies had to follow the same principles as were applied in the mother country, and hence the Colonial Act had provided for greater centralization of power and a policy of co-ordination and integration of the several parts of the Portuguese nation in a more cohesive whole: a single unit with several forms. The overseas achievements of the past generation had proved the worth of these principles, and it was naive to try to apply to Portuguese countries, with their own special character and needs, systems which had been perfectly appropriate for the British Commonwealth. The background and history were totally different.

The speech did little to ease the situation, but it served to harden Portuguese self-confidence. The months dragged by uncertainly, and then in August 1955, the Indians decided on a repeat performance of the previous year's demonstrations on the border – but this time with a difference. This time the march on Goa would not be the march of Goanese returning to the land of their birth to free it from the oppressor, but of Indians out to save their neighbours by a non-violent conquest. So on 15 August, some 5,000 Indians appeared as *satyagrahis* on the border, but with troops standing by. The Portuguese police tried to play it cool, but were not prepared to allow Indian nationals to 'invade' Goanese territory. Under pressure, however, they eventually opened fire, and it is estimated that fifteen Indians were killed and thirty-eight wounded. The rest melted away and, according to Lawrence,[1] later tried to storm the Bombay Government Secretariat in a demand for the payment they had been promised. The police mowed hundreds down with machine-guns. Many others had been in trouble with the railway police for trying to travel home without tickets. Everyone was thoroughly disillusioned. The next move was a series of terrorist raids across the border by the *Azad Gomantak Dal*, from training camps at Belgaum and Nasik among others. Nehru brushed these incidents off as the inescapable casualties of a struggle for freedom. Meanwhile, Goa continued to prosper with a boom in the iron-ore industry which made her one of the world's biggest exporters of that commodity. Nehru came out in his true colours when he told the Indian Parliament on 6 September, that 'we are not prepared to tolerate the presence of the Portuguese in Goa, even if the Goans want them to be there'. He received a little comfort from Britain's foreign secretary, Lord Home, who told him that NATO's commitment to Portugal probably did not extend to the Goa crisis – it would be 'pushing it' to argue that it did – and, so far, the Portuguese had not invoked their alliance with Britain in regard to the Goa dispute.[2]

[1] Lawrence, *op. cit.*, p. 58; see also p. 278.
[2] In August 1954, Mr Selwyn Lloyd, Minister of State at the Foreign Office, London, had told the Portuguese Ambassador, Theotónio Pereira, that Her Majesty's Government would urge the Indian Government not to use or provoke the use of force.

Nothing substantial happened, however, for six years, partly because the world was busy with a series of crises elsewhere, and in any case both Portugal and India awaited the final decision of the International Court over Dadrá and Nagar Aveli, which was not pronounced until 2 April 1960. In March 1961, the Angolan War broke out, and world pressure on Portugal started to build up fast, while India's eastern frontier came under peril from China. On 23 October, the Afro-Asian seminar on the future of the Portuguese possessions opened in New Delhi. In November, Nehru visited President Kennedy in Washington, and, in the light of subsequent events, observers have wondered whether the President gave him some kind of assurance that the United States would take no action if Goa were invaded. It seems clear that, after the New Delhi seminar, India was pledged to oust the Portuguese from the East as the Africans were trying to do in Angola, and it seems unlikely that Nehru and Kennedy talked without a single reference to this issue. Moreover, immediately after the invasion, the United States condemned the aggression but stated that it would not affect the passage of aid to India. Schlesinger tells us that, up to the last minute, the United States made it plain that she was against aggression, and he complains that this was not counterbalanced by a lecture to Portugal on the wrongs of colonialism. It seems that after the invasion the State Department promised Salazar to restrict its official reactions to the issue of aggression, without mentioning colonialism at all. Adlai Stevenson was ordered, against his own judgment, to trim his U.N. speech accordingly. However, the pledge to Salazar was apparently given without consultation with the White House. President Kennedy's personal position remains in some ways obscure, but the fact is that, in addition to all the other diplomatic approaches, he sent Nehru a personal message on 13 December, urging him to desist from the use of force, and on 16 December, the United States government made a further appeal to the Indian Premier 'to suspend preparations for the use of force in connection with a direct offer of U.S. help in seeking a peaceful solution to the problem', as Stevenson later put it in the Security Council.[1] The truth of the matter is that neither the United States nor anyone else could have deflected Nehru from his purpose at this time except by a straight promise to get Portugal out of India in some other way, and this would hardly have been a feasible way for the United States to treat Portugal,

[1] Schlesinger, pp. 486-90; Keesing's Contemporary Archives, p. 18660.

her ally in NATO. The U.S. Ambassador in New Delhi, Professor Galbraith, succeeded in getting the invasion postponed for three or four days, but that was all.

For some weeks prior to the invasion, Portugal and India charged each other with border provocations and violations, massing of troops, and hostile overflights. Nehru had also been accusing Goa of an internal reign of terror and torture against pro-Indian nationalists. The eventual campaign itself, however, showed that there had been no Portuguese military build-up in Goa, and that Indian allegations about African reinforcements from Mozambique were utterly baseless. India claimed that the strength of the Portuguese forces was anything up to 12,000. The campaign showed that the total was 3,500, none of whom was African.[1] Two days after the invasion, *The Times* correspondent in Panjim reported:

> The number of actual Portuguese soldiers captured belies the Indian propaganda which before the invasion spoke of 'massive reinforcement' of the garrison. Much else of the propaganda which preceded the assault can now be seen to have been baseless. The Indian authorities had said that the colony was falling into 'anarchy and chaos' and that the invasion was necessary to save Goa from a mass exodus and extermination, but even after the sporadic shooting of yesterday [19 December] and the excitement of the invasion Panjim is calm and orderly.[2]

The *Guardian* correspondent reported from Bombay:

> Granted the moral distinction between the ends in view, the whole propaganda operation reminded a British observer irresistibly of Suez. A different story was trotted out each day, and later events have demonstrated that at least some were flatly untrue. . . . A *satyagrahi* tortured to death last month has turned up alive and well. Correspondents near the border at Belgaum were treated to a farrago of anti-Portuguese charges, undetailed . . . unsubstantiated, and even inconsistent. A day before the attack we learned within the space of 10 minutes both that the Portuguese troops were withdrawing from the borders and that they were massing menacingly. For the massacre and holocaust story no evidence has been produced whatever. As for the breakdown of law and order, perhaps the

[1] Keesing's, *op. cit.*, 18638.
[2] *The Times*, 20 December 1961.

fewer unflattering parallels drawn the better. The pity is that these trivialities masked and discredited India's real case.[1]

On 11 December, the Portuguese had informed the U.N. Security Council that Indian troops were building up on the borders of Goa. The next day the Governor-General of Goa, General Manuel Antonio Vassalo e Silva, announced the evacuation of women and children. Several hundred families went by sea and air to Portugal, most of them being wives and children of Portuguese officials and military personnel. Notes were exchanged between Portugal and India through the embassies of other powers, and Portugal proposed the despatch of an international mission to study the situation on the Goan border and determine responsibility for the incidents. The Indians ignored this suggestion, stating simply that the Indian people were determined to ensure that there were no more vestiges of colonial rule on their territory.[2] On 15 December, U Thant sent messages to Dr Salazar and Mr Nehru urging them not to let the situation deteriorate and to enter into immediate negotiations. Salazar replied to the effect that his forces in Portuguese India had been rigorously instructed not to commit or even reply to acts of provocation, and that Portugal had always been willing to negotiate with India to find solutions for all the problems arising from the Portuguese presence in the sub-continent, including the possibility of an international guarantee that Portuguese territory would not be used against the security of the Indian Union. The offer was still open.[3] Nehru replied that the only solution was for Portugal to get out and to obey U.N. resolutions on ending colonialism. Portuguese officials in Goa, he alleged, were being withdrawn, and a state of chaos threatened. Intensive diplomatic activity ensued in London and New Delhi, and both the U.K. High Commissioner, Sir Paul Gore-Booth, and the American Ambassador, Mr J. K. Galbraith, saw Mr Nehru and his Foreign Minister, Mr M. J. Desai, to urge them not to resort to force. The Portuguese Ambassador in London, Dr Manuel Rocheta, called on the Lord Privy Seal, Mr Edward Heath, who told him that Her Majesty's Government deplored this tension between a member of the Commonwealth and one of Britain's allies. In a subsequent statement, the Foreign Office said that Portugal, as well as India,

---

[1] *Guardian*, 26 December 1961.
[2] Keesing's, *op. cit.*, 18636.
[3] *Ibid.*

had been urged to use restraint, and that Britain would favour the despatch of international observers to Goa or any similar move acceptable to both sides. A spokesman added that Britain had no standing in the dispute as neither side had asked her to mediate. Asked what effect an Indian attack would have on the Anglo-Portuguese Alliance, which pledged Britain to protect all Portuguese territories, the spokesman said there would be no question of Britain engaging in hostilities with India.

In fact, on 11 December, Portugal had formally invoked the Alliance by asking, in terms of the 1899 Treaty between the two countries, what measures Britain would be able to adopt to co-operate with Portuguese forces to stem the Indian aggression. Her Majesty's Government replied that there would be 'inevitable restrictions' on the aid that Britain could give in a struggle with a member of the Commonwealth. Salazar later recalled:

> We also asked the British government for permission to use some airfields necessary for connections with Goa. I am sorry to say that the British government took a week to inform us that we could not use them. Had it not been for this delay we should certainly have found alternative routes, and we could have rushed to India reinforcements in men and material for a longer sustained defence of the territory.[1]

In other words, Portugal wanted air stages en route to Goa. Britain's failure even to reply to the request until it was too late deeply wounded Salazar and he never quite got over it. It is true that, even if Britain had responded favourably, it would not have made much difference to the outcome, but it was the silence that hurt.

The invaders struck at midnight on 17-18 December. Some 30,000 Indian troops under Lt.-Gen. Chaudhuri, with tanks and heavy artillery, attacked from three directions: southward from Savantadi into northern Goa, a northward thrust from Karwar into southern Goa, and south-westwards from Belgaum towards Sanqualim and Ponda, which covered the approaches to Goa's capital, Panjim, and the port of Mormugão. The Indian air force went for the airport and also dropped leaflets. The Portuguese mined roads and bridges. Heavy fighting took place at six points in the north and three in the south,[2] and the governor-general tried to establish a redoubt at

---

[1] Salazar's address to the National Union, 3 April 1962.
[2] Lawrence, *op. cit.*, p. 155.

Fort Vasco da Gama, near Mormugão. The only Portuguese warship in the area, the 1,700-ton frigate *Afonso de Albuquerque*, fought gallantly with three Indian warships, a cruiser and two destroyers, before shellfire drove her aground, with her brave Captain Cunha Aragon badly wounded. At Damão, the whole population rallied round the local governor, whose wounds caused both of his legs to be amputated, while another brave effort at Diu brought posthumous glory to Lieutenant Oliveira e Carmo, who, with only two gunners to help him, stood out in a launch, the *Vega*, though both his knees were shattered. But, of course, it was no use. The Portuguese were outnumbered by ten to one, and by 11.10 a.m. on 19 December, it was all over. The governor-general, whose instinct was to carry on, was persuaded by his advisers that it would simply be suicide, and he surrendered to Chaudhuri. Lawrence claims that the Indians then moved in to rape and plunder, and certainly many of Goa's art treasures were carted off to India. But the *Daily Telegraph* correspondent reported from Bombay on 20 December, that he had been in Panjim only a few hours after the Portuguese surrender and had been impressed by the 'swift, efficient and orderly' take-over by the Indians. Everything was peaceful and there was no fighting. The population seemed immensely relieved that it was all over so quickly. Within a month of the occupation, the Brazilian embassy in New Delhi, acting for Lisbon, issued thousands of Portuguese passports to Goanese anxious to leave their homes on Indian soil because of Indian harassment, and many others from within Goa itself applied to go to Portugal and her other overseas territories. On 14 March 1962, the Lok Sabha passed legislation incorporating Goa into the Union. Nehru promised considerable autonomy to the region and that the predominant language, Konkani, would have its proper place in Indian life. He estimated that, in the fighting, forty-five Portuguese had been killed and fifty-five wounded, with one missing; while India had sustained twenty-two deaths with fifty-three wounded. Portugal interned thousands of Indians in Mozambique, froze their assets and deported them. General Vassalo e Silva returned to Portugal to face court-martial. There was was much bitterness in Portugal at the ease with which the defences had fallen, especially as foreign critics used this as a pretext for asserting that Goa really favoured the invader. In fact, the people of Goa had rallied to the Portuguese troops as best they could, and only a few days before the invasion, had gone off in their thousands to St Francis Xavier's shrine once more to pray for deliverance from India. Vassalo e Silva had done his best in organizing a retreat which must have saved many lives. It would have been an empty gesture to offer more martyrs to the inevitable. His officers were not experienced and the plans for a redoubt were ended when some of the troops, believing that by this time their main job was to avoid leaving useful equipment behind, destroyed their weapons and turned up empty-handed. In the outcome the case was dropped and Vassalo e Silva retired.

In London, the Labour Opposition leader, Hugh Gaitskell, while deploring the Portuguese presence in India, also expressed profound regret that force had been used. In the House of Commons, he asked the Commonwealth Secretary, Mr Duncan Sandys, whether any attempt had been made to secure a combined Commonwealth approach to Mr Nehru to head the invasion off, and whether anything had been done to encourage Portugal to leave India. Mr Sandys replied:

> I do not think it would have been really a case when it would have been suitable to try and get a ganging-up, so to speak, of all the Commonwealth members. I think this was essentially a case when each Commonwealth government expresses its views to the Indian government, and we were not the only ones to do so. We have made our views known to the Portuguese government on a number of occasions, and ... we have very recently urged upon them to avoid any action in Goa which might be regarded as provocative.

Mr John Hynd (Lab.) asked what effect these events would have on the alliance with Portugal. Mr Sandys replied that 'we made it clear to the Portuguese government as long ago as 1954 that it would be impossible for Britain to be engaged in hostilities against a fellow member of the Commonwealth.'

As soon as the invasion started, the Portuguese delegate at the U.N., Dr Vieira Garin, requested an immediate meeting of the Security Council in view of this 'clear and flagrant violation of the sovereign rights of Portugal and of the U.N. Charter'. By seven to two votes, with two abstentions, the Council agreed to a debate, and Mr Adlai Stevenson, for the United States, strongly criticized India, while Mr Zorin, for the U.S.S.R., supported her. Stevenson was grieved by the thought that a man like Nehru, a disciple of one of the world's great saints of peace, and one who had been looked up to as an apostle of non-violence, could have performed an aggressive act of a kind specifically forbidden by the Charter. It was shocking that the Indian Minister of Defence, Mr Krishna Menon, 'so well known in these halls for his advice on peace and his tireless enjoinders to everyone else to seek the way of compromise', was on the borders of Goa inspecting his troops at the zero hour of invasion:

> If it is to survive, if the United Nations is not to die as ignoble a death as the League of Nations, we cannot condone the use of force in this instance, and thus pave the way for forceful solutions of other disputes which exist in Latin America, Africa, Asia and Europe. In a world as interdependent as ours, the possible results of such a trend are too grievous to contemplate.[1]

Stevenson then urged that India should withdraw from Goa, and insisted that India and Portugal should negotiate on the basis of the principles of the Charter. Mr Zorin argued that the issue was wholly within India's domestic jurisdiction. Portugal was creating a threat to peace and security in various parts of the world by her continuing colonialism. Britain and America had not denounced her for 'annihilating scores of thousands in Angola' nor suggested a cease-fire there, nor the withdrawal of troops.

Liberia, Ceylon and the United Arab Republic presented a resolution calling for a declaration that the enclaves were a threat to peace and to the unity of India, rejecting Portugal's charges of aggression against India, and calling on the Portuguese to terminate their hostile action and co-operate with India in the liquidation of her colonial possessions. This resolution was backed by the U.S.S.R. but rejected by the other seven powers on the Council. An alternative resolution supported by Britain, the United States, France and Turkey called for an immediate cessation of hostilities, and for India to withdraw to the positions occupied before 17 December; it urged the disputants to work out a permanent solution of their differences by peaceful means, and requested the Secretary-General of the U.N. to be available to help them. Chile, Ecuador and Nationalist China supported the proposers, while only four resisted the resolution: Russia, Ceylon, Liberia and the United Arab Republic. Russia's dissent operated as a veto, so that the resolution, though carried by a majority, failed.

[1] Keesing's, *op. cit.*, 18660-1.

This was the ninety-ninth time that the U.S.S.R. had used its vetoing powers. In a subsequent statement, Adlai Stevenson warned:

> The failure of the Security Council to call for a cease-fire tonight in these simple circumstances is a failure of the United Nations. The veto of the Soviet Union is consistent with its long role of obstruction. But I find the attitude of some other members of the Council profoundly disturbing and ominous, because we have witnessed tonight an effort to rewrite the Charter, to sanction the use of force in international relations when it suits one's own purposes. This approach can only lead to chaos and to the dis integration of the United Nations.[1]

Yet Nehru could write, as he shortly did, to President Kennedy to say that Cardinal Gracias and other Catholic dignitaries in India had supported the invasion and approved of India's decision.

The extent of integration in Goa had been clearly marked by the fact that Goanese held all the higher posts of administration in their hands apart from the governor-generalship, and there had even been an exception in that case when in 1835, Bernardo Pereo da Silva, a native of Neura near Old Goa, held the post with the title of Prefect. At the time of the invasion the secretary-general, the director of civil administration, the chief justice and all other senior officials had been born locally, and Lawrence points out with some justice that in British India no Indian had ever been chief justice, nor was any Indian a British citizen in the sense that the Goanese were citizens of Portugal. Portuguese India had always been represented in the parliamentary assemblies in Lisbon, and many Goanese had become ministers, provincial governors and ambassadors in Lisbon and overseas. They had risen to the top in Portuguese universities. The mingling within Goa of white, brown and black had never had a counterpart on the other side of the Indian border, and while many Indians had married white women, it had been rare for white men to marry Indian girls.

After the invasion, the Indians appointed a military governor and chief civil administrator who purported to be of Goanese extraction, but their genealogies were dubious. The secretary-general had his job scrapped and was personally threatened with a trial for treason,

[1] *Ibid.*

because he had given shelter to the captive governor-general's wife. The Goanese attorney-general and the doyen of the judiciary were removed from office, the former being dragged from his house, kicked and spat upon. Schools were closed. Hundreds of Goanese officials and civil servants, 350 in the Board of External Trade alone, lost their jobs. Churches and shrines were desecrated and an attempt was made to seize the patriarch. Priests especially were harassed, and few parish clergy risked celebrating Midnight Mass that Christmas. Lawrence testifies that 11,000 Indian police were drafted in and many suspects arrested. The integration of Goa's economy with that of the Union could only reduce the local standard of living. During the next few years complaints poured out of Goa, as the residents made their grievances known to Portuguese friends abroad. There had been wholesale confiscation of land, in many cases for military installations. Teachers' salaries had been drastically cut and journalists were under pressure from the authorities. Unemployment had risen steeply, though the cost of living doubled itself within three years, and cheap Indian labour had been drafted in despite the large numbers of jobless Goanese. Production in the iron mines had slowed down. There were complaints that relations between Christians, Hindus and Moslems had sharply deteriorated, and that the position of the Catholic Church was reflected in the drop in the number of seminarians from 156 in 1961 to only 12 in 1964. Eventually, the Indian government held a plebiscite on 16 January 1967, to ascertain whether the people favoured the incorporation of Goa into the State of Maharashtra, and of Damão and Diu into the State of Gujerat. Although the vote was allowed to many Indians who had entered Goa since the invasion and in practice denied to many Goanese outside the annexed territories, the government's proposals were rejected by a large majority.

On 18 January 1967, the Portuguese government issued a statement, communicated to the U.N. Secretary-General, in which it referred to a Note it had received from the Indian government, dated 14 January 1963. This stated that the culture, language, laws and customs of the inhabitants of Goa would be preserved, and no alterations would be made save with the people's consent. Indeed, even before the invasion, on 4 May 1961, Mr Nehru had told the Indian parliament that Goa would remain 'an independent entity'. In fact, the Portuguese statement continued, after the occupation the Indian government revoked the local system of law, substituted Indian for local officials, initiated religious discrimination, introduced the caste system, forbade the Portuguese language to be taught, and harassed people who asked to keep their Portuguese nationality. Poverty, unrest and revolt took hold, the statement alleged. When, in 1966, the Indian Bill to mount the referendum was introduced, an Indian deputy, Dr Dandekar, asserted: 'This law is fraudulent and dishonourable, and is calculatedly worded to secure a pre-determined result.' Public reaction was such that in Goa itself the police arrested 3,000 people. The Portuguese statement ended with an accusation that India was planning social and cultural genocide.

Even apart from this sorry tale, the mere fact of annexation may mean that an identity has been lost. A society which was, for all its imperfections, a sign of reconciliation between Europe and the Orient has ceased to be. It is all the sadder at a time when the world is threatening to harden its divisions along racial lines. Goa was small, but still a living proof of what men of very different races can make of the business of living together, despite false starts. One must sympathize with a newly reborn India which feels that a European presence on its fringe is a sign of contradiction to all it has achieved at high cost. The tragedy is that an inter-racial settlement like Goa or the much smaller Gibraltar should be unacceptable to Indian or Spanish nationalists simply because of geography, or because the settlement depends on another power elsewhere. Absorption need not inherently mean the disintegration of the absorbed community, and the departure of a colonizing power can even stimulate inter-racial living, as in parts of former British Africa. But if, in practice and because of special circumstance, an absorbed community has its identity blurred, then some of its message to the world at large will be lost. In any event, absorption should depend at least as much on the will of the smaller entity's people as much as on that of the adjoining 'giant', especially when the enclave or colony offers no threat to its powerful neighbour. Undoubtedly, there were those in Goa, as in the *diaspora*, who wanted change, but for some of them, at least, the object was disapproval of the Portuguese regime, not Portugal's presence. Even if they had been in the majority, whether Goa should have had autonomy or independence is not the same question as whether it should be incorporated into India. As for religion, the Hindu-Christian dialogue in Goa was worth preserving in its own right. To support the annexation for motives relating to the Church's status in India might seem to suggest an appeal to an end to justify an indefensible means. One assumes that Cardinal Gracias acted in conscience, and as a major figure of the Vatican Council he commands world-wide respect. But one cannot help asking how far his views were coloured by the residual conflict between the *Padroado* and *Propaganda*. As a bishop he was entitled to speak out on the moral issues affecting even a political question, but his partisanship does not seem to' have taken this form. On the Christmas Eve after the annexation he preached in the Bombay pro-Cathedral in these terms:

> It is not for you or me – if we are to be sensible – to pass judgment on the measures adopted by our government in securing freedom for Goa. The leaders of the nation, who are in full possession of the facts, are in the best position to assess the situation and to take decisions. . . . In the face of violent criticism in the West, we have the profoundest sympathy for Mr Nehru. It is not a case of entering into a discussion of the moral issues. . . . He was, so to speak, between the devil and the deep sea – on the one hand to be sensitive to opinion abroad, and on the other to pressure at home.[1]

Could some compromise have been struck, and was Salazar wrong in refusing to talk about sovereignty? The trouble is that there seems to have been so little room for compromise. In the case of Gibraltar, many solutions have been proposed: condominium, for instance, or the return of sovereignty to Spain followed by a 'perpetual lease' to Britain. It is not conceivable that any such answer would have made sense in New Delhi; all the indications are that nothing but Portugal's departure from Goa would have satisfied Indian nationalist feeling. Although the port of Mormugão and the mineral deposits doubtless had their appeal, and there was genuine Indian feeling that Indian unity was impaired by Portuguese Goa, the underlying issue at stake was the whole principle of Portuguese 'colonialism' in the modern world, wherever it might be found.

[1] *The Examiner*, Bombay, 7 January 1962.

CHAPTER 11

The Opposition

With political parties banned and the corporations still inchoate, effective opposition was never possible as long as Salazar controlled events. In the later years of his regime, speeches in the National Assembly began to take a more critical turn, and the Corporative Chamber's committee work had some effect on legislation, especially in its technical aspects. But the conditions in which elections were held made it virtually impossible for the hardline opposition to secure seats in the Assembly, especially as the electorate was unable to vote for individual candidates. Voting was, and is, for entire lists of candidates, the National Union's or the opposition's, and, even when individual aspirants looked attractive, the thought of overturning the regime daunted many people for many years, particularly those who remembered what life had been in the last few years before Salazar.

There were other problems. Candidates favoured by the National Union had an organization to help them in their campaign, while opposition candidates had to finance themselves and, in trying to organize meetings and propaganda, could find themselves breaking the censorship and anti-association laws at every turn of the road. The month before the elections was supposed to be free of restrictions on campaigning, but owners of halls were chary of hiring them out to the opposition, the censorship obviated press publicity, and the broadcasting media were state-controlled. For many years, too, the condition that voters had to be literate or show a minimum property qualification kept half the adult population off the electoral rolls, and made it easy for unscrupulous officials to exclude known dissidents. Opposition candidates could not get access to the rolls, or at least could not take copies, nor were they allowed to be present at the scrutiny. Anti-government campaigners who went too far were liable to arrest, and were subjected to all kinds of petty hindrances. There were instances of police interference with the distribution of ballot papers, and time and again the opposition simply withdrew their lists in despair.

This type of conduct has deep roots in Portuguese history, and only extremists would suggest that Salazar personally ordered police or returning officers to cheat, forge and destroy ballot papers. Yet all these things did occur, and, the ideals of the *Estado Novo* being what they were, one would have hoped for a systematic drive to clean up electoral behaviour. Salazar could hardly have been in total ignorance of what went on.[1] Even his friends discerned in him at times, as one of them puts it, 'the prejudice that dulls the ears to evidence'.

One can only guess at what went on in his mind. With his grasp of the papal encyclicals, he knew, and honestly believed, that the people's right to share in national decision went to the roots of natural law. But there was always his abiding fear of regression to disorder, a fear by no means unfounded, but liable to swell to disproportion. This fear, coupled with his paternalistic and authoritarian nature, inhibited him from giving life to what he had conceived. His overriding dread was of Communism. Its denial, in practice and principle, of human rights, its atheism, its evangelical imperialism, its effects on the family, its economic misguidedness – all continued to make it for him a sort of Anti-Christ. It also stood, as he saw it, for the death of Europe and her civilization, and he foresaw its predatory interest in Africa. These were, after all, the days of confrontation, not co-existence. The years after the Second World War were the era of the oppressed Cardinals: Stepinac, Mindszenty and Wyszynski; of thousands of jailed prelates and clergy; of the suppression of Christian education and the closing down of churches. Salazar not only detested the system of thought, its effects on the family, its economic fantasies; he had no illusions about the skill of its prophets, or the swiftness with which it could appeal in a country as poor as Portugal.

A Portuguese Communist Party existed and was always active. It had to work outside the law, and was professedly subversive and violent, the only really well-organized group among the opposition. Thus, though small and unrepresentative, it exerted an influence out of proportion to its numbers, with a special appeal to rural workers in the Alentejo. The result was that, in Salazar's mind, any and every

[1] In reporting to Salazar, Ministers doubtless tried to gild the lily, but Salazar's flair for cross-examination would have cut through that. He was always ready to use his personal friends as a grapevine, and Maria, his housekeeper, kept him abreast of popular gossip. He told Christine Garnier, author of *Vacances avec Salazar*, that many people who felt shy of writing to him direct would write to Maria instead, and Maria complained that the volume of correspondence impeded her domestic chores!

expression of opposition came to be seen as a Communist plot, or as something the Communists could exploit, and was treated as a threat to the state.

Paradoxically, it was precisely the restrictions on non-subversive opposition, coupled with the moderates' inability to coalesce, that gave the Communist Party its role. With its coherence and internal unity, it became, symbolically at least, the spearhead of opposition. The tragedy is that the Portuguese Socialists failed to establish a working-class movement of their own, and, like the Republicans, they found their strength in the intellectual middle-class. By this default, the dissentient element in the working-class had only the Communist Party to turn to, if it wanted to be militant at all, until in more recent years a Catholic workers' movement began to sniff above the ground. In practice, however, the Communist Party failed to secure a hold on the industrial workers, but has been effective among some intellectuals and university students. If, at any time in the post-war years, the opposition as a whole had effectively combined to try and overthrow the regime, it could only have been under Communist leadership. In such ways, over-reaction to opposition becomes counter-productive.

There were grounds for acute anxiety over the Communists during the Spanish Civil War, when the Spanish and Portuguese underground parties were aiming at a unitary Iberian nation, in which Portugal would simply have been absorbed as a region or province. But the Spanish Left was defeated, and, during the Second World War, Portugal was too preoccupied with survival against a potential invader with a massive war machine to have much time for internal politics, other than pro-British and pro-German rivalries. After the war a lively attempt was made to co-ordinate all opposition groups, including the Communists, in the movement known as MUD (*Movimento de Unidade Democrático*) until, true to form, it splintered into fragments. An unsuccessful bid to recoup its losses emerged in 1953 in the MND (*Movemento Nacional Democrático*), but the *MUD Juvenil* continued to work effectively among university students.

Although by the time of the Second World War it was clear that Salazar was there to stay, and the era of Republican revolutions faded, former Republican ministers continued after the war to be the rallying point for discontented intellectuals and professional men. Among these respected figures were Dr Mario Azevedo Gomes, Dr António Sergio, Col. Norton de Matos and the distinguished mathematician, Professor Ruy Luis Gomes. The last two withdrew their candidatures from the presidential elections of 1949 and 1951 respectively, because of the frustrations their campaigns ran into. The repression of opposition tended to go in waves, with police activity sometimes more intensive than at others. The government's critics felt they were constantly being watched by a network of informers, paid by the PIDE (some of whose officials had received their training from the Germans in pre-war days).[1] After the war, the PIDE were primarily concerned with the Communists, the likeliest source of outright subversion, but they continued to harass all forms of opposition and to assume that all critics were subversive. They paid special attention too, to university students, among whom the Communists were notably active, and were particularly suspicious of certain girl students whom the Communists were keen to use as agents on the grounds that they were more likely than men to escape police surveillance.

The London *Observer* in 1954, spoke of the 'quietly efficient and comparatively gentle apparatus of dictatorship' in Portugal. Progress had been made in many spheres but at a snail's pace, and 'the father of his people has dedicated his life to their welfare, but refuses to give them opportunities to grow up'.[2] In the following year *The Times* said that the Portuguese system was not Fascist but 'a Portuguese effort to solve a Portuguese problem'. The period 1920-6 had been the shameful years of faction, disorder and corruption, but now 'a wide variety of political opinions are openly expressed'. Republican Day celebrations were permitted to the opposition as a gesture, Monarchists made themselves felt, the Pretender was not exiled, the Church was disestablished but the social encyclicals guided the state. It was, however, a corporative state without corporations. Half the funds of the six-year development plan had been earmarked for the overseas territories, and at home, substantial progress had been made in building hydro-electric works, irrigation, agriculture, power industries and the building of schools, hospitals and roads.[3] Salazar was quoted as saying:

> The truth is, I am profoundly anti-parliamentarian. I hate the speeches, the verbosity, the flowery, meaningless interpolations,

[1] Allegations of PIDE brutality will be fully discussed later in this chapter.
[2] *Observer*, 29 August 1954.
[3] *The Times*, 25 October 1955 (special supplement).

the way that we waste passion, not found any great idea, but just about futilities.

All this appeared in a special supplement geared to the state visit to London of the Portuguese President Craveiro Lopes. At that time, too, Professor Hugh Trevor-Roper was writing:

> Dr Salazar is himself neither monarchist nor republican; he is merely a monarch: illiberal, paternal, religious. As such he has restored order and solvency to his country, given it some useful institutions, steered it past some formidable crises in which other, more ambitious monarchs have foundered, asserted its prestige, preserved its independence, raised its standards of life. Can any ruler, liberal or illiberal, do more than this for his country?[1]

Yet there was another side to the coin. In January 1954, some fifty members of the opposition were arrested on their way home from the peace meeting in Vienna. They included Professor António José Saraiva, the writer Dr Jaimé Cortezão, the poet Alexandre O'Neil, and the painter Maria Keil. Sixteen of them were brought to trial in 1955, accused of subversive propaganda. Eight were acquitted, but the remainder received sentences ranging from one to three and a half years. In the same year, Professor Ruy Luis Gomes headed a group sentenced to terms of imprisonment ranging from nine to nineteen months. Their offence was trying to disseminate propaganda aimed at urging the government to negotiate with India over the Goa question. Some of the accused were members of the MND central committee. They were originally accused of treason, but this extremist charge was dropped. In the autumn, 100 young men and girls of the *MUD Juvenil* were seized; seventy were released, thirty put on trial. Of these, twenty-four were bailed, six detained in custody. Among them was a nineteen-year-old student named Herminio Marvão, who, according to *L'Humanité*, was kept in a damp dungeon, despite his tubercular condition, and was subjected to long hours of questioning and torture. Another of the group was Agostinho Neto, later to figure prominently in the African rebel movements. It was at this time that accusations relating to PIDE's use of the 'statue' torture began to become prominent in foreign headlines: the system of keeping a prisoner on his feet under questioning for long periods. A group of fifty-three distinguished foreign

[1] *Sunday Times*, 16 October 1955.

writers, including Mauriac and Sartre, petitioned the Portuguese government for clemency for Herminio Marvão.

In the spring of 1956, *Le Monde* criticized Salazar for being too slow and cautious in his development policies, but spoke of his system as a dictatorship safeguarding itself from excesses.[1] Yet in the following month, a resolution in Salazar's own movement, the National Union, shook the national conscience in these terms:

> The rich are richer, while new signs of poverty appear daily, thus indicating that the standard of living of the working-classes is becoming steadily lower.

The Portuguese industrialist was

> not concerned with improving the standard of living of the workers. He makes his profits by exploiting labour instead of attaining them through an increased production from his enterprises.

Industrialists should be educated for a life of 'work and responsibility, not of luxury, arrogance and impunity'.[2] In July 1956, a group of opposition leaders, including three former prime ministers and one of the revolutionary group who brought Salazar to power, presented a manifesto to President Craveiro Lopes. This demanded an amnesty for political prisoners, freedom of association and expression, the abolition of censorship, the ending of police restrictions on political liberty, and free discussion of national problems. The same year had seen the arrest of the journalist David de Carvalho, the lawyer Costa Gomes (and his wife Natalia), and Americo de Sousa, a militant Communist who had been sent to the Cape Verde islands camp of Tarrafal in 1936, when he was only seventeen years old. His health was said to have deteriorated seriously on the island, where he was held for five years without trial. Now he was in prison again. There was anxiety, too, about the secretary-general of the Communist Party, Alvaro Cunhal, sentenced to seven years in 1949, with a period of 'security measures' to follow.[3] He was also said to be seriously ill and deprived of medical treatment. Finally, in 1956, four members of the *MUD Juvenil* were sent to prison for two years with security measures to follow. When Professor Ruy Luis Gomes tried to give evidence on their behalf, he found himself in prison for contempt.

[1] *Le Monde*, 28 May 1956.
[2] Meeting of the National Union, 27 June 1956.
[3] Preventive detention.

The defence lawyers were so angered that they left the court in protest.

In February 1957, Queen Elizabeth and the Duke of Edinburgh were received with delirious enthusiasm by the Portuguese people, and the state visit was marked by all sorts of happy impromptu incidents. When the time came for the royal couple to fly home, the crowds broke loose and it looked as though the plane would never leave the ground. The same month saw fifty-two people brought to trial for political offences; thirty of them were acquitted, but the rest were sentenced to prison terms varying from six months to two years. At this time the students' syndicates were dissolved by Dr Leite Pinto, Minister of Education, and thousands of students demonstrated in the streets. In Lisbon, some 3,000 of them massed around the parliament building, the palace of S. Bento, and, although the gathering was peaceful, the police started to break it up roughly. A message was sent to the Minister of the Presidency, Professor Marcello Caetano,[1] who took immediate steps to have the police withdrawn. The students then thronged into the Assembly chamber and warmly applauded deputies who criticized the decree suppressing the syndicates. The decree was then sent to the Corporative Chamber for modifications. The whole incident contrasted sharply with the student demonstrations of the previous autumn against the Russian invasion of Hungary. On that occasion the police did not interfere.

It is not easy to form a clear picture of what was really going on in Portugal at this time. Only a few months later, the *Guardian* in London was reporting that Salazar governed, 'not as a flamboyant autocrat, but as a diligent and commanding national manager'. The paper added:

A small list of people said to have suffered the death penalty circulates among his opponents, But at a recent mass political trial, most were acquitted and no heavy sentences were imposed.[2]

[1] Professor Caetano, one of Portugal's leading lawyers, had held a succession of high offices under Salazar, and had been closely concerned with the establishment of the youth movement, the *Moçidade*. The Presidency is the Prime Minister's (i.e. the President of the Council's) department, and is headed by a senior minister other than the Premier himself. This minister is responsible for the preparation and implementation of the national development plans, and carries high influence in the government. Caetano had also been one of the architects of the New State legislation.

[2] *Guardian*, 4 July, 1957.

Portugal had abolished the death penalty a century before, and the suggestion had been that opponents of the government had been murdered by the police.

Later in the same year, however, the *Guardian* carried a series of articles by Mr Gerald Gardiner, Q.C., then a leading member of the English Bar, and later to become Lord Chancellor in the Labour government. He had been to Portugal privately to investigate the allegations of repression, and he began his report[1] with a reference to the presidential election of six years before. This was the 1951 election for the President of the Republic, and the two opposition candidates had come to grief. The candidature of Professor Ruy Luis Gomes had been rejected by the Council of State, while Admiral Quintão Meireles had withdrawn from the contest because, he said, conditions had been such as to inhibit a free election. In the 1955 elections for the National Assembly, Mr Gardiner continued, no one had been elected from the opposition groups. Half the nation was disfranchised because of the would-be voter's need to prove himself literate or tax-paying, and the disqualified classes were so loosely defined that the government had wide discretion in compiling the electoral rolls. The twenty-eight opposition candidates were not allowed to be present at the count, nor could they issue publications without government approval.[2] A rigid censorship was in force in Portugal, and no association could be set up without government approval. Though Portugal was by this time a member of the United Nations, the government had, in April 1957, turned down an application to start a Portuguese United Nations Association. Officials and employees in public service could be dismissed if they opposed the fundamental principles of the 1933 Constitution, or failed to co-operate in achieving the aims of the state.[3] There were no free trade unions in the sense generally accepted in the West; that is, they could not be formed outside the corporative framework.

Gardiner then turned to the penal system, especially the mode of imprisonment known as 'security measures' (a form of preventive detention after a substantive sentence has been served). He was concerned here with laws which provided penalties for issuing publications without government approval,[4] for illegal associa-

[1] 18 October 1957.
[2] Decree-Law 26,599.
[3] Decree-Law 25,317.
[4] Decree-Law 26,589 (s.2).

tion,[1] and for striking (two to eight years' imprisonment). There were also penalties for printing subversive material,[2] and police were empowered to close premises identified in their view with subversive activities.[3] The basic idea behind these laws was to control the avowedly violent Communist underground, but in practice anything showing elements in common with Marxist principles (e.g. socialism in the Western European sense) tended to attract the rigours of the law. Gardiner pointed out that arrested persons could be held for three months without trial, and, by permission of the Minister of the Interior, for two further periods of forty-five days each, making a total of six months in all. Writs of *habeas corpus* were not granted in practice. The result was that a man could be held for a few months, released and re-arrested, and thus spend many months in custody without a trial. There had been cases of this, and some of the prisoners concerned had finally been acquitted by the courts.[4] Imprisonment 'as a measure of security' (preventive detention) could be imposed for one to three years, and it was the duty of the police to apply or extend security measures.[5] These could be extended by successive periods of three years as long as the prisoner continued to be 'dangerous'.[6] Persons regarded as a danger to state security could be deported for years without trial.[7] Under these laws, many persons had been arrested by the PIDE and imprisoned or deported to Timor or the Tarrafal Camp in Cape Verde. Mr Gardiner had personally met a jurist who had thus been held on Timor for seventeen years.

This account seems to suggest that, although life sentences as such have been abolished under Portuguese law, the PIDE can, on their own exclusive initiative, keep people in jail or exile indefinitely without trial. In fact, this is not so. It is true that offenders can be *deported* by government decree and thus without trial, though this rarely happens nowadays. It is true that the police can hold a man by various devices for many months before trial, and can themselves conduct the *preliminary* 'judicial' investigation leading to security

---

[1] Law 1, 901.
[2] Decree-Law 37,447 (s. 24).
[3] *Ibid.* (s. 23).
[4] Decree-Law 35,042.
[5] Decree-Law 37,447 (ss. 20-2).
[6] Decree-Law 40,550 (s. 7). Section 8 allows for security measures to be imposed on a 'dangerous' person, e.g. a known Communist, even if the substantive allegations in the trial are not proceeded with.
[7] Decree-Law 37,749.

measures. But, as a careful reading of Decree-Law 37,447 shows, they cannot pass a sentence; nor can they apply or extend security measures without at least a confirmatory court order, from which there is a right of appeal. The court may impose a sentence of, say, three years' imprisonment plus three years' security measures. After the six years the prisoner cannot be detained further unless the court so orders. Police evidence carries great weight, and a prisoner will find it very difficult to win the court's sympathy if the police evidence is that he is unrepentant. It is not, however, impossible to defeat the police, and it has been done. Talking to lawyers of all political views, one forms the impression that the extension of security measures for a second term has for a long time been comparatively rare, and a third term extremely rare. Lord Russell of Liverpool, as will be seen, found in 1963 that, of 325 people imprisoned for security offences, only three were serving a second term of security measures. In recent years the courts have occasionally released prisoners even before the end of the *first* term of security measures, and second terms are mainly reserved now for hardline Communists. The more flexible non-Communist can often avoid an extension by promising 'good behaviour' in future, though this may involve a reluctant abandonment of his principles. The practice of deportation has dwindled almost to nothing, and it was a striking exception for the socialist lawyer, Dr Mario Soares, to be sent to São Tomé early in 1968. One of Professor Marcello Caetano's first acts on becoming prime minister in the autumn of that year was to allow Soares to return, and the latter has resumed his legal practice in Lisbon, though this means starting all over again at the age of forty-four. The tragedy of these penalties is that they play such havoc with family and professional life.

On the whole, sentences have not been heavy, and in phases when many arrests were being made there were many acquittals. Gardiner referred to a case in Oporto where fifty-two young persons were brought to trial. Only three were over the age of thirty, the average age was twenty-two, two-thirds were students, seven were women, the youngest was seventeen. Some were jailed, most were acquitted. Fryer and McGowan Pinheiro tell us[1] that in 1959 'there were 3,811 trials leading to convictions for crimes against religion or the security of the state, or for other political offences; 1,586 of these trials were

1 Fryer and McGowan Pinheiro, *op. cit.*, p. 183.

initiated by the secret police (PIDE)'. We are not told how many of these persons were actually convicted or what sentences were passed, and the figures probably include a great many minor offences against public order, especially as the figures the authors give for the following year are less intimidating: 103 persons tried between March and July 1960 received sentences totalling 138 years, with an aggregate of 123 years' security measures. The resident *Times* correspondent, reporting from Lisbon, stated that a total of 167 men and women were sentenced in 1960 for political offences, with sentences varying from a few months to several years.[1] A closer look at the sentences shows that most of them ranged from fifteen months to two years, with a minimum of four months and a maximum of eight years. The picture is not a happy one, but contrasts with the popular impression abroad that the Portuguese prisons are stuffed with political offenders running into thousands. In fact, Lord Russell of Liverpool's investigation in 1963 revealed that the total number of people actually serving sentences for security offences throughout Portugal was 353.[2] At the time of writing, the figure is under 100.

In the mass trial of young people at Oporto, the accused had been arrested in the first few months of 1955, but did not come to trial until June 1957, though Portuguese law demands that the definitive trial should take place within a year. Gardiner spoke of disquieting evidence that some students had been tortured. He understood that one of the accused had undergone the 'statue' torture for seven days and nights, and he had spoken to students who claimed that they had endured it for five days and nights. In another context he referred to two (unnamed) men said to have died under torture, also at Oporto. In March 1957, seventy-two jurists of Lisbon and Oporto had petitioned the government for an inquiry into PIDE conduct. According to Amnesty International,[3] 'an inquiry was opened, but when, on the 23/10/57, the first signatory, Fernando de Abranches Ferrão, who had been asked for his evidence, was able to name 26 specific cases, the inquiry was discontinued'. Another thirty-three jurists, this time of Coimbra, also petitioned for investigations to be held. They included an important local official of the regime,

[1] *The Times*, 5 June 1961.
[2] Lord Russell of Liverpool, *Prisons and Prisoners in Portugal: an Independent Investigation*, 1963.
[3] Prison Conditions in Portugal: a factual report compiled by Amnesty International, London, September 1965, p. 24.

Dr Martin Afonso de Castro, deputy civil governor of Coimbra. In June of that year, Gardiner attended the second trial of Professor Ruy Luis Gomes and four others, who were accused of trying to publish an article which not only called for human rights at home but urged the government to negotiate with Premier Nehru over India's claim to Goa, and to hold a referendum there. They were arrested in August 1954, and held until their conviction in April 1955. They appealed, and in August 1956, the appeal court ordered a re-trial. The accused were then re-arrested and detained until the final hearing in June 1957.[1] Though they had not seen their lawyers for the best part of a year, they were allowed only one hour's conference with them before going into court. The proceedings were held without any record being made of the evidence or arguments, and, in the end, four of the accused were jailed for two years, and one for ten months.

It is accepted that the PIDE later mellowed, but the accusations current in the 1930s and at times in the 1950s were dreadful. Fryer and McGowan Pinheiro mention solitary confinement in 'refrigerator' cells, the 'statue' for ten days, and murder. They had heard, they say, of a pregnant woman beaten on the belly, of a miner whose head was beaten against the wall until he went mad, and of two men nailed to the wall by their genitals.[2] In its 1965 report, Amnesty International spoke of a change in climate after the late 1940s:

> Later statements seem to indicate that beatings or electrical torture are much less frequently used, and that the only means of physical torture which is frequently employed is the 'statue'.[3]

This, too, had changed. Long periods of standing, aided by beatings, had been discontinued in favour of simply keeping the prisoner awake for days on end, apart from ten-minute intervals of sleep here

---

[1] Such time-lags are common enough in the slow legal processes of a number of European countries, and, in Portugal, the time served in jail awaiting trial is at least deducted from the ultimate sentence (though this is not of much help to those who are finally acquitted). In view of his personal standing, one would have expected Ruy Luis Gomes to have been given bail pending trial, at least in the last phase when a re-trial had been ordered. Public opinion was inflamed over Goa at that time, however, and suggestions of compromise were seen as something akin to treason. Some of the opposition, without wanting to abandon Goa, did think that a reasonable compromise could be attempted.

[2] Fryer and McGowan Pinheiro, *op. cit.*, pp. 196-8.

[3] Amnesty International, *op. cit.*, p. 23.

and there, while using techniques like alternate cajoling and bullying. It is no slur on the memory of the brave or their subsequent champions to point out the problems of assessing the truth of these allegations, or of deciding how far the particular incident reflected the general practice. In any closed society, rumour is rife. Inevitably, much of the evidence is hearsay. Some of it is vague. The rest comes from 'interested' parties, the captor's word clashing with the captive's; and there are villains on both sides. In fairness to the police, one must recognize the almost unique Portuguese propensity for hyperbole. In fairness to the prisoner, no one who has met the opposition over the years can pretend that the charges are wholly baseless. The only solution to this dilemma is to stage the kind of public inquiry which will subject all the evidence to merciless cross-examination, especially the evidence of the police. The Amnesty report, to which we shall return, marshalled some of the evidence without passing judgment. But it put its finger on the heart of the matter by urging the Portuguese government to make provision for a suitable inquiry, and pointing out that failure to do so would lend credibility to what was alleged.

In October 1957, 100 former Republican ministers, retired officers and intellectuals published a manifesto in which they declared their intention of abstaining from the November elections for the National Assembly, as there was no chance of their being genuinely free. The signatories included Dr Mario de Azevedo Gomes, Dr Jaime Cortesão, and Admiral José Mendes Cabeçadas. On the eve of the elections,[1] the *New York Times* reported that the electorate numbered a million or so. He described the regime as a velvet glove dictatorship, stated that a lot of criticism of the government had been allowed to appear in the press over the previous month, but that the opposition had found themselves hampered, badgered and ridiculed. Some opposition meetings had been allowed, and there had been complaints of the country's economic backwardness, not to mention the lack of civil liberties. The opposition had not been allowed to examine the electoral rolls, could not find adequate meeting halls, and there had been some skimping of their press and radio (pre-election) privileges. The result was that virtually all opposition candidates had withdrawn, and these included right-wingers and Catholics. They had thought it suspicious when, in 1953, the opposition had polled 20 per cent of

[1] Benjamin Welles in *New York Times*, 2 November 1957.

the votes in Aveiro and Lisbon, yet won no seats. Would the same thing happen again? The only redeeming feature was that half the National Union's candidates were under fifty, and thirty of them were under forty, so at least the Assembly would not be composed of ageing diehards. Commenting after the ballot, the London *Observer*'s correspondent described the opposition as not even radical.[1] Most of them believed in the *assimilado* system in the African provinces and in Portugal's stand on Goa. They were more easy-going than their counterparts in Spain, and much less frightening than the critics of General Peron in Argentina. Their essential plea was simply for civil rights. The election had finally brought a high percentage of the electorate to the polls, varying from 60 to 80 per cent in different districts. The *New York Times* wound up by asserting that Salazar was incorruptible and self-sacrificing – within his lights.[2] He was a sort of tribal chief, patriotic and unselfish. On the whole, the writer thought, the Portuguese seemed satisfied, or at least resigned.

It was in January 1958, that the name of Captain Henrique Galvão began to appear in the headlines of the foreign press. He had been a government official who, in the previous decade, had presented a highly critical report on conditions in Portuguese Africa to the National Assembly in Lisbon. He was arrested in 1952 for trying to plan a *coup d'état*, appealed against his conviction and secured a re-trial. In March 1953, he was sentenced by a military court to three years' imprisonment. Having already been in prison for some time, he should have been freed at the end of 1954, but it seems that, while in prison, he had managed to keep in touch with the conspiracy outside the walls, and to keep it alive. Leaflets had been circulated, inciting to civil war and containing scurrilous attacks on the government, not to mention threats to the head of state. Galvão was therefore detained for further charges to be heard, and the definitive trial opened up only in January 1958. This trial was held *in camera* and Galvão was sentenced to sixteen years' imprisonment, with civil rights suspended for twenty years. He was then sixty-three. His appeal failed, and at the end of the year he contrived to escape and make his way to South America. He was to come into the news again early in 1961.

Galvão had been in close touch with the extraordinary man who, in the 1958 presidential election, became the spearhead of the

[1] J. Halcro Ferguson, 3 November 1957.
[2] *New York Times*, 4 November 1957.

Portuguese opposition, and in the end the only opposition candidate to bid for the presidency of the Republic. This was General Humberto Delgado, then fifty-two, an eccentric, but a man of ability and boundless energy. His exaggerated, sometimes clownish behaviour made him the sort of man the serious opposition would normally have spurned, but his energy and dynamism supplied them with the fire they knew they lacked at the time. Delgado was the son of a Republican officer, and in 1926 had been among his country's first pilots, showing himself to be a man of immense physical bravery. In the early days he supported Salazar, and later recalled with disgust the series of Republican governments which, in pre-Salazar days, had lasted for less than two months, including those led by men as highly respected as Azevedo Coutinho and Cunha Leal. In 1944, Delgado became Director-General of Civil Aviation, and in 1947, went to Canada to represent his country with the International Civil Aviation Organization. He also served as military liaison officer with NATO, and in 1957, returned to his earlier post in charge of civil aviation at home. During the Second World War, he had completed a brilliant survey of the Atlantic islands, and taken a leading part in the London negotiations with the Allies prior to their taking over the Azores bases. He was always proud of his well-earned British decoration, not to mention his membership of the Athenaeum, the exclusive London club, and that King George VI had spoken well of him.

But by 1958, Delgado was a frustrated man, convinced that his gifts were not being properly used. But he also felt honestly irked by what he saw as the slow tempo of Salazar's policies, and felt that the time had come for someone to give the country a new inspiration. What would have happened to Portugal if this exhibitionist had won the dictatorial powers he avowedly sought is not clear. Yet his criticisms had substance. Writing later in his *Memoirs*, he exasperates the unsuspecting reader with his conceit, but offers a factual assessment of the country's condition which it is hard to fault.[1] The Portuguese worker was still spending between 67 and 87 per cent of his income on food. A worker employed for the whole year in 1958, could not have fed his family properly on his average daily wage, and, said Delgado, there would have been an overall 2 per cent deficit in his budget. The national mortality rate for the first year of life was 88 per 1,000, as against an average of 50 in 102 other countries.

[1] Delgado, pp. 69-78.

There was only one doctor per 1,000 people as against one per 800 in Italy. Some 40 per cent of the industrial turnover went to wages, leaving 60 per cent for capital profits as compared with 70 per cent for wages and 30 per cent for profits in advanced countries. The *per capita* income was 182 dollars as against 209 in Turkey, and 1,453 in the United States. Farm labourers in the Alentejo could scrape about 4s. a day when they could get work. The national product per head was rising at only 3 per cent per annum. Portugal still possessed considerable wealth, but it was concentrated in very few hands.[1] While the country was spending 32 per cent of its revenue on defence, only 9 per cent went to education and 4 per cent to public assistance. Half the nation was still illiterate.[2] Grim though this indictment seems, it has to be viewed in the perspective of what went before and what has happened since: the chaos and beggary of 1930; the need to build the basic infrastructures – transport, telephones, water and power supply, and the like – before even a start could be made on boosting industrial output; the problem of defending huge regions in the overseas provinces; the consequently slow growth rate between 1930 and 1958, the at times dramatic growth between 1958 and today. The picture painted by Delgado's book in 1964 bears little relation to the facts of 1969. As for the 1950s themselves, Delgado overlooked such items as Portugal's obligations to NATO, and the visible results achieved in state housing, school and hospital building, and communications. For instance, between 1930 and 1955, illiteracy among children of school age (then seven to eleven) was reduced from a level of 73.1 per cent to less than 10 per cent, while the overall illiteracy level had fallen from 61.8 to 40.3 per cent. A total of 13,555 state schools had been opened, and half a million people had flocked to the special courses provided by the 1952 adult education scheme. Large municipal hospitals had appeared in urban centres to cater for thousands of patients, with a network of cottage hospitals in the countryside. Sir Alfred Bossom described in *The Times*, the imaginative building of houses and flats for workers.[3]

Delgado, however, still had grounds for complaint in terms of the tempo of growth. Salazar still believed that the country had to pull itself up by the bootstraps and by suffering, paying its way as it went,

---

[1] It used to be said that most of the wealth was commanded by the 'eleven families'. Delgado put it at 50. Others were calling it 200.

[2] Figueiredo, pp. 67-77.

[3] *The Times Supplement*, 25 October 1955; *Daily Telegraph*, 28 December 1955.

without recourse to 'artificial' injections of aid from abroad. True, wealth was unfairly distributed, but at that time Portugal had not developed her 'third class' of technocratic non-proprietors. The owner was still the manager, and to break with the one might be to lose the other. So the answer as Salazar saw it was, not to despoil the rich, but to pressurize them into investment for industrial expansion. The result should be an increase in earnings to benefit wage-earner and shareholder alike. While this process was going on, of course, the industrialist still lived in comfort, while to people already short of calories each extra sacrifice was a crucifixion, without benefit of a sufficient welfare state to relieve the people's poverty. The State had money and reserves, but these were the guarantee of the stable escudo. So the prescription had to be hard work, sacrifice and patience, and, to give him credit, he asked nothing of the people that he did not ask of himself. In 1958 as now, a strong currency was essential for Portugal's overall growth, but how far can a nation keep wealth tied up in banks while, in Salazar's own words, a child cries for a crust of bread? There are no easy answers to questions like this, especially when, as in Portugal, it can be an uphill task to persuade the rich to put their money to work. Salazar's 'pay as we go' formula was unpopular with a generation born into a post-Keynesian world liberally flowing with credits. But Salazar clung to his course, convinced that anything else would shatter an economy too fragile to risk experiments tailored for more advanced countries. His defenders would argue that a number of modern economists are in some respects back-pedalling. Not all that is pre-Keynesian is inherently inopportune. Moreover, underlying the economic considerations was Salazar's own endemic distrust of imported ideas; and imported money could bring ideas with it. He did not believe that there could be aid without strings, and feared that foreign influences might at worst impel a downhill plunge into Communism, or at best a return to the chaos of corrupt party politics.

It was as a sign of contradiction to what he represented as a slow, plodding economy, that Delgado decided to stand as opposition candidate in the presidential election of 1958. He announced in unambiguous terms that, if elected, he would dismiss Salazar. Writing in his *Memoirs* some years later, he put his economic criticisms with much force and with a fair degree of conviction. But it is one thing to quote other people's figures, another to define policy. There is little to show that, in 1958, he really knew what the country needed. Then, and later, he adopted the stance that some initial chaos, even a civil war, might be inevitable, and that a new dictatorship would have to be established. But at no time did he outline a convincing blueprint for solving the country's ills. Moreover, even while preparing for a constitutional election, he was not above planning revolution. He had been involved in a conspiracy in 1956, and then:

> On the night of 2/3 June (five days before the election) and the 18/19 December 1958, the problem of Portugal was meant to be and should have been settled by armed revolutions which I was to command. Unfortunately, the officers taking part refused at the last moment to go forward in this patriotic venture.[1]

Some of the hindrances put in the way of his electoral campaign may well have been prompted by intelligence reports about his plans for revolution. This does not, however, justify all that was done to obstruct him. He announced his candidature in April 1958, and within a month the other opposition candidates had yielded to him. Admiral Quintão Meireles was the first to withdraw, giving as his reason the impossibility of a fair election. He was, in any event, an ageing man. So was Dr Cunha Leal, who also stood down in Delgado's favour, not wishing to fragment the opposition effort. Dr Arlindo Vicente, despite his outspoken criticisms of Delgado, followed suit. The Communists were dead against the quixotic general, but their numbers were too small to affect the election. It therefore became a straight fight between Delgado and the candidate backed by the National Union. This was not President Craveiro Lopes, whose term of office was ending, but who might have been expected to stand again. It is known that he was seriously at odds with the Minister of War, Lieutenant-Colonel Santos Costa, who exerted great influence in the government, and who was a stern traditionalist. It has even been suggested that Craveiro Lopes was in some way involved in the abortive Delgado plan for a June coup, and it is certain that his own fairly liberal instincts were at variance with the way the country was being run. The 'official' candidate turned out to be Admiral Américo Tomás, and the election became a straight fight between him and Delgado.

---

[1] Delgado, *op. cit.*, preface, page x; and pp. 131-42.

Admiral Tomás was supported by the National Union's organizational network, which gave him certain advantages over an individual opponent without comparable backing. Delgado alleged that copies of the electoral register were made available to the National Union campaigners, while his own people could only take handwritten copies from a single original, and that the National Union received official help in distributing ballot papers. His own papers, he asserted, were sometimes seized or delayed by the police, while the censorship blocked his propaganda.[1] For all that, Delgado succeeded in inflaming the public imagination, not so much by his programme as by his sheer exuberance. On the eve of the election, the *New York Times* correspondent reported from Lisbon that by no stretch of the imagination could it be said that the electorate was aflame with discontent, even though there were real grievances.[2] Some days later he added that, if elected, Delgado would not last a month. He had no programme and was a complete egoist. But he had retained the courage he had shown in the air in the 1920s, and he had woken Portugal up – the best thing that had happened to the country in thirty years.[3, 4] The London *Observer* noted that Delgado behaved like a clown, but added that many people who would not in the ordinary way have supported him, had rallied to him as a symbol of change.[5] This was the key to it. Change was in the wind, and change was something the people had not known for a long time. Everywhere he went, Delgado found the crowds awaiting him, whether in the town or countryside. In Oporto, the police diverted his car into side streets, but his meeting that same night was packed. There had been fighting and shooting in the streets of Oporto, and there was an ugly incident in a Lisbon demonstration, too, when the Republican Guard lost its head and charged into a crowd in the *Rossio*, fired into it and wounded a number of people. At Beja, Delgado was carried shoulder high. In the fishing villages of the south, the people held their emaciated children up for him to see. At Braga, on the other hand, Santos Costa had turned out the Legion, and Delgado went to the city against his friends' advice that the Legionnaires would attack him on arrival. In fact, this did not

---

[1] *Ibid.*, pp. 116-70.
[2] *New York Times*, 5 June 1958.
[3] *New York Times*, 9 June 1958.
[4] In his *Memoirs*, Delgado carefully quotes the complimentary part of this assessment, while omitting the rest.
[5] *Observer*, 8 June 1958.

occur, and most of the people stayed indoors while Santos Costa was denouncing Delgado and his friends for their lack of patriotism. The probability is that Santos Costa knew a good deal about the abortive June conspiracy. At any rate, he alerted the troops from the start of the campaign and was prepared for all eventualities. As we saw it, Delgado was playing on the feelings of unenlightened people who could all too easily be whipped into frenzy in the service of one man's ambition.

Santos Costa was never a popular figure in Portugal. Few would deny his immense ability as Under-Secretary for War, and later, as Minister of Defence, not to mention his contribution to NATO during the first decade of its existence. But he was never a man to handle others with velvet gloves, and his ruthlessness won him many enemies. They saw him as an archetypal reactionary whose ambition, in the 1950s, sought to dominate the government and the country through the army. Be that as it may, Santos Costa was also a professional soldier. He had been an adult in the days when blood flowed in the city streets, and the fact is that there are young men in Lisbon today who turned out in 1958 to cheer for Delgado, yet remember that some of his closest supporters showed themselves up pretty badly. A former law student told the present writer that he had seen an inoffensive, country bumpkin type of uniformed policeman, not a PIDE agent, brutally beaten up and trampled. For good measure, his assailants had 'put the boot in', and smashed his face to pulp. Nor is one reassured by Delgado's references in his *Memoirs* to his own desire, and even once his own attempt, to strangle people. Did gratuitous repression make men lose their heads? Or did some of them invite repression in the first place? Or was it both? What is clear is that, when crowds are aroused in Portugal, anything can happen, and that, while interference with the ballot or with honest campaigning is unpardonable, the fear that Delgado's boys were spoiling for a massive confrontation was not without foundation.

At the end of the day, the victory went to Admiral Tomás, who won 758,998 votes against Delgado's 236,528. Even by official estimates, Delgado secured a quarter of the vote. Had the election been fair, he argued, he would have won it outright. The *Guardian* reported that, while the Portuguese dictatorship was less harsh than others, it did not trust its own popularity enough to hazard it in a fair fight.[1]

---

[1] *Guardian*, 5 June 1958.

The foreign press in general saw the whole affair as a farce. The *New York Times* summed up:

> General Delgado naturally lost by a large majority of votes to the candidate chosen by António de Oliveira Salazar, dictator and Prime Minister. The name of the victor happens to be Rear-Admiral Américo Tomás, but this is of no importance whatsoever. He will have no power, and Dr Salazar could just as well have chosen the first traffic policeman he came across.[1]

This was far from fair to the new President who, ten years later, handled the interregnum after Salazar's physical collapse with a strength and dignity that won him universal admiration and may have saved his country. For the time being, however, Delgado was defeated, the regime breathed again, and a weary reporter quoted Caesar: 'There came to the much tormented nations of the Mediterranean a tranquil evening after a sultry day.'

There is no way of deciding what Delgado's chances would have been in a straight-up fight. The odds probably are that he would not have won, but would have secured a higher percentage of the poll. For reasons which he explicitly and mysteriously declines to explain in his *Memoirs*, he did not seek constitutional redress from the courts, as he was entitled to do. Instead, he petitioned President Craveiro Lopes for a fresh election.[2] The President had no powers in the matter and turned the petition down, but the document is important for the details it gives of what Delgado calls the shameful methods used by the Salazarists. In the first place, the official estimate of the strength of the total electorate was given as 1,001,138, while Delgado claimed that more than 2,000,000 people were entitled to vote. If he was wrong about this, it was hardly his fault, since he had no proper access to the electoral rolls. What surprised him specifically was that, in Lisbon, with 900,000 citizens, the voters were numbered at only 105,978, while in Oporto, it seemed, only 27,107 had voted out of 400,000 citizens. Even though men had to prove literacy or that they were taxpayers, and the female vote was confined to certain categories, it still seemed that the official figures were out of step with all the enthusiasm, and what looked to the naked eye like a very large turn-out. In Luanda, the capital of Angola, it was said that only 40 per cent of the total roll took the trouble to vote, yet the size of the ballot

[1] *New York Times*, 10 June 1958.
[2] Delgado, *op. cit.*, pp. 116-70.

in previous elections had reached twice that level. Unfortunately, this kind of suspicion is always hard to pin down, but in other connections Delgado was on stronger ground. His ballot papers for the Azores and Madeira had been held up by the authorities, he said. He gave instances where officials seized ballot papers and tore them up in the polling booth, and where returning officers had been guilty of various irregularities. Thirty of Delgado's team had been arrested, including his chief assistant, Dr Vieria de Almeida, and two men trying to distribute voting papers among potential supporters.

After the election, Delgado was swiftly sacked from his posts in civil aviation and the Ministry of Communications, and told to return to the army. On 27 July, he wrote to four high-ranking generals with a plan for a *coup d'état*.[1] Botelho Moniz did not reply. Lopes da Silva sent a verbal message saying he agreed with Delgado, but could not accept his suggestions. Costa Macedo said he disagreed with most of what Delgado said, and thought he was exaggerating. Beleza Ferraz replied: 'We have different conceptions both of politics and of loyalty, and therefore we cannot meet on the same ground nor follow the same paths.' Delgado comments:

> It might be thought that these gentlemen were observing regulations or being loyal, but ask the officers, cadets, sergeants, corporals or privates if any one of them was a better professional soldier than myself. As for loyalty, which at times is completely inopportune, every one of them had taken part in the 28 May revolt as I had done.[2]

It was at this time Salazar made two important changes in the government. For all his energetic support in the election, Santos Costa was replaced as Minister of Defence by General Julio Botelha Moniz, while Professor Marcello Caetano was replaced as Minister of the Presidency by Ambassador Theotónio Pereira. One version is that pressure was put on Salazar to liberalize his cabinet, but this rings oddly in relation to Caetano, whose more liberal attitudes brought him into conflict with Salazar at this time. Santos Costa had been in office for twenty-two years, and may well have felt the time had come to move to new pastures. In fact he sat down to pass his final promotion test, and became a general. (Today he holds a

[1] Delgado, *op. cit.*, pp. 131-42.
[2] *Ibid.*, p. 142.

key directorship in an oil firm.) There were, however, other factors. Both Santos Costa and Caetano were spearheads of important pressure groups, and Salazar doubtless felt some kind of challenge in this.

The opposition continued to tread a dangerous path. On 6 October, a crowd of 3,000 turned out peacefully in Lisbon to lay a wreath on the monument of a former President. It was the forty-eighth anniversary of the founding of the Republic, and the mild celebration was led, not only by Delgado, but by distinguished men of letters like Arlindo Vicente, António Sergio, Jaime Cortesão and Azevedo Gomes. The police broke up the demonstration with tear gas and in doing so made a stupid mistake. There was no need for it, and their action only created more bad will. Later in the year, a group of oppositionists tried to invite the British Labour militant, Mr Aneurin Bevan, to Lisbon to give a lecture. The Portuguese government not only stopped the visit, but arrested Azevedo Gomes, Vieira d'Almeida, Jaime Cortesão and António Sergio, all of whom were over seventy years old. The allegation was that they had been distributing leaflets claiming that the government was planning to take action against Delgado. After some days, they were released on bail.

In the new year, Delgado was brought before a military tribunal, accused of insulting the President and government, and dismissed from the army. He was, however, allowed the maximum pension: 75 per cent of his pay. He obtained sanctuary in the Brazilian embassy, where he was befriended by the Brazilian Ambassador, Dr Alvaro Lins, who tells the story in his book, *Mission in Portugal*. The Portuguese government claimed that this was unnecessary, as Delgado was in no danger of arrest, but, during his ninety-eight days in the embassy, the PIDE kept a careful watch outside. After negotiations, it was agreed that he should have safe conduct out of the country, and on 21 April 1959, he left for Rio de Janeiro, where he established his National Independence Movement. His final gesture, a month before his departure, had been an attempted coup in Lisbon planned with Galvão. It was aborted on 19 March. Fr Perestrelo, a priest who had given refuge to some of the conspirators in the cathedral cloisters, was arrested and found to be carrying guns under his cassock.[1] Figueiredo tells us that 'Latin American embassies in Lisbon were kept busy giving asylum to scores of opposition leaders,

[1] His father was director of the naval shipyard.

while others were escaping into exile abroad'.[1] Among them was Manuel Serra, then President of Catholic Youth, who safely reached Brazil, and Major Luis Calafate, who reached Venezuela but proceeded to fall out violently with Galvão. The conspirators caught in Lisbon during the March 1959 attempt, were later sentenced to fairly light terms ranging from three to twenty months. Eight were acquitted. Serra and Calafate had their cases deferred. Rumours again ran rife, and the names of Craveiro Lopes and even that of Defence Minister Botelho Moniz, were mentioned in connection with the plot.

Delgado spent the rest of the year in Rio, planning his next move with caution, as the current Brazilian government under Kubitschek was regarded as well disposed to Salazar; certainly, it did not recognize the Portuguese opposition. In November, Delgado came to Britain, one of a series of journeys abroad to arouse foreign sympathy and co-ordinate the Portuguese exiles. He was received by members of all three major parties, and wrote articles for leading British journals. The press, though a little taken aback by his melodramatic performance recalled Britain's debt to him for the part he had played in the wartime negotiations over the Azores. After visiting Amsterdam he returned to Rio and there, in the following April (1960), he received a letter from Galvão in Venezuela, proposing the seizure of the Portuguese luxury liner *Santa Maria*. The idea was to sail it to the West African coast, attack São Tomé and northern Angola, and then seek asylum in Ghana. This was all to be done under the aegis of the Iberian Revolutionary Directory for Liberation (DRIL) which also included Spaniards. Delgado comments that, after the *Santa Maria* arrived in Brazil, he found that not even Galvão really knew what DRIL was:

> It certainly did not live up to the claims of its leaders who, when they arrived in Recife, said they had 2,500 suicide commandos. They overdid it there, even if one makes allowances for Iberian 'elaboration'.[2]

The plan was considerably modified, and the seizure was planned to coincide with President Kennedy's accession to power in the U.S. on 20 January 1961, and the forthcoming inauguration in Brazil of President Quadros, who was known to favour the Portuguese

[1] Figueiredo, *op. cit.*, p. 87.
[2] Delgado, *op. cit.*, p. 187.

opposition. When the time came, the conspirators, led by Galvão, managed to get on board the ship as third-class passengers or stowaways, bringing their guns with them in a coffin accompanied by a lady in mourning. A woman member of the ship's company had supplied them with full details and timing of the shipboard routine and the crew's movements. Once in the Caribbean, the ship was easily seized at gunpoint, though one officer resisted and was killed. Renamed the *Santa Liberdade*, the ship sailed to Recife, on the north-east coast of Brazil, and there Delgado came aboard, having gone out to the ship clandestinely in a little boat, with doused lights, commandeered by the *Time* magazine reporters. The conspirators were penniless, and even had to rely on money collected by Brazilian students to clear their bills in the ship's bar, which they honourably did. But it was plain the adventure could go no further, and the ship surrendered to the Brazilian authorities. At least the gesture had been made. The world was in no doubt that a Portuguese opposition was alive and had something to say for itself. The world's press spent a lot of money covering the incident, and the sheer audacity of the gesture won a lot of sympathy.

Galvão claimed that the passengers on board the ship had for the most part sympathized with his aims. Public opinion in Britain and the United States had veered towards him. At Salazar's request, British and American naval vessels at first pursued the *Santa Maria*, but the Labour opposition in the British House of Commons argued that Galvão had not committed an act of piracy; he was, they maintained, leading a legitimate revolt against a dictatorship. The British vessels gave up the chase on the ground that the distance between them and the Portuguese ship was too great. The American vessels caught up with the *Santa Maria* but did not hinder it, though American planes flew over it for reconnaissance purposes, and with a view to passing information to the naval ships sent by Lisbon to destroy the *Santa Maria*. The local U.S. commander, Admiral Dennison, finally entered into negotiations with Galvão, who claimed that the U.S. was now in effect treating him as a legitimate belligerent. Lawyers of the U.S. State Department had apparently pointed out that there was no piracy in the case of persons rebelling against a government, provided they 'confined their activities to the nation in question'. The French government had not complied with a request from Lisbon to join in the hunt. President Kennedy had decided that even the presence of American passengers on board the ship did not give the U.S. the right to board her. When the *Santa Maria* was surrendered, Quadros was already in power, and Galvão and his friends received a warm welcome in Brazil.[1]

Shortly after this incident, the war in Angola broke out, and the rebels in South America took heart. They fell out among themselves, however, and in October 1961, Delgado, acting in Rabat after establishing a North African headquarters, dismissed Galvão as secretary-general of the National Independence Movement on grounds of 'treason' and 'exhibitionism', and issuing 'theatrical propaganda' harmful to the cause. Galvão is still alive in exile, a permanently sick man. Strangely enough, the events of 1961 strengthened Salazar's position at home. An *Associated Press* despatch reported in March from Lisbon that both the *Santa Maria* incident and Angolan flare-up had been received by opposition leaders at home with chagrin, and there was a tendency to say that, while they disliked the dictatorship, they were even more afraid of what might come after it.[2] It was about this time that the Portuguese opposition at home formed the *Directorio Republicano*, which temporarily brought together some right-wingers, angry young professionals, radicals, socialists, dissatisfied officers, and some Catholics. This 'national front' was not interested in Delgado and indeed found him an embarrassment, especially now that he had become tied up with rebellious elements in Spain. *The Times* correspondent reported in June: if Salazar keeps order in Africa, nothing can shake him.[3] In October, even the *Guardian*, the severest among the high-quality British papers in its criticisms of Portuguese Africa, commented that the regime remained 'stubbornly authoritarian in an old-fashioned way, but a good way short of the full thoroughness of modern totalitarianism'.[4]

Delgado, however, was not finished. His next move was to plan the military coup at the Beja garrison in the south of Portugal. He arrived back in Portugal clandestinely via North Africa and Spain at the end of the year, and reached Beja in the early hours of New Year's Day, 1962. The project was disastrously mismanaged. The attack on the garrison had begun before Delgado arrived. He had been relying on the 'neutrality' of some troops outside Beja, but

---

[1] Henrique Galvão, *My Crusade for Portugal*, Weidenfeld & Nicolson, London, 1961.
[2] *Christian Science Monitor*, 1 March 1961.
[3] *The Times*, 5 June 1961.
[4] *Guardian*, 28 October 1961.

rapidly discovered that this had been a false hope. He kept clear of the garrison himself and managed to escape. The leader of the attack, Captain Varela Gomes, was seriously wounded, and all the attackers were either killed, or, like Manuel Serra, the Catholic Actionist, arrested. The survivors, other than Delgado himself, came to trial in July 1964. Of eight-six defendants, sixty-five were found guilty and sentenced to terms ranging from seventeen months to ten years. The shortest sentence was passed on Captain Gomes's wife, and, having been held in jail pending trial, she was released at once. Gomes himself received six years, and Serra ten.

During the next three years, Delgado kept his flag flying, but his movement weakened through internal dissension, not unconnected with his own authoritarianism. He transferred his headquarters to North Africa in 1964, after the Brazilian authorities had begun to hedge him in, and travelled widely, under a number of passports and usually armed, until at last, on 24 April 1965, his bludgeoned body was found in a shallow grave on Spanish soil near Badajoz, a few miles from the Portuguese border. With him was his secretary, the thirty-year-old Brazilian D. Arajaryr Campos, who had supported him bravely for a number of years and had even been to Beja with him in 1962. Five days earlier, the battered body of an unknown man had been found nearby, in the River Caia. The Spanish authorities held an inconsequential inquiry. The Portuguese authorities said they would put no obstacles in the way of an international inquiry. Lawyers representing the Delgado family crossed the Spanish border to try and find some evidence of what had really happened, but on their return were held by the Portuguese police for several days or weeks. Some oppositionists took the view that Delgado had been murdered by the PIDE, and in May 1965, the distinguished Portuguese exile, Professor Emilio Guerreiro, came from Paris to London where he held a press conference and asserted that a man had been found in Italy who had been involved in a PIDE plot. Delgado, said the professor, had been killed as a birthday present for Salazar, and the secretary had been killed as well because Salazar was a misogynist. Yet it could well be argued that by 1965 Delgado was a spent force and hardly worth a major scandal. A well-known oppositionist in Lisbon suggested to the author that the PIDE may have staged an ambush with a view to arrest, that Delgado may have pulled a gun, and that in the ensuing fight he was killed; the unknown man in the river could have been a policeman. Officials in Lisbon suggested at the time that Delgado had been killed by rival oppositionists in exile, possibly by the Communists. The circumstances were ambiguous. Why did somebody try to remove all traces of Delgado's identity except the ring with its HD engraving? Why was the body hidden, yet in such a way that discovery was certain sooner rather than later? The Delgado family's lawyer, Dr Mario Soares, tried to pursue the inquiry in Italy, but in doing so ran into trouble with the PIDE. At one stage he was stopped from going abroad, and later, as already mentioned, was deported for some months. Official hypersensitivity to foreign reaction could account for this, and Dr Soares was hardly the PIDE's favourite person, having been in their prisons a dozen times. Yet any sort of restraint in such a context only serves to sharpen the questions. All one can say with certainty is that Delgado had a rare facility for making enemies, that his activities in his last year or two were devious and are still mysterious, and that more agencies than one had reasons for wanting to be rid of him.

With all Delgado's faults, it seems a pity that he could not have been better utilized in the service of his country. After the election, he refused a government offer to send him to Canada to study economics, which he regarded as a device for getting him out of the way. In aiming for the highest position, he was really out of his class, and his overweening vanity may have made it unlikely that he could ever have been content with a middle-range job. It is also the tragedy of the opposition that he was the most effective candidate they could produce. They deserved better. Oddly enough, it was Salazar himself who pronounced a kind of epitaph, when, in a speech at the end of the year, he referred to Delgado's dynamism and sincerity, but added that the General had had a genius for creating trouble.

No discussion of the Portuguese opposition can ignore the role of the modern Church, and to this we shall turn our attention before examining the role of the opposition at large from the time of Delgado onwards. Until a few years ago, political opposition on the part of the Church was usually identified with Communist countries where the Christian faithful fought against persecution; but in the past decade things have changed, and a new generation of younger priests, and certain bishops, has emerged to criticize right-wing governments. This quite untraditional tendency has been most noticeable in Spain and South America, but the 'renewed' Catholic Church in Portugal also has its clergy and active laity whose consciences owe much to the social encyclicals of John XXIII: *Mater et Magistra* and *Pacem in Terris*; to the Vatican Council's Constitution *Gaudium et Spes*; and to Pope Paul VI's *Populorum Progressio*. Prior to the Republic, the Portuguese Church had degenerated. Historically, she had had her saints, from Queen Elizabeth and Anthony of Padua to John de Brito; nor was she ever identified with any of the major European schisms and heresies. The Catholic faith was endemic to the Portuguese character, and, as in Spain, the anti-clericalism which developed in and after the Age of Reason was the bitter reaction of men let down by something they had loved and trusted in. The clergy, concerned for order and the *status quo*, had become identified with the privileged classes. Their post-Reformation defensiveness, the 'state of siege' mentality, had led to a static theology unable to interact with dynamic secular scholarship and the signs of the times. Association with the corridors of power sapped the spirituality of the priest and created a worldly, comfortable clergy. The Church's political influence with the monarchy proved corrupting for both institutions. The life of the Church was not eclipsed, and in some parts of the country religious practice flourished even during the nineteenth century, but it was Pope Pius IX who described the state of the Portuguese Church as deplorable.[1] In the second half of the century, outstanding men like Cardinal Ferreira dos Santos Silva and Cardinal Sebastião Neto tried to save something from the impending wreck, but the rot had set in too deeply. In 1910, the new Republic seized the Church's property, savaged her liberties, and bundled her, so to speak, into the vestry. The religious orders were outlawed. It was licit to shoot a Jesuit on sight. And to safeguard Lisbon's Irish nuns, a British gunboat showed its nose in the Tagus.

The new government, however, was well aware that the force of religious faith can survive the institution. While Afonso Costa made the death of religion a prime objective, he and his colleagues knew it would have to be the work of generations. So the Church, albeit restricted, was not dismantled. Their approach achieved the opposite of their intentions; it is now a historical platitude that the way to purify the Roman Catholic Church at any given time is to remove her temporal privileges. Forced back by this deprivation to her own interior resources, the Portuguese Church began to rediscover her

[1] M. de Oliveira: *História Eclesiastica de Portugal*, 2nd edition, p. 391, Lisbon 1948.

primitive spirit and to examine her conscience. The process has been slow. Many Catholics in the early part of the century resisted the enlightenment offered by Leo XIII, as we have seen. Some of them, in Portugal, resented Leo's refusal to give a privileged moral status to monarchy, and it was partly because of their attitude that Salazar, always Leo's disciple, declined to join the Catholic Party.

But there were signs within the Church of an honest renewal, a process powerfully strengthened by events in 1917 at the Cova da Iria. It was in this year, the year of the Russian revolution, that an alleged manifestation of the Blessed Virgin appeared to three shepherd children on a hillside near Fatima, a town in Salazar's 'bailiwick', warning them among other things against the rise of Communism. It has been said that, for believers, no explanation is necessary, and that, for unbelievers, no explanation is possible. This is not the place to argue about it, and the story was well enough told by the English Jesuit scholar, Fr C. C. Martindale,[1] who reformed the art of hagiography, and made holy war on false mysticism. He was the least likely man in the world to be impressed by visions. The incident was studied, too, by Fr Karl Rahner, S.J., today the Catholic Church's leading theologian. He left it convinced that a glimpse of eternity had been granted. If Fatima could impress that sceptical, German mind, it was more than a charade foisted on a stupid peasantry. If it is said that Salazar used it to keep the starving masses quiet, the fact is that it had gripped them, and many others, for many years before he came to power. It had also reached out to the wider world. Some of the circumstances around the event are unsatisfactory. For the present writer, this 'happening' has always been less convincing than what happened to Bernadette at Lourdes. But the fact remains that some kind of spiritual experience was received and made an impact which, as a matter of recorded fact, gave new life to the Church in Portugal. The Fatima shrine is a cold, bleak place. The local bishops have always set their faces against crude and emotional exploitation, and the only survivor of the children has spent her life in a Carmelite convent. At times of pilgrimage, thousands of poor people make their way to the shrine from all over the country, and they are joined by thousands more from abroad. There is that in their faces which belies superstition and fraud. If the Virgin's alleged warning against Communism has been exploited, her message of

[1] Fr C. C. Martindale, S.J.: *The Meaning of Fatima*, New York, 1950.

prayer and penance also survives. Pattee tells us that it has changed the face of the Portuguese nation, not because of spectacular cures at the shrine, but by the subtle infiltration of a new spirit. He quotes Antero de Figueiredo: 'For years Our Lady of Fatima has been touching the hearts of the Portuguese people from the humblest to the most cultivated, and, it would seem, most particularly the cultivated.'[1] Whatever happened at the Cova da Iria, it has at least enabled Portugal to assert, nationally, the primacy of the spirit. 'A whole nation', said an Italian observer in 1942, 'has been shaken out of its torpor and touched by a supernatural wave.'[2]

When Salazar came to power he maintained the separation of Church and State. His friend Cerejeira, as Patriarch of Lisbon, saw the wisdom of not asking for material concessions, and in fact the Church's lost property was not restored to her, nor even claimed. She exists today, not without government help in specific cases, such as the building of a church, but basically on the people's voluntary offerings. This helps to keep the clergy healthily poor and insecure, and thus able to identify themselves more credibly with the under-privileged classes. In the 1933 Constitution, Article 45 provided for freedom of public and private worship for all religions, together with the right to establish Church organizations and associations 'in accordance with the norms of law and order'. Salazar was wholly sincere in his wish to reinstate the Church to her proper place in Portuguese life:

> We return, with all the force of a nation reborn, to the great source of our national life . . . and, without any sacrifice of the material progress of our time, we aim to place ourselves on the same spiritual level as eight centuries ago.[3]

But he intended the Church to know her place and keep it. Speaking of Church-State separation, he said:

> Better a Church ruled by her own institutions in harmony with her needs and aims than one governed by the State through its ordinary administrative channels. It is better for the State to define and accomplish those things which are of national interest in its proper

---

[1] Pattee, op. cit., p. 328; and Antero de Figueiredo, Fatima, Graça, Segredos, Misterios, Lisbon, 1936.
[2] Luigi Moresco, Gli occhi che videro la Madonnal, p. 18, Rome, 1942.
[3] Commentary on the Concordat, 7 May, 1940; SNI, Lisbon.

sectors of activity, than to borrow from the Church any political
force which it may lack. . . . The State will abstain from dealing in
politics with the Church, and feels sure that the Church will
equally refrain from any political action in relation to the State. . . .
It must be so, because political activity corrupts the Church.[1]

In practice, of course, he expected the Church to support him, and
was to show much annoyance in 1958, when Catholics were showing
signs of restiveness. The institutional Church, that is to say the
bishops, for the most part have supported him over the years, and the
Catholic opposition of recent times has criticized this fact severely.
Under the Concordat, episcopal appointments are submitted to the
government for consideration, and, while Rome is not absolutely
bound by government rejection of a candidate, she does not see
much joy in making appointments in the teeth of official hostility.
The result is to make the appointment of bishops too dependent
on the will of the state. In July 1958, however, the Bishop of Oporto,
Dom António Ferreira Gomes, wrote a letter to Salazar whom he
knew quite well, and to whom he had made his critical representations
before. This letter criticized the restrictions on human rights in
Portugal and Spain, rebuked parish clergy for using their sermons
to urge the people to back the regime in elections, and complained
of the harshness of Portugal's poverty, her beggars, and her under-
nourished children. It was time, he said, for the Church to come out
of the catacombs and speak her mind. The letter in itself need not
have caused a break in relations. Though not easily argued out of his
point of view, Salazar was capable of facing a private showdown.
The bishop, however, doubtless because he thought it the only way
to get something done, had copies made and widely distributed.
This was another matter, and Salazar was furious. Whether because
he expected to be arrested, or simply to draw the world's attention
to the situation in Portugal, the bishop left the country. It is believed
that, while his arrest was unlikely, he was certainly under surveillance,
and that he was not prepared to carry on under such circumstances.
He was never formally exiled, nor officially ordered not to return,
but it seems quite sure that Lisbon made it clear to Rome that his
presence in Portugal would not, for the moment, be opportune.
He remained abroad until 1969, and is now back in Oporto, exercising his episcopal functions once more. Rome had not replaced him,

[1] Egerton, *op. cit.*, p. 301.

but had simply appointed a temporary administrator during his absence.

Another bishop who struck an independent line was the saintly Dom Sebastião de Resende of Beira, in Mozambique. He always maintained his personal links with Salazar and secured his help to redress certain grievances. But, in the 1950s, when abuses of the African labour system were still rife, he issued some aggressive pastoral letters denouncing the current practices, especially where the African worker found himself forced to leave home to work, with disastrous effects on family life and unity. One, at least, of these letters was suppressed by the PIDE, but nobody dared touch the bishop whose integrity and sincerity were beyond question. Substantial reforms in subsequent years undoubtedly owed a lot to his intervention, and he had the generosity to tell the present writer, in 1963, that the material conditions of the African people in his country had greatly improved, and that in some respects they compared favourably with other African countries. He also made it clear, however, that given further abuses, he would act again as he had before. He was a great champion of education for the Africans, and lashed the government into action. Above all, he longed for a local university, and urged the government to ride abreast of current Catholic thought by hinging its educational work, not on 'Europeanization', but on the indigenous African cultures.[1]

There is no doubt that the Church has come to life again in Portugal. The Republican era left its mark, of course, and many middle-aged intellectuals are not believers. However, a recent survey by the *Juventude Universitária Católica* showed that only 14.5 per cent of all university students (19.3 per cent of the men) described themselves as established atheists or agnostics.[2] The practice of religion varies and is hard to assess, but many churches are full on Sundays, and the congregations include many more men than they used to. When young people practise, it can safely be said they do so because they want to, and no longer out of convention. The *Cursos de Cristiandade*, a kind of admixture of retreat course and group therapy, have brought many lapsed Catholics back to the sacraments. These gatherings

---

[1] The University of Lourenço Marques as yet has only a small minority of African students, but they are increasing annually. The bishop did not live to see it start. He died, tragically young, of cancer five years ago.

[2] Juventude Universitária Católica: *Situação e Opinião dos Universitarios*, Lisbon, 1967.

bring men and women of all classes and political shades together for a few days of intensive discussion, clerics and laity talking together, and social topics are primary themes. The most important development is the rise of a younger generation of clergy, who have prayed their theology through in the context of social inquiry, and who have been deeply influenced by the thought of Pope John and the work of the Vatican Council. They tend to be sharply critical of the government, and plead for an open society. Their major stronghold, the Oliveis seminary near Lisbon, has been teaching an up-to-date theology, and it came as a sharp setback when, in the autumn of 1968, the Rector and several professors resigned because the Cardinal Patriarch wished to send some of their students to the new Catholic University in Lisbon, where they presumably feared that a less progressive theology might be taught. A former Oliveis teacher, Fr Felicidades Alves, the pastor of Belem, an outspoken critic of social injustice, finally came to grief with his ecclesiastical superiors last year. He was said to favour a non-institutional Church and to be interested in the 'theology of revolution', but the crux came with a charge of disrespect and insubordination. He was suspended and now works and lives as a layman.

The overall trend, however, remains encouraging, though a majority of the country does not go to church. The work of the priests and nuns for the poor and under-privileged in the parishes is effective and edifying. The quality of the clergy has substantially improved, and Fryer and McGowan Pinheiro tell us:

Today far more people go to church, and the clergy are often better educated and lead more pious lives than used to be the case.[1]

There is no question of discrimination against the Jewish and Protestant minorities in Portugal, and the ecumenical movement flourishes. Besides Catholic students and workers who favour a socialist stance, there is an important body of educated Christian-Democrats who have been highly vocal in opposition. In 1965, a group of one hundred Catholic liberals published a statement condemning the government's policy, backing the views of the social-democrat movement, and accusing the government of using the faith as a cloak for nationalism and totalitarian attitudes. Later, a cultural group of Catholics known as *Pragma* was suppressed.

One of the most heartening signs is that, over the past decade or

[1] Fryer and McGowan Pinheiro, *op. cit.*, pp. 209-13.

so, the *aggiornamento* identified with Pope John and Vatican II has not only encouraged a social conscience in priests, but has given rise in the Portuguese working-class to a Catholic element standing for Christianized socialism. Its voice is heard in such movements as the *Liga Operaria Católica*, the *Centro de Cultura Operaria*, and the Young Christian Workers. While many Catholics support the regime or regard it as the least of all available evils, the events of recent years have fostered the growth of a Christian Democrat movement among the Catholic intellectuals, some of whom work within the regime, while others, like the distinguished lawyer Dr Francisco Sousa Tavares, are frankly oppositionist. Events in the Church's life have overtaken Salazar. But the restoration of the Church as a factor to be reckoned with in Portuguese life cannot wholly be dissociated from the new lease of life he gave to the Church from the start of his public life.

Police activity under Salazar is a topic demanding special treatment, for in no respect has his personal reputation been more vulnerable. While, for many years, the world regarded him as a dictator, but a reasonably benevolent one, accusations against his security police came to impair that judgment, and the name of the PIDE became a byword for fear and repression. Those who believe that Salazar gave his country a place in the world again, and started something that could still lead to a stable and prosperous future remain bewildered that under such a man the enforcement of law could have taken such a brutal turn. Few would suggest that Salazar personally ordered torture or set out to establish a reign of terror, but it is suggested that he was too prone to believe what his policemen told him, and to disregard complaints against them, especially in the light of his obsession with the Communist threat. Even apart from outright cruelty in the physical sense, he must have known, and up to a point encouraged, the frequent short detentions and night-time interrogations which seem to have been designed at times, not so much for normal police purposes, but rather as a means of rebuke and warning. This treatment inflicted its own kind of psychological pain and disturbance, and reduced to a state of nerves many who did not deserve it. All this, however, assumes that the facts are proven. In fact, the story is fraught with obscurity and contradiction.

There is nothing harder than to judge situations where a policeman's word is pitted against a prisoner's, even when the latter is a man of conscience, for both of them are interested parties and it is rare to find an impartial witness of what went on in a police station on any given occasion. The problem afflicts the most enlightened countries. As we have seen, Salazar admitted police abuses in the 1930s, ordered disciplinary action, yet felt that ill-treatment of prisoners had to be seen in the context of saving the innocent from terrorists. Certain allowances, indeed, can be made for what may have happened in the early days of his regime when the nation had to be rescued from anarchy and violence. But, as the years passed, these dangers were reduced. Foreign press reports in the 1950s vary, but on the whole they do not suggest an endemic climate of terror in Portugal. In any closed society, rumour is always rife and hard to refute, though, in the absence of the public inquiry system, the regime has only itself to blame for this. Salazar was to complain in 1963[1] that he was still receiving complaints from abroad about the Tarrafal camp as though it was still flourishing, yet in fact it had been closed down for years. One has also to bear in mind the Portuguese flair for hyperbole, and that much of the evidence is, inevitably, hearsay. It seems doubtful whether prisoners could have survived some of the treatment alleged, and whether so many people could have stood up to ten days of the statue torture. Even while investigating the Nazi war crimes, Lord Russell of Liverpool came to doubt the feasibility of the statue technique in its worst alleged forms. On the other hand, no one who has known Portugal for a long time can doubt that extreme measures were sometimes used in the 1930s, and that while, in the past twenty years, there have been fewer suggestions of outright torture, some prisoners have been beaten up in PIDE headquarters, especially when they were working-class people and thus unprotected by 'influence'. Eventually, the commonest technique was prolonged interrogation without sleep, and this was reserved mainly for hardline Communists, including some students. Some particularly unpleasant complaints have been made about the treatment of girls.

The foreign visitor, of recent years, saw little on the surface to suggest a police state, and it appeared to be fairly safe to voice one's opinions provided one avoided suspicion of being involved in associations.[2] After the Angola crisis of 1961, oppositionists of all kinds were often pulled in for a few days or weeks of questioning and

[1] António de Oliveira Salazar, 'Realities and Trends of Portugal's Policies', *International Affairs*, vol. 39, no. 2, April 1963, p. 176.
[2] Fryer and McGowan Pinheiro, *op. cit.*, p. 205.

'solitary', and then released. Psychological pressures included sudden police visits at night, and one heard, for example, of secretaries being quizzed about their employers' associates. From 1965 onwards, all this began to ease off, and political arrests began to be confined to clear cases of involvement with groups regarded as revolutionary. The author was told by diplomats in Lisbon in the summer of 1967, that the nocturnal police visits had almost become a thing of the past. Soon after Professor Caetano came to power in 1968, he dispensed with the traditional PIDE bodyguard and was reported to have ordered the police not to arrest anyone simply on the ground that he had openly opposed the government. At all times, police behaviour has been erratic and irrational, some oppositionists getting away with daring indiscretions, while others, often less dangerous, have attracted the attention of the police. Much seems to depend on the official mood of the moment. An absurd and, one hopes, residual incident occurred in 1968, when Dr Raul Rêgo published his booklet *Towards a Dialogue with the Cardinal Patriarch of Lisbon*.[1] It rebuked the Church for being too closely tied to the government, and made familiar pleas for the Church to use her influence to secure a wider measure of social justice. Rêgo was detained for a week, given the usual hectoring, and then, on the Cardinal's intervention, released.

On such occasions, one police officer might deliver a bullying address, with threats of exile, while others would give advice more in sorrow than in anger. Middle-aged prisoners were astonished to be told they were too precocious and anxious for notice, and intellectuals were urged to find outlets for their energies within the prescribed structures. Some of the dialogue seems to have been quite cultivated, which only serves to heighten its absurdity. But the agony of mind this sort of thing stimulates, not only for the prisoner alone in his cell without a book for days, but also for his family, who may not even know where he is, is something to which the authorities have been singularly insensitive. A lawyer in practice on his own simply cannot afford the luxury of these absences. In all these situations the note of paternalism, of prefects putting naughty boys into detention where the headmaster's picture hangs on the wall, is something that has to be taken very seriously. It is not just a piece of technique, any more than the solemn charge of 'disrespect to authority', so baffling to those who live in irreverent democracies. These attitudes in a humourless people

---

[1] Raul Rêgo, *Para um Diálogo com O Sr Cardeal Patriarca de Lisboa*, Lisbon, 1968.

have very deep roots of fear. A young PIDE inspector, once asked by the author why he harassed the non-revolutionary critics, gave this significant answer: 'If there is one thing I fear more than a Communist,' he said, 'it is a progressive Catholic.' This fear is still real among many Portuguese: the fear that any disruption of the *status quo* will disintegrate the country again. Hence the PIDE network of informers, often very efficient, but probably falling short of the army of spies it was often said to be. Most Portuguese people live and die without any direct awareness of it, and it seems odd that a country, notorious for inefficiency, should have found its organizational flair uniquely in the police force – even if a few of its early chiefs were trained in pre-war Germany. All police forces have their informers, of course, and whether more Portuguese than British or Frenchmen are ready to 'grass' on their fellows is open to doubt. Be that as it may, it was for many years widely assumed that 'the PIDE are everywhere', and it is certain that they secured results.

Much has been written in journals of several countries on the subject of torture and ill-treatment by the PIDE in their prisons and police stations. Some of it is not well backed by detailed evidence, yet official denials from Lisbon also seem to lack the ring of conviction. Perhaps the fairest, and indeed the only, thing to do for the purposes of this narrative is to select the only two systematic attempts by British sources to get to the truth of the matter, and to summarize the findings. The first, favourable to the Portuguese authorities, is the report on the Portuguese prisons and prisoners by the late Lord Russell of Liverpool, who, in March 1963, was invited by the Portuguese government to carry out an independent investigation.[1] Russell made his name as a senior member of the judge advocate general's department of the British army in the Second World War, and whose comprehensive study of the Nazi war crimes became a best-seller under the title, *The Scourge of the Swastika*. He later wrote an account of *The Trial of Adolf Eichmann*. He spent ten days of intensive inquiry in the PIDE prisons and headquarters, and had long sessions with various ministers. In the prisons he was allowed to talk freely to inmates. The other report was published two years later by Amnesty International,[2] the wholly independent and highly respected organization set up by a number of British lawyers eight

[1] Russell, *op. cit.*
[2] Amnesty International, *op. cit.*

years ago to work for political prisoners everywhere, provided they were genuinely being penalized because of their honestly held beliefs. This report contains accounts given by former Portuguese prisoners, and, without passing final judgment, calls on the Portuguese authorities to hold a full inquiry and to give more facilities to independent and international bodies to conduct their own investigations. It argues that, whereas Russell spoke only to prisoners still in custody and therefore perhaps inhibited in their answers, Amnesty's sources were ex-prisoners or exiles who were not thus inhibited. It also declares that Russell dealt mainly with the cases of convicted men, whereas in fact the ill-treatment complained of took place during the pre-trial or interrogation period. It adds that Russell had experience of only a few cases, whereas the interrogations were numerous.

For the sake of clarity, it should be explained that, in the early part of the present decade, Lisbon prisoners were interrogated in PIDE headquarters and, during that stage, were housed in the Aljube prison in the city centre, which, so far as PIDE purposes are concerned, has since been closed. The drill was that the prisoner spent his time basically in isolation in the Aljube, but was taken to police headquarters for the actual questioning. When interrogation was complete, the prisoners awaiting trial were then housed a few miles out of town in the prison at Caxias, where conditions were good. The Aljube was a very old prison, and the conditions there were bad.

While many allegations had been made about the interrogation stage, there was also a general impression that all PIDE prisons were suspect, and Russell had to look into this. He by no means ignored the interrogation stage, he disapproved of the Aljube, and his subsequent recommendations seem to have led to its closure.[1] In his favour it must be pointed out that, although he was talking to men and women in custody, his special skill and experience should have been enough to enable him to see through appearances and at least to sense when something was being hidden or falsified. Some of the things he quotes as having been said by prisoners do not suggest a general climate of inhibition on their part. The Amnesty report also has strengths and weaknesses. One has to rely on the team's perspicacity, but one cannot help asking how far the investigators were convinced about what they

[1] It has recently been reopened to take an overspill of ordinary criminal, non-political prisoners from the local penitentiary.

were told, and how effective their cross-examination was. They do not, in fact, pass judgment on what they were told, but simply indicate that it is enough to make a full-scale inquiry imperative. As in Russell's case, one has to assume that men like Lord Gardiner, as he was by 1965, and Mr Paul Johnson, now editor of the *New Statesman*, were percipient enough to know whether a good *prima facie* case had been made out or not. Russell had the advantage of being able to demonstrate that some accusations were manifestly inaccurate. Gardiner had the advantage of having personally questioned a substantial number of people who complained of what had been done to themselves by the police.

First, then, Lord Russell of Liverpool's report. He began by visiting two non-political prisons for the sake of later comparisons. At the Lisbon penitentiary the prisoners were working, not on mailbags, but on making furniture, cardboard boxes, plumbing requisites, and chromium plating. They also had a large printing press on which they produced government publications. Every cell had its own radio set and the prisoners had a radio room from which they could broadcast their own programmes and records. He saw nearly all of them and spoke to whom he wanted. He was left with a very favourable impression. Cells were roomy, and prisoners were allowed to have their own ornaments brought in. There was ample provision for games. Russell also saw the school prison at Leiria, equivalent to a British Borstal institution. The bedrooms, dining and recreation rooms were all good, and the boys were not locked in. They worked mostly in agriculture and the prison tended its own vineyards. A number of boys were either pursuing the trades they had practised outside or were learning crafts as apprentices. The prison records showed that only 6 per cent of the intake at Leiria later 'graduated' to prison.

Turning to the PIDE establishments, Russell was shocked by the Aljube, in Lisbon, and the inspector who accompanied him confessed that the police themselves were ashamed of it. Plans were being made to transfer the prisoners to Caxias, when one wing there, at the time in process of renovation, was ready. There were thirty-nine prisoners in the Aljube, all awaiting trial, thirteen of them in small, dark, narrow cells, the others in rooms which were rather better. Some of these could take four beds, and the rooms on the top floor were the best of all. Apart from the top floor, however, the general air was one of gloom and despondency. The men in the cells looked like caged animals. One of them, a coloured youngster from Angola, was plainly terrified at Russell's approach until it was carefully explained to him who Russell was. His cell was pitch dark, and, even when the light was turned on, it was impossible to read. This young man did say, however, that he had not been physically ill-treated. There was no reading or recreation allowed, and nowhere to exercise. However, Russell was satisfied, with the aid of a drawing made by a prisoner, that there were no more than thirteen of the dark cells, and these, Russell asserts, were not as bad as had been suggested by Fr Andrade.[1] The priest had told Russell at Caxias that, when he had been in the Aljube, he had been in a cell where he could not raise his knees or sit on the bed. Russell was satisfied, after a thorough inspection, that none of the cells was less than twelve feet high. But they were bad enough for men who, because they had to be isolated during interrogation, could be kept there for as long as two to three months.[2] An article in the London *Observer*[3] had stated that a thousand prisoners were crammed into the Aljube and Caxias. Russell says that this would have been utterly impossible. At the time the article was written, the figure for the two prisons was 233. When Russell himself went there, it was 153. The total number of people convicted of security offences and at that time in custody was 353.

At PIDE headquarters in Lisbon, Russell was able to go through the building from top to bottom. The interrogation rooms were plain rooms about eight feet by twelve with a desk and two chairs, and a large window. He watched some interrogations and was able to speak privately to the prisoners. Most of them were not in serious trouble and were likely to be released.[4] He met there the young man from Angola whom he had seen in such a pitiable state in the Aljube. Now he was much more cheerful. It had been established that he had not done anything serious, and Russell was told that he was going to be sent back to Coimbra University to continue his law studies. An

---

[1] Cf. *infra*, this chapter; and also Chapter 9.
[2] A friend of the author's, a liberal who has never been tried or convicted, but has been pulled in for questioning two or three times, once spent a month in a cell like this. He was struck once, never beaten up, but pointed out that a month in the cell was torture in its own right.
[3] 4 March 1962: by Michael Moynihan, quoting Mr Neville Vincent.
[4] This is the least satisfactory part of Russell's account. Obviously, the police would be on their best behaviour while he was there, and one has to ask whether they would have been quite so gentle with prisoners facing more serious accusations.

article in the London *Spectator*[1] had stated that prisoners 'practically out of their minds' were put into rooms where the walls were mainly yellow but blue at the top, and that the demented prisoners thought the blue was the sky, took a running jump at it, and injured themselves. Russell found that the rooms most nearly approximating to this description were the interrogation rooms, where the walls were yellow and the ceilings blue. He added that many houses in the south of France are painted in the same way, and he found it difficult to believe that prisoners would have behaved in the way described. While at the police office, Russell made a number of recommendations for improving the lot of the people detained in the Aljube. Not long after his visit, the PIDE closed it down, and prisoners undergoing interrogation today are housed at Caxias, where there are no old-fashioned cells.[2]

When Russell went to Caxias, he found an extremely well-equipped hospital of 184 beds. There were only three prisoners in it at the time, but he was satisfied that anyone needing hospital treatment got it there. One prisoner had been brought down from Peniche for surgery for cancer, and was in a comfortable room equivalent to a hospital private ward outside. At that time, the north wing of the prison was being renovated, but Russell was able to see that the rooms were going to be very spacious, with good medical and sanitation arrangements. While the work was going on, the south wing was overcrowded, with eighteen men in a room meant for ten. But while the prison lacked the recreational facilities enjoyed in the Lisbon penitentiary, and was generally inferior to the prison at Peniche where sentences were served, the overall conditions were acceptable and the wing was due to be closed when the other one was ready. There were a number of women prisoners, all of whom had proper beds with sheets. Prisoners could have extra food and drink sent in.

Peniche lies fifty miles to the north of Lisbon and externally is a sixteenth-century fort. It is here that political prisoners serve their sentences after trial. Russell found the interior up to date, with ten men in each well-lit room. Though they did not have the radio sets or games available in Lisbon, they had facilities for exercise, could spend two hours a day in the library, had access to hot water for

---

[1] 13 April 1962; by Neville Vincent, quoting an informant.
[2] The author once visited Caxias, and found the prisoners in large airy rooms, able to take about a dozen at a time, with modern flooring and with toilet facilities, including showers, completely shut off from the 'cell'.

two hours every morning, and enjoyed two baths a week. The prison could hold 140, but the number of prisoners there at the time was 114. The small sick-bay handled routine cases, while more serious cases went to Caxias.[1] Most of the prisoners were serving sentences of less than three years (plus security measures). Two or three were serving ten-year sentences, but for treasonable offences, while one man, who had been involved in a plot to kill Salazar, was serving twenty years. There is no death penalty or life sentence in Portugal. The quarters and all facilities were impeccable, except that prisoners had no privacy from each other in the visiting room. Prisoners wore their own clothes. Finally, Russell visited the small PIDE prison at Oporto, where he found thirty-six prisoners, fourteen of whom were 'in' for illegal emigration only, and were facing slight sentences of about a month, and in some cases were likely to be bound over.[2]

Russell also gives an account of conversations he had with half a dozen prisoners, of special interest. An article in the March 1963 Amnesty bulletin had said that Mario Pedroso Gonçalves had suffered terribly in regard to his health in prison, that he had been severely beaten and tortured while in prison, and that other prisoners had staged a hunger strike because of his screams, induced by pain in the kidneys. Gonçalves told Russell that he had been hit on the face a couple of times, but nothing else. He was on special diet, and his kidney trouble was being treated. It was not due to ill-treatment. He had been told that he would be sent from Peniche, where Russell saw him, to Caxias if his condition did not improve. The Amnesty bulletin had said that he had had an operation in the end but that he had then been returned to damp quarters. This, he told Russell, was not true.

[1] An English expert on prisons and penology has told the author of his visit, some years ago, to Caxias, where he was exceptionally impressed with the senior medical officer, not only as a doctor, but for his understanding of prisoners and their problems.

[2] The Amnesty report accepts that on the whole 'the (Portuguese) government are endeavouring to improve the physical conditions within the prisons' but it says that Russell makes no reference to solitary confinement cells, and adds that statements taken from exiles suggest that there are or were such cells. An exile is quoted as saying that in 1950, he was confined for twelve days in a concrete box 3 ft × 4 ft × 5 ft, with no light or window, and that he was forced to urinate on the floor. Another exile (no date mentioned) said he spent twenty days in underground cells which were 3 ft wide and 9 yards long. The author could find nothing of this sort when he visited Caxias in 1963, and it seems likely that, if such cells once existed, they were no longer being used. The whole trend of prison policy would seem to be against it.

The *Spectator* article already quoted had said that Dr Orlando Ramos had been tortured for five days and five nights. Ramos told Russell that he had been interrogated in a cell in the Aljube for ten days incessantly without being allowed any sleep, but had not been 'physically ill-treated in any way'. (This presumably means he was not tortured, in the ordinary sense of the word.) Russell seems to doubt whether the interrogation was as long as ten days, but does not say why. This may be connected with his general doubts, expressed elsewhere, about the feasibility of the 'statue'. Because of Ramos's fears that the security measures imposed on him might keep him in prison indefinitely, Russell made careful inquiries and concluded that it was very rare for a prisoner to serve more than one three-year term. Only three of the 325 political prisoners then serving sentences were doing so, and in those cases the offences were very serious. The *Spectator* article spoke of Ramos as being confined in the Caxias Fortress, in an atmosphere of terror and under appalling conditions. But not even the Amnesty report speaks of Caxias in this way. When Russell saw Ramos, he was at Peniche. He was an important official in the Communist Party.

Also at Peniche, Dr Humberto Lopes, a lawyer of standing and a highly cultured man, said that when he was first arrested in 1953 he was interrogated with some brutality, had sustained the 'statue' for several hours, and had been beaten with a truncheon. The first time, he lay in prison for a year and four months before being acquitted. Later, he was charged in connection with incriminating papers allegedly found in the room in which he had been detained in prison. He disclaimed all knowledge of these, but admitted that a paper, on which he had written legal advice for another prisoner, was his. It contained nothing incriminating. His admission about this paper was used by the prosecutor as proof that the other papers were also his. He was sentenced to two-and-a-half years, plus security measures, on 23 July 1957. According to the same *Spectator* article, he had been sentenced for giving legal advice to another prisoner. This was not so. Russell had reservations about the 'statue' allegation, but, in this case, his objection is hard to understand, because, while ten days might seem to be beyond human endurance – the period often quoted in allegations against the PIDE – the 'several hours' referred to by Dr Lopes would seem feasible.

In Caxias, Russell spoke to Dr Julieta Gandra, a doctor from Angola, who in 1965 was to be Amnesty's prisoner of the year. The

Spectator article had stated that she was in continual pain from a serious liver disease and denied proper medical care. Russell discovered from the PIDE inspector with him that prisoners could see a specialist of their own choice, if they wished. Dr Gandra told Russell, apparently, that she was suffering from a gastric ulcer. She added that she would have liked to see a certain doctor, but felt it was wrong for her to do so when her fellow prisoners were unable to afford this privilege. She named three other prisoners who, she said, needed specialist treatment. Russell found that two of them had seen specialists while in prison.

In Caxias at that time, the PIDE were holding Fr Joaquim Pinto de Andrade, who they believed had been involved in the Angolan uprising. (His brother was a leader of one of the movements concerned.) A Leopoldville news agency had said that he was in a flea-ridden bed, suffering from a liver complaint, deprived of his glasses, and unable to move because the cell was so narrow. This story evidently referred to the period of his prior confinement in the Aljube. He repeated most of it to Russell, who says that doubtless some of it was true. But the priest was now in good health, and his description of the Aljube cell was 'grossly exaggerated'. He was in perfectly good health when Russell saw him, and had had his glasses and watch restored. He was well dressed, and was reading a book. On the day that Russell saw him, a Radio Moscow broadcast stated that Fr Andrade was gravely ill. The present writer also saw Fr Andrade in Caxias a couple of months before Russell did, and found him in the condition Russell describes. He had some books, and had been allowed out at Christmas to say Mass in the cathedral.

In the Aljube, Russell saw José Bernardino, a leading Communist Party official, who did not dispute that he was secretary of some student organizations regarded by the government as subversive. He broadly confirmed reports that he had been subjected to the 'statue' for two periods of nine and seven days, and that his hearing was seriously impaired. Russell thought the allegations referred to something like the Stehzelle punishment used at Auschwitz. This means standing or kneeling for hours or days on end in a dark narrow cell specifically designed for the purpose. Russell states:

I searched every nook and cranny in all the prisons and had every door opened which might conceivably be concealing something, but there was nowhere this punishment could have been carried out, though it is, of course, possible to keep a person standing to attention for a length of time, though it would not be long before he fainted.

From his visit to PIDE headquarters, Russell was convinced that it would have been physically impossible for the 'statue', as described by Dr Ramos and Sr Bernardino, to have been carried out there. He thought it a little more than coincidental that the only allegations made to him of this form of punishment had been made by three prisoners who were important Communist Party members.[1] Finally, Miss Judith Hart, the British M.P., had reported five months earlier that Bernardino's health was broken and his hearing seriously impaired. When Russell saw him, his hearing was normal, his mind perceptive, and his health seemed excellent. Sr Bernardino himself agreed that it was.[2]

Amnesty International published its report in September 1965. It contains a discussion of the limitation of freedom in Portugal at that time, of the power of the police and the courts, PIDE methods and the political prisons. Much of this ground has also been covered in the present chapter, including Lord Gardiner's report of 1957. The report on the conditions of imprisonment was put together by taking statements from Portuguese exiles in London and Paris who had at some time been in the PIDE prisons, and it included statements taken by Mr Paul Johnson, editor of the *New Statesman*, from Portuguese exiles in Brazil, who had declared their willingness to

---

[1] This could mean either that it was Communist Party policy to make such complaints or that the PIDE reserved this treatment for Communist militants; there is probably truth in both.

[2] The Amnesty report refers to a letter received from a man who said he was a prisoner at Caxias when Russell went there. He claimed that Russell saw only one of three rooms where political prisoners were held, and only ten out of the fifty men housed there, as the other forty were on the recreation ground. The other cells held fifty-four and twenty-seven men respectively. The present writer visited Caxias shortly before Russell did, and finds it hard to understand this letter. Fifty men in any of those rooms would turn it into an asphyxiating pig-sty. No one would be able to sleep. It would be impossible to remove all traces of this even for a naive visitor. At any moment Russell might have asked for the other room doors to be opened (one can hardly believe that he did not), or have seen the men on the recreation ground. In any case, the Portuguese authorities would not have risked inviting him during a period of such over-crowding when all they had to do was to wait a few months until the north wing was completed.

testify under oath in London. An analysis of some of these statements will be useful.

One section deals with the problems of defence lawyers, the pressures put on students, and the weight the PIDE's evidence carries with the Plenary Tribunal which hears political cases. In 1955, three lawyers, Drs Arnaldo Mesquita, Sousa Castro and Vilaca, were arrested in court and held for six months. Later, Mesquita was re-arrested and held for fourteen months before he was acquitted. The repeated arrests of Mario Soares, discussed earlier in this chapter, are also referred to. There is mention of Manuel João da Palma Carlos, a lawyer who, disgusted with the way a trial was being run, threw up his hands and told the judges to do what they liked, 'proof or no proof'. For this, he was sentenced to seven months. Many students are said to have complained that they were often intimidated by the police shortly before their examinations and threatened with termination of their studies. A number of cases are cited in which, it is alleged, proof of guilt was slender. Francisco Miguel is reported as testifying that, after serving a ten-year sentence, he was given a further five-and-a-half years' security measures for organizing Communist cells in Caxias prison in 1953. But, said Miguel, in 1953 he had been in the Tarrafal camp.[1] In 1963, a British barrister, Miss Audrey Sander, reported on a trial she had attended in Portugal. She stated that slight evidence was given by six witnesses, who were not cross-examined. Two PIDE officers followed, and their statement that evidence of the accused's involvement with the Communists was in their files was accepted as valid testimony for the purposes of the court. Defence counsel declined to make a final plea: a common device of the lawyers for showing their contempt for the futility of the proceedings. In the same year, an American lawyer, Mr Patrick Hallinan, witnessed José Bernardino's trial. One PIDE officer gave evidence that the accused had made a confession and added that documents to show his involvement with the Communists were available. (Bernardino admitted his involvement to Russell, but the issue for Amnesty is the paucity of evidence adduced in court and accepted by the judges.) Bernardino, it is alleged, was kept without sleep for seven days and again for another nine. He was in custody

[1] This appears on p. 9 of the Amnesty report, yet on p. 13 it states that Tarrafal was closed in 1945. This can hardly be a misprint because, if it were, it would make nonsense of its context. On the other hand, Fryer and McGowan Pinheiro also speak in their book, cited above, as though the camp was closed in the mid-1950s.

for six months before seeing a lawyer. The principal defence witness was arrested on the day of Bernardino's trial. An informant, whose name is not stated, told Amnesty of a student who, in 1964, was twice shot by the police. The only witness was a taxi driver who was arrested on a technical charge, held for three months, and was then too frightened to give evidence.

In 1965, another British barrister, Ian Macdonald, attended a trial of thirty-one students in Portugal. The prosecution evidence was a batch of twenty-five confessions allegedly made by the students, but they were based on the information supplied by a man called Nunes Alvares Pereira, who had been arrested a month before the thirty-one, said Mr Macdonald. When the trial came on, Pereira was in Brazil. Thus a key witness – said by the PIDE to be chief Communist organizer in the universities – was absent, and there was no corroboration of the confessions. A PIDE witness said he had seen fifteen of the accused sign confessions, but, under cross-examination, could identify only one or two of them. The Amnesty report also refers to difficulties which prisoners claimed to have had in establishing communication with their lawyers, and to allegations that prisoners had often had to talk to their legal advisers in the presence of an official. Students had also complained that, once they had acquired any sort of a police record, they were barred from all hopes of a career or even a job in the public sector, and even in some of the larger companies. There were allegations, too, of teachers being dismissed because they were politically suspect, and of prisoners having their syndicate cards withdrawn so that, on release, they could not practise their trades again. Miss Sacuntala Miranda, an exile in London, had said that her cousin had lost a teaching job simply because he (or she) was related to Miss Miranda. João dos Santos Baleizão had alleged that the police had detained him to stop him taking up an option on a government job, and in the end he had emigrated to South America.

The section of the report dealing with interrogation by the PIDE asserts that 'psychological pressures to threats of torture and outright brutality' had been used, not merely against the Communists, but also against teenage students. It refers to Lord Gardiner's interviews, already quoted in this chapter, with students who claimed to have suffered the 'statue'. In general, Amnesty is disposed to accept that police methods underwent a change after the first twenty to twenty-five years of the Salazar regime, when they had been much more brutal. Statements on events occurring after 1947 had shown that beatings and electrical tortures were much less frequent, and that in the end the 'statue' was the only technique to be used. Arnaldo Mesquita indicated that by the time he was arrested in 1955, the 'statue' had been reduced to continual sleeplessness without blows and making the subject stand all the time. It was, he stated, still bad enough to make men lose their reason.

About half the cases quoted relate to the pre-war period. For instance, Francisco de Oliveira Pio, an exile in Brazil, claimed that in 1931 (before Salazar became prime minister), fellow prisoners of his in the Aljube had been tortured and bore the marks of it. Some people had had electric wires attached to their pelvis and genitals. At Oporto, there had been whipping, kicking and electrical burning. One man had died after his release as a result of this treatment. This was during the period 1933-4. In the 1932-9 period, Armando Correia de Magalhaes had been threatened with torture and death, but his connections with influential people had saved him. He had witnessed burns on the pelvis or genitals of other prisoners. Arlindo Augusto da Costa Chiu, another exile in South America, had been beaten and kicked, his kidneys had suffered from beating with sandbags, and his testicles had been twisted. As late as 1959, he had had to undergo an operation to deal with the continuing effects of the damage to his sexual organs. In the period around 1947, Augusto Filipe Aragão dos Santos had been kicked and repeatedly beaten in the Oporto prison, dragged out during the night for interrogation, and kept in solitary confinement for two months. Another prisoner, he claimed, had hanged himself as a result of ill-treatment.

It was about this period that the name of Fernando Gouveia began to crop up: a senior PIDE official with a bad reputation for brutality. Later, he appears to have left the PIDE and gone into oblivion without explanation. His name was mentioned to Amnesty by Duarte Mendes, who claimed to have endured the 'statue' for 273 hours with one interval of twenty hours, and also several beatings, before being acquitted by the courts. Gouveia was also referred to in the case of Francisco Miguel who had spent many years in prison for his Communist activities. His various sufferings were alleged to include a savage beating by six PIDE agents using a cat-o'-nine-tails, a four-edged stick, two doors, a chair and their hands and feet. The prisoner was handcuffed all the time. He also claims to have sustained seven months' solitary confinement. Another time, he said, he was kept standing and awake for thirty days and nights, with one forty-hour

interval. The 'non-violent' form of 'statue' had been inflicted on
Arnaldo Mesquita for six days and nights, also under the supervision
of Gouveia.

As to the later period, a number of cases are mentioned in relation
to a batch of students arrested in 1964 and tried in June 1965. Nicolas
Jacob, a French lawyer, went to Lisbon to inquire about it in 1964,
and a British barrister, Ian Macdonald, went the year after. They
reported that Maximino Vaz de Cunha, a medical student, had had
to go to hospital after sixty hours of questioning; Baeta Neves had
tried to swallow the lens of his spectacles after being threatened with
the truth drug; Mario António Figueiredo Neto had been questioned
for four days and five nights; António Jose Borrani Crisostomo
Teixeira had sustained the same treatment for four or five successive
periods of several days each. Even a seventeen-year-old had suffered
fifty-four hours of it. One of the girls involved was visited in
December 1964 by her father, who subsequently wrote to the Minister
of the Interior to complain about her condition:

> Her face was that of a corpse; she could not co-ordinate her ideas
> and had difficulty in the articulation of words. Besides this, she
> could not stand up properly, but walked clutching the walls.

Six months later she was brought to trial and *The Times* reported:

> The presiding judge accepted the request of Maria de Azevedo's
> parents that a police doctor who attended their daughter be called
> to give evidence, as well as an inspector who had dealt with her
> case. The girl is still under psychological treatment in hospital,
> and came to court from there.[1]

Amnesty adds that the father was threatened by the PIDE that he
might be prosecuted for disseminating false information and injuring
the nation's reputation abroad. In another case, Col. Luis Blanqui
Teixeira, a retired army officer, filed a complaint against the Director
of the PIDE, asserting that his son Fernando had been tortured,
beaten and kept awake for thirteen consecutive days.

On 1 March 1959, a group of prominent Catholics had asked
Salazar to inquire into allegations of police brutality. They said:

> Everybody has heard of recurrent instances of political trials where
> the judges inexorably silence lawyers, witnesses and defendants

[1] 22 June 1965.

whenever they try to describe any kind of physical violence used during the detention period of the preparatory phase of a case. . . . None of these hearings ever led to the opening of a judicial inquiry into the police methods denounced by the defence.

There are obvious problems about both these reports. Russell was under official auspices, and one would like to know more about Amnesty's sources and some of those who questioned them. The present writer's belief, as to the post-war years, is that some of the allegations made in this period are exaggerated, though not groundless. Repeat a charge often enough, and everyone assumes it to be true; but doctors manifest considerable scepticism about the possibility of keeping people awake for several days at a time, standing up or otherwise, let alone several week-long periods with only a short break between them. It seems more probable that the PIDE frequently questioned prisoners for very long hours, but with more intervals for sleep than the PIDE's accusers suggest. They have undoubtedly used the techniques of rousing people in the night, alternate threats and promises, solitary confinement, and brutality (as distinct from torture). Days, or weeks, of solitary confinement with nothing to read can be agony enough, of course, especially for cultured men. Equally, it seems certain that the working-class prisoner and the student often stood to get a 'bashing' if he was difficult or aggressive, especially at times when plots were in the wind, or when Communist activity was especially acute and known to be one of the elements in the African wars. It has to be remembered that groups similar to the Irish Republican Army have always existed in Portugal, whether Republican or Communist, and that the Portuguese Communist Party, unlike its counterparts in other Western countries, is avowedly committed to the overthrow of the state. There is a long tradition of ill-treating prisoners held for political reasons in Portugal, and the allegations made in 1913 by the 'Amnesty' of those days about Republican ill-treatment of their opponents are in some ways worse than what in modern times has been said of the PIDE.

At the same time, Amnesty International is perfectly right in pointing out that moral law applies no less to Communist prisoners than to anyone else. It also pointed out that the only way to handle the clash of evidence was to hold an inquiry. It urged that the prisons should be opened to inspection by the International Red Cross, as such an investigation would do more good than the findings of individuals. It went on:

> It is most important also that the Portuguese government should instigate a full inquiry into the many allegations which have been made about the interrogation methods of the PIDE. The allegations have been frequent enough to constitute a grave condemnation of the government, should they be true. By choosing to ignore them, or to prosecute those who make them, the government is not only showing a total disregard for the basic human rights of the individual, but is also lending truth to the allegations.

Most countries would resent internal investigation by outsiders, but a public internal inquiry, conducted by men of impeccable integrity, would have swung world opinion to Portugal's side, even had the findings been adverse, provided the proper steps had then been taken to remedy the situation. However, the Portuguese have often been the victims of their own hypersensitivity, and inquiries of this kind have not been part of their tradition.

At the present time, these questions are much less live than they were, and it will be said, with some truth, that the Portuguese police were not unique in the Western world for irregularities in interrogation. But, above all in an authoritarian regime, eternal vigilance is essential to protect policeman and prisoner alike, and one hopes that in future all such matters will be exposed to the full force of public inquiry and opinion. As regards Salazar himself, it is hard for those who know him personally to believe that he could ever have ordered or even permitted deliberate and gratuitous brutality. It is, however, possible that his own abstractedness and detachment from the ordinary emotions of day-to-day living may have combined with his distaste for scandals to make him an easy prey to hot denials by those entrusted with the security of the state, when allegations were made against them.

In 1963, the author secured permission to talk to some PIDE officers in an attempt to find out how their minds worked, and has tried ever since to gather evidence to add to first impressions.[1] There are among them a number of highly efficient officers who work competently for Interpol, contain the really violent elements in Portugal, and whose

[1] The PIDE's name has now been changed to The Directorate-General of Security.

intelligence work for the army in the African wars has been courageous and effective. Some have lost their lives in the process. The senior PIDE officer tends to be a strange, humourless, lonely and morbidly dedicated character, with a strong *esprit de corps*. Some of the inspectors seem to be cultivated and civilized, and they include men who, for one reason or another, have been unable to finish a university course. The PIDE, in fact, is said to be something of a refuge for men with interrupted careers. The lower ranks have their thugs, of course, but the inspector tends to be a different kettle of fish. To dismiss his sense of dedication is to misread the position; the really disturbing thing about him is that he is a man with a mission, convinced that the state's security rests on his shoulders, and is always in imminent peril, even from moderate oppositionists. He can enter into serious dialogue with his prisoners, relying, in appropriate cases, on the university background he shares with them. This is only an impression, but one is left with the feeling that officers on the inspectorate level have not, in recent years, approved outright brutality; that, if they entered a room where a prisoner was being knocked about, the performance would quickly stop. This is certainly true of the present Director, Major Silva Pais, though it is hard to say how far his senior assistants would turn a blind eye to what goes on in their absence. When asked outright, senior officers do not pretend that nothing irregular ever happens, but they put it down to loss of tempers and angry exchanges. If you ask them about extended interrogation, they ridicule suggestions that the statue is employed, and, as to the rest, refer you to police methods in New York, Paris and Rome; even, they may gently hint, at times in England. They also point out, correctly, that there are still dangerous revolutionaries in Portugal, and others who come in from abroad from time to time.

What ought to be done? The general conduct of the PIDE has ameliorated, and any country has to have its Special Branch or FBI. The weakness in Portugal may lie in this body's subjection to the Ministry of the Interior. The procedures of the non-political courts and the ordinary Judicial Police, and the conduct of the non-political prisons, are subject to the Ministry of Justice, and this department's record is exemplary. Its prisons are almost ahead of their time, especially where the treatment of young offenders is concerned. Prisoners are engaged in skilled work, can save money and help their families – and have been able to do so for many years. Everything possible is done to maintain the family bond, the prisoner's family has generous access to him, and voluntary agencies prepare him for rehabilitation. Foreign visitors select the prison hospitals for special praise, and are generally impressed by the quality of the officials, the physical conditions and the food. The educational opportunities are not lost. Illiterates are taught to read and write, and more advanced students can prepare for examinations. A British social worker of strong left-wing views, who has seen both Scandinavian and Portuguese prisons, told the author that he favoured the latter because of their 'climate of humanity'. There is a long, pre-Salazar tradition behind all this, but Salazar also made his contribution to it.

The PIDE, despite its responsibility to the Minister of the Interior, contrasts with the judicial police because, over many years, it seemed to be a law unto itself. This may have been nurtured by Salazar's habit of receiving the Director of the PIDE, and his reports, in person, and one of Professor Caetano's earliest acts on coming to power was to stop this practice. Reports now go to the Minister of the Interior only, and it is up to the minister to let the Premier know what he needs to know. But something more radical than this is required. Officers suffer from not being trained initially as ordinary policemen in a normal police force. In Britain, the Special Branch personnel come from the same ranks and belong to the same force as policemen concerned with ordinary crime, and acquire the humanity and flexibility their colleagues in other departments have grown up with. The PIDE would be all the better for a similar policy, and the way they have developed in Africa, where they have to work with the army, may well be a proof of this. Their approach to the resettlement villages, their encouragement of early release of captured rebels,[1] and their pragmatic attempt to win the confidence of the disaffected, contrast with their Lisbon record and show what can be done. If the army's influence, in Africa, served to restrain settlers from taking the law into their own hands, and communicated itself to the local PIDE, it seems reasonable to hope for similar results from an amalgamation of the security force with the normal criminal police. The essential idea must be to reserve police activity for those who break relevant and acceptable laws, and to abolish restraints on honest critics who pose no threat to the nation's security. Repression of opinion and fresh ideas has asphyxiated Portugal, and it will take

[1] In August 1967, the author was shown a batch of applications for release addressed to the Governor-General and signed by the Chief of the PIDE in Lourenço Marques. See Chapter 9.

some time to reverse the process to the point where an adult Portuguese nation can take its proper place in the international order.

The story of the opposition from 1959 onwards has revealed its major weakness, its unpreparedness for technical planning in the technological age. This is hardly the fault of men who, living in a monolith, have not enjoyed the stimulants of effective political life. Some of them have been living on an outworn past. The tough old Republican father-figures have faded away – Dr Cunha Leal is an octogenarian – and there seems to be no one of quite their stature to take their place. Visiting Portugal in the 1960s, one has found that older people tend to extremes. Either they are old-style Republicans, bitterly anti-Salazar and anti-clerical, or else they are 'ultras' who still regard Salazar with a kind of mystical awe, and believe that, without the firm hand of authority, Portugal must return to its dismembered history. On both sides, these great old diehards fight the battles of yesterday, with more than a touch of hereditary romanticism, while the less significant Monarchists support the regime but continue to dream of pre-Republican days. The younger and more progressive Republicans have now split off from the school of Cunha Leal, and, as joint manifestos have shown from time to time, are achieving a measure of common cause with the Socialists and the Catholics. Anti-Catholic positions have ceased to be relevant, and the changes in the modern Church have removed some of the sting from traditional anti-clericalism. Some of the middle-aged, professional men who, until 1968, continued to brave the police and the prisons are bound to command admiration, and, if awards for courage were in question, two of the highest would go to the Socialist lawyer, Dr Mario Soares, and the Socialist journalist, Dr Raul Rêgo. There are, on this level, plenty of capable men who would make good parliamentarians, but they do not include an obvious national leader; and, while commanding the sympathy of most professional men, they do not to any great extent attract the young, whose imagination has been caught by modern revolutionary trends abroad. (In the October 1969 elections there emerged an impressive alliance of Catholics and Socialists under the young, moderate and highly intelligent Francisco Pereira de Moura, a Lisbon professor of economics. It has been welcomed as a group with a clear capacity for the future.)

It was in January 1959 that the *Guardian* remarked that while, as dictatorships go, the Portuguese variety was not excessively harsh, the rule of law was a façade, and the rules were so arranged that the opposition could not attain power.[1] Salazar, a month or so before, had sadly recalled 'the respect and loving care lavished on the Church during the past thirty years', and grieved at the tendency of some Catholic elements to oppose him. Even the Cardinal Patriarch, a respected but conservative figure, had been saying that, while the spiritual and temporal spheres were separate, the former had to shed light on the latter, and not vice versa. The overriding suspicion of Communist and other foreign influences continued to affect the official mind, and in May 1959, Salazar declared that 'a long time ago the government was warned that in 1959 an international campaign of greater scope and violence would be unleashed against the two states of the Iberian peninsula'. In June, 402 students of Portugal's three universities issued a statement urging Salazar to retire and complaining that only 3 per cent of all university students came from working-class families. They also quoted a complaint by the head of the science faculty in Lisbon: 'In 1911, a chemistry student enjoyed five times more laboratory facilities than he does today.' July saw sentences of two to five years passed on ten people accused of belonging to secret organizations, and shorter sentences were passed on another thirteen for the same offence towards the end of the year. At the end of the year, Manuel Serra escaped from prison, sought refuge in the Cuban embassy, and thence made his way to South America.

The slow tempo of educational development was a primary cause of opposition complaint at this time. The *Guardian* reported that 80 per cent of children left school at or before the age of eleven. One in six went to secondary school. Government spending on education amounted to 9s. per head (as against £9 in Britain). In 1950, some 40 per cent of people over seven years old were illiterate. Under the current £800 million, six-year development plan, less than 1 per cent had been allotted for technical education and scientific research.[2] Salazar's defenders pointed out that it was still a question of first things first, and recalled his answer when once he was asked to give a bursary to a girl with a rare operatic voice. 'How can I,' he had said, 'give money to those who sing, when I don't have enough for those who cry?' The anomalies of Portuguese life appear in the most bewildering way if one glances at foreign press reports for the year 1960.

[1] *Guardian*, 15 January 1959.
[2] *Ibid.*, 28 November 1960.

In May the *New York Times* correspondent reported that President Eisenhower's recent visit to Portugal had dismayed the opposition there, and then came out with this surprising statement:

> The clandestine opposition also expresses respect for the elderly dictator. Opposition leaders praise his selflessness, his honesty and his devotion to Portugal's interests as he sees them.[1]

The writer added that the severest criticisms were reserved for the men around Salazar, and that the critics wanted Salazar himself to retire with honour, making way for a new democratic regime.[2] Another view was that of Captain Galvão who, on 9 January 1960, wrote in *The Nation*:

> It is his talent for fraud which alone distinguishes Salazar from other dictators and gives his own dictatorship a different appearance. He has always been a constant and clever liar. Under the guise of paternalism, Premier Salazar has robbed [the people] of their fundamental liberties, degraded them to the status of a flock herded by police, sterilized them in spirit, and kept a fifth of them in hunger and sickness.

Galvão thought that Portugal should stay in Africa, but, of course, without Salazar. Another curious light on Portuguese anomalies came from reports of the trial, held in July 1960, of those involved in the attempted coup of March 1959, which had been led by Calafate and Serra, both of whom had now fled the country. The conspirators who eventually faced trial received very short sentences (three to twenty months), in view of the seriousness of the charge and all of them, bar one, were released at once, as they had served their time while awaiting trial. All the prisoners made a very good impression on observers, and even the prosecutor said they were not in any way linked with the Communists. An extraordinary procession of priests, generals and other dignitaries went into the box to give evidence of good character. The defence speeches were brilliant. One advocate spent a whole afternoon attacking Portuguese justice. Another selected the controlled press for his target. A third went as far as to

---

[1] *New York Times*, 29 May 1960.
[2] Some of Salazar's closest acquaintances say today that he often showed signs in the 1950s of wanting to retire, but that what finally drove him off this course was the Delgado affair, followed three years later by the flare-up in Africa. At that time a change of regime would obviously have been too disruptive.

say that he would have welcomed a successful coup. Nothing seems to have happened to him, yet in the following November, the president of the Oporto Bar, Dr António Macedo, was arrested with several other lawyers. All they had done was to sign a petition about some elderly women who had been in prison for some years and were not receiving the hospital treatment they needed.

The year 1961 will for ever be remembered as the year of the war in Angola. But other events of importance occurred in that year, and in January, President Tomás met three opposition leaders, Dr Mario de Azevedo Gomes, Dr Acadio de Gouveia and Dr Eduardo de Figueiredo. Subsequently, a mixed group of Republican and Socialist intellectuals issued the most constructive and detailed proposal to come in a comprehensive way from the opposition side in many years. This document is known as the *Programme for the Democratization of the Republic* and was dated 31 January 1961. There were sixty-one well-known signatories, and some of the recommendations, especially in the fields of education and economic planning, have since come to pass. Briefly, the *Programme* called for the legalization of parties and strikes, the abolition of the PIDE and the political courts, the abandonment of the corporative organization in favour of a decentralized administration, with more powers for municipal authorities.

As regards the overseas provinces, the *Programme* did not propose that they should be given independence. But it demanded the liberties of the United Nations Charter for them, decentralized government, a labour statute (they now have a good one), lay educational systems with missionary help, and freedom of religion. Measures were demanded to correct injustices in the prices paid for the overseas provinces' raw materials (there is now a common market system in operation between Portugal and the *ultramar*).

The Programme stipulated that censorship and security measures should be abolished throughout Portuguese territory, with free speech assured. The president and vice-president of the Supreme Tribunal should be elected by the judges and not appointed by the government. Education should be a prime concern of government planning, and a national commission should be established for its reform. Students should be represented in the university senates. Official education should be secular, though there would be complete freedom for religious schools to cater for those who wanted them. There should be a system of free meals and books for schoolchildren, and families suffering hardship because their children's education debarred them from working should be compensated. The universities should be autonomous and their rectors elected. The signatories asked for a Superior Council of Scientific Investigation to be set up. This, like the educational commission, has now come into being. A demand for a new press law was accompanied by an interesting suggestion that all papers should publish the sources of their incomes.

Another set of proposals which have now become actual, related to the setting up of special planning boards to regulate national development.[1] Taxation, says the *Programme*, should fall on income, not production and there should be a system of progressive taxation, with no tax on capital investment. The co-operative principle should be developed, especially in the countryside, and a programme of agrarian reform should aim to convert current properties, when they are too small or too big, into average-size holdings, A special credit system should be available for farmers. The welfare system should be run by elected workers, who should also have a share in the control of industry. There should also be wholly free, trade unions.[2] Suggestions were also offered for the health service and the provision of social welfare, including cheap housing. In this connection, the government has already done a great deal, and workers can buy cheap homes by paying a modest rent for a period of years, after which the houses become their own. Portugal, however, is up against the same problem that even prosperous countries like Britain have to face: that of building enough houses to keep pace with the needs of the growing population. Extensive provision for cheap housing is one of the outstanding achievements of Salazar's government, but presumably the opposition would give it a higher priority claim on national resources.

This *Programme* of the opposition is a distinguished document. It does not offer detailed blueprints for its implementation, of course, but is an indication of the contribution the opposition could make in initiating policies, say, in the National Assembly. It is in this connection that the opposition gains credibility, especially as it includes

[1] Today there is a *Conselho de Plano Económico* and a *Commissão Tecnica do Planeamento e Integração Económica*.
[2] As matters stand today, the labour syndicates can conclude bargains with the employers without government intervention, unless they fail to reach agreement. Professor Caetano has also abolished the system whereby syndical officials had to be approved by the government. The opposition, however, want the unions to be relieved of all connection with corporative structures.

professional men with the kind of expertise required for detailed planning and action. It is of the utmost importance that they should have their chance to make a contribution.

It was in the spring of 1961, just after the outbreak of the troubles in Angola, that an extraordinary attempt was made to oust Salazar from within the regime. It was an officers' conspiracy, though confined to a small minority, and seems to have stemmed from a sort of panic induced by the bloodshed in Africa. It began towards the end of March when a senior officer, believed to be General Albuquerque de Freitas (Commander-in-Chief, Air), sent a memorandum to the Minister of Defence, General Botelho Moniz, stating that Portuguese youth would not want to fight a losing battle against savages, that Portuguese isolation must be ended, and that the government needed new blood – though not Delgado or Galvão.[1] A group of officers, acting with the minister, planned to pass a vote of 'no confidence' in Salazar at a meeting of the Defence Council on 8 April. General Luis Camara Pina, Army Chief-of-Staff, is said to have discovered this and to have warned Salazar not to attend the meeting. A delegation of the malcontents saw President Tomás on 11 April, and when he told them that 'I won't dismiss the only great statesman of the century after Churchill', they intimated that they would be satisfied if Salazar would resign. Tomás managed to play for time, and the next day Salazar had the Republican Guard deployed at strategic points and alerted the PIDE. On 13 April, the conspirators assembled in the Ministry (they were said to include the Defence Chief of Staff, General José António Beleza Ferraz, and the minister for the army, Lieutenant-Colonel Almeida Fernandes), and agreed that at 4 p.m. the army would start taking over key government positions. At noon, Salazar dismissed Botelho Moniz. Later the public squares were deserted, and at 4 p.m., Salazar went on the air. The rebellion was over. Most of the defence chiefs were unsympathetic and certainly had no wish to risk civil war. No proceedings were taken, but Moniz was said to be under surveillance in his home, and again the rumours went around that former President Craveiro Lopes had been in some way involved. Salazar then proceeded to clear out most of the government and to appoint a new cabinet, mostly men of university background with an average age of forty-three. The two most significant changes brought the tempestuous Adriano

[1] De Freitas had been appointed to study Delgado's activities in 1960.

Moreira to the Overseas Ministry, and Alberto Franco Nogueira to the Foreign Ministry. In August, David Holden, writing in the *Guardian*,[1] took the view that the nation had tended to rally behind Salazar after the Angolan rising. The *Sunday Times* had also reported that the opposition favoured holding on in Angola, and had begun to discuss the possibilities of reunion with Brazil.[2]

This did not stop the opposition, led by Azevedo Gomes, from pressing the recommendations of the *Programme for Democratization* as hard as they could, with special stress on the need for a vast educational plan for the indigenous Africans and for freedom for the Africans to develop according to their own culture and traditions. The *Times* reported from Lisbon in May that, if Salazar could keep order in Africa, nothing would be able to dislodge him. There had been four major plots against him over the past fourteen years, and they had all failed. Some forty-eight officers and civilians had been tried, most of them receiving only short sentences. There was no air of general unrest or depression, the nation was industrious, docile and decently fed. The docility was partly due, the report continued, to a fear of undoing all that had been achieved. The government's policy was one of make haste slowly, but tremendous strides had been made in building roads, developing the power industries, in educational, health and housing services. Industry was steadily growing, the shops were full, there was a busy international airport, and the seaport served vessels from all over the world.[3]

Early in 1962, the students showed themselves to be not so docile. There was uproar in Lisbon University when the police clamped down on a traditional annual celebration, and, when the police, in defiance of the university's constitutional rights, invaded the university precincts, the Rector, Professor Marcello Caetano, resigned in protest.[4] Though previously a leading minister of the regime for many years, he now went into private legal practice and remained there until called to the premiership in 1968. In 1963, Cunha Leal and Azevedo Gomes formed the *Acção Democrato-Social*, which brought all the moderate opposition together, apart from the Catholics and Monarchists. The Catholic intelligentsia, however, have frequently

---

[1] *Guardian*, 17 August 1961.
[2] *Sunday Times*, 2 May 1961.
[3] *The Times*, 5 June 1961.
[4] He has now, as Prime Minister, forbidden police harassment of non-subversive critics of the Government.

identified themselves with this social democrat group and its objectives. An attempt in 1964 to secure recognition for the new group failed.[1] During the early 1960s, the PIDE continued to be very active, and at the end of 1964, some seventy students were arrested, the PIDE were again accused of brutality, and middle-class parents fumed when their children were branded with the Communist smear. In July 1965, a Christian Movement of Democratic Action appeared, including many young priests and intellectuals. The same month saw a presidential election, which returned Admiral Tomás for another term. This time he was elected under procedures established by a change in the Constitution made by the government after the Delgado campaign in 1958. An Electoral College of 585 was formed of members of the National Assembly and Corporative Chamber, and delegates from provincial and municipal councils. The opposition presented no candidates. Sixteen members of the social democrat group wrote to Salazar in the following September, accusing him of turning the Portuguese into a nation of sleepwalkers. They protested against censorship and the repression of ideological systems other than Salazar's own, and they demanded recognition of their own group. It was led, they said, by men in their seventies who had served their country well and repudiated 'any suggestion of insurrection and subversion'. It had taken Salazar twenty-eight years to give the economy a real impetus, and this had been too long. Two months later, the National Assembly elections were held. All 130 seats went to the National Union, as the opposition had withdrawn their forty candidates for the usual reason that they saw no possibility of a genuinely free election in the absence of proper campaigning with full press and radio facilities. One slight concession had been made, in that the opposition had been told that this time they could supervise the scrutiny of the ballot. Also, when the list of opposition candidates for Braga was rejected, the Supreme Court overrode the decision. But when the opposition then asked for the election day to be put back a bit to give them time for a full month's campaigning, the request was refused. There were one or two curious incidents at this time, including some demonstrations by government supporters in Lisbon and Africa, who seemed to be exceptionally bitter about the opposition at a time when, as the official side saw it, national unity was of paramount importance. The lesson is that Portugal will not

---

[1] The only officially recognized group other than the *União Nacional* is the small *Causa Monárquica* which supports the regime.

easily learn the *mores* of comradely opposition. For them, life is made up of light and darkness, and opposition too often tends to be synonymous with total mutual rejection.[1]

It was after this election that Salazar made the speech in which he regretted that the opposition had not played a more prominent part, and referred to the sincerity and dynamism of Delgado. The tragedy is that he never found a way of bringing them into dialogue with himself, though anyone who knows both them and him can see how much they might have been able to give each other, even in informal talks. Five opposition personalities wrote to Salazar in October 1966, asking for permission to give a series of lectures on the theme of 'celebrating the past and building the future'. The topics proposed including the evolution of Portuguese democracy, the national economy, justice and individual liberty, the university crisis of 1962, forty years of censorship, and the situation of the artist. The signatories were Dr Mario Soares; Dr António Alçada Batista, a Catholic publisher; Dr Francisco de Sousa Tavares, a distinguished Catholic lawyer; Dr Francisco Salgado Zenha, a lawyer outstanding for his advocacy in defence of political prisoners; and Sr Francisco Lino Neto, a former royalist. Their petition was unsuccessful. In the following month, a mixed group of businessmen and intellectuals, nearly 200 in all, petitioned the President, asking him to dismiss the Prime Minister and dissolve parliament. The present regime, they declared, depended on 'the systematic use of force, of suppression, of formation of public opinion' by the police, the para-military Legion and other official organizations. It was a 'personal dictatorship built upon an ideologic-political reaction, and within a sociologically backward society'. Finally, the manifesto criticized what it called the state's policy of 'sacrificing the working-classes, maintaining a low salary policy, with generalized poverty, in order to pile up capital'.

A year later, another 235 intellectuals appealed to the National Assembly. They were led by eight prominent socialists and liberal Catholics, and they called for a press law which, though provided for under the Constitution, had never been given effect. They urged the abolition of press censorship and of the practice of seizing books without warrant from competent authorities. The signatories spoke

[1] In the 1965 elections, there were 1,209,580 registered electors, out of a Metropolitan population of 9,000,000, while in the overseas provinces 150,000 had a vote out of a combined population of 13,000,000. The turnout in Portugal itself was 74.1 per cent.

of those who, because of fear, wrote 'with prudence, metaphors, omissions or half-truths', and deplored the insecurity, anxiety, even despair that resulted from the censorship of creative activity.

Early in 1968, the PIDE interrogated, in a prison in Madrid, a number of men alleged to belong to an organization dedicated to the overthrow of the Salazar regime. This is the clandestine military body known as LUAR, whose Portuguese initials stand for the League of Union and Revolutionary Action. Organized abroad, it was said to be planning from Paris a revolutionary uprising in Portugal. The early summer of 1968 saw a further mixed group of intellectuals petitioning the Assembly again for an end to censorship, reminding the delegates that in 1963, Salazar himself had said that he was not averse to the idea. The petition quoted Pope John and the present Pope on man's 'inviolable right to be informed'.

It would not be true to suggest that Portugal, late in 1968, was seething under the surface with subversive intent. Even at the time of the Delgado campaign in 1958, the *New York Times* reported that by no stretch of the imagination could it be said that all the electorate was aflame with discontent, though there were real grievances.[1] In 1961, after the outbreak of violence in Angola, the ranks seemed to close a little more than usual, and even oppositionists told the present writer that, granted a free and unobstructed referendum, it was not at all clear that Salazar would be rejected by the nation. Five years later, moderate oppositionists thought that a referendum would dismiss him, not so much because the nation was anti-Salazar as because the younger generation wanted to have its chance. Repeated visits to Portugal in the current decade have produced the impression that the majority of thinking people knew the time had come for radical changes, that few had a clear idea of what precisely ought to be done, that very few would have favoured subversive methods. Feeling about Salazar himself was very mixed. Many were conscious of his achievements, but felt the time had come for Portugal to get into the modern world, and into Europe. Others, who felt that Salazar's day was long since done, were uncertain and unhappy about the alternatives.

The sad fact is that, outside the circle of professional intellectuals and students, most Portuguese had, by the time Salazar's illness ended his public life in September 1968, become politically apathetic.

[1] *New York Times*, 5 June 1958.

Living standards were rising, and a new lower middle class with them. The stress was on material improvement and competition with the neighbours. Ideas were at a discount. It was a high price to pay for stability. Fryer and McGowan Pinheiro, however, while paying tribute to the old Republicans for keeping faith with their ideals in spite of penal restrictions, criticize them for not having an adequate programme.[1] Some have a personal following, especially in the northern, traditional centres of Republicanism, and it is remembered that in the 1930s, they tried repeatedly to overthrow the Salazar regime. On the other hand,

> they speak always with emotion of 'the people' – but with few exceptions they are totally uninterested in the political organization of workers and peasants. The masses of the people are merely crowds to be manipulated by leaders.[2]

The dissidents have so far been neutralized by the law and the police. Though it is some time since an oppositionist in a restaurant needed to look over his shoulder before speaking, censorship and the ban on parties have obviated effective combination. It must also be admitted, however, that, apart from the somewhat general terms of the 1961 Programme, the Republicans and Socialists have failed to produce convincing blueprints for the overhaul of the social order and the economy. While some of them are rightly respected, it is very difficult to ascertain exactly what they are after, and they do not strike one as men of statesmanlike calibre. As we have seen, this may have as much to do with the lack of opportunity for practising politics as with the individual's inborn qualities. The Socialists are now by far the more energetic of the dissidents, and have broken off from Cunha Leal's Republicans (the *Acção Democrato-Social*).

As a matter of fact, some of the best and most constructive criticism today comes from a stratum of men in their thirties and early forties who are not committed to political ideologies, but speak as technicians and practical men of fairly balanced views. These are the bright young Turks of industry, boardroom and bank, and they have their counterparts in the civil service, even in the government and the diplomatic corps. Their outlook is expansionist and European, and their present preoccupation is to foster investment programmes, change the credit system, and invite more foreign capital into Portugal.

[1] Fryer and McGowan Pinheiro, *op. cit.*, pp. 200-8.
[2] *Ibid.*, p. 201.

Many of them show signs of a sharpened social conscience – they include a number of practising Catholics – and they often make more of an appeal to the younger intelligentsia than the more traditional oppositionists do. But this is not to say that the traditional opposition is quiescent.

Among the socialists Dr Mario Soares, now forty-five, is one of the best-known names, though it has been said that he is better known abroad than he is in Portugal. As a courageous man who has suffered for his convictions, he has attracted the interest of the foreign press, and his foreign connections have made him suspect, especially in view of his activities abroad in connection with the Delgado affair. Yet he is a man of basically moderate views. In Britain, he would probably be identified with the left wing of the Labour Party. He grew up in a home where opposition was part of the furniture, yet it is a matter for real regret that he remains alienated from authority. His professional and political colleagues do not all seem to see him as a natural party leader, but there is no doubt he would have a lot to give as a parliamentarian. Nor can one say what he might prove to be if really given a chance to show his mettle. There is a similar problem among the Christian Democrats. Men like Sousa Tavares, Alçada Batista, Lino Neto, Nuno Pereira (leader of the ill-fated *Pragma*) and Sidónio Pais, are interesting personalities, but no one stands out head and shoulders as the largely undisputed leader of a potential party. They are extremely intelligent men. Like the socialists they include a number of lawyers whose courage over the years, in and out of the courts, has been inspiring and exemplary. Some of the Christian and socialist writers, too, would make a rich contribution to the country's literature if censorship were removed. There are also journalists in Lisbon and Oporto – one thinks especially of men like Raul Rêgo, a socialist writer on the *Diário de Lisboa* – who could make the Portuguese press one of the most interesting in Europe.

Not all who use the label Catholic or socialist are moderates, but most of them are utterly non-subversive. In private discussion they show far more balance, common sense and fairness than one would expect from the ranks of the frustrated. They often do justice to Salazar's achievements, and they strike one as men of integrity and constructive intention who grieve at their exclusion from public life, not because of unbridled ambition, but because, on the whole, they are law-abiding, patriotic characters who want to do something useful.

It is impossible to know the traditional opposition and not to feel respect, affection and sorrow for them. They have often disarmed themselves by an excess of mutual criticism and they lost opportunities in the election for the National Assembly in October 1969 when they seemed to be fighting outworn battles. They lost some support by adopting a new approach to the African question, and favouring negotiation with the guerrilla leaders. The government's African policy was also attacked by Pereira de Moura's new grouping which includes militant young socialists and Catholic progressives, who favour independence for the African provinces, with African majority rule at an early date. This is still a minority view in Portugal, but the new group offered a well argued programme for the whole of Portugal's needs in the 1970s. These stimulating 'new men' include some extremists, but generally they stand for policies similar to those of the British Labour Party, including a measure of nationalization, and the leadership is totally non-subversive. They offer, in fact, the prospect of something quite new in Portuguese life: that of a stable and 'loyal' opposition; and they maintain a dialogue with the young progressives who have now emerged even within the National Union and secured at least a fifth of the seats in the new Assembly. In the 1969 election the oppositionists won no seats, but may stand a better chance next time. Portugal, meanwhile, still has its subversives to watch, including, for instance, the LUAR movement, but the way to defeat them plainly is to give the moderate stratum its head.

The Portuguese feeling for British institutions contrasts with the national flair for invective and superlatives. The light and shade of compromise, the mottled beauty of blended ideals, are not in the landscapes of Portuguese history. The present Prime Minister, while anxious to give a voice to the critics, would have them speak, as it were, within the family: that is, within the National Union. Oppositionists, however, do not share his faith in an institution which they regard as, at best, outmoded. Whether the time has come to think in terms of political parties presents Professor Caetano with his hardest domestic puzzle. For as he undoubtedly sees it, to create, suddenly, a pluralist political structure after forty years of the monolith, could be to invite disaster.

What has to be understood is that the dilemma is real. History does not suggest that the old-style party system offers much hope for Portugal.

It is true that African countries with one-party systems hope to branch out again one day into pluralist patterns. If their first experiments in party democracy failed, they are still young enough to try again. But Portugal had parties for a century, and the results, though mixed, were frequently tragic. Dare she try again? The alternative, Salazar's corporative dream, had never been properly tried. But could it really work? Has it ever worked anywhere? Is it consonant with human nature?

The ideal is noble enough: the search for truth and decision through the interaction of minds within an organic unity, dedicated to the common good, as distinct from the tensions of sectional competition. It is also true that the tempo of modern life and the highly sophisticated decisions that have to be taken in a computerized age have forced more 'corporatism' on everyone: joint planning by former antagonists, government by technocracy within a democratic framework, more ministerial legislation, the ascendancy of the executive. Yet there are great dangers in this. How, in such situations, can the right of the average man to share in decisions affecting his life be exercised? Can a borderline be effectively drawn between state intervention and state interference? Can there be communion without absorption? When Britain's trade unions fight against anti-union legislation it is their identity and survival they are afraid for. Subject to differences of stress, the choices facing Portugal today are not wholly foreign to the problems afflicting democratic countries. But if both the party system and the corporative, unitary formula are found unsatisfactory, Portugal must find an alternative. A compromise might be possible, with a party system for the National Assembly while the Corporative Chamber keeps its character; but the formation of the corporations would have to be completed at once, and they would have to enjoy immediate rights to elect their representatives in the Chamber. Whether this or some other solution is sought, it is here that the opposition, if it is to be credible now, must show what it is made of. It has got to come up with a new way of life. It must be primarily creative, and what it produces must be, not a pale imitation of anyone else's system, but something essentially Portuguese. This is what opposition is about.

CHAPTER 12

The Last Lap

The seizure of Goa, the *Santa Maria* and the outbreak of war in Africa, far from toppling Salazar's 'throne', tended to close the nation's ranks behind him.[1] Internal dissension was muted in the homeland, and the non-Communist opposition were almost at one with Salazar in the defence of the nation's integrity. If Salazar had hoped to retire about this time, there could be no question of it now, when signs of division and instability at home would have given joy to the common foe. The name that dominated the public imagination in Portugal was not that of Andrade and his friends who simply wanted independence, but that of Holden Roberto, the mind behind the terror, who wanted the white man out of Portuguese Africa, lock, stock and barrel.

It was against the background of national unity and resolution that Salazar gave a confident interview to *Life* magazine early in 1962. In this he sought to show that his policy was not to deny the concept of autonomy and self-determination, but that the Portuguese interpretation of those terms was geared to a situation unparalleled in countries governed by other colonizing powers. There was, he said, no single canon of autonomy, and it already existed in Angola and Mozambique to a very large extent, though certain issues were reserved to Lisbon. Autonomy had to adapt itself to the local people's capacity for self-administration in a way that respected the unity of the nation, a unity which the provinces did not want to dissolve. Would there one day be separate sovereign states in Angola and Mozambique? Salazar did not know, but it was not impossible:

> The fact of a territory proclaiming its independence is a natural phenomenon of human societies and therefore it is a hypothesis that is always admissible, but indeed no one can or ought to set a time-table for it.

[1] *Guardian*, 17 August 1961.

Sovereignty had to be responsible, and it was in the interests of the indigenous Africans that progress should be slow and deliberate. The United States, Salazar felt, wanted speedier action. The Americans seemed to be preoccupied with anti-Communism and felt that the one way to scotch it in Africa was to grant independence. The result would be that the new states would reject the Soviet bloc and enter the U.S. orbit. But events had proved that, in fact, precipitate independence only served to open the door to Communism.

In the following year, he analysed his thinking further in an article for *International Affairs*.[1] His policies at home, he said, had had to take account of the abnormal individualism of the Portuguese who were shy of communal alignment and of subordinating their convictions to the will of a minority. Their acute critical sense tended to rest on the negative aspects of people and affairs. They found it hard to co-operate and hence the failure of the parties. At the same time, their generous spirit could lay them open to the call of the demagogue. Then, when the achievement betrayed the promise, they could be cast into deep discouragement. It had seemed to him that the only way to meet these problems was to establish (corporativist) forms of 'associative life' which in fact was now more intense than it had ever been:

> We have endeavoured to follow a course of action in accordance with which, bearing in mind the character of our people, public liberties are regulated with a view to their effective exercise and not as a function of an ideal which experience would show to be unattainable.[2]

As regards Africa, Salazar did not doubt the capacities of African leaders, but there were not enough of them at all levels to enable

[1] *International Affairs:* vol. 39, no. 2, April 1963, 'Realities and Trends of Portugal's Policies', by António de Oliveira Salazar. (Review published in London by the Royal Institute of International Affairs, Chatham House.)
[2] In March 1958 Salazar had told the National Assembly: 'With her parties which alternately come into power or collaborate with the government, with her parliament and free elections, in short with her democracy, Great Britain appears to have the fullest expression of political wisdom as suited to the British people. But she thinks, and this is questionable, that she has found the ideal formula for all other countries.'
In September of the same year he further declared: 'If democracy means levelling down by refusing to admit the natural inequalities of men, if it consists in believing that power is derived from the masses, that government should be the business of the masses and not of elites, then I certainly consider democracy to be a fiction.'

them to assume, alone, the complex functions of a modern state. When nationals of the former colonial power stayed in the new states to run economic enterprises, they remained there in a new role: that of an alien. In this way, the new states ran the risk 'of finding themselves in the throes of a subjection graver than that from which they claim to have liberated themselves'. If, on the other hand, the colonizers left the country, there tended to follow 'a process of retrogression in economic and social life, and a return to certain practices which are incompatible with the desired prosperity and progress'.

The root of the trouble was that the African leaders were unsupported among their own peoples by the engineers, economists, technicians and men trained for public service who were indispensable for growth:

Since a nation's economy cannot be invented or improvised, and professional training is an extremely slow process (as is being acknowledged even by economically strong countries as regards their own plans for development), it would seem that the peoples in question have been set on a road along which they will not succeed in keeping pace with the rest of the world, and will thus perpetuate their backwardness and compromise their national independence.

Then comes this crucial paragraph:

The independence of the African nations has, in general, rested on two errors which will work to their detriment: anti-white racialism and the alleged unity of the peoples of that continent. This latter supposition will tend to subordinate the Negro to the Arab; black racialism will tend to bring about the rejection of all that the more progressive white man had brought in capital, labour and culture. It would be wiser to replace racial exclusiveness by the collaboration which we have seen to be indispensable. It is for this reason that we hold that the economic, social and political advancement of those territories will only be possible on a multi-racial basis in which the responsibilities of leadership in all fields fall to those most suited to them, irrespective of their colour.

However much the critic may disagree with these sentiments, nobody who has met Salazar has ever argued that they were not sincerely held, or that they were just a crude gloss on a white man's determination to go on exploiting the African. He meant it all, and he meant it passionately. Writers like Schlesinger can talk about Salazar's 'medieval certainties' if they will, but certainties they were, however paternalistic or oblivious to the tempo of modern events. For Salazar, it was not for man to be blown off-course by winds of change, as though they could not be denied. It was for man to order change and to resist fashions that did not correspond to his truest and deepest human needs.

In September 1963, President Tomás paid a visit to Angola, where protocol flew to the winds, and he walked about freely in crowds of all races. This happened, not only in Luanda, but even in townships and villages like Quitexe, 'Ngaga and Aldeia Vicosa where former freedom fighters have returned and settled down. About this time, *Le Monde* reported that the United Nations seemed to realize that there would be no decolonization in Portuguese Africa until there was a revolution in Lisbon;[1] Dr Alfred Broughton, a British Labour M.P., was sufficiently impressed by what he saw in Mozambique to report that the world would do better to leave Portugal at peace to get on with the job; and the West German Vice-President, Dr Richard Jaeger, after a similar visit, commented in glowing terms to the *Reinischer Merkur*. In October, the Portuguese Foreign Minister, Dr Franco Nogueira, met representatives of the African states in New York for conversations which were reasonable and constructive in spirit. The Africans' view was reported to be that, even granting a certain progress in the social and economic spheres in Angola and Mozambique, their task was to insist on the political issues of self-determination and independence. Franco Nogueira told a press lunch at this time that, while Portugal was on good terms with South Africa and had many trading interests in common, Portuguese policy was diametrically opposed to apartheid. A month later, two new universities, with high-powered staffs and ultra-modern equipment, opened in Luanda and Lourenço Marques, and the first students included a number of Africans. Confidence in Lisbon remained high, with a level of gold and foreign exchange reserves sufficient to cover Portugal's imports for sixteen months (corresponding figures were twelve months for the U.S., six for France and Germany, three for Britain).

The year 1964 was one of steady growth, but it also saw the start of the war in Mozambique. President Tomás went there in the

[1] 17 September 1963.

summer, however, and was acclaimed as warmly as he had been in
Angola. In May 1965, the Portuguese-Dutch-Swedish consortium
LISNAVE announced it was to build, in Lisbon, Europe's biggest
shipyard. Today its dry-dock receives Gulf Oil's 340,000-tonners,
and the next stage of expansion will make it large enough to take
million-ton tankers. By the summer of 1965, too, Salazar was able
to announce that, in spite of the wars, the 1964 balance-of-payments
had shown a surplus of £97 million, a substantial increase on 1963.
The *New York Times* had reported[1] that the African bloc had
softened their anti-Portuguese campaign and seemed to be giving
less help to the rebels; Western diplomats were tending to look on
Portuguese Africa as an anti-Communist bulwark. Some weeks
later, Archduke Otto von Habsburg, the Austrian journalist,
reported that he had visited Portuguese Guinea, where hostilities
had broken out in 1963, and that rebel prisoners to whom he had
talked had no wish to return to the rebel side. Meanwhile, Portugal's
trade with Britain had risen by 76 per cent, and, with the aid of German
investment, a huge irrigation project had been started for 420,000
acres in the Alentejo, whose low-yield crop would eventually be
multiplied by six. It was announced, too, that 2,600,000 workers
would now qualify for free medical services, while the school population had risen to 900,000. An Indian court declared that Goa belonged
to India by right of conquest, not liberation, and with this piece of
irony ringing in his ears, Franco Nogueira went off again to New York
to extend the hand of friendship to Portugal's African neighbours.
They were not seen to respond, at least in the Chamber; the atmosphere in the corridors, on the other hand, could have been much worse.

On 11 November 1965, the Smith government in Rhodesia pronounced its 'unilateral declaration of independence'.[2] As a result,
Anglo-Portuguese relations, already strained, moved into their most
uncomfortable phase since the days of blockade and pre-emption in
the Second World War. Some months before, Britain's new Labour
government, under Harold Wilson, had imposed a ban on exporting
certain classes of arms to Portugal. Portugal's answer, in effect, was to
place orders for naval shipping with France at a time when Britain's
shipyards would have welcomed them. British sources pointed out that
no one in Britain was banned from supplying ships to the Portuguese,

[1] 16 March 1965.
[2] UDI.

and that having recourse to France was conduct unbecoming in a trading partner. At this point, official humour in Lisbon became a shade heavy-handed. As a senior civil servant put it: 'We couldn't have Mr Wilson losing sleep over whether a British destroyer might be used against freedom fighters in the bush.' It only needed the Rhodesian crisis to reduce relations between the two oldest allies from the cordial to the barely correct.

Official Portuguese policy was one of neutrality. The quarrel was between Rhodesia and Britain. UDI and the subsequent Constitution were illegal, and Portugal would do nothing to help or hinder the Smith regime, or any sanctions which might be invoked against it. She had, however, an overriding duty to allow her landlocked African neighbours access to the sea: a duty established by a long series of international conventions. Soon after UDI, Portugal held talks with Zambia and Malawi over a possible Beira-Lusaka airlift for oil supplies. In the event, a rail and road alternative was preferred and effected. Meanwhile, the R.A.F. and the Royal Navy started to police the Mozambique channel, and Britain was pressurizing Lisbon to adopt a positive anti-Rhodesia stance. Was this the wrong way round? Should Britain have invited Portugal to act as a bridge between London and Salisbury, where she commanded respect? Franco Nogueira is one of the shrewdest diplomats in the West, and, while his threats would have had little effect on Smith as long as the latter could count on South Africa, his mediation would have been another matter. It would have been in Portugal's own interest to supply this service at a time when her main objective was to avoid tensions in southern Africa. What happened in the event was that, instead of Portugal bridging the London-Salisbury divide, the Rhodesian issue became a block to Anglo-Portuguese friendship at a time when Anglo-Portuguese trade was rising to record heights. It has also been argued that the costly airlift of oil, at Britain's expense, from Tanzania to Zambia might have been avoided if Britain had been prepared to rely on Portuguese ports and railways. No doubt, from Britain's point of view, a high degree of dependence on Portugal would have been politically unacceptable in view of the African states' hostility to Portugal's presence in Africa. It seems, nonetheless, a pity that the Anglo-Portuguese Alliance could not have been instrumental in the search for solutions.

While Portugal, and many other countries, may be criticized for subsequent failure to implement sanctions against Rhodesia, it has to be seen that her case is based on a legal position which seems to be more concerned with letter than spirit, perhaps, but is certainly not without substance. Before examining this, however, it also has to be said that Britain's handling of Portugal in the early stage was less than masterly. At the end of March 1966, Lord Walston left London for Lisbon to discuss the Rhodesian crisis. The talks seemed to be making headway when, out of the blue, came the news that Britain had taken the issue to the United Nations. Whatever the rights and wrongs of this, Lisbon was badly affronted. The move had been made without warning, and right in the midst of seemingly useful talks. In the Security Council debate, it seemed to the Portuguese that Britain had marked them down as the scapegoats. But events took a curious turn. Britain's proposal was to blockade the Mozambique port of Beira, so that shipments of oil for Rhodesia could be barred from the Beira-Umtali pipeline. The pipeline's closure was plainly going to mean a serious loss of revenue for Mozambique, while the blockade of a Portuguese port by the British navy was bound to offend the oldest ally's sensitivities. Pressure for the debate had not come from the African states. Indeed, they succeeded in postponing it for three days. In the debate itself, Sierra Leone and Mali seemed half-sympathetic to Portugal, and the Russian delegate stated flatly that Portugal was the party least responsible for the crisis. Such feelings were doubtless more anti-British than pro-Portuguese, but the African countries may also have felt that they had enough problems without new confrontations in the south. Damage to the Rhodesian economy would affect that country's African neighbours, and, if the blockade did not bring Smith to his knees, Rhodesian attitudes might harden irreversibly. Such misgivings did not, however, prevail, but when, on 9 April, the Security Council sanctioned the Beira blockade, Russia and France abstained from the vote. So did Mali, Uruguay and Bulgaria. All this occurred at a time when Portugal was already trading with the Soviet bloc, and her relations with her African neighbours had been softening towards normality.

On 27 April, Franco Nogueira informed the U.N. Secretary-General, U Thant, that Portugal had grave doubts about the legality of the Beira resolution. Could such a resolution be effective when two permanent members of the Council, Russia and France, had abstained? His argument[1] was basically that recent amendments to the U.N.

[1] António Patrício: *Efeito do voto de abstenção de um membro permanente de Conselho de Segurança sobra matéria não processual*, Coimbra, 1968.

Charter[1] had increased the Security Council's membership from eleven to fifteen. The permanent members still numbered five, but the non-permanent 'sector' was increased by four. As amended, Article 27 (s. 3) of the Charter provided that Security Council decisions 'shall be made by an affirmative vote of nine members including the concurring vote of the permanent members'. Did this not mean that a resolution could not be effective without the concurring vote of all five permanent members; that an abstention by one permanent member would amount to an exercise of its veto? If this were not true, as the Portuguese saw it, then nine minor powers, as non-permanent members of the Council, could make peace and war without the concurrence of the five major powers (unless one of them formally used the veto). This was surely not the Charter's intention. In fact, before the recent amendments, it would have been impossible without ambiguity. For when the Council's membership stood at eleven, seven affirmative votes were needed to pass a resolution, and the abstention of the five permanent members would have defeated it by sheer force of arithmetic. What Portugal was really saying amounted to: (a) the recent amendments were meant to enlarge the Security Council, but not to weaken the permanent members' role; and (b) 'including the concurring vote of the permanent members' implies that all five major powers must concur for a resolution to be effective. In a paper on the effect of abstentions written in 1969 by Dr António Patricio, a senior official of the Portuguese Foreign Ministry,[2] the author shows how over the years the Security Council's work has largely turned on the major powers' unanimous support. He recalls how doubts about the legal meaning of abstentions by the major powers have emerged within the Council itself and in the writings of British, French, Danish, American and South African jurists. He pleads for a consultative opinion from the International Court of Justice.

Franco Nogueira also pointed out to the secretary-general that, under a series of international conventions, Portugal (in Mozambique) is obliged to grant free access to the sea to her landlocked neighbours, and he asks whether the Security Council really has power to pass a resolution which negates those conventions. In a Lisbon press conference on 3 May, the foreign minister described the resolution as a frontal attack on the principle of freedom of the seas and

[1] Effective from 31 August 1965.
[2] António Patricio, op. cit.

added that it was strange that such an attack should come from Britain:

> Throughout the centuries the United Kingdom has always battled for the freedom of navigation on the high seas: in our time, it has refused to recognize the blockade on Cuba; British ships transport 60 per cent of the supplies to North Vietnam; but the British government thought it right that the Security Council should institute a blockade of our port of Beira. If this principle is to be accepted, one does not know to what extremes it may lead. A ship suspected of transporting fuel for Rhodesia can as well be stopped on entering the port of Beira as on leaving the port where the fuel was shipped; and so the ports of carrying countries with large merchant navies, such as Norway, Sweden, Greece or Panama, or the ports of oil-supplying countries, like Venezuela, or Persia, or Iraq, can tomorrow be subjected to blockade, on the allegation that the ships which sail from those ports carry merchandise for destinations which do not accord with the objectives of one or other power with a powerful navy. We shall then find ourselves on the way to pure arbitrariness and to impositions arising from imperialistic policies.[1]

Chapter VII of the Charter, dealing with U.N. action to keep or restore peace, had been invoked when there was no war in prospect and no threat to peace. Finally, Franco Nogueira continued, the Council's resolution seemed to imply that no one was now entitled to proclaim neutrality in a dispute. Would this come to mean that even a country like Switzerland might one day be called upon to abandon its neutral status?

At the end of the year, the Security Council passed a resolution imposing a wide range of economic sanctions on Rhodesia. Member states were required not to receive certain classes of Rhodesian exports, including iron-ore, sugar, tobacco and chrome; and they were not to export to Rhodesia, machinery, motor vehicles or oil. Again, France and Russia abstained, together with Mali and Bulgaria. France gave as her reason that she considered the Rhodesian question as one that fell within the domestic competence of the United Kingdom. The Russian delegate attributed his abstention to the absence from the amended resolution of five amendments earlier proposed

---

[1] Information Bulletin of the Portuguese Embassy, London, 20 May 1966.

by the African states. These had been designed to prevent oil from reaching Rhodesia, to condemn South Africa and Portugal, to urge the withdrawal of all British offers to Salisbury, to prohibit the purchase of coal[1] and manufactured goods from Rhodesia, and to deplore Britain's refusal to use force. The resolution's implications for Mozambican trade and communications services were serious. However, it must have been some consolation that, in the current session of the General Assembly, a resolution directed against Portugal was, for its proposers, no more than a Pyrrhic victory. It included attacks on international financial and banking organizations for assisting Portugal and met with sharp reactions from those bodies, whose policies were concerned, they said, with economic, not political problems. The resolution received scant attention from the world's press. Some of the Afro-Asian countries abstained or were deliberately absent. In all, forty-five nations declined to vote against Portugal, and those voting in Portugal's favour included Australia, Austria, Brazil, Belgium, Canada, Spain, the United States, the United Kingdom, Holland and South Africa.

On 17 December, U Thant sent out his questionnaire to member nations inquiring what steps they were taking to implement sanctions against Rhodesia. Ten days later, Franco Nogueira gave another press conference in Lisbon in which he referred to supplies of oil. Portugal, he said, was not a world producer of oil (at that time), she was not buying, had not bought, nor did she propose to buy oil for Rhodesia. Portugal was not an exporter of oil, nor did she transport it:

> It is known that the consumption of [oil in] Mozambique is about half that of Rhodesia – and it would be difficult therefore, to conceive how Rhodesia's consumption could be taken from Mozambique's own supply. Everyone knows, on the other hand, that we have neither increased our purchases, nor instituted in Mozambique, or in any other part of the national territory, any rationing with regard to oil consumption.[2]

On 13 January 1967, U Thant sent out another questionnaire, to which Franco Nogueira replied on 3 February, pointing out that he had received no satisfaction regarding his queries on the legality

---

[1] Imports of coal from Rhodesia were and are of vital significance for Zambia, which, quite correctly, continues to receive them.
[2] Information Bulletin of the Portuguese Embassy, London, 30 January 1967.

of the Security Council's Beira resolution. He had written to the secretary-general on 27 April 1966, and again on 14 May. U Thant had replied on 21 June, to the effect that he thought the objections were unfounded but that the Secretariat could express an opinion only if asked to by one of the major powers. Franco Nogueira had, therefore, written to the Security Council on 29 July, asking it to take the matter up, and again on 20 September. Apart from a formal acknowledgment to the first letter, no reply had been received. Franco Nogueira also indicated that losses to the Portuguese economy resulting from the blockade had totalled £10 million and he claimed compensation under Article 50 of the United Nations Charter.

Portugal's official attitude to supplies for Rhodesia was one thing; what happened on her soil was another, and there is no doubt that Portuguese nationals in Mozambique have acted in defiance of the Security Council's sanctions resolution. So far as oil is concerned, however, the position is somewhat obscure. On 7 June 1967, a British Labour M.P., Mr Ben Whitaker, asked Mr George Thomson, then Minister of State at the Commonwealth Office, about oil reaching Rhodesia through Lourenço Marques. Mr Thomson replied that the origin of the oil reaching Rhodesia along the railway line from Lourenço Marques was obscure because of the complexity of oil deliveries at that port, which not only serves the local refinery at Matola, but is also the *entrepôt* for traffic to Swaziland, Botswana and the Northern Transvaal. Deliveries to the port consisted of both crude oil and refined products, hence the problem of identifying individual vessels with shipments earmarked for Rhodesia, or which would later arrive there.

A Portuguese government statement on 13 June, claimed that, between April 1966 and May 1967, 169 oil tankers had reached Lourenço Marques, of which fifty-eight were British and in the service of British companies. Not one was Portuguese, or serving any Portuguese company. Britain's retort was to point out that, of the fifty-six tankers delivering at Lourenço Marques in the first five months of the year, only six had been operating for British companies. Moreover, a reference to public shipping information showed that the Portuguese figures for the period April 1966 to May 1967 were not correct. A total of 141 tankers had arrived during that time. Of these, twenty-nine were British, of which only thirteen were carrying for British oil companies. Nine calls were paid by Portuguese vessels. Between forty and fifty tanker deliveries were made by vessels of no fewer than nine countries to supply crude oil for the Lourenço Marques refinery and to supply the refining companies' deficiencies of refined-oil products which could not be produced locally. (In fact, Britain suspected that Matola had sufficient capacity to supply Rhodesia's limited requirements of 250,000 tons of oil per annum.) But the main point was that, whatever the origin of the supplies, and whether or not the Portuguese administration was formally cognizant of their destination, the Security Council resolution of 16 December 1966, paragraph 2(e), required Portugal and the other member states to prevent the 'participation in their territories or territories under their administration or in land or air transport facilities or by their nationals or vessels of their registration in the supply of oil or oil products' to Rhodesia. Britain was satisfied that 'the bulk of the oil reaching Rhodesia travels along the railway line between Lourenço Marques and Gwelo', as one spokesman in London put it to the author, that 'the Portuguese government make no attempt to deny' it, and that no British companies were involved in the delivery of oil to Rhodesia via Lourenço Marques.

About this time, the *Sunday Times* 'Insight' team were conducting an investigation into the way sanctions were being broken by various countries. Its report[1] did not specifically accuse Portugal of being involved in oil supplies for Rhodesia, but it revealed that, where other commodities were concerned, Rhodesian exports and imports were passing through Mozambique. A Rhodesian firm would place an order with an agent in Mozambique, who in turn would place it with the suppliers as though he wanted it for himself. Overseas suppliers could be counted upon to mark the consignments really intended for Rhodesia with an agreed code. The Beira-Umtali railway did the rest, including the delivery of motor cars. Exports from Rhodesia travelled on the same railway, which links with the Malawi-Beira network. With the aid at times of compliant Malawi officials, it could be made to look as though the appropriate trucks were really coming from Malawi. In Beira, it could be shown that Rhodesian exports came from Malawi or Mozambique, as the local Chamber of Commerce was quite prepared to issue bogus certificates of origin. Between April and June, 65,000 tons of Rhodesian pig-iron had been exported from Rhodesia from the ports of Beira and Lourenço Marques.

It was an unsavoury business all round. OECD figures, reproduced

[1] 27 August 1967.

in the *Spectator* on 23 June, showed the following increases in exports to Rhodesia during the first two months of 1967, as compared with the same period of 1966: West Germany 62 per cent; Japan 62 per cent; France (during the first three months) 100 per cent; the EEC as a whole 15 per cent; and EFTA (excluding Britain) 16 per cent. Exports to South Africa had also risen considerably, those from the EEC by 60 per cent, and it was clear that South Africa was now operating an extensive *entrepôt* trade on behalf of Rhodesia. As Mr George Thomson, M.P., Minister of State at the Commonwealth Office, later pointed out, such figures could be misleading, especially if their relevance to a shorter period were applied to a longer one. There was, however, no doubt that many countries were evading their obligations under the sanctions resolution.

It is not pertinent here to discuss the wisdom or otherwise of using sanctions as a means of defeating UDI. These facts are simply to show how two old allies failed to establish a meeting of minds. Britain was preoccupied from the start with her overriding duty to protect Rhodesia's Africans from a regime determined to block their progress to majority rule, and which now has adopted apartheid as a way of life. Many criticisms can be made of the way London has handled the situation. Perhaps, in the early stages, the white Rhodesians were bullied when they might still have been open to persuasion and reassurance. Sanctions have not achieved their objective, and harm the African more than the white man. But it is felt that Portugal, whose policies are inconsistent with apartheid, might have shown more understanding of her ally's intent. Events on her frontiers and elsewhere in Africa may have caused her to fear the emergence of another African state in the 'southern third'. But why, if she means what she says about giving her African peoples their proper place in government? It is on them she has to depend at the end of the day, and if they are, and remain, content, there is little that outsiders can do to unhinge the Portuguese 'presence'. Internal peace will be assured if Portugal follows her own logic. At the same time, Portugal has always been in a difficult position, and has lost far more than she can afford through sanctions and the blockade (well over £20 million). What she feels most acutely is that she has been treated as a scapegoat by her British ally who seems to show less hostility to South Africa, a country which has done more than anyone else to keep Rhodesia viable; and it is hard to escape the conclusion that South Africa is handled with care because of the massive British and

U.S. investments there. Why, too, should Portugal be singled out for 'the treatment' when so many of Britain's allies, and others, are merrily trading away with Salisbury?

There has been a Rhodesian mission in Lisbon for five years, and while it enjoys no diplomatic status, it receives a great many facilities. A Rhodesian trade delegation to Lisbon in July 1969 aroused new fears that events are driving Portugal far too closely into the arms of her racialist neighbours in Africa. If Portugal is to act consistently with her anti-apartheid stance, she might yet set out to deflect the Rhodesian regime into new ways of thinking. There is plenty to bargain with, and the constant contacts between Rhodesia and Mozambique offer a means of encouraging those Rhodesians who know in their hearts that their leaders are wrong.

Portugal has more than played her part in supplying aid to countries less fortunate than herself. An International Monetary Fund review, at the start of 1967, showed she was sixth out of thirteen nations in the aid she supplied per head of her population to developing countries. In terms of the ratio of aid to national income, she emerged at the top of the list. Her Minister of Economics, Dr Corrêa de Oliveira, formerly president of the EFTA Ministerial Council, was now elected to the corresponding post in the OECD. The Iberian-Atlantic Command of NATO was established near Sintra in February, and, in the following month, two ministers came from Malawi, Mr Msonlhi and Mr Tembo, to conclude agreements on transport and communications. Domestically, it was shown that the gross internal product had risen from £728.9 million with a growth rate of 4.5 per cent in 1956 to £1,170 million and a growth rate of 7 per cent in 1965. At this time, too, the Salazar Bridge, built with American aid across the Tagus, was opened with high celebration. It is a fine suspension bridge and the longest bridge in Europe, constructed by Portuguese workers, though under American management. In May, Pope Paul VI visited the shrine at Fatima. The intent was non-political, the Pope's policy being to visit centres where international groups of pilgrims assemble in large numbers, but some sought to discern in his choice of Fatima some recompense for the sense of injury felt when he went to Bombay in 1964, so soon after India's invasion of Goa. The cardinals who accompanied the Pope took the occasion to urge the need for African bishops in Angola and Mozambique, which are not even technically missionary countries. It appears that the Portuguese government fears the exposure of African bishops to pressures from rebel movements, and with that in view, it is understood, has suggested that Angolan bishops should be named for Sees in Mozambique, and vice versa. Officials maintain that African bishops would even be welcome in Portugal itself, but, according to some sources, the obstacle here would be the Portuguese hierarchy.

There is no doubt that the Portuguese bishops are out of date in their thinking, with a few outstanding exceptions, and these include auxiliary bishops, whose appointments do not require consultation between the Holy See and the government, and who found their way into office through the former and highly progressive Nuncio, now Cardinal Furstenberg. Some critics believe that the government has more reservations than it admits about appointing African bishops, and there seems to be some trouble about replacing Cardinal Cerejeira as Patriarch of Lisbon. He is well past the retiring age of seventy-five, but his offer to resign has not as yet been accepted by the Pope. This may be because of problems over his successor. Rome is rumoured to want a progressive who is not favoured by Lisbon. However, though not notably progressive, Cardinal Cerejeira is a man of undoubted spirituality who has won the respect of his clergy by his efforts to keep step with the Vatican Council's thinking, and by his energetic support of liturgical and pastoral reform. The all too easy judgment that he has always been Salazar's instrument is unfair to both of them. For many years their meetings were confined to a single annual event, and the cardinal has often made plain his concern for human rights. It is known that his relations with the Premier were at times distinctly cool.

In the summer of 1967, it was announced that Anglo-Portuguese trade was up again – exports to Britain by 13 per cent – with a Portuguese deficit of £13 million. In May, Malawi's Minister of Finance was in Lisbon to discuss the services his country might derive from the Cabora Bassa project, and the LISNAVE shipyard opened on schedule. By 1968, it was employing 5,000 workers and now receives some of the world's largest tankers. The Arab-Israeli war of that summer of 1967 put Portugal in an awkward position. Although she has relations with some Arab states, she has none with either Israel or the United Arab Republic, both of which have bitterly opposed her African policy, the Israelis going so far as to train anti-Portuguese nationalist fighters in their country. Britain and the United States approached Lisbon for a signature to a proposed declaration supporting freedom of the seas in the Gulf of Aqaba and the Tiran straits, but Portugal, in common with other countries, declined to sign. The matter was under discussion in the United Nations, and, in view of Portugal's delicate relationship with that body and the absence of relations with the disputant countries, it was felt better not to be involved. An additional reason, given by Franco Nogueira, was that the declaration was too narrowly phrased, and that, if freedom of the seas were to be asserted in the Gulf straits, it should also have been maintained for the Mozambique channel. In August, Franco Nogueira toured southern Africa, and was well received by Dr Banda in Malawi, as well as in the South African Republic. On 7 September, he issued a fifth invitation to U Thant to visit Portuguese Africa.[1] The Secretary-General was shortly due to visit other African countries, and it was hoped he would take in Angola and Mozambique. As usual, he declined politely. He would have, he said, no time. During these summer months, on the other hand, five more British M.P.s went to Portuguese Africa, and returned with favourable impressions: Messrs Ronald Bell and Edward Taylor (Conservative), and Messrs J. F. Bellenger, Evelyn King and Desmond Donnelly (then Labour, now Independent Labour).

Early in 1968, soon after the President's visit to Portuguese Guinea, Portugal claimed that Rhodesian sanctions had cost her £17 million. On a more cheerful note, Anglo-Portuguese trade struck a record total of £125 million, with Portugal's deficit reduced to £4 million in relation to Britain. At this stage Britain was Portugal's biggest customer, taking 21 per cent of her exports. May figures showed that, in metropolitan Portugal, real wages for men in the transforming industries had risen in six years by 19.8 per cent (as against 16.7 per cent in Britain). Consumer prices in the past seven years had risen by only 20.8 per cent as distinct from:

	Per cent
Denmark	45.2
Britain	27.7
Sweden	32.5
Switzerland	27.5
Finland	40.4
Norway	32.1
Austria	27.8

[1] Previous invitations had been extended on 29 August 1963, 6 February 1964, 25 May 1964, and 25 June 1966.

all of whom are Portugal's partners in EFTA (Finland having associate status). In June a further stage of the Alentejo project was completed with the opening of the Roxo Dam. On 17 July, Salazar gave his last major interview to an Argentinian paper, *Extra*, in which he asserted that Portugal's gross national product had risen by 65 per cent in the past ten years, and that industrial production had been multiplied six times since 1938. This interview showed he was near the end of his working life. His sense of historical timing had weakened considerably. African maturity he saw in terms of centuries rather than decades. It was the voice of a tired and aged man.

He was, however, moving a little faster towards a reinflationary policy. Measures were being planned to introduce export credit and credit insurance, and to enable commercial banks to extend medium- and long-term credit. It had been announced in June that, in future, they would be permitted to make loans of more than two years and up to five for farming, industry and exports. But businessmen, unable to get on with the job of setting up their factories, and anxiously waiting for the promised measures to be given concrete form, were becoming really impatient. Foreign firms with access to funds outside were coming into Portugal and setting their factories up at once – thus beating their Portuguese competitors on the latter's own ground. In August, Salazar made a number of drastic changes in his government, some of them promising. Motta Veiga remained in charge of planning, but the governor of the Bank of Portugal, Sr João Augusto Dias Roas, became Finance Minister. The formidable Alfredo dos Santos, who, as Minister of the Interior, had been in charge of the PIDE, was replaced by the more expansive António Gonçalves Rapazote, a lawyer and landowner.

On 6 September 1968, Salazar was rushed to the Red Cross hospital in Lisbon with an intracranial subdural haematoma: a clot on the brain. It later transpired that some weeks before he had had a bad fall at his summer house on the road to Estoril, and forbidden those who knew of it to speak of it outside. One version, from a usually impeccable source, states that the fall occurred while Salazar's chiropodist was tending the ageing Premier's feet, and that Salazar later wrote him a letter, in an unusually clear hand, confirming his order to keep the incident secret. This letter was evidently meant to cover the poor chiropodist in case the facts should come out later with heavy recriminations for the man who had held his tongue. Be that as it may, an operation to remove the clot was performed by the leading

Portuguese brain surgeon, Dr A. Vasconcelos Marques, a well-known oppositionist, and he was assisted by Professor Almeida Lima, in the presence of Salazar's personal doctor and friend of many years, Dr Eduardo Coelho, a distinguished heart specialist. Some days later it seemed that the operation had been a complete success, but within twenty-four hours of an optimistic bulletin, the news broke that the patient had suffered a stroke. General Eisenhower's physician, Dr Houston Merritt, flew from the United States to see what he could do. He agreed with the Portuguese doctors' diagnosis which meant, in effect, that Salazar's working life was done.

Newspapers all over the world were alerted for what they half-expected to be a Portuguese revolution. At the least, there would be chaotic upheavals, and much jockeying for position. One wild rumour was that President Johnson, concerned for the bases in the Azores, was sending in his paratroops to quell the Lisbon riots. But there were no riots, and a cynic remarked in Lisbon that, had it been Eusebio who was ill, wailing crowds would have mobbed the hospital. In fact, business as usual was the theme of Lisbon life, and there seemed to be more reporters than anyone else outside the Red Cross building. Fairly constant streams of cars drew up. Distinguished and not so distinguished people entered the hall to sign the visitors' book, and a run-of-the-mill Lisbonian found himself lining up with a visiting foreign minister to take his turn with the pen. Dona Maria, Salazar's housekeeper, seemed to stay there night and day. She had become a celebrity overnight, and now faced the cameras and questions with dignity. All sorts of apocrypha started to gain currency. The cardinal was at the bedside absolving the dying statesman from the excommunication incurred by his expulsion of the Bishop of Oporto. In fact, of course, the bishop was never expelled, and Salazar never incurred a papal sanction. All the cardinal did was to take the hand of his former fellow-student. A chaplain gave him the last sacraments – in the normal form. A more poignant, and perhaps a likelier story was that, in a moment of consciousness, Salazar murmured the question: 'Am I a prisoner?'

In the country at large, Salazar's strongest supporters grieved and were fearful. Those who had seen the best in him but felt the time for change was long overdue were full of mixed feelings. The opposition neither gloated nor fooled themselves that the day of revelation was at hand. Many a malcontent, in fact, spoke with a curious kind of subdued nostalgia. They had suffered, yet did not forget that Salazar had given their country a place in the modern world. Grudging admiration for his tenacity in times of national crisis clashed with exasperation at the endemic state of internal intellectual stagnation. The cynical marksmanship of the taxi-drivers, hawking traditional gobbets of phlegm through the windows, seemed to waver a little and fall quite short. It was sad, they said, with a shrug.

In the Council of State, tensions were high. The President of the Republic, Admiral Tomás, had to decide whether to dismiss the unconscious Salazar and whom to appoint in his place. A certain fastidious hesitation at sacking a prostrate man after forty years of service clashed with the country's urgent need. The Council of State's role was advisory only, but, with a lesser man in the President's chair, events could have got out of hand. It is to the lasting credit of the admiral, hitherto thought of as a figurehead, that in fact they did not. Argument, by all accounts, was feverish. The council included ex-officio members, like the presidents of the parliamentary chambers, and men whose past service entitled them to lifelong membership. They included General Santos Costa, said to be bidding for power with support from military quarters and the ultra-conservative elements. Professor Marcello Caetano, also a Council member, was reported to be his prime opponent. Franco Nogueira's name was canvassed. He was known to be tired after years of doing battle in international forums. He remained, however, severely aloof from the power game. There was talk of a triumvirate of Caetano, the brilliant Kaulza de Arriaga (then head of the nuclear programme and now Commander-in-Chief, Mozambique), and Antuñez Varela, a liberal Catholic who in the previous year had resigned as Minister of Justice. Why had he resigned? Was he weary for liberalization? Was it true that, in a notorious vice case, charges against important men had been suppressed against his will? Or was he just hard up, unable to keep nine children on his ministerial pittance? There were other questions. Would Adriano Moreira, despite a clash with Caetano, return to high office, and might General Deslandes, the former Angolan Governor-General, be a possible Premier? The full story will not be known for some time. What is certain is that the President's solid determination to keep the temperature down proved to be the catalyst for something approaching a consensus. At one stage, he is said to have made it plain that the final decision was his and his alone. That decision could not be postponed much longer. It was now clear that Salazar, though flatly refusing to die, would never be able to work again. His left side was irrevocably paralysed. He was conscious for only odd moments. The country had to be governed.

So it was, on 25 September, that the President talked to the nation on television. Salazar, he said, had 'served with genius and with total and unflagging dedication for more than 40 years', but he must now be replaced. The new Prime Minister was Professor Marcello José das Neves Alves Caetano. In the strange, indefinable way that these things happen, the country had come to much the same conclusion. Lisbon remained calm, almost sluggish in the airless heat. There was a guarded expectancy, a quiet approval that a highly respected man had been chosen, one who would not let Portugal down in the eyes of the world and might even move the country into new orbits of growth. The opposition, if not too sanguine, hoped for some measure of liberalization. The take-over was as smooth as glass, and men in the streets said bluntly that Salazar had never served his country better than he was now doing by dying slowly. The long prohibition of politics, heightened by the new preoccupation with an infant affluence, had long since yielded a fatalistic apathy. Yet it was also true that the Salazar mystique was not dead, and an uncomfortable sense of the *paterfamilias* brooding through his coma over the scene, and wagging the well-known finger, arrested the irresponsible. Even oppositionists confessed to a willingness to wait and see.

Marcello Caetano was sixty-three and looked very much less. Spare and lithe, he was cold and cerebral, yet capable of affection. He was aloof, proud and ambitious, yet without a trace of vanity. He was conservative and sceptical of the opposition's calibre, yet concerned, as an honest lawyer should be, for the rule of law and personal freedoms. A Salazarist who had nonetheless clashed with the master in certain respects, yet a man of unquestioned integrity, he had above all been exposed to international influences.[1] The slightly unsuitable cut of his glasses gives his eyes a glowering look at odds with the thin-lipped smile. He is every inch the scholarly jurist, yet also the man of action, the practical company lawyer, the keen negotiator, and the capable minister. The son of a primary teacher,[2] he won his law degree at the age of twenty-one, and became well known as a right-wing Catholic writer. He edited *A Época, A Ideia*

---

[1] Once he was Prime Minister, Salazar never strayed beyond Spain.
[2] Salazar had always favoured youngish men of humble origin. Franco Nogueira's father was a shepherd, Moreira's a policeman. In 1963 the average age of the government was a little under forty.

Nacional and *A Voz*. Later he wrote for the *Jornal de Comércio e das Colonias*, and was secretary of the review *Naçao Portuguesa*, founded by Pedro Theotónio Pereira. At the age of twenty-three, Caetano was legal adviser to the Finance Ministry under Salazar, and played a major role in drafting the legal instruments of the New State, notably its Administrative Code. He became a doctor of law in 1931, a professor of Lisbon University in 1933. Throughout his life he maintained as far as he could his teaching work in the faculty of law, and, even when he was running a high-powered legal practice, was scrupulous in his attendance at lectures, all of which he minutely prepared. From 1940 to 1944, he was National Commissioner for the *Mocidade*, the youth movement; from 1944 to 1947, Minister for the Colonies; then President of the National Union's executive, and in 1949 a full-time teacher again. In 1950, he was appointed President of the Corporative Chamber, and, five years later, Minister of the Presidency in charge of the National Plans. After the 1958 election and the Delgado campaign, he was dropped from the government,[1] and returned to private practice and academic life. In 1959, Caetano became Rector of Lisbon University, but resigned in 1962, in protest against police action in the university precincts. He then devoted himself to teaching and legal work again, advising some of the country's major companies, until he was called to the Premiership.

Marcello Caetano has been a prolific writer on subjects ranging from law, politics and administration to colonial questions, education and youth. As a jurist his fame is international. He remains convinced of the corporative principle, and is concerned to support traditional forms of Church authority. He maintains Salazar's stand over Africa, and the principle of tutelage for the subject peoples. He can be accused of an intellectual snobbery, yet is much more open to demands for personal freedoms than Salazar ever was. He is a practising Catholic, and married the daughter of a Republican minister and poet, João Barros. There are several children of the marriage, one of them a leading architect.

In his first broadcast speech to the nation, Caetano declared on 27 September:

> The nation has for long accustomed itself to being led by a man of genius; from today it must adapt itself to government by men like other men.

[1] See Chapter 11, *supra*.

He needed, he said, 'the help of the nation'. His aim was to establish a climate of normality and to reduce the national crisis to a minimum, yet also to accelerate the rhythm of national life. He would have to ask for sacrifices from all, 'including the sacrifice of some liberties which we would like to restore'. He would foster reciprocal toleration of ideas, but there would be no room for Communism or anarchy. The demands of public order were inexorable. On the other hand, continuity

> implies an idea of movement, of sequence, and of adaptation. Fidelity to the doctrine brilliantly taught by Dr Salazar should not be confused with obstinate attachment to formulas or solutions which he once might have adopted.

The speech seemed to be concerned to reassure yet stimulate the conservative, while offering modest encouragement to the progressive. One of Caetano's first moves, widely approved, was to appoint Dr Alfredo de Queiroz Vaz Pinto as Minister of the Presidency in charge of the National Plan. It was Vaz Pinto who had turned Portuguese Airways (TAP) into one of Europe's finest airlines, which now carries 700,000 passengers annually. In a later reshuffle, he also appointed Dr Valentim Xavier Pintado, the young and brilliant economic adviser to the *Banco Português do Atlântico*, as Secretary of State for Commerce, in a combined department linking commerce and finance under Dr Dias Rosas. Xavier Pintado was a critic of Salazar's deflationary policies, and had constantly urged the need for more foreign investment and radical reform of the domestic credit system. With Dr Costa André as Secretary of State for Finance, and the lively team supporting Vaz Pinto in the planning departments, it seemed that the economy was getting into the hands of energetic, European-minded expansionists. Caetano has been accused, in fact, of surrounding himself with technocrats, but, in a 1969 interview with the Barcelona paper *Vanguardia*, he retorted that the men he had gathered round him were 'of humanistic training with a Christian-social background and a thorough technical grounding'.

Another of the new Prime Minister's early decisions was to bring the socialist lawyer Mario Soares back to Portugal from exile in São Tomé. Press censorship was drastically reduced, but later tightened up again. This may have been prompted by the news of recurring disturbances in Spain, to which Portugal is always sensitive.

By the summer months of 1969, however, oppositionist activities were being given unprecedented coverage in the Portuguese press. On 19 November, the domestic and foreign press were, to their astonishment, invited to PIDE headquarters when Dr Rapazote presented a decoration to the Director, Major Silva Pais. In his speech, the Minister of the Interior said that in metropolitan Portugal at that time there were only 124 'political' prisoners, and no one was serving more than a first term of security measures after the substantive sentence. Thirty-one prisoners were under interrogation, twenty-one were being held for illegal emigration, and eleven had been charged and were being held pending trial. By this time, too, Caetano had forbidden the police to impede anyone simply because he had openly criticized the government, and he had refused to keep the Prime Minister's traditional PIDE bodyguard. Reports from the PIDE were to be submitted to the Minister of the Interior only, not to the Prime Minister, and the suspicion of direct control by the Premier of the security police had been allayed.

On 10 October 1968, the *Diario Popular* published a widely discussed article dividing the population into those who opposed 'movement' in the nation's life, those who were in a hurry, and those who were waiting, prepared to give the new government a certain amount of credit. (This was certainly the attitude of the responsible opposition.) The paper added that the credit thus put at Caetano's disposal would be repaid only when 'Portugal has given up her place at the tail end of European statistics', and when press and other liberties had been assured. The test would come in the elections for the National Assembly in November 1969. The first year of the new administration could hardly be expected to solve all the problems heaped up on its plate, and it is known that Caetano's first and most difficult task was to reorganize the administrative machinery itself. It was not easy to find the men to do it, as nobody wanted to commit himself to the new situation until it was clear that there was some future in it. Hence the conservatives accused Caetano of going too fast, while the opposition thought him too slow.

Towards the end of 1968, the Brazilian Foreign Minister, Dr Magalhaës Pinto, visited Lisbon, to be followed shortly by Mr Harry Oppenheimer, one of the business kings of South Africa. In his November address to the National Assembly, Caetano flatly denied that Portugal had any secret pact with Rhodesia or South Africa, but the question must have become live again in many people's minds when, in the following March, the South African Minister of Defence, Dr Pieter Botha, also visited Lisbon.

In December 1968, Dr José Guilhermo de Melo e Castro became president of the National Union's executive, and this was seen as a further sign of a new flexibility in the country's institutions. Caetano also reasserted his confidence in the corporative system and its trade unions, which, in the past eight years, had achieved 400 collective bargains affecting a million workers. December, however, was also marked by unrest in Lisbon's technical university, with student strikes and a strident anarchical theme. Many of the students, however, were simply concerned with the urgent need for radical reforms in the university system: more teachers, better facilities, new teaching methods. Portuguese universities have a high reputation in certain subjects, notably law, medicine and pure science, but there is a serious dearth of equipment and laboratories essential for the applied sciences. Many of the courses, too, are too long and cumbersome, requiring as much as seven years for the basic degree. The general state of unrest in academic circles prompted the government to cancel arrangements for the 1969 World University Games to be held in Lisbon. The official explanation was that the Games would clash with the Portuguese elections.

Caetano's visit to Portuguese Africa in April 1969 was an outstanding success, and his reception was even warmer than the President's had been, for this was the first time for at least forty years that the effective head of the Portuguese government had visited these countries.[1] Fresh university troubles broke out at home, this time at Coimbra. On 13 May, the socialist opposition issued a manifesto, with 200 signatures, demanding an end to *Salazarismo* – even without Salazar. The remarkable fact was that the manifesto was reported in the press, the first time in many years that the censors had allowed publicity to oppositionist activities. On 14 May, a great Republican Congress opened at Vieiro in the north of Portugal under the chairmanship of Dr Arlindo Vicente, with a special message from the veteran Republican leader, Dr Cunha Leal. The themes were familiar and the demands included the release of political prisoners and free debate on the African question. Some 900 guests sat down to

---

[1] An interesting footnote to the visit was the announcement that, in 1928, there were 5,000 cases of sleeping sickness in Angola, while in 1963 the total was nine. This tribute to Portuguese mastery of tropical diseases acknowledges the success of one of the most advanced faculties in the university system.

a Congress dinner, and the entire event was extensively reported in the newspapers. Though one statement, signed earlier in the year by 250 intellectuals, had not been reported in the press, coverage had been given to a demand for civic liberties signed by 800 businessmen, and also to the remarks of Dr Mario Soares at the Socialist International conference at Eastbourne. In the past, it had been his readiness to speak his mind abroad that had laid Soares open to imprisonment and exile.

On 22 May, the first Ecumenical Centre in Portugal was opened at Figueira da Foz, with an address by Dr Eugene Carson Blake, Secretary-General of the World Council of Churches. By this time, the elections due in November were becoming a burning issue. Caetano had already commended himself to the nation in a series of televised fireside chats, and, on 29 June, Dr Rapazote appeared to discuss the election arrangements. Fair treatment would be extended, he said, to all sides. All elements would have equal access to the voting lists. There would be no restraints on voters, and all candidates would have a share in the control of the ballot itself. Oppositionists would be free to meet in order to prepare their lists of candidates. The minister warned, however, that no one should attack the Constitution or the foundations of the regime. All literates, including women, would be entitled to vote, and it was disappointing that so far only 1,816,148 voters had registered; this was a breach of duty on the electorate's part. Finally, all permissions to hold meetings so far requested had been granted, and the candidates' right to unrestricted freedom of speech, assembly and propaganda in the month before the election would this time be respected.

An election for the National Assembly cannot directly affect the government, which answers only to the president. But a hostile Assembly could bring the government's work to an early halt. So the election this year, even in a one-party system, was of the highest importance: the biggest test to date of Caetano's intentions. In the event, it was not wholly free in the sense understood elsewhere in the West, but it was freer than any other for thirty-five years, and as such represented an evolutionary landmark. As always, the officially supported National Union and the opposition groups presented for election in each constituency, not individuals, but lists of candidates, and the voter's task was to choose a whole list. Broadly speaking, all literate Portuguese adults of either sex, who were not insane or had not been deprived of their civil rights by a court, were entitled to stand for election and to vote. Candidates could be disqualified if their opposition amounted to a challenge to the foundations of the state. This provision, essentially designed to defeat the Communist, has always been capable of a much wider application. However, of 172 opposition candidates put forward in 1969, only twelve were disallowed. Unhappily, this included the entire opposition list in Mozambique (seven names), who, it was said, had failed to establish their Portuguese citizenship. The most important departure from the practice under Salazar was that this time the opposition were allowed to form commissions for the purpose of putting up lists and fighting a campaign. Censorship was maintained on the ground that Portugal is still a nation at war, and that after forty years of strict control a period of transition is required before the country can be let loose with total liberty of the press. The opposition, unlike Marcello Caetano, had no access to the broadcasting media, nor could meetings be held in the big assembly halls.

At the same time, the opposition were able to make many public speeches and to give a number of press conferences which were reported at considerable length in the newspapers. Some of their propaganda was censored, but a great deal of it was successfully circulated. There were no stories of ballot papers being seized by the police or of interference with voters at the polling booths. The ballot was supervised by mixed juries including the opposition, and, astonishingly, on polling day there was hardly a policeman in sight and not a trace of the all too familiar election disorders. Representatives of the opposition were freely distributing ballot papers outside the polling stations. The opposition had formed commissions which amounted to coalitions of Catholics with traditional Republicans and Socialists, or with other left-wingers under Pereira de Moura, who is himself a Catholic. His group, the Democratic Electoral Commission (CED), won many more votes than the traditional opposition in the United Democratic Electoral Commission (CEUD). Cunha Leal's Social Democratic Action group, a dwindling force, withdrew from the campaign. The rest of the opposition saw it through, with candidates in most of the major centres.

It was a mark of the political apathy which the long years of restriction had induced among the people that probably well under half of those entitled to vote took the trouble to register, and this was particularly marked in the African provinces. In metropolitan Portugal, excluding the Atlantic islands, 1,043,982 of the 1,670,685 registered voters actually went to the polls, a proportion of 62.4 per cent. None of the opposition groups won a constituency. Of the total vote, 88 per cent went to the National Union, 10.3 to the CED and 1.5 to the CEUD, while the almost negligible Monarchists' group secured only 0.1 per cent. Dr Pereira de Moura of the CDE afterwards expressed a degree of satisfaction with the results, which, he said, would make it 'impossible for the government to ignore the strength of the democratic movement', but socialist leader Dr Mario Soares declared that the elections proved the impossibility of a successful fight against a one-party regime.

While it is true that the results may seem to betray Caetano's earlier promise of a wholly free election, it is equally true that the campaign was more free than any in living memory. Opposition demands that the government should negotiate with the African rebels simply did not accord with popular feeling. No one spending any length of time in Portugal today can pretend that there is any widespread demand for an immediate and unconditional reversal of the African policy, and it is of special interest to talk to young men returning from military service there. The experience seems to add much to their stature and their sense of responsibility, and, although many of them suffer career problems because of the break in their studies, they do not for the most part show any sign of rebellion. The people at large are increasingly anxious to settle the wars which inhibit national growth, but there is no evidence of a crumbling morale. If defence costs account for over 40 per cent of the Budget, this is still only 7 per cent of the gross national product, and, while the burden is heavy, it is not intolerable. The main complaint of the thoughtful conscripts is that the African peoples' development is still too slow.

There have also been changes within the National Union itself which cut the ground from under the feet of the opposition. Many of the Union's candidates in this election were young progressive-conservatives belonging to the new class of technocrats and white-collar workers. They are men with ideas, and in many respects have stolen their opponents' ideas. Even sceptics allow that at least 20 of the 130 men now sitting in the National Assembly represent this progressive trend, and some put it much higher.

Finally, there was the personal stature of Marcello Caetano, who stands head and shoulders above all potential challengers as the one reliable man endowed with the gifts to update Portuguese life. He moves too fast for some and much too slow for others. The

opposition accuse him of breaking his earlier promises but, taking
the country as a whole, there seems to be not a single name to command
the respect and confidence that Caetano does. There were really only
two wholly vital opposition groups at work in the Portuguese
nation last autumn: the progressive Catholic minority and the new,
post-Communist 'revolutionaries' in the universities, whose inspiration derives from Ché, Mao, Ho, the 'French Revolution' of 1968,
Mr Danny Cohn-Bendit, and Professor Herbert Marcuse. Both
groups, which share as in South America a surprising degree of
common ground, will doubtless become more important as time
goes on, but as yet lack high-powered prophets. The traditional
middle-class opposition had nothing to offer them, and nothing to
offer the working-class, which has yet to become a potent political
force in its own right.

Caetano's future will turn in part on how he handles the new young
militant intellectuals and on how he shapes the workers now finding
their feet with more education and better living conditions; for it will
be a major tragedy if the new preoccupation with hire purchase
payments damps down the political sense of the working-class in
Portugal as it has already done to a high degree in Spain. The continuing 'presence' of even a helpless Salazar acts as a sign and inspiration for an older generation of 'ultras' who still inhibit Caetano's
liberalizing instinct. Between such forces and the impatience of the
young, he has to move with tact and delicacy. His modernization
of a cumbersome bureaucracy will take some time, and the credit
extended to him by public opinion may have to be renewed. Two years
ago he told the author that the young Portuguese *désirent avoir la
chance*, but he also believes that too drastic and rapid a surgery would
be more than the nation's nerves could stand. His approach is to
put teeth into existing institutions, and to give the young an opening
within them. Whether he can still put meaning into a corporative
system, as he hopes at a time when party democracy has failed to
serve a number of 'younger' nations, or whether his role, however
dynamic, is going to be transitional is something time alone can tell.

October 1969 saw the resignation of Dr Franco Nogueira as
Portugal's Foreign Minister. This does not imply a radical change in
African policy. Franco Nogueira's wish for a change was well known,
and no one begrudges him a chance to serve in other ways with a few
rewards of the kind he has hitherto sacrificed. He could yet be a
future candidate for the premiership. But Franco Nogueira, in recent

years, has come to fix his eyes exclusively on an African future for
Portugal, and to play down her European involvement. Caetano and
those around him may be more inclined to polarize the two concerns
and to look to a future that will be at least as European as African,
with a continuing 'feel' for relations with Brazil. How far and how
fast they will move towards African self-determination remains an
open question. But at least they are realists, and the dominant
theme in Portuguese politics now is how to strike the right balance
between the European and African involvement. The more European influences get to work in Portugal the faster her African policy
will evolve.

And what of Salazar himself, half-paralysed in retirement in his
home at São Bento which the government has allowed him to retain.
On his eightieth birthday in April, he received some Coimbra students
and managed a few painful words in front of the TV cameras. In
autumn a correspondent of the French journal *L'Aurore* had an
interview with him, and subsequently reported that Salazar had not
been told that he was no longer Prime Minister. In November, the
former leader was brought by car to the polling booth. It all smacks
of rather poor taste. By every rule in the book, however, he ought to
have died last year, and it is a measure of his indomitable will that
he has simply refused to relinquish his life.

Few modern statesmen have been so hard for the modern world to
interpret. What was his motivation, and how did his elusive mentality
work? A leading oppositionist once complained to the author that
Salazar would have been more intelligible, had his weaknesses been
more human. His life was devoid of scandals. Riches to him were less
than nothing. His family-sized home behind the São Bento Palace,
where the National Assembly meets and he had his office, was
anything but luxurious. In summer he would spend a few months at
a tough little fortress near Estoril, whose only redeeming feature was
that it virtually stood on the sea, travelling into the office by car
each day. He was never closely guarded. A policeman or two stood
at the gate and a personal detective appeared on public occasions.
Access to the house was easy. You had to have an appointment, but
you only had to give your name to be admitted at once. At São Bento
you would walk across the garden alone, ring the bell, and be let in
by a tiny maid. Salazar had some trouble with his eyes, and the sitting-
room, heavily tapestried, would often be curtained and dimly lit

on a summer's afternoon. Salazar would enter, smiling, but plainly making an effort. The usual courtesies were dispensed, but they rarely included refreshment. Smoking he could not stand, complaining that the smell clung to the curtains. He would also expect some courtesies from the visitor. A Minister who once arrived without a hat and said he never wore one, was invited to do so in future, please.

Though he read and understood English, Salazar preferred, when talking to foreigners, to use his excellent French. Once he had warmed up, he would lean back in his chair, put his finger tips together, and proceed to talk in plain and lucid terms, didactically, as though he were back in Coimbra giving a lengthy tutorial. Having decided to see you, he would settle down to a couple of hours' uninhibited exposition. A polite request here and there for your opinion had the ring of an oral examination. As he sat there in his buttoned boots, a rug across his knees, discoursing quietly and with an old-world charm, it was hard to believe he was a national leader, but, as the time went on, one began to sense the power, the purpose, the unforgiving nature. He could be a spell-binder, and the effect could be paralytic, almost comatose. It was not until the visitor was well away from the house that his critical faculty started to unwind. Salazar's style was friendly and sceptical, with a touch of astringent irony. Whatever is said of him, his concern for the poor was genuinely consuming, but mention the opposition and he would make them sound like precocious striplings. He came across, in fact, more as a headmaster than a dictator. His world view was severely pragmatic: 'We're talking politics,' he would say, 'so I won't speak of honour.' He showed an uncanny nose for the next moves in the world's most sensitive sectors – his wartime diplomacy set new classical standards – and a curious understanding of statesmen he had never met. The one Communist country he could talk about with sympathy in later years was China, which intrigued him, as did Japan. His feeling for Britain was a blend of admiration for her traditions, courage and skills; grief that she had lost her empire and, he was too polite to say outright, her morals; sadness at her failure to understand her oldest ally, and an irritation with efforts to impose the British way of life in nations ill-attuned to it. The winds of change were 'a meaningless phrase'. It was for men to make history, not to be pushed around by it. The hero-figure was Churchill. Lord Avon was 'a gentleman'. It was not for him, Salazar, to comment on later political leaders. He just felt puzzled sometimes.

In 1955, during the Royal visit, Salazar was greatly taken with Queen Elizabeth. What baffled him was a system of constitutional conventions which could compel 'a woman of sensitivity and refinement, with a delicate conscience and keen intelligence, not to say four children of her own, to sign, contrary to all her instincts, an Act of Parliament legalizing homosexuality'. The eternal love-hate relationship that has always marked the old alliance came out in him every time. At a low ebb in Britain's fortunes he could turn to a colleague and cry out miserably: 'Do you think it means nothing to me that Britain is weak?' Yet he felt he could understand the weakness. 'I'm not surprised that Britain is tired and disillusioned,' he was to tell the present writer in the post-war years. 'In two world wars you gave all you had to the world, and your allies in gratitude took your empire away.' But he could not forget that when, on the eve of the rape of Goa, Portugal wanted to send troops out by air and asked London for Middle East fuelling stages, there came, not a refusal, but simply no reply. A 'yes' would not have saved Goa; but no reply! If Britain's departure from Africa had been hard for him to take, America's African policy under President Kennedy really perplexed him. He was not lacking in admiration for individual Americans nor in gratitude for what the United States had done for the post-war world, but he plainly felt that young America also needed tutelage. He feared that her technological culture, for all its genius, was in some way deforming, and needed re-connection to the primordial roots of Europe's civilization. He also resented the contrast of America's anti-colonial message with her neo-imperial thrust.

Like most young Portuguese of his day, Salazar was exposed in his formative years to French rather than British cultural influences, and his oldest friends think he was rather pro-German in the First World War. Not so, they add, in the Second World War. They never doubted his brilliance, but felt it took a practical, not a creative turn. Dr Eduardo Coelho speaks of his acute and logical mind, but the logic, he says, was mathematical rather than juridical. Underneath the cold surface, they found a man of sensibility, affection and strong emotion. As a Catholic he would speak nostalgically of the primitive Church with its strong sense of community, and resented the Church's later intrusion into politics. In the realm of theology, on the other hand, he expected the Church to be dogmatic, admired Pope Pius XII, and thought Pope John's decision to summon the Second Vatican

Council was a major error, reducing the Church's power to the will of the people, and weakening papal authority. The Roman Curia, the Vatican's civil service, he dismissed with a gentle contempt as 'a kind of *Terreiro de Paço*'. His clashes with the Sacred Congregation *De Propaganda Fide* were to come into the open during the Goa crisis.

His gradualism was strongly marked in his approach to Africa. He believed the African needed closer association with Europeans in order to reach full maturity. It troubled him to hear that African students in Portuguese universities found it hard to master abstract subjects like mathematics. In interviews with the foreign press he always stressed that evolution in Africa would have to be what he called 'natural', carefully nurtured, based on merit, never artificially forced. He felt that slogans like democracy or liberty were simply a cover for the programme of ambitious, self-appointed leaders who were little concerned for the actual needs of the masses, and were largely unrepresentative of them. Visiting statesmen would urge Salazar to give a deadline for self-determination in Portuguese Africa, or to bring Africans at once into the highest executive *échelons*. He rejected none of this in principle, but other countries had damaged their former colonies by making unrealistic predictions and acting upon them; Portugal meant to be guided by evidence. All would depend on education (her responsibility) and merit (the citizen's response). A black governor-general, minister of state, or bishop? Why not? But promotion and qualification belonged together, and the self-determining options had to be a graduation prize.

It was, perhaps, this preoccupation with merit which did more than anything else to cut Salazar off from the modern world. To see it as a way of stalling world opinion is at best an over-simplification, at worst a total misreading. There are many ways in which Portugal could satisfy African and world opinion without long-term material loss. But Salazar could not, and would not, come to terms with an age so unreflective that the young seek to forge their creeds through the act of revolt, and reject revolutions based on preconceived dogma; in which the fact of being and aspiring is sufficient title to a share in control, with questions of competence left unasked and seen as irrelevant. In some ways, Salazar's thought had plainly become anachronistic, yet the visitor found himself asking whether in other respects the ageing leader saw ahead of his time. There was something about the unsoldierly Salazar that reminded one of Lord Montgomery:

the same austerity, concentration, absorption, eye for detail and abnormal lucidity; the same sense of his own inerrancy, the same trait of sleeping well on monumental decisions.

It is strange to think that the adoptive father of Micas and Maria Antonia is the man who, over the African question, has stood his ground in the teeth of world opinion for a decade. The more the pressures mounted, the more he refused to buy approval. Time and again his critics have urged him to make a conciliatory gesture, and have hinted at what they might do for him in financial terms by way of reward. The answer was always no. Events in Angola and Mozambique certainly touched the official conscience. The development process has been stepped up in recent years to the point where some observers hope that a dream eluding the rest of us might yet be realized there. But on matters of principle, Salazar would not budge. He showed the same toughness in wartime diplomacy – there are those who well remember his 'terrifying silences' in those days – and, although he could sometimes display a barely controlled fury, the overriding memory is that of his massive calm.

Strangest of all his personality contrasts is that a man of his principles could allow the security police to crush even the innocent opposition. Non-subversive liberals were often as liable to arrest, interrogation and detention as the hard-core, underground Communist. Things happened in police headquarters which would not have happened in Salazar's presence, of course, but there is a feeling that, when complaints were made, he was prone to believe what he wanted to hear: a tendency which gave the advantage to the policeman's side of the story. Some of those who knew him well, speak of his 'compartmentalized' mind. Like others of his generation, he was overborne by the past with its tale of upheavals and violence. He reacted with genuine fear to things which seem harmless to those whose experience is different. His detachment from ordinary living, too, may well have established within him a certain insensitivity to personal griefs and frustrations which, on a person-to-person basis, he would have sought to redress. He has been known to intervene in cases brought to his notice by those he could not ignore. But his mind was that of a man who ruled as a monarch, and whose training had intellectual roots in an age when men, out for zeal for souls, saw heresy as social disorder and sought to redeem the erring through pain. Salazar would not have subscribed precisely to this; the allusion is not to be laboured. But his view of the social order owes something to the medieval schoolmen from whom he derived his philosophy. It has both merits and demerits.

If there is a single key to Salazar, it probably has to do with the fact that he is a pre-Conciliar Catholic: one for whom philosophy ended with Aquinas, and for whom Pope John and the Vatican Council had no message. For complex historical reasons, the pre-Conciliar Church tended to be paternal, defensive, entrenched, exclusive, dogmatic and monolithic. The Second Vatican Council proclaims a fraternal, pilgrim Church, with a message to give but plenty to learn, dynamic and open, ready to take its chance in a pluralist world, and to seek common cause with right-minded men of all creeds and none. The Catholic view of secular society has undergone great changes, and the history of this development over the centuries, as described in 1936 by Maritain,[1] has a startling bearing on Salazar. As such, it merits a glancing summary.

The medieval Church saw temporal civilization as a force in the service of God, a function of the sacred. God's relation to the world was that of the *sacrum imperium,* and this demanded an organic unity in society. There was scope for a degree of diversity and pluralism, but spiritual unity was the basis for the temporal city. Because the role of the temporal was to minister to the spiritual, it followed that spiritual leaders could invoke the apparatus of temporal government in holding society's spiritual unity fast. There arose a paternalist concept of monarchy, the king as the *paterfamilias* of the state, a reflection of the divine fatherhood. The anointed king was the vicar of the people and of God (or of God only), the whole concept of father and family became a kind of superior essence, the corporation was a family of the second degree, and society was organized in a structure of rigorous hierarchies. Hence the high value set on the virtue of obedience, enshrined in the life of the monastic order. The ultimate effort to express this unitary form of society was the Holy Roman Empire, which in practice was none of the things its name suggests. The ideal was noble, even sublime; but perhaps, in the human condition, unrealizable. As the Middle Ages advanced, the stress on organic unity degenerated into absolutism. Such unity as was achieved tended to be mechanical rather than organic, while political motives overcame the primacy of the spiritual.

[1] Jacques Maritain, *True Humanism*, pp. 121-204, Geoffrey Bles, London, 1938.

The primacy of politics found its prophet in Machiavelli, its slogan in *cuius regio eius religio*. A last-ditch effort to save the primitive, unitary concept produced, in the Counter-Reformation, an absolutist reaction. Its prophet was Ignatius Loyola, whose heroic will set out to bend all energies, through the hierarchical structures, to the service of charity and God's greater glory. In this view, the monarch was no longer a *vices gerens multitudinis*, but derived his authority straight from God – that is to say, it was not routed through the popular will. Self-immolation through obedience became the brightest star in the Ignatian firmament. But it was too late to do more than stem the tide. The corporations had become rich, oppressive, despotic and regressive. Disenchanted with organic solutions, men began to look to themselves. Nationalism and liberalism proclaimed the individual and his opinions as the source of right and truth. The formula worked as a rejoinder to reaction, but did not offer a new sense of direction to society. Its free-for-all spirit ran amok in the age of industrial capitalism, and a cancerous state of social injustice revived the call to transform society, to give it a new coherence and identity. So there arose another 'counter-reformation', this time in the form of the dictatorship of the proletariat; a new, materialist absolutism in which the state imprints its anonymous visage on the obedient multitude. Lenin became the Loyola of his day, but with society, not God, for his centre of gravity. In the struggle to recapture organic unity, however, the new system overspilled and became collective and standardized. Other totalitarian systems arose in competition, Fascism hinging on the state, National Socialism on the race.

Now the world has to think again, and try again: to find a way for freedom and unity to harmonize. One way involves a total rejection of dogma, whether Marxist or Christian: an anarchistic search for truth through revolution. The Christian search, on the other hand, is for a theocentric humanism, or a theological anthropology, hinging, not on a *sacrum imperium*, but on the liberty of the creature united by grace to God. This involves an organism, but one with a far wider scope for pluralism than the unitary theme of the Middle Ages allowed. Then, pluralism simply meant a multiplicity of jurisdictions and a diversity of customary law. Now it must mean a new organic heterogeneity: a diversity of groups and social structures incarnating positive liberties. Society should be seen as composed, not just of individuals, but of particular societies formed by them – each group enjoying as much autonomy as possible. The diversity is part of the structure, not an infrastructure of the monolith. The unifying principle will lie, not in a common profession of faith, but in that field where believers of all kinds and unbelievers can find common cause in their common human nature (as Pope John XXIII was to put it).[1]

Maritain's account of the historical process may or may not commend itself, but what he says of the modern Christian approach accords with the thought of the modern popes and the Second Vatican Council, whereas what he says of the 'monarchical' concept of the Church and religion exactly describes the mind of Salazar. The Council accepted the growing role of the state in an age of increasing complexity, but held to the limitations of the subsidiarity principle. Though never exposed to Jesuit influence, Salazar's own instincts were undoubtedly Ignatian: the emphasis on authority, obedience, hierarchy, the dread of national fragmentation, the attempt to recapture the unitary ideal through a closely-knit discipline. He saw in theory that the freedoms implied by pluralism constitute basic human rights, and that the individual's right to share in decisions affecting his life are not to be sunk in a plea for obedience. The life of total obedience may be chosen by the monk; it cannot be imposed on the nation. Salazar would have been the first to say that the state must serve the people, not the reverse. But in practice, while admiring it in others, he did not believe that Portugal could run a social democracy based on the parliamentary party. His solution was the corporative state, and it may have been because of subconscious fears that the principle might prove to be unworkable that he never brought himself to test it fully. Equally, the wholesale education required for wholly active corporativism was slowed down by his financial policies. To this indictment he would doubtless enter a plea of *force majeure*.

Part of the purpose of this analysis has been to expose the differences between Salazar's ideas and Mussolini's. Whatever descriptions Salazar may deserve, Fascist is not one of them. Admittedly, despotism, benign or otherwise, always inhibits liberties, and it may be felt that at the end of the day, labels are unimportant. Yet among the various authoritarian systems there are differences of spirit which affect the people who live under them. To see this is essential for any balanced judgment of Salazar himself and of what he has made of his country.

[1] Pope John XXIII, *Pacem in Terris*, pp. 56-7, Catholic Truth Society, London, 1963.

CHAPTER 13

Portugal Today

No sense of propriety can alter the fact that Salazar's epitaph has to be written soon. This book, it is hoped, may be a contribution towards it. He is neither a saint nor a sinner beyond recall, but he has been one of the most extraordinary men to walk across this century's history, a man of power and vision with obstinate limitations, a scholar who could shape national destinies, a poor man who knew how to handle the wealth he despised, a half-recluse who could weep for those he burdened, a man in whom pride and humility constantly fought for the mastery. He has left an indelible mark on Portugal, Europe and Africa, and attracted more hatred and adulation than rulers of much larger nations. Whatever history says of him, it cannot disregard him. To understand his significance, one has to compare the Portugal of 1928 with what she is today, her strengths and weaknesses then and now. A feature that won a lot of dislike was his uncanny, ironical way of seeing through other people's ideals, his hatred of fashionable slogans. Was this shrewdness or cynicism? For himself, he said at the start: 'I know quite well what I want and where I am going.' He would probably ask to be judged in pragmatic terms. As he said to a Lisbon reception in April 1935:

> I do not hide, nor do I minimize, the difficulties of those systems which do not exploit the passions but rather address themselves to the highest qualities in man. It was rather to emphasize those difficulties that I have mentioned them. It is, however, in the interests of truth and necessity that we should not yield to tendencies or suggestions that would drag us again into that arena of competition and artifice recognized by all as the root of mediocrity where not long since we were floundering, and out of which we have painfully struggled.

Salazar was always a financier rather than an economist, yet current developments are in a sense a natural follow-up to his work rather than a total break with it. What the young technocrats really disapproved of was the slowness of the advance, the fear of injecting inflationary stimuli, and the sacrifice of industrial growth to financial stability. The Portuguese economy today must risk a measure of over-heating. The key to it all is stepped-up investment, the encouragement of foreign capital, and the provision of medium- and long-term credit for expansion. As has been said, Salazar had already begun to move in this direction, but it was not until April 1969, seven months after his first illness, that measures were introduced to provide for export credits and insurance. Under the new regulations, short-term credits, some of which have been kept alive by renewals, can now be channelled into medium-term arrangements. Differential discount rates have been introduced: 2¼ per cent for export bills (a completely new departure) and 2½ per cent for further- ing imports of capital equipment, raw materials and essential foods. The modest bank rate of 3 per cent now applies to loans secured by shares or bonds quoted on the Stock Exchange, and on bank loans to credit institutions for up to 180 days. Loans can be granted for up to five years if production can thus be stimulated. The scope of the principal credit institution, the *Caixa Geral de Depositos*, has been widened, and the new *Companhia de Seguros de Creditos* can issue insurances covering up to 85 per cent of the goods or services involved in export transactions. The government allotted 3 billion escudos for new investments in 1969, with a further 2.5 billion to come from local authorities or other public funds, if the options were taken up.

It will be as well to take a brief look at the Portuguese economy as a whole. The population of metropolitan Portugal in 1967 was 9,440,000, with a gross national product of £1,925 million and £204 *per capita* (the second lowest *per capita* rate in Europe). In the third quarter of 1968, gold and foreign reserves stood at 35,750 million escudos (£533 million)[1], two-thirds of it in gold. The nation's *per capita* income has risen from £74 in 1959 to £135 in 1966 (as against £237 in Spain and £539 in Britain), and again to £184.45 in 1968. Agriculture accounts for 34 per cent of the labour force, but only 17 per cent of the gross national product.

[1] Portugal did not devalue her currency after the 1967 devaluation of sterling. The rate of exchange in midsummer 1969, was 69 escudos to the £.

Trade figures in 1968 showed:

	£ million
Exports to Britain	74.3
Imports from Britain[1]	59.7
All exports	306.0
All imports	435.0

Exports were up by 4.4 per cent, but this represented only half their rate of growth the year before, while a 2 per cent drop in imports was insufficient. However, the trading deficit of £129 million was 6.6 per cent less than in 1967, and trade has more than doubled since 1960. Exports consist mainly of primary products or those which require a minimum of 'transformation'. Some of the leading commodities exported include cork, tinned fish, wine, wood products, tomato paste and textiles. Leading imports include machinery, raw materials, foodstuffs and consumer goods. Exports to Portugal's EFTA[2] partners have risen 400 per cent since the association was formed in 1960. Her dealings abroad can be shown as follows:

Exports		Imports	
	Per cent		Per cent
To EFTA	33.6	From EEC	34.2
Portugal Overseas	25.4	EFTA	23.1
EEC[3]	16.8	Portugal Overseas	15.4
OECD[4]	15.6	OECD	13.0
Others	9.6	Others	14.3

Exports rose by 109.2 per cent from 9,048 million escudos in 1960 to 19,685 million in 1967, while imports rose by 96.5 per cent from 15,695 million to 29,130 million.

Portugal's traditional balance of payments surplus is achieved by a regular metropolitan surplus on invisibles, including tourist receipts and emigrants' remittances, and on the overseas provinces'

---

[1] Britain takes 20 per cent of all Portugal's exports, but as Portugal's principal supplier has lost her place to Germany.
[2] European Free Trade Area.
[3] European Economic Community.
[4] Organisation for Economic Co-operation and Development.

trade with the outside world. Thus the balance of payments for the whole escudo area has developed thus:

Current Account

1964:	+ 482 million escudos
1965:	− 991 million escudos
1966:	+1,588 million escudos
1967:	+3,880 million escudos

After the devaluation of sterling, tourist receipts dropped considerably and in 1969 are expected to be 25 per cent less than in 1968. But the current Development Plan aims to give the tourist trade its biggest boost to date. Defence accounts for over 42 per cent of the Budget and 7 per cent of the gross national product. The labour supply has been reasonably adequate and its quality is high. Portuguese workers are also very flexible and accept the concept of labour mobility and the need to change one's skills to adapt to new industry with a facility that more prosperous Western countries envy. Heavy emigration, however, and the needs of the army now dangerously imperil the expanding need for industrial labour.[1] Agricultural labour is at such a high premium that wages in that sector leaped by 20 per cent in 1968. The need for workers at home has to be balanced against the advantage of emigrants' remittances to the balance of payments, but it is growing more and more urgent, and the Development Plan envisages a substantial increase in special vocational training for adults. Top management in Portugal varies, but at its best is as good as anywhere else. Weak management usually goes with firms which have grown lazy in an over-protected domestic market and supply goods of indifferent quality, unable to compete effectively abroad. Perhaps the biggest problem lies with middle management, and the language is a barrier to an easy solution by way of 'importing' managers.

Before 1966, Portugal's average growth rate was one of the highest in Europe (8 per cent). But 1966 was a bad year. There was a certain sluggishness in European trade, bad weather affected crops disastrously, and this combined with Portugal's deflationary monetary measures and poor capital market yielded a growth rate of only 3 per cent, less than half the rate prescribed for the gross domestic product by the Interim Plan of 1964-7. The period 1968-9 has seen

[1] It is difficult to assess the rate of emigration as some of it is clandestine. But a fair figure for 1966 is 120,000 and some would put it at 150,000.

no more than a growth of 5 per cent, but it is hoped to raise this to 7 per cent under the current Plan. The money is there for expansion, and indeed one of Portugal's major problems has been an excess liquidity.

Private investment is still modest and constitutes one of Caetano's biggest problems. He is urging all firms to put themselves on a competitive basis and offers a welcome to foreign investors. The Plan looks for a 9 per cent expansion rate for the manufacturing industries, with special stress on engineering, new chemical industries, the processing of agriculture and forestry products, and textiles. The bulk of foreign investment at present – there are 600 foreign firms operating in Portugal – comes from Holland, Belgium, Sweden and Japan, focusing on clothing, electronic equipment and car assembly. German, American and British firms are also active, while Nippon is prospecting for copper in Angola. The limited number of major projects now developing in metropolitan Portugal include the new SACOR refinery near Oporto which should in the end yield 4,000,000 tons a year; the expansion of the national steelworks, the *Siderurgia Nacional*, which produced 600,000 tons in 1969 and aims to double this and more by 1974; the expansion of tourist facilities; and the development of the LISNAVE shipyard, whose workers, within a decade, expect to achieve wage parity with Western Europe. The important textile industry has been hit by current British restrictions on imports, and the government is offering to convert short-term to long-term borrowing provided that the firm's equipment and management are up to standard. Tax concessions are available for mergers, but only if obsolete plant is replaced within two years. The Plan aims at replacing half the industry's equipment by 1973. Textiles account for a labour force of 72,000. Between 1964 and 1967, imports dropped from £44.7 million to £40.8 million, while exports rose from £48.2 million to £68.3 million.

Membership of EFTA has been of enormous importance to Portugal, especially as it allows her concessions not available to the other partners. Under this arrangement, Portugal's tariffs on a wide range of goods have been cut by only 40 per cent. This has to be increased to 50 per cent in 1970 and to 100 per cent by 1980. So, while infant industries have so far been protected, there is now no ground for undue protection against the demand for modernization. EFTA markets have provided important outlets for Portugal's textiles, clothing and footwear. In 1960, exports to EFTA covered only 60 per cent of imports, today they exceed them by 3 per cent. For some time, Portugal has had a request for association with the EEC on the table, but is not pressing it very hard. Its effects today would be very uncertain, and some of the advantages reaped from the EFTA involvement would certainly disappear. The EEC, moreover, is unlikely to admit Portugal to any form of association until her political institutions are freer, and as matters stand, Angola and Mozambique could hardly fit into the Yaounde Convention involving the eighteen African states now associated with the Six. If Britain enters the Common Market and her EFTA partners follow suit to any degree, Portugal will be exposed to the fiercest competition. However, as the OECD Report put it in 1966:

> Despite the continuing high levels of military expenditure and the increased effort required to finance productive investment in the overseas provinces, there are at present great possibilities for rapid economic growth in metropolitan Portugal. There are some basic favourable conditions – i.e. large potential domestic savings, a strong balance of payments and comparatively high foreign reserves. But the present substantial emigration of workers to more industrialized countries illustrates the need to speed up economic development and the creation of adequate employment opportunities.

The Report made a number of strong anti-deflationary recommendations which have now begun to bear fruit, but there is an increasing doubt about how long the military expenditure can really be allowed to burden the Budget when there is such an urgent need, not only for industrial growth, but also for improved social services.

The 1968-73 Development Plan envisages a total investment of 167,480 million escudos (£2,700 million), four times as much as the Interim Plan of 1965-7, even when adjustment is made for the difference in the number of years involved. The first Plan, for 1953-8, gave pride of place to infrastructures, the second to the growth of the national product and the standard of living, the third (interim) to trading with EFTA and EEC. The current Plan envisages a 7 per cent rise in the growth rate each year, with the main stress on industry, and with transport, communications and agriculture following on. Aims include establishing more equality among the different regions, an increase of private consumption at the rate of 5.9 per cent a year to £1,600 million by 1973. The twenty-five training centres existing in 1967, will be more than doubled. While manufacturing should rise by 9 per cent annually, the figure for electricity, gas and water is 9.5 per cent, with 3 per cent for agriculture and forestry. Tourism, construction and the manufacturing industries are the dominant themes. Of the total investment, 123,000 million escudos will go to metropolitan Portugal,[1] 44,480 million to the overseas provinces. Substantial tax concessions are offered to foreign investors, especially for new industries in under-developed rural zones and regional development schemes.

Agriculture suffers from bad structures, traditional harvesting of low-yield crops, and too little investment in fruit growing and stock breeding. Where crops are concerned, 1 per cent of the land-holding covers half the arable area. In the south, rural workers have had to scrape a bare living on huge landed estates owned by the wealthy few, while in the north the problem has been how to persuade large numbers of small-holders to merge their holdings or even to combine for marketing and the purchase of modern equipment. A degree of progress has been achieved, but grain yields are the lowest in Europe. The £80 million irrigation of the Alentejo, now forging ahead with German investment, should raise production in the affected areas from a level of £35,000 a year to £670,000. There has also been a huge increase in the wine trade, with exports totalling £20 million in 1967. Portugal also supplies half the world's cork consumption, and it is here that the programme of afforestation over the years has borne fruit. The number of tractors has risen by two-thirds in five years, but by the end of 1966, was still under 18,000. On the other hand, the effect of the grants for mechanization offered in 1968 should see some early improvement in the modernization of farming

---

[1] The metropolitan programme is as follows:

	Million Escudos
Agriculture, forestry, stock-raising	14,600
Fisheries	1,842
Mining and manufacturing	31,150
Rural improvement schemes	2,880
Electrical power	17,607
Transport, communication, meteorology	27,090
Housing and town planning	8,050
Tourism	11,850
Education and research	5,643
Health	2,338
	123,050

techniques. The real problem is the social and educational backwardness of the peasant farmer, who as matters stand is reluctant to change
his traditional ways. While crop and cereal yields remain below par,
however, a degree of progress has been made, not only in the vineyards and forestry, but also in the olive groves and fisheries. Agricultural products accounted, in 1963, for 41 per cent of all exports.
The figure for 1967 was 27.9 per cent, a change which reflects the
growth of industry. But in absolute terms, there is ample scope for
agricultural development.

   Portugal will have to work hard. Exports to Britain and France are
down, and these countries account for a quarter of Portugal's export
transactions. At home, family allowances were increased last year,
together with other social benefits, and it all has to be paid for.
The potential is there, but so are the wage demands, and such
competitiveness as Portugal can show abroad today depends in part
on her low wage levels. In such circumstances, foreign investment
is important, not only in terms of finance, but also in terms of the
technical and managerial know-how that comes with it. The achievements of the Portuguese worker to date, in the building of hydro-
electric schemes, for instance, prove that he can do the job – given the
right direction and training.

Though Portugal remains, by European standards, a poor country,
the worker's standard of living has risen beyond comparison with
his lot ten years ago, at least so far as the skilled man is concerned.
Craftsmen today can command relatively high figures, and one of
the outstanding features of recent years has been the emergence of
a stabilizing lower middle-class, with increased purchasing power.
The small motor car and the motor cycle are the symbols of improved
status and earnings, though, as in Spain, too many people are trying
to do two jobs to keep abreast of the neighbours. The beggars who
used to roam the city streets have now largely disappeared, and it is fair
to say that in Portugal today there is no longer any outright hunger,
though the diet may seem rudimentary by some Western standards.
It still turns largely on fish. Between 1960 and 1966, agricultural
wages rose by 89 per cent and factory wages by 39. Between 1961
and 1967, the average increase in real terms was an annual 3 per cent
in Lisbon and 4·5 per cent in Oporto for the whole of industry, and
7 per cent for the manufacturing and construction sectors. In 1968,
overall industrial wages rose by 7 per cent, agricultural wages by

20 per cent. All of which, together with improved social benefits, stimulates consumption and purchases of foreign durables, and is a spur to modernization. On the whole, wages have kept well ahead of prices, which have been rising at an average of 2.5 per cent a year since 1965, but in the last quarter of 1968 they had risen by 7 per cent over the same period for the year before. Whereas, in the period 1963-8, consumer prices rose in Spain by 44 per cent, the corresponding figure for Portugal was 24 per cent. The figures[1] taken from the

[1] *Comparisons of Per Capita Income in 1965 (in dollars)*

Portugal	377
Britain	1,451
Italy	883
Spain	594
Greece	566

The Portuguese figure has now increased to 442.68 (1968). The figure which, in 1962, Delgado so rightly and bitterly complained about was 182.

Growth of wages in industry (including transforming industries)

	Lisbon		Oporto	
	Nominal (per cent)	Real (per cent)	Nominal (per cent)	Real (per cent)
1963	5.1	2.9	4.0	2.2
1964	4.6	1.2	7.2	3.6
1965	5.8	2.3	11.9	7.3
1966	8.0	2.8	10.9	3.5
1967	8.51	2.8	11.0	6.3

Rural Wages (percentage growth)

	Men	Women
1963	5.1	4.0
1964	12.1	12.5
1965	6.5	7.4
1966	16.8	14.9
1967	9.9	10.8
1968	18.8	15.9

The overall division of incomes works out at 44.3 per cent to wages, and 55.7 per cent to profits and dividends.

Cost of Living Index

1963	100
1964	103
1965	108
1966	112
1967	119
1968	124

National Accounts (published by the Institute of Statistics, Lisbon) and the U.N. Yearbook of National Account Statistics (1966), give some idea of the way the standard of living has progressed. The advance, if not dramatic, is solid.

Health services, too, have improved slowly, and today more than half the population is covered by some form of insurance; this should rise to three-quarters by the end of the current Plan. There is still a shortage of doctors, partly because of the expense of the medical courses in the university, not to mention their length. Ten years ago, Portugal had only one doctor for every 1,400 people. Latest figures in the U.N. Statistical Year Book show that by 1965 the comparative situation was as follows:

Average number of inhabitants per doctor

Portugal	1,180 (1,129 today)
Austria	550
France	900
Holland	860

Portugal's figures for adult deaths (the crude death rate) are roughly average for Europe: worse than in Italy, Holland, Spain and Greece; a little better than in Austria, Belgium and even Britain and Germany. In terms of infant mortality (under the age of one), however, Portugal shows up very badly. Her 1953 figure of 95.5 per thousand has been reduced to 59, but the 1966 European average was about 30. Portugal's infant deaths are mostly due to diseases of the digestive organs, and there is now an energetic drive to build clinics all over the country to try and defeat this tendency. Overall expectation of life at the time of birth has improved in a decade from 49 years to 60.7 for men and 66.3 for women (1962), while the average European figure was 67 for men and 72.3 for women. In 1964, there were 170 people per hospital bed (as against 250 in 1952), while the figure for England and Wales, and France, was 120, for Germany 90, for Italy 100, and for Sweden 70. In Greece it was 180. Average intake of calories in 1951-54 was only 2,350 daily (95.5 per cent of minimum needs). By 1963 it had risen to 2,550 (3.7 per cent over the minimum) and it now stands at 3,000. In 1963, Portugal's average of 103.7 per cent of the minimum contrasted with the European average of 116 per cent.

As regards medical treatment today, workers who are employed in industry are well insured by the *Caixas de Previdência e Abono e Família*, organizations run by mixed boards of employers' and workers' representatives. This insurance supplies free medical care and three-quarters of the cost of drugs, which in Portugal are very expensive. Hospitalization is free and teams of doctors are available for urgent and night calls. Workers' requirements are met in accordance with the provisions of the ILO Convention, No. 102 of 1952. Sick benefit amounts to 60 per cent of wages. Workers in the major firms, like SACOR or the mammoth *Companhia União Fabril* (*CUF*), which has fifty subsidiary companies in a wide variety of leading industries, insurance and banking, and an annual turnover of £150 million, are exceptionally well looked after, and enjoy special arrangements made by their firms in addition to the state-organized insurances. In rural areas and the fishing communities, medical care is more haphazard. *Casas de Povo* and *Casas dos Pescadores* theoretically correspond to the urban Caixas, but doctors and hospital beds are harder to come by. People who are not covered by these formal arrangements, whether in town or in the country, depend on charity medical services and hospitals associated with the *Misericordia* organization, and a number of Church and parish bodies, some of which are very energetic. Doctors rarely refuse to treat the poor for nothing, but such patients need charity help to buy the prescribed drugs. State ambulance services are very good, and few sick people in Portugal today need go altogether unattended. Charity bodies have to cater for other needs as well, however, for, although there are family allowances, there are as yet no old age pension or ordinary unemployment benefit schemes.[1]

In an article published in 1968, by a former Minister of Education, Dr Veiga da Maçedo, it was estimated that the illiteracy rate had dropped from 61.8 per cent in 1930 to 40.4 per cent in 1950 (the figure that is usually quoted by foreign critics). Today, the writer believed, only 7.9 per cent of those under forty were illiterate, while the overall percentage was 15-18 per cent. All children of the appropriate age now go to primary school. The 1960 census found that only 34.6 per cent of the population had received primary education, 4.4 per cent had attended secondary schools, and 1.2 per cent had pursued higher studies. Illiteracy among the working population was 31.2 per cent. The past nine years have therefore seen a substantial advance.

Official statistics for 1968-9 show that 1,350,000 students attend

[1] Health statistics from the U.N. Demographic Year Book, Statistical Year Book and Compendium of Social Statistics.

schools and higher institutes, and in higher education there has been a 7 per cent increase in recent years. The university population (1967) was:

Coimbra	7,646
Lisbon (academic)	11,131
Lisbon (technical)	5,911
Oporto	5,368

The total of 30,056 represented 0.35 per cent of the total population, and has now risen to 38,000. The 1968-9 figures for attendance at school and other courses, excluding vocational training centres and kindergartens, are as follows:

Ciclo Preparatorio[1]	44,000
Grammar schools	40,000
Technical schools	100,000
Telescola (adults)	25,000
Primary	910,000
	1,119,000

There is little in the way of state provision for scholarships to secondary schools and universities, but grants can be obtained from bodies like the Gulbenkian Foundation, which has made a major contribution to Portuguese education, and provides bursaries for exceptionally able students to pursue post-graduate courses abroad. It is probably true to say that, if a boy or girl shows promise, he or she will, one way or another, receive education beyond the primary stage, if all concerned are willing to make special efforts. A friend of the author's, for instance, who is a taxi-driver, has sent his son and daughter to secondary schools, and the son, after army service, is likely to go to university. All this has involved the father in heavy sacrifices, including working all the hours he can without endangering his passengers. This is a common enough story in modern Portugal, but emphasizes the tragedy of having to spend 40 per cent of the Budget on defence, when so many promising youngsters are lining up for limited opportunities. The 1966 UNESCO Statistical Yearbook offers the following comparative figures (the first stage is the 5-14 age group, the second stage the 15-19 group, but, as the basic figures relate to courses rather than age groups, and the length of the courses

---

[1] This is an intermediate course between primary and secondary levels.

varies from country to country, an adjusted ratio is provided to yield a true comparison):

Ratio of school enrolment to school age population (1964)

	First stage (%)	Second stage (%)	Combined figure (%)	Adjusted ratio (%)
Austria	61	56	60	69
Belgium	65	142	85	106
France	60	118	72	91
Germany	75	77	76	88
Greece	63	54	60	75
Holland	55	112	71	88
Portugal	52	41	49	67
Spain	73	35	59	73
England and Wales	61	144	86	93

From all the above statistical data it is easy to see how Salazar's policy has worked out. Social and educational services have advanced fairly steadily, but slowly. So far as Salazar was concerned, the nation had to tighten its belt and not live on credit. It had to wait for advances until it could pay for them. Meanwhile, the people had to cling together and stick it out. Against that background, the profits earned by the wealthy companies offer a striking contrast, yet, in Salazar's thinking, it was through their development that the country would haul itself up by the boot-straps. The theory may be open to a wide range of criticisms, yet in a way it has worked – at the price of one generation sacrificing itself for the next. The trouble is that the world is moving fast, and Portugal cannot view her situation in isolation from the rest. The tempo of development now must multiply, if it is to glimpse the prospect of catching up in the end with Europe. In all fairness, however, the poverty, degradation and internal confusion of Portugal in 1928 was so bad that, if Salazar had not assumed office, Portugal might have become by now a province of Spain. There are those who favour a unitary Iberia. The Portuguese do not.

It has been hard to talk about Salazar's last years of power without seeming to disregard him. With the eruption of the African question, Portugal stood almost alone against the onslaughts of the Afro-Asian

bloc and the disapproval of much of the West, and with the rise of
Franco Nogueira, a Portuguese voice other than Salazar's was heard
upon the international stage. Its tone was the right blend of logic and
aggression, showing a single-minded purpose, indeed, yet with under-
tones of a flexibility foreign to Salazar. Franco Nogueira's speeches
in the United Nations, spoken in fluent English, are masterpieces
of their kind, and his unofficial relations with those whose job it is
to attack him in the Chamber may be shown one day to have made a
contribution to history. His openness with the press has made him
something rare in Portuguese circles: a newsman's man. Yet, while
Franco Nogueira was never just 'his master's voice', and in some
respects was his master's teacher (which few ministers managed to
be), the country's foreign policy in the 1960s has borne the imprint
of Salazar's vision as truly as it did in the Second World War. Between
them, these two men have made a formidable team, the one in his
seventies, the other in his forties, and for ten years they have with-
stood a barrage of world opposition which few small powers could
survive.

The fruits are now being reaped. Portugal is not under the diplomatic pressures now which a few years ago seemed implacable. It
has been said that it was Salazar's master-stroke to keep the Americans
in the Azores on a day-to-day basis, and that U.S. opposition to
Portugal in the United Nations changed on that account. This is
only part of the story. The United States, even in President Kennedy's
time, was not prepared to back the more extreme and unrealistic
anti-Portuguese motions. State Department attitudes have become
more reflective and mellow, and some officials are willing to say that
perhaps insufficient attention was paid to the Portuguese argument
in the turbulent days of 1961. The State Department stands by the
principle that people should have the right to determine their own
futures, and it would doubtless respond happily if a dateline for self-
determination were established for Portuguese Africa. But it does
not seek to impose a specific method or timetable on Lisbon, and,
once Portuguese Africa was re-established on lines acceptable to
world opinion, it would be anxious to channel such aid as it could
to further an evolution there. American business men with African
interests obviously tend to favour the white man's stand, but there is a
section of official opinion in the United States which is willing to see
that the Portuguese have a distinctive contribution to make in
Africa, while convinced that a programme of self-determination

would do as much good to Portugal as to the African peoples concerned.[1]

Relations with France and Germany have been constantly strengthened over the past few years, notably through increasing trade and investment, and a number of French and German statesmen, including Dr Kiesinger, have visited Lisbon. President De Gaulle was naturally well disposed, but Portugal's potential in Europe and Africa, and through her links with Brazil, has attracted European attention, and Germany is now Portugal's main supplier, quite apart from her investment in the Alentejo and the Krupps organization's involvement in the Angolan iron-ore industry. As we have seen, it was a Franco-German consortium which won the Cabora-Bassa contract. Portugal has been hurt by the Spanish African policy which has denied to Lisbon the support it had hoped to receive from Madrid, and which may have a bearing on the unfriendliness of some South American countries. It is, however, recognized that Spain's own position in Africa was very different from Portugal's, and relations, though strained, are far from breaking-point. Belgian and Italian hostility has mollified in recent years, and, though liberal Holland opposes Portuguese policy overseas and Sweden is bitterly hostile, Dutch and especially Swedish business concerns have important stakes in the Portuguese economy. Relations with Britain have eased and Anglo-Portuguese trade continues to rise, but a British writer is bound to regret the failure of the British bid for Cabora-Bassa, which doubtless bore some relation to political uncertainties. Until the Rhodesian question is settled, some tensions must remain.

Marcello Caetano officially visited Brazil last year. Though hallmarked by a basic Portuguese culture, the Brazilians have long since developed their own identity, and tend to feel nettled when Portugal points to Brazil as her gift to the world. Today, the prospects for Brazil's economy seem almost limitless, while Portugal in Europe stays near the bottom of the league. Relations have varied in tune with changes in the Brazilian government. The present Brazilian leadership, right-wing and partly military, is better disposed to Portugal than some others have been. It seems, however, to be in the grip of United States advisers who urge deflationary policies, perhaps to protect United

[1] The Nixon administration's statement on its African policy, issued in March 1969, while standing for self-determination in Portuguese Africa, added that the absence of apartheid policies there had to be seen as an important factor in the equation.

States imports, when Brazil should be developing her own untapped resources and creating new jobs for the masses. The government there is supported by those middle-class Catholics who seem to lack all social conscience in the teeth of the workers' grinding poverty, and it dreads the dynamic movements among the clergy and workers for radical social reforms. The militant leader, Archbishop Helder Camara of Recife, is especially hated, though he rejects the path of violence, and he has been banned from the radio. One of his closest associates, a young university chaplain, was recently murdered horribly by extremists. Twenty progressive bishops and ten times as many priests are known to be under police surveillance, and, on the eve of Caetano's departure for Rio, two Catholic Portuguese workers' groups sent a message urging him to wait until the Brazilian government changed its approach to the Catholic Church. Caetano's own attitude doubtless is that talking to people does more good than ostracism, and that Portugal's future is at stake. Enthusiasm for stronger links between Brazil and Portugal is probably stronger on the Portuguese side, and, while the dramatic boom in Angola's economic prospects may have given new life to the old political dream of a link between South America and Africa, it also posits new rivalries between these South Atlantic powers. It is said that Brazilian statesmen fuss over Lisbon to attract the votes of Brazilians whose Portuguese origins are more recent and whose links with the Portuguese are more direct. Yet there is more to it than this. Even when mixed, blood stays thicker than water. Portugal and Brazil take a common pride in what they regard as their special understanding of 'tropical man'; both respond to the 'luso-tropicalism' of Gilberto Freyre, the Brazilian anthropologist, which, despite its mythical overtones and quasi-mystical language, is at worst a doubtful synthesis of authentic observable fact, and at best represents the optimistic and aspirational side of the Portuguese character.

Inter-racialism in Brazil is relative. Though often impressive in prosperous urban centres, it acquires another hue in the poverty-stricken north where the Negro's condition recalls the days of slavery. In their weaknesses, as in their strengths, however, the two countries doubtless find common ground: the inter-racial dream has never been completely achieved in either, yet. In the hope that some day it will, there is much to be said for the vision of a Portugal serving in some way as a natural link between continents: Europe, Africa and South America, with still a tiny foothold in the East. The little

Portuguese island of Macao, off the mainland Chinese coast, has had its troubles in recent years, and Portugal's continuing presence there is attributed to the forbearance she has now had to show to the Chinese Communists, after years of receiving refugees from the mainland. If the disturbances of some years ago have not been repeated recently, it is said to be because of a paradox: that the Portuguese, of all people, have established a working *modus vivendi* with the Communists in Macao for the present. There may have been a capitulation here, and refugees are no longer received. Yet Mao's China depends on the Portuguese presence for one of her few sources of gold and foreign exchange.

Oddly enough, it was Mao himself who once said that the only people who really understood the inter-racial theme were the Portuguese. There was a stage, indeed, in 1961, when Portugal nearly took a quota of Chinese immigrants into Angola from Formosa, but it came to nothing for fear of angering Peking. Yet the suggestion was consistent with Portugal's preparedness for any sort of racially mixed society provided it existed within the framework of a distinct and independent nation. A racially mixed nationalism is not an exclusively Portuguese dream, but what this book has tried to suggest is that Portugal has it in her to give the concept a living form more easily than many, probably than most.

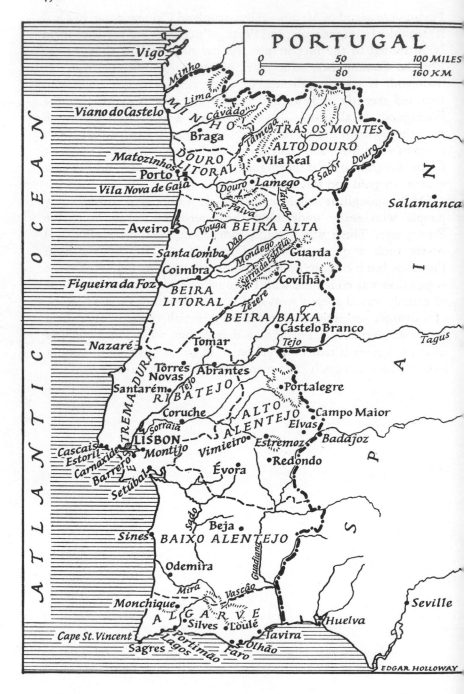

PORTUGAL

| 0 | 50 | 100 MILES |
| 0 | 80 | 160 KM |

Vigo

Minho

Lima

MINHO

Cávado

Braga

DOURO LITORAL

Viano do Castelo

Matozinhos

Porto

Vila Nova de Gaia

Tâmega

TRÁS OS MONTES

ALTO DOURO

Vila Real

Douro

Sabôr

Douro

Lamego

Távora

Paiva

SPAIN

Salamanca

Aveiro

Vouga

BEIRA ALTA

Dão

Santa Comba

Mondego

Guarda

Coimbra

Serra da Estrela

Covilhã

Figueira da Foz

BEIRA LITORAL

Tézere

BEIRA BAIXA

Cástelo Branco

Nazaré

Tomar

Tejo

Tejo

Tagus

ESTREMADURA

Tôrres Novas

Abrantes

Santarém

Tejo

RIBATEJO

Portalegre

Coruche

ALTO ALENTEJO

Campo Maior

Elvas

Cascais

Estoril

Carnaxide

Sorraia

LISBON

Montijo

Vimieiro

Estremoz

Badájoz

Barreiro

Setúbal

Évora

Redondo

Sado

Beja

BAIXO ALENTEJO

Odemira

Guadiana

Sines

Mira

Vascão

Seville

Monchique

ALGARVE

Silves

Loulé

Cape St.Vincent

Sagres

Lagos

Portimão

Faro

Olhão

Tavira

Huelva

ATLANTIC OCEAN

EDGAR HOLLOWAY

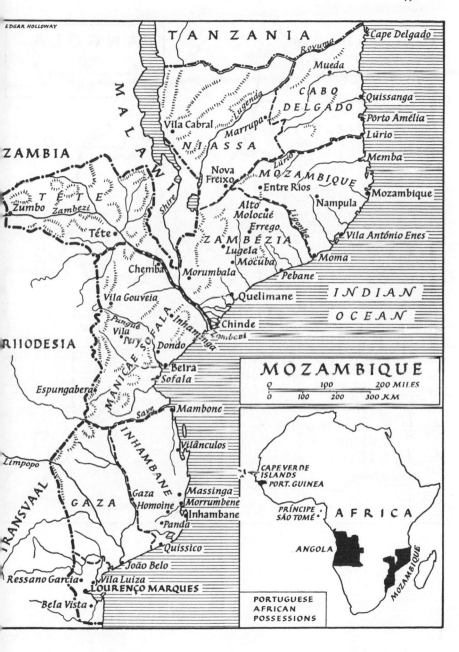

EDGAR HOLLOWAY

TANZANIA

Cape Delgado

Rovuma

Mueda

MALAWI

CABO
DELGADO

Quissanga

Lugenda

Pörto Amélia

Vila Cabral

Marrupa

Lúrio

NIASSA

Memba

Lúrio

Nova
Freixo

MOZAMBIQUE

Entre Rios

Mozambique

Ligonha

Nampula

ZAMBIA

Alto
Molocué

Shire

Errego

Vila António Enes

TÉTE

ZAMBÉZIA

Zumbo

Zambezi

Lugela

Mocuba

Moma

Téte

Chemba

Morumbala

Pebane

Vila Gouveia

Quelimane

INDIAN

Pungué

Chinde

OCEAN

RHODESIA

Vila
Pery

Inhamissa

Zambesi

Dondo

Espungabera

MANICA E SOFALA

Belra

Sofala

MOZAMBIQUE

0   100   200 MILES

0   100   200   300 KM

Save

Mambone

Vilânculos

INHAMBANE

Limpopo

CAPE VERDE
ISLANDS

PORT. GUINEA

Massinga

TRANSVAAL

GAZA

Gaza

Morrumbene

Homoine

Inhambane

Panda

PRÍNCIPE
SÃO TOMÉ

AFRICA

Quissico

ANGOLA

Ressano Garcia

João Belo

Vila Luiza

LOURENÇO MARQUES

MOZAMBIQUE

Bela Vista

PORTUGUESE
AFRICAN
POSSESSIONS

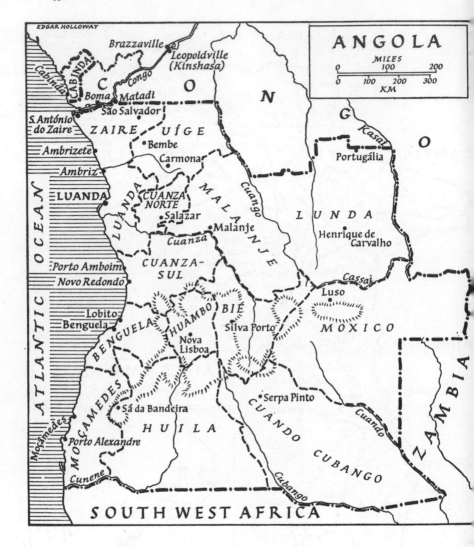

EDGAR HOLLOWAY

ANGOLA

MILES
0   100   200

0   100   200   300
KM

Brazzaville
Leopoldville
(Kinshasa)
Cabinda
CABINDA
Congo
C
Boma Matadi
São Salvador
S. António
do Zaire
ZAIRE
UÍGE
Ambrizete
Bembe
Carmona
Ambriz
LUANDA
LUANDA
CUANZA
NORTE
Salazar
Cuanza
CUANZA-
SUL
Porto Amboim
Novo Redondo
Lobito
Benguela
BENGUELA
HUAMBO
Nova
Lisboa
MOÇAMEDES
Sá da Bandeira
HUILA
Porto Alexandre
Cunene
MALANJE
Cuango
Malanje
BIÉ
Silva Porto
Serpa Pinto
CUANDO
CUBANGO
Cubango
Cubango

C
O
N
G
O
Kasai
Portugália
LUNDA
Henrique de
Carvalho
Cassai
Luso
MOXICO
Cuando
ZAMBIA

ATLANTIC OCEAN

SOUTH WEST AFRICA

Appendices
Table of Events
Bibliographical Note
Index

Report of the Six

In 1959, the United Nations Committee of Six outlined 12 Principles, subsequently adopted by the General Assembly, as those 'principles which should guide Members in determining whether or not an obligation exists to transmit the information called for in Article 73(e) of the Charter of the United Nations'. In other words, the 12 Principles are the standard for testing whether or not a country is a non-self-governing territory, i.e. a colony to which the governing power should be prepared to grant independence, unless the subject peoples themselves determine otherwise. The text of the Report of the Six set the Principles out as follows:

Principle I

The authors of the Charter of the United Nations had in mind that Chapter XI should be applicable to territories which were then known to be of the colonial type. An obligation exists to transmit information under Article 73 (e) of the Charter in respect of such territories whose peoples have not yet attained a full measure of self-government.

Principle II

Chapter XI of the Charter embodies the concept of Non-Self-Governing Territories in a dynamic state of evolution and progress towards a 'full measure of self-government'. As soon as a territory and its peoples attain a full measure of self-government, the obligation ceases. Until this comes about, the obligation to transmit information under Article 73 (e) continues.

Principle III

The obligation to transmit information under Article 73 (e) of the Charter constitutes an international obligation and should be carried out with due regard to the fulfilment of international law.

Principle IV

Prima facie there is an obligation to transmit information in respect of a territory which is geographically separate and is distinct ethnically and/or culturally from the country administering it.

Principle V

Once it has been established that such a *prime facie* case of geographical and ethnical or cultural distinctness of a territory exists, other elements may then be brought into consideration. These additional elements may be, *inter alia*, of an administrative, political, juridical, economic or historical nature. If they affect the relationship between the metropolitan State and the territory concerned in such a manner which arbitrarily places the latter in a position or status of subordination, they support the presumption that there is an obligation to transmit information under Article 73 (*e*) of the Charter.

Principle VI

A Non-Self-Governing Territory can be said to have reached a full measure of self-government by:

    (*a*) Emergence as a sovereign independent State;
    (*b*) Free association with an independent State; or
    (*c*) Integration with an independent State.

Principle VII

(*a*) Free association should be the result of a free and voluntary choice by the peoples of the territory concerned expressed through informed and democratic processes. It should be one which respects the individuality and the cultural characteristics of the territory and its peoples, and retains for the peoples of the territory which is associated with an independent State the freedom to modify the status of that territory through the expression of their will by democratic means and through constitutional processes.

(*b*) The associated territory should have the right to determine its internal constitution without outside interference, in accordance with due constitutional processes and the freely expressed wishes of the people. This does not preclude consultations as appropriate or necessary under the terms of the free association agreed upon.

Principle VIII

Integration with an independent State should be on the basis of complete equality between the peoples of the erstwhile Non-Self-Governing Territory and those of the independent country with which it is integrated. The peoples of both territories should have equal status and rights of citizenship and equal guarantees of fundamental rights and freedoms without any distinction or discrimination; both should have equal rights and opportunities for representation and effective participation at all levels in the executive, legislative and judicial organs of government.

Principle IX

Integration should have come about in the following circumstances:

(*a*) The integrating territory should have attained an advanced stage of self-government with free political institutions, so that its peoples would have the capacity to make a responsible choice through informed and democratic processes;

(*b*) The integration should be the result of the freely expressed wishes of the territory's peoples acting with full knowledge of the change in their status, their wishes having been expressed through informed and democratic processes, impartially conducted and based on universal suffrage. The United Nations could, when it deems it necessary, supervise these processes.

Principle X

The transmission of information in respect of Non-Self-Governing Territories under Article 73 of the Charter is subject to such limitation as security and constitutional considerations may require. This means that the extent of the information may be limited in certain circumstances, but the limitation in Article 73 (*e*) cannot relieve a Member State of the obligations of Chapter XI. The 'limitation' can relate only to the quantum of information of economic, social and educational nature to be transmitted.

Principle XI

The only constitutional considerations to which Article 73 (*e*) of the Charter refers are those arising from constitutional relations of the territory with the Administering Member. They refer to a situation in which the constitution of the territory gives it self-government in economic, social and educational matters through freely elected institutions. Nevertheless, the responsibility for transmitting information under Article 73 continues, unless these constitutional relations preclude the Government or parliament of the Administering Member from receiving statistical and other information of a technical nature relating to economic, social and educational conditions in the territory.

Principle XII

Security considerations have not been invoked in the past. Only in very exceptional circumstances can information on economic, social and educational conditions have any security aspect. In other circumstances, therefore, there should be no necessity to limit the transmission of information on security grounds.

APPENDIX B

Franco Nogueira's argument was that a series of Resolutions which, in effect, changed the Charter of the United Nations in regard to the future of Non-Self-Governing Territories in order to bring Portugal to heel had been passed illegally, in that they had been passed by a simple majority vote. In fact, the Charter had laid down the procedures to be adopted when amendments to the Charter were proposed. These were contained in Articles 108 and 109 of the Charter as follows:

Article 108

Amendments to the present Charter shall come into force for all Members of the United Nations when they have been adopted by a vote of two-thirds of the Members of the General Assembly and ratified in accordance with their respective constitutional processes by two-thirds of the Members of the United Nations, including all the permanent Members of the Security Council.

Article 109

1. A General Conference of the Members of the United Nations for the purpose of reviewing the present Charter may be held at a date and place to be fixed by a two-thirds vote of the Members of the General Assembly and by a vote of any seven [now nine] Members of the Security Council. Each Member of the United Nations shall have one vote in the conference.

2. Any alteration of the present Charter recommended by a two-thirds vote of the conference shall take effect when ratified in accordance with their respective constitutional processes by two-thirds of the Members of the United Nations including all the permanent Members of the Security Council.

3. If such a conference has not been held before the tenth annual session of the General Assembly following the coming into force of the present Charter, the proposal to call such a conference shall be placed on the agenda of that session of the General Assembly, and the conference shall be held if so decided by a majority vote of the Members of the General Assembly and by a vote of any seven Members of the Security Council.

2 H

Table of Events

1934	December 17	Election returns government supporters only to the National Assembly.
1935	January 11	National Assembly inaugurated.
	February 18	President Carmona re-elected.
1936	July 18	Spanish Civil War begins.
	September 30	Portuguese Legion formed.
	October 24	Salazar announces severance of diplomatic relations with Republican Spain.
	October	Formation of Portuguese *Mocidade* (youth movement).
1937	July 5	Attempted assassination of Salazar.
1938	April 28	Salazar announces recognition of General Franco's Nationalist Government in Spain.
1939	March 17	Treaty of Non-Aggression (Iberian Pact) signed between Portugal and Spain.
	September 2	Portugal announces her neutrality in impending world conflict, but reasserts loyalty to the Anglo-Portuguese Alliance.
	September 3	Britain declares war on Germany.
1940	June 10	Italy enters the war on Germany's side.
	July 29	Protocol confirming Iberian Pact is signed; Salazar and Franco meet.
	October 23	Franco meets Hitler at Hendaya.
1941	June 21	Germany attacks Russia.
	December 7	Japanese attack Pearl Harbour.
1942	January 29	General Delgado in London to discuss survey of the Azores.
	February 17	Salazar meets Franco at Seville.
	October 23	Battle of Alamein.
	November 8	Operation Torch.
1943	July 25	Fall of Mussolini.
	August 18	Portugal signs agreement giving Britain and her allies the use of the Azores bases.
	October 12	Churchill announces final details of Azores agreement to the House of Commons.
1944	June 7	Eden tells House of Commons that Portugal has now banned the export of wolfram to the Axis powers.
	August 23	Portugal severs diplomatic relations with Vichy government.

2H*

1945	November 18	Portuguese opposition (MUD) boycotts National Assembly elections.
1946	October 10	Abortive *revolução da Mealhada.*
1947		Galvão compiles his report on Africa.
	April	Abortive revolt of army officers. Britain passes Indian Independence Act.
1948	March 15-16	Portugal joins OEEC.
1949	February 13	President Carmona returned unopposed after withdrawal of Norton de Matos.
	April 4	Portugal joins NATO.
	November 13	Opposition again boycotts elections for National Assembly.
1951	April 18	President Carmona dies.
	July 22	President Craveiro Lopes elected.
1954		Dispute with India over Goa comes to a head.
1955	July 25	India closes mission in Lisbon.
	October	President Craveiro Lopes's state visit to Britain.
1957	February	Queen Elizabeth's state visit to Portugal.
	October	Opposition again boycotts Assembly elections.
1958	March 18	Galvão sentenced to sixteen years' imprisonment.
	June 8	Presidential election: Delgado loses to Admiral Tomás.
	July	Bishop of Oporto's letter to Salazar publicized, and Bishop goes into virtual exile.
1959	January 15	Galvão escapes from prison and flees to South America.
	June	Princess Margaret visits Portugal.
1960	Early	U.S.S.R. Ambassador Solod arrives in Conakry, Guinea, and helps preparations for nationalist movement in Angola.
	January 12	OEEC becomes OECD.
	May 30	Portugal joins EFTA.
	July 14	A fortnight after Congolese independence, U.N. Security votes military aid to Leopoldville to help the country now torn by disorders and the Katangese secession.

1960	December	U.N. Declaration on Colonialism; Portuguese overseas possessions held to be non-self-governing territories.
1961	January 22	Galvão's men seize the *Santa Maria*.
	January 31	Portuguese opposition produces its *Programme for Democratization of the Republic*.
	February 4	Disorder flares up in Luanda, capital of Angola.
	February 13	Congo hears of the death of Lumumba while allegedly escaping from custody in Katanga.
	March 15	African nationalists strike in northern Angola. Angolan War begins (UPA and MPLA attack from Congo).
	April 13	After abortive attempt at a coup in Lisbon, Salazar reshuffles his government and takes over as Minister of Defence. Franco Nogueira becomes Foreign Minister and Adriano Moreira Overseas Minister.
	June	Congo: Adoula becomes Prime Minister.
	September 6	Portuguese government ends *assimilado* system.
	September 18	U.N. Secretary-General Dag Hammarskjöld dies in air crash.
	December 18	Indian army invades Goa.
1962	January 1	Delgado's attack on Beja garrison fails.
	April	ILO Report on Portuguese Africa.
1963	January 15	Tshombe surrenders to U.N. troops and Katanga secession ends. PAIGC rebels begin operations in Portuguese Guinea under Amilcar Cabral.
	September	President Tomás visits Angola.
	November 22	Assassination of President Kennedy.
	December 31	Britain dissolves Central African Federation.
1964	July	President Tomás visits Mozambique.
	August	Mondlane's FRELIMO starts the nationalist war on the northern frontier of Mozambique (working from Tanzania).
1965	April 24	Delgado's body found on the Spanish side of the Portuguese border near Badajoz.

1965	November 11	Rhodesia's UDI.
	November	Opposition in Portugal boycotts Assembly elections.
1966	January 14	Assassination of Nigerian Premier, Abubakar Tafawa Balewa. Beginnings of Nigerian revolt.
	March	Britain takes Rhodesia question to the U.N.
	April 9	Security Council authorizes Beira blockade.
	December 16	Security Council votes economic sanctions against Rhodesia.
1968	September 6	Salazar collapses with a clot on the brain.
	September 25	Marcello Caetano named Prime Minister.
1969	February 3	Mondlane assassinated in Dar-es-Salaam.
	February 5	Salazar returns home from hospital.
	July	Bishop of Oporto returns to his diocese.
	October 26	National Assembly elections. Opposition present lists of candidates. National Union wins all seats.

Bibliographical Note

The principal documentary sources on which this book relies are itemised in footnotes and other references throughout the text. But some further observations may be helpful. A valuable work, published at the end of 1969 and thus too late for me to make any proper use of it, is perhaps the most comprehensive account of Portuguese Africa as it is today to appear in any language so far. It is entitled *Portuguese Africa: a handbook*, and is edited by D. M. Abshire and M. A. Samuels of the Centre for Strategic and International Studies, Georgetown University, Washington, D.C. (published in Great Britain by Pall Mall Press). The result of several years' work by a well-qualified team, who toured the countries concerned, the book offers a credible piece of objective reporting without any attempt at special pleading. It offers a wealth of political, social and economic data, with a wide range of statistics. It also provides useful perspectives for judgments on the racial question and the guerrilla wars.

Then there is another new work which belies its emotive title and, while published in South Africa, is strictly factual and takes no sides. This is *The Terror Fighters: a profile of guerrilla warfare in Southern Africa*, by Al J. Venter (published in Cape Town and Johannesburg by Purnell). Venter is a hard-headed newsman who went into the fighting areas with the Portuguese army in Angola. From that side of the fence he can offer a first-hand service which may be usefully compared with on-the-spot reports of life among the guerrillas in Portuguese Guinea by Basil Davidson (*The Liberation of Guiné*, Penguin African Series, London, 1969). Davidson has now been challenged by John Biggs-Davison, M.P., who also knows the area well, in a booklet: *Portuguese Guinea: nailing a lie* (Congo African Publications, London, 1970).

For an understanding of Portuguese Africa until very recent times, the works of Professor James Duffy, to whom I have frequently referred in this book, offer the most comprehensive guide to the available documentation, and in this connection I would refer especially to his *Portuguese Africa* (Cambridge, Mass., and London, 1959). I have also referred to Dr Richard Pattee's *Portugal and the Portuguese World*, and this contains several pages of very useful bibliography relating to Portugal's historical and cultural background. Finally, the man who probably knows more than anyone else outside Portugal about the history of Portuguese racial relations, Professor C. R. Boxer, has recently produced: *The Portuguese Seaborne Empire, 1415-1825* (Hutchinson, London, 1969).

Index